HAYEK ON MILL

F. A. HAYEK

THE COLLECTED WORKS OF

F. A. Hayek

HAYEK ON MILL

The Mill-Taylor Friendship and Related Writings

F. A. HAYEK

Edited by Sandra J. Peart

Liberty Fund

This book is published by Liberty Fund, Inc., a foundation established to encourage study of the ideal of a society of free and responsible individuals.

The cuneiform inscription that serves as our logo and as a design element in Liberty Fund books is the earliest-known written appearance of the word "freedom" (*amagi*), or "liberty." It is taken from a clay document written about 2300 B.C. in the Sumerian city-state of Lagash.

Hayek on Mill: The Mill-Taylor Friendship and Related Writings is volume 16 of The Collected Works of F. A. Hayek, published by The University of Chicago Press.

This 2024 Liberty Fund paperback edition of *Hayek on Mill: The Mill-Taylor Friendship and Related Writings* is licensed by The University of Chicago Press, Chicago, Illinois, U.S.A., and published by arrangement with Routledge, a member of the Taylor & Francis Group, an Informa Business.

Frontispiece: Friedrich Hayek by Bettmann; Bettmann via Getty Images © Bettmann
Cover photo: Friedrich Augustus Von Hayek by Hulton Deutsch; Corbis Historical via Getty Images © Dulton-Deutsch

Printed in the United States of America

24   25   26   27   28   P   5   4   3   2   1

Library of Congress Cataloging-in-Publication Data can be found on the Library of Congress website at https://lccn.loc.gov/2023018023.

Liberty Fund, Inc.
11301 North Meridian Street
Carmel, Indiana 46032
libertyfund.org

Printed on paper that is acid-free and meets the requirements of the American National Standard for Permanence of Paper for Printed Library Materials, Z39.48-1992. ⊗

Cover design by Erin Kirk, Watkinsville, Georgia
Printed and bound by Sheridan Books, Inc., Chelsea, Michigan

THE COLLECTED WORKS OF F. A. HAYEK

Founding Editor: W. W. Bartley III
General Editor: Bruce Caldwell

The University of Chicago Press edition
was published with the support of

The Hoover Institution on War, Revolution,
and Peace, Stanford University

The Cato Institute

The Earhart Foundation

The Pierre F. and Enid Goodrich Foundation

The Heritage Foundation

The Morris Foundation, Little Rock

CONTENTS

HAYEK ON MILL: THE MILL-TAYLOR FRIENDSHIP AND RELATED WRITINGS

PART I.   *John Stuart Mill and Harriet Taylor: Their Friendship and Subsequent Marriage*

PART II. *Related Writings*

CONTENTS

ILLUSTRATIONS

EDITORIAL FOREWORD

Volume 16 of *The Collected Works of F. A. Hayek* has been rather a long time in the making. Not long after I accepted the assignment for this collection, my administrative responsibilities expanded, first at Baldwin-Wallace College, then with the History of Economics Society, and finally in my current capacity as Dean at the Jepson School of Leadership Studies. Each successive role rendered the blocks of time required to make substantial progress on a work such as this more infrequent. But whenever I was able to return to the collection, I enjoyed the respite from the decanal schedule and lost myself in the intertwined stories of John Stuart Mill, Harriet Taylor Mill, and Friedrich Hayek. It is thus with considerable relief but also much pride that I present this collection to the reader. I note in passing that Francis E. Mineka also found decanal pressures weighing on him as he prepared *The Earlier Letters of John Stuart Mill*.

Part 1 republishes Hayek's book *John Stuart Mill and Harriet Taylor: Their Friendship and Subsequent Marriage*, which first appeared in 1951 under the title *John Stuart Mill and Harriet Taylor: Their Correspondence and Subsequent Marriage*. The Editor's Introduction explains my choice to use the *Friendship* subtitle in this collection. The short explanation is that Hayek subsequently included an errata sheet that listed the title with the word 'Friendship' replacing 'Correspondence'.

Part 2 collects essays and correspondence by Hayek related to the Mill-Taylor book. These are presented in chronological order; conceptually they fall into three categories. In the first category, we observe Hayek describing the difficulties associated with collecting the materials for the volume. Included in this category are 'J. S. Mill's Correspondence' (1943), prepared for the *Times Literary Supplement*; the previously-unpublished 'Dispersal of the Books and Papers of John Stuart Mill' (1944); and much of the correspondence in the present collection. Second, Hayek's 1942 Introduction to *The Spirit of the Age*, 'John Stuart Mill at the Age of Twenty-Five', and the previously-unpublished essay 'J. S. Mill, Mrs. Taylor, and Socialism' reveal his early interest in Mill. Here emerge the themes of the later Mill-Taylor book: Hayek's interest in the influence of Harriet Taylor Mill and Gustave d'Eichthal on Mill, in Mill's methodology and his shifting position on socialism, and in Mill's *Political*

Economy. The third category includes the reviews or introductions that in large measure owe their publication to Hayek's Mill-Taylor volume. Hayek's Introduction to Francis E. Mineka's magisterial edition of *The Earlier Letters of John Stuart Mill, 1812–1848* (1963) constitutes the crowning example of this.

Hayek's erudition immediately becomes evident as one takes up *John Stuart Mill and Harriet Taylor*. He worked with large quantities of published as well as unpublished materials. As editor of the present collection, my first immediate challenge was to locate the published works used by Hayek and then to assess what among the materials unpublished in 1951 remains unpublished today and where, if at all, the rest has appeared in print. Fortunately, the project he began brought to light sufficiently the significance of Mill's manuscripts and letters so that the University of Toronto's *Collected Works of John Stuart Mill* became a reality between the publication of the Mill-Taylor book and the commencement of this project. My first editorial decision, then, was to read and verify Hayek's presentation of the Mill side of the correspondence against the University of Toronto collection. Second, I verified Harriet Taylor Mill's correspondence against *The Complete Works of Harriet Taylor Mill*. Third, Hayek quotes from or refers to an extensive set of nineteenth- and twentieth-century works about John Stuart Mill, and I checked each of those quotations and citations against the edition used by Hayek.

Irrespective of the sources on which Hayek relied in his text, in this edition typographical errors in Hayek's edition are silently corrected, and punctuation and spelling are silently rendered consistent with the published collections mentioned above. Slight errors on Hayek's part are silently corrected as well. Exceptions to the rule of verifying against *The Collected Works of John Stuart Mill*, *The Complete Works of Harriet Taylor Mill*, or other published sources used by Hayek are few: in the event that a fragment or letter remains unpublished, it was compared to the original in an archival setting; and when I suspected the wording was incorrect either in *The Collected Works of John Stuart Mill* or *The Complete Works of Harriet Taylor Mill*, I verified the text against the original. Such exceptions, which occur rarely, are noted in the text. For materials referred to by Hayek that have been subsequently published or republished, Hayek's original source (e.g., an older, published collection of Mill's writings or an archival listing) has been verified, and the information about the subsequent publication (e.g., volume and page numbers in *The Collected Works of John Stuart Mill*) is included in square brackets. In particular, all entries to the *Autobiography* are collated with volume 1 of *The Collected Works of John Stuart Mill*, and the location in the aforementioned collection of any and all letters, essays, passages, or books by Mill are noted in square brackets, generally as an editor's addition to Hayek's already-existing footnote.

Early on, I decided to convey to the reader not simply the number and complexity of Hayek's sources but also his skill as a collector and editor. Hence followed an editorial decision to note more-substantial errors in the text rather than to silently correct all but the most egregious errors. Words omitted by Hayek are added in square brackets, and words that should not be included are struck through. Instances of Hayek's occasional use of square brackets are noted in the text to avoid confusion; when he used a query—that is, (?) or [?]—in his presentation of a letter and the word has been supplied in the subsequently-published version, that version is included and Hayek's query is noted in a footnote. When Hayek's quotation differs substantially from the subsequently-published version, the subsequently-published wording is used and Hayek's version is provided in a footnote. A rare exception to this rule occurred when, upon review, Hayek seemed clearly correct and the subsequent publication incorrect; in this case Hayek's version is retained and the other version is noted in an editorial footnote. Errata noted by Hayek are silently changed in the text, and footnotes remind the reader of Hayek's original.

The presentation of the correspondence in *John Stuart Mill and Harriet Taylor* follows Hayek's presentation. Some of the correspondence Hayek quoted from, especially that by Harriet Taylor Mill, was quite apparently written in haste, with sentences added to one side of the main text or wrapped around the edge of a letter. In such cases the position of various sentences is noted in an editorial footnote.

On the rare occasion that Hayek incorrectly cited an archival source, the correct citation is provided in the text with an editorial note containing Hayek's original citation. On the rare occasion that Hayek misstated a source or page number, the correct source or page number is noted.

When Hayek referred to a secondary source, he rarely provided full publication information; such information is silently added when Hayek first refers to the source. Titles, publishers, and dates of publications are corrected silently unless the title has been substantially abbreviated by Hayek, in which case the addition to the title is provided in square brackets. Full publication information on journal articles, when not provided by Hayek, has been added in square brackets.

Since Hayek worked with such an extraordinary amount of unpublished material containing multiple types of handwriting, as well as an enormous library of published secondary sources, the small number of mistakes is absolutely astounding.

EDITOR'S ACKNOWLEDGEMENTS

Preparation of this volume began during a sabbatical year spent at George Mason University. I am grateful to Baldwin-Wallace College for the sabbatical time and for summer research grants in 2004 and 2005, to the Mercatus Foundation, Earhart, and the Pierre E. and Enid Goodrich Foundation for sabbatical support, and to colleagues at George Mason University for allotting me office space in the lovely Buchanan House.

I thank the following individuals and institutions for permissions to reproduce or quote from materials for which they hold the copyright: the Estate of F. A. Hayek for permission to quote from his unpublished correspondence and papers; Stephen Kresge for permission to quote from transcripts of interviews conducted by W. W. Bartley III with F. A. Hayek; and the London School of Economics, the Hoover Institution Archives, Johns Hopkins University, the Yale University Library, and King's College Cambridge for permission to quote from materials contained in their archives.

Editing a volume of this sort inevitably entails a great deal of assistance from archivists and librarians. I am grateful for the time and efforts provided by the following: Carol Leadenham, Archivist, and Barbara Zoeller at the Hoover Institution Archives; Silvia Gallotti, Archives Assistant, and Sue Donnelly, Archivist, at the London School of Economics; Elizabeth Ennion, Assistant Archivist, at King's College, Cambridge University; Kelly Spring, Assistant Curator of Manuscripts, Special Collections, Johns Hopkins University; Jennifer Gunter King at Mount Holyoke; Jonathan Morgan at Dr. Williams' Library; and Cynthia Ostroff, Manager, Public Services, Manuscripts and Archives, Yale University Library.

In addition, I had the good fortune to receive partially edited versions of some of the essays included in Part 2 below. W. W. Bartley undertook the project in his role as general editor of the works of F. A. Hayek, and his successor Bruce Caldwell passed these materials on to me. Bartley's version of *The Spirit of the Age* was particularly helpful to my work. Two published collections, John Stuart Mill's *Collected Works* and Harriet Taylor Mill's *Complete Works* were invaluable resources for me, providing identifications and contextual information for the material below. The reader will find many specific acknowledgements to these publications in the editor's footnotes. It is only fitting that a republication of Hayek's 1951 book on Mill and Taylor, a work that was instrumental to the subsequent publication of Mill's letters and on which the *Collected Works* editors relied, should now have been helped by the *Collected Works* he did so much to encourage in the first instance.

Several conferences proved helpful to this work. In May 2005, I directed a conference titled 'Hayek on Mill: Consequences for Liberty and Responsibility'. I thank the Liberty Fund for supporting the conference, as well as Liberty Fund Fellow Claire Morgan and participants Richard Boyd, Bruce Caldwell, Ross Emmett, Andrew Farrant, Evelyn Forget, Ali Khan, Chandran Kukathas, David Levy, Loren Lomasky, Leonard Liggio, Ann Robson, and Alan Ryan for very good discussions and comments. A follow-up conference in December 2006, 'Hayek and the Liberal Tradition', proved just as helpful; I thank Liberty Fund Fellow Mark Yellin for his support, and Bruce Caldwell, Henry Clark, Steven Durlauf, Ross Emmett, Andrew Farrant, Roberta Herzberg, Hartmut Kliemt, Deirdre McCloskey, Leonides Montes, Claire Morgan, Ann Robson, Eric Schliesser, and Vernon Smith for their comments and discussions.

Early versions of the material that eventually formed the Editor's Introduction were presented at a seminar in the Buchanan House (fall 2005) and as plenary lectures at L'Associazione Italiana per la Storia dell'Economia Politica ('Did J. S. Mill Ruin Classical Liberalism?', Lecce, June 2006), the History of Economics Society ('We're All "Persons" Now: Classical Economists and Their Opponents on Marriage, the Franchise, and Socialism', Presidential Address, Toronto, June 2008), and the Summer Institute for the Preservation of the History of Economic Thought ('Editor's Introduction', Richmond, June 2012). I thank participants for the lively discussions that ensued.

I am grateful for the assistance of the following individuals as I prepared the collection: Bruce Caldwell, whose patience and good humor have been exceptional; David M. Levy, whose encouragement, assistance, and comments on the Editor's Introduction have been enormously important; Andrew Farrant, who read and commented on drafts of the Editor's Introduction; Pam Khoury, who transcribed the unpublished texts; Emily Nowlan, who read the *John Stuart Mill and Harriet Taylor* typescript against the published book and found herself fascinated by the story; Tammy Tripp, who assisted with obtaining materials and permissions; and Craig, Nathan, and Matthew, who have endured even longer absences from our home than the usual decanal pressures dictate so that I could finish this labour of love!

EDITOR'S INTRODUCTION

John Stuart Mill was, perhaps, the quintessential liberal of the nineteenth century. He was also the great social reformer of the century. So it was entirely fitting that the twentieth-century scholar most responsible for reviving ideas from the period of classical liberalism, F. A. Hayek, undertook the difficult challenge of situating Mill not only within the complicated social and intellectual milieu of nineteenth-century Europe but also within the mid-twentieth-century debates on socialism and planning.[1] In so doing, he began 'the new era of Mill scholarship' that has since borne much fruit.[2] Certainly the correspondence that first appeared in Hayek's 1951 collection was a key precondition for any reexamination of the foundation of liberalism, the sources of Mill's Radicalism, and the influence of the woman who was first and foremost his good friend and afterwards his wife, Harriet Taylor Mill.[3]

[1] In an interview later in life, Hayek linked his discovery and subsequent publication of the 'fascinating' Mill-Taylor correspondence to the unfinished *Abuse of Reason* project. See F. A. Hayek, *Hayek on Hayek: An Autobiographical Dialogue*, eds. Stephen Kresge and Leif Wenar (Chicago: University of Chicago Press; London: Routledge, 1994), pp. 128–29. For the definitive discussion of the *Abuse of Reason* project, see Bruce Caldwell's Introduction to *Studies on the Abuse and Decline of Reason*, ed. Caldwell, vol. 13 (2010) of *The Collected Works of F. A. Hayek* (Chicago: University of Chicago Press; London: Routledge), pp. 1–45. Philippe Légé, 'Hayek's Readings of Mill', *Journal of the History of Economic Thought*, vol. 30, June 2008, p. 200, suggests that Hayek 'considered his work as being written right in the middle of a period of decline of liberalism and of western civilization'.

[2] Albert William Levi, 'Review of *John Stuart Mill and Harriet Taylor: Their Correspondence and Subsequent Marriage*', *Ethics*, vol. 62, January 1952, p. 146. Levi's review commences with the announcement, 'From the publication of this book begins the new era of Mill scholarship'. Hayek's book filled the 'precondition' for a new biography of Mill that had been 'wandering about in search of an author' (*ibid.*, p. 146). Michael St. John Packe's biography, *The Life of John Stuart Mill* (London: Seeker and Warburg), appeared in 1954. Lionel Robbins, 'Packe on Mill', *Economica*, n.s., vol. 24, August 1957, p. 254, offers the following judgment: 'Recollecting the fine scholarship, the deep understanding and the admirable literary restraint of Professor Hayek's own contribution, it is difficult to repress a regret that it was not he who attempted the definitive life as well'.

[3] Lewis S. Feuer, 'Review of *John Stuart Mill and Harriet Taylor: Their Correspondence and Subsequent Marriage*', *Philosophy and Phenomenological Research*, vol. 13, December 1952, p. 246, correctly emphasized the significance of Hayek's book in enabling a reexamination of the foundations of liberal principles and Mill's Radicalism.

For those who know the complexities of Mill's life and work, it is perhaps unsurprising that Hayek did not provide a once-and-for-all resolution to the challenge of locating Mill with respect to the nineteenth- or twentieth-century debates.[4] Even as the book appeared, reviewers were divided, climbing on board to address one of Hayek's major themes, that Harriet's influence on Mill was substantial, with a 'yes of course!' or 'not so!' Herbert Finer was unconvinced that Mill's writings on socialism were a result of Harriet's influence, while Albert William Levi agreed with Hayek in the main, that Harriet's influence strengthened the rationalist element in Mill's thought.[5]

There is also evidence that Hayek's views on Mill changed over time and that, even at roughly the same time, Hayek emphasized different threads in Mill's writing.[6] On 1 April 1947 Hayek gave the opening address, entitled '"Free" Enterprise and Competitive Order', at the founding meeting of the Mont Pèlèrin Society.[7] There, he characterized Mill as 'still a true liberal'[8] who held 'that the abandonment of all harmful or unnecessary state activity was the consummation of all political wisdom'.[9] Two years earlier, however, Hayek had referred to Mill as a 'false individualist' whose ideas tended to develop into 'socialism or collectivism'.[10] One theme that emerges from the correspon-

---

[4] Remarking on the complexity of assessing Hayek's views on Mill, Caldwell rightly notes that 'part of the problem is that Mill, like Hayek, made so many different contributions' (p. 689). Bruce Caldwell, 'Hayek on Mill', *History of Political Economy*, vol. 40, Fall 2008, pp. 689–704.

[5] Herbert Finer, 'Review of *John Stuart Mill and Harriet Taylor: Their Friendship and Subsequent Marriage*', *Annals of the American Academy of Political and Social Science*, vol. 279, January 1952, pp. 232–33; Levi, 'Review', p. 146. See also Charles C. Gillespie, 'Review of *John Stuart Mill and Harriet Taylor: Their Correspondence and Subsequent Marriage*', *Journal of Modern History*, vol. 24, December 1952, pp. 430–31; Robert T. Harris, 'Review of *John Stuart Mill and Harriet Taylor: Their Friendship and Subsequent Marriage*', *Western Political Quarterly*, vol. 5, March 1952, pp. 151–52; and Bruce L. Kinzer, 'Review of *The Complete Works of Harriet Taylor Mill*', *Albion*, vol. 31, Autumn 1999, pp. 518–20.

[6] For a thoroughgoing examination of how Hayek's views towards Mill changed over time, see Légé, 'Hayek's Readings of Mill'.

[7] The lecture was published as '"Free" Enterprise and Competitive Order', in Hayek, *Individualism and Economic Order* (Chicago: University of Chicago Press, 1948), pp. 107–18.

[8] *Ibid.*, p. 109.

[9] *Ibid.*, p. 110. Hayek continues: 'But little was in fact done to make the rules of property conform better to its rationale, and Mill himself, like so many others, soon turned his attention to schemes involving its restriction or abolition rather than its more effective use'.

[10] F. A. Hayek, *Individualism: True and False* (Dublin: Hodges, Figgis & Co.; Oxford: Basil Blackwell, 1946), reprinted with extensive editorial commentary in *Studies on the Abuse and Decline of Reason*, vol. 13 of *The Collected Works of F. A. Hayek*, p. 50 (page references are from the *Collected Works* version). In *The Road to Serfdom*, first published in 1944, Hayek located Mill within the broad English liberal tradition that transcended parties: 'And even today the English conservative or socialist, no less than the liberal, if he travels abroad, though he may find the ideas and writings of Carlyle or Disraeli, of the Webbs or H. G. Wells, exceedingly popular in circles with which he has little in common, among Nazis and other totalitarians, if he finds an intellectual island where the tradition of Macaulay and Gladstone, of J. S. Mill or John Morley, lives, will find kin-

dence and essays included in this volume is that Mill's flirtations—if flirtations they were—with socialism were the source of much of Hayek's sometimes-evident frustration with Mill's life and work and with Mill's relationship with Harriet Taylor (later Harriet Mill).[11]

Among the many liberal causes associated with Mill, we may consider the following: the defense of the abolition of slavery, repeal of the Corn Laws, the extension of the franchise and property rights to women, the Governor Eyre controversy, and the question of birth control.[12] Mill was at the center of each of these, sometimes on the winning side (Corn Laws, abolition of slavery, franchise, birth control) and sometimes in a losing coalition (Governor Eyre). Mill's position on property rights and socialism bears particular emphasis: perhaps because only it remained as a live problem for twentieth-century intellectuals in Europe and elsewhere, it was this, more than any other topic, that keenly interested Hayek throughout his own long career.[13]

---

dred spirits who "talk the same language" as himself'. F. A. Hayek, *The Road to Serfdom* (Chicago, University of Chicago Press, 1944), reprinted as *The Road to Serfdom: Texts and Documents—The Definitive Edition*, ed. Bruce Caldwell, vol. 2 (2007) of *The Collected Works of F. A. Hayek*, p. 219.

[11] Andrew Farrant asserts that Hayek and Ludwig von Mises have a 'decidedly negative view of J. S. Mill'. Farrant, 'A Renovated Social Fabric: Mill, Hayek, and the Problem of Institutional Change?', in *Hayek, Mill, and the Liberal Tradition*, ed. Farrant, Studies in the History of Economics (London: Routledge, 2011), p. 81. Caldwell suggests that Hayek's teacher, Wesley Clair Mitchell, influenced Hayek's view of Mill. Caldwell, 'Hayek on Mill', p. 691. In Caldwell's view, Mitchell's assessment of Mill 'as a reform-minded socialist who had shown that questions of distribution were subject to human control, may well have started Hayek on this long, and ultimately highly ambivalent, relationship with ideas of Mill and Harriet Taylor'. Caldwell, Introduction to *Studies on the Abuse and Decline of Reason*, vol. 13 of *The Collected Works of F. A. Hayek*, p. 24. In the transcribed interview published in 1994, Hayek remarked that he devoted 'a great deal of time to John Stuart Mill, who in fact never particularly appealed to me'. Hayek, *Hayek on Hayek*, p. 128. Légé, 'Hayek's Readings of Mill', provides evidence of Hayek's increasingly critical stance toward Mill after 1962. Hayek's frustration with Mill is sometimes evident below, but he also found much to admire in Mill and that, too, will be evident in what follows.

[12] For an account of Mill's role in the birth control movement, see James Huzel, *The Popularization of Malthus in Early Nineteenth Century England* (Aldershot, UK: Ashgate Publishing Limited; Burlington, VT: Ashgate Publishing Co., 2006).

[13] Partly as a by-product of that interest (but also, as noted below, partly because of the extraordinary drama involved in the relationship), Hayek soon also became interested in Mill's relationship with Harriet Taylor. He concluded in his unpublished essay on Mill and Taylor, 'J. S. Mill, Mrs. Taylor, and Socialism', 'That Mill was at that time completely under Mrs. Taylor's dominance and that she proved to be the much stronger character of the two is shown beyond doubt by the letters we have'. Hayek, this volume, p. 305. In my view, the conclusion to be drawn from the Mill-Taylor correspondence below, Hayek's more mature view, and the one that emerges from Hayek's published words, is one of influence and partnership but not domination.

Hayek's interest in Mill was evident early on and spanned much of his career. However 'unintentionally' this came about,[14] by the end of WWII he had established himself as a Mill scholar of significant stature. In 1948 he wrote to Austin Robinson, then Secretary of the Royal Economic Society, about the possibility of two sorts of publications: one, which would become the Mill-Taylor volume edited by Hayek,[15] and a second, more voluminous correspondence project to be edited by a person then unnamed.[16] The minutes of the Royal Economic Society dated 19 May 1949 record that the Secretary of the society 'had also discussed with Professor Hayek the possibility of assistance in the preparation of his edition of Mills' [sic] Letters. It was agreed to appoint a Committee composed of the President [D. H. Robertson], the Secretary [Austin Robinson], Mr. Harrod and Professor Robbins to make recommendations to the Council as to its future policy with regard to these and other publications'.[17]

The undertaking was enormous. Included in this volume is an essay penned by Hayek in 1944, 'The Dispersal of the Books and Papers of John Stuart Mill', in which he described just how widely Mill's letters had been dispersed and from which we glean a sense of how much collecting remained for Hayek to do.[18]

John Stuart Mill and Harriet Taylor appeared in 1951. More than a decade later Hayek wrote the Introduction, republished below, to the definitive Uni-

[14] See below, note 18, for Hayek's use of the adverb.

[15] Both Hayek and Robinson referred to the Mill-Taylor project at this time as the Mill-Taylor 'letters', and Hayek himself referred to the 'correspondence' (see note 16 below); it must have been later that Hayek decided to use the word 'friendship' in the book's title.

[16] 'In the course of my work I have also come across a good deal of correspondence between Mill and the famous Mrs. Taylor who was ultimately to become Mrs. Mill. For a number of reasons these letters are not suitable for inclusion in a straightforward edition of his letter[s]: both sides of the correspondence must be given, a good deal of it is unsuitable for publication because it deals with ordinary household matters or contains interminable discussions of their health, a great deal of explanatory text is required, and the series extend[s] far beyond the year 1848. . . . I have therefore decided to take this part of the correspondence out of the general collection and to make a separate book of it on which I am now working' (brackets indicate editorial insertions). Hayek offered to help find a 'suitable' editor for the larger collection, to 'turn over' his materials to that person, and to 'assist with my advice' for the project. Hayek to E. A. G. Robinson, 2 October 1948, Royal Economic Society Minute Book, 1938–1955, RES/2/1/3, London School of Economics (LSE) Library's Collections.

[17] Minutes of the Royal Economic Society, 19 May 1949, Royal Economic Society Minute Book, 1938–1955, RES/2/1/3, LSE Library's Collections.

[18] Hayak described the difficulties in the later interview, remarking that he 'unintentionally' earned the reputation for being 'one of the foremost experts' on Mill 'through my noticing in tracing Saint-Simonian influence on England how much of the important correspondence of John Stuart Mill which threw light on this issue was either available only widely dispersed among many publications, often in places difficult to find, or only in manuscript'. Hayek, *Hayek on Hayek*, p. 129.

versity of Toronto edition of Mill's early letters that appeared under the editorship of Francis E. Mineka.[19] Albert William Levi's assessment of the significance of Hayek's achievement was surely no exaggeration.[20]

Hayek's Early Interest[21]

Written at the same time as Hayek's 'The Counter-Revolution of Science', the 1942 essay 'John Stuart Mill at the Age of Twenty-Five' is reproduced in this collection.[22] Here Hayek remarked that though 'John Stuart Mill may not have been an original thinker of the very first rank',[23] 'he was certainly not, as is now sometimes suggested, merely a late representative of a once powerful school'.[24] The question of Mill's originality—and of his susceptibility to the influence of others[25]—has bedeviled commentators, Hayek included, for

[19] Hayek described how he transferred the materials to Francis E. Mineka: 'But after publishing the correspondence between John Stuart Mill and Harriet Taylor [1951] and putting all my material at the disposal of Mill's successful biographer, Michael Packe, I unloaded all my accumulation of transcripts of Mill letters on Dr. Francis Mineka of Cornell University who, I am sure, will do the job of editing much better than I could have done'. Hayek, *Hayek on Hayek*, p. 129. Correspondence between Packe and Hayek reveals Packe's deep appreciation for Hayek's support and assistance as Packe prepared the biography. Packe remarked upon completing the manuscript: 'May I once more express to you my sincere gratitude for all your help and encouragement'. Packe to Hayek, 7 April 1953, Folder 30, Hoover Institution Archives.

[20] The Mill-Taylor book also contains evidence that Hayek worked with three versions of Mill's *Autobiography* (the early draft, the World Classics edition, and the Columbia edition), which would be collated only in 1981 with the publication of volume 1 of the University of Toronto's *Collected Works of John Stuart Mill*. See Levi, 'Review', for commentary.

[21] Having learned of Hayek's early interest in John Stuart Mill, Jacob Viner pointed Hayek to *The Spirit of the Age* as well as correspondence with Saint-Simon. See the correspondence below dated 7 December 1941 on p. 332.

[22] The essay was published as the Introduction to John Stuart Mill, *The Spirit of the Age* (Chicago: University of Chicago Press, 1942), pp. v–xxviii.

[23] This volume, p. 273. Légé, 'Hayek's Readings of Mill', p. 202, suggests that Hayek 'kept relativizing' Mill's independence by 'insisting on the new influences to which Mill had been exposed', first James Mill, then Comte and the Saint-Simonians, and then Harriet Taylor Mill. For a fine discussion of intellectual influences on Mill, see also Alan Ryan, *Mill: Texts and Commentary* (New York: Norton, 1975), pp. xv–xxvi.

[24] This volume, p. 273.

[25] The question of whether Mill was 'overly' susceptible to the influence of Harriet Taylor Mill or others was raised even in Mill's time, when—as is clear below on p. 75—Carlyle and others found Harriet's influence to be excessive. In portraying Mill the reformer as a woman, the popular press took this to an extreme: in cartoons and caricatures Mill is shown to have been so profoundly influenced by women that he became one with them. Sandra J. Peart, 'We Are All "Persons" Now: Classical Economists and Their Opponents on Marriage, the Franchise, and

many years.[26] As Hayek remarked, there was, first, the question of Mill's 'extraordinary education':

> A warning, however, may be necessary, not only against overstressing the influence of this education on his later views but also against overestimating the length of the period during which he remained completely under the sway of the views he had been taught. It is sometimes difficult to remember that the extensive literary activity and the participation in the various debating groups between 1822 and 1828 were all the work of a young man between sixteen and twenty-two years of age. Mill himself, by devoting more than forty percent of his *Autobiography* to the first twenty-two years of his life, gives a rather misleading impression. The 'reasoning machine' as which he appears there, the 'made man' as which he was known to his contemporaries, was, after all, little more than a boy, carefully trained, and continuing to train himself, as an instrument of propaganda of the views of his unquestioned intellectual masters. It would probably not be unjust to say that he was then rather less original or independent in thought than many a brilliant young man of the same age.[27]

Second, even at this early stage, Hayek was struck by the question of Mill's relationship with Continental thinkers.[28] In Hayek's view, Mill was overly open to ideas on the Continent, France especially: 'In fact, if one may speak of prej-

---

Socialism', *Journal of the History of Economic Thought*, vol. 31, March 2009, pp. 3–20, reproduces cartoons from *Judy* and *Punch* that show Mill as a woman.

[26] 'Now, the anti-Mill myth, which persisted in my young days, and which was not only held by Edwin Cannan, but all sorts of other people in my sphere of work, used to dwell upon the fact that Mill was not original'. Lionel Robbins, *A History of Economic Thought*, eds. Steven G. Medema and Warren J. Samuels (Princeton, NJ: Princeton University Press, 1998), p. 225. In Robbins' view, George Stigler did much to correct the long-held view that Mill was unoriginal: 'I think that Mill has been underrated as an economist, particularly perhaps in the oral tradition of the London School of Economics, myself a bad culprit at one stage. But this is a side issue and Professor Stigler has dealt with it very effectively'. Robbins, 'Packe on Mill', p. 259. Stigler wrote: 'In terms of identifiable theories, [Mill] was one of the most original economists in the history of the science. I shall list his major contributions, each of which was at least original to him as any important theory is to the person with whom it is chiefly associated'. George J. Stigler, 'The Nature and Role of Originality in Scientific Progress', *Economica*, n.s., vol. 22, November 1955, pp. 296–97.

[27] 'John Stuart Mill at the Age of Twenty-Five', this volume, p. 275. Hayek had come to a similar conclusion in the 1940's; in the previously-unpublished essay below 'J. S. Mill, Mrs. Taylor, and Socialism', he countered the claim that Mill was a great child prodigy: 'There was in fact nothing of a Gauss in him'. This volume, p. 301.

[28] While noting the usefulness of Hayek's distinction between the Scottish Enlightenment thinkers and the Continental constructivists, Caldwell rightly notes that it fails to illuminate the full richness of nineteenth-century positions. Caldwell, Introduction to *Studies on the Abuse and Decline of Reason*, vol. 13 of *The Collected Works of F. A. Hayek*, p. 40.

udices of so singularly candid a mind, there can be little doubt that Mill had acquired something like prejudice and even contempt not only for English society, which he little knew, but also for the contemporary development of English thought and especially of English political economy, which he neglected to a surprising extent'.[29]

Yet Hayek was too sophisticated to conclude in this essay that Mill was simply 'representative' of his 'age or country': 'It is a mistake that we all at times make to think of the great men of the past as "representative" of their age or country. The temptation to do so is particularly strong in regard to our near intellectual forebears, the men who have to a large extent fashioned our own outlook'.[30] Throughout 'John Stuart Mill at the Age of Twenty-Five', in 'J. S. Mill, Mrs. Taylor, and Socialism', and then especially in the Mill-Taylor book, Hayek attempted to make sense of Mill on Mill's terms rather than those of a century later.

Hence began the serious effort to locate and collect Mill's letters, documented below in the essays and correspondence related to the Mill-Taylor volume. Jacob Viner, who himself owned one of Mill's letters and who knew of others in private possession, remarked in correspondence that the task was 'huge'.[31] In the *Times Literary Supplement* of 13 February 1943 Hayek listed twenty-one different collections holding significant quantities of Mill's letters, and he sought information on additional unpublished materials. Already the significance of the early correspondence with Auguste Comte and Gustave d'Eichthal was clear to him: 'How important many of Mill's other letters of this early period are, not only for the understanding of his own development, but for the intellectual history of the time in general, is shown by the numerous smaller collections and single letters which have been published at various dates. They include, apart from the comparatively well-known collections of his correspondence with Auguste Comte and Gustave d'Eichthal, many others, no less interesting, which have fallen into undeserved oblivion'.[32] Pub-

---

[29] 'John Stuart Mill at the Age of Twenty-Five', this volume, p. 274. The problem was exacerbated by Mill's fairness as demonstrated by his willingness to consider and perhaps adopt the sensible arguments of others. Stigler writes that 'Mill was not trying to build a new system but only to add improvements here and there to the Ricardian system. The fairest of economists, as Schumpeter [*History of Economic Analysis* (New York: Oxford University Press, 1954), pp. 528–30] has properly characterized Mill, unselfishly dedicated his abilities to the advancement of the science'. Stigler, 'The Nature and Role of Originality', p. 299.

[30] 'John Stuart Mill at the Age of Twenty-Five', this volume, p. 273.

[31] Viner to Hayek, 22 September 1942, this volume, p. 334. The Viner-Hayek correspondence reveals how substantially important Viner's suggestions and guidance were to the project. One also senses from the correspondence that both Hayek and Viner enjoyed the 'pleasure of the hunt'. For Hayek's use of this phrase, see his Introduction to *The Earlier Letters of John Stuart Mill, 1812–1848*, this volume, p. 331.

[32] Hayek, 'J. S. Mill's Correspondence', this volume, p. 289.

lished collections revealed a curious gap in the letters, one that Hayek found most important to fill: letters from the period leading up to the publication of Mill's *Political Economy* were lacking. Not surprisingly, it was these years which especially interested Hayek.[33]

Finding correspondence from these years proved to be no simple task. In 'The Dispersal of the Books and Papers of John Stuart Mill', Hayek recounted how 'the greater part of Mill's books and papers' were disposed of after his death.[34] In March 1904, Mill's step-daughter Helen Taylor was still living at his Avignon cottage. Helen's niece, Mary (Algernon, or 'Haji', Taylor's daughter) was by then living with Helen, and she 'succeeded in rescuing the old and apparently somewhat senile lady from the clutches of designing French servants and to take her to England'. In February 1905 the Avignon household was liquidated: 'Half a ton of letters to be sorted, all manner of rubbish to be separated from useful things, books to be dusted and selected from, arrangements to be made for sale, and 18 boxes to be packed'.[35] Letters were then sold to an Avignon bookseller, while some of Mill's books and furniture were sold in autumn 1905 by Mary Taylor on behalf of Helen Taylor; the library was later offered to Somerville College, Oxford. After Helen Taylor's death in 1907, more of Mill's effects were disposed of in a sale at Torquay, and Mary Taylor soon afterwards placed the editing of the Mill letters in the hands of Hugh S. R. Elliot.[36] Two additional major sales followed the death of Mary Taylor: in 1922 and 1927, at Sotheby's, Mill's letters and pamphlets made their way to libraries in England, Scotland, and the United States, as well as the private collections of Harold Laski and John Maynard Keynes.[37]

Mill's early letters were published as part of the magnificent University of Toronto *Collected Works of John Stuart Mill* series.[38] Hayek's Introduction to *The*

---

[33] Hayek's letter to Robinson dated 2 October 1948 refers to these years as 'the more interesting part of [Mill's] life'. Royal Economic Society Minute Book, 1938–1955, RES/2/1/3, LSE Library's Collections.

[34] This volume, p. 293. See Hayek's 12 February 1944 letter to Jacob Viner in which Hayek allows that he is disgusted by the dispersal of Mill's letters and finds himself unable 'to speak my mind publicly about it'.

[35] 'The Dispersal of the Books and Papers of John Stuart Mill', this volume, p. 293.

[36] *Ibid.*, p. 294.

[37] *Ibid.*, p. 296. Correspondence from Hayek to Robinson dated 2 October 1948 reports that Hayek had by then located 'well over 400 letters': 'I have got together well over 400 letters by Mill belonging to the period, some of them very interesting and throwing much light on his development and the politics of the times. Of these only some thirty have been published by Elliot, about 200 have been published in some thirty other places, while the rest are unpublished'. Royal Economic Society Minute Book, 1938–1955, RES/2/1/3, LSE Library's Collections.

[38] *The Earlier Letters of John Stuart Mill, 1812–1848*, ed. Francis E. Mineka, vols. 12–13 (1963) of *The Collected Works of John Stuart Mill* [hereafter cited as *Collected Works*] (Toronto: University of Toronto Press, 1962–1991). The later letters were published as *The Later Letters of John Stuart Mill, 1849–1873*, eds. Francis E. Mineka and Dwight N. Lindley, vols. 14–17 (1972) of *Collected Works*.

Earlier Letters of John Stuart Mill, 1812–1848, reproduced below, rightly commended Francis E. Mineka for 'the solid hard work' in bringing the extraordinary collection to fruition.[39] He there criticized Helen Taylor for contributing to the difficulties associated with bringing the collection together, difficulties which the foregoing suggests were almost insurmountable and which Hayek himself greatly helped overcome: 'John Stuart Mill has not been altogether fortunate in the manner in which his memory was served by those most concerned and best authorized to honour it'.[40]

> There are few figures of comparable standing whose works have had to wait nearly a hundred years for a collected edition in English to be published. Nor, while his reputation was at its height, did any significant information become available that would have enabled another hand to round off the somewhat angular and fragmentary picture Mill had given of himself. He had been quite aware that his more public activities would be of interest to later generations and had begun to mark some of the copies of his letters which he had kept as suitable for publication. But Helen Taylor appears increasingly to have been more concerned to prevent others from encroaching upon her proprietary rights than to push on with her own plans for publication.[41]

In his 1951 Introduction to *John Stuart Mill and Harriet Taylor*, Hayek emphasized the difficulty of understanding Mill's relationship with his longtime friend, later his companion and still later wife, Harriet Taylor Mill. The book's two subtitles perhaps reflect the difficulty. It was published by Routledge and Kegan Paul in Britain under the title *John Stuart Mill and Harriet Taylor: Their Correspondence and Subsequent Marriage*. The University of Chicago Press publication of the same year retains the title on the spine and title page. The errata, however, contains an entry: 'On the title page instead of *Their Correspondence* read *Their Friendship*'. Erratum seems a misnomer: perhaps, in light of his decision to pass on the full correspondence for an additional publication, Hayek

---

[39] This volume, p. 331. There, Hayek refers to the 'pleasure of the hunt' being largely his own (*ibid.*). One cannot but be impressed by Hayek's persistence in the early going. Related correspondence between Piero Sraffa and J. M. Keynes suggests that for them, too, the pleasure of the hunt was tangible. More than this, it allowed Keynes, Sraffa, and Hayek to speak across their ideological divide. On 7 May 1943, Sraffa began a letter to Keynes: 'My dear Maynard, / This is the most sensational news there has ever been about Ricardo. *His letters to [James] Mill have been found!* And a MS by Ricardo in addition. / . . . I should add that this letter of Mill is in reply to one of Hayek in which he told him that I was editing Ricardo for the R.E.S. & was anxious to find these letters, and enquired on my behalf' (italics in original; brackets indicate editorial insertions). Folder no. 3, Hoover Institution Archives.

[40] This volume, p. 322.

[41] *Ibid.*

reconsidered, and changed, the original title.[42] By March 1951, when the work was advertised in the *Times Literary Supplement*, 'Friendship' was used in the subtitle.[43]

The difficulty of finding Mill's 'centre of gravity'[44] arose partly because Hayek had come to know Mill's temperament—as well as anyone might know another's—but it became clear to him that temperament was insufficient to fully explain or characterize Mill's intellectual positions. So, in the Introduction to the Mill-Taylor volume, Hayek wrote: 'Not by temperament but out of a deeply ingrained sense that this was his duty did Mill grow to be the 'Saint of Rationalism', as Gladstone once so justly described him'.[45] We are left with a Mill who wrote volumes, including an *Autobiography*, but who remained something of a puzzle through the mid-twentieth century and beyond. Indeed, Hayek recognized that the existence of the *Autobiography* itself proved singularly unhelpful:[46]

> There is thus perhaps no other instance where an autobiography had so much to tell us and where at the same time such a purely intellectual account of a man's development is so misleading. The *Autobiography* is as remarkable for what it leaves out as for what it discusses—what it leaves out not in any desire to suppress but because Mill thought it genuinely irrelevant. It is one of the most impersonal accounts of a mental development ever attempted, an account in which only the factors found a place that in Mill's view ought to have influenced it. Of what in the ordinary sense of the word we should call his life, of his human interests and personal relations, we learn practi-

[42] To emphasize that what Hayek finally produced is a work about the correspondents' friendship, the later title is used below. Additional warrant for doing so is provided by Hayek's own hand on a presentation copy given to Margit von Mises. There, Hayek stroked out the word 'correspondence' and inserted instead 'friendship' in the title.

[43] See *Times Literary Supplement* (London), 30 March 1951, issue 2565, p. 195. Interestingly, the advertisement refers to Hayek as the 'editor'.

[44] Samuel Hollander notes, 'There is some difficulty in getting a grip on Mill's centre of gravity'. Hollander, *The Economics of John Stuart Mill* (Oxford: Basil Blackwell, 1985), p. 638.

[45] This volume, p. 13.

[46] As noted above, Hayek used several drafts of Mill's *Autobiography*. Indeed, his exhaustive search also greatly clarified scholarship concerning the process by which the *Autobiography* was written and revised, with the early draft (the basis for Jacob Hollander's manuscript) being written after Mill's marriage to Harriet Taylor and before her death, and the more complete version, which became the basis for the Columbia 1924 edition, being revised after 1861. Levi, who notes his indebtedness to Hayek for collecting the relevant correspondence, convincingly argues that the revisions did not, however, substantially change what Mill wrote about his relationship with Harriet Taylor Mill. Levi, 'The Writing of Mill's *Autobiography*', *Ethics*, vol. 61, no. 4 (July 1951), pp. 284–96. For a close examination of Harriet Taylor Mill's influence on the *Autobiography*, see Jack Stillinger, 'Who Wrote J. S. Mill's *Autobiography*?', *Victorian Studies*, vol. 27, Autumn 1983, pp. 7–23.

cally nothing. Even the account of 'the most valuable friendship of his life' is scarcely an exception to this; the feeling of incongruity which this account of Mill's greatest experience conveys is not least due to its being represented as a purely intellectual experience. It would certainly be a mistake to believe that Mill really was like that, that what he regarded as deserving of a public record gives us a picture of the whole man.[47]

Hayek set out to clarify the character of that 'most valuable friendship' using Mill's words and those of Harriet Taylor Mill.[48] Two points require emphasis. First, as noted above and as the essays below attest, the task of locating the letters, let alone the additional requirement of organizing the words to tell a coherent story, was simply unprecedented. Second, Hayek's deliberate tactic of letting Mill and Harriet Taylor Mill speak almost exclusively in their own words, was an extraordinary—perhaps unique—choice at the time, one that puts Hayek at the forefront of literary criticism, a field in which he has yet to receive due recognition.[49]

As Bruce Caldwell rightly notes, Hayek was keenly aware of the difficulty of assigning 'influences' on Mill's thought, whether that of Harriet Taylor, Gustave d'Eichthal, the Saint-Simonians, Auguste Comte, or any other of the many sources of intellectual stimulus and debate for Mill.[50] Hayek of course chose from the correspondence to which he had access. Yet, remarkably, he was willing to let the correspondence, along with Mill's own assessments in the *Autobiography* and elsewhere, speak for itself. The account that emerges in what

[47] Hayek, Introduction to *John Stuart Mill and Harriet Taylor*, this volume, p. 13.

[48] Without wishing to push the argument too far, it is interesting to note the similarities between Hayek's life and Mill's. See Caldwell, *Hayek's Challenge* (Chicago: University of Chicago Press, 2004), p. 297; and Légé, 'Hayek's Readings of Mill', p. 207.

[49] One reviewer noted Hayek's 'restraint and absence of pedantry' in 'permit[ting the reader] to judge the rest'; see Noel Annan, 'Review of *John Stuart Mill and Harriet Taylor: Their Friendship and Subsequent Marriage*', *Economic Journal*, vol. 61, December 1951, pp. 872–74. Gwendolen Freeman remarked on Hayek's 'somewhat unfamiliar role of literary historian', *Times Literary Supplement* (London), 4 May 1951, issue 2570, p. 272. This is not to suggest that Hayek's voice is absent from the Mill-Taylor correspondence below. He situates and provides context for the letters, and he weighs in especially on Mill's claims as they relate to Taylor's influence on Mill, remarking that Taylor's 'influence on his thought and outlook, whatever her capacities may have been, were quite as great as Mill asserts' (Introduction to *John Stuart Mill and Harriet Taylor*, this volume, p. 14). The question of Taylor's influence on Mill has been long studied; see Alice S. Rossi, ed., *Essays on Sex Equality by John Stuart Mill and Harriet Taylor Mill* (Chicago: University of Chicago Press, 1961); Janet Seitz and Michèle Pujol, 'Harriet Taylor Mill', *American Economic Review*, vol. 90, March 2000, pp. 476–79; Evelyn Forget, 'John Stuart Mill, Harriet Taylor and French Social Theory', in *The Status of Women in Classical Economic Thought*, ed. Robert Dimand and Chris Nyland, pp. 285–307 (London: Routledge, 2003); and Légé, 'Hayek's Readings of Mill'.

[50] Caldwell, Introduction to *Studies on the Abuse and Decline of Reason*, vol. 13 of *The Collected Works of F. A. Hayek*, p. 25.

follows is consequently one largely of Mill's (and Taylor's and d'Eichthal's) own telling.[51]

Mill and Taylor

Sometime in the 1940's Hayek penned the previously unpublished essay 'J. S. Mill, Mrs. Taylor, and Socialism', reproduced below.[52] He begins the essay by remarking, 'How far it is always justified to pry into the intimate life of the great man of the past is a question on which opinions will probably differ'.[53] He continues to state that the question of Taylor's influence on Mill underscored his interest in the relationship.[54] Parts of the essay duplicate Hayek's 1942 essay 'John Stuart Mill at the Age of Twenty-Five'. Certainly its title suggests that Hayek's interest was primarily in Taylor's intellectual contributions to Mill's views on socialism; yet Hayek was also interested in how Taylor's influence carried over to key ideas of his own time: 'If what Mill himself has told us about Mrs. Taylor's gifts and the influence she exerted on him is anywhere near the objective truth, she would not only be one of the most remarkable women who ever lived but also have played a decisive part in shaping the opinions which govern our own time'.[55]

It also bears emphasis, however, that the full story in the Mill-Taylor volume tells an enduring tale of love and the deep cost that came with their rela-

---

[51] So, too, when Hayek comes to assess Comte's influence on Mill, he warns of this difficulty and then relies on Mill's own words as a summary judgment; see Hayek's essay 'Sociology: Comte and His Successors', in *Studies on the Abuse and Decline of Reason*, vol. 13 of *The Collected Works of F. A. Hayek*, pp. 277–78.

[52] The manuscript was discovered by Caldwell in the study of Hayek's son, Laurence Hayek, after Laurence's death, and has since been deposited in the Hayek papers at the Hoover Institution. See Caldwell, 'Hayek on Mill', p. 697. In the correspondence with Jacob Viner, dated 7 February 1948, reproduced below on p. 348, Hayek writes of presenting a paper concerning Mill and Taylor at a seminar in Princeton.

[53] This volume, p. 298. Robbins, too, was aware of this question; see 'Packe on Mill', p. 255: 'There can be no doubt that the discovery of their correspondence was one of the great literary finds of the century—a revelation of a story of enduring human interest. What Mill and Harriet would have said of its publication scarcely bears thinking of. But this is no condemnation of those who published it. Time wipes out the entitlement to privacy'.

[54] Here, as in *John Stuart Mill and Harriet Taylor*, Hayek focused on Taylor's influence as it relates to Mill's writings on socialism as well as *On Liberty*: 'Whatever she was, there is no reason to doubt that she had great influence on some of Mill's work, that she had closely collaborated with him in writing his famous, and in many ways his finest book, *On Liberty*, and that she is in some measure responsible for Mill's gradual movement towards socialism. For good or bad she has thus taken some part in the development of modern ideas'. 'J. S. Mill, Mrs. Taylor, and Socialism', this volume, p. 299.

[55] 'J. S. Mill, Mrs. Taylor, and Socialism', this volume, p. 298.

tionship.[56] Sometimes in the attempt to pin down influence, credit, and blame, the overwhelming power of the story becomes obscured. Despite his interest in the economic and social thought of Mill and Taylor, Hayek was apparently also deeply taken by the love story; certainly the collection here attests to how he deliberately conveyed the drama and heartbreak associated with the romance.[57]

Letters from Taylor to Mill, dated provisionally in the summer of 1833, bear witness to the emotional turmoil associated with the relationship, culminating in Harriet's declaration: 'I am glad that you have said it—I am *happy* that you have—no one with any fineness or beauty of character but must feel compelled to say *all*, to the being they really love, or rather with any *permanent* reservation it is not *love*—while there is reservation, however little of it, the love is just *so much* imperfect'.[58]

The relationship cost them dearly: friends and family alike followed convention and judged Mill and Taylor accordingly. Harriet predicted as much in the above letter: '*Yes*—these circumstances *do* require greater strength than any other—the greatest—that which you have, & which if you had not I should never have loved you, I should not love you now'.[59] Mill alludes to the cost in a letter to W. J. Fox from the same time: 'What ought to be so much easier to me than to her, is in reality more difficult—costs a harder struggle—to part company with the good opinion of the world, and with my former modes of doing good in it'.[60]

For the student of relationships, the Mill-Taylor story is one of great drama and much mystery. Hayek's collection does little to clear up with finality the mystery of whether the relationship was platonic or sexual before or even

---

[56] Though the situations differed, Hayek, too, bore a cost for his second marriage. See James Buchanan, 'Buchanan Workshop: Hayek, Part 2' (unpublished transcription, George Mason University, 6 April 2005).

[57] Levi comes to a similar conclusion upon his close reading of the *Autobiography*: 'Those who find [the *Autobiography*] a purely intellectual exercise are not sufficiently diligent in their quest. . . . The sections dealing with Mrs. Mill before and after their marriage exhibit an unmeasured love'. Levi, 'The Writing of Mill's *Autobiography*', p. 295.

[58] Harriet Taylor to John Stuart Mill, 6 September 1833, this volume, p. 49. Hayek quotes the same passage in 'J. S. Mill, Mrs. Taylor, and Socialism', this volume, p. 303.

[59] Harriet Taylor to John Stuart Mill, 6 September 1833, this volume, pp. 49–50.

[60] Mill to W. J. Fox, 7 September 1833, this volume, p. 51. Hayek provides evidence from the period before Mill knew Taylor that Mill was intensely susceptible to loneliness: 'By loneliness I mean the absence of that feeling which has accompanied me through the greater part of my life, that which one fellow traveler, or one fellow-soldier, has towards another—the feeling of being engaged in the pursuit of a common object, and of mutually cheering one another on, and helping one another in an arduous undertaking. This, which after all is one of the strongest ties of individual sympathy, is at present, so far as I am concerned, suspended at least, if not entirely broken off' (Mill to John Sterling, 15 April 1829, this volume, p. 34). Hayek attributes this in part to Mill's education; see this volume, p. 33.

after their marriage.[61] More recently, commentators continue to speculate. Mill's first modern biographer, Michael Packe, made the strong claim that Mill and Taylor 'never went to bed together' before they were married.[62] Jo Ellen Jacobs, Harriet's biographer and editor of her letters, argues that the couple lived in abstinence not because of social conventions but because Harriet was infected by her first husband with syphilis.[63] Mill biographers Nicholas Capaldi and Richard Reeves remain agnostic about the hypothesis as well as the nature of the relationship before and after the marriage.[64]

At first blush it seems the letters might speak for themselves on this matter. If, in private correspondence, Mill and Taylor wrote that they had abstained from sexual relations, then this would seem unequivocal. As Mill's biographer Reeves notes, however, and as Hayek himself confirmed (above, p. xxvii), Taylor and especially Mill were public figures sensitive to the possibility of a wider audience even for their private letters. Professions of abstinence then might be meant for this potential audience.[65] Reeves finds the stated rationale for abstinence in the *Autobiography*—avoidance of conduct that might 'bring discredit on her husband, or therefore on herself'—to be 'risible'.[66] It seems plausible nonetheless that this was a couple who wished to uphold *their own* standard of morality, a standard that was less about what gossip actually ensued as about moral conduct and desert. The distinction between blameworthiness and blame, from Adam Smith's 1759 *Theory of Moral Sentiments*, was well known to both Mill and Taylor.[67] Their conduct throughout the relationship

---

[61] Hayek was, however, convinced that the relationship was platonic; this volume, p. 305.

[62] Packe, *The Life of John Stuart Mill*, p. 317. Robbins, 'Packe on Mill', p. 253, criticizes Packe for systematic evidence-free reconstruction: 'Lytton Strachey may have done this sort of thing but Boswell did not. And, for serious biography, I submit, Boswell is the better model'.

[63] *The Complete Works of Harriet Taylor Mill*, ed. Jo Ellen Jacobs (Bloomington: Indiana University Press, 1998), pp. xxx–xxxii.

[64] Capaldi writes that 'not a scrap of evidence exists' that the relationship was sexual before marriage or platonic afterwards. Nicholas Capaldi, *John Stuart Mill: A Biography* (Cambridge: Cambridge University Press, 2004), p. 230. Reeves surveys the literature while recognizing the difficulty of making a definitive judgment on the matter. Richard Reeves, *John Stuart Mill: Victorian Firebrand* (London: Atlantic Books, 2007), pp. 149–55.

[65] Reeves, *John Stuart Mill*, p. 152: 'Given this sensitivity to the broader audience for whom they were often writing, it is necessary to take much of what they said on the issue of their relationship with at least a pinch of salt'.

[66] *Ibid.* The phrase 'bring discredit' is found in John Stuart Mill, *Autobiography and Literary Essays*, eds. John M. Robson and Jack Stillinger, vol. 1 (1981) of *Collected Works*, p. 236.

[67] The distinction appears in Part 3, chapter 2: 'Of the love of Praise, and of that of Praise-worthiness; and of the dread of Blame, and of that of Blame-worthiness'. Adam Smith, *Theory of Moral Sentiments* [1759], ed. D. D. Raphael and A. L. Macfie (Indianapolis: Liberty Fund, 1982), pp. 113–34. See Mill's comments on the passage on 'praiseworthiness' in John Stuart Mill, 'Notes', in James Mill, *Analysis of the Phenomena of the Human Mind* (London: Baldwin and Cradock, 1829; repr., with notes by J. S. Mill, Alexander Bain, George Grote, and Andrew Findlater, London: Longmans, Green, Reader, and Dyer, 1869), pp. 298–99: 'The idea of *deserving*

seems to have been governed by a covering law that as long as they did nothing to warrant blame, they could endure the harms the relationship brought to each secure in the knowledge that they had done nothing to deserve the maliciousness of their friends and acquaintances. So their actions seem to have been aimed at avoiding Smithian 'blameworthiness' as opposed to blame itself; if this is so, then abstinence is perhaps believable.

Certainly Hayek presents his readers with a stark story of real or perceived hurt and rejection. He collects together contemporary reactions in a full chapter of the Mill-Taylor book entitled 'Friends and Gossip (1834–1842)'. Here we learn, in John Roebuck's words, of the 'suppressed titter [that] went round the room' when Mill and Taylor arrived at a dinner party in 1835.[68] Mill's friendship with Roebuck was, Hayek tells us, the first casualty of the affair. Hayek provides evidence that the Carlyles were initially most amused by the relationship; even the destruction of Carlyle's *French Revolution* manuscript in 1835, though it tested their friendship, did not estrange them from Mill and Taylor.[69] Carlyle seems to have appreciated the toll on Mill associated with the arrangement between Mill and Taylor: 'They are innocent says Charity: they are guilty says Scandal: then why in the name of wonder are they dying broken-hearted?'[70] Two years later, Carlyle speculated—carelessly as Hayek informs us—about whether Harriet Taylor had come to a decision to live away from her husband while in town.[71] Relations between the Carlyles and Mill became superficial by the early 1840's and an open break between them occurred in 1846.[72] Hayek attributes the break to Carlyle's gossip, of which the above description is but one instance, about Harriet Taylor's estrangement from John Taylor.[73]

---

praise is but a more complex form of the association between our own or another person's acts or character, and the idea of praise. To deserve praise, is, in the great majority of the cases which occur in life, the principal mode of obtaining it; though the praise is seldom accurately proportioned to the desert. And the same may be said of blame. A powerful association is thus, if circumstances are favourable, generated between deserving praise and obtaining it'.

[68] This volume, p. 73.

[69] This volume, p. 78.

[70] Thomas Carlyle to John Sterling, 3 October 1836, this volume, p. 80.

[71] This volume, p. 81.

[72] This volume, p. 83.

[73] A second reason for the continued strain in the relationship between Carlyle and Mill was Carlyle's position regarding slavery and his call, in 1849, for the re-enslavement of former West Indian slaves. See Sandra J. Peart and David M. Levy, *The 'Vanity of the Philosopher': From Equality to Hierarchy in Post-Classical Economics* (Ann Arbor: University of Michigan Press, 2005); and [Thomas Carlyle], 'Occasional Discourse on the Negro Question', *Fraser's Magazine for Town and Country*, vol. 40, December 1849, pp. 670–79. For Mill's response, see [John Stuart Mill], 'The Negro Question', *Fraser's Magazine for Town and Country*, vol. 41, January 1850, pp. 25–31, reprinted in John Stuart Mill, *Essays on Equality, Law, and Education*, ed. John M. Robson, vol. 21 (1984) of *Collected Works*, pp. 85–95.

In the years that followed their isolation from friends and family, Mill and Taylor formed an intense friendship. And so it was that in the mid-1840's, they began to withdraw from their acquaintances: Sarah Austin, Harriet Martineau, Mrs. Grote, and Lady Ashburton.[74] Beginning in 1846 with regard to a newspaper article and then recurring frequently thereafter, Mill attributed his work as a 'joint production' with Taylor. Perhaps not surprisingly then, in Mill's list of his publications he described the *Political Economy* as 'a joint production with my wife'.[75] The *Autobiography* provides an account of the writing, focused on the incredibly short period during which the *Political Economy* was written:

> The *Political Economy* was far more rapidly executed than the *Logic*, or indeed than anything of importance which I had previously written. It was commenced in the autumn of 1845, and was ready for the press before the end of 1847. In this period of little more than two years there was an interval of six months during which the work was laid aside, while I was writing articles in the *Morning Chronicle* (which unexpectedly entered warmly into my purpose) urging the formation of peasant properties on the waste lands of Ireland. This was during the period of the Famine, the winter of 1846/7.[76]

Hayek concludes that 'we have practically no documentary evidence of the part which Mrs. Taylor took in the composition of the first edition of the work. What little light the existing papers throw on the period tend on the whole to confirm Mill's account'.[77]

When Mill first published the *Political Economy*, he included this dedication to Harriet Taylor on a limited number of copies: 'To Mrs. John Taylor as the most eminently qualified of all persons known to the author either to originate or to appreciate speculations on social improvement, this attempt to explain and diffuse ideas many of which were first learned from herself, is with the highest respect and regard dedicated'.[78] Not surprisingly, we learn below that Harriet Taylor's husband, John Taylor, was not pleased; when Harriet Taylor wrote to ask for his views on the matter, he protested that the dedication would 'revive recollections now forgotten' and 'create observations and talk that cannot but be extremely unpleasant to me'.[79] Upon John Taylor's death after a long illness through which Harriet Tay-

---

[74] This volume, p. 85.

[75] Ney MacMinn, J. R. Hainds, and James McNab McCrimmon, *Bibliography of the Published Writings of John Stuart Mill* (Evanston: Northwestern University, 1945), pp. 59 and 69. Stillinger, 'Who Wrote J. S. Mill's *Autobiography*?', p. 11, finds a total of twenty examples of the phrase 'joint production' in this bibliography and Mill's *Autobiography*.

[76] Mill, *Autobiography*, vol. 1 of *Collected Works*, p. 243.

[77] This volume, p. 116.

[78] This volume, p. 119.

[79] John Taylor to Harriet Taylor, 3 April 1848, this volume, p. 118.

lor nursed him, the question arose as to whether Mill should attend the funeral. Again, for Harriet Taylor the matter turned on propriety and the perception thereof: 'Then again the public in some degree & *his* public too have heared or are sure to hear (through Arthur if no other way) of the Dedication—of our intimacy. . . . Does not therefore *absence* seem much more noticeable than coming?'[80]

Fallout from the relationship continued; Mill's brother George Grote Mill broke off relations with them. Harriet Taylor wrote to him on 5 July 1851, 'I do not answer your letter because you deserve it—that you certainly do not—but because tho I am quite inexperienced in the best way of receiving or replying to an affront I think that in this as in all things, frankness and plain speaking are the best rule'.[81] Mill followed up a month later with 'I have long ceased to be surprised at any want of good sense or good manners in what proceeds from you'.[82] A 18 July 1851 letter from his sister Mary Elizabeth Colman conveys only a fraction of the tragedy that ensued: 'And now Good Bye. . . . If this should close all intercourse between us as I think possible it will be to me very painful, but at least the sting will be wanting of thinking that I have shrunk from the duty of honesty towards you'.[83]

So much for the emotional toll of the relationship. As noted above, Hayek's interest in the Mill-Taylor correspondence extended to his interest in assessing Taylor's intellectual influence on Mill. Like many others, Hayek attributes Mill's wavering on socialism to the romantic entanglement with Taylor:[84] 'Despite the great harm done by his work, we must probably forgive Mill much for his infatuation with the lady who later became his wife—upon whose death, in his opinion, "this country lost the greatest mind it contained" and who, according to his testimony, "in the nobleness of her public object . . . never stopped short of perfect distributive justice as the final aim, implying therefore a state of society entirely communist in practice and spirit."'[85]

---

[80] Taylor to Mill, 19 July 1849, this volume, p. 160. Taylor continued: 'My first impulse was against—my present is *for*—but the reasons are so nearly balanced than an opinion of yours would turn the scale' (this volume, p. 161). It is not known whether Mill attended the funeral; *ibid.*

[81] This volume, p. 172.

[82] 4 August 1851, this volume, p. 173.

[83] This volume, p. 171. The full letter is extraordinarily candid.

[84] Ludwig von Mises in 1927 blamed Taylor for influencing Mill, who then purportedly merged socialism and liberalism itself. Mises, *Liberalism in the Classical Tradition*, 3rd ed., trans. Ralph Raico (Irvington-on-Hudson,NY: Foundation for Economic Education, [1927] 1985): 'John Stuart Mill is an epigone of classical liberalism, and, especially in his later years, under the influence of his wife, full of feeble compromises. He slips slowly into socialism and is the originator of the thoughtless confounding of liberal and socialist ideas that led to the decline of English liberalism and to the undermining of the living standards of the English people'.

[85] *The Fatal Conceit: The Errors of Socialism*, ed. W. W. Bartley III, vol. 1 (1988) of *The Collected Works of F. A. Hayek*, p. 149. Packe's judgment is harsh, referring to 'Harriet's astounding, almost hypnotic control of Mill's mind', *The Life of John Stuart Mill*, p. 317.

Hayek also attributes Mill's interest in the subjects of marriage and divorce and the broader topic of women's rights at least partly to the difficult situation in which Taylor and Mill found themselves over the years. Here again, Hayek allowed Mill to speak for himself. Mill's early manuscript on the subject—reprinted in full as chapter three of *John Stuart Mill and Harriet Taylor*—confirms on the whole the case made in the *Autobiography* that it was 'so far from being the fact' that his views on the equality of the sexes were in any way influenced by Harriet Taylor.[86] On the contrary, Mill's conclusion, reproduced below, was that his own views on the subject attracted Harriet to him: 'Those convictions were among the earliest results of the application of my mind to political subjects, and the strength with which I held them was, as I believe, more than anything else, the originating cause of the interest she felt in me'.[87] More than thirty years before the publication of *The Subjection of Women* Mill urged that women must be educated in order to become fully independent:

> It is not law, but education and custom which make the difference [between men and women]. Women are so brought up, as not to be able to subsist in the mere physical sense, without a man to keep them: they are so brought up as not to be able to protect themselves against injury or insult, without some man on whom they have a special claim, to protect them: they are so brought up, as to have no vocation or useful office to fulfil in the world, remaining single; for all women who are educated for anything except to *get* married, are educated to *be* married, and and what little they are taught deserving the name useful, is chiefly what in the ordinary course of things will not come into actual use, unless nor until they are married.[88]

'All this' Mill attributed to the current state of marriage laws, which were themselves determined by a yet larger question: 'what woman ought to be'.[89] Mill's Radical egalitarianism prevailed: 'If nature has not made men and women unequal, still less ought the law to make them so'.[90]

In the Mill-Taylor book Hayek also included Harriet Taylor's essay of about the same time in which she suggested that nineteenth-century social arrangements served to keep women uneducated: 'In the present system of

---

[86] Mill, *Autobiography*, vol. 1 of *Collected Works*, p. 253; this volume p. 57. His views were nonetheless in line with those of Harriet Taylor who in 1848 wrote that the 'women question' was more significant than that of the labouring classes as it 'goes deeper into the mental and moral characteristics of the race than the other & it is *the race* for which I am interested' (Harriet Taylor to W. J. Fox, 12 May 1848, this volume p. 120).

[87] Mill, *Autobiography*, vol. 1 of *Collected Works*, p. 253; this volume p. 57.

[88] This volume, pp. 61–62.

[89] This volume p. 62.

[90] *Ibid.*

habits & opinions, girls enter into what is called a contract perfectly ignorant of the conditions of it, and that they should be so is considered absolutely essential to their fitness for it!'[91] Almost twenty years later, two letters from Mill to Taylor discussed events in America—the Convention on Women in Ohio—with great hope: 'I really do now think that we have a good chance of living to see something decisive really accomplished on that of all practical subjects the most important'.[92] Out of these conversations emerged the 'Emancipation of Women', published in the *Westminster Review* in 1851.

In 1851, too, Mill formally pledged not to use the rights, to which he and Taylor so strenuously objected, associated with marriage: 'I, having no means of legally divesting myself of these odious powers (as I most assuredly would do if an engagement to that effect could be made legally binding on me), feel it my duty to put on record a formal protest against the existing law of marriage, in so far as conferring such powers; and a solemn promise never in any case or under any circumstances to use them'.[93] All in all, the evidence Hayek brings to light below on the 'women question' suggests strongly that their views were congruent early on and throughout their lives, as opposed to Taylor moving Mill towards an interest in or sympathy for women.

Mill and d'Eichthal

The second characteristic of Mill's life and work that stands out over the years is his shifting relationship with French socialist thought. Both Hayek's book *John Stuart Mill and Harriet Taylor* and essay 'John Stuart Mill at the Age of Twenty-Five' demonstrate that Hayek was also intrigued by the ebb and flow of this influence on Mill. Mill's relationship with the French socialists, most notably Gustave d'Eichthal, predated that with Harriet Taylor. Hayek correctly notes that Mill's acquaintance and then friendship with d'Eichthal had 'a much greater influence on Mill than the single reference to him in the *Autobiography* would suggest'.[94]

On 30 May 1828, the French publicist Gustave d'Eichthal (1804–1880), then still an enthusiastic supporter of Auguste Comte, attended a meeting of the London Debating Society. On that occasion Mill impressed d'Eichthal. In 'John Stuart Mill at the Age of Twenty-Five', Hayek described how the acquaintance rapidly grew into a friendship. Thus began the correspondence which for Hayek represented an 'important, though little-known' source of

[91] This volume, pp. 71–72.
[92] Mill to Taylor, October/November 1850, this volume, p. 163.
[93] Mill to Taylor, 6 March 1851, this volume, p. 165.
[94] Hayek, 'John Stuart Mill at the Age of Twenty-Five', this volume, p. 278. Mill mentions d'Eichthal in the *Autobiography* (Mill, *Autobiography*, vol. 1 of *Collected Works*, p. 173).

information about Mill's views on socialism.[95] D'Eichthal soon joined the Saint-Simonian group (from which Comte had separated) and became one of its most ardent and active apostles. From that point on, he 'spared no pains to convert his young English friends to the new creed'.[96]

Mill eventually voiced a thorough criticism of Comte's theoretical and political views in which he relied on the lesson learned from Macaulay about the dangers associated with using deductive reasoning in politics.[97] As Hayek notes with interest, in an early reaction addressed to d'Eichthal Mill recognized one of the most vulnerable spots in Comte's political doctrines: supposing the government were to direct 'all the forces of society' towards 'some one end', how is society or the government to settle on one single end for all:[98]

> The very first and fundamental principle of the whole system, that government and the social union exist for the purpose of concentrating and directing all the forces of society to some one end. He cannot mean that government should exist for more than one purpose, or that this one purpose should be the direction of the united force of society to more than one end. What a foundation for a system of political science this is! Government exists

[95] Hayek, 'John Stuart Mill at the Age of Twenty-Five', this volume, p. 280.

[96] *Ibid.* For Hayek's assessment of the reception of Saint-Simonian ideas in England in the 1820's and 1830's, in particular with respect to Carlyle and Mill, see 'Saint-Simonian Influence', in *Studies on the Abuse and Decline of Reason*, vol. 13 of *The Collected Works of F. A. Hayek*, pp. 235–55. Caldwell reports (p. 222, note 15) that upon reading Carlyle's *Signs of the Times* (1829), d'Eichthal sent Carlyle a copy of Saint-Simon's *Le nouveau Christianisme* and issues of the Saint-Simonian periodical, *L'Organisateur*.

[97] Hayek, 'John Stuart Mill at the Age of Twenty-Five', this volume, p. 281. See [Thomas Babington Macaulay], 'Mill's *Essay on Government*: Utilitarian Logic and Politics', *Edinburgh Review*, vol. 49, March 1829, pp. 159–80; 'Bentham's Defence of Mill: Utilitarian System of Philosophy', *Edinburgh Review*, vol. 49, June 1829, pp. 273–99; and 'Utilitarian Theory of Government, and the "Greatest Happiness Principle"', *Edinburgh Review*, vol. 50, Oct. 1829, pp. 99–125. All three articles are reprinted in James Mill and Thomas Babington Macaulay, *Utilitarian Logic and Politics: James Mill's 'Essay on Government', Macaulay's Critique, and the Ensuing Debate*, ed. Jack Lively and John Rees (Oxford: Clarendon Press, 1978), pp. 77–178.

[98] This is Hayek's concern in *The Road to Serfdom*, vol. 2 of *The Collected Works of F. A. Hayek*, p. 162: 'It is entirely in the spirit of collectivism when Nietzsche makes his Zarathustra say: "A thousand goals have existed hitherto, for a thousand people existed. But the fetter for the thousand necks is still lacking, the one goal is still lacking. Humanity has no goal yet. But tell me, I pray, my brethren: if the goal be lacking to humanity, is not humanity itself lacking?"' In 'Socialist Calculation: The Competitive "Solution"', *Economica*, n.s., vol. 7, May 1940, pp. 125–49, republished in *Socialism and War: Essays, Documents, Reviews*, ed. Bruce Caldwell, vol. 10 (2007) of *The Collected Works of F. A. Hayek*, pp. 117–40, Hayek traced the twentieth-century search for a planning goal to Saint-Simon: 'In a planned system all economic questions become political questions, because it is no longer a question of reconciling as far as possible individual views and desires, but one of imposing a single scale of values, the "social goal" of which socialists ever since the time of Saint-Simon have been dreaming' (p. 138).

for all purposes whatever that are for man's good: and the highest and most important of these purposes is, the improvement of man himself, as a moral arid intelligent being, which is an end not included in M. Comte's category at all. The united forces of society never were, nor can be directed to one single end, nor is there, so far as I can perceive, any reason for desiring that they should. Men do not come into the world to fulfill one single end, and there is no single end which if fulfilled even in the most complete manner would make them happy.[99]

As noted above, d'Eichthal continued to try to answer all criticism, informing Mill about Saint-Simonian views as well as the organization of the Saint-Simonians.[100] Yet, whatever affection Mill felt towards d'Eichthal or attraction towards the Saint-Simonian program, we learn from Hayek that Mill stopped short of endorsing Saint-Simonianism wholesale or recommending Saint-Simonian arrangements as a policy prescription. He did so on the grounds that such sectarianism was incompatible with individual liberty. In 1830, he conceded that being completely 'cured of those *habitudes critiques*, which, you seem to suppose, are the only obstacle to my adopting the entire doctrine of your school', a debt owed 'partly, though not entirely, to the St Simonian school. I had much changed from what I was before I read any of their publications; but it was their works which gave order and system to the ideas which I had already imbibed from intercourse with others, and derived from my own reflexions'.[101] Always scrupulously fair, Mill now retracted some of 'the objections I formerly urged against the St. Simonian school, as some of the points which I objected to, appeared from a perusal of the *Producteur* (every word of which I have read with as great a care and interest as any book I ever saw) never to have been held by them in the sense in which I thought them objectionable, & as you informed me in answer to my two letters the other points had been given up'.[102]

Notwithstanding this concession, it seemed to Mill that widespread adoption of Saint-Simonian recommendations required a people who generally were different than those who currently lived and worked in nineteenth-century England. His continued refusal to collaborate with Saint-Simonians was now based largely on the rationale that it appeared 'utterly hopeless and

---

[99] Mill to d'Eichthal, 8 October 1829, in Mill, *Earlier Letters*, vol. 12 of *Collected Works*, p. 36.

[100] D'Eichthal to Mill, 23 November and 1 December 1829, *Lettres inédites de John Stuart Mill à Auguste Comte*, ed. L. Levy-Bruhl (Paris: F. Alcon, 1899), pp. 59–89.

[101] Hayek, 'John Stuart Mill at the Age of Twenty-Five', this volume, p. 282; the full letter from Mill to d'Eichthal dated 9 February 1830 is reproduced in Mill, *Earlier Letters*, vol. 12 of *Collected Works*, pp. 44–49.

[102] Hayek, 'John Stuart Mill at the Age of Twenty-Five', this volume, p. 282. In this essay, Hayek transposed 'them' as 'him'.

chimerical to suppose that the regeneration of mankind can ever be wrought by means of working on their opinions'.[103] This was particularly true in England, where 'Englishmen habitually distrust the most obvious truths, if the person who advances them is suspected of having any general views'.[104] Until a generalized change in character occurred, Saint-Simonian ideas might be adopted on a small scale, experimentally, and spread voluntarily by example. By no means were they to be imposed from without, by an agency that had somehow divined the common good.[105]

Hayek's view, expressed in the 1942 essay 'John Stuart Mill at the Age of Twenty-Five', is that while Mill's 1834 review of *St. Simonism in London* for the *Examiner* was infused with Saint-Simonian language pertaining to 'natural' and 'transitional' states of society, he here never went as far as to endorse the details of the Saint-Simonian argument as they pertained to property, inheritance, or other socialist measures of reform.[106] Whatever shifting emphases we see in Hayek's work on Mill, he maintained this position throughout his later (1951) commentary on Mill and d'Eichthal in the *John Stuart Mill and Harriet Taylor*.

Mill's Political Economy: *Property and Socialism*

Whatever influence Taylor and d'Eichthal exercised on Mill was wrapped up in Mill's shifting position on property enumerated in the chapters at the start of Book 2 of his *Political Economy*. There Mill famously distinguished between the laws of production ('physical truths') and of distribution ('a matter of human institution solely').[107] Laws of distribution might be altered by

---

[103] *Ibid.*

[104] *Ibid.* The full letter from Mill to d'Eichthal appears in *Cosmopolis*, vol. 6, 9 February 1830, pp. 350–53, and is reprinted in Mill, *Earlier Letters*, vol. 12 of *Collected Works*, pp. 45–48. Mill concludes, 'You imagine that you can accomplish the perfection of mankind by teaching them St Simonism, whereas it appears to me that their adoption of St Simonism, if that doctrine be true, will be the natural result and effect of a high state of moral and intellectual culture previously received' (p. 48).

[105] See Mill's review of *St. Simonism in London* in the *Examiner*, 2 February 1834, pp. 68–69. There Mill argued that, at least as it related to the 'community of women', Saint-Simonism had evolved into despotism: 'Theirs was a system much nearer to despotism than to licentiousness, or even rational liberty'. The review is reprinted in John Stuart Mill, *Newspaper Writings*, eds. Ann P. Robson and John M. Robson, vols. 22–25 (1986) of *Collected Works*, 23:674–80. It is of interest also for its discussion of marriage and divorce especially as Mill and Taylor had just spent time in Paris (see below, p. 283).

[106] Hayek, 'John Stuart Mill at the Age of Twenty-Five', this volume, p. 287. See also note 104 above.

[107] John Stuart Mill, *The Principles of Political Economy with Some of Their Application to Social Philosophy*, ed. John M. Robson, vols. 2–3 (1965) of *Collected Works*, 2:199. Here is Hayek's judgment

'consent of society': 'any disposal whatever of them can only take place by the consent of society, or rather of those who dispose of its active force. . . . The distribution of wealth, therefore, depends on the laws and customs of society. The rules by which it is determined, are what the opinions and feelings of the ruling portion of the community make them, and are very different in different ages and countries'.[108] Beginning in the mid-twentieth century, this now-famous distinction generated considerable interest and much criticism.[109] Hayek concluded that Mill thereby denied any relationship between production and distribution, the 'size of the product' being 'independent of its distribution'.[110]

Notwithstanding Hayek's conclusion, it bears noting that Mill insisted such changes will have consequences on the amount to be distributed: 'Human beings can control their own acts, but not the consequences of their acts either to themselves or to others. Society can subject the distribution of wealth to whatever rules it thinks best: but what practical results will flow from the operation of those rules, must be discovered, like any other physical or mental truths, by observation and reasoning'.[111] He was, as Samuel Hollander has demonstrated at length, much preoccupied with the resulting potential impact on production of various institutional arrangements for land tenure, inheritance, and poor relief.[112]

The first edition (of 1,000 copies) of the *Political Economy* sold out in less

---

in *The Fatal Conceit*: 'It is probably John Stuart Mill as much as anyone who is responsible for spreading' this 'error'. Mill 'overlooks the dependence of size on the *use* made of existing opportunities'. *The Fatal Conceit*, vol. 1 of *The Collected Works of F. A. Hayek*, pp. 92–93.

[108] Mill, *Political Economy*, vol. 2 of *Collected Works*, p. 220.

[109] The technical point relating to the purported independence of production and distribution was largely unnoticed before the Cambridge controversies directed scrutiny towards Ricardo's (and Mill's) economics. See Piero Sraffa, *Production of Commodities by Means of Commodities* (Cambridge: Cambridge University Press, 1960); and Pedro Schwartz, *The New Political Economy of J. S. Mill* (London: Weidenfeld and Nicolson, 1972). For Sidney Webb, Mill's separation of production and distribution marked the beginning of a new sort of economic analysis: 'The publication of John Stuart Mill's "Political Economy" in 1848 marks conveniently the boundary of the old individualist economics. Every edition of Mill's book became more and more socialistic'. Sidney Webb, 'Historic', in *Fabian Essays in Socialism*, ed. George Bernard Shaw (London: Fabian Society, 1889; repr., Garden City, NY: Doubleday, 1961), p. 80.

[110] *The Fatal Conceit*, vol. 1 of *The Collected Works of F. A. Hayek*, p. 93.

[111] Mill, *Political Economy*, vol. 2 of *Collected Works*, p. 200. For a review of the literature on what, precisely, Mill meant by his famous distinction, see Hollander, *The Economics of John Stuart Mill*. On one side of this are those who, like Hayek and others before and after Hayek, take Mill to mean that there are 'no productive consequences to a change in distribution'. Ludwig von Mises, *Socialism: An Economic and Sociological Analysis*, trans. Jacques Kahane from the 1922 German ed.(London: Jonathan Cape, 1936; repr., Indianapolis, IN: Liberty Classics, 1981), p. 155. On the other side are those who, like Hollander and more recently Farrant ('A Renovated Social Fabric', pp. 82–84), argue that Mill connected distribution and aggregate output.

[112] Hollander, *The Economics of John Stuart Mill*, pp. 218–19.

than a year, and Mill urgently wished to prepare a second and revised edition. The main discussion of institutional arrangements associated with socialism was contained in the chapter 'On Property' at the beginning of Book 2. In the edition that followed, Mill revised this chapter more than any other. As Mill explained in the *Autobiography*, the revolution of 1848 had made the public more willing to consider new social arrangements, and he and Harriet Taylor had consequently acquired a renewed interest in French socialism: 'In the first edition the difficulties of Socialism were stated so strongly, that the tone was on the whole that of opposition to it. In the year or two which followed, much time was given to the study of the best Socialistic writers on the Continent, and to meditation and discussion on the whole range of topics involved in the controversy: and the result was that most of what had been written on the subject in the first edition was cancelled, and replaced by arguments and reflexions which represent a more advanced opinion'.[113]

Hayek provides an account of these revisions in the Mill-Taylor volume. He tells the reader that the first installment of the revised proofs, containing major revisions to the chapter on socialism, was sent to Harriet Taylor in February 1849. Through Hayek's lens we see Mill struggling to answer Taylor's objections to his reflections on whether socialism can succeed given his own perception of the relative fixity of human nature:

> *J. S. M. to H. T.:* 15 / Monday / 19 Febr. [1849] / I received your dear letter 11[114] on Saturday & this morning the first instalment of Pol. Ec. This last I will send again (or as much of it as is necessary) when I have been able to make up my mind about it. The objections are I think very inconsiderable as to quantity—much less than I expected. . . . In the new matter one of the sentences you have cancelled is a favourite of mine, viz 'It is probable that this will finally depend upon considerations not to be measured by the coarse standard which in the present state of human improvement is the only one that can be applied to it.' What I meant was that whether individual agency or Socialism would be best ultimately—(*both* being necessarily very imperfect now, & *both* susceptible of immense improvement) will depend on the comparative attractions they will hold out to human beings with all their capaci-

---

[113] Mill, *Autobiography*, vol. 1 of *Collected Works*, p. 241. Cf. also the paragraph added to the Preface of the second edition of the *Political Economy*: 'The additions and alterations in the present edition are generally of little moment; but the increased importance which the Socialist controversy has assumed since this work was written, has made it desirable to enlarge the chapter which treats of it; the more so, as the objections therein stated to the specific schemes propounded by some Socialists, have been erroneously understood as a general condemnation of all that is commonly included under that name. A full appreciation of Socialism, and of the questions which it raises, can only be advantageously attempted in a separate work'. Mill, *Political Economy*, vol. 2 of *Collected Works*, p. xcii.

[114] Mill and Taylor numbered their letters.

ties, both individual & social, infinitely more developed than at present. I do not think it is English improvement only that is too backward to enable this point to be ascertained for if English character is starved in its social part I think Continental is as much or even more so in its individual, & Continental people incapable of entering into the feelings which make very close contacts with crowds of other people both disagreeable & mentally & morally lowering.[115]

Two days later Mill wrote to Taylor that should she find 'the objections as now stated to Communism' were not valid in the revision, he 'certainly' would 'not print it'.[116]

Mill now closely examined the different distributional systems proposed by the Saint-Simonians and Charles Fourier. In his view, the current state of human nature and the consequent improbability of limiting population growth presented a key stumbling block to socialist schemes. In a market economy, where the cost of children was borne by parents, the material inducements to limiting numbers were strong. Under communism and the social arrangements advocated by Charles Fourier and the Saint-Simonians, the material inducements were much weakened. Mill concluded that for a system without property to succeed the labouring classes would need to become sufficiently willing to limit their numbers absent the material incentive to do so.[117] Mill worried that Fourier and his followers had ignored these issues and had relied 'wholly on such an arrangement of social circumstances as without any inculcation of duty or of "ought", will make every one, by the spontaneous action of the passions, intensely zealous for all the interests of the whole'.[118] He was under no illusion as to the difficulty of the task, writing to Harriet Taylor, 'To make people really good for much it is so necessary not merely to give them good intentions & conscientiousness but to unseal their eyes—to prevent self flattery, vanity, irritability & all that family of vices

---

[115] This volume, pp. 132–34.

[116] This volume, p. 135.

[117] Mill acknowledged that in a system in which public opinion were more powerful socialistic schemes might serve to induce the poor to limit their numbers; see Mill, *Political Economy*, vol. 2 of *Collected Works*, p. 206. Ludwig von Mises, *Socialism*, p. 157, denied Mill's hypothesis that human nature might alter and claimed instead that motivation would be the same under both settings: 'It is not impossible that under Socialism the public spirit will be so general that disinterested devotion to the common welfare will take the place of self seeking. Here Mill lapses into the dreams of the Utopians and conceives it possible that public opinion will be powerful enough to incite the individual to increased zeal for labour, that ambition and self-conceit will be effective motives, and so on. It need only be said that unfortunately we have no reason to assume that human nature will be any different under Socialism from what it is now'.

[118] Mill to Taylor, 31 March 1849, this volume, p. 148.

from warping their moral judgments as those of the very cleverest people are almost always warped now'.[119]

Human nature being what it was, Mill foresaw difficulties under socialism. Without some sort of additional restraint on population (such as disgrace associated with having children that one could not support), he foresaw that the pressure of population growth would be more severe under socialism than under a system of private property.[120] Mill concluded in favour of small scale and voluntary experimentation—schemes, he writes, that are 'capable of being tried on a moderate scale': 'It is for experience to determine how far or how soon any one or more of the possible systems of community of property will be fitted to substitute itself for the "organization of industry" based on private ownership of land and capital. In the meantime we may, without attempting to limit the ultimate capabilities of human nature, affirm, that the political economist, for a considerable time to come, will be chiefly concerned with the conditions of existence and progress belonging to a society founded on private property and individual competition'.[121]

As for a system in which property pertained, Mill called for improvements to the existing system of private property (by, for instance, restricting the amount one might inherit) alongside individual agency.[122] He was 'not charmed' (as he put it in his famous chapter on the stationary state) by the outcomes of unbridled competition: 'I confess I am not charmed with the ideal of life held out by those who think that the normal state of human beings is that of struggling to get on; that the trampling, crushing, elbowing, and treading on each other's

---

[119] Mill to Taylor, 21 March 1849, this volume, p. 145. Peart and Levy, *'Vanity of the Philosopher'*, p. xiii, argue that much of Mill's analytical machinery was developed to address 'the problem of self-motivated human development in the context of institutional change'. Mill wrote that the future well-being of the labouring classes depended on the 'degree in which they can be made rational beings' (Mill, *Political Economy*, vol. 3 of *Collected Works*, p. 763).

[120] This, too, Mill moderated in view of Taylor's comments: 'The alteration I have made in that sentence of the P.E. was instead of "placard their intemperance" to say "placard their enormous families"'. Mill to Taylor, 31 March 1849, this volume, p. 147. Mill warned in the *Political Economy* against reforms that failed to address self-restraint with the predicted result of 'a more numerous, but not a happier people'. Mill, *Political Economy*, vol. 2 of *Collected Works*, p. 159; cf. pp. 341–61.

[121] Mill, *Political Economy*, vol. 2 of *Collected Works*, pp. 213–214.

[122] For Mill on inheritance laws, including his argument that inheritance could properly be taxed, see Mill, *Political Economy*, vol. 2 of *Collected Works*, pp. 220–26. Mill's 1861 *Utilitarianism* later made clear the presupposition that 'one person's happiness . . . is counted for exactly as much as another's'. J. S. Mill, *Utilitarianism*, *Fraser's Magazine*, October–December 1861; reprinted in John Stuart Mill, *Essays on Ethics, Religion, and Society*, ed. John M. Robson, vol. 10 (1985) of *Collected Works*, p. 257. See Hollander's assessment in *The Economics of John Stuart Mill*: Mill's 'overriding concern was social justice—which can be interpreted, as Mill came to interpret it, as the highest category of utility—and by which he understood respect for individuality to be satisfied by equality of opportunity' (p. 826).

heels, which form the existing type of social life, are the most desirable lot of human kind, or anything but the disagreeable symptoms of one of the phases of industrial progress'.[123] Yet, significantly, no general policy stance followed upon that observation.

All in all, Mill foresaw a 'better distribution of property' would follow upon a combination of altered choices by individuals coupled with a change in inheritance laws consistent with claims to the fruits of one's labour. As such, he favoured a modified form of capitalism over socialism, modifications that would lead to a 'better distribution of property': 'On the other hand, we may suppose this better distribution of property attained, by the joint effect of the prudence and frugality of individuals, and of a system of legislation favouring equality of fortunes, so far as is consistent with the just claim of the individual to the fruits, whether great or small, of his or her own industry'.[124] Comparing 'individual agency in its best form' and 'Socialism in its best form' Mill held that the conclusion would 'depend mainly on one consideration', 'which of the two systems is consistent with the greatest amount of human liberty and spontaneity'.[125]

The Saint of Rationalism

Hayek was sharply critical of Mill's position on institutional change for two reasons. The first was part of his longstanding methodological position that institutions evolve best without direction by ill-informed (or partially-informed) human designers.[126] Here, rather than directing his disapproval at any specific institutional reform, Hayek criticized institution-making (or institutional reform) as a policy or methodological stance.[127] He did so on now-famous Austrian methodological grounds, that no one centrally-located policy maker possessed the requisite information to design the con-

[123] Mill, *Political Economy*, vol. 3 of *Collected Works*, p. 754.

[124] *Ibid.*, p. 755.

[125] Mill, *Political Economy*, vol. 2 of *Collected Works* p. 208.

[126] In the context of policy analysis this is the analogue to Hayek's 1945 argument about the price system; see 'The Use of Knowledge in Society', *American Economic Review*, vol. 35, September 1945, pp. 519–30, repr, in Hayek, *Individualism and Economic Order*, pp. 77–91.

[127] For a recent treatment that compares Mill, Hayek, and James Buchanan, see Sandra J. Peart and David M. Levy, 'Discussion, Construction and Evolution: Mill, Buchanan and Hayek on the Constitutional Order', *Constitutional Political Economy*, vol. 19, March 2008, pp. 3–18. Peart and Levy argue that Mill is closer to Buchanan in this regard than Hayek. For the case that Frank Knight falls on the Mill-Buchanan side of this spectrum, see Ross Emmett, 'Discussion and Evolution of Institutions in a Liberal Democracy: Frank Knight Joins the Debate', in Farrant, *Hayek, Mill, and the Liberal Tradition*, pp. 57–77.

stitutional order; and he linked Mill's 'rationalistic individualism' to 'socialism or collectivism'.[128]

Hayek famously distinguished between 'law' and 'legislation', and he argued that the constitutional order, 'law', is best left unarticulated and evolving, outside the realm of planning or human design. Though Mill ultimately advocated for an improved form of capitalism he was, by contrast, willing to examine the outcomes of various institutions, including socialism. Rather than ruling out institutional reforms on methodological grounds, Mill's policy stance was a matter of his considered view on which set of institutional arrangements would yield the best set of outcomes. Importantly, he came to these considered views after a careful examination of the evidence; in his view local variation and experimentation were the means by which specific institutional arrangements would come to flourish and, if successful, spread by example.

Hayek, perhaps somewhat harshly, placed Mill in a long line of rationalist thinkers, 'false individualists' as he put it in the 1945 lecture 'Individualism: True and False'. There, Hayek made the case that 'true' individualism traced its roots from Adam Smith to David Hume, Edmund Burke, Alexis de Tocqueville, and Lord Acton, in contrast with the Continental rationalists, in whose ranks he included J. S. Mill. True individualists trace 'the combined effects of individual actions' in order to 'discover that many of the institutions on which human achievements rest have arisen and are functioning without a designing and directing mind'.[129] By contrast, the rationalists held that 'social processes can be made to serve human ends only if they are subjected to the control of individual human reason'.[130] Here, rules and institutions are designed by rational human action, a methodology that 'always tends to develop into the opposite of individualism, namely, socialism or collectivism'.[131]

---

[128] F. A. Hayek, 'Individualism: True and False', p. 4.

[129] *Ibid.*, p. 7. See Caldwell's assessment in Caldwell, Introduction to *Studies on the Abuse and Decline of Reason*, vol. 13 of *The Collected Works of F. A. Hayek*, pp. 1–45: 'The distinction between the hubris of the scientistic approach and the humility of individualism would be a major theme of Hayek's "Individualism: True and False", and would reappear in later writings as the contrast between constructivist rationalism and the evolutionary way of thinking' (p. 13).

[130] Hayek, 'Individualism: True and False', p. 10.

[131] *Ibid.*, p 4. There was in Hayek's view yet another problem with such rationalism—its narrow conception of economic man: 'It would be only a slight exaggeration to say that, in the view of those British philosophers, man was by nature lazy and indolent, improvident and wasteful, and that it was only by force of circumstances that he could be made to behave economically or would learn carefully to adjust his means to an end. The *homo oeconomicus* was explicitly introduced, with much else that belongs to the rationalist rather than the evolutionary tradition, only by the younger Mill'. *The Constitution of Liberty: The Definitive Edition*, ed. Ronald Hamowy, vol. 17 (2011) of *The Collected Works of F. A. Hayek*, p. 121. Leonidas Montes, 'Is Friedrich Hayek Rowing Adam Smith's Boat?', in Farrant, *Hayek, Mill, and the Liberal Tradition*, p. 19, argues that Hayek

How did the Mill-Taylor correspondence fit into this perspective? The foregoing has revealed that Hayek had developed an interest in seeing whether and how Mill's connections with the French so-called utopian socialists influenced Mill's economic thought. But secondly, Hayek attempted to sort out how it was that, steeped in the empiricist tradition, Mill came to be a rationalist. Significantly, the collection below suggests that Hayek came to believe that it was Taylor, more than Mill, who was the rationalist at heart.[132] Hayek came to this conclusion notwithstanding Mill's own claim in the *Autobiography* to the opposite effect: 'What was abstract and purely scientific [in the *Political Economy*] was generally mine; the properly human element came from her'.[133]

So, for Hayek, Harriet Taylor Mill moved John Stuart Mill in precisely the wrong methodological direction: from the Scottish empiricist tradition to a rationalist, constructivist, and hence interventionist position.[134] Her influence on Mill was *not*—as Mill claimed—to make Mill more sentimental but rather less, to move Mill towards the rationalist position that Hayek found so problematical:[135] 'Her influence on his thought and outlook, whatever her capacities may have been, were quite as great as Mill asserts, but that they acted in a way somewhat different from what is commonly believed. Far from it having been the sentimental it was the rationalist element in Mill's thought which was mainly strengthened by her influence'.[136]

Just how far Mill was moved towards rationalism by Taylor remains an open question, one that is exacerbated, as George J. Stigler remarked, by Mill's fair-

---

suggests that Mill here departed from Adam Smith. In this respect, it now seems fair to say that Hayek was mistaken; Mill's conception of economic man is much more Smithian than that of late nineteenth-century economists such as William Stanley Jevons. See Sandra J. Peart, Introduction to *W. S. Jevons: Critical Responses*, ed. Peart, (London: Routledge, 2004), vol. 1, pp. 1–26; and note 134 below.

[132] Hayek alludes to Harriet Taylor's 'rationalist revolt against the tyranny of public opinion'. This volume, p. 22.

[133] This volume, p. 14.

[134] There has been a long debate on whether Mill's methodology remained within or departed from the empiricist tradition; see Sandra J. Peart '"Disturbing Causes", "Noxious Errors", and the Theory-Practice Distinction in the Economics of J. S. Mill and W. S. Jevons', *Canadian Journal of Economics*, vol. 28, November 1995, pp. 1194–1211; and Samuel Hollander and Sandra J. Peart, 'John Stuart Mill's Method in Principle and in Practice: A Review of the Evidence', *Journal of the History of Economic Thought*, vol. 21, December 1999, pp. 369–98. Robbins' review of Hayek's *Constitution of Liberty* (Lionel Robbins, 'Hayek on Liberty', *Economica*, n.s., vol. 28, February 1961, pp. 66–81), placed Bentham and the two Mills squarely in the British empiricist (not rationalist) tradition. The key issue for Robbins was whether laws and institutions are to be judged by how they conform to abstract rights deduced by reason, or by their utility, something known outside of reason (p. 72).

[135] Packe's biography contains a similar judgment. *The Life of John Stuart Mill*, pp. 316–17. By contrast, Kinzer asserts, 'Harriet Taylor cared less for the life of the mind than for the life of the heart'. Kinzer, 'Review', p. 518.

[136] This volume, p. 14.

ness, his openness to arguments of all sorts and perhaps especially to those made by Harriet Taylor Mill.[137] Yet on the question of human improvement, it is fair to say that Mill remained cautious in spite of her suggestions. So he wrote in 1849, 'I cannot persuade myself that you do not greatly overrate the ease of making people unselfish. Granting that in "ten years" the children of the community might by teaching be made "perfect" it seems to me that to do so there must be perfect people to teach them'.[138] Mill continued in objection to Taylor's argument that the labouring classes might soon be remade by a process of education, writ large:[139] 'You say "if there were a desire on the part of the cleverer people to make them perfect it would be easy"—but how to produce that desire on the part of the cleverer people?' The task would prove impossible even under the extreme assumption of absolute power to build institutions: 'I must say I think that if we had absolute power tomorrow, though we could do much to improve people by good laws, & could even give them a very much better education than they have ever had yet, still, for effecting in our time anything like what we aim at, all our plans would fail from the impossibility of finding fit instruments'.[140]

In short, there is no doubt that Mill's political economy is capacious enough to include institutional change and that he advocated for specific institutional reforms to spread by voluntary adoption. The subsequent question is whether Mill must then be categorized as a 'rationalist' as Hayek used the term. Suppose by 'rationalist' Hayek intends one who would advocate for the construc-

---

[137] See Stigler's remark: 'The one conspicuous exception to the rule of overestimation of the importance of one's own ideas was John Stuart Mill, whose rectitude was so extreme as to be painful: He played down his own contributions—and was rewarded for a century with an undeserved reputation for noncreativity. So modesty and respect for received knowledge would be most dubious assets for a scientific innovator. This lesson, on reflection, should be obvious enough; one cannot communicate effectively with other people unless one uses the language to which they are accustomed'. George J. Stigler, *Memoirs of an Unregulated Economist* (Chicago: University of Chicago Press, 1988), p. 216.

[138] Mill to Taylor, 21 March 1849, this volume, p. 144.

[139] For Taylor, as for Mill, education encompasses much more than simple schooling; as Mill put it in his 1845 'The Claims of Labour', education instead consisted of 'whatever acts upon the minds of the labouring classes' or 'the whole of their social circumstances'. J. S. Mill, 'The Claims of Labour', in John Stuart Mill, *Essays on Economics and Society*, ed. John M. Robson, vols. 4–5 (1967) of *Collected Works*, 4:376. See Farrant, 'A Renovated Social Fabric', p. 103; and E. G. West, 'Private versus Public Education: A Classical Economic Dispute', *Journal of Political Economy*, vol. 72, October 1964, republished in *The Classical Economists and Economic Policy*, ed. A. W. Coats, (London: Methuen, 1971), pp. 123–43.

[140] Mill to Taylor, 31 March 1849, this volume, pp. 144–45. Any 'change from wrong to right', Mill held, 'is not so easy to make, as to wish for, and to talk about'; in 1845 Mill warned in 'The Claims of Labour' that 'Society' 'has a long and difficult apprenticeship yet to serve'. Mill, *Essays on Economics and Society*, vol. 4 of *Collected Works*, p. 366. He reiterated this position in the 'Chapters on Socialism' where he warned that socialism could not be imposed by coercion or an 'Act of Parliament'. Mill, *Essays on Economics and Society*, vol. 5 (1967) of *Collected Works*, p. 750.

tion of the constitutional order; it does seem clear that Mill proceeds with more caution than Hayek grants. Certainly in the case of cooperatives or other socialist experiments, for instance, Mill advocates trial on a small scale and voluntary adoption, by collection of empirical evidence and competition among local and variable arrangements. Most significantly, in no case does Mill allow that those in charge have the ability to foresee how institutional change should proceed or evolve. Nor does he suggest that policy makers might specify how human nature should evolve or human wants be satisfied.

Conclusion

Hayek took the position—in line with Mill—that democracy is insufficient to block institutional reform.[141] For Mill, this is a good feature of democracy,[142] but for Hayek, it is highly problematical because it feeds the hubris of institution-makers and the imposition of ill-conceived institutional reforms on locales. The significant difference, perhaps, is to be found in Mill's Smithian virtue ethics heritage, a heritage that was lost at the end of the nineteenth century until the latter quarter of the twentieth century. For Smith, as for Mill, individuals are connected by bonds of sympathy and a desire to be praiseworthy. It is this which, in Mill's view, would constrain the more numerous labouring classes from unjust taking.[143] By contrast, Hayek's notion of sympathy is more akin to following behaviour or imitation; there is less room for virtue ethics in his conception of human nature.[144]

[141] Late in his life Hayek faulted Mill for passing on to twentieth-century intellectuals the 'delusion' that democratic politics is sufficient to limit government. In a 1978 interview with James Buchanan, he attributed this 'delusion' to the Utilitarians, Jeremy Bentham, James Mill and John Stuart Mill; F. A. Hayek, 'Nobel Prize Winning Economist', ed. Armen Alchian (transcript of an interview conducted in 1978 under the auspices of the Oral History Program, University Library, University of California, Los Angeles, 1983 [transcript no. 300/224, Department of Special Collections, Charles E. Young Research Library, UCLA]). See also *The Fatal Conceit*, vol. 1 of *The Collected Works of F. A. Hayek*, p. 149.

[142] See David M. Levy and Sandra J. Peart, 'The Theory of Economic Policy in British Classical Political Economy: A Sympathetic Reading', in 'The Role of Government in the History of Economic Thought', supplement, *History of Political Economy*, vol. 37, 2005, pp. 120–42. Hayek's notion of sympathy is more akin to following behaviour or imitation; there is no room for virtue ethics in his conception of human nature.

[143] See Sandra J. Peart and David M. Levy 'Hayek's Sympathetic Agents', in Farrant, *Hayek, Mill, and the Liberal Tradition*.

[144] *Ibid.* Hayek takes the additional and well-known position that some reform might lead to full-blown socialism, but here he engaged less with Mill than with twentieth-century collectivists. On the calculation debate, see David M. Levy and Sandra J. Peart, 'Socialist Calculation Debate', in *The New Palgrave Dictionary of Economics*, 2nd ed., ed. Steven N. Durlauf and Lawrence E. Blume (New York, Palgrave Macmillan, 2008), doi:10.1057/9780230226203.1570.

It bears emphasis in closing this introduction that Hayek agreed with Mill's longstanding and hard-and-fast position—which he shared with Taylor—that the labouring classes, the Irish, and women were all capable of making economic and political decisions. In Mill's time that position was widely and successfully attacked late in the nineteenth century, and Mill was criticized by Thomas Carlyle, among others, for holding it. It cost him dearly.[145] But by 1951, the debate about human capacity had largely disappeared from public discourse: Hayek (like Ludwig von Mises before him) did not take up the capacity arguments that had been so central to the late nineteenth-century debates about economic arrangements and human agency. Hayek's objections to socialism contain no hint of argument made by Mill's opponents in the nineteenth century that the poor are inferior and lack the self-restraint to behave prudently.[146] Reaching back to Mill from the twentieth century to engage with him in a debate over socialism, Hayek instead focused in large measure on whether and how the constructivist Taylor moved Mill towards rationalism and hence interventionism and on how Mill was read and perhaps misread in the twentieth century by those who favoured collectivism.

---

[145] See Peart and Levy, 'Vanity of the Philosopher', for a detailed account of the debates over human rationality and presumed homogeneity. That account places Mill on the side of Smith and political economists such as William Nassau Senior; and Thomas Carlyle and John Ruskin on the side of human difference and the presumed inferiority of the Irish, former slaves, and women.

[146] This is not to say that capacity arguments did not persist. See Maurice Dobb, 'Economic Theory and the Problems of a Socialist Economy', Economic Journal, vol. 43, December 1933, pp. 588–98.

HAYEK ON MILL

The Mill-Taylor Friendship and Related Writings

JOHN STUART MILL AND HARRIET TAYLOR
Their Friendship and Subsequent Marriage

ACKNOWLEDGEMENTS

The originals of most of the letters and other documents reproduced in this volume are preserved in the Yale University Library and in the British Library of Political and Economic Science and my greatest obligation is to the Library Committees of these two institutions for their permission to reproduce these documents which has made this volume possible. I am similarly indebted to the Provost and Fellows of King's College, Cambridge, who have not only allowed me to use some letters bequeathed to them by the late Lord Keynes but have also presented to the British Library of Political and Economic Science a set of letters by Mrs. Mill when it was noticed that at some earlier stage these had become accidentally detached from a larger collection of similar documents now in the latter Library; to the National Library of Scotland and to the Huntington Library in Pasadena, California. The National Provincial Bank, Ltd. (as representatives of the late Miss Mary Taylor), and Mr. Stuart Mill Colman of Galmpton, Devonshire, have made substantial contributions to this volume by presenting documents in their possession to the British Library of Political and Economic Science; and Mrs. Hugh Gemmel of East London, S.A., and Mrs. Vera Eichelbaum of Wellington, New Zealand, have similarly assisted by their permission to reproduce or use documents in their possession.

Of those who have helped in other ways I must in the first place mention Professor Jacob Viner of Princeton University, who originally drew my attention to the collection at Yale University Library. To Professor Arthur H. Cole, Librarian of Harvard University, I am under a special obligation for his help in procuring in war-time from British Columbia, where it had strayed, the portrait of Harriet Taylor reproduced facing page 127 of this volume. Mrs. Z. J. Powers, Librarian of Historical Manuscripts of Yale University Library, and Mr. W. Park and Mr. J. S. Ritchie of the Department of Manuscripts of the National Library of Scotland have been good enough more than once to supply copies or to check transcriptions when I was not able myself to inspect documents in their care.

Finally I must mention Dr. Ruth Borchardt and Mrs. Dorothy Hahn, who in different stages of the work on the collection of John Stuart Mill's general correspondence have assisted me for long periods and on the result of whose work I have been able to draw to a large extent in preparing this volume. To all these as well as to the many others who have more indirectly helped in its production I wish to express my most sincere thanks.

ABBREVIATIONS AND SYMBOLS USED

J.S.M.: John Stuart Mill.

H.T.: Harriet Taylor (Mrs. John Taylor—until 1851).

H.M.: Harriet Mill (Mrs. John Stuart Mill—from 1851).

MTColl.: Mill-Taylor Collection in the British Library of Political and Economic Science (London School of Economics). The references (e.g. XXVII/233) are to the volume and the number of the item (*not* the folio), unless they refer expressly to one of the boxes separately numbered in Roman numerals.

Letters (ed. Elliot): *The Letters of John Stuart Mill*, edited with an Introduction by Hugh S. R. Elliot, two volumes (London: Longman's Green and Co., 1910).

Letters of T. C. to J. S. M.: Letters of Thomas Carlyle to John Stuart Mill, John Sterling and Robert Browning, edited by Alexander Carlyle (London: T. Fisher Unwin Ltd., 1923).

MacMinn, *et al.*, *Bibliography: Bibliography of the Published Writings of John Stuart Mill*. Edited from his Manuscript with Corrections and Notes by Ney Mac-Minn, J. R. Hainds and James McNab McCrimmon. (Evanston, Illinois: Northwestern University Press, 1945).

Autobiography: J. S. Mill, *Autobiography*. The page references are to the 'World's Classics' edition (Oxford: Oxford University Press, 1924), except where they are expressly to the complete edition published in 1924 by Columbia University Press.[1]

D.D.: J. S. Mill, *Dissertations and Discussions* (London: Longman's, Green, Reader, and Dyer, 1858 and later).

[ ] Square brackets are used to indicate editorial insertions in the text of documents.

[?] and [??] indicates a gap of one or more words.

(?) and (??) indicates that the reading of the preceding word or words is doubtful.

. . . indicates omissions or parts missing from the manuscript.

---

[1] [John Stuart Mill, *Autobiography of John Stuart Mill*, with a preface by John Jacob Coss (New York: Columbia University Press, 1924).—Ed.]

INTRODUCTION

I

The literary portrait which in the *Autobiography* John Stuart Mill has drawn for us of the woman who ultimately became his wife creates a strong wish to know more about her. If Harriet Taylor, to give her the name which she bore during the greater part of her life, was anything like what Mill wished us to believe, we should have to regard her as one of the most remarkable women who ever lived. Even if merely her influence on Mill was as great as he asserts, we should have to think of her as one of the major figures who shaped opinion during the later Victorian era. Yet until now it has been solely Mill's account on which we have had to rely in forming an estimate; and the very extravagance of the language he employed in her praise has generally produced more disbelief than conviction. It is natural to dismiss as the product of an extraordinary if not singular delusion a description which represents her as more a poet than Carlyle,[1] more a thinker than Mill himself and as the only equal to his father in 'the power of influencing by mere force of mind and character, the convictions and purposes of others, and in the strenuous exertion of that power to promote freedom and progress'.[2] The best known version of Mill's estimate of his wife's genius in the *Autobiography* is too long to be quoted in full, and it would probably be unnecessary to do so. A few sentences will recall the general tone of a description which extends over many pages:[3]

---

[1] [Thomas Carlyle (1795–1881), Scottish essayist. His first work of importance was *Sartor Resartus*. He was, early on, a close friend of J. S. Mill, but that friendship became strained over Mill's relationship with Harriet Taylor (noted by Hayek in chapter 4 below) and ultimately ended. Hayek does not emphasize that Mill and Carlyle also disagreed over the issue of slavery, with Mill writing a sharply critical response in 1850 to Carlyle's 1849 'An Occasional Discourse on the Negro Question'.—Ed.]

[2] John Stuart Mill, *Autobiography*, pp. 149 and 174. [*Autobiography and Literary Essays*, eds. John M. Robson and Jack Stillinger, vol. 1 (1981) of *The Collected Works of John Stuart Mill* [hereafter cited as *Collected Works*] (Toronto: University of Toronto Press, 1962–1991), pp. 183, 213.—Ed.]

[3] *Ibid.*, pp. 158–59. [Mill, *Autobiography*, vol. 1 of *Collected Works*, p. 195.—Ed.]

In general spiritual characteristics, as well as in temperament and organisation, I have often compared her, as she was at this time, to Shelley: but in thought and intellect, Shelley, so far as his powers were developed in his short life, was but a child compared with what she ultimately became. Alike in the highest regions of speculation and in the smaller practical concerns of daily life, her mind was the same perfect instrument, piercing to the very heart and marrow of the matter; always seizing the essential idea or principle. The same exactness and rapidity of operation, pervading as it did her sensitive as [well as] her mental faculties, would with her gifts of feeling and imagination have fitted her to be a consummate artist, as her fiery and tender soul and her vigorous eloquence would certainly have made her a great orator, and her profound knowledge of human nature and discernment and sagacity in practical life, would [the] in times when such a *carrière* was open to women, have made her eminent among the rulers of mankind. Her intellectual gifts did but minister to a moral character at once the noblest and the best balanced which I have ever met with in life. Her unselfishness was not that of a taught system of duties, but of a heart which thoroughly identified itself with the feelings of others, and often went to excess in consideration for them, by imaginatively investing their feelings with the intensity of its own.

Though this fullest expression of his feelings did not appear until the posthumous *Autobiography*, Mill had not hesitated to announce them earlier in similar tones. The prefaces to *On Liberty* and to the reprint of the article on 'The Enfranchisement of Women' in *Dissertations and Discussions*,[4] both published shortly after her death, are in a similar strain. A few sentences from the latter may also be quoted:[5]

[4] [The article was written following the first National Women's Rights Convention held in 1850 in Worcester, Massachusetts, and was published in 1851 in the *Westminster Review*. It was reprinted soon after in America, where it was used to support the women's rights movement. *Dissertations and Discussions* was a collection of Mill's essays that was first published in two volumes in 1859 and expanded to four volumes in the third edition by 1875. These essays had mostly appeared in the *Westminster Review* and the *Edinburgh Review*. They have since been republished in various volumes of Mill's *Collected Works* to which the reader is referred throughout below.—Ed.]

[5] *D.D.*, vol. 2, p. 411. [The essay is republished in *The Complete Works of Harriet Taylor Mill*, ed. Jo Ellen Jacobs (Bloomington: Indiana University Press, 1998), pp. 51–73, with an editorial remark (p. 30) that it is the 'best known example of Harriet Taylor Mill's writing'. From Mill's *On Liberty*, we have the following: 'To the beloved and deplored memory of her who was the inspirer, and in part the author, of all that is best in my writings—the friend and wife whose exalted sense of truth and right was my strongest incitement, and whose approbation was my chief reward—I dedicate this volume. Like all that I have written for many years, it belongs as much to her as to me'.—Ed.]

All that excites admiration when found separately in others, seemed brought together in her: a conscience at once healthy and tender; a generosity, bounded only by a sense of justice which often forgot its own claims, but never those of others; a heart so large and loving, that whoever was capable of making the smallest return of sympathy, always received tenfold; and in the intellectual department, a vigour and truth of imagination, a delicacy of perception, an accuracy and nicety of observation, only equalled by her profundity of speculative thought, and by a practical judgment and discernment next to infallible.

But it was not only in the anguish and grief over her loss that Mill expressed himself in such terms. He used similar language to others and, as we shall see, to her before they were married, and in the Dedication of his *Principles of Political Economy* had expressed his admiration in print, though confined to a limited number of copies, while her first husband was still alive.

Was all this sheer delusion? Some of Mill's friends evidently thought so and their views, especially Carlyle's, have largely determined the opinions of later generations. Yet even if it had been nothing more it would not only present us with a curious psychological puzzle, but also leave open the question how far Mill's ideas, and especially his changes of opinion at a critical juncture of European thought, may have been due to this delusion. Yet it is not altogether easy to accept the view that so eminently sober, balanced and disciplined a mind, and a man who chose his words as deliberately and carefully as Mill, should have had no foundation for what he must have known to be unique claims on behalf of any human being. Before one accepts that view and all that it implies for our judgment of the man and of the *Autobiography*, one would like some independent evidence. Apart from Mill none of those who expressed views about Harriet Taylor's qualities have really had much grounds on which to base them, except W. J. Fox, whose is also the only other voice that joins in her praise.[6]

Mill himself, however, on one occasion, has emphatically denied that a proper memoir of his wife could be written. In a letter sent in 1870 to Paulina Wright Davies [Davis], the American champion of women's rights, he wrote:

[6] On receipt of the news of Mrs. Mill's death Fox wrote to Mrs. P. A. Taylor (16 November 1858): 'Mrs. Mill gone! So lovely once! So superb ever!' and on the next day he wrote to his daughter: 'Mrs Mill died on the 3rd at Avignon. She would not have objected to being buried there, in the ground which Petrarch has given a wide-world fame; and of which it might (if she remains) be said, "A greater than Laura is here"' (Richard Garnett, *The Life of W. J. Fox*, London: John Lane, The Bodley Head; New York: John Lane Company, 1910, p. 99). [William Johnson Fox (1786–1864) was a Unitarian, supporter of the Anti-Corn Law movement, gifted orator, and M.P. (Oldham) from 1847 to 1863. He contributed to the *Westminster Review* and served as editor of the *Monthly Repository*, where he published articles by J. S. Mill as well as Harriet Martineau.—Ed.]

Were it possible in a memoir to have the formation and growth of a mind like hers portrayed, to do so would be as valuable a benefit to mankind as was ever conferred by a biography.

But such a psychological history is seldom possible, and in her case the materials for it do not exist. All that could be furnished is her birth-place, parentage, and a few dates! and it seems to me that her memory is more honored by the absence of any attempt at a biographical notice, than by the presence of a most meagre one.

What she was, I have attempted, though most inadequately, to delineate in the remarks prefaced to her Essay, as reprinted with my 'Dissertations and Discussions'.[7]

We have of course even less information about Mrs. Taylor now than was in Mill's possession, and if our main aim were to reconstruct a full-scale picture of her person that task would indeed be impossible. It is little that we can do to give life to the improbable picture of a paragon of all excellencies which he has drawn for us. But though we may not be able to do justice to her, and though we may not be able to learn much about her person, we must welcome all independent evidence on the character of their relation and the nature of her influence on his work. Mill has given us his picture of this connexion as it appeared to him and he was perhaps entitled to feel that he had nothing to add to it. This does not mean that there may not be material which is of interest to us because of the light it throws on that picture.

II

Whether the existence of an autobiography always means that we know its author better than we would without it is a question on which different opinions are possible. No doubt almost any autobiography tells us much that without it we should never know. A self-portrait as candid and patently truthful as Mill's enables us to see some aspects of his person as is possible with few other figures of the past. Yet in some respects the existence of an autobiography may be the cause of our knowing less about its subject. The more successful it is the more it is apt to discourage biographical studies by others. It

---

[7] E. C. Stanton, S. B. Anthony and J. A. Gage, *History of Woman Suffrage* (New York: Charles Mann, 1889), vol. 1, pp. 219–20. [The full letter, dated 22 July 1870, is published in *The Later Letters of John Stuart Mill, 1849–1873*, eds. Francis E. Mineka and Dwight N. Lindley, vols. 14–17 (1972) of *Collected Works*, 17:1747–48. Paulina Kellogg Wright Davis (1813–1876) was a writer, speaker, social reformer, and suffragist. In 1835, she and her first husband, Francis Wright, participated in the Utica anti-slavery convention. See Mill, *Later Letters*, vol. 17 of *Collected Works*, pp. 1668–70, note 1.—Ed.]

certainly makes us see the author more as he saw himself, often looking back from old age, than as he appeared to his contemporaries. Even where there was no intention to mislead, as there certainly was not in the case of Mill, the impression conveyed may be very one-sided. What seems most important to the man himself need not appear so to others, and what he has left out may be as characteristic of him as what he has included.

All this is in a high degree true of John Stuart Mill's *Autobiography*. It is probably the one among his works which will live longest, through which he has already exercised the greatest influence, and which is likely to determine his permanent place in the history of ideas. It may well prove that his purely scientific achievements, his *Logic* and his *Political Economy*, will occupy more modest places in that history than seemed probable to his contemporaries, and that even *On Liberty* and his other contributions to political philosophy will represent a more rapidly passing phase of thought than they would have thought possible. But even if in the final estimate Mill should not be ranked as an original thinker of the first order, I believe that his reputation will emerge from its present eclipse; he will again be recognized as one of the really great figures of his period, a great moral figure perhaps more than a great thinker, and one in whom even his purely intellectual achievements are mainly due to his profound conviction of the supreme moral value of unrelenting intellectual effort. Not by temperament but out of a deeply ingrained sense that this was his duty did Mill grow to be the 'Saint of Rationalism', as Gladstone once so justly described him.

There is thus perhaps no other instance where an autobiography had so much to tell us and where at the same time such a purely intellectual account of a man's development is so misleading. The *Autobiography* is as remarkable for what it leaves out as for what it discusses—what it leaves out not in any desire to suppress but because Mill thought it genuinely irrelevant. It is one of the most impersonal accounts of a mental development ever attempted, an account in which only the factors found a place that in Mill's view ought to have influenced it. Of what in the ordinary sense of the word we should call his life, of his human interests and personal relations, we learn practically nothing. Even the account of 'the most valuable friendship of his life' is scarcely an exception to this; the feeling of incongruity which this account of Mill's greatest experience conveys is not least due to its being represented as a purely intellectual experience. It would certainly be a mistake to believe that Mill really was like that, that what he regarded as deserving of a public record gives us a picture of the whole man. It is even doubtful whether we can fully appreciate the significance or the lesson of the *Autobiography* until we know much more of the very human being whose strongest beliefs have led him thus to depict himself.

If, however, the existence of the *Autobiography* increases rather than lessens the need for an adequate biography, it is no accident that three-quarters of a century after Mill's death no such work exists. Without additional knowledge on what, according to his own account, was the decisive factor in his life, such a biography could not be written. It is not the only but the most important point on which the essential material for such a biography was wanting.

The present volume is no more than an attempt to fill this particular gap— material for a future biography rather than an attempt at an appreciation. But since, for reasons immediately to be explained, I have in the book itself refrained from any interpretation or estimate of this new material, I may per- haps here express the conclusions I have formed on the significance of Harriet Taylor in Mill's life. They are, that her influence on his thought and outlook, whatever her capacities may have been, were quite as great as Mill asserts, but that they acted in a way somewhat different from what is commonly believed. Far from it having been the sentimental it was the rationalist element in Mill's thought which was mainly strengthened by her influence. I know of only one study, a little known essay by the Swedish writer Knut Hagberg, which has correctly seen the nature of this influence as it now reveals itself.

'[I]t is obvious', writes Hagberg, 'that it was this woman who made him into a Radical rationalist. She has given the impress of her personality to all his greater works; to all her opinions Mill has given the form of philosophic maxims. But even in his most arid reflexions on woman's similarity with man and on the nature of Logic, Mill is in reality a romantic'.[8]

III

The present book is the outcome of work originally undertaken without any such design. It grew unexpectedly out of an effort to bring together Mill's cor- respondence during the earlier part of his life, which had never been system- atically collected. A considerable number of these letters have been assembled and are waiting to be edited and published. In the course of this work the mate- rial now presented has come to light and it soon became clear that it would not fit into the contemplated edition of Mill's professional correspondence. These private letters clearly demanded a treatment different from the simple chronological presentation with a few explanatory footnotes which would suf- fice for his more formal letters. To be intelligible most of them require much more knowledge of the circumstances in which they were written. Those let- ters of Harriet Taylor to Mill which have been preserved, and certain other pieces of family correspondence, were clearly of as much interest in this con- nexion as Mill's own. On the other hand, a considerable part of their corre- spondence, belonging to the period following their marriage and dealing with

[8] Knut Hagberg, *Personalities and Powers* (London: John Lane, 1930), p. 196.

purely domestic matters, is hardly of sufficient interest to justify publication. Neither their maids' meat consumption, nor their neighbour's rats, nor all the voluminous reports about the momentary state of their health are suitable for printing. Some selection thus became imperative. Finally, much of this correspondence belongs to the period after 1848, which is so fully represented in H. S. R. Elliot's edition of *The Letters of John Stuart Mill* (1910) that a new collection of Mill's general correspondence for this period is not called for.

It soon appeared that the most satisfactory solution of these problems would be to take the private letters out from the general correspondence and to combine them with certain other material in a volume of a somewhat different character. There was some temptation to go beyond such a mere presentation of the documents, and to use them instead as the foundation for a book about Mill and Harriet Taylor. I have deliberately refrained from attempting this. To some readers this volume will therefore appear as the material for a book rather than the finished product. The justification for presenting the documents in this fashion is that they could provide the material for several different books which might be written around them; thus any attempt at interpretation would almost inevitably have interfered with the impartial presentation of the documents. Not all the fragments which accident has preserved can be made to fit into one coherent story which at the same time they are sufficient to justify. Yet any selection guided by an interpretation would have been likely to omit documents which from a different point of view might prove significant.

I have therefore endeavoured to reproduce for the first eighteen years of Mill's friendship with Harriet Taylor, for which the material is scanty, practically every available scrap of correspondence which I have been able to date with any degree of confidence. To this I have added whatever other contemporary material throws light on these letters, including a collection of the comments of their friends and acquaintances. Most of the latter have already appeared in print and the picture of the relationship now generally held is mainly derived from them.

For the period from 1849 onwards we possess one continuous set of notes of Harriet Taylor to Mill and two long and several shorter series of letters by Mill written to his wife after their marriage in 1851. Of these only selected passages are reproduced. Any selection of this sort is bound to be arbitrary in some measure and at least Mill's accounts of his journeys might deserve to be printed at greater length in a different context. If that part of the volume was not to grow to disproportionate size, however, only a few samples of his descriptions of his travels could be included, to secure space for passages which bear more directly on the interests which he shared with his wife.

A few words should be said here about the method of transcription and the principles of editing which have been followed. Full observation of the strictest canons of literary editorship would in this case have unduly impaired readability. The character of the manuscripts, many of them hastily written informal notes, and certain habits of both Mill and Mrs. Taylor, made some editorial emendations indispensable if the printed text was to be read with ease. If every possible doubt about the correct reading of a word, or every punctuation sign which had to be inserted, had been indicated, the text would have been intolerably encumbered. Where, as is true of most of their letters, the same kind of mark, which might be a full stop, a comma, or a hyphen, is made to serve for all three, where punctuation is often altogether absent (Mill practically always omitted punctuation signs at the end of a line), or its need indicated only by the spacing of the words, and where capital letters are employed in the most haphazard manner, it would have been merely irritating if every full stop inserted had been enclosed in square brackets or every other sign of punctuation queried as possibly intended for something else. A reasonable compromise between faithfully reproducing the general character of the manuscripts and achieving easy readability was necessary. Where there could be no real doubt about the meaning I have not hesitated to make the needed corrections without at the same time eliminating those peculiarities and idiosyncrasies which did not affect the readability. Where the spelling, grammar, or punctuation is unusual the reader may therefore assume that it follows the manuscript, even though no 'sic' or exclamation mark draws special attention to these peculiarities and though in other places similar defects have been tacitly corrected.

IV

It remains to give a brief account of the sources of the material which is here presented. Most of it derives from Mill's own papers, which were left by him to his stepdaughter Helen Taylor, who jealously guarded them during her life. A full account of the later fate and ultimate dispersal of these documents will have to be given in the edition of Mill's general correspondence, and for the present a brief sketch may suffice. Some of the papers were probably destroyed and others dispersed when in 1905 Helen Taylor gave up the cottage at Avignon where Mill had spent the greater part of the last fifteen years of his life, and, after he had left the house at Blackheath Park, presumably kept most of his documents. Parts of the contents of the cottage were then hurriedly disposed of by some friends.[9] Most of Mill's papers were however pre-

[9] See the Diary kept by Mary Taylor from 20 February 1904 to 4 July 1906 in MTColl. LVIII/B and Jules Véran, 'Le Souvenir de Stuart Mill à Avignon', *Revue des Deux Mondes*, September 1937 [pp. 212–22]. [Hayek provided a more detailed discussion of the fate of Mill's estate, including his correspondence, in the Introduction to *The Earlier Letters of John Stuart Mill*,

served and shipped to England and on Helen Taylor's death in 1907 passed to her niece Mary Taylor. It was while the papers were in the latter's possession that Mr. H. S. R. Elliot was given an opportunity to prepare, mainly from the drafts of his letters which Mill kept from about 1848 onwards, the two-volume edition of the *Letters of John Stuart Mill* published in 1910. But although Elliot was allowed to see, he was not permitted to print any of Mill's intimate letters, which Mary Taylor reserved for publication by herself at a later date.[10] This intention, to which she repeatedly referred, was never carried out. Shortly before her death in November 1918 she was corresponding with a literary agent about a volume of such letters[11] which seems to have existed in typescript and which probably contained most of the material in the present volume and perhaps also other documents which have since been lost. It has not been possible to trace this typescript and since the offices of the literary agency as well as those of the publisher who had been approached, of Mary Taylor's solicitors, and the depository where her executors kept some of the papers concerning her, were destroyed by fire during the London 'Blitz' in December 1940, there is little likelihood that it has survived.

Excepting only some, the more intimate family letters, the whole of the Mill documents which had been in Mary Taylor's possession were sold, at the instruction of her executors, at two auctions at Messrs. Sotheby's of London, on 29 March 1922 and 27 July 1927.[12] Almost all the items were bought in the first instance by various booksellers but, excepting only a few pieces which probably went to private collectors, seem sooner or later to have found a permanent resting-place in one or another of a number of University Librar-

---

1812–1848, ed. Francis E. Mineka, vols. 12–13 (1963) of *Collected Works,* 12:xviii–xxiii, republished in this volume, pp. 322–31. Hayek there reports that in her will Mary Taylor left all copyrights and letters and correspondence referring to Mill and Harriet Taylor to the National Provincial Bank as the legatees and literary executors of the estate.—Ed.]

[10] See the letter of H. S. R. Elliot to Lord Courtney, dated 8 May 1910, in MTColl. III/69. [Lord Courtney (1832–1918) was a British politician and, from 1897 to 1899, President of the Royal Statistical Society.—Ed.]

[11] See the letter by Messrs. A. P. Watt & Son to Mary Taylor, dated 30 January 1918, in MTColl. XXIX/315, in which it is estimated that the proposed volume would run to 272 printed pages. This probably included the extensive correspondence between Mrs. Mill and Helen Taylor now among the MTColl. but not reproduced in the present volume. That typed copies of most of these letters must have existed appears from [the] word 'typed' on many of the envelopes in which they had been kept.

[12] [In his Introduction to the *Earlier Letters,* Hayek reports that the sale on 29 March 1922 yielded a gross amount of £276.19, much of which was due to the sale of letters by Carlyle to Mill. The bulk of the Mill manuscripts was sold in 1926 to the Library of the London School of Economics. The 27 June 1927 Sotheby's sale, described as 'The Property of Miss Mary Taylor, dec.', containing some 132 letters to his wife signed by Mill, became part of the material at Yale University Library as well as part of J. M. Keynes' collection, which eventually was deposited at King's College, Cambridge. See this volume, p. 329.—Ed.]

ies in Great Britain and the United States. Major parts of the collection are now at the Libraries of the London School of Economics, Leeds University, Johns Hopkins University, Yale University, and North-Western University. Of these the 'Mill-Taylor Collection' of the British Library of Political and Economic Science (as the Library of the London School of Economics is correctly described) is much the largest, and in the course of the work on Mill's correspondence it has been possible to acquire for it a good deal of additional material, deriving from the same and from other sources, including the family letters retained by Mary Taylor's executors at the time of the sales, and a number of letters preserved by the descendants of some of Mill's relatives and of some of his other correspondents. But, although the London collection is probably the richest so far as Mill's general correspondence is concerned, the smaller collection at Yale University Library has made the greatest contribution to the present volume. Almost all of Mill's letters to his wife which have been preserved and the most important of his letters to W. J. Fox are in that collection. Other Libraries have of course also contributed and a full list of these will be found above under *Acknowledgements* and in the notes giving the whereabouts of the individual letters.

ONE

HARRIET TAYLOR AND HER CIRCLE
1830

John Stuart Mill probably met Harriet Taylor for the first time in the summer or early autumn of 1830 when she was still in her twenty-third year but already married for more than four years and the mother of two sons.[1] The special register, kept at the time for the voluntary use of Dissenters at Dr. Williams' Library, records on 10 October 1807, the birth at No. 18, Beckford Row, Walworth, in the South of London, of Harriet, daughter of Thomas Hardy, 'surgeon and man-midwife'. Her granddaughter Mary Taylor states[2] that the Hardys had for some centuries been lords of the manor of Birksgate, near Kirkburton, where Thomas Hardy lived in retirement for the last ten years or so of his life before he died in 1849. If this is more than an unfounded affectation of gentility he was probably a younger son who early went to London to take up a profession. He appears at any rate to have practised at Walworth for many years since at least 1803, and even earlier to have married the daughter of a citizen of Walworth; other members of the Hardy family also seem to have lived in London. Thomas Hardy's practice apparently was sufficiently lucrative to enable him to give his numerous children a fairly good education. Occasional glimpses of him which we get in the family letters do not show him as an altogether amiable character. The impression they leave is of a somewhat domineering and difficult person, and since at least in later life Harriet Taylor's relations to her parents were not too cordial, the tradition that it was an unhappy home which drove her into an early marriage is at least credible.

John Taylor, to whom she was married on 14 March 1826, only five months after her eighteenth birthday, was eleven years her senior. He was

---

[1] In the *Autobiography* (p. 156). [*Autobiography and Literary Essays*, eds. John M. Robson and Jack Stillinger, vol. 1 (1981) of *The Collected Works of John Stuart Mill* [hereafter cited as *Collected Works*] (Toronto: University of Toronto Press, 1962–1991), p. 193.—Ed.] Mill himself gives 1830 as the year when they became acquainted and adds that he was then in his twenty-fifth and she in her twenty-third year, which, taken literally, would fix the date between May and October of that year. That it was 1830 (and not 1831 as Bain says) is confirmed by a letter of Mrs. Mill of 14 February 1854, quoted on p. 191.

[2] *Letters* (ed. Elliot), vol. 1, p. xi. For further information and the Hardy, Taylor and Mill families see the genealogical tables in Appendix III. [Elliot mentions Mary Taylor on p. xi, but there is no mention there of Birksgate.—Ed.]

a junior partner of David Taylor & Sons, a firm of wholesale druggists or 'drysalters' that had been carrying on a prosperous business in the City for at least fifty years. The firm had long been established in Finsbury Square and the adjoining Cross Street, and had already been conducted there by John Taylor's grandfather, that 'fine specimen of the old Scotch puritan; stern, severe, and powerful, but very kind to children, on whom such men make a lasting impression',[3] who, as Mill tells us, had lived in his childhood in the next house to James Mill's at Newington Green and had sometimes invited young John to play in his garden. At least three of the sons of this old man, David, George and John Taylor, succeeded him in the firm, and by the time his grandson, John the younger, married, 'uncle David' appears to have been the senior partner and to have remained in that position during his nephew's life.

What we know about John Taylor on the whole tends to support the description of him given in the *Autobiography*: 'a most upright, brave, honourable man, but without the intellectual or artistic tastes which would have made him a companion' for his wife.[4] Carlyle's characterization of him as 'an innocent dull good man',[5] though perhaps less fair, is probably also not quite wrong. But if John Taylor was above all a prosperous business man who enjoyed the good things of life, his interests extended beyond this limited sphere. He devoted a good deal of time to the management of the finances of the Unitarian congregation to which the Taylors as well as the Hardys belonged, and conducted the occasionally difficult negotiation with its strong-willed minister, William Johnson Fox. As a convinced radical he took an active interest in politics; there is also some evidence that on behalf of the Unitarians he concerned himself with the affairs of the new University of London.[6] In 1836 we find him among the original members of the Reform Club, which suggests that he was

---

[3] *Autobiography*, p. 156. [Mill, *Autobiography*, vol. 1 of *Collected Works*, p. 193.—Ed.]

[4] [Harriet Taylor softened Mill's initial characterization somewhat. Mill's draft read, 'of liberal opinions but of no intellectual or artistic tastes, nowise a companion for her'; see Jack Stillinger, 'Who Wrote J. S. Mill's *Autobiography*?', *Victorian Studies*, vol. 27, Autumn 1983, p. 17. Harriet Taylor's revision, accepted by Mill and published as the 1924 Oxford edition of the *Autobiography* (p. 157) from which Hayek quotes, reads: 'Married at any early age, to a most upright, brave, and honourable man, of liberal opinions and good education, but without the intellectual or artistic tastes which would have made him a companion for her'. Hayek omitted the phrase 'of liberal opinions and good education'. The passage occurs in Mill, *Autobiography*, vol. 1 of *Collected Works*, p. 193. The 1924 Columbia edition of the *Autobiography* has a note to the text after the word 'or'. The note reads, 'Pencil note by H. T. [Helen Taylor] on MS. "not true"'. See Mill, *Autobiography* (New York: Columbia University Press, 1924), p. 130.—Ed.]

[5] Thomas Carlyle, *Reminiscences of Thomas Carlyle*, ed. Charles Elliot Norton (London: Macmillan and Co., 1887), vol. 1, p. 110.

[6] MTColl. XXIX/328.

regarded as one of the more important radical business men.[7] He also seems to have made a special point of looking after the interests of the numerous political exiles from France and Italy who had arrived in London.

For the first five years after their marriage John Taylor and his wife lived in the City in a house at 4, Christopher Street, Finsbury Circus, in close vicinity both to the firm and W. J. Fox's new chapel at South Place. Their first son, Herbert, was born there on 24 September 1827, and a second son, Algernon, invariably called Haji, followed on 2 February 1830. The third and last child, Helen (usually called Lily), was born on 27 July 1831. One or two surviving letters exchanged between husband and wife during the first few years of their married life show Mrs. Taylor as a devoted young wife and happy mother.[8] But there is no reason to doubt that a certain disparity of tastes made itself felt long before her friendship with Mill began.

The only description of Harriet Taylor's appearance at that time comes from W. J. Fox's daughter, who, if she really refers as she says to about 1831, would then have been a small girl of about seven. As it mentions Mrs. Taylor's age as about twenty-five, it probably dates from two or perhaps even more years later and is practically contemporaneous with the portrait reproduced opposite page 127[9] which it singularly well confirms:

> [Mrs John] Taylor at this date, when she was, perhaps about five and twenty years of age, was possessed of a beauty and grace quite unique of their kind. Tall and slight, with a slightly drooping figure, the movements of undulating grace. A small head, a swan-like throat, and a complexion like a pearl. Large dark eyes, not soft or sleepy, but with a look of quiet command in them. A low sweet voice with very distinct utterance emphasised the effect [and enhanced the charm] of her engrossing personality. Her children idolised her.[10]

[7] [Following the passage of the Reform Bill of 1832, the Reform Club was founded in 1836 by Edward Ellice (1781–1863) to promote discussion of liberal reforms. Members included W. E. Gladstone, William Thackeray, and, later, Sir Winston Churchill.—Ed.]

[8] MTColl.XXVIII/143, 144. [*The Complete Works of Harriet Taylor Mill* reports that only one letter to John Taylor, written 28 July 1828, survives from the period before their separation. This letter, which is Hayek's XXVIII/143, is reproduced in *ibid.* on pp. 439–41 and shows Harriet to be happy in marriage at this time. XXVIII/144 is a letter from John Taylor to Harriet of which only the envelope survives. See *The Complete Works of Harriet Taylor Mill* [hereafter cited as *Complete Works*], ed. Jo Ellen Jacobs (Bloomington: Indiana University Press, 1998), p. 295, note 95. Harriet wrote the poem, 'Mermaid's Song' (reproduced in *ibid.*, pp. 215–16) on another envelope.—Ed.]

[9] [Hayek's presentation states that the portrait is 'given as a frontispiece to this volume'.—Ed.]

[10] Quoted by Richard Garnett, *The Life of W. J. Fox* (London: John Lane, The Bodley Head; New York: John Lane Company, 1910), p. 98, from the manuscript recollections of Mrs. E. F. Bridell Fox, the original of which does not seem to have been preserved. The reference to her children idolizing Mrs. Taylor also suggests a later date than 1831 when the youngest would only just have been born and the two boys have been very small.

21

This delicate frame evidently harboured very strong convictions and emotions which during these early years however were still seeking an outlet and adequate means of expression. It is probable that from an early stage her character and outlook had been shaped by a violent revolt against the social conventions which not only, at the time of life when she did not comprehend what it meant, had placed her in permanent dependence on a man whom she regarded as her inferior in intellect and general culture, but which also excluded her from almost all those activities for which she regarded herself fit. There is almost certainly an autobiographical element in a passage of one of her early literary efforts in which she complains that 'in the present system of habits and opinions, girls enter into what is called a contract perfectly ignorant of the conditions of it, and that they should be so is considered absolutely essential to their fitness for it!'[11] But if the conditions of women, their education and their position in marriage were at the time Mrs. Taylor's main concern and probably the starting point of her other reflections, they were by no means the limit of her rationalist revolt against the tyranny of public opinion.

What we know about her views and interests during these early years must be derived from a sheaf of notes and drafts which seem to belong mostly to the time just before or soon after she met Mill, but none of which can be dated with any certainty. There is no clear evidence that she attempted any prose composition before she met Mill or before, soon afterwards, she began to contribute to Fox's *Monthly Repository*.[12] But the variety of drafts and scraps on the position of women, on education and various social usages and conventions, which date from about the same period, suggest that these problems must have been occupying her for some time. The most interesting of these essays, which in parts curiously anticipates some of the arguments of *On Liberty*, is reprinted as Appendix II to the present volume.[13]

Mrs. Taylor had however tried her hand at poetry for some time before 1830. The six poems of hers that have been preserved, three of them printed in the *Monthly Repository*, are of unequal quality. They suggest the inspiration

[11] MTColl., Box III/79, reprinted below in chapter 3. Compare also a similar passage, *ibid.*, 77. There is also, *ibid.*, Box III/113, a draft of part of a review of *The Life of William Caxton* by W. Stevenson which appeared in 1833 as no. 31 of 'The Library of Useful Knowledge'. This draft is partly in her and partly in John Taylor's hand. [The first item mentioned by Hayek is reproduced under the title 'On Marriage' in full in Harriet Taylor Mill, *Complete Works*, pp. 21–24; the second appears under the title 'The Nature of the Marriage Contract', *ibid.*, pp. 17–20; the third is reproduced under the title 'Life of William Caxton', *ibid.*, pp. 273–87.—Ed.]

[12] [In 1831, W. J. Fox, who by then served as editor of the *Monthly Repository*, purchased the journal. Alfred Lord Tennyson and Robert Browning contributed verse to the journal; contributors of articles included John Stuart Mill, Leigh Hunt, William Bridges Adams (who, as Hayek notes below, married Fox's friend, Sarah Flower), and Harriet Martineau.—Ed.]

[13] [The essay is published under the title 'Sources of Conformity' in Harriet Taylor Mill, *Complete Works*, pp. 137–42.—Ed.]

of Shelley and the best show some real poetic gift, though in execution they are probably not much superior to the production of many young women of her time. Two of her published and one of her unpublished poems are also printed in Appendix I.[14]

The only members of Mrs. Taylor's circle of whom we can form a distinct picture, and probably the only ones who mattered in connexion with Mill, were William Johnson Fox and the two remarkable young women with whom he had become closely associated only a short time before: Eliza and Sarah Flower. In 1830 Fox was a man of forty-four and at the height of his fame as a Unitarian preacher but, as editor of the *Monthly Repository* since 1827, already at the beginning of a transition to an even more influential position as a radical journalist and politician. He had risen from a small farmer's son, and later a weaver's boy and bank clerk in Norwich, to be a considerable public figure mainly through that eloquence which in later years made him famous as one of the most powerful orators of the Anti-Corn-Law League. At the time he was however still one of the leading figures of the Unitarian Association, but this connexion soon became looser, and in later years, though he continued to preach at South Place Chapel, it was more as a precursor of the Ethical Movement of his successor Moncure Conway than as the representative of any Christian denomination.[15] The alienation from the more strict body of Unitarians was partly the result of his connexion with Eliza Flower.

Fox was unhappily married and had been brought in close contact with the two beautiful and highly gifted sisters when on the death of their father in 1829 he had become their trustee. Aged twenty-seven and twenty-five respectively in 1830, and thus only slightly older than Mill and Harriet Taylor, Eliza and Sarah Flower must have been fascinating persons. Eliza was a composer of some distinction and Sarah wrote poetry of merit and is to-day remembered as the author of the hymn 'Nearer, my God, to Thee'. After the early death of their mother they had been educated solely by their father and had developed their natural gifts without systematic training or much discipline of any sort. There can be little doubt that it was Eliza Flower to whom Mill

---

[14] ['Written at Daybreak' (Appendix 1 to the *John Stuart Mill and Harriet Taylor*, reprinted in this volume, pp. 261–62) is reproduced in Harriet Taylor Mill, *Complete Works*, p. 209 (along with various drafts of the poem, pp. 210–12). 'To the Summer Wind' (this volume, p. 262) is republished in *ibid.*, pp. 218–19, and 'Nature' (this volume, p. 263) is republished in *ibid.*, p. 219. A total of twelve poems, including drafts of several, are reproduced in Harriet Taylor Mill, *Complete Works.*—Ed.]

[15] [Moncure Conway (1832–1907) was a Virginian whose uncompromising anti-slavery position and disillusion with the Unitarian Church caused him to lose some credibility in America and prompted him to take a speaking tour to England in 1863. There, he found an affinity with the ideas of the South Place Ethical Society, which had evolved when the Unitarian Association split and South Place became the center of progressive social causes. He returned to America in 1884. *Oxford Dictionary of National Biography*, s.v. 'Conway, Moncure Daniel', by John d'Entremont, accessed 16 May 2014, http://www.oxforddnb.com/view/article/47686.—Ed.]

refers in the *Autobiography* when he speaks of Mrs. Taylor's 'life [. . .] of inward meditation, varied by familiar intercourse with a small circle of friends, of whom one only (long since deceased) was a person of genius, or of capacities of feeling or intellect kindred with her own'.[16] A series of informal notes by Eliza Flower to Mrs. Taylor which have survived[17] show that for some years in the early 'thirties the two women were fairly intimate and that the fragile and somewhat unstable Eliza Flower was rather looking up to the younger but more self-possessed and more happily circumstanced married woman. Known as 'Ariel' in her intimate circle, Eliza Flower seems indeed to have had in her something of that ethereal spirit. Fox's biographer describes her as

> Emphatically a child of nature, open and transparent as the day. She worshipped Mozart, Shakespeare, Milton, Burns, Byron, but if these had never existed, Eliza Flower would still have been Eliza Flower. While this independence and spontaneity gave an indescribable charm to her character, they were not wholly favourable to her in the world of Art. Music came so naturally to her that she never realised the importance of strenuous study, and such a professional training as, indeed, it would probably have been beyond her means to procure.[18]

Eliza Flower became Fox's closest friend, devoting all her energies to assist him in his literary work, and after his separation from his wife in 1835 came to superintend his household, inevitably causing scandalous talk which for a time made Fox's position in the congregation difficult. This may also have been one of the reasons which made it appear inadvisable for Mrs. Taylor to maintain the connexion when her own position came under similar criticism, although Eliza Flower's increasing eccentricity probably also made the two women gradually drift apart.

In her way the younger sister, Sarah Flower, seems to have been no less remarkable a person and by her marriage in 1834 to William Bridges Adams[19]

---

[16] *Autobiography*, p. 157. That this passage refers to Eliza Flower is confirmed by a pencil note of Helen Taylor on the original manuscript of the *Autobiography*, reproduced in the Columbia University Press edition of 1924, p. 130. [The passage appears on p. 195 of Mill, *Autobiography*, vol. 1 of *Collected Works*, where an editor's note confirms that it refers to Eliza Flower.—Ed.]

[17] MTColl. XXVII/10–39. [Hayek lists this as MTColl. XXXII/10–39.—Ed.]

[18] Richard Garnett, *The Life of W. J. Fox* (1910), p. 66. It seems that unfortunately all the papers of W. J. Fox, collected for his biography by his daughter Mrs. Bridell Fox and including a biographical sketch by her, have been destroyed during the last war excepting only the collection of letters by Mill to Fox which were acquired by Lord Keynes and are now in the Library of King's College, Cambridge, and an autobiographical sketch by Fox himself which is now in Conway Hall, London.

[19] [William Bridges Adams (1797–1872) was a Radical author and, from 1832 to 1836, a major contributor to the *Monthly Repository*. He wrote on political reform under the pen name

brought another strong personality into the closer circle of friends in which Mrs. Taylor and Mill moved. W. B. Adams, who had been married before to a daughter of Francis Place,[20] was then mainly active as a radical writer and for several years was one of the most frequent contributors to the *Monthly Repository*. He later became a successful carriage manufacturer and eminent railway engineer. For some time he seems to have been on cordial terms with Mill, who took great trouble to draw attention to a book, *The Producing Man's Companion*, which Adams had published under the pseudonym of 'Junius Redivivus'.[21]

Around this inner group there gathered in the early eighteen-thirties a number of minor literary and artistic figures, mostly contributors to the *Monthly Repository* and including a considerable number of women. For some time Harriet Martineau,[22] then at the very beginning of her literary career, was among Fox's most regular contributors. Two other gifted sisters, Margaret Gillies, the miniature painter, and Mary Gillies, the novelist, also appear to have belonged to the somewhat unconventional and strongly feminist group of whose members Leigh Hunt has drawn a picture in his *Bluestocking Revels*.[23]

Junius Redivivus (Junius reborn), a reference to a political letter writer of the previous century. He was also an engineer and later invented the fish joint used in railway rails. *The Earlier Letters of John Stuart Mill, 1812–1848*, ed. Francis E. Mineka, vols. 12–13 (1963) of *Collected Works*, 12:123, note 1.—Ed.]

[20] [Francis Place (1771–1854) was a London tailor, friend to Bentham and James Mill, reformer, and early supporter of contraception. In 1822, he published *The Principles of Population* in which he advocated the use of contraceptive devices. His work helped overturn the anti-union Combination Laws in 1824, he was an early leader of the Chartists, and he later organized a campaign against the Corn Laws. See Sandra J. Peart and David M. Levy, *The 'Vanity of the Philosopher': From Equality to Hierarchy in Post-Classical Economics* (Ann Arbor: University of Michigan Press, 2005), p. 233.—Ed.]

[21] Mill reviewed the *Producing Man's Companion* both in the *Monthly Repository* (vol.7, April 1833) and in *Tait's Edinburgh Magazine* (June 1833). [These are republished in Mill, *Autobiography*, vol. 1 of *Collected Works*, pp. 369–77 and pp. 381–90. Ed.]

[22] [Harriet Martineau (1802–1876) was the daughter of a textile manufacturer from Norwich whose parents were Unitarians with progressive views. In 1823, she published an anonymous article, 'On Female Education', in the *Monthly Repository*, and in 1829, after the death of her father, she moved to London where William Fox paid her a small wage. In 1832, she rose to fame with the publication of the first tale in her *Illustrations of Political Economy*. She then travelled to America, and upon her return, she published *Society in America* (1837) in which she criticized the American system of slavery and also argued that women were treated like slaves in America. In 1852, she joined the staff of the *Daily News*, for which she wrote over 1,600 articles during the next sixteen years. See Mill, *Earlier Letters*, vol. 12 of *Collected Works*, p. 140, note 19.—Ed.]

[23] First published in the *Monthly Repository* (July 1837) [n.s., vol. 11, pp. 33–57]. [James Henry Leigh Hunt (1784–1859) was an essayist and poet whose friends included many artists: John Keats, Percy Bysshe Shelley, and Lord Byron. He helped his brother start the political journal the *Examiner* in 1808, an outlet to promote Radical reform ideas. Mill, *Earlier Letters*, vol. 12 of *Collected Works*, p. 135, note 20.—Ed.]

The *Monthly Repository* itself during Fox's editorship, especially after he had purchased it in 1831 and largely divorced it from its predominantly Unitarian character, was an organ of very considerable distinction and influence both in its political and literary department.[24] Some of the articles, especially Crabbe Robinson's series on Goethe,[25] are landmarks of the literary history of the period. But the feature which distinguished it from the other radical periodicals of the time and which, while it alienated its Unitarian supporters, must have made it particularly congenial to Harriet Taylor, was its strong feminist bias. Both W. J. Fox, whose views on divorce show a Miltonian strain, and W. B. Adams wrote in it extensively on the subject, and their arguments often so closely resemble some of Mrs. Taylor's manuscript drafts of the period that one wonders whether it was merely that she imbibed her ideas from them or whether her somewhat unpolished drafts did not perhaps serve as the basis for the articles of the more skilled writers.

It is probable that John Stuart Mill was in close contact with Fox's circle for some time before he met Mrs. Taylor. It has even been said that he was supposed at one time an aspirant for Eliza Flower's hand.[26] There existed many connexions between the group of the Utilitarians and Fox's Unitarian congregation, which included such immediate disciples of Jeremy Bentham as Dr. John Bowring and Dr. Southwood Smith[27]; Fox himself in 1826 had contributed to the first number of the *Westminster Review*.

The impressions we derive from the *Autobiography* are rather misleading when we try to form a picture of John Stuart Mill at the age of twenty-four when he was introduced to Mrs. Taylor. That work conveys to us mainly, on the one hand, an image of the object of that extraordinary educational experiment which is its main theme, and on the other, of the author when he wrote it in late middle age. But the Mill of the intermediate period who concerns us

---

[24] See Francis E. Mineka, *The Dissidence of Dissent, the Monthly Repository, 1806–38* (Chapel Hill: University of North Carolina Press, 1944).

[25] [Henry Crabbe Robinson (1775–1867) was an expert on German literature who wrote articles on Goethe for the *Monthly Repository* in 1832–1833. Mill, *Earlier Letters*, vol. 12 of *Collected Works*, p. 127, note 11.—Ed.]

[26] Moncure D. Conway, *Centenary History of the South Place Society* (London: Williams & Norgate, 1894), p. 89.

[27] [John Bowring (1792–1872) was an influential Unitarian who met and became Bentham's disciple in 1821. He edited the *Westminster Review* since its inception in 1824. From 1841 to 1848, he served as M.P. for Bolton, where he advocated for free trade. He was Bentham's literary executor. See *Oxford Dictionary of National Biography*, s.v. 'Bowring, Sir John', by Gerald Stone, accessed 16 May 2014, http://www.oxforddnb.com/view/article/3087. Dr. Southwood Smith (1788–1861) was a sanitary reformer and Bentham's physician. In 1827, he published *The Use of the Dead to the Living* in which he argued that the current burial system was wasteful and proposed that dissection would be a more productive use of bodies. Bentham bequeathed his body to Southwood along with instructions for its use after his death. For details, see the University College London's Bentham Project (http://www.ucl.ac.uk/museums/jeremy-bentham).—Ed.]

here was in many ways a very different person from either. He was no longer simply the creation of his father, the perfectly constructed intellectual instrument zealously serving the cause for which his father had designed him. That period had ended with the 'crisis in his mental development' which occurred in his twentieth year. Nor was he yet the austere, secluded and severe philosopher he became soon after the age of thirty. Even in appearance we must imagine him very different from the familiar picture which we derive mainly from Watt's portrait painted in the last year of his life or from the photographs of not much earlier date. Long before then ill health, overwork and constant nervous strain had prematurely made him look old. No early portrait of Mill as a young man exists and we must try to reconstruct his appearance from the few descriptions by contemporaries.

Carlyle, first meeting him in 1831, described him as 'a slender, rather tall and elegant youth, with small clear Roman-nosed face, two small earnestly smiling eyes; modest, remarkably gifted with precision of utterance, enthusiastic, yet lucid, calm; not a great, yet distinctly a gifted and amiable youth'.[28] Much later he remembered him as 'an innocent young creature, with rich auburn hair and gentle pathetic expression, beautiful to contemplate'.[29] The earliest portrait which has been preserved, the medallion reproduced here,[30] is also of a later date. It would appear to represent him in his late thirties and is probably identical with the portrait done by a certain Cunningham in Falmouth in 1840 which Caroline Fox describes as 'quite an ideal head, so

[28] J. A. Froude, ed., *Thomas Carlyle, A History of the First Forty Years of His Life* (London: Longman's, Green, and Co., 1882 edition), vol. 2, p. 190.

[29] C. G. Duffy, *Conversations with Carlyle* (London: Sampson, Low and Marston, 1892), p. 167. A somewhat earlier description of Mill given in the *Autobiography of Henry Taylor, 1800–75* (London: Longman, Green and Co., 1885), vol. 1, p. 79, referring to the years 1824–1827:

> He was pure-hearted—I was going to say conscientious—but at that time he seemed so naturally and necessarily good, and so inflexible, that one hardly thought of him as having occasion for a conscience, or as a man with whom any question could arise for reference to that tribunal. But his absorption in abstract operations of the intellect, his latent ardours, and his absolute simplicity of heart, were hardly, perhaps, compatible with knowledge of men and women, and with wisdom in living his life. His manners were plain, neither graceful nor awkward; his features refined and regular; the eyes small, relatively to the scale of the face, the jaw large, the nose straight and finely shaped, the lips thin and compressed, [and] the forehead and head capacious; and both face and body seemed to represent outwardly the inflexibility of the inner man. He shook hands with you from the shoulder. Though for the most part painfully grave, he was as sensible as anybody [to] [for] Charles Austin's or Charles Villier's sallies of wit, and his strong and well-built body would heave for a few moments with half-uttered laughter. He took his share in conversation, and talked ably and well, of course, but with such a scrupulous solicitude to think exactly what he should and say exactly what he thought, that he spoke with an appearance of effort and as if with an impediment of the mind.

[30] [The medallion is printed on p. 145 of this volume.—Ed.]

expanded with patient thought, and a face of such exquisite refinement'.[31] But by then Mill had already passed through his first bout of severe illness, lost most of his hair and acquired that nervous twitch over his eyes which he retained during the remainder of his life. If, however, after his thirtieth year Mill was permanently handicapped by ill health, and though he may even never have fully recovered from the nervous breakdown of ten years before, he appears to have been naturally endowed with a splendid constitution, which enabled him not only to overcome these handicaps but to continue to perform an amount of work and to remain even during acute illness capable of an amount of physical exertion which sometimes seem scarcely credible.

The story of his education is too well known to need retelling even in outline. On the basis of the full account of this education which we possess, he has, in a recent study of child geniuses,[32] been awarded the highest intelligence quotient of all recorded instances of specially precocious children; but, as the author of that study rightly suggests, this may well be merely the result of our knowing so much more about Mill's childhood performances than about those of most others. Indeed, astounding as the speed is with which he passed as a child through a course of education which normally lasts into early manhood, and amazing as are his powers of retention and the discipline of orderly thought and exposition which he acquired, there is little sign of originality or creative powers in his early years. His own natural modest estimate of his innate capacities indeed may be nearer the truth. In the *Autobiography* he represents his father's educational experiment as conclusive precisely because in

> natural gifts I am rather below than above par. What I could do, could assuredly be done by any boy or girl of average capacity and healthy physical constitution: and if I have accomplished anything, I owe it, among other fortunate circumstances, to the fact that through the early training bestowed upon me by my father, I started, I may fairly say, with an advantage of a quarter of a century over my cotemporaries.[33]

That when this education ended John Mill was for some years little more than the 'reasoning machine' depicted in the *Autobiography* we need not

---

[31] Caroline Fox, *Memories of Old Friends* (new enlarged edition in one volume; London: Smith, Elder and Co., 1883), p. 110. John Sterling in an unpublished letter to Mill of 1840 now in the Library of King's College, Cambridge, refers to this portrait as a 'medaillon'. [Here and elsewhere Hayek used this spelling for the word 'medallion'.—Ed.]

[32] Catherine Morris Cox, *The Early Mental Traits of Three Hundred Geniuses* (*Genetic Studies of Genius*, ed. Lewis Madison Terman, vol. 2, Stanford, CA: Stanford University Press, 1926).

[33] *Autobiography*, p. 26. [Mill, *Autobiography*, vol. 1 of *Collected Works*, p. 33.—Ed.]

doubt.[34] The description given of him at the age of eighteen or nineteen by his friend John Roebuck is probably very just; he writes that when he first met Mill he found that:

> although possessed of much learning, and thoroughly acquainted with the state of the political world, [he] was, as might have been expected, the mere exponent of other men's ideas, those men being his father and Bentham; and that he was utterly ignorant of what is called society; that of the world, as it worked around him, he knew nothing; and, above all, of *woman*, he was as a child. He had never played with boys; in his life he had never known any, and we, in fact, who were now his associates, were the first companions he had ever mixed with.[35]

When one reads the chapters of the *Autobiography* devoted to these years and the prodigious amount of work accomplished, it is only too easy to forget that Mill was still only twenty years of age when the period terminated in a severe and prolonged attack of melancholia. That one of the main causes of the acute dejection, from which he emerged only gradually over a period of years, was, in addition to overwork, the struggle to emancipate himself from the complete intellectual sway which his father had held over him, one may readily believe without subscribing to the full to the psycho-analytical interpretation given of it recently in an interesting study.[36] To that essay we are indebted also for an important passage omitted from the published version of the *Autobiography*. It is taken from the manuscript of an early draft, quite possibly the same which we shall later find Mill discussing with his wife in 1854, which was in the possession of the late Professor Jacob H. Hollander and is presumably still among his library:

[34] [See Mill, *Autobiography*, vol. 1 of *Collected Works*, p. 111: 'I conceive that the description so often given of a Benthamite, as a mere reasoning machine, though extremely inapplicable to most of those who have been designated by that title, was during two or three years of my life not altogether untrue of me'.—Ed.]

[35] *Life and Letters of John Arthur Roebuck: with Chapters of Autobiography* (ed. Robert Eadon Leader, London: E. Arnold, 1897), p. 28. Cf. Mill's own statement to Caroline Fox: 'I never was a boy; never played at cricket' (*Memories of Old Friends*, p. 107) [Hayek added the bracketed word in the quoted text. British politician John Arthur Roebuck (1801–1879) met Mill in 1824 at the India House. Roebuck, George John Graham (1801–1888), and Mill were close friends who at this time called themselves the 'Trijackia'. Roebuck and Mill became estranged in the 1830s as a result of Mill's attachment to Harriet Taylor. See Mill, *Earlier Letters*, vol. 12 of *Collected Works*, p. 20, note 2.—Ed.]

[36] A. W. Levi, 'The "Mental Crisis" of John Stuart Mill', *The Psychoanalytical Review*, vol. 32, spring, 1945, pp. 86–101. Cf. p. 98: 'The real cause [of the mental crisis] was those repressed death wishes against his father, the vague and unarticulated guilt [feeling] which he had in consequence, and the latent, though still present dread that never now should he be free of his father's domination!' [Hayek added the bracketed phrase 'of the mental crisis' using parentheses.—Ed.]

But in respect to what I am here concerned with, the moral agencies which acted on myself, it must be mentioned as a most [baneful] ~~shameful~~ one that my father's ~~older~~ children neither loved him, nor, with any warmth of affection, anyone else. [. . .] That rarity in England, a really warm hearted mother, would in the first place have made my father a totally different being, and in the second would have made the children grow up loving and being loved. But my mother, with the very best intentions, only knew how to pass her life in drudging for them. Whatever she could do for them she did, and they liked her, because she was kind to them, but to make herself loved, looked up to, or even obeyed, required qualities which she unfortunately did not possess.

I thus grew up in the absence of love and in the presence of fear; and many and indelible are the effects of this bringing up in the stunting of my moral growth. [. . .] I grew up with an instinct of closeness. I had no one to whom I desired to express everything which I felt; and the only person I was in communication with, to whom I looked up, I had too much fear of, to make the communication to him of any act or feeling ever a matter of frank impulse or spontaneous inclination.[37]

Another evil I shared with many of the sons of energetic fathers. To have been, through childhood, under the constant rule of a strong will certainly, is not favourable to strength of will. I was so much accustomed to [expect to] be told what to do either in the form of direct command or of rebuke for not doing it that I acquired ~~the~~ [a] habit of leaving my responsibility as a moral agent to rest on my father, ~~and~~ my conscience never speaking to me except by his voice.[38]

This passage is significant not only because of the candid description of Mill's attitude towards his father but no less because of the reference to his

[37] [This material appears in Mill, *Autobiography*, vol. 1 of *Collected Works*, pp. 612–13. It is part of a set of 'Rejected Leaves for the Autobiography, R31–37'. These first attempts became the 'Early Draft of the *Autobiography*', published in Mill, *Autobiography*, vol. 1 of *Collected Works*, p. 50, line 22, to p. 58, line 15. According to the commentary at *ibid.*, p. 611, beginning at 52.14, Mill condensed this material into a single paragraph.—Ed.]

[38] *Ibid.* [Levi, 'The "Mental Crisis"'], pp. 92–93. Judging from this passage, which is almost the only one that is available, this early draft of the *Autobiography* is likely to be of very considerable importance in connexion with the subject of this book. Repeated applications to the Executors of the late Professor Hollander for permission to examine the manuscript have, however, been unsuccessful. [The full passage, along with notes concerning Harriet Taylor Mill's marginalia, are reproduced in Mill, *Autobiography*, vol. 1 of *Collected Works*, pp. 612–13. Of particular interest in this respect is this sentence (p. 613): 'I thus acquired a habit of backwardness, of waiting to follow the lead of others, an absence of moral spontaneity, an inactivity of the moral sense and even to a large extent, of the intellect, unless roused by the appeal of some one else'. Harriet may indeed have activated Mill's moral sense. See 'A Joint Production', this volume, p. 148.—Ed.]

mother, whose complete absence from the *Autobiography* has so often been commented upon. Yet it is doubtful whether the harsh judgment expressed in it, very probably written during the period of his estrangement from his mother following his marriage, truly represents his feelings as a young man. There is some testimony to the contrary by contemporaries, and even though the unfavourable comments evoked by the *Autobiography* may have led them to overemphasize this point, they agree too well to be dismissed.

H. Solly[39], who had been a classmate of John's younger brother James at University College and in the summer of 1830 had spent a week with the Mills at their cottage at Mickleham, near Dorking in Surrey, says that

> John Mill always seemed to me a great favourite with his family. He was evidently very fond of his mother and sisters, and they of him; and he frequently manifested a sunny brightness and gaiety of heart and behaviour which were singularly fascinating.[40]

Elsewhere Solly remembers

> the impression he made on us by his domestic qualities, the affectionate playfulness of his character as a brother in the company of his sisters, and of the numerous younger branches of the family.[41]

J. Crompton, another member of the same class at University College, records his impressions from similar visits in almost the same words:

> In these days John was devotedly attached to his mother and exuberant in his playful tokens of affection. Towards his father he was deferential, never venturing to controvert him in argument nor taking a prominent part in the conversation in his presence.[42]

---

[39] [Henry Solly (1813–1903) was a British Unitarian minister and social reformer. He supported the Chartist movement and worked to instigate three important social organizations—the Working Men's Club, the Charity Organization Society, and the Garden City movement—that provided for the working classes in late Victorian Britain. He married, in 1841, Rebecca Shaen (1812–1893) at the Presbyterian (Unitarian) Chapel, High Street, Stourbridge, Worcestershire. They had one son and four daughters; one of their daughters married the economist Philip Wicksteed. See *Oxford Dictionary of National Biography*, s.v. 'Solly, Henry', by Alan Ruston, accessed 16 May 2014, http://www.oxforddnb.com/view/article/37991.—Ed.]

[40] H. Solly, *These Eighty Years* [*or, the story of an Unfinished Life*] (London: Simpkin, Marshall, & Co., Limited, 1893), vol. 1, p. 148.

[41] H. Solly, in *The Workman's Magazine* (1873), p. 385. [The full article appears in the *Workman's Magazine*, ed. Henry Solly, no. 7, July 1873, pp. 384–88.—Ed.]

[42] Manuscript notes by A. S. West of a conversation with the Rev. J. Crompton in the Library of King's College, Cambridge [JMK/PP/87/20A].

John Mill was then, of course, living at his parents' home and continued to do so after James Mill's death in 1836 until his marriage fifteen years later. At the time of which we are speaking he shared that home with eight younger brothers and sisters, ranging down to George who must have been nearly twenty years his junior.[43] John had then taken over from his father most of the task of instructing the younger members of the family, a duty which must have made considerable inroads on his time but of which he makes practically no mention in the *Autobiography*.[44] But though Mill continued these duties, the home must have become increasingly uncongenial to him as he slowly detached himself from the beliefs of the father whose strong personality dominated it. His position was not made easier by the fact that since 1823, when he had entered the offices of the East India Company, his father had become also his official superior with whom he must have been in constant close contact after, in 1828 and at the age of twenty-two, he had himself been promoted to a senior position. He could expect no sympathy from the older man for the many new impressions and ideas which he readily absorbed in those years and

[43] Mill, in a letter to be quoted later [this volume, p. 174] indeed refers to George as being twenty years his junior, but that may not have to be taken quite literally. The exact dates of the births of most of the children of James Mill are unknown, as they never seem to have been baptized and in consequence, in the then state of affairs, their births never to have been registered.

[44] A comment of one of his sisters on this has been preserved in a letter now in the Library of King's College, Cambridge [JMK/PP/87/20A].

> *Harriet I. Mill to the Rev. J. Crompton, 26 October 1873:* My poor mother's [Her] married life must have been a frightfully hard one, from first to last: I hope and think that the eighteen following years, always excepting the desertion of her eldest son, were years of satisfaction and enjoyment. Here was an instance of two persons, as husband and wife, living as far apart, under the same roof, as the north pole from the south: from no 'fault' of my poor mother certainly: but how was a woman with a growing family and very small means (as in the early years of the marriage) to be anything but a German Haŭsfraŭ? how could she 'intellectually' become a companion for [such a mind] as my father? *His* great want was 'temper', though I quite believe circumstances had made it what it was in our childhood, both because of the warm affection of his early friends, and because in the latter years of his life he became much softened and treated the younger children [very] differently. What would be thought *now* if the fate of *our* childhood were known? You will perhaps be surprized to hear that that mention of teaching a younger sister Latin is the sole allusion to any member of the family, except my father: that sister must have been the eldest, Willie, (Mrs King). *I* have no recollection of John's ever teaching me Latin—the only thing my father professed to teach us, expecting us, however, to know everything else and abusing us for our ignorance if we did not! *I* have no distinct recollection of John prior to his return from France in 1821, when we were at Marlow for the summer and he at once wrote out and pinned on the walls the way in which the hours of the day were to be passed by the four of us,—my two elder sisters, myself and James. Any regular teaching we had was from him, and he carried some of us very far in mathematics and algebra. Indeed I have been told that he said I could have taken the Senior Wrangler's degree at Cambridge.

which led him more and more away from the utilitarian faith. It was particularly in these years following the 'crisis in his mental history' that he proved that exceptional capacity of which he justly prides himself in the *Autobiography*, his 'willingness and ability to learn from everybody'.[45] But few systems of thought can have been more antipathetic to James Mill than those by which in these years his son was most attracted, those of Coleridge and his German inspirers, of the French Saint-Simonians,[46] and soon of Carlyle. For a time we feel in his correspondence with some of his contemporaries, particularly in his letters to John Sterling[47] and Adolphe d'Eichthal,[48] how he suffered from the intellectual isolation in which he has been led and how he longed for a real companion with whom he could fully share his new interests. But, although this is the one period in his life when he went out of his way to seek friendships with other men and when he freely mixed in various kinds of society, he remained essentially lonely. There is a significant letter to John Sterling which bears quoting at some length since it better than any other document describes his emotional state not long before he met Harriet Taylor.

J. S. M. to John Sterling, 15 April 1829.[49] I am now chiefly anxious to explain to you, more clearly than I fear I did, what I meant when I spoke to you of the comparative loneliness of my probable future lot. Do not suppose me

[45] *Autobiography*, p. 205. [Mill, *Autobiography*, vol. 1 of *Collected Works*, p. 253.—Ed.]

[46] [Claude Henri de Rouvroy, Comte de Saint-Simon (1760–1825), founded the French socialist school of thought. He was much influenced by revolutionary France. He joined the French army at age seventeen and was sent to aid the colonists in the American Revolution. After his return to France (1783), he made a fortune in land speculation but gradually dissipated it. He turned to the study of science and technology as the solution to society's problems and wrote 'On the Reorganization of European Society' (1814) and (with Auguste Comte) 'Industry' (1816 1818) in which he envisioned an industrialized state directed by modern science. In *New Christianity* (1825), he stated that religion should guide society towards improving life for the poor. For more on the influence of Saint-Simon on Mill, see this volume, pp. 276–86.—Ed.]

[47] [John Sterling (1806–1844) was a writer and, in 1828, editor of the *Aethenæum* with Frederick Denison Maurice. Maurice and Sterling were both followers of Coleridge who joined the London Debating Society as liberals in opposition to Bentham. Mill became an ally and friend of Sterling. See Mill, *Earlier Letters*, vol. 12 of *Collected Works*, pp. 28–29, note 1; and for a list of their correspondence published in Mill, *Earlier Letters*, vols. 12–13 of *Collected Works*, see 13:784.—Ed.]

[48] [Gustave d'Eichthal (1804–1886), son of a wealthy Jewish banking family, became interested in the ideas of Saint-Simon through the influence of his mathematics teacher, August Comte. D'Eichthal visted England and saw Mill speak on 30 May 1828. They soon became friends and longtime correspondents. See Mill, *Earlier Letters*, vol. 12 of *Collected Works*, p. 26, note 1; and for the list of their correspondence published in Mill, *Earlier Letters*, vols. 12–13 of *Collected Works*, see 13:781.—Ed.]

[49] *Letters* (ed. Elliot), vol.1, p. 2. [This is a portion of the letter which is reproduced in full in *The Letters of John Stuart Mill*, edited with an Introduction by Hugh S. R. Elliot, two volumes (London: Longman's Green and Co., 1910), pp. 1:1–3, and in Mill, *Earlier Letters*, vol. 12 of *Collected Works*, pp. 28–30.—Ed.]

to mean that I am conscious at present of any tendency to misanthropy—although among the various states of mind, some of them extremely painful ones, through which I have passed ~~through~~ [during] the last three years, something distantly [approximating to] ~~approaching~~ misanthropy was *one*. At present I believe that my sympathies with society, which were never strong, are, on the whole, stronger than they ever were. By loneliness I mean the absence of that feeling which has accompanied me through the greater part of my life, that which one fellow traveler, or one fellow soldier has towards another—the feeling of being engaged in the pursuit of a common object, and of mutually cheering one another on, and helping one another in an arduous undertaking. This, which after all is one of the strongest ties of individual sympathy, is at present, so far as I am concerned, suspended at least, if not entirely broken off. There is now no human being (with whom I can associate on terms of equality) who acknowledges a common object with me, or with whom I can cooperate even in any practical undertaking without the feeling, that I am only using a man whose purposes are different, as an instrument for the furtherance of my own. *Idem sentire de republicâ*, was thought by one of the best men who ever lived to be the strongest bond of friendship: for *republicâ* I would read 'all the great objects of life,' where ~~all~~ the parties concerned have at heart any great objects at all. I do not see how there can be otherwise that *idem velle, idem nolle*, which is necessary to perfect friendship. Being excluded therefore from this, I am resolved hereafter to avoid all occasion for debate, since they cannot now strengthen my sympathies with those who agree with me, & are sure to weaken them with those who differ.

Unsettled though Mill's mind was in these years, they were nevertheless one of the periods of his greatest productivity and perhaps that of his most original thought. Indeed it seems that most of the ideas which he later developed in his major works were first conceived during the few years following his recovery from the period of dejection. It was in 1829 that Macaulay's famous attack on James Mill's *Essay on Government*,[50] perhaps together with some of the early works of Auguste Comte which John Mill read at the same time, started the train of thought which led to his characteristic ideas on Logic on which he began to work at the beginning of the following year. About the same time he wrote his first and most original work on economic theory, the *Essays on Some Unsettled Questions of Political Economy*. He also continued to steep himself in the history of the French Revolution on which he had started to work

[50] [Thomas Babbington Macaulay (1800–1859) was a Whig lawyer and writer who opposed slavery and, in 1829, published an article in the *Edinburgh Review* that successfully criticized James Mill's argument for democracy on utilitarian grounds. Macaulay entered Parliament in 1830 and was instrumental in the passage of the Reform Bill of 1832. See note 52 below.—Ed.]

when, early in 1828, he had reviewed Walter Scott's *Life of Napoleon* and which a few years later still seemed his favourite topic of conversation.[51] His interest in French politics had then been rekindled by a visit to Paris immediately after the Revolution of July 1830, and therefore either just before or just after he first met Mrs. Taylor; and for some time thereafter French affairs greatly occupied his attention until they were partly superseded by the even more direct concern with the Reform Bill[52] agitation at home into which he threw much of his energy.

[51] Compare the entry in J. L. Mallet's diary under the date of 2 March 1832 in *Political Economy Club, Centenary Volume* (London: Macmillan and Co., 1921), vol. 6, p. 231, and Henry Crabbe Robinson's Diary (Typescript in Dr. Williams' Library, vol. 14) under the date of 27 March 1832. [Crabbe, *Diary, Reminiscences and Correspondence of Henry Crabbe Robinson*, ed. Thomas Sadler, 2 vols. in 1 (Boston: Houghton, Mifflin and Company, 1898). The entry in question is dated 3 March and appears on p. 169 of vol. 2.—Ed.]

[52] [The Reform Bill of 1832 extended voting rights to previously-disfranchised citizens, reapportioning representation in Parliament towards the cities of the industrial north, and doing away with 'rotten' and 'pocket' boroughs like Old Sarum, in which seven voters still sent two members to Parliament. In addition to reapportioning, the act extended the right to vote to any man who owned a household worth £10, adding 217,000 voters to an electorate of 435,000. *Encyclopædia Britannica Online, s.v.* 'Reform Bill', accessed May 19, 2014, http://www.britannica .com/EBchecked/topic/495344/Reform-Bill. For Mill's account of the agitation for the bill, see his letter to Sterling, dated 'From the 20th of October to the 22nd, 1831' in Mill, *Earlier Letters*, vol. 12 of *Collected Works*, pp. 74–88.—Ed.]

TWO

ACQUAINTANCE AND EARLY CRISES
1830–1833

Even if we do not accept all of Thomas Carlyle's later adornments of the story,[1] there is no reason to doubt the tradition that it was W. J. Fox who brought Mill to Mrs. Taylor. To the dinner-party at the home of the Taylors at which the introduction was effected not only Mill but the whole 'Trijackia' was invited, that is, he and his closest friends of the preceding years, John Roebuck and George John Graham.[2] Harriet Martineau was also of the party and later appears to have been fond of telling the circumstances, but Bain's discretion has refrained from passing her story on to us.[3] Apparently a strong mutual attraction was at once felt. In the *Autobiography* Mill says that 'it was years after my introduction to Mrs. Taylor before my acquaintance with

---

[1] This account was given orally by Carlyle to Charles Eliot Norton in 1873 after the receipt of the news of Mill's death and is recorded verbatim in *Letters of Charles Eliot Norton* (London: Constable & Co., 1913), vol. 1, pp. 496–97: 'A verra noble soul was John Mill, quite sure, beautiful to think of. I never could find out what more than ordinary there was in the woman he cared so much for; but there was absolute sincerity in his devotion to her. She was the daughter of a flourishing London Unitarian tradesman, and her husband was the son of another, and the two families made the match. Taylor was a verra respectable man, but his wife found him dull; she had dark, black, hard eyes, and an inquisitive nature, and was ponderin' on many questions that worried her, and could get no answers to them, and that Unitarian clergyman you've heard of, William Fox by name, told her at last that there was a young philosopher of very remarkable quality, whom he thought just the man to deal with her case. And so Mill with great difficulty was brought to see her, and that man, who, up to that time, had never looked a female creature, not even a cow, in the face, found himself opposite those great dark eyes, that were flashing unutterable things while he was ~~discoursing~~ [discoursin'] the utterable concernin' all sorts o' high topics'. A similar conversation with Carlyle is recorded by C. G. Duffy, *Conversations with Carlyle* (London: Sampson, Low and Marston, 1892), p. 167.

[2] Alexander Bain, *J. S. Mill: A Criticism with Personal Recollections* (London: Longman's, Green, and Co. 1882), p. 164, and R. E. Leader, *Life and Letters of J. A. Roebuck* (London, 1897), p. 38. John Arthur Roebuck (1801–1879), barrister and leading radical politician, had become a close friend of Mill on his arrival from Canada in 1824. George John Graham (1801–1888) probably had become acquainted with Mill about the same time but in 1830 had only just returned from five years' service as Military Secretary of Bombay. He became Registrar-General of Births and Deaths in 1838. [See note 35 in chapter 1 above.—Ed.]

[3] Alexander Bain, *J. S. Mill*, p. 164, and Gordon S. Haight, *George Eliot and John Chapman* (New Haven: Yale University Press, 1940), p. 213.

her became at all intimate or confidential'.[4] But though we know little about the first two years after the meeting, the connexion seems even then to have been closer than these words suggest. There are no dated documents before the birth of Mrs. Taylor's last child, Helen, on 27 July 1831, and if it were not for one curious fact one would be inclined to assign the few undated early letters referring to Mill to a date after this. There exists, however, a note by Eliza Flower to Mrs. Taylor in which, with reference to an article on Lord Byron in the *Edinburgh Review*, she asks 'Did you or Mill do it?'[5] This must refer to the review of Thomas Moore's *Letters and Journals of Lord Byron* which appeared in the *Edinburgh Review* for June 1831, and since the date of the letter seems to be 30 June 1831, it would appear as if at this early date Mrs. Taylor's closest friend was already so familiar with the similarity of her and Mill's views as to believe (without justification) that the article must be by either of them.[6]

This circumstance gives one more confidence than one might feel otherwise for assigning the earliest letters relating to their connexion to the preceding winter, when the Saint-Simonian Bontemps[7] who is mentioned in one of them is known to have been in London. These early letters are all connected with a certain Monsieur Desainteville, a Frenchman living in London and occasionally contributing to the *Monthly Repository*.[8] The earliest extant letter by Mrs. Taylor to Mill refers to him.

H. T. to J. S. M., Winter 1830/31 (?)[9] Friday Morning / My dear Sir / You may imagine how much we were afflicted by this sad story of our poor

---

[4] *Autobiography*, p. 156. [*Autobiography and Literary Essays*, eds. John M. Robson and Jack Stillinger, vol. 1 (1981) of *The Collected Works of John Stuart Mill* [hereafter cited as *Collected Works*] (Toronto: University of Toronto Press, 1962–1991), p. 193.—Ed.]

[5] MTColl. XXVII/32. The date is taken from the postmark on what appears to be the continuation of this letter, *ibid.*, XXVII/37.

[6] That by that time Mill was already well known to Eliza Flower may be concluded from his first but not last friendly puff he gave some of her hymns in the *Examiner* of next month. 'Musical Illustrations of the Waverley Novels . . .' by Eliza Flower, in the *Examiner*, 3 July 1831, pp. 420–21. Similar notes by Mill on songs by Miss Flower appeared in the *Examiner* for 8 April 1832 and 17 February 1833. See MacMinn, *Bibliography*, pp. 17, 20 and 25. [These are published in John Stuart Mill, *Newspaper Writings*, eds. Ann P. Robson and John M. Robson, vols. 22–25 (1986) of *Collected Works*, 22:331–33, 23:436–38, and 23:554–55.—Ed.]

[7] [Bontemps was one of the hierarchy of seventy-eight Saint-Simonians organized by Enfantin in 1831. See *The Earlier Letters of John Stuart Mill, 1812–1848*, ed. Francis E. Mineka, vols. 12–13 (1963) of *Collected Works*, 12:71, note 2.—Ed.]

[8] F. E. Mineka, *The Dissidence of Dissent, the Monthly Repository, 1806–38* (Chapel Hill. University of North Carolina Press, 1944), p. 405. [*Dissidence* lists one contribution by Desainteville in the *Monthly Repository*, vol. 6, pp. 528–36.—Ed.]

[9] MTColl. L/3. [According to *The Complete Works of Harriet Taylor Mill* [hereafter cited as *Complete Works*], ed. Jo Ellen Jacobs (Bloomington: Indiana University Press, 1998), the note is written on paper 'watermarked 1828' and was 'probably written in 1830 or 1831', possibly the 'first year' of their meeting. It is addressed to 'John Mill Esq'. It is reproduced on p. 323.—Ed.]

friend M. Desainteville the *first* intelligence of which I got from your *two* notes which I received *together* yesterday: how unkind and neglectful we must have appeared? Pray express to him my sympathy and best wishes. Mr. Taylor has seen him and found him better than he expected: what a terrible state of emotion he must have suffered so to have [so] reduced him.

in haste yours very truly

H. Taylor

B. E. Desainteville to John Taylor, early 1831 (?):[10] Desainteville en acceptant avec plaisir l'invitation de Monsieur Taylor croit devoir l'informer que M. Bontemps connait parfaitement Mill et que ce dernier ne serait pas à la table de M. Taylor l'un des convives les moins intéressants pour M. Bontemps. Si Monsieur Taylor n'y voit aucun inconvénient, Desainteville le prier d'inviter Mill à diner avec nous, ce serait en outre le vrai moyen de sceller *joliment* la réconciliation qui s'est opéré entre Monsieurs Taylor et Mill.

We have no knowledge why a reconciliation between John Taylor and Mill should have been necessary at so early a date.[11]

Whether these documents belong to the first or to the second year of the acquaintance, they at least agree with the strong probability that at the end of two years it had become fairly intimate. If we correctly interpret the reference to the 'Nouvelle Forêt' in the following undated note by Mill, it would appear that at the beginning of August 1832, when he returned from a walking tour in Hampshire, West Sussex, and the Isle of Wight, ending up in the New Forest,[12] he found a letter from Mrs. Taylor telling him that they must not meet again.

J. S. M. to H. T., late July 1832 (?):[13] Benie soit la main qui a tracé ces charactères! Elle m'a écrit—il suffit; bien que je ne dissimul pas c'est pour me dire un éternel adieu.

[10] MTColl. XXIX/257.

[11] The following invitation which has also been preserved (MTColl. II/300) somewhat confirms the impression that these documents belong to January 1831, when Monsieur Bontemps is known to have been in London: 'Mr and Mrs Taylor request the pleasure of Mr. Mill's company at dinner on Tuesday next at 5 o'clock when they expect to see Mr. Fox and some friends of M. Desainteville / Finsbury Square / Jan[uary] 28th'. [Harriet Taylor Mill, *Complete Works*, p. 323.]

[12] See Mill's Diary of this walking tour in Mount Holyoke College, South Hadley, Mass. [MS 0049].

[13] MTColl. IX/16. [The letter is reproduced in Mill, *Earlier Letters*, vol. 12 of *Collected Works*, p. 114, where it is dated August 1832?. Packe, who dates the letter July 1832, has a translation; see Michael St. John Packe, *The Life of John Stuart Mill* (London: Secker and Warburg, 1954), p.

Cette adieu, qu'elle ne croie pas que je l'accepte jamais. Sa route et la mienne sont séparées, elle l'a dit: mais elles peuvent, elles doivent, se rencontrer. A quelqu' époque, dans quelqu' endroit, que ce puisse être, elle me trouvera toujours ce que j'ai été, ce que je suis encore.

Elle sera obéie: mes lettres n'iront plus troubler sa tranquillité, ou verser une goutte de plus dans sa coupe des chagrins. Elle sera obéie, par les motifs qu'elle donne,—elle le serait quand même elle se serait bornée à me communiquer ses volontés. Lui obéir est pour moi une nécessité.

Elle ne refusera pas, j'espère, l'offrainde de ces petites fleurs, que j'[ai] apportée[s] pour elle du fond de la Nouvelle-Forêt. Donnez-les lui s'il le faut, de votre part.

A few weeks later, however, normal relations between them seem to have been re-established. At least on 1 September Mill wrote to John Taylor the only letter exchanged between the two men which has been preserved.

J. S. M. to John Taylor, 1 September 1832:[14] Saturday / I.H. / My dear Sir / Two acquaintances of mine, MM. Jules Bastide and Hippolyte Dussard,[15] distinguished members of the republican party in France, have been compelled to fly their country for a time in consequence of the affair of the fifth & sixth of June. They were not conspirators, for there was no conspiracy, but when they found the troops and the people at blows, they took the side of the people. Now I am extremely desirous to render their stay here as little disagreeable as possible, and to enable them to profit by it, and to return with a knowledge of England and with those favourable sentiments towards our English *hommes du mouvement* which it is of so much importance that they and their friends should entertain. I am particularly desirous of bringing them into contact with the better members of the Political Union, that they ~~might~~ [may] not suppose our men of action to be all of them like the Revells[16] and [the] Murphys whom they saw and heard on Wednesday

139. Since the walking tour to which Mill refers ends in New Forest on 6 August, August seems the more likely month. See note 1 to letter 55 in Mill, *Earlier Letters*, vol. 12 of *Collected Works*, p. 114.—Ed.]

[14] Yale University Library, postmarked 1 September 1832. [MS 350, Box 1, Folder 2. The letter is published in Mill, *Earlier Letters*, vol. 12 of *Collected Works*, p. 115. Ed.]

[15] Jules Bastide, French publicist (1800–1879), had been condemned to death because of the part he had taken in the street disturbances which had taken place in Paris on 5 June 1832, on the occasion of the funeral of General Lamarque. He returned to Paris in 1834. Hippolyte Dussard, French economist (1798–1876). Mill had almost certainly made the acquaintance of the two men on his visit to Paris two years earlier.

[16] Major Revell was apparently one of the officers of the 'National Political Union' founded in October 1831 to assist in the agitation for the Reform Bill.

last.[17] Yourself and Mr. Fox are the persons I should most wish them to see. But I do not like to give them a letter of introduction to you without first ascertaining whether it would be agreeable to yourself. Will you therefore oblige me with a line to say, if possible, that you will allow me to tell them to call upon you, or otherwise[18] to say that you would rather not. I have not mentioned the matter to them, nor shall I do so until I have the pleasure of hearing from you.

Ever truly yours
J. S. Mill.

Apparently Mr. Taylor at once sent an invitation to the two Frenchmen, who were, however, unable to accept it, and a little later M. Desainteville asked Mrs. Taylor to renew it.

B. E. Desainteville to H. T., September 1832:[19] De retour de la campagne j'apprends la mort de mon pauvre ami Crawley et j'avai, comme vous pouvez le concevoir, le coeur brisé. Le volume des oeuvres de Platon que je vous ai prête lui appartient et je vous serai infiniment obligé, si vous n'en faites plus usage, de me l'envoyer, afin de le restituer à qui de droit.

Mill me parait extrêmement heureux de la cordialité avec laquelle M. Taylor, qu'il estime beaucoup, l'a reçu et j'en ressens moi-même la plus vive satisfaction. Il me dit que MM. Bastide et Dussard n'ont pas perdu l'espoir que vous renouvellerez l'aimable invitation que vous avez eu l'extrême bonté de leur faire et que des circonstances tout à fait indépendants d'eux ne leur ont pas permis d'accepter: ou, comme Mill quitte Londres vendredi prochain, auriez vous la bonté de prier de Mr. Taylor d'inviter ces messieurs avec Mill à prendre le thé jeudi prochain chez vous? cela contenterai tout le monde.

---

[17] [On 29 August 1832, Murphy made a 'fiery attack' on the government's Irish policy, and the meeting passed a resolution to support 'the People of Ireland in their efforts to throw off the galling and oppressive imposts of Tithes and Church-cess'. See Mill, *Earlier Letters*, vol. 12 of *Collected Works*, p. 115, note 4.—Ed.]

[18] Page torn. [Mill, *Earlier Letters*, vol. 12 of *Collected Works*, p 115, note 5, notes 'part covered by seal'.—Ed.]

[19] MTColl. XXVII/4. This note can be approximately dated from the fact that Mill left for Cornwall (where he spent the second part of his vacation) on Thursday, 20 September, and that according to the *Gentlemen's Magazine* for September 1832, (p. 283) 'Francis Edward Crawley esq. of Dorset Place' died on 5 September, aged twenty-nine. This was probably the same Crawley who in July 1828 with Horace Grant and Edwin Chadwick had accompanied Mill on his walking tour in Berkshire, Buckinghamshire and Surrey (see the Diary of this walking tour in Yale University Library [MS 350, Box 2, Folder 41]; and the Diary of tour to Cornwall in MTColl. [XXXVII]).

Je me fais un véritable plaisir de vous envoyer çi-joint le dernier numéro d'Ten[20] qui contient le discours de l'excellent M. Fox avec des observations sur lui qui me font bien plaisir.

J'ai l'honneur d'etre, madame,

V.t.h.e.t.b.A.[21]

B. E. Desainteville

During 1832 and the years immediately following the one common interest in which we can follow Mill's and Mrs. Taylor's activities are their contributions to Fox's *Monthly Repository*. This journal Fox had bought in 1831, perhaps with financial help from Mr. Taylor, after he had already been editing it for three years, and for a time Mrs. Taylor lent the help of her pen to assist him in the effort of turning it from a denominational organ into a general literary and political periodical. Practically all her known publications appeared in the *Monthly Repository* for 1832, and in the following year Mill also became a regular contributor and at the same time entered a new field as a critic of poetry.

Mrs. Taylor's contributions[22] of 1832 include her three printed poems,[23] probably written some time before and already mentioned, six reviews of

---

[20] [Hayek has 'St, (?)' here instead of 'd'Ten'. Desainteville appears to be referring to a review of Tennyson in the *Westminster Review* in the summer of 1832, with a commentary by Fox defending Bentham. I thank Evelyn Forget for her help with the identification here and in note 21 below.—Ed.]

[21] [The original letter has no periods after the initials, which stand for 'votre très humble et très bien aimé'.—Ed.]

[22] The identifications of the articles in the *Monthly Repository* are taken from the manuscript key in the set of this journal which originally belonged to a member of the Fox family and is now preserved in the Library of Conway Hall, London. It seems that both the identification in Richard Garnett's *Life of W. J. Fox* (London: John Lane, The Bodley Head; New York: John Lane Company, 1910) and in the copy of the *Monthly Repository* in the British Museum, which has served F. E. Mineka's study *The Dissidence of Dissent* (Chapel Hill: University of North Carolina Press, 1944), also derive from this source. Apart from a brief review of a book on Australia (Robert Dawson, *The Present State of Australia*, London: Smith, Elder and Co., 1830, whose author was probably a relative of Mrs. Taylor's), which appeared already in the issue for January 1831 (vol. 5, pp. 58–59), and the contributions mentioned in the text and fully listed by Mineka, that key also ascribes to Mrs. John Taylor, but with a '?', two articles signed 'Theta' in vol. 8 (1834), namely one on 'Female Education and Occupation' (pp. 489–98) and one 'On Tithes' (pp. 525–29). These attributions seem very doubtful, however, and the note on tithes at least is almost certainly by Mill, even though in a letter to Fox of February 1834 (King's College, Cambridge) he wrote, with reference to an earlier note on the same subject, 'You will have received today from her, the note on Tithe'. [The letter to Fox, dated 24 February 1834, is published in Mill, *Earlier Letters*, vol. 12 of *Collected Works*, p. 215. See also Mill's earlier letter, dated 22 February 1834, *ibid.*, p. 214. On the attribution, see Mill to Fox, 4 July 1833, *ibid.*, p. 160: 'I like the new number of the M.R. very much, except the article on the education of women'. A footnote dates the article in question as July 1833, author unidentified.—Ed.]

[23] ['The Snow-Drop', *Monthly Repository*, n.s., vol. 6, 1832, p. 266; 'To the Summer Wind', *Monthly Repository*, n.s., vol. 6, 1832, p. 617; and 'Nature', *Monthly Repository*, n.s., vol. 6, 1832. Reproduced in Harriet Taylor Mill, *Complete Works*, pp. 218–19.—Ed.]

books and one small essay. It cannot be said that there is anything very remark-able about her prose compositions of this time. They begin in May with a review of Sarah Austin's translation of Prince Puckler-Muskau's *Tour of a Ger-man Prince* where she finds something to praise because 'in this land of "caste" he avows his sympathy with the *paria*'.[24] In June appeared a somewhat more ambitious discussion of Mrs. Trollope's *Domestic Manners of the Americans* with which she dealt severely:

> It has unfortunately chanced that, with few exceptions, the descriptions of the United States have been those of persons either of small intellect, and incapable, with their best efforts, of judging between that which is essential and that which is accidental, as instance Basil Hall; or, worse, those whose prejudices make their principles, and whose long-formed habits of subservi-ency make them fancy servility refinement, and its absence coarseness: and of this latter class is the author before us.[25]

Three more reviews by Mrs. Taylor, like the others well written and express-ing strong radical sentiments, appeared in July and September,[26] and in November followed one more, of a translation[27] of B. Sarrans' *Louis Philippe and the Revolution of 1830* in which one is inclined to detect signs of Mill's hand, though it may be that merely his writings on the subject had served as a model. The review ends:

> There can be no doubt that the state of things in France is again slowly tend-ing towards a great moral or physical revolution. That the former may suffice, all friends of humanity must desire; but, should that force of itself be insuf-ficient to produce agreement between the spirit of the government and the spirit of the time, they will not be [no] true friends of humanity who shall not welcome any power which, by means of some evil, may work the regeneration of the people who head [lead] the political regeneration of Europe. As need-ful is it to be kept in mind by nations, as by individuals, *Aide toi, le ciel t'aidera*.[28]

[24] *Monthly Repository* (second series), vol. 6, 1832, p. 354. [The poem appears at pp. 353–54 of the *Monthly Repository*. It is reprinted in Harriet Taylor Mill, *Complete Works*, pp. 179–80.—Ed.]

[25] *Ibid.*, p. 402. [The review, which appeared at pp. 401–6 of the *Monthly Repository*, is reprinted in Harriet Taylor Mill, *Complete Works*, pp. 180–85.—Ed.]

[26] 'Some Memorials of John Hampden, his Party and his Times. By Lord Nugent', *ibid.*, pp. 443–50; 'Mirabeau's Letters during his Residence in England', *ibid.*, pp. 604–8, and 'The Mysti-cism of Plato or Sincerity rested upon Reality', *ibid.*, pp. 645–46. [Harriet Taylor Mill, *Complete Works*, pp. 185–92, 192–96, and 196–98.—Ed.]

[27] Erroneously ascribed by Mrs. Taylor to Sarah Austin. [Harriet Taylor Mill, *Complete Works*, pp. 198–204.]

[28] *Ibid.*, pp. 761–62. [The full essay appears at pp. 756–62. It is republished in Harriet Taylor Mill, *Complete Works*, pp. 203–4.—Ed.]

Mrs. Taylor's last known contribution to the *Monthly Repository*, in December, is a pleasant little essay on the rival attractions of 'The Seasons' of which the only noteworthy passage is perhaps the startling assertion that

> Flowers are Utilitarians in the largest sense. Their very life is supported by administering to the life of others—producers and distributors, but consumers only of what, unused, would be noxious.[29]

Mill's contributions are more interesting, even from our particular point of view. When, early in 1832, Fox had first urged him to contribute he had committed himself no further than to a guarded half-promise that whenever he had anything suitable he would be glad to let Fox have it for the *Monthly Repository*.[30] The first result of this was an essay 'On Genius' which appeared in the form of a Letter to the Editor in September 1832.[31] But his regular contributions did not begin until his article 'What is Poetry' appeared in January of the following year.[32]

There could be little doubt that this new strong interest was due to Mrs. Taylor's influence even if we had not Mill's own statement that this was so. Before that time he had appeared to his friends as a distinctly unpoetical nature[33] and in his account of his discovery of Wordsworth he himself explains Wordsworth's appeal to him by the fact that Wordsworth was 'the poet of unpoetical natures'.[34] In another available fragment of that early draft of the *Autobiography* which has already been mentioned Mill says:[35]

[29] *Ibid.*, p. 827. [The full essay appears at pp. 825–28. It is republished in Harriet Taylor Mill, *Complete Works*, pp. 204–8.—Ed.]

[30] See the letter of J. S. M. to W. J. Fox, of 3 April 1832, in the Library of King's College, Cambridge, and reprinted in Richard Garnett's *Life of W. J. Fox*, p. 100. [The letter appears at 100–101. It is reprinted in Mill, *Earlier Letters*, vol. 12 of *Collected Works*, pp. 97–98.—Ed.]

[31] *Monthly Repository* (second series), vol. 6, 1832, pp. 649–59, reprinted in *Four Dialogues of Plato*. Translation and Notes by John Stuart Mill, edited by Ruth Borchardt (London: Watts & Co, 1946), pp. 28–40. [Reprinted in Mill, *Autobiography*, vol. 1 of *Collected Works*, pp. 329–39. The letter appeared in the October issue of the *Monthly Repository*.—Ed.]

[32] *Monthly Repository* (second series), vol. 7, 1833, pp. 262–70, reprinted [as 'Thoughts on Poetry and Its Varieties'] in *D.D.*, vol. 1, p. 63 [pp. 63–94], and in *Early Essays by John Stuart Mill*, edited by J. W. M. Gibbs (London: George Bell & Sons, 1897), pp. 201–20.

[33] Thomas Carlyle, after meeting Mill for the second time on 12 September 1831, had described him as 'a fine clear enthusiast, who will one day come to something; yet [to] nothing poetical, I think: his fancy is not rich' (J. A. Froude, ed., *Thomas Carlyle, A History of the First Forty Years of His Life* (London: Longman's, Green, and Co., 1882), vol. 2, p. 200). J. A. Roebuck similarly wrote of Mill that 'in reality he never had poetical emotions, and the lessons of his early childhood [and youth] had chilled his heart and deadened his spirit to all the magnificent influences of poetry' (R. E. Leader, *Life and Letters of J. A. Roebuck*, p. 38).

[34] *Autobiography*, p. 126. [Mill, *Autobiography*, vol. 1 of *Collected Works*, p. 153.—Ed.]

[35] The following unpublished passage from the early draft of the *Autobiography* in the library of the late Professor Jacob Hollander is produced from notes taken some years ago by Mr. A. W.

The first years of my friendship with her were, in respect of my own development mainly years of poetic culture. . . . I did cultivate this taste as well as a taste for paintings and sculptures, and did read with enthusiasm her favourite poets, especially the one whom she placed far above all others, Shelley.

From a much later source we know that among Shelley's poems they particularly admired the 'Hymn to Intellectual Beauty', and the same authority reports that their strong preference for Shelley was accompanied by an equally strong aversion to Byron, the lowness of whose ideals Mill deplored while Mrs. Mill then described the popular enthusiasm for him as 'a mere popular delusion'.[36]

Of the two essays of poetry which were among the first fruits of Mill's new interest it has not unjustly been said that

> while clear and strenuous as most of his thoughts were, [they] are neither scientifically precise, nor do they contain any notable new idea not previously expressed by Coleridge, except perhaps the idea, that emotions are the main links of association in the poetic mind: still his working out of the definition of poetry, his distinction between novels and poems, and between poetry and eloquence, is interesting as throwing light upon his own poetical susceptibilities. He holds that poetry is the 'delineation of the deeper and more secret workings of human emotion'.[37]

In Mill's next excursion into criticism of poetry it is fairly certain that Mrs. Taylor took a direct part; and, although it saw the light of print only in recent times, it was destined to play some role in the development of a major poet. Robert Browning had some years before, when still a boy, made the acquaintance of W. J. Fox and the Misses Flower. Eliza Flower is even reputed to have inspired both Browning's lost early poem *Incondita* and his *Pauline*, the first of his poems to be printed. When it appeared in March 1833, Browning turned to Fox for help in making it known, and Fox not only reviewed it himself in the *Monthly Repository* but also passed a copy on to Mill for review elsewhere.

Levi when the manuscript was still accessible. I am especially indebted to Mr. Levi for putting these notes at my disposal. [Hayek met Levi while Levi was conducting research at the London School of Economics; see Levi 'The Writing of Mill's *Autobiography*', *Ethics*, vol. 61, July 1951, p. 296. The fragment is from a series of rejected leaves that are published in Mill, *Autobiography*, vol. 1 of *Collected Works*, RII.1–8; the series of leaves is discussed on p. 616. The passage above appears at p. 623.—Ed.]

[36] Theodor Gomperz, *John Stuart Mill: Ein Nachruf* (Vienna: Verlag von Carl Konegen, 1889), p. 44.

[37] W. Minto in *John Stuart Mill: Notices of His Life and Works* (London: E. Dallow, 1873), p. 33. [The word in brackets is Hayek's addition. The contribution by William Minto, pp. 31–35, is entitled 'His Miscellaneous Criticisms'.—Ed.]

A short article which Mill wrote on it for the *Examiner* could not be inserted[38] and an attempt to alter and enlarge it for Tait's *Edinburgh Magazine*[39] met with no better fate. This article is lost. But Mill also freely annotated his copy[40] on the margin, marking 'all the passages where the meaning is so imperfectly expressed as not to be easily understood', and summed up his opinion on the flyleaf. Some of these marginal notes are in a different hand, which is almost certainly Harriet Taylor's, and though the notes which can be ascribed to her with any confidence do not go beyond short exclamations like 'most beautiful' and 'deeply true', there can be little doubt that she and Mill fully discussed the poem before Mill returned the annotated copy to Fox with the remark that 'on the whole the observations are not flattering to the author—perhaps too strong in the *expression* to be shewn to him'.[41] The copy nevertheless reached Browning soon afterwards and the young poet was so deeply mortified by the criticism that he resolved never again by premature publication to expose himself to similar censure. Although Mill's critique has been printed in the standard *Life of Robert Browning*, it has never been included in any publication concerning Mill and therefore may be given a place here:[42]

> With considerable poetic powers, the writer seems to me possessed with a more intense and morbid self-consciousness than I ever knew in any sane human being. I should think it a sincere confession, though [of] a most unlovable state, if the 'Pauline' were not evidently a mere phantom. All about her is full of inconsistency—he neither loves her nor fancies he loves her, yet insists upon *talking* love to her. If she *existed* and loved him, he treats her most ungenerously and unfeelingly. All his aspirings and yearnings and regrets point to other things, never to her; then he *pays her off* toward the end by a piece of flummery, amounting to the modest request that she will love him and live with him and give herself up to him *without* his *loving her*

[38] See the letter by J. S. M. to W. J. Fox of 19 May 1833 in the Library of King's College, Cambridge. [Mill, *Earlier Letters*, vol. 12 of *Collected Works*, pp. 157–58. The letter is dated 19 May but postmarked 18 May.—Ed.]

[39] See the letter of J. S. M. to W. J. Fox of June 1833 in the same collection. [Mill, *Earlier Letters*, vol. 12 of *Collected Works*, p. 159.]

[40] The copy of *Pauline* containing Mill's notes came later into the possession of John Forster and with his library reached the Victoria and Albert Museum, London, where it is now preserved in the Forster and Dyce Collection (pressmark 48.D.46). [The Forster Collection, where the annotated copy of *Pauline* resides, is accessible at http://www.vam.ac.uk/content/articles/n/national-art-library-forster-collection/.—Ed.]

[41] J. S. M. to W. J. Fox, 10 October 1833, in the Library of King's College, Cambridge. [The full letter appears in Mill, *Earlier Letters*, vol. 12 of *Collected Works*, pp. 185–89; the passage above is at p. 185.—Ed.]

[42] W. H. Griffin and H. C. M. Minchin, *The Life of Robert Browning* (1938), p. 59. [W. Hall Griffin, *The Life of Robert Browning with Notices of His Writings, His Family & His Friends*, 3rd ed., ed. Harry Christopher Minchin (London: Methuen & Co. Ltd., 1938), pp. 59–60.—Ed.]

moyennant quoi he will think her and call her everything that is handsome, and he promises her that she shall find it mighty pleasant. Then he leaves off by saying that he knows he shall have changed his mind by to-morrow, and 'despite these intents which seem so fair', but that having been thus visited once no doubt he will be again—and is therefore 'in perfect joy', bad luck to him! as the Irish say. A cento of most beautiful passages might be made from this poem, and the psychological history of himself is powerful and truthful—*truth-like* certainly, all but the last stage. *That*, he evidently has not yet got into. The self-seeking and self-worshipping state is well described—beyond that, I should think the writer has made, as yet, only the next step, viz. into despising his own state. I even question whether part even of that self-disdain is not *assumed*. He is evidently *dissatisfied*, and feels part of the badness of his state; he does not write as if it were purged out of him. If he once could muster a hearty hatred of his selfishness it would *go*; as it is, he feels only the *lack* of *good*, not the positive evil. He feels not remorse, but only disappointment; a mind in that state can only be regenerated by some new passion, and I know not what to wish for him but that he may meet with a *real* Pauline.

Meanwhile he should not attempt to show how a person may be *recovered* from this morbid state, for *he* is hardly convalescent, and 'what should we speak of but that which we know'.

Mill took a much deeper interest in the other rising great poet of the time, Alfred Tennyson. Although the review of the second volume of Tennyson's poems, on which Mill had been working at about the time when he wrote on Browning, at first did not grow beyond an introduction which he later turned into his second article on poetry for the *Monthly Repository*,[43] it was, when it ultimately appeared two years later,[44] still the first full recognition of a great poet.

That at this time Mill's interests were inspired and shared by Mrs. Taylor we may also feel assured from the closeness of their contacts. At least by the spring of 1833 Mill seems to have been spending most of his free time at the new home of the Taylors at 17 Kent Terrace, Park Road, on the western edge of Regent's Park, to which they had moved from the City at some time during the preceding winter. In reply to W. J. Fox's mentioning that he had hoped to meet Mill there on a certain Wednesday, Mill explained:

---

[43] 'Two Kinds of Poetry' in *Monthly Repository* for November 1833, reprinted *D.D.*, vol. 1, p. 77, and in *Early Essays by John Stuart Mill*, ed. J. W. M. Gibbs (1897), pp. 221–26. ['Two Kinds of Poetry' appeared in the October 1833 *Monthly Repository*, and in *D.D.*, pp. 77–91. It is reprinted in Mill, *Autobiography*, vol. 1 of *Collected Works*, pp. 354–65, and in *Early Essays*, ed. Gibbs, pp. 219–36.—Ed.]

[44] 'Tennyson's Poems' in the *London Review* (July 1835), reprinted in *Early Essays* [ed. Gibbs], pp. 239–67. [Republished in Mill, *Autobiography*, vol. 1 of *Collected Works*, pp. 397–418.—Ed.]

J. S. M. to W. J. Fox, 19 May 1833:[45] I seldom go there without [some] special reasons on that day of the week, for as it cannot be right in the present circumstances to be there *every* evening, none costs so little to give up than [as] that in which there is [a] much shorter time and that [only] in the presence of others. Had I known of your going I would have gone—

And in another letter to Fox, only a week or two later, Mill said that he was 'going to Kent Terrace today, despite of its being Wednesday'.[46]

During the following summer Mill seems to have continued his visits at some place in the neighbourhood of London at which Mrs. Taylor was staying and there exist a few notes by her to him which may conjecturally be assigned to this period.

H. T. to J. S. M., summer 1833(?):[47] In the beautiful stillness of his lovely country—and with the fresh feeling of all the enjoyment it has been to him—and so soon after that which to him is such a quick-passing pleasure—he is perhaps feeling again, what he once said to me, that 'the less human the more lovely' I seemed to him. do you remember that my love? *I* have, because I felt that whatever such a feeling was, it was not love—and since how perfectly he has denied it,—or that may not be exactly the feeling, but only his old 'vanity of vanities' may have come back? neither one nor the other would grieve *me*, but for his own dear sake—for me I *am* loved as I desire to be—heart and soul take their rest in the peace of ample satisfaction after how much [calm] & care which of that kind at least has [have] passed for ever—o this sureness of an everlasting spiritual home is itself the blessedness of the blessed—& to that being added—or rather that being brought by, this exquisiteness which is & has been each instant since, & seems as if with no fresh food it would be enough for a long llfes [*sic*] enjoyment. O my own love, whatever it may or may not be to you, you need never regret for a moment what has already brought such increase of happiness and can in no possible way increase evil. If it is right to change the 'smallest chance' into

---

[45] King's College, Cambridge. [The full letter, dated 19 May and postmarked 18 May, is published in Mill, *Earlier Letters*, vol. 12 of *Collected Works*, pp. 157–58, with the passage above at p. 158.—Ed.]

[46] King's College, Cambridge, undated, probably June 1833. [Mill, *Earlier Letters*, vol. 12 of *Collected Works*, p. 159. The letter is dated June 1833, and the sentence in the text above reads, in full: 'As for *me*, I am going to K.T. today, despite its being Wednesday'.]

[47] MTColl. II/324, watermarked '1831'. Where dated letters by Mrs. Taylor are on paper with a dated watermark, the years usually agree or are at least not more than a year apart, and though this letter is not likely to be of 1831 it may well be of 1832. [Hayek added the material in brackets at the end of this quotation. Harriet Taylor Mill, *Complete Works*, p. 325. Note 10 states that although Mill, *Earlier Letters*, vol. 12 of *Collected Works*, dates the letter as 1833, there is no evidence on the letter itself to confirm that date.—Ed.]

a '*distant certainty*' it w^d surely show want of intellect rather than use of it to [breaks off before end of page].

H. T. to J. S. M., summer 1833(?):[48] Far from being unhappy or even *low* this morning, I feel as tho' you had never loved me half so well as last night—& I am in the happiest spirits & quite *quite* well part of which is owing to that nice sight this morng. I am taking as much care of your robin as if it were your own sweet self. If I do not succeed in making *this* live I shall think it is not possible to tame a full grown one. It is very well but so was the other for two days. . . .

[& so I shall do] adieu darling. How *very* nice next month will be. I am quite impatient for it.

These letters may or may not belong to the summer of 1833 when the relation was evidently approaching a new crisis. We can watch some of the developments in Mill's letters to Carlyle, whom he had promised to visit at Craigenputtock[49] during his month's vacation in September. In a letter of 2 August he for the first time hinted mysteriously that this visit would remain in some measure uncertain 'because the only contingency which would prevent it may happen at any time, and will remain possible to the very last'.[50] A month later he wrote that the plan was definitely off:

J. S. M. to Thomas Carlyle, 5 September 1833:[51] There were about twenty chances to one that I should [see you in the autumn], but it is the twenty-first which has taken effect in Reality. I was mistaken, too, when I said that if I went not to Craigenputtoch I should go nowhere: I am going to Paris: the same cause which I then thought, if it operated at all, would [operate to] keep me here, now sends me there. It is a journey entirely of duty; nothing else, you will do me the justice to believe, would have kept me from Craigenputtoch after

---

[48] MTColl. II/316. The second sheet is torn off, and the conclusion given after the dots follows [sideways] on the margin after a few words concluding a sentence from the missing part. [Harriet Taylor Mill, *Complete Works*, p. 325.]

[49] ['A high moorland farm on the watershed between Dumfriesshire and Galloway' (Froude, *Thomas Carlyle, The First Forty Years*, vol. 1, p. 108), Craigenputtock was the ancestral home of Jane Welsh Carlyle, to which the couple moved in the face of financial pressures. See *ibid.*, pp. 385ff.—Ed.]

[50] *Letters* (ed. Elliot), vol. 1, p. 61. [The full letter is at pp. 57–62 and is reprinted in Mill, *Earlier Letters*, vol. 12 of *Collected Works*, pp. 169–73, with the passage above at p. 172.—Ed.]

[51] *Ibid.*, pp. 62–63. [Hayek added '[see you in the autumn]' to this passage. The full letter is at pp. 62–65 and is reprinted in Mill, *Earlier Letters*, vol. 12 of *Collected Works*, pp. 174–77, with the passage above at pp. 174–75.—Ed.]

what I have said & written so often; it is duty, and duty connected with a person to whom of all persons alive I am under the greatest obligations.

It seems that on the very day when he wrote this letter Mill must have spoken or written to Harriet Taylor more openly than before. All we have is the following note of hers to him, posted on the following day.

H. T. to J. S. M., 6 September 1833:[52] I am glad that you have said it—I am *happy* that you have—no one with any fineness & [or] beauty of character but must feel compelled to say *all*, to the being they really *love*, or rather with any *permanent* reservation it is *not* love—while there is reservation, however little of it, the love is just *so much* imperfect. There has never, *yet*, been *entire* confidence *around* us. The difference between you and me in that respect is, that *I* have always *yearned* to have *your* confidence with an intensity of wish which has *often*, for a time, swallowed up the naturally stronger feeling. The affection itself—you have not given it, not that you *wished* to reserve—but that you did not *need* to give—but not having that need of course you had no perception that I had & so you had discouraged confidence from me 'till the habit of *checking first thoughts* has become so strong that when in your presence timidity has become almost a *disease* of the nerves. It would be absurd only it is so painful to notice in myself that every word I ever speak to you is detained a second before it is said 'till I am quite sure I am not by implication asking for your confidence. It is but that the only being who has ever called forth all my faculties of affection is the only one in whose presence I ever felt constraint.[53] At times when that has been strongly felt *I* too have doubted whether there was not possibility of disappointment—that doubt will never return. You can scarcely conceive dearest what *satisfaction* this note of yours is to me for I have been depressed by the fear that I w^d ~~wish~~ most [wish] altered in you, *you* thought quite well of, perhaps [thought] the best in your character. I am quite sure that want of energy *is* a defect, would be a defect if it belonged to the character, but that thank Heaven I am sure it does not. It is such an opposite to the *sort* of character.

Yes—these circumstances *do* require greater strength than any other—the greatest—that which you have, & which if you had not I should never have

---

[52] MTColl. L/4. [The full letter is published in Harriet Taylor Mill, *Complete Works*, pp. 326–28. The notes about the placement of the final paragraphs are provided at p. 328.—Ed.]

[53] There is in MTColl. II/321 also an undated fragment of a note by Mrs. Taylor expressing a similar idea and probably of about the same time: 'I on the contrary never did either "write or speak or look as I felt at the instant" to you. I have always suffered an instinctive dread that mine might be a foreign language to you. But the future must amend this, as well as many other things'. [The fragment, which is undated, is reprinted in Harriet Taylor Mill, *Complete Works*, p. 326.—Ed.]

loved you, I should not love you now. In this, as in all these [most] important matters there is no medium between the *greatest*, *all*, and none [nothing]— anything less than all being insufficient. there might be just as well none.

If I did not know them to be false, how heartily I should scorn such expressions, 'I have ceased to will'! then to *wish*? for does not *wish* with the power to *fulfill* constitute *will*? It is false that your 'strength is not equal to the circumstances in wh you have placed' yourself.—It is quite another thing to be guided by a judgment on which you can rely & which is better placed for judgment than yourself.

Would you let yourself 'drift with the tide whether it flow or ebb' if in one case every wave took you further from me? Would you not put what strength you have into resisting it? Would you not *wish* to resist it, would you not *will* to resist? Tell me—for if you would not, how happens it that you will to love me or any *most dear*!

However—since you tell me the evil & I believe that [the] evil, I may truly [surely] believe the good—and if all the good you have written in the last two or three notes be *firm truth*, there is *good enough*, even for me. The most horrible feeling I ever know is when for moments the fear comes over me that *nothing* which you say of yourself is to be absolutely relied on—that you are not *sure* even of your strongest feelings. Tell me again that it is *not*.

[perpendicular to rest of text] If it were certain that 'whatever one thinks best the other will think best' it is plain there *could* be no unhappiness—if that were certain want of energy could not be *felt*, could not be an evil, unless both wanted energy—the *only* evil there could [can] be for me is that you should *not* think my best your best—or should not agree in *my* opinion of my best.

[across the edge of p. 5] *dearest* I have but five minutes in w^h to write this or I should say more—but I was *obliged* to say something before to-morrow. t'was so long to wait *dearest*.

Of what must have preceded this we get a glimpse from a letter by Mill to Fox, written on the next day, in which he suggests that he might transfer to Fox's *Monthly Repository* the paper on Poetry which he had thought of putting at the head of the review of Tennyson.

J. S. M. to W. J. Fox, Saturday, 7 September 1833.[54] If you like the idea, and if you see *her* before Monday, will you mention it to her—you know it is hers—if she approves, it shall be yours. I shall see her on Monday myself,

[54] King's College, Cambridge. [Mill, *Earlier Letters*, vol. 12 of *Collected Works*, p. 178; the full letter is at pp. 178–79. Hayek added the bracketed material and notes that the page is torn at 'Yes' and 'herself'; *Earlier Letters* notes a tear also at 'out'.—Ed.]

and then I shall speak of the matter to her. [Ye]s[55]—she is like hers[elf][55] if she is ever ou[t] of spirits it is always something amiss in *me* that is the cause—it is so now—it is because she sees that what ought to be so much easier to me than to her, is in reality more difficult—costs a harder struggle—to part company with the opinion of the world, and with my former modes of doing good in it; however, thank heaven, she does not doubt that I can do it—

It seems that as the outcome of long discussions Mr. Taylor had been persuaded to agree to an experimental separation from his wife for six months, and in the course of September Mrs. Taylor left for Paris. Mill followed her there on the 10th of October for a stay of somewhat over six weeks. One of the letters which he wrote thence to Fox has been preserved and must be quoted in full.

J. S. M. to W. J. Fox, Paris, 5 or 6 November 1833:[56] I could have filled a long letter to you with the occurrences and feelings and thoughts of any one day since I have been here—this fortnight seems an age in mere duration, and *is* an age in what it has done for us two. It has brought years of experience to us—good and happy experience most of it. We never could have been so near, so perfectly intimate, in any former circumstances—we never could have been together as we have been in innumerable smaller relations and concerns—we never should have spoken of all things, in all frames of mind, with so much freedom and unreserve. I am astonished when I think how much has been restrained, how much untold, unshewn and uncommunicated till now—how much which by the mere [new] fact of its being spoken, has disappeared—so many real unlikenesses, so many more false impressions of unlikeness, most of which have only been revealed to me since they have ceased to exist or those which still exist have ceased to be felt painfully. Not a day has passed without removing some real & serious obstacle to happiness. I never thought so humbly of myself compared with her, never thought & [or] felt myself so little worthy of her, never more keenly regretted that I am not, in some things, very different, for her sake—yet it is so much to know as I do now; that almost all which has ever caused her any misgivings with regard to our fitness for each other was mistaken in point of fact—that the mistakes no longer exist—& that she is now (as she is) quite convinced that we are perfectly suited to pass our lives together—better suited indeed for that perfect than for this imperfect companionship. There will never again I believe be any obstacle to our being together entirely, from the slightest doubt that the

---

[55] Page torn.

[56] Yale University Library [MS 350, Box 1, Folder 2]. The English postmark is dated 7 November 1833. [Mill, *Earlier Letters*, vol. 12 of *Collected Works*, pp. 185–89.—Ed.]

experiment would succeed with respect to ourselves—not, as she used to say, for a short time, but for our natural lives. And yet—all the other obstacles or rather the one obstacle being as great as ever—our futurity is still perfectly uncertain. She has decided nothing except what has always been decided—not to renounce the liberty of sight—and it does not seem likely that anything will be decided until the end of the six months, if even *then* finally. For me, I am certain that whatever she decides will be wisest and rightest, even if she decides what was so repugnant to me at first—to remain here alone—it is repugnant to me still—but I can now see that perhaps it will be best—the future will decide that.

When will you write again—she shewed me your letter—is beautiful in *you* to write so to any one, but who could write otherwise to her?

I am happy, but not *so* happy as when the future appeared surer.

I had written thus far before receiving your letter, and I am glad of it. I have now taken a larger sheet and copied the above ~~unto~~ [into] it.

Your letter does indeed show that you do not at all 'understand her state' and never have understood it—this I have only lately begun to suspect, & never was quite sure of it till now—and I see that under the presumption that you were more aware than I perceive you are of the real state of her feelings, I myself have said & written things which have confirmed you in the wrong impression.

You seem to think that she *was* decided, and *is* now undecided—that the state of feeling which led to the separation has been as you say 'interrupted' and is to be 'recommenced'. Now this is an incorrect and so far a lower idea of her than the true one—she *never* had decided upon anything except not to give up either the feeling, or the power of communication with me—unless she did so, it was *Mr. Taylor's* wish, and seemed to be necessary to his comfort that she should live apart from him. When the separation had actually taken place, the result did as you say seem certain—not because we had willed to make it so, but because it seemed the necessary consequence of the new circumstances if the feelings of all continued the same. This was the sole cause & I think cause enough for the hopefulness and happiness which I felt almost all that month and which must have made a false impression on you. I never felt sure of what was to be after the six months, but I felt an immense increase of the chances in my favour. When I came here, I *expected* to find her no more decided than she had always been about what would be best for all, but *not* to find her as for the first time I did, doubtful about what would be best for our *own* happiness—under the influence of that fact and of the painful feelings it excited, I wrote to you. *That* doubt, thank heaven, lasted but a short time—if I had delayed my letter two days longer I should never have sent it.

If Mr. Taylor feels as you believe he does, he has been very far from telling her 'all he feels'; for his last letter to her, which came by the same post as this of yours (the first she has ever shewed me) is in quite another tone. He is most entirely mistaken in all the facts. Her affection to [for] him, which originated in gratitude for his affection & kindness, instead of being weakened by this stronger feeling, has been greatly *strengthened*, by so many new proofs of *his* affection for *her*, & by the unexpected & (his nature considered) really admirable generosity & nobleness which he has shewn under so severe a trial. Instead of *reviving* in absence, her affection for him has been steady throughout; it is of quite another character from *this* feeling, & therefore does not in the least conflict with it *naturally*, & now when circumstances have thrown the two into opposition she can no more overcome, or wish to overcome the one, than the other. The difference is, that the one, being only *affection*, not *passion*, would be satisfied with knowing him to be happy though away from her— but if the choice were absolutely between giving up the stronger feeling, & making him (what he says he should be) durably wretched, I am quite convinced that either would be [more(?)][57] than she could bear. I know it is the common notion of passionate love that it sweeps away all other affections— but surely the *justification* of passion, & one of its greatest beauties & glories, is that in an otherwise fine character it weakens *no* feeling which deserves to subsist, but would naturally strengthen them all. Because her letters to Mr. Taylor express the strong affection she has always felt, and he is no longer seeing, every day, proofs of her far stronger feeling for another, he thinks the affection has *come back*—he might have seen it quite as plainly before, only he refused to believe it. *I* have seen it, and felt its immense power over her, in moments of intense excitement with which I am sure he would believe it to be utterly incompatible.

Her affection for him, which has always been the principal, is now the sole obstacle to our being together—for the present there seems absolutely no prospect of that obstacle's being got over. She believes—& she knows him better than any of us can—that it would be the breaking-up of his whole future life—*that* she is determined never to be the cause of, & as I am as determined never to urge her to it, & [as] convinced that if I did I should fail. Nothing could justify it but 'the most distinct perception' that it is not only 'necessary to the happiness of both', but the only means of saving both or either from insupportable unhappiness. That can never be unless the alternative were entire giving up. I believe he is quite right in his impression that the worst for him which is to be expected at the end of the six months is her remaining permanently here. She will, if it is in human power to do so, make him understand the exact state of her feelings, and will as at present minded, give *him* the choice of every possible arrangement except entire giving-up, with the strong wish that her remaining here may be his choice;

---

[57] Page torn. [The square brackets are in Hayek's text.—Ed.]

with a full understanding however that the agreement whatever it be, is to be no longer binding than while it is found endurable. This seems but a poor result to come of so much suffering & so much effort, but for *us* even so the gain is great.

She has seen and approved all that precedes, therefore it is as much her letter as mine. So now you know the whole state of the case.

She is on the whole far happier than I have ever known her, and quite well physically though far from strong—I have many anxious *thoughts* of how she is to bear the being again alone with so little of hope to sustain her. I am so convinced of all I have written above, that if the final decision were already made (whatever it might be) I am certain that the fact of Mr. Taylor's being to be here so soon after I am gone would be a real & great good to her—but *now*, I am afraid unless she sees her way clearly to some tolerably satisfactory arrangement in the first few days of his visit she will only be made more unhappy by being made to feel [still] more keenly the impossibility of avoiding great unhappiness to him.

You know, perhaps, that her brother has been here—nothing could have been better or sweeter than all he said & did—he was even *friendly*.

Can I do anything for you here—see anyone, or bring over anything for you—I shall leave Paris probably Friday week.

It is idle, almost, to *say* any thanks for all you are saying and doing for our good & for such part of the interest you feel in it, as regards me personally—I may be able some time or other to make some return to you for it all, more than by invoking as I do, all the blessings earth is heir to upon you [and yours].

~~Yours~~

J. S. M.

A small slip of paper which was probably enclosed with this letter carried a note from Mrs. Taylor to Fox and Eliza Flower:[58]

I had written to you dearest friends both,—as you are—but now that I have seen that letter[59] of yrs, I cannot send mine. It is sad to be misunderstood by you—as I have been before—but it will not be always so—my own dear friends. O what a letter was that! but my head & soul bless you both.

He tells you quite truly our state—all at least wh. he attempts to tell—but there is so much more might be said—there has been so much more pain than

---

[58] Yale University Library [MS 350, Box 1, Folder 2. The letter is dated 5? November 1833.—Ed.]

[59] [Hayek has a query in the text here.—Ed.]

I thought I was capable of, but also O how much more happiness. O this being seeming as tho God had willed to show the type of the possible elevation of humanity. To be with him wholly is my ideal of the noblest fate for all states of mind & feeling which are lofty & large & fine, he is the companion spirit and heart desire—we are not alike in trifles only because I have so much more triviality[60] than he. Why do you not write to me my dearest Lizzie? (I never wrote that name before) if you w^d say on the merest scrap what you are talking about—what the next sermon is about where you walked to, & such like, how glad I should be! You must come here—it is a most beautiful paradise. O how happy we might all be in it. You will see it with me, bless you! won't you?

When Mill returned to London about 20 November he at once saw Fox and a few days later again wrote to him.

J. S. M. to W. J. Fox, London, 22 November (?) 1833.[61] I have the strongest wish, and some hope, that there will some day arrive a sketch of Paris, in the manner of some of your local sketches—if there does, it will be the most beautiful thing ever written—she has spoken quite enough to me at different times, to shew what it would be.

Have you seen Mr. Taylor? he has received a letter by this time, part of which she has sent to me, and which if he was still in the state in which you last saw him, will certainly put him completely out of it. Ed. Hardy[62] while he confirms all you told me of the impression her precious letter made upon him when it came, bringing back his old hopes and theories, affirms positively that all this had quite gone off before he received any other letter, & that his acquiescence in her return to him is *not* given under the influence of those hopes and theories but of a real intention of being with her as a *friend and companion*. His conduct & feelings *now*, will shew whether this is correct. I shall be anxious to know your impression when you shall have seen him in his present state.

It seems he had written to her *again* since I left Paris—she writes 'I had yesterday one of those letters from Mr Taylor which make us admire & love him. He says that this plan & my letters have given him delight—that he has been selfish—but in future will think more for others & less for himself—but still he talks of this plan being good *for all*, by which he means *me*, as he says he is sure it will "prevent after misery" & again he wishes for complete confidence. I have written exactly what I think without reserve'.

---

[60] [Hayek has 'frivolity' in the text here.—Ed.]

[61] Yale University Library. The beginning of the letter, dealing with other matters, is not reproduced. [Mill, *Earlier Letters*, vol. 12 of *Collected Works*, p. 189. The letter is dated 22 November 1833.—Ed.]

[62] Mrs. Taylor's brother.

We do not know what 'this plan' was, but apparently some sort of compromise solution was agreed upon not long after. From another letter by Mill to Fox written within a week of this[63] we learn that Mill still did not expect to remain in England and for this reason felt unable to pursue a suggestion of taking a share in the control of the *Examiner*, which was in difficulties. At the same time, in a very full report to Carlyle on conditions in Paris,[64] which the latter intended to visit, Mill expressed the hope of seeing him there in the following summer. It seems however that Mrs. Taylor returned to England long before the end of the six months and probably even before the end of 1833. The understanding seems to have been that while Mr. Taylor agreed to the continuance of the friendship, the external appearances of married life should be preserved. Perhaps it was to this date that Mrs. Taylor referred when, some twenty years later, she gave a foreign visitor emphatically to understand that since the beginning of her friendship with Mill she had been to neither of the two men *more* than a *Seelenfreundin*.[65] We do not know whether it was already at that time or only a few years later that she commenced to live most of the time in the country[66] with her small daughter, only occasionally visiting Kent Terrace, while the two boys were apparently placed in some boarding school.

[63] Dated 26 November 1833 and partly published in Richard Garnett, *The Life of W. J. Fox*, pp. 151–52. [Mill, *Earlier Letters*, vol. 12 of *Collected Works*, p. 198.—Ed.]

[64] J. S. M. to Thomas Carlyle, 25 November 1833. *Letters* (ed. Elliot), vol. 1, pp. 71–80. [The letter is published in Mill, *Earlier Letters*, vol. 12 of *Collected Works*, pp. 190–97. In the Elliot edition, it is found at pp. 71–81.—Ed.]

[65] H. Gomperz, *Theodor Gomperz, Briefe und Aufzeichnungen ausgewählt, erlätert und zu einer Darstellung seines Lebens verknüpft von Heinrich Gomperz*, vol. 1 (Vienna: Gerold & Co., 1936), p. 233.

[66] For some time during the 1830's she appears to have taken a house in Kingston-on-Thames, before about 1839 she moved to Walton-on-Thames, where she lived during most of the next ten years.

THREE

ON MARRIAGE AND DIVORCE
about 1832

The situation and the natural inclinations of both parties must have combined from the beginning to make the position of women and their position in marriage one of the main topics of common interest to Mill and Harriet Taylor. The principles at issue are not touched upon in any of the early letters which have survived, but we have two manuscript essays which they wrote for each other at a very early date. Since Mill's and an earlier draft of Harriet Taylor's are on paper watermarked '1831' and a later version of hers on paper watermarked '1832' we shall probably not go far wrong in attributing them to the latter year. Mill's is much the longer and may be given first. It tends to confirm his claim in the *Autobiography* that contrary to what an uninformed person would probably suspect, this was not one of the subjects on which he was mainly indebted to her for his ideas. He says there that

> it might be supposed, for instance, that in my strong convictions on the complete equality in all legal, political, social and domestic relations, which ought to exist between men and women, may have been adopted or learnt from her. This was so far from being the fact, that those convictions were among the earliest results of the application of my mind to political subjects, and the strength with which I held them was, [as] I believe, more than anything else, the originating cause of the interest she felt in me. What is true is, that until I knew her, the opinion was, in my mind, little more than an abstract principle. . . . I am indeed painfully conscious of how much of her best thoughts on the subject I have failed to reproduce, and how greatly that little treatise [*The Subjection of Women*] falls short of what would have been [given to the world] if she had put on paper her entire mind on this question, or had lived to revise and improve, as she certainly would have done, my imperfect statement of the case.[1]

[1] *Autobiography* pp. 206–7, footnote. [*Autobiography and Literary Essays*, eds. John M. Robson and Jack Stillinger, vol. 1 (1981) of *The Collected Works of John Stuart Mill* [hereafter cited as *Collected Works*] (Toronto: University of Toronto Press, 1962–1991), p. 253 note. The *Collected Works* (but not the Oxford) edition reads: 'falls short of what would have been given to the world if she had put on paper'. Hayek supplies the title in brackets.—Ed.]

Here are his ideas on the subject as he expressed them for his friend about thirty-seven years before he stated them in print:[2]

> She to whom my life is devoted has wished for a written exposition of my opinions on the subject which, of all connected with human Institutions, is nearest to her happiness. Such as that exposition can be made without *her* to suggest and to decide, it is given in these pages: she, herself, has not refused to put into writing for *me*, what she has thought and felt on the same subject, and *there* I shall be taught all perhaps which I have, and certainly all which I have not, found out for myself. In the investigation of truth as in all else, 'it is not good for man to be alone'.[3] And more than all, in what concerns the relations of Man with Woman, the law which is to be observed by both should surely be made by both; not, as hitherto, by the stronger only.
>
> How easy would it be for either me or you, to resolve this question for ourselves alone! Its difficulties, for difficulties it has, are such as obstruct the avenues of all great questions which are to be decided for mankind at large, and therefore not for natures resembling each other, but for natures or at least characters tending to all the points of the moral compass. All popular morality is as I once said to you a compromise among conflicting natures, each renouncing a certain portion of what its own desires call for, in order to avoid the evils of a perpetual warfare with all the rest. That is the best popular morality, which attains this general pacification with the least sacrifice of the happiness of the higher natures, who are the greatest, indeed the only real, sufferers by the compromise; for *they* are called upon to give up what would really make them happy; while others are commonly required only to restrain desires the gratification of which would bring no real happiness. In the adjustment, moreover, of the compromise, the higher natures count only in proportion to their number, how small! & [or] to the number of those whom they can influence: while the conditions of the compromise weigh heavily upon them in the ~~states (?)~~ [ratio] of their greater capacity of happiness, and its natural consequence, their keener sense of *want* and disappointment when the degree of happiness which they know would fall to their lot but for untoward external circumstances, is denied them.
>
> By the higher natures I mean those characters who from the combination of natural and acquired advantages, have the greatest capacity of feeling happiness, and of bestowing it. Of bestowing it in two ways: as being beautiful to contemplate, and therefore the natural objects of admiration and love;

[2] MTColl.XLI/I. [The callout for note 2 is missing in Hayek's original. The essay, reproduced in full by Hayek, is catalogued as 'Paper on woman's position in society', MTC XLI, Folio 1–14. It is published as 'On Marriage', dated 1832–1833?, in Mill, *Essays on Equality, Law, and Education*, ed. John M. Robson, vol. 21 (1984) of *Collected Works*, pp. 35–49.—Ed.]

[3] [Genesis 2:18.—Ed.]

and also as being fitted, and induced, by their qualities of mind and heart, to promote by their actions, and by all that depends upon their will, the greatest possible happiness of all who are within the sphere of their influence.

If all persons were like these, or even would be guided by these, morality ~~would~~ [might] be very different from what it must now be; or rather it would not exist at all as morality, since morality and inclination would coincide. If all resembled you, my lovely friend, it would be idle to prescribe rules for them. By following their own impulses under the guidance of their own judgment, they would find more happiness, and would confer more, than by obeying any moral principles or maxims whatever; since these cannot possibly be adapted beforehand to every peculiarity of circumstance which can be taken into account by a sound and vigorous intellect *worked* by a strong *will*, and guided by what Carlyle calls 'an open loving heart'.[4] Where there exists a genuine and strong desire to do that which is most for the happiness of all, general rules are merely aids to prudence, in the choice of means; not peremptory obligations. Let but the desires be right, and the 'imagination lofty and refined':[5] and provided there be disdain of all false seeming, 'to the pure all things are pure'.[6]

It is easy enough to settle ~~to~~ [the] moral bearings of our question upon such characters. The highest natures are of course impassioned natures: to such, marriage is but one continued act of self-sacrifice where strong affection is not, every tie therefore which restrains them from seeking out and uniting themselves with some one whom they can perfectly love, is a yoke to which they cannot be subjected without oppression: and to such a person when found, they would natural[ly,] superstition apart, scorn to be united by any other tie than free and voluntary choice. If such natures have been healthily developed in other respects, they will have all other good and worthy feelings strong enough to prevent them from pursuing this happiness at the expense of greater suffering ~~of~~ [to] others, and that is the limit of the forbearance which morally[7] ought in such a case to enjoin.

But will the morality which suits the highest natures, in this matter, be also best for all inferior natures? My conviction is, that it will, but this can be only a happy accident. All the difficulties of morality in any of its ~~brands~~ [branches], grow out of the conflict which continually arises between the highest morality and even the best popular morality which the degree of development yet ~~achieved~~ [attained] by average human nature, will allow to exist.

[4] [Thomas Carlyle, 'Biography', *Fraser's Magazine*, vol. 5, April 1832, p. 259.   Ed.]

[5] [William Wordsworth, 'Weak is the will of Man, his judgment blind", in *The Poetical Works*, 5 vols. (London: Longman, Rees, Orme, Brown, and Green, 1827), 2:285.—Ed.]

[6] [Titus 1:15.—Ed.]

[7] [Hayek offers the correct word, 'morality', in the errata.—Ed.]

If all, or even most persons, in the choice of a companion of the other sex, were led by any real aspiration towards, or sense of, the happiness which such companionship in its best shape is capable of giving to the best natures, there would never have been any reason why law or opinion should have set any limits to the most unbounded freedom of uniting and separating: nor is it probable that popular morality would ever, in a civilized or refined people, have imposed any restraint upon that freedom. But, as I once said to you, the law of marriage as it now exists, has been made *by* sensualists, and *for* sensualists, and *to bind* sensualists. The aim and purpose of that law is either to tie up the sense, in the hope by so doing, of tying up the soul also, or else to tie up the sense because the soul is not cared about at all. Such purposes never could have entered into the minds of any to whom nature had given souls capable of the higher degrees of happiness: nor could such a law ever have existed but among persons to whose natures it was in some degree congenial, and therefore more suitable than at first sight may be supposed by those whose natures are widely different.

There can, I think, be no doubt that for a long time the indissolubility of marriage acted powerfully to elevate the social position of women. The state of things to which in almost all countries it succeeded, was one in which the power of repudiation existed on one side but not on both: in which the stronger might cast away the weaker, but the weaker could not fly from the [yoke of the] stronger. To a woman of [an] impassioned character, the difference between this and what now exists, is not worth much; for she would wish to be repudiated, rather than to remain united only because she could not be got rid of. But the aspirations of most women are less high. They would wish to retain any bond of union they have ever had with a man to whom they do not prefer any other, and for whom they have that inferior kind of affection which habits of intimacy frequently produce. Now, assuming what may be assumed of the greater number of men, that they are attracted to women solely by sensuality or at best by a transitory *taste*; it is not deniable, that the irrevocable vow gave to women when the passing gust had blown over, a permanent hold upon the men who would otherwise have cast them off. Something, indeed *much*, of a community of interest, arose from the mere fact of being indissolubly united: the husband took an interest in the wife as being *his* wife, if he did not from any better feeling: it became essential to his respectability that his wife also should be respected; and commonly when the first revulsion of feeling produced by satiety, went off, the mere fact of continuing together, if the woman had anything loveable in her and the man was not wholly brutish, could hardly fail to raise up some feeling of regard and attachment. She obtained also, what is often far more precious to her, the certainty of not being separated from the [her] children.

Now if this be all that human life *has* for women, it is little enough: and any woman who feels herself capable of great happiness, and whose aspirations have not been artificially checked, will claim to be set free from *only* this, to seek for more. But women in general, as I have already remarked, are more easily contented. And this I believe to be the cause of the general aversion of women to the idea of facilitating divorce. They have a habitual belief that their power over men is chiefly derived from men's sensuality; and that the same sensuality would go elsewhere in search of gratification, unless restrained by law and opinion. They, on their part, mostly seek in marriage, a home, and the state or condition of a married woman, with the addition or not as it may happen, of a splendid establishment &c. &c. These things once obtained, the indissolubility of marriage renders them sure of keeping. And most women, either because these things [really] give them all the happiness they are capable of, or from the artificial barriers which curb all spontaneous movements to seek their greatest felicity, are generally more anxious not to peril the good they have than to go in search of a greater. If marriage were dissoluble, they think they could not retain the position once acquired; or not without practising upon the ~~attention~~ [affections] of men by those arts, disgusting in the extreme to any woman of simplicity, by which a cunning mistress sometimes establishes and retains her ascendancy.

These considerations are nothing to an impassioned character; but there is something in them, for the characters from which they emanate—is not that so? The only conclusion, however, which can be drawn from them, is one for which there would exist ample grounds even if the law of marriage as it now exists were perfection. This conclusion is, the absurdity and immorality of a state of society and opinion in which a woman is at all dependent for her social position upon the fact of her being or not being married. Surely it is wrong, wrong in every way, and on every view of morality, even the vulgar view, that there should exist any motives to marriage except the happiness which two persons who love one another feel in associating their existence.

The means by which the condition of [a] married ~~women~~ [woman] is rendered artificially desirable, are not any superiority of legal rights, for in that respect single women, especially if possessed of property, have the advantage, the civil disabilities are greatest in the case of the married woman. It is not law, but education and custom which make the difference. Women are so brought up, as not to be able to subsist in the mere physical sense, without a man to keep them: they are so brought up as not to be able to protect themselves against injury or insult, without some man on whom they have a special claim, to protect them, they are so brought up, as to have no vocation or useful office to fulfil in the world, remaining single; for all women who are educated [for anything except to *get* married, are educated] to *be* married, and what little they are taught deserving the name useful, is chiefly what in the ordinary course of things will not come into actual use, unless nor until they are married. A single woman therefore is felt both by herself and others as a kind of excrescence on the surface of society, having no use or function or office there. She is not indeed precluded from useful and honorable exertion of various kinds, but a married woman is *presumed* to be a useful member of society unless there is evidence to the contrary; a single woman must establish, what very few either women or men ever do establish, an *individual* claim.

All this, though not the less really absurd and immoral even under the law of marriage which now exists, evidently grows out of that law, and fits into the general state of society of which that law forms a part; nor could continue to exist if the law were changed, and marriage were not a contract at all, or were an easily dissoluble one. The indissolubility of marriage is the keystone of woman's present lot, and the whole comes down and must be reconstructed if that is removed.

And the truth is, that this question of marriage cannot properly be considered by itself alone. The question is not what marriage ought to be, but a far wider question, what woman ought to be. Settle that first, and the other will settle itself. Determine whether marriage is to be a relation between two equal beings, or between a superior and an inferior, between a protector and a dependent; and all other doubts will easily be resolved.

But in this question there is surely no difficulty. There is no natural inequality between the sexes; except perhaps in bodily strength; even *that* admits of doubt: and if bodily strength is to be the measure of superiority, mankind are no better than savages. Every step in the progress of civilization has tended to diminish the deference paid to bodily strength, until now when that quality confers scarcely any advantages except its natural ones: the strong man has little or no power to employ his strength as a means of acquiring any other advantage over the weaker in body. Every step in the progress of civilization has similarly been marked by a nearer approach to equality in the condition of the sexes; and if they are still far from being equal, the hindrance is not now in the difference of physical strength, but in artificial feelings and prejudices.

If nature has not made men and women unequal, still less ought the law to make them so. It may be assumed, as one of those presuppositions [propositions] which would almost be made weaker by anything so ridiculous as attempting to prove them, that men and women ought to be perfectly coequal: that a woman ought not to be dependent on a man, more than a man on a woman, except so far as their affections make them so, by a voluntary surrender, renewed and renewing at each instant by free and spontaneous choice.

But this perfect independence of each other for all save affection, cannot be, if there be dependence in pecuniary circumstances: a dependence which in the immense majority of cases must exist, if the woman be not capable, as well as the man, of gaining her own subsistence.

The first and indispensable step, therefore, towards the enfranchisement of woman, is that she be so educated, as not to be dependent either on her father or her husband for subsistence: a position which in nine cases out of ten, makes her either the plaything or the slave of the man who feeds her; and in the tenth case, only his humble friend. Let it not be said that she has an equivalent and compensating advantage in the exemption from toil: men think it base and servile in men to accept food as the price of dependence, and why do they not deem it so in women? solely because they do not desire that women should be their equals. Where there is strong affection, dependence is its own reward: but it must be voluntary dependence; and the more perfectly voluntary it is,—the more exclusively each owes every thing to the other's affection and to nothing else,—the greater is the happiness. And where affection is not, the woman who will be dependent for the sake of a maintenance, proves herself as low-minded as a man in the like case—or *would* prove herself so, if that resource were not too often the only one her education has given her, and if her education had not also taught her not to consider as a degradation, that which is the essence of all prostitution, the act of delivering up her person for bread.

It does not follow that a woman should *actually* support herself because she should be *capable* of doing so: in the natural course of events she will *not.* It is not desirable to burthen the labour market with a double number of competitors. In a healthy state of things, the husband would be able by his single exertions to earn all that is necessary for both; and there would be no need that the wife should take part in the mere providing of what is required to *support* life: it will be for the happiness of both that her occupation should rather be to adorn and beautify it. Except in the class of actual day-labourers, that will be her natural task, if task it can be called which will in so great a measure, be accomplished rather by *being* than by *doing.*

We have all heard the vulgar talk that the proper employments of a wife are household superintendence, and the education of her children. As for household superintendence, if nothing be meant but merely seeing that servants do their duty, that is not an occupation, every woman that [who] is capable of doing it at all can do it without devoting anything like half an hour every day to that purpose peculiarly. It is not like the duty of a head of an office, to whom his subordinates bring their work to be inspected when finished: the defects in the performance of household duties present *themselves* to inspection: skill in superintendence consists in knowing the right way of noticing a fault when it occurs, and giving reasonable advice and instruction how to avoid it; and more depends [up]on establishing a good *system* at first, than upon a perpetual and studious watchfulness. But if it be meant that the mistress of a family shall herself do the work of servants, *that* is good and will naturally take place in the rank in which there do not exist the means of hiring servants; but nowhere else.

Then as to the education of children: if by that term be meant, instructing them in particular arts or particular branches of knowledge, it is absurd to impose that upon mothers: absurd in two ways: absurd to set one-half of the adult human race to perform each on a small scale, what a much smaller number of teachers could accomplish for all, by devoting themselves exclusively to it; and absurd to set all mothers doing that for which some persons must be fitter than others, and for which average mothers cannot possibly be *so* fit as persons trained to the profession. Here again, when the means do not exist for [of] hiring teachers, the mother is the natural teacher: but no special provision needs to be made for that case. Whether she is to teach or not, it is desirable that she should *know*; because knowledge is desirable for its own sake; for its uses, for its pleasures, and for its beautifying influence when not cultivated to the neglect of other gifts. What she knows she will be able to teach to her children if necessary: but to erect such teaching into her occupation whether she can better employ herself or not, is absurd.

The education which it *does* belong to mothers to give, and which if not imbibed from them is seldom obtained in any perfection at all, is the training of the affections; and through the affections, of the conscience, and the whole moral being. But *this* most precious, and most indispensable part of education, does not take up *time*; it is not a business, an occupation; a mother does not accomplish it by sitting down with her child for one or two or three hours to a task. She effects it by *being* with the child; by making it happy, and therefore at peace with all things, by checking bad habits in the commencement; by loving the child, and by making the child love her. It is not by particular effects [efforts], but imperceptibly and unconsciously that she makes her own character pass into the child; that she makes the child love what she loves, venerate what she venerates and imitate as far as a child can, her example. These things cannot be done by a hired teacher; and they are better and greater, than all the rest. But to impose upon mothers what hired teachers *can* do, is mere squandering of the glorious existence of a woman fit for woman's highest destiny. With regard to such things, her part is to see that they are rightly done, not to do them.

The great occupation of woman should be to *beautify* life: to cultivate, for her own sake and that of those who surround her, all her faculties of mind, soul, and body; all her powers of enjoyment, and powers of giving enjoyment; and to diffuse beauty, and elegance, and grace, everywhere. If in addition to this the activity of her nature demands more energetic and definite employment, there is never any lack of it in the world. If she loves, her natural impulse will be to associate her existence with him she loves, and to share *his* occupations; in which, if he loves her (with that affection of *equality* which alone deserves to be called love) she will naturally take as strong an interest, and be as thoroughly conversant, as the most perfect confidence on his side can make her.

Such will naturally be the occupations of a woman who has fulfilled what seems to be considered as the end of her existence, and attained what is really its happiest state, by uniting herself to a man whom she loves. But whether so united or not, women will never be what they should be, nor their social position what it should be, until women, as universally as men, have the power of gaining their own livelihood: until, therefore, every girl's parents have either provided her with independent means of subsistence, or given her an education qualifying her to provide those means for herself. The only difference between the employments of women and those of men will be, that those which partake most of the beautiful, or which require delicacy and taste rather than muscular exertion, will naturally fall to the share of women: all branches of the fine arts in particular.

In considering, then, what is the best law of marriage, we are to suppose that women already are, what they would be in the best state of society; no less capable of existing independently and respectably without men, than men without women. Marriage, on whatever footing it might be placed, would be wholly a matter of choice, not, as for a woman it now is, something approaching to a matter of necessity; something, at least, which every woman is under strong artificial motives to desire, and which if she attain not, her life is considered to be a failure.

These suppositions being made; and it being no longer any advantage to a woman to be married: merely for the sake of being married, why should any woman cling to the indissolubility of marriage, as if it could be for the good of one party that it should continue when the other party desires that it should be dissolved?

It is not denied by anyone, that there are numerous cases in which the happiness of both parties would be greatly promoted by a dissolution of marriage. We will add, that when the social position of the two sexes shall be perfectly equal, a divorce if it be for the happiness of either party, will be for the happiness of both. No one but a sensualist would desire to retain a merely animal connexion with a person of the other sex, unless perfectly assured of being preferred by that person, above all other persons in the world. This certainty never can be quite perfect under the law of marriage as it now exists: it would be nearly absolute, if the tie were merely voluntary.

Not only there are, but it is in vain to hope that there will not always be, innumerable cases, in which the first connexion formed will be one the dissolution of which if it *could* be, certainly would be, and ought to be, effected.

It has long ago been remarked that of all the more serious acts of the life of a human being, there is not one which is commonly performed with so little of forethought or consideration, as that which is irrevocable, and which is fuller of evil than any other act of the being's whole life if it turn out ill. And this is not so astonishing as it seems: The imprudence, while the contract remains indissoluble, consists in marrying at all: If you *do* marry, there is little wisdom shewn by a very anxious and careful deliberation beforehand. Marriage is really, what it has been sometimes called, a lottery; and whoever is in a state of mind to calculate chances calmly and value them correctly, is not at all likely to purchase a ticket. Those who marry after taking great pains about the matter, generally do but buy their disappointment dearer. ~~Then (?)~~ [For] the failures in marriage are such as are naturally incident to a first trial; the parties are inexperienced, and cannot judge. Nor does this evil seem to be remediable. A woman is allowed to give herself away for life, at an age at which she is not allowed to dispose of the most inconsiderable landed estate what then? if people are not to marry until they have learnt prudence, they will seldom marry before thirty: can this be expected, or is it to be desired? To direct the immature judgment, there is the advice of parents and guardians: a precious security! The only thing which a young girl can do, worse than marrying to please herself, is marrying to please any other person. However paradoxical it may sound to the ears of those who are reputed to have grown wise as wine grows good, by *keeping*, it is yet true, that A, an average person can better know what is for his own happiness, than B, an average person, can know what is for A's happiness. Fathers and mothers as the world is constituted, do not judge more wisely than sons and daughters; they only judge differently: and the judgments of both being of the ordinary strength, or rather of the ordinary weakness, a person's own self has the advantage of a considerably greater number of *data* to judge from, and the further one of a stronger interest in the subject. Foolish people will say, that being interested in the subject is a disqualification; strange that they should not distinguish between being interested in a cause as a party before a judge, i.e., interested in deciding one way, right or wrong,—and being interested as a person is in the management of his own property, interested in deciding right. The parties themselves are only interested in doing what is most for their happiness; but their relatives may have all sorts of selfish interests to promote by inducing them to marry or not to marry.

The first choice, therefore, is made under very complicated disadvantages. By the fact of its being the *first*, the parties are necessarily inexperienced in the particular matter; they are commonly young (especially the party who is in ~~the~~ greatest peril from a mistake) and therefore inexperienced in the knowledge and judgment of mankind and of themselves generally: and finally, they have seldom had so much as an opportunity ~~offered~~ [afforded] them, of gaining any real knowledge of each other, since in nine cases out of ten they have never been once in each other's society completely unconstrained, or without consciously or unconsciously acting a part.

The chances therefore are many to one against the supposition that a person who requires, or is capable of, great happiness, will find that happiness in a first choice: and in a very large proportion of cases the first choice is such that if it cannot be recalled, it only embitters existence. The reasons, then, are most potent for allowing a subsequent change.

What there is to be said in favor of the indissolubility, superstition apart, resolves itself into this: that it is highly desirable that changes should not be frequent; and desirable that the first choice should be, even if not compulsorily, yet very generally, persevered in: That consequently we ought to beware lest in giving facilities for retracting a bad choice, we hold out greater encouragement than at present for making such a choice as there will probably be occasion to retract.

It is proper to state as strongly as possible the arguments which may be advanced in support of this view in [of the] question.

Repeated trials for happiness, and repeated failures, have the most mischievous effect on all minds. The finer spirits are broken down, and disgusted with all things: their susceptibilities are deadened, or converted into sources of bitterness, and they lose the power of being ever *contented*. On the commoner natures the effects produced are not the less deplorable. Not only is their capacity for [of] happiness worn out, but their morality is depraved: all refinement and delicacy of character is extinguished; all sense of any peculiar duties or of any peculiar sacredness attaching to the relation between the sexes, is worn away; and such alliances come to be looked upon with the very same kind of feelings which are now connected with a passing intrigue.

Thus much as to the parties themselves, but besides the parties, there are also to be considered their children; beings who are wholly dependent both for happiness and for excellence upon their parents; and who in all but the extreme cases of actual profligacy, or perpetual bickering and discussion [disunion], *must* be better cared for in both points if their parents remain together.

So much importance is due to this last consideration, that I am convinced, if marriage were easily dissoluble, two persons of opposite sexes who unite their destinies would generally, if they were wise, think it their duty to avoid having children until they had lived together for a considerable length of time, and found in each other a happiness adequate to their aspirations. If this principle of morality were observed, how many of the difficulties of the subject we are considering would be smoothed down! To be jointly the parents of a human being, should be the very last pledge of the deepest, holiest, and most desirable [durable] affection, for *that* is a tie which independently of convention, is indeed indissoluble: an additional and external tie, most precious where the souls are already indissolubly united, but simply burthensome while it appears possible to either that they should ever desire to separate.

It can hardly be anticipated, however, that such a course will be followed by any but those who to the greatest loftiness and delicacy of feeling, unite the power of the most deliberate reflexion. If the feelings be obtuse, the force of these considerations will not be felt; and if the judgment be weak or hasty, whether from inherent defect or [from] inexperience, people will fancy themselves in love for their whole lives with a perfect being, when the case is far otherwise, and will suppose they risk nothing by creating a new relationship with that being, which can no longer be got rid of. It will therefore most commonly happen that when circumstances arise which induce the parents to separate, there will be children to suffer by the separation: nor do I see how this difficulty can be entirely got over, until the habits of society allow of a regulated community of living, among persons intimately acquainted, which would prevent the necessity of a total separation between the parents even when they had ceased to be connected by any nearer tie than mutual goodwill, and a common interest in their children.

There is yet another argument which may be urged against facility of divorce. It is this. Most persons have but a very moderate capacity of happiness; but no person ever finds this out without experience, very few even with experience: and most persons are constantly wreaking[8] that discontent which has its source internally, upon outward things. Expecting therefore in marriage, a far greater degree of happiness than they commonly find; and knowing not that the fault is in their own scanty capabilities of happiness— they fancy they should have been happier with someone else: or at all events the disappointment becomes associated in their minds with the being in whom they had placed their hopes—and so they dislike one another for a time—and during that time they would feel inclined to separate: but if they remain united, the feeling of disappointment after a time goes off, and they pass their lives together with fully as much [of] happiness as they could find either singly or in any other union, without having undergone the wearing of repeated and unsuccessful experiments.

Such are the arguments for adhering to the indissolubility of the contract, and for such characters as compose the great majority of the human race, it is not deniable that these arguments have considerable weight.

That weight however is not so great as it appears. In all the above arguments it is tacitly assumed, that the choice lies between the absolute interdiction of divorce, and a state of things in which the parties would separate on

---

[8] [Hayek has a query after the word 'wreaking'.—Ed.]

the most passing feeling of dissatisfaction. Now this is not really the alternative. Were divorce ever so free, it would be resorted to under the same sense of moral responsibility and under the same restraints from opinion, as any other of the acts of our lives. In no state of society but one in which opinion sanctions almost promiscuous intercourse (and in which therefore even the indissoluble bond is not practically regarded,) would it be otherwise than disreputable to either party, the woman especially, to change frequently, or on light grounds. My belief is, that in a tolerably moral state of society, the first choice would almost always, especially where it had produced children, be adhered to, unless in case of such uncongeniality of disposition as rendered it positively uncomfortable to one or both of the parties to live together, or in case of a strong passion conceived by one of them for a third person. Now in either of these cases I can conceive no argument strong enough to convince me, that the first connexion ought to be forcibly preserved.

I see not why opinion should not act [with] as great efficacy, to enforce the true rules of morality in these [this] matters, as the false. Robert Owen's definitions[9] of chastity and prostitution, are quite as simple and take as firm a hold of the mind as the vulgar ones which connect the ideas of virtue and vice with the performance or non-performance of an arbitrary ceremonial.

The arguments, therefore, in favour of the indissolubility of marriage, are as nothing in comparison with the far more potent arguments for leaving this like the other relations voluntarily contracted by human beings, to depend for its continuance upon the wishes of the contracting parties. The strongest of all these arguments is that by no other means can the condition and character of women become what it ought to be.

When women are [were] merely slaves, to give them a permanent hold upon their masters was a first step towards their evolution [elevation]. That step is now complete: and in the progress of civilization, the time has come when women may aspire to something more than merely to find a protector. The position [condition] of a single woman has ceased to be dangerous and precarious: the law, and general opinion, suffice without any more special guardianship, to shield her in ordinary circumstances from insult or inquiry [injury]: woman in short is no longer a mere property, but a person, who is counted not solely on her husband's or father's account but on her own. She is now ripe for equality. But it is absurd to talk of equality while marriage is an indissoluble tie. It was a change greatly for the better, from a state in which all the obligation was on the side of the weaker, all the rights on the side of the physically stronger, to even the present condition of an obligation

---

[9] *Chastity*, sexual intercourse *with* affection. *Prostitution*, sexual intercourse *without* affection. (J. S. M.'s footnote). [In Mill's manuscript, the text of the note is placed to the left of the main text and the note is marked by a superscript 'x' in the text. See the note to the text in 'On Marriage', in Mill, *Essays on Equality, Law, and Education*, vol. 21 of *Collected Works*, p. 48.—Ed.]

nominally equal on both. But this nominal equality is not real equality. The stronger is always able to relieve himself wholly or in a great measure, from as much of the obligation as he finds burthensome: the weaker cannot. The husband can ill-use his wife, neglect her, and seek other women, not perhaps altogether with impunity, but what are the penalties which opinion imposes on him, compared with those which fall upon the wife who even with that provocation, retaliates upon her husband? It is true perhaps that if divorce were permitted, opinion would with like injustice, try the wife who resorted to that remedy, by a harder measure[10] than the husband. But this would be of less consequence. Once separated she would be comparatively independent of opinion: but so long as she is forcibly united to one of those who *make* the opinion, she must to a great extent be its slave.

Several scraps or drafts of Harriet Taylor on the same subject have been preserved of which the following is the most complete and may well be the one which in fulfillment of her promise she gave to Mill.[11]

If I could be Providence for [to] the world for a time, for the express purpose of raising the condition of women, I should come to you to know the *means*—the *purpose* would be to remove all interference with affection, or with any thing which is, or which even might be supposed to be, demonstrative of affection—In the present state of womens mind, perfectly uneducated, and with whatever of timidity and dependance is natural to them increased a thousand fold by their habits of utter dependance, it would probably be mischievous to remove at once all restraints, they would buy themselves protectors at a dearer cost than even at present—but without raising their natures at all, it seems to me, that once give women the desire to raise their social condition, and they have a power which in the present state of civilization and of mens characters, might be made of tremendous effect. Whether nature made a difference in the nature of men and women or not, it seems now that all men, with the exception of a few lofty minded, are sensualists more or less—Women on the contrary are quite exempt from this trait, however it may appear otherwise in the cases of some—It seems

---

[10] [Hayek has a query here in the text.—Ed.]

[11] MTColl., Box III/79, on paper watermarked '1832'. An earlier draft on part of the same on paper watermarked '1831', *ibid.*, Box III/17. [Two versions of this essay appear in *The Complete Works of Harriet Taylor Mill*, ed. Jo Ellen Jacobs (Bloomington: Indiana University Press, 1998), as 'On Marriage' (pp. 21–24) and 'Legislative Interference in Matters of Feeling' (pp. 20–21). The latter is there identified as Hayek's source but the text above is closer to that in 'On Marriage'. The essay is also reproduced as 'Appendix A: Harriet Taylor, On Marriage (1832–1833?)', in Mill, *Essays on Equality, Law, and Education*, vol. 21 of *Collected Works*. The text above has been rendered consistent with the version that appears in the *Collected Works*.—Ed.]

strange that it should be so, unless it was meant to be a source of power in demi-civilized states such as the present—or it may not be so—it may be only that the habits of freedom and low indulgence on [in] which boys grow up and the contrary notion of what is called purity in girls may have produced the appearance of different natures in the two sexes—As certain it is that there is equality in nothing, now—all the pleasures such as they are being mens, and all the disagreeables and pains being womens, as that every pleasure would be infinitely heightened both in kind and degree by the perfect equality of the sexes. Women are educated for one single object, to gain their living by marrying—(some poor souls get it without the churchgoing—It's [in] the same way—they do not seem to [me] be a bit worse than their honoured sisters)—To be married is the object of their existence and that object being gained they do really cease to exist as to anything worth calling life or any useful purpose. One observes very few marriages where there is any real sympathy or enjoyment of companionship between the parties—The woman knows what her power is, and gains by it what she has been taught to consider 'proper' to her state. The woman who would gain power by such means is unfit for power, still they do lose (?) use this power for paltry advantages and I am astonished it has never occurred to them to gain some large purpose: but their minds are degenerated by habits of dependance—I should think that 500 years hence none of the follies of their ancestors will so excite wonder and contempt as the fact of legislative restraint as to matters of feeling—or rather in the expressions of feeling. When once the law undertakes to say which demonstration of feeling shall be given to which, it seems quite [in]consistent not to legislate for all, and to say how many shall be seen, how many heard, and what kind and degree of feeling allows of shaking hands—the Turks is the only consistent mode—

I have no doubt that when the whole community is really educated, tho' the present laws of marriage were to continue they would be perfectly disregarded, because no one would marry—The widest and perhaps the quickest means to do away with its evils is to be found in promoting education—as it is the means of all good—but meanwhile it is hard that those who suffer most from its evils and who are always the best people, should be left without remedy. Would not the best plan be divorce which could be attained by *any, without any reason assigned*, and at small expence, but which could only be finally pronounced after a long period? not *less* time than two years should elapse between suing for divorce and permission to contract again   but what the decision will be *must* be certain at the moment of asking for it—*unless* during that time the suit should be withdrawn—

(I feel like a lawyer in talking of it only! O how absurd and little it all is!)—In the present system of habits and opinions, girls enter into what is called a contract perfectly ignorant of the conditions of it, and that they should be so is considered absolutely essential to their fitness for it!—But after all the one argument of the matter which I think might be said so as to strike both high and low natures is—Who would wish to have the person without [the] inclination? Whoever would take the benefit of a law of divorce must be those whose inclination is to separate and who on earth would wish another to remain with them against their inclination? I should think no one—people sophisticate about the matter now and will not believe that one '*really would wish to go*'. Suppose instead of calling it a 'law of divorce' it were to be called 'Proof of affection'—They would like it better then—

At this present time, in this state of civilization, what evil would be caused by, first placing women on the most entire equality with men, as to all rights and privileges, civil and political, and then doing away with all laws whatever relating to marriage? Then if a woman had children she must take [the] charge of them, women would not then have children without considering how to maintain them. Women would have no more reason to barter person for bread, or for anything else, than [men] have ~~men.~~—public offices being open to them alike, all occupations would be divided between the sexes in their natural arrangement. Fathers would provide for their daughters in the same manner as for their sons—

All the difficulties about divorce seem to be in the consideration for the children—but on this plan it would be the women's *interest* not to have children—*now* it is thought to be the womans interest to have children as so many *ties* to the man who feeds her.

~~Love~~ [*Sex*] in its true and finest meaning, seems to be the way in which is manifested all that is highest best and beautiful in the nature of human beings—none but poets have approached to the perception of the beauty of the material world—still less of the spiritual—and [there] ~~hence~~ never yet existed a poet, except by [the] inspiration of that feeling which is the perception of beauty in all forms and by all [the] means which are given us, as well as by *sight*. Are we not born with the *five* senses, merely as a foundation for others which we may make by them—and who extends and refines those material senses to the highest—into infinity—best fulfils the end of creation—That is only saying—*Who enjoys most, is most virtuous*—It is for *you*—the most worthy to be the apostle of all ~~the highest~~ [loftiest] virtue—to teach, such as may be taught, that the higher the *kind* of enjoyment, the *greater* the *degree*—perhaps there is but one class to whom this *can* be *taught*—the poetic nature struggling with superstition: *you* are fitted to be the saviour of such—

FOUR

FRIENDS AND GOSSIP
1834–1842

Much of the information we have about Mill and Harriet Taylor during the early years after their friendship had become intimate comes at second hand. For a few years in the middle of the 1830's they apparently made little attempt to conceal their intimacy until they became aware of the inevitable gossip which they had caused and withdrew almost completely from all social contacts. At that early stage Mill introduced Mrs. Taylor to a few friends, particularly the Carlyles, and it is from their numerous and in the later years not always too friendly comments that the now generally accepted picture of their relationship is mainly derived. It may be useful to interrupt the presentation of the new manuscript material and to bring together in a separate chapter the more important references by contemporaries.

The story told by John Roebuck, who for about ten years had been one of Mill's most intimate friends and who seems to have been the first with whom he broke completely on account of Mrs. Taylor, is characteristic. Roebuck had been present at the dinner party at which Mill first met Mrs. Taylor, but then lost sight of her until at a party at Mrs. Buller's, the mother of Mill's friend Charles Buller, he one day saw

> Mill enter the room with Mrs. Taylor hanging [up]on his arm. The manner of the lady, the evident devotion of the gentleman, soon attracted universal attention, and a suppressed titter went round the room. My affection for Mill was so warm and sincere that I was hurt by anything which brought ridicule upon him. I saw, or thought I saw, how mischievous might be this affair, and as we had become in all things like brothers, I determined, most unwisely, to speak to him on the subject.[1]

[1] R. E. Leader, *Life and Letters of J. A. Roebuck* (London, 1897), pp. 38 39. The party at the Bullers may well have been the soirée given on 15 June 1835, mentioned in *Letters and Memorials of Jane Welsh Carlyle*, ed. J. A. Froude (London: Longman's, Green, and Co., 1883) vol. 1, p. 21 [note 1]. It cannot have been before 1835, since it was only at the beginning of that year that the Bullers came to live in London. There exists a letter by Roebuck to Helen Taylor dated 23 August 1873 (MTColl. VIII/28) which confirms Roebuck's printed account of his alienation from Mill as not due, as Mill suggests in the *Autobiography* (p. 127) [*Autobiography and Literary*

Roebuck goes on to tell how he went to see Mill at India House to remonstrate with him, how Mill silently listened but by the reception he gave him on the next occasion made it clear that he regarded their friendship at an end.

We do not know precisely when this incident occurred, but by the spring of 1834 the connexion seems to have been freely talked about among Mill's friends. It was the first piece of gossip which the Carlyles then learnt on their return to London after two years' absence. They both in their inimitable ways at once passed on the news to Carlyle's brother in Italy, and then kept him abreast of developments when they themselves made the new acquaintance.

Thomas Carlyle to Dr. John Carlyle, May 1834:[2] Mrs. Austin had a tragical story of his [John Mill's] having fallen *desperately in love* with some young philosophic beauty (yet with the innocence of two sucking doves), and being lost to all his friends and to himself, and what not; but I traced nothing of this in poor Mill; and even incline to think that what truth there is or was in the [his] adventure may have done him good. Buller also spoke of it, but in the comic vein.

Jane Carlyle to Dr. John Carlyle, May 1834:[3] The most important item [of news learnt from Mrs. John Austin] was that a young Mrs. Taylor, tho' encumbered with a husband and children, has ogled John Mill successfully so that he was desperately in love.

Thomas Carlyle to Dr. John Carlyle, 22 July 1834:[4] Our most interesting new friend is a Mrs. Taylor, who came here for the first time yesterday, and stayed long. She is a living romance heroine, of the clearest insight, of the royallest

---

Essays, eds. John M. Robson and Jack Stillinger, vol. 1 (1981) of *The Collected Works of John Stuart Mill* [hereafter cited as *Collected Works*] (Toronto: University of Toronto Press, 1962–1991), pp. 152, 154], to mere differences of their views on the respective merits of Byron and Wordsworth.

[2] J. A. Froude, ed., *Thomas Carlyle, A History of the First Forty Years of His Life* (London: Longman's, Green, and Co., 1882), vol. 2, p. 430. [Hayek supplies the bracketed name. *The Carlyle Letters Online* corrects Froude: 'with some young ill-married philosophic Beauty'; see Thomas Carlyle to John Carlyle, 18 May 1834, *The Collected Letters of Thomas and Jane Welsh Carlyle*, 7:158–67, doi:10.1215/lt-18340518-TC-JAC-01.—Ed.]

[3] [Hayek supplies the material in brackets. I have been unable to locate this letter. It is not in *Letters and Memorials of Jane Welsh Carlyle*, ed. J. A. Froude; *New Letters and Memorials of Jane Welsh Carlyle*, ed. Alexander Carlyle (London: John Lane, 1903); or *The Carlyle Letters Online*, http://carlyleletters.dukejournals.org/. Since Hayek appears to have seen the letter, my conclusion is that it was held privately; perhaps it continues to be so.—Ed.]

[4] J. A. Froude, *ibid.*, vol. 2, p. 441. [*The Carlyle Letters Online* offers the following: 'Our most interesting new friend is a Mrs. Taylor (thro' Mill, who is said to be in love with her,—in platonic love, *versteht sich* [understood] who came here' and 'Jane is to go and pass a day with her soon (about the Regent's Park)'; see Thomas Carlyle to Margaret A. Carlyle, 5 August 1834, *Collected Letters*, 7:256–61, doi:10.1215/lt-18340805-TC-MAC-01.—Ed.]

volition, very interesting, of questionable destiny, not above twenty-five. Jane is to go and pass a day with her soon, being greatly taken with her.

Of course, Mrs. Taylor was nearly twenty-seven at the time. Apparently Jane went, and a fortnight later we get another report.

Thomas Carlyle to his Mother, 5 August 1834:[5] We have made, at least Jane has made, a most promising acquaintance, of a Mrs. Taylor; a young beautiful reader of mine and 'dearest friend' of Mill's, who for the present seems 'all that is noble' and what not. We shall see how that wears. We are to dine there on Tuesday, and meet a new set of persons, said, among other qualities, to be interested in *me*. The editor of ~~the~~ Fox['s] Repository (Fox himself) is the main man I care for.

Thomas Carlyle to Dr. John Carlyle, 15 August 1834:[6] We dined with Mrs. (Platonica) Taylor and the Unitarian Fox (of the Repository if you know it) one day. Mill was also of the party, and the husband—an obtuse, most joyous-natured man, the pink of social hospitality. [. . .] Mrs. Taylor herself did not yield unmixed satisfaction, [I think,] or receive it. She affects, with a kind of sultana noble-mindedness, a certain girlish petulance, and felt that it did not wholly prosper. We walked home, however, even Jane did, all the way from [the] Regent's Park, and felt that we had done a duty. For me, from the Socinians, as I take it, *wird Nichts.* Here too let me, wind up the Radical Periodical Editorship[7] which your last letter naturally speculates upon. Mill I seem to discern has given it to this same Fox (who has just quitted his Preachership and will, like myself, be out on the world); partly I should fancy by Mrs. Taylor's influence, partly as himself thinking him the safer man.

---

[5] Manuscript letter in the National Library of Scotland, incompletely published in *Letters of Thomas Carlyle 1826–1836* (ed. C. E. Norton, London: Macmillan and Co., 1888), vol. 2, pp. 200[–201]. [The full letter is published in *The Collected Letters of Thomas and Jane Welsh Carlyle*, eds. Charles Richard Sanders and Kenneth J. Fielding, vol. 7, *October 1833–December 1834* (Durham: Duke University Press, 1977), pp. 256–61, with the quoted passage at pp. 259–60.—Ed.]

[6] J. A. Froude, *Thomas Carlyle, The First Forty Years*, vol. 2, pp. 448–49, and *Letters of Thomas Carlyle 1826–1836* (ed. Norton), vol. 2, p. 207. See also Carlyle's entry in his *Journal* on 12 August 1834 (the day of the dinner) quoted in *Reminiscences* (ed. Norton), vol. 1, p. 114, note [1]. ['Mill, I discern, has given Fox the Editorship of that Molesworth periodical; seems rather ashamed of it. *A la bonne heure*: is it not probably *better* so? Trust in God and in thyself! O could I but; all *else* were so light, so trivial'. *Reminiscences by Thomas Carlyle*, ed. Charles Eliot Norton (London: Macmillan and Co., 1887), vol. 1, p. 114, note 1.—Ed.]

[7] There had been preliminary discussions about the creation of a new Radical Review, which in the following year led to the establishment of the *London* (later *London and Westminster*) *Review*.

A few weeks later, on the 8th of September, the Carlyles set out to call on Mrs. Taylor, but before reaching her house he broke down on a seat in Regent's Park when[8] 'Mrs. Taylor with her husband make their appearance, walking; pale she, and passionate and sad-looking: really felt a kind of interest in her'.

When shortly afterwards *Sartor Resartus* appeared, a copy was presented to Mrs. Taylor by the author, whose interest in her was however not unmixed with concern for Mill.

> *Thomas Carlyle to Dr. John Carlyle, 28 October 1834:*[9] Mill, himself, who were [far] the best of them all [of Mill's usual set] is greatly occupied of late times with a set of quite opposite character, which the Austins and other friends mourn much and fear much over. It is that fairest Mrs. Taylor you have heard of; with whom, under her husband's very eyes, he is (Platonically) over head and ears in love! Round her come Fox the Socinian and a flight of really wretched-looking 'friends of the species', who (in writing and deed) struggle not in favour of Duty being *done*, but against Duty of any sort almost being *required*. A singular creed this; but I can assure you a very observable one here in these days: by me 'deeply hated as the GLAR,[10] which is its colour (die seine Farbe ist)', and substance likewise mainly. Jane and I often say: 'Before all mortals, beware of a friend of the species!' Most of these people are very indignant at marriage and the like; and frequently indeed are obliged to divorce their own wives, or be divorced: for tho' the *world* is already blooming (or is one day to do it) in everlasting 'happiness of the greatest number', these people's own *houses* (I always find) are little Hells of improvidence, discord, unreason. Mill is far above all that, and I think will not sink in it; however, I do wish him fairly far from it, and tho' I cannot speak of it directly would *fain* help him out: he is one of the best people I ever saw, and—surprisingly attached to *me*, which is another merit.

At the beginning of the next year Mrs. Taylor appears again in the Carlyle letters.

> *Jane Welsh Carlyle to Dr. John Carlyle, 12 January 1835:*[11] There is a Mrs. Taylor whom I could really love, if it were safe and she were willing; but she is a

---

[8] J. A. Froude, *Thomas Carlyle, The First Forty Years*, vol. 2, p. 466.

[9] Manuscript letter in National Library of Scotland, incompletely published in *Letters of Thomas Carlyle 1826–1836* (ed. Norton), vol. 2, p. 240–41. [The full letter is published in *The Collected Letters of Thomas and Jane Welsh Carlyle*, 7:322–30, with the quoted passage at 7:326–27.—Ed.]

[10] 'Glar', mud or any moist sticky substance. [Hayek supplies the phrase in brackets.—Ed.]

[11] *New Letters and Memorials of Jane Welsh Carlyle*, ed. Alexander Carlyle (London: John Lane, 1903), vol. 1, p. 49, also J. A. Froude, *Carlyle's Life In London* (new edition), vol. 1, p. 24. [*Thomas Carlyle: A History of His Life in London, 1834–1881*, 2 vols., ed. J. A. Froude (London: Longmans,

dangerous looking woman and engrossed with a dangerous passion, and no useful relation can spring up between us.

Thomas Carlyle to Alexander Carlyle, 27 February 1835:[12] The party we had at the Taylors' was most brisk, the cleverest (best gifted) I have been at for years: Mill, Charles Buller (one of the gayest, lightly-sparkling, lovable souls in the world), *Repository* Fox (who *hotches*[13] and laughs at least), Fonblanque, the *Examiner* Editor,—were the main men. It does one good; though I buy it dear, dining so late: towards eight o'clock!

These friendly relations could not but be somewhat clouded by the famous incident which occurred a few days later, however admirable the spirit in which Carlyle at first bore the blow. Mill had shortly before borrowed the manuscript of the first volume of Carlyle's *French Revolution* and on 6 March had to go and break to Carlyle the news that the whole manuscript had been accidentally burnt. He arrived at the Carlyle's house in the evening in a carriage with Mrs. Taylor and rushing up the steps alone at first merely begged Mrs. Carlyle to go down and speak to Mrs. Taylor. Although it is probably later embroidery that on first seeing the carriage Mrs. Carlyle exclaimed to her husband, 'Gracious Providence, he has gone off with Mrs. Taylor!',[14] this seems indeed to have been so much the first thought of both the Carlyles that they appear to have been curiously relieved when they learnt the true reason for the visit. After Mrs. Taylor drove off Mill sat with the Carlyles until late at night while they did what they could to assure him that the loss was not too serious. Later, however, they seem to have conceived the idea that Mrs. Taylor was responsible for the destruction of the manuscript and their various hints to that

---

Green, and Co., 1884) The passage to which Hayek refers occurs on p. 25. There, a note from Jane Carlyle is appended to the letter of 16 February 1836 from Thomas to John. Hayek quotes its contents in note 12 below. *The Carlyle Letters Online* has Jane Welsh Carlyle misspelling Harriet Taylor's name: 'There is a Mrs. Tailor'; see Thomas Carlyle to John A. Carlyle, 12 January 1835, *Collected Letters*, 8:7 16, doi:10.1215/lt-18350112 TC JAC 01. Ed.]

[12] *Letters of Thomas Carlyle 1826–1836*, vol. 2, pp. 283–84. On 16 February, the day before the party, Mrs. Carlyle had written to Dr. John Carlyle: 'We are going to-morrow to Mrs. [Taylor's] whom I should like that you knew, and could tell me whether to fall desperately in love with or no' (J. A Froude, *Carlyle's Life in London* (new edition), vol. 1, p. 25). [Hayek supplies the name in brackets. The *Carlyle Letters Online* supplies: 'one of the gayest, highly sparkling', and for 'hotches' (below, note 13), inserts 'heaves'; see Thomas Carlyle to Alexander Carlyle; 27 February 1835, *Collected Letters*, 8:58–64, doi:10.1215/lt-18350227-TC-AC-01.—Ed.]

[13] 'Hotches' = fidgets.

[14] C. G. Duffy, *Conversations with Carlyle* (London: Sampson, Low and Marston, 1892), p. 169. The contemporary account of the episode given by Carlyle in his *Journal* (*Reminiscences*, ed. Norton, vol. 1, p. 106) makes no mention of this.

effect[15] were later exaggerated by others[into the scarcely veiled allegation that Mrs. Taylor had deliberately destroyed it. Any suggestion that Mrs. Taylor was responsible for the accident seems however to be clearly disproved by the very letter of Mill's in which he told Carlyle that Mrs. Taylor had also seen the manuscript and which appears to have been the basis for their later suspicions. Mill, the most truthful of persons, would certainly not have written as he did a few days after the catastrophe in refusing Carlyle's good-natured offer to lend him the manuscript of part of the second, volume of the *French Revolution*, 'provided you durst take it'.[16]

> *J. S. M. to Thomas Carlyle, 10 March 1835:*[17] I will not take the *Fête des Piques*—not that I believe such a thing could possibly happen again, but for the sake of retributive justice I would bear the badge of my untrustworthiness. If however you would give me the pleasure of reading it give it to Mrs. Taylor—in her custody no harm could come to it—and I can read it aloud to her as I did much of the other—for it had not only the *one* reader you mention[ed] but a second just as good.

Carlyle, however, seems not to have accepted this suggestion and Mill to have seen no more in manuscript. For a while cordial relations continued not only with Mill but also with Mrs. Taylor.[18] But after 1835 Mrs. Taylor's illness and absence from town during the greater part of the year prevented much further contact and perhaps there also occurred about that time a definite clash between the two ladies which strained the relations. Something like that at least is suggested in Carlyle's *Reminiscences* when he says that Mrs. Taylor had

> at first considered my Jane to be a rustic spirit fit for rather tutoring and twirling about when the humour took her; but got taught better (to her lasting memory) before long.[19]

[15] See particularly Carlyle's account in *Letters of Charles Eliot Norton*, eds. S. Norton and M. A. de Wolfe Howe (London: Constable & Co., 1913), vol. 1, p. 496, and Alfred H. Guernsey, *Thomas Carlyle* (London: D. Appleton & Co., 1879), pp. 86–87.

[16] *Letters of T. C. to J. S. M.*, p. 109, letter dated 9 March 1835.

[17] National Library of Scotland, published in *Letters* (ed. Elliot), vol. 1, p. 10. See also the letter by Mill's sister Harriet written to Carlyle shortly after Mill's death (*Letters of T. C. to J. S. M.*) in which she states that 'as far as my recollection goes, the misfortune arose from my brother's own inadvertence in having given your papers among[st] wastepaper for kitchen use', p. 107. [The letter from Mill to Carlyle in the text above is republished in *The Earlier Letters of John Stuart Mill, 1812–1848*, ed. Francis E. Mineka, vols. 12–13 of *Collected Works*, 12:253. Mill had offered to compensate Carlyle for his time lost as a result of the incident, to which Carlyle had responded that Mill might do so. Mill begins the letter: 'Nothing which could have happened, could have been at this time so great a good to me as your note, received this morning'.—Ed.]

[18] See Carlyle's letter to Mill of 30 October 1835, promising to call at Kent Terrace, in *Letters of T. C. to J. S. M.*, p. 119.

[19] Thomas Carlyle, *Reminiscences* (ed. Norton), vol. 1, p. 104.

Mill's regular visits and Sunday walks with Carlyle, however, continued for some years. In the spring of 1836 we find Mrs. Carlyle greatly concerned about the news of two of their 'dearest friends' John Mill and John Sterling being 'dangerously ill'.[20] A little later, soon after James Mill's death and shortly before Mill left for France in the summer of the same year, Carlyle visited the Mills at their summer house in Mickleham near Dorking in Surrey and sent a full report to his wife in Scotland.

> *Thomas Carlyle to Jane Welsh Carlyle, Chelsea, 24 July 1836:*[21] There was little sorrow visible in their house, or rather none, nor any human feeling at all; but the strangest *unheimlich* kind of composure and acquiescence, as if all human spontaneity had taken refuge in invisible corners. Mill himself talked much, and not stupidly—far from that—but without emotion of any discernible kind. He seemed to me [to be withering or] withered into the miserablest metaphysical *scrae*,[22] body and mind, that I had almost ever met with in the world. His eyes go twinkling and jerking with wild lights and twitches; his head is bald, his face brown and dry—poor fellow after all. It seemed to me the strangest thing what this man could want with me, or I with such a man so *unheimlich* to me. What will become of it? Nothing evil; for there is and there was nothing dishonest in it. But I think I shall see less and less of him. Alas, poor fellow! It seems possible too that he may not be very long seeable: that is one way of its ending.

It is difficult to remember that Mill, of whom Carlyle here speaks, had only a few weeks before completed his thirtieth birthday. Mrs. Carlyle's reply to this deserves also to be quoted.

> *Jane Welsh Carlyle to Thomas Carlyle, 2 August 1836.*[23] Poor Mill! he really seems to have '*loved and lived*'; his very intellect seems to be failing him in its strongest point:—his implicit admiration and subjection to you.

For a time after Mill's departure what news Carlyle had about his movements on the Continent came at second hand and Carlyle lost no time in passing on the gossip which made the round.

---

[20] *Letters and Memorials of Jane Welsh Carlyle*, ed. Froude, vol. 1, p. 57.

[21] J. A. Froude, *Thomas Carlyle, A History of his Life in London* (1004), vol. 1, pp. 74–75. James Mill had died on 23 June, Carlyle's visit took place on 16–18 July, and Mill left for France on 30 July. [*Carlyle Letters Online* supplies 'composure and acquiescence,—as if under a deadly pressure of Fear, all human' and translates 'unheimlich' as 'dismal'. See Thomas Carlyle to Jane Welsh Carlyle, 24 July 1836, *Collected Letters*, 9:16–23, doi:10.1215/lt-18360724-TC-JWC-01.—Ed.]

[22] 'Scrae', Dumfriesshire dialect for 'an old shoe'.

[23] *New Letters and Memorials of Jane Welsh Carlyle* (ed. Alexander Carlyle, London: John Lane, 1903), vol. 1, p. 60.

Thomas Carlyle to John Sterling, 3 October 1836:[24] Mill, they say, writes from Nice: he is not going into Italy, owing to ~~the~~ Cholera and quarantine: his health is a little, and but a little, improved. Mrs. Taylor, it is whispered, is with him, or near him. Is it not [very] strange, this pining away into dessication and nonentity, of our poor Mill, if it be so, as his friends all say, that this Charmer is the cause of it? I have not seen any riddle of human life which I could so ill form a theory of. They are innocent says Charity: they are guilty, says Scandal: then why in the name of wonder are they dying broken-hearted? One thing only is painfully clear to me, that poor Mill is in a bad way. Alas, tho' he speaks not, perhaps his tragedy is more tragical than that of any of us: this very item that he does not speak, that he never could speak, but was to sit imprisoned as in ~~the~~ thick ribbed ice, voiceless, uncommunicating, is it not the most tragical circumstance of all?

Six days later, however, a long and friendly letter was despatched by Carlyle to Mill at Nice on the urging of their common friend Horace Grant.[25] On Mill's return in November close contacts were promptly resumed and for another year or so, mainly in connexion with the *London and Westminster Review*, continued fairly regular if less cordial than before.

Thomas Carlyle to John Sterling, 17 January 1837:[26] John Mill, as perhaps you know, is home again, in better health, still not in good. I saw him the day before yesterday; sitting desolate under an *Influenza* we all have. I on the whole see little of him. He toils greatly in his Review; sore bested with mismanaging Editors, Radical discrepancies, and so forth. His *Platonica* and he are constant as ever: innocent I do believe as sucking doves, and yet suffering the clack of tongues, worst penalty of guilt. It is very hard; and for Mill especially as unlucky as ever. The set of people he is in is one[—that] I have to keep out of. No ~~class~~ [clan] of mortals ever profited me less. There is a vociferous platitude in them, a mangy hungry discontent,—their very joy like that of a thing, scratching itself under disease of the itch. Mill was infinitely too good for them; but he would have it, and his fate would. I love him much, as a friend *frozen within ice* for me!

---

[24] *Letters of T. C. to J. S. M.*, pp. 197–98.

[25] *Letters of T. C. to J. S. M.*, p. 136. Horace Grant (1800–1859), Mill's junior colleague in the Examiner's office at India House, 1826–1845.

[26] National Library of Scotland, incompletely published in *New Letters of Thomas Carlyle* (ed. Alexander Carlyle, 1904), vol. 1, p. 53, and part of the missing passage by J. A. Froude, *Thomas Carlyle, A History of his Life in London*, vol. 1, p. 108, tacked on to a letter of different date. [The passage quoted in Froude commences: 'Mill is in better health, still not in good. The set of people he is in, is one that I have to keep out of. No class of mortals ever profited me less'. This is part of a letter to Sterling dated 7 June 1837.—Ed.]

In 1838 they evidently drifted apart.[27] When Mill left again for Italy at the end of that year he seems to have given the Carlyles as his other friends to understand that he was going to Malta, but as both Carlyle's brother John and John Sterling were at Rome[28] at the time and seem to have seen Mill, the pretence, if kept up at all, cannot have been effective for long. Though Carlyle, once more at the urging of Horace Grant, sends a long epistle to Rome,[29] his comments to Sterling when he meets Mill some time after the latter had returned are in a changed tone.

> *Thomas Carlyle to John Sterling, 29 September 1839.*[30] Mill, whom I had not seen till that day (before yesterday) at the India House, was looking but indifferently; he confessed [professed] not to be sensibly better at all by his last-year's journeying. Mrs. Taylor, he farther volunteered to tell me, is not living in [at] the old abode in the Regent's Park, but in Wilton Place, a street where as I conjecture there are mainly wont to be *Lodgings*. Can it be possible? Or if so, what does it betoken? I am truly sorry for Mill: he has been a most luckless man since I came hither, seeming to himself all the way to be a lucky one rather.

This is a rather bad instance of careless gossip on the part of Carlyle. It is true that after her return from Italy Mrs. Taylor lived for a time at 24 Wilton Place, Belsize Square. But so did Mr. Taylor.[31] They had probably either let or closed their house in Kent Terrace because of Mrs. Taylor's long absence, or the house was merely being redecorated. There is no sign whatever that in town Mrs. Taylor ever lived apart from her husband, although of course her

[27] See *New Letters of Thomas Carlyle* (ed. Alexander Carlyle, 1904), vol. 1, pp. 116 and 133 (letters dated 9 March and 18 July 1838), and in *Life in London*, vol. 1, pp. 142–43 (letter dated 27 July 1838). [The letter of 18 July reads in part: 'Mill I saw last night; borrowing some Books from him. Friendly as ever when we meet, but that is now rarely: our paths diverge more and more; to me he is nearly altogether barren'.—Ed.]

[28] See Thomas Carlyle, *Life of John Sterling* (1851), in *Carlyle's Works* (Boston: Dana Estes and Charles E. Laureat, 1884), p. 221 [The full letter from Sterling to Carlyle, dated 19 May 1849, is at pp. 219–22.—Ed].

[29] *Letters of T. C. to J. S. M.*, p. 165. [The letter is dated 23 March 1839 and appears in full at pp. 165–69.—Ed.]

[30] *Ibid.*, pp. 225–26. Cf. also Sterling's reply, dated 30 September 1839, given by A. K. Tuell, *John Sterling* (New York: The Macmillan Company, 1941), pp. 70–71: 'Yesterday's post brought a pleasant letter from Mill along with yours. But he says no word of that miserable matter you hint at. I think it is a good sign of a man that he feels strongly that kind of temptation, but a far better one that he both feels it and conquers it, which I trust that Mill has done and will do'.

[31] See the letters in MTColl. XXVIII/149–51, to her husband, the first of 27 July 1839, announcing her return, apparently from Brighton, to Wilton Place, the others of October addressed to her husband at that address. [The letters, of which the first is dated 26 July 1839, are published in *The Complete Works of Harriet Taylor Mill* [hereafter cited as *Complete Works*], ed. Jo Ellen Jacobs (Bloomington: Indiana University Press, 1998), pp. 445–48.—Ed.]

stays in her husband's house seem to have been little more than occasional visits between her sojourns in the country.

In 1841 Mill appears to have sent to Carlyle Sarah Flower Adams' drama *Vivia Perpetua* with a request to express his opinion on it to Mrs. Taylor, but before Carlyle can write to her he has to enquire from Mill her address.[32] In the following year Mrs. Taylor approached Carlyle in a different matter.

H. T. to Thomas Carlyle:[33] Walton. July 9 (1842) / Dear Mr Carlyle, / I am going to ask you to do for me what if you consent to, I shall feel to be a great favour.

It is to be trustee to a little settlement made at the time of my marriage upon me—& upon the children. of the present two trustees, one, a M^r. Travers, a brother in law of M^r. Taylor's, is going to leave England to live abroad & I am anxious to have the vacancy filled so that I shall leave this portion of my young ones interests in the surest hands:

Au reste it is a very simple matter & could in no way cause any trouble or inconvenience, otherwise I should hardly feel entitled to ask it. May I hope that you will not disappoint me in this?

> Dear Mr Carlyle
> Most truly yrs
> H. Taylor

Pray present my kind regards to Mrs Carlyle. M^r. Taylor joins in this request & proposes to take an early opportunity ~~for~~ [of] calling at Chelsea to make it in person.

In reply to this and to Mr. Taylor's personal appeal Carlyle could truthfully plead in a letter of four days later that Mrs. Taylor could not find 'any person, possessed of common sense and arrived at years of discretion, who is so totally unacquainted with every form of what is called Business' as he himself was.[34] To make sure that he would escape the unwelcome burden he offered to walk

---

[32] *Letters of T. C. to. J. S. M.*, p. 174. [The full letter, dated 24 February 1841, appears at pp. 173–74.—Ed.]

[33] MTColl. XXVII/2. [Hayek added the year in parentheses above. The letter is published in Harriet Taylor Mill, *Complete Works*, pp. 412–13, where note 67 remarks that the trusteeship was debated in 1842.—Ed.]

[34] *Letters of T. C. to J. S. M.*, p. 179 [the full letter, dated 13 July 1842, appears at pp. 179–80], letter of J. S. M. to T. Carlyle of 24 February 1841 [there is no letter from Mill to Carlyle on 24 February 1841; the context of Hayek's discussion suggests that he intended to refer to Carlyle's 24 February 1841 letter to Mill in which Carlyle asked for Harriet Taylor's address], and of T. Carlyle to Mrs. Taylor of 7 ~~July~~ [March] 1841. [Brackets here indicate editorial insertions.—Ed.]

over from Richmond to her house at Walton to talk the matter over. This produced an invitation and Carlyle together with Mill spent two days at Walton.[35]

Although a few more notes were exchanged between Mill and Carlyle after this, and an inscribed copy of *Past and Present* was sent by the author to Mrs. Taylor when it appeared in 1843,[36] the relations seem to have become very superficial even before at last some of Carlyle's talk about them came to their ears. In October 1846 the break became open: when Carlyle went to call on Mill at India House to ask him to a dinner he was giving in honour of an American visitor, and met Mill on the way in the street, 'he received me like the very incarnation o' the East Wind, and refused my invitation peremptorily'.[37] That seems for many years to have been the end of their regular intercourse.[38] After Mill's marriage some superficial contacts appear to have been resumed and even the two ladies once more to have met. At least Mrs. Carlyle's last recorded comment on Mrs. Mill seems to refer to some date after the Mills were married. In a conversation with Gavan Duffy in 1851 she described Mrs. Mill as

a peculiarly affected and empty body. She was not easy unless she startled you with unexpected sayings. If she was going to utter something kind and affectionate, she spoke in a hard, stern voice. If she wanted to be alarming or uncivil, she employed the most honeyed and affectionate tones. 'Come down to see us', she said one day (*mimicking her tone*), 'you will be charmed with our house, it is so full of rats'. 'Rats!' cried Carlyle, 'Do you regard *them* as an attraction?' 'Yes' (*piano*), 'they are such dear, innocent creatures'.[39]

Carlyle never seems to have quite understood that it had been his unrestrained talk about Mill and Mrs. Taylor which had caused the estrangement, and even many years later his remarks to C. E. Norton when he received the

---

[35] The visit took place on 18 and 19 July 1841. See Helen Taylor's Diary in M I Coll. XLIV and *Letters of C. E. Norton*, eds. G. Norton and M. A. de Wolfe Howe (London, 1913), vol. 1, p. 498. [The visit took place on 18 and 19 July 1842.—Ed.]

[36] This copy of *Past and Present* is now with the remnants of Mill's library in Somerville College, Oxford.—According to Carlyle's account Mill's 'great attachment' to him 'lasted about ten years, and then suddenly ended, I never knew how' (*Letters and Memorials of Jane Welsh Carlyle*, ed. J. A. Froude, vol. 1, p. 2).

[37] *Letters of C. E. Norton*, vol. 1, p. 499.

[38] In 1848, however, Mill sent to Carlyle a presentation copy of the *Political Economy* (Francis Espinasse, *Literary Recollections* (London: Hodder and Stoughton, 1893), p. 218). [Carlyle annotated Mill's *Political Economy*; see Murray Baumgarten, 'Parameters of Debate: A Reading of Carlyle's Annotations of Mill's *Principles of Political Economy*', in *Carlyle: Books & Margins* (Santa Cruz: University Library of the University of California, 1980).—Ed.]

[39] C. G. Duffy, *Conversations with Carlyle* (1892), p. 169. [The passage has been changed to the past tense as it appears in Duffy; Hayek used the present tense for Jane Carlyle's description of Harriet Taylor.—Ed.]

news of Mill's death show that he only half suspected what was undoubtedly the truth:

> Many's the time I've thought o' writin' to him and sayin' 'John Mill, what is it that parts you and me?' But that's all over now. Never could I think o' the least thing, unless maybe it was this. One year the brother o' that man Cavaignac who was ruler for a time in France,—Godefroi Cavaignac, a man o' more capacity than his brother,—was over here from Paris, an' he told me o' meeting Mill and Mrs. Taylor somewhere in France not long before, eatin' grapes together off o' one bunch, like two love birds. And his description amused me, and I repeated it, without thinking any harm, to a man who was not always to be trusted, [Charles Buller], a man who made trouble with his tongue, and I've thought he might perhaps have told it to Mill, and that Mill might have fancied that I was making a jest o' what was most sacred to him; but I don't know if it was it, but it was the only thing I could ever think of that could ha' hurt him.[40]

Carlyle's letters show that this was probably not the only occasion when he had talked rather freely on the matter. It seems at any rate that at some time in the middle 'forties Mill and Mrs. Taylor had suddenly become aware of the talk that was going on about them and not only broke radically with all those whom they suspected of gossip but altogether withdrew from society. To have offended in this connexion was the one thing that Mill never forgave. His intimate motherly friend Sarah Austin, who had taught him German when he was fifteen and whom for twenty years afterwards he had regularly addressed in his frequent letters as his *Liebes Mutterlein*, he seems to have regarded, probably with some justification, as the chief offender. She was not only well known as a gossip but also in a special position to know since for some years the Austins had lived at Regent's Park with their garden adjoining that of the Taylors and separated from it only by a hedge through which the children were constantly creeping.[41] In her case the ban was so complete that the mere fact that the Austins had come to live in the neighbourhood was in 1848 sufficient reason for Mrs. Taylor not wishing again to go to Walton.[42] Even after his wife's death, in 1859, when John Austin died, Mill could still not bring himself to write to her an ordinary letter of condolence but wrote

[40] *Letters of Charles Eliot Norton*, vol. 1, pp. 499–500. The name in square brackets is omitted in the printed version and has been kindly supplied by the Librarian of the Houghton Library, Harvard University, where C. E. Norton's papers and his diary are now preserved.

[41] Janet Ross, *Three Generations of English Women* [*Memoirs and Correspondence of Susannah Taylor, Sarah Austin, and Lady Duff Gordon*], new revised and enlarged edition, (London: T. Fisher Unwin, 1893), p. 432.

[42] See below, p. 126.

instead to her granddaughter Janet Duff Gordon (a girl of seventeen living at the time with Mrs. Austin), who later described how 'the evidently intentional slight cut her to the heart'.[43]

Another old acquaintance who had even better grounds for knowing the whole history of the relationship and who talked freely about it, Harriet Martineau, became the object of Mill's most intense dislike. Two other ladies who at one time had known Mill well, Mrs. Grote and Harriet Baring (Lady Ashburton), fared not much better. And a number of other persons appear for the same reason to have been placed under a complete ban.[44]

[43] Janet Ross, *The Fourth Generation* (London, 1912), p. 73.

[44] [In a letter dated 11 March 1839 to his brother John, Carlyle indicated his belief that the relationship was platonic: 'It is a mad and unhappy business that; one cannot see any reason in it at all, or even any right unreason: for I do believe the whole thing is strictly Platonic still! . . . For me I have never whispered to Mill anything about it; I have had no call to go minutely into that or other affairs of his: if you see the lady herself, you will find her very clever, but not at all attractive as I judge; a most morbid piece of brilliancy. Poor Mill!' See Thomas Carlyle to John Carlyle, 11 March 1839, *Collected Letters*, 11:42–51, doi:10.1215/lt-18390311.—Ed.]

FIVE

THE YEARS OF FRIENDSHIP
1834–1847

The survey of the accounts given by contemporaries has led us far beyond the date at which we interrupted the presentation of the main documents. We must return to the time when, after Harriet Taylor's return from Paris, some new *modus vivendi* was agreed between her and her husband. It seems not probable, however, that the more stable form which her relationship to Mill ultimately assumed was at once found. The few fragments of correspondence which we have for the years immediately following this return give glimpses of recurring internal and external difficulties. Very few of the notes which seem to belong to the next two or three years can be dated with certainty. But what is probably the earliest happens to be dated.

> *H. T. to J. S. M. (?), 20 February 1834:*[1] *Happiness* has become to me a word without meaning—or rather the meaning of the word has no existence in my belief. I mean by Happiness the state wh I can remember to have been in when I consciously used the word—a state of *satisfaction*, by satisfaction meaning not *only* the *mind made up*, not only having *conviction* of some sort on every large subject, but *cheerful* hopeful *faith* about all wh I could contemplate & not understand & this along with the great & conscious enjoyment from my own emotions & sensations—that Happiness I had often a year ago—I believe that if the world were as well directed as human beings might direct it, & may be expected to direct it, that all might be *Happy*, in proportion to their capacity for Happiness & that those with *great* capacity might be *actually* happy—live in a *satisfied* state, without *need* for [of] more but with, for their *forward* view, a placid contemplation of the probability of still greater capacity in some other existence—I do not believe I shall ever again feel that— the *most* this world can do for me is to give present enjoyment sufficient to make me forget that there is nothing else worth seeking—for the great mass

[1]MTColl. L/5. The date is given only on a typed envelope of later date, probably by Mary Taylor. [Mary Taylor was Harriet Taylor's grandniece and the date was typed early in the twentieth century. It may be unreliable. Hayek has a question mark after 'consistent'. The letter is published in *The Complete Works of Harriet Taylor Mill* [hereafter cited as *Complete Works*], ed. Jo Ellen Jacobs (Bloomington: Indiana University Press, 1998), p. 329.—Ed.]

of people I think wisdom would be to make the utmost of sensation while they are young enough & then die—for the very few who seem to have an innate incomprehensible capacity of emotion, more enjoyable than any sensation but consistent with & adding to all pleasurable sensation for *such if* such there be wh. I greatly doubt, *their* wisdom like the others is to *live out* their pleasures & die—*now* I believe that such beings w^d not c^d not live out those enjoyments but that I think is because they come to them late thro' struggle & suffering generally, wh gives an artificial depth and tenacity to their feeling, for those who come to such feelings at all are those of the most imagination—& so hold them firmest. I do not believe *affection* to be natural to human beings—it *is* an instinct of the lower animals for their young— but in humans it is a made up combination of feelings & associations wh will cease to exist when artificiality ceases to exist: only passion is natural that is temporary affection—but what we call affection will continue so [as] long as there is dependance.

During the next few months some passages of Mill's letters to W. J. Fox give us some indication of the prevailing state of affairs. The other two members of the group mentioned in the first were probably Eliza and Sarah Flower.

J. S. M. to W. J. Fox, about April 1834:[2] I hope we shall meet oftener—we four or rather five—as we did on Tuesday—I do not see half enough of you— and I do not, half enough, see *anybody* along with her—*that* I think is chiefly what is wanting now—that, and other things like it—

J. S. M. to W. J. Fox, 26 June 1834:[3] Our affairs have been gradually getting into a more & more unsatisfactory state—and are now in a state which, a very short time ago, would have made me quite miserab[le] but now I am altogether in a higher state than I was & better able to conquer evil & to bear it. I will tell you all about it some day—perhaps the first time we meet—but by that time perhaps the atmosphere will be clearer—adieu—

I have not spoken to you about our affairs lately, as I did while she was away; partly because I did not need so much [*need*] to give confidence & ask support when she was with me, partly because I know you disapprove & cannot enter with the present relation between her & me & him. but a time per-

[2] King's College, Cambridge. [The letter is published in *The Earlier Letters of John Stuart Mill, 1812–1848*, ed. Francis E. Mineka, vols. 12–13 (1963) of *The Collected Works of John Stuart Mill* [hereafter cited as *Collected Works*] (Toronto: University of Toronto Press, 1962–1991), 12:213–14, where it is tentatively dated 14 February 1834.—Ed.]

[3] King's College, Cambridge. [The letter is published in Mill, *Earlier Letters*, vol. 12 of *Collected Works*, pp. 226–27, with note 5 stating that the page is torn at 'miserable' and note 8 stating that 'the postscript is written at the top of the verso'.—Ed.]

haps is coming when I shall need your kindness more than ever—if so, I know I shall always have it—

The remaining notes exchanged between Mill and Mrs. Taylor which seem to belong to this time must be given in a more or less arbitrary order.

J. S. M. to H. T.:[4] I have been made most uncomfortable all day by your dear letter sweet & loving as it was dearest one—because of your having had that pain—& because of my having given you pain. You cannot imagine dearest how very much it grieves me now when even a small thing goes wrong now that thank heaven it does not often happen so, & therefore always happens unexpectedly. As for my saying 'do not let us talk of that now' I have not the remotest recollection of my having said so, or what it was that I did not want to talk about—but I am sure that it was something which I considered to be settled & done with long ago, & therefore not worth talking any more about, a reason which you yourself so continually express for not explaining to me or telling me about impressions of yours, uncertainty about the nature of which is tormenting me—& I have latterly learnt sufficient self sacrifice, sometimes to yield to that feeling, & leave off asking you questions which you tell me it is unpleasant to you to answer. But whatever it was that we were talking about on the common I am sure if I had thought that anything remained to be said about it, much more if I had thought that such a matter as whether we can or cannot be in complete sympathy, had depended on what remained unsaid, I should have been a great deal more anxious to have everything said, than you would have been to say it. O my own love, if you were beginning to say something which you had been thinking [of] for days or weeks, why did you not tell me so? why did you not make me feel that you were saying what was important to you, & what had not been said or had not been exhausted before? I am writing you [know] in complete ignorance about what it was—but I am sure ~~that~~ I have tormented you enough & long enough by refusing to acquiesce in your seemingly determined resolution that there *should be* radical differences of some sort in some of our feelings, and now having found, & convinced you, that there are none that need make us unhappy, I have learnt from you to be able to bear that there should be some—consisting chiefly in the want of some feelings in me which you have. But I thought we perfectly knew & understood what those were, & that neither of us saw any good in discussing them further—& when I ask you questions which you do not like to answer, it is only to know what is paining you

---

[4] Yale University Library [MS 350, Box 1, Folder 2]. [The letter is published in Mill, *Earlier Letters*, vol. 12 of *Collected Works*, pp. 227–28. It is dated tentatively as summer 1834. Hayek inserts a query after 'and now having found'.—Ed.]

I have been made most uncomfortable all day by your dear letter sweet & loving as it was dearest one — because of your having had that pain — & because of my having given you pain. You cannot imagine dearest how very much it grieves me now when even a small thing goes wrong now that thank heaven it does not often happen so, & therefore always happens unexpectedly. As for my saying "do not let us talk of that now" & I have not the remotest recollection of my having said so, or what it was that I did not want to talk about, but I am sure that it was something which I considered to be settled & done with long ago & therefore not worth talking any more about.

a reason which you yourself so continually
express ~~as your reason~~ for not explaining
to me or telling me about impressions of yours,
& uncertainty about the nature of which is
tormenting me — & I have lately learnt
sufficient self sacrifice, sometimes to yield to
that feeling, & ~~venture~~ leave off asking you
questions which you tell me it is unpleasant
to you to answer. But whatever it was
that we were talking about on the common
I am sure if I had thought that anything
remained to be said about it, much more
if I had thought that such a matter as
whether we ~~could~~ can or cannot be in complete
sympathy, had depended on what remained
unsaid, I should have been a great deal
more anxious to have ~~the whole subject~~ everything said,
~~said~~, than you would have been to say it.
O my own love, if you were beginning to
say something which you had been
thinking of for days or weeks, why did

you not tell me so? Why did you not make me feel that you were saying what was important to you, & what had not been said or had not been exhausted before? I am writing you know in complete ignorance about what it was - but I am sure I have tormented you enough & long enough by refusing to acquiesce in your seemingly determined resolution that there should be radical differences of some sort in some of our beliefs. & now having found, & convinced you, that there are none that need make us unhappy, I have learnt from you to be able to bear that there should be some - consisting chiefly in the want of some feelings in me which you have. But I thought we perfectly knew & understood what those were, & that neither of us saw any good in discussing them further & when I ask you questions which you do not like to answer, it is only to know what is paining you at the time.

not meaning to discuss feelings any more if it is feelings & not facts that are annoying you

I know darling it is very doubtful if you will get this before I see you — but I cannot help writing it & perhaps I shall feel easier afterwards. at present I feel utterly unnerved & quite unfit for thinking or writing or any business — but I shall get better. & dont let it make you uncomfortable mine own —

o you dear one

my own adored one!

at the time—not meaning to discuss feelings any more if it is feelings and not facts that are annoying you.

I know darling it is very doubtful if you will get this before I see you—but I cannot help writing it & perhaps I shall feel easier afterwards. at present I feel utterly unnerved & quite unfit for thinking or writing or any business—but I shall get better, & don't let it make you uncomfortable mine own—o you dear one.

Below the last four words which Mill had enclosed between two lines at the foot of his letter there is a further line in Harriet Taylor's hand: 'my *own adored* one!'.

H. T. to J. S. M.:[5] I don't know why I was so low when you went this morning. I was *so* low—I could not bear your going my darling one; yet I should be well enough accustomed to it by now. O you dear one! dear one!

They are not coming to-day nor at all at present & I am not sorry for it. I shall get on very well, I have no doubt, until Thursday comes & *you*. I wish to-morrow were Thursday, but I do not wish you were coming before Thursday because I know it would be so much harder to bear afterwards.

If I knew where at Sevenoaks L & Sallie are I would go in the chaise & see them. but that will do any time.

be well & happy dearest—but *well* before everything. dearest I cannot express the sort of dégout I feel whenever there comes one of these sudden cessation of life—my only spiritual life—being much with you—but never mind—it is all well & right & very happy as it is. only I long unspeakably for Saturday. This place is very lovely but it both looks & feels to me quite lifeless. farewell darling mine.

H. T. to J. S. M.:[6] This is one thing so perfectly admirable to me, that you never in any mood, doubt the worth of enjoyment or the need of happiness—one less fine w^d undervalue what he had not reached. does not this *prove* that you have the poetic principle? for me my hope is so living and healthy that it is not possible to me to doubt that it will increase more & more until it assumes some new and higher form—going on towards perfection.

Those words yesterday were *cold* and distancing, *very*, at *first*—Do you not know what it is to receive, with an *impulse* of thankfulness and joy and comfort, the packet which proves at first sight only a collection of *minerals*—one feels somewhat like a *mineral*—but this comes & must come from the uncongenial circumstances The circumstances wh. *tend* to elate or to despond do

---

[5] MTColl. XXVIII/235, on paper watermarked '1833'. [Harriet Taylor Mill, *Complete Works*, p. 330. The reference to 'L and Sallie', which Hayek has as 'L[izzie] and Sallie' is to Eliza and Sarah Flower.—Ed.]

[6] MTColl. II/323. [Harriet Taylor Mill, *Complete Works*, pp. 325–26. No date is provided.—Ed.]

not come at the same time to both—and tho' such things in no degree *alter* ones mind, they *have* their effect in deciding which state of mind shall be for the time uppermost—and always will have as long as it pleases Heaven to endow us with a body and senses.

Yes—dearest friend—things as they are now, bring to me, beside *moments* of quite complete happiness, a *life* & how infinitely to be preferred before all I ever knew! I never for an instant could wish that this had never been on my own account, and only on yours if you c^d think so—but why do I say *mine* & *yours*, what is good for the one must be so for the other & will be so always—*you* say so—& whatever of sadness there may sometimes be, is only the proof of how much happiness there is by proving the capacity for so much more.

You say that what you think virtue, 'the wise & good' who have long known and respected you, wont think vice—How can you think people wise, with such opposite notions? You say too that when those who profess different principles to the vulgar, *act* their principles, they make all worse whom they do not make better & I understand you to believe that they would make many worse & few better in your ~~own~~ case—Is not this then the 'thinking with the wise, & acting with the vulgar' principle? And does not this imply compromise & insincerity? *You* cannot mean that, for that is both base & weak—if made a rule, & not an occasional hard necessity.

I was not *quite* wrong in thinking you feared opinions.—I never supposed you dreaded the opinions of fools but only of those who are otherwise wise & good but have not your opinions about Moralities.[7]

Two more notes by Mrs. Taylor are both on paper watermarked 1835 and were probably written in that or the following year.

H. T. to J. S. M.:[8] Tuesday eveng / Dearest—You do not know me—or perhaps more truly you do not know the best of me—I am not one to 'create chimeras about nothing'—you should know enough [of] ~~about~~ the effects of petty annoyances to know that they are wearing & depressing not only to body but mind—these, on account of our relation, I have & you have not—& these make me morbid—but I can say most clearly & surely that I am *never* so without being perfectly conscious of being so—that I always know that in a better state of health all those morbid & weakly feelings & views & thoughts would go. So far from your two instances being like this—those women took the life with the men they loved at once as a desperate

---

[7] [Hayek has a query in the text here. Harriet Taylor Mill, *Complete Works*, p. 326, notes that the last paragraph is 'written in crosshatch' and completes the sentence with the word 'Moralities'.—Ed.]

[8] MTColl. L/7, on two sheets watermarked '1835'. [Harriet Taylor Mill, *Complete Works*, pp. 330–32.—Ed.]

throw without knowing anything of those men's characters—if I had done that do you think that I should not have been blindly devoted? of course I should—in such a case the woman has absolutely nothing to make life of but blind implicit devotion—It is not true that my character is 'the extreme of anxiety and uneasiness' if my circumstances do not account to you for all or more of anxiety & uneasiness which I show to you, why there is nothing to be said about that—you do not know the natural effect of those circumstances.[9] If it is true that so long as you concealed your feelings from me for fear of paining me, I can only say I am sorry for it because I know you too well not to know that no real feelings of yours would ever pain me. Then as to your inquiring of how I should like that you sh^d go for a walk without me I can only say that I am not a fool—& I should laugh at, or very much dislike the thought, that you sh^d make your 'life obscure insignificant & useless' pour les beaux yeux & I cannot think it was consistent with love to be able to think or wish that. If it is true, & I suppose you know yourself, that then 'you would never speak a true word again' never 'express natural liking' never 'dare to be silent or tired' why I can but say that if you would take such a life as that you must be mad. That one *might* never be wholly satisfied with the finite is possible but I do not believe that I sh^d ever show that—I think it would & must be true of persons of intellect & cultivation without acute feelings—but I have always observed where there is strong feeling the interests of feeling are always paramount & it seems to me that personal feeling has more of infinity in it than any other part of character—no ones *mind* is *ever* satisfied, nor their imagination nor their ambition—nor anything else of that class—but feeling *satisfies*—All the qualities on earth never give happiness without personal feeling—personal feeling always gives happiness with or without any other character.[10] The desire to give & to receive feeling is almost the whole of my character.

With the calmest, coldest view I believe that my feeling to you would be enough for my whole life—but of course only if I were conscious of having æ [as] good [a] feeling.

I have always seen & balanced in my mind all these considerations that you write about therefore they do not either vex or pain me. I know *all about* all these chances—but I know too what you do not, but what I have always told you, that once having accepted that life I should make the very best of it. I used long ago to think that in that case I should have occasional fits of the deepest depression, but that they would not affect our happiness, as I should not let you see them—for long now I have been past thinking that.

[9] [A note is added to the *Complete Works* here suggesting that Harriet Taylor may be referring to her 'estrangement from her husband', or to 'her life with syphilis'. See Harriet Taylor Mill, *Complete Works*, p. 331, note 20.—Ed.]

[10] [Hayek has queries in the text beside the words 'paramount' and 'character'.—Ed.]

I shall always show you & tell you *all* that I feel. I always do, & the fact that I do so proves to me that I should have but little that was painful to show. as to the rash & blind faith & devotion of those women you instance look at the result to them! & that is the natural result of such an engagement entered into in that way. If when first I knew you I had given up all other life to be with you *I* sh^d gradually have found if *not* that you did not love me as I thought at least that you were different[11] to what I had thought & so been disappointed—there would never be disappointment now. I do not know if 'such a life never succeeds' I feel quite sure that it would succeed in our case. You may be quite sure that if I once take that life it will be *for good.*

With not only all that you write—but more *all* that can be said, fully before me I should without hesitation say 'let it be', I do not hesitate about the certainty of happiness—but I do hesitate about the rightfulness of, for my own pleasure, giving up *my* only earthly opportunity of 'usefulness'. *You* hesitate about your usefulness & that however greater in amount it may be, is certainly not like mine *marked out* as duty. I should *spoil* four lives & injure others. This is the only hesitation. When I am in health & spirits I see the possibilities of getting over this hesitation. When I am low & ill I see the improbabilities. Now I give pleasure around me, I make no one unhappy, & I am happy tho' not happiest myself. I think any systematic middle plan between this & all impracticable. I am much happier not seeing you continually here, because then I have habitually enough to make me able to always be wishing for more, when I have that more rarely it is in itself an object & a *satisfaction.*

I think you have got more interest in all social interests than you used to have, & I think you can be satisfied, as I can at present perhaps with occasional meeting—but then [thro'] ~~for~~ every moment of my life you are my one sole interest & object & I would at any instance give up all, were it ten thousand times as much, rather than have the chance of one iota of diminution of your love.

This scrawl[ed] literally in the greatest haste—because you said write—but in the morng I shall see you. *mine.*

H. T. to J. S. M.:[12] Wednesday / Dear one—if the feeling of this letter of yours were your *general* or even *often* state ~~of mind~~ it would be very unfortunate for—may I say *us*—for *me* at all events. Nothing I believe would make me love you less but certainly I should not admire one who could feel in this way except from mood. Good heaven have *you* at last arrived at fearing to be '*obscure & insignificant*'! What *can* I say to that but 'by all means pursue your brilliant and important career'. Am *I* one to choose to be the cause that the

---

[11] [Harriet Taylor Mill, *Complete Works*, has a query beside the word 'different'.—Ed.]
[12] MTColl. L/6, watermarked '1835'. [Harriet Taylor Mill, *Complete Works*, pp. 332–33]

person I love feels himself reduced to 'obscure & insignificant'! Good God what has the love of two equals to do with making obscure & insignificant if ever you *could* be obscure & insignificant you *are* so whatever happens & certainly a person who did not feel contempt at the very idea the words create is not one to brave the world. I never before (for years) knew you to have a mesquin feeling. It is a horrible want of unanimity between us. I know what the world is,[13] I have not the least desire either to brave it or to court it—in no possible circumstances sh^d I ever do either—those imply some *fellow-feeling* with it & that I have only in case I could do it or any individual of it any good turn—then I should be happy for the time to be at one with it—but it is to me as tho' it did not exist as to any ability to hurt me—it could not, & I never could feel at variance with it. how I long to walk by the sea with you & hear you tell me the whole truth about your feelings of this kind. There seems a touch of Common Place vanity in that dread of being obscure & insignificant—you will never be that—& still more surely *I* am not a person who in any event could give you cause to feel that *I* had made you so Whatever you [may] think *I* could never be either of those words.

I am not either *exceedingly* hurt by your saying that I am [of] an anxious and uneasy character. I know it is false and I shall pity you if . . . [14]

From the winter of 1835/6 illness becomes a constant feature in the lives both of Mill and Mrs. Taylor, never again quite to disappear. Mrs. Taylor appears to have been in delicate health even for some time before this, but the first references to this occur only about that time: 'she is well, that is as well as

---

[13] [Hayek has 'I know what the root (?) is'; Harriet Taylor Mill, *Complete Works*, p. 333, replaces the queried 'root' with 'world'. Ed.]

[14] Continuation missing. Another note of Harriet Taylor's of uncertain date but probably of the same period in MTColl. II/317 may be given at least as a note.

H. T. to J. S. M. Yes dear I will meet you, [in the chaise,] some where between this and Southend—the hour will depend on what your note says to-morrow (that is supposing the chaise is to be had of which there is very little doubt.)

bless you dearest! I did not write yesterday. I wish I had for you seem to have expected it. I have been quite well & quite happy since that delicious eveng & I may perhaps see the to-day, but if not I shall not be disappointed—as for *sad* I feel since that eveng as tho' I shall never be that again.

I am very well in all respects, but more especially in spirits.

Bless thee—to-morrow will be delightful & I am looking to it as a [the] very great[est] treat

so dear if you do not meet me on [your] road from Southend you will know I could not have the chaise.

Friday.

[Hayek has a query in place of the '[your]' supplied above; see Harriet Taylor Mill, *Complete Works*, pp. 323–24.—Ed.]

she ever is', wrote Mill to. W. J. Fox on 2 February 1836,[15] adding that he himself was still out of health. He had been suffering from a nervous head complaint affecting his eyes since the end of the preceding year and his family and his friends seem to have attributed this to the continued emotional strain. His father, already confined at home by his last illness, wrote on 9 March 1836 to his younger son James, who shortly before had left for India, that 'John is still in a rather pining way; though, as he does not choose to tell the cause of his pining, he leaves other people to their conjectures'.[16] That the suspected cause was avoided by the family as a subject of conversation is only too likely from the story told by Bain that James Mill, on learning of John's connexion with Mrs. Taylor, had 'taxed him with being in love with another man's wife. He replied, he had no other feelings towards her, than he would have towards an equally able man. The answer was unsatisfactory, but final'.[17]

At the same time it seems that the heavy burden of work which John Mill had carried for years and continued to impose upon himself provides a sufficient explanation for the breakdown of his health. Just then the absence of his father from India House had thrown still more work on him after for a year, in addition to his normal activities, he had acted as editor of the new *London Review* and in consequence of the inefficiency of his subordinate, the nominal editor,[18] had had to run the journal practically single-handed. For some time he tried to get over his illness by allowing himself occasional short breaks, such as an excursion to Gravesend with Carlyle, at which, as the latter tells us, Mill hoped 'to go, and "get better" (in six and thirty hours) at a place out there; and would not go without me'.[19] Later in the spring however he was forced to spend some weeks at Brighton, from where he was apparently brought back by the approaching death of his father. James Mill died on 23 June and we have seen how sadly changed Carlyle found Mill's appearance shortly afterwards. Soon he was ordered away for three months by his doctor and at the end of July he took his two young brothers Henry and George to the Continent. In Paris they met Mrs. Taylor with her son Herbert and probably also the two younger children, who had travelled two days ahead of them. To the first reports which George and Henry Mill sent home to their sisters John added a few lines on the same sheet.

[15] King's College, Cambridge. [Mill, *Earlier Letters*, vol. 12 of *Collected Works*, p. 298. The date provided there is 23 February 1836. Mill adds to this, 'I am still out of health'.—Ed.]

[16] Alexander Bain, *John Stuart Mill: A Criticism, With Personal Recollections* (London: Longmans, Green, and Co., 1882), p. 43.

[17] Alexander Bain, *John Stuart Mill*, p. 163.

[18] Thomas Falconer (1805–1882). [Falconer was the brother-in-law of J. A. Roebuck. Mill, *Earlier Letters*, vol. 12 of *Collected Works*, p. 249, note 6.—Ed.]

[19] *New Letters of Thomas Carlyle* (ed. A. Carlyle, 1904), vol. 1, p. 2. [*New Letters of Thomas Carlyle*, ed. Alexander Carlyle, 2 vols. (London and New York: John Lane, The Bodley Head, 1904).—Ed.]

J. S. M. to Clara Mill, Paris, 3 August 1836:[20] One having written to W[illie] &
one to H[arriet] I must write to Clara—so here goes—We are all quite as
well, perhaps rather better than was to be expected. George & Henry do not
seem at all struck with Paris—they are I think too young to care much about
it or to be impressed by it at all. They seemed pleased with the country, & on
the whole the excursion has been hitherto tolerably successful. But the only
piece of thorough solid delight that George seemed to have was in meeting with a playfellow about his own size [age][21] whom he likes & who likes
him very much. Nothing is settled yet about our travelling further—it is not
finally settled whether we shall go alone or with our friends here, much less
when we shall go & how—the places are all taken by the diligence for nearly
a week to come, & posting so far is very expensive—but we shall see. One
thing seems certain—that both Derry & I can stand travelling. We have not
tried any night work to be sure yet. We will write again from Geneva.

ever affectionately yours

J. S. M.

The two parties proceeded to Geneva and Lausanne where Henry and
George Mill and probably the Taylor children remained while Mill and Mrs.
Taylor went on to Northern Italy. As they left Lausanne his brothers reported
home that[22] 'his head is most obstinate; those same disagreeable sensations
still, which he has tried so many ways to get rid of, are plaguing him'. Three
weeks later Henry passes on news received from Italy:[23] 'John wrote [to] us a
very desponding letter, saying that if he had to go back without getting well,
he could not again go to the India House, but must throw it up, and try if a
year or two of leisure would do anything'. After spending two months in Pied-
mont and on the bay of Genoa, and after they had been prevented from going
further south by the quarantine imposed because of an outbreak of cholera,
John Mill and Mrs. Taylor returned to Switzerland via Milan and the Italian
lakes. At the end of October they picked up the children at Lausanne, and
early in November[24] Mill at least was back in London and at his work at India
House, in only slightly better health and with his head in particular no bet-

---

[20] MTColl. XLVII/3. [Mill, *Earlier Letters*, vol. 12 of *Collected Works*, pp. 307–8. Hayek supplied
the bracketed names.—Ed.]

[21] Herbert Taylor, who was only a year or two George Mill's junior. This acquaintance led to a
lasting friendship between George Mill and the two Taylor boys.

[22] Alexander Bain, *John Stuart Mill*, p. 44.

[23] *Ibid.*

[24] See the letter of Henry and John Stuart Mill to their mother and sisters, postmarked Paris,
4 November 1836, MTColl. XLVII/4. [Mill, *Earlier Letters*, vol. 12 of *Collected Works*, p. 308]

ter than before. It was from this time that 'he retained to the end of his life an almost ceaseless spasmodic twitching over one eye'.[25]

For some months after his return Mill was exceedingly busy working up arrears at India House. He had been absent in effect for five months and during his absence had been promoted, on the death of his father, to the third place in the Examiner's Office. His salary had in consequence risen to £1,200 a year, the figure at which it remained for the next eighteen years.

But most of Mill's energies during the little over two years which separate this from the next long Continental journey were devoted to the editorship of the *London and Westminster Review*. The death of his father had made it possible for him to free it from the all too close connexion with the more doctrinaire type of Utilitarianism and to use it as a vehicle for inspiring into the Radical movement his own somewhat different ideals. Especially in 1838, after he had bought the *Review* from Sir William Molesworth[26] and when he devoted it largely to the support of Lord Durham's Canadian mission, in the hope that Lord Durham would become the leader of a new Radical movement,[27] his interests were more deeply engaged in current politics than almost at any other period of his life, excepting only the years of the Reform agitation.

There can be little doubt that Mrs. Taylor interested herself in Mill's editorial activities but there is little evidence to show how far this interest went. That she was currently reputed to exercise some influence on the policy of the *Review* appears from the story told by Mrs. Carlyle that their friend Godefroy Cavaignac used to call Mrs. Taylor 'the Armida of the "London and Westminster"'.[28] Cavaignac, the elder brother of General Louis Cavaignac, was then living in London as a refugee and probably contributed to the *Review* and thus presumably knew why he compared Mrs. Taylor to the beautiful enchantress of Tasso's *Gerusalemme Liberata* who estranged crusading knights from their duty and who to that generation had become a familiar figure through the

[25] Alexander Bain, *John Stuart Mill*, p. 44.

[26] [William Molesworth (1810–1855) was born in London and became the eighth baronet in 1823. He was elected Member of Parliament for East Cornwall in 1832. He became acquainted with George Grote and J. S. Mill, and in 1835, with John Roebuck, he founded the *London Review* as an organ of the Philosophical Radicals. He soon after purchased the *Westminster Review*, and for some time, with J. S. Mill, he edited the united magazines. In 1836 he helped found the Reform Club. *Oxford Dictionary of National Biography*, *s.v.* 'Molesworth, Sir William', by Peter Burroughs, accessed 19 May 2014, http://www.oxforddnb.com/view/article/18902.—Ed.]

[27] [John George Lambton, first Earl of Durham (1792–1840), was sent to British North America in 1838 as Governor-General following the rebellions of 1837 in Upper and Lower Canada. In 1839 he published the Durham Report in which he recommended that Upper and Lower Canada be united under a form of representative government.—Ed.]

[28] Jane Welsh Carlyle to John Sterling, January–February 1842, in *Letters and Memorials of Jane Welsh Carlyle* (ed. J. A. Froude, 1893), vol. 1, p. 138. [*Letters and Memorials of Jane Welsh Carlyle*, ed. James Anthony Froude, 3 vols. (London: Longmans, Green, and Co. 1883).—Ed.]

operas of Gluck and Rossini. But the only document referring to Mrs. Taylor's connexion with the *Review* is a letter of hers to her husband, answering an inquiry on behalf of some of his Italian friends. John Taylor, who had introduced Mazzini to Carlyle in the preceding year,[29] seems to have continued to exert himself on his behalf and for other political refugees, and on one of his visits to his wife in the neighbourhood of London to have charged her with an inquiry in their interest. On the next day, a Saturday, when Mill probably arrived, Mrs. Taylor replied.

H. T. to John Taylor, 23 September 1837:[30] My dear John, / I find that Usiglio's article is to be in the next number of the 'London'—Robertson it seems meets the contributors at the publisher's Hooper Pall Mall—& ~~Mr.~~ Mill went in there as he passed a day or two since & found both Usiglio & Mazzini there with Robertson[31]—he had a good deal of talk with both of them & liked both very much—he has undertaken to do all the revising that is ~~necessary~~ [required] to Usiglio's article & has engaged him to write another on new Italian books & Mazzini to write one on Italian politics since 1830 at which time he was involved in them[32] & I do not know how they are paid but I believe at the old rate of 16 guin[s] the sheet. & I do not know how soon. There seems by a letter from Greece in the Chronicle yesterday[33] to be a man named Usiglio engaged in politics there. perhaps it is a brother or relation of this man.

[29] T. Carlyle, *Reminiscences*, ed. Charles Elliot Norton, vol. 1 (London: Macmillan and Co., 1887), p. 110. [Carlyle remembered Mazzini as 'the most *pious* living man I now know'. *Ibid.* Ed.]

[30] MTColl. XXVIII/135. [Harriet Taylor Mill, *Complete Works*, p. 441. There it is noted that this was 'probably written in 1836 or 1837'.—Ed.]

[31] Angelo Usiglio [1802–1875], a refugee from Modena and intimate friend of Mazzini. [John Robertson once served as the sub-editor of the *Westminster Review* under John Stuart Mill, and Guiseppe Mazzini (1808–1875) was an exile who sought to establish an independent and united Italy. See Harriet Taylor Mill, *Complete Works*, p. 441, note 4.—Ed.]

[32] The first issue of the *London and Westminster Review* brought out by John Robertson (c. 1010–1875) had been that for July 1837. An article on Italian Literature since 1830, signed 'A. U.', appeared in the issue for October of that year, an article on Paolo Sarpi, signed 'J. M.', in April 1838 and an article on 'Prince Napoleon Bonaparte', signed 'J. M.', in December 1838. In Mill's identification of the articles in the copy given to Caroline Fox and reproduced in the 1883 edition of her *Memories of Old Friends* (pp. 102–4, note) all three articles are ascribed to Mazzini, but here Mill's memory must have been at fault, since there is also a reference to the article by Usiglio in one of the letters written by Mill to John Robertson referred to below. See also Mazzini's letter to his mother of 15 September 1837 in *Epistolario di Guiseppe Mazzini* (Imola, 1912), vol. 2, p. 85. [Fetter dates the transition to Robertson's 'nominal' editorship, with Mill becoming 'active' in the management and editing of the newly-named *London and Westminster Review*, in time for the April 1836 volume. See Frank W. Fetter, 'Economic Articles in the *Westminster Review* and Their Authors, 1824–51', *Journal of Political Economy*, vol. 70, December 1962, pp. 570–96.—Ed.]

[33] *Morning Chronicle*, 22 September 1837, which refers to the expulsion from Greece of a refugee Emile Usiglio, who had arrived in Athens as an emissary of Mazzini to form a branch of 'Young Europe'. [The article is at columns 4 and 5, on p. 2.—Ed.]

I hope you had a pleasant ride yesterday. I am quite well. I hope you will soon come again, before long. Good bye.

Your affectionate

H. T.

Mill on this occasion probably spent the beginning of a short vacation with Mrs. Taylor since a few days later he wrote to Robertson[34] from a walking tour in South Wales which lasted into October.

Of the several notes and fragments of notes by Harriet Taylor to Mill which appear to belong to these years the only two which seem to be complete may be inserted here:

H. T. to J. S. M.:[35] I went this morning there in the hopes of your word my delight & there it was. believe all I can [ever] say when I tell you how happy I am, that is, how happy you make me.

This sweet letter has been with me at every moment since I had it & it keeps me *so* well *so* happy *so* in spirits—but I cannot tell thee how happy it made me when first I read it on the highest point of the nice common with those glorious breezes blowing. It has been like an equinoctial tempest here ever since you left. Mama and C[aroline][36] are here—I like it & it does me good—in the absence of the only good I ever wish for.

Thank God however the promised summer which was to be so much is come & will be all it was to be—has been already so much. I am to see you on Saturday. indeed I could not get on without.

I can not write better to-day—tho' I never *felt* better or more.

Adieu my only & most precious—till Saturday—dear Saturday

H. T. to J. S. M.:[37] You will want to know how she is before you go shall you not dear—so I write—I want so much to hear how you got on last night that you were not tired or uncomfortable in that, I should think, very tiresome expedition? I did so hate your leaving me—yet that little visit made me very happy—perhaps that is the reason I am better as I am this morng—not very much but really *somewhat* better & that *is* much. I do not think I shall see you before Tuesday—that is

---

[34] See the letters by Mill to John Robertson written from that tour in C. D. M. Towers, 'John Stuart Mill and the *London and Westminster Review*', *Atlantic Monthly*, vol. 69, 1892 [pp. 58–74]. [These are published in Mill, *Earlier Letters*, vol. 12 of *Collected Works*, pp. 349–57.—Ed.]

[35] MTColl. XXVIII/238, watermarked '1837'. [Harriet Taylor Mill, *Complete Works*, p. 333. Hayek has queries in the text after 'letter' and 'point'.—Ed]

[36] [Harriet's sister, Caroline Ley. Hayek supplies the bracketed name.—Ed.]

[37] MTColl. XXVIII/234, watermarked '1838'. [Harriet Taylor Mill, *Complete Works*, pp. 334–35.—Ed.]

a *terrible* long time, but it does not feel to me longer than Monday. It is your going away that makes it feel so long but that cannot be avoided. Only do *you* my darling be well & happy & I shall be well as I am happy, the *happiest* possible—(*no* not *possible*—there *is* a happier possibility always)—but I am perfectly happy. I do not see exactly how to manage going to the sea—so I give it up at present.

When I think that I shall not hold your hand untill Tuesday the time is so long & my hand so useless. Adieu my delight.

je baise tes jolies pattes[38]

cher cher cher

Towards the end of 1838 both Mill and Mrs. Taylor were again ailing seriously and preparing for a long journey to Italy. Mill was suffering from pains in the chest and severe dyspepsia, and although his family does not seem to have regarded his illness as very serious,[39] some of his friends had already little doubt that he was threatened with consumption. Both Mill and Mrs. Taylor appear this time to have taken great care not to let it be known that they were to travel together. Mill let it be understood that he was going to Malta,[40] while Mrs. Taylor was ostensibly proposing to visit one of her brothers and his Italian wife at Pisa.[41] None of the letters and other documents of the period make

[38] [Harriet Taylor Mill, *Complete Works*, p. 335, note 33, has the following translation: 'I kiss your pretty paws [or sideburns]'.—Ed.].

[39] Alexander Bain, *John Stuart Mill*, pp. 44–45, quotes a letter of Henry Mill of 17 January 1839, who writes: 'As to John's health, none of us believe that it is anything very serious; our means of judging are his looks when he was here, and also what we have heard from Dr. Arnott. We are told, however, that his sending him away is because the pains in the chest, which are the symptoms, make it seem that a winter in Italy just now will afford him sensible and permanent benefit for the whole of his life'.

[40] E. G. Wakefield to W. Molesworth, 27 November 1838: 'Our noble friend Mill is ordered to Malta. His lungs are not organically diseased but will [be] if he remains here. He thought till the other day that his disease was mortal, but yet he lagged away at [this] ~~the~~ Durham case, as if he had expected to live for ever' (A. J. Harrop, *The Amazing Career of Edward Gibbon Wakefield* (London: George Allen & Unwin, 1928), p. 109).

In his Autobiography (p. 211) [John Stuart Mill, *Autobiography and Literary Essays*, eds. John M. Robson and Jack Stillinger, vol. 1 (1981) of *Collected Works*, p. 247] Mill calls his illness of 1854/5 the 'first attack of the family disease', and his letters of that period show that he himself then thought it was a first attack. But he certainly must have been aware at the earlier date that he was threatened by it. Caroline Fox (*Memories of Old Friends* (new and revised edition, 1883), pp. 97–98) records an interesting conversation with Mill when he was in Falmouth in the spring of 1840 attending his brother Henry, who was dying of consumption: 'On consumption, and why it was so connected with what is beautiful and interesting in nature. The disease itself brings the mind as well as the constitution into a state of prematurity, and this reciprocally preys on the body. After an expressive pause, John Mill quietly said "I expect to die of consumption"'.

[41] Letter by John Taylor to Messrs. G. H. Gower of Leghorn, 19 December 1838, MTColl. XXIX/271.

any allusion to the joint journey, but the complete identity of the itinerary,[42] so far as it is known, could leave no doubt about it even if Mill had not sixteen years later in his letters to his wife from Naples referred to their earlier joint visit.[43]

Mrs. Taylor and her daughter Helen, then a little over seven years old, were just before Christmas taken by Mr. Taylor as far as Paris and Mill apparently joined them there a few days later. The following letter to his mother was sent a day or two after his arrival.

J. S. M. to Mrs. James Mill:[44] Paris / 28th Dec[r] 1838 / Dear mammy / Please send the first page of this scrawl to Robertson[45]—it saves double postage.

I am about as well, I think, as when I left London. I had a wretched passage—for want of water the boat could not get into Boulogne till half past two in the morning—it set off at 1/2 past eight & spent the whole 18 hours in going as slowly as it could. My already disordered stomach stood the sickness very ill & I arrived very uncomfortable & was forced to start for Paris a very few hours afterwards. The first day I was uncomfortable enough, but as the effect of the sea went off I got better & arrived at Paris after 30 hours of the diligence much less unwell than I thought I possibly could. Unless I could have got to Marseilles by the 30th it was [of] no use getting there before the 9th so I do not start till Sunday morning & shall not travel any more at night, but post to Chalons (expensive as it is) & then go down the Saone & Rhone to Avignon. Letters put in the post on the 2nd directed to M. J. S. Mill Poste Restante à Marseille France, will be sure to reach me in time. After that direct Poste Restante à Pise, Italie.—I cannot tell if I shall have time to write to you from Marseille but I will endeavour. The weather has not got very cold yet & I dare say I shall get into the mild climate first.

They call England's a bad climate but the north and east of France have certainly a worse. What I most dread is the sea passage from Marseille to Leghorn—seasickness is so bad with me now. Love to all—

yours affectionately
J. S. Mill

[42] Mrs. Taylor's itinerary can be reconstructed in great detail from her passport in MTColl. Box III. [The passports are items 66, 67, and 68 in Box III.—Ed.]

[43] Carlyle was also told by Mrs. Buller that Mill was going to Malta and promptly passed this on to John Sterling (T. Carlyle to John Sterling, 7 December 1838, in *Letters of T. C. to J. S. M.*, p. 217).

[44] MTColl. XLVII/6. [Mill, *Earlier Letters*, vol. 13 of *Collected Works*, p. 392.—Ed.]

[45] A letter to John Robertson (c. 1810–1875), editor of the *London and Westminster Review* on the affairs of the Review, printed in C. D. M. Towers, 'John Stuart Mill and the *London and Westminster Review*', *Atlantic Monthly*, vol. 69, 1892. [The letter is published in Mill, *Earlier Letters*, vol. 13 of *Collected Works*, pp. 393–34.—Ed.]

From a letter of Mrs. Taylor's to her husband from Chalons on 3 January[46] we know that she had left Paris on the same Sunday, 30 December, which Mill had set for his departure, and had travelled in extremely cold weather via Fontainebleau, Sens and Auxerre and was to continue down the rivers to Marseilles and thence by sea to Leghorn. In Pisa[47] her brother and sister-in-law proved to be away and the journey was soon continued to Rome and, after only a short stop, to Naples where they spent most of February. During a fortnight's stop at Rome on the return journey in the early part of March Mill reports home on the state of his health.

> *J. S. M. to ?, Rome, 11 March 1839:*[48] I have returned here after passing about three weeks very pleasantly ~~at~~ [in] Naples, and the country about it. I did not for some time get any better, but I think I am now, though very slowly, improving, ever since I left off animal food, and took to living almost entirely on macaroni. I began this experiment about a fortnight ago, and it seems to succeed better than any of the other experiments I have tried.

Ten days later on the way north another report is rather more gloomy.

> *J. S. M. to ?, 21 March 1839:*[49] As for me I am going on well too—not that my health is at all better; but I have gradually got quite reconciled to the idea of returning in much the same state of health as when I left England; it is by care and regimen that I must hope to get well, and if I can only avoid getting worse, I shall have no great reason to complain, as hardly anybody continues after my age (33) to have the same vigorous health they had in early youth. In the meantime it is something to have so good an opportunity of seeing Italy.

From the last part of the journey we have a few observations by Mrs. Taylor pencilled in a notebook[50] which for the earlier part gives merely the names of some of the places visited. Florence is described as

> quite worthy ~~of~~ its reputation for beauty—the valley so exactly the right size to frame the city, which from whatever point of view one sees it is very beau-

---

[46] MTColl. XXVIII/146. [Harriet Taylor Mill, *Complete Works*, pp. 442–43.—Ed.]

[47] MTColl. XXVIII/147.

[48] Alexander Bain, *J. S. Mill*, p. 45. [The letter, to 'an unidentified correspondent', is published in Mill, *Earlier Letters*, vol. 13 of *Collected Works*, p. 395.—Ed.]

[49] Alexander Bain, *J. S. Mill*, p. 45. [The letter is published in Mill, *Earlier Letters*, vol. 13 of *Collected Works*, p. 395, note 2, where the parenthetical addition '(33)', which is omitted by Hayek, is attributed with high likelihood to Bain.—Ed.]

[50] MTColl. Box II. [Harriet Taylor Mill, *Complete Works*, pp. 170–75, reprints these under the title 'The Arts in England', and ascribes the fragments to Box III/105. The portion quoted above appears at p. 171.—Ed.]

tiful. The best view is from the bank of the Arno opposite the ~~Corsini~~ [Cascini], in the eveng. The Appenines are less beautifully shaped here than at any point at which I have seen them. I think the view of Florence from Fiesole the least pretty, as I think Fiesole the least pretty suburb of Florence. it quite agrees with continental notions of country going that even the plague sh^d drive Boccacio's company no further than Fiesole. Florence is the most indeed the only middle age looking place in Italy.

There are also some brief comments on the galleries and similar notes on Bologna, Padua and Venice where the party arrived in the middle of May.

J. S. M. to Mrs. James Mill.[51] Venice / 19th May 1839 / My dear mother—I have been some days in this strange & fine old place, the most singular place in Italy—& I write to say that I am going to set out almost immediately on my return. I shall go by the Tyrol, & through Germany, slowly; if you write very soon, write to Mannheim; if not, to Brussels. As to how far the object of my journey has been attained, that is rather difficult to say, & I shall probably be able to say more about it after I have been for some time returned & have resumed my regular occupations. I certainly have not recovered my former health; at the same time I have no very troublesome complaint & no symptoms at all alarming & I have no doubt that by proper regimen & exercise I shall be able to have as good health as people generally have, though perhaps never again so good a digestion as formerly. In this however I shall be no worse off than three fourths of all the people I know. I am not in the least liable to catch cold—I never was less so in my life, & all idea of the English climate being dangerous for me may be entirely dismissed from all your minds. I shall in time find out how to manage myself—indeed I think I have in a great measure found it out already.—I have found no letters at Venice except one old one from Robertson. I do not know if any have been written but I shall leave word to send them after me to Munich where at any rate I hope to find some. Will you shew this or tell the contents of it to Grant[52] & thank him warmly from me for his unwearied obligingness & kindness—& will you or the boys tell Mr. Robertson that his letter without date, but bearing I think the postmark 1st April, & directed to Rome, did not for some reason or other reach me there, but has followed me here, & is the last I have had from him & I am hoping for another with fresher news about himself & all other matters—also that I have not yet seen the review, for although they take it at the reading room in Florence, they had not yet got the last number.

---

[51] MTColl. XLVII/7. [Mill, *Earlier Letters*, vol. 13 of *Collected Works*, pp. 398–99.—Ed.]

[52] [Horace Grant (1800–1859) worked alongside Mill in the Examiner's office at the India House from 1826 to 1845. Mill, *Earlier Letters*, vol. 12 of *Collected Works*, p. 17, note 2.—Ed.]

I have been unusually long without English news having neither had any letters nor seen any newspapers but of very old date. But I shall make it all up six weeks hence.—I have had a most pleasant stay in Italy & may say that I have seen it pretty thoroughly—I have left nothing out except Sicily, & a few stray things here & there. I have been last staying at the baths of Albano in the Euganean hills, not far from Padua—most lovely country, more of the English sort than Italy generally is—but the weather for a month past has been as bad as a wet English summer except that it has never been cold. Italy is a complete disappointment as to climate—not comparable as to brightness & dryness to the South of France, though I can easily believe that some parts of it are more beneficial to certain complaints. Among other fruits of my journey I have botanized much, & come back loaded with plants. By the bye among those I want Henry to dry for me, I forgot to mention the common elder. Italy is no disappointment as to beauty, it is the only country I have ever seen which is more beautiful than England—& I have not seen a mile of it that is not beautiful. I expect to enjoy the passage of the Alps exceedingly if the weather will let me, & there seems to-day some chance of its clearing—it is the first day without rain for a fortnight past.—Let me hear from some of you soon.

affectionately
J. S. Mill

From Venice the party proceeded through Bassano and the Val Sugana into the Tyrol where for a short while Mrs. Taylor's notes become a little fuller:[53]

> Trent on the Adige most beautiful & imposing as we approached it from Borgo [di Val Sugana—the last stop before Trent]. a very fine town with German spaciousness cleaness & *pleasant eatables*. delightful to find oneself in Germany again. At Borgo the inn people spoke german & there was german frankness niceness simplicity & honest charges. and from an opposite house, for the first time for six months the great pleasure of hearing the sound of german music played with german touch on a german piano-forte. Certainly the Italians have no taste for music.

Taking about a week going over the Brenner to Innsbruck and via Mittenwald into Bavaria the party arrived at the end of May in Munich. Mrs. Taylor's notes conclude:[54]

---

[53] [Hayek supplies the below material in brackets. Harriet Taylor Mill, *Complete Works*, pp. 174–75.—Ed.]

[54] [Harriet Taylor Mill, *Complete Works*, p. 175.—Ed.]

altogether Munich is a most cheerful happy looking place & if as dissipated
as people say presents an argument for dissipation.

The journey through Germany via Heidelberg and Aachen and finally
through Brussels to Ostend took another month and Mill arrived in London
just in time to resume his duties at India House on July 1st while Mrs. Taylor
seems to have gone at once to Brighton.

The years from about 1840 to 1847 are an almost complete blank in our
knowledge of Mill's private life and the character of his connexion with Mrs.
Taylor. We have scarcely any documents belonging to this period and few
other contemporary sources of interest. It is probable that it was at the beginning of this time that they had become aware of the scandalous talk about
them, had learnt to exercise caution, and that they withdrew almost completely from society. There were other reasons present with both of them
which contributed to this retirement. With the abandonment of the editorship
of the *London and Westminster Review* in 1840 Mill had also given up the attempt
to inspire an active radical group to effective political action, and thereafter devoted all his free time to the composition of his major theoretical treatises. The *Logic* was completed at the end of 1841, although it appeared only
in March 1843, and part of it was rewritten in the interval. After some years
of abortive endeavour to write a treatise on 'Ethology', he turned in 1845 to
work on the *Political Economy*. Severe financial losses which he had suffered
through the American repudiation of 1842 forced him to economize and to
save in an endeavour to make good losses on the capital which he held in trust
for his mother and sisters. This considerably reduced his mobility, and according to Bain,[55] he took no holiday at all during the first three or four years of
the decade. He also seems to have suffered during these years renewed bouts
of illness.

The forms of his intercourse with Harriet Taylor had by then presumably
settled down to a recognized routine. Since the end of the 1830's Mrs. Taylor
lived mainly in a house at Walton on Thames where Mill appears regularly to
have spent the week-ends. It is to the beginning of this period, more precisely
to the summer of 1842 and the following years, that Bain's often quoted story
refers, that Mill went regularly to dine with her at her husband's house about
twice a week, Mr. Taylor himself dining out.[56] This must have been confined
to the short periods of Mrs. Taylor's visits to town, which seem to have been
few during the time to which Bain refers. Bain also mentions their attend-

[55] Alexander Bain, *J. S. Mill*, p. 164. [Bain makes this observation on p. 78.—Ed.]

[56] [*Ibid.*, p. 164: 'In the summer of 1842, and for some of the following summers, I cannot
say how many, I knew that he went to dine with her at her husband's house, in Kent Terrace,
Regent's Park, about twice a-week (Mr. Taylor himself dining out)'.—Ed.]

ing together Carlyle's courses of lectures which were given in 1838 to 1840. One letter of Mrs. Taylor's referring to the last of these courses has been preserved.

> *H. T. to Miss Eliza Fox, May or June 1840:*[57] My dear Miss Fox, not having heard from L[izzie?] & thinking it a pity the card should lie here idle I sent it on Monday to Miss Gillies. But I know Mr. Mill has one, which I do not think he will use, & which I am sure he will be very glad to send to her.
>
> I am very glad she liked the lectures; I did not expect it; it is the highest flattery when she *likes*; I heard a *mot* of H. Mar[tineau] very charactiristic, she wrote to Mr. Carlyle approving the syllabus but reminding him that he had omitted the 'Hero' as 'Martyr' to which he replied that if he had not considered him that in every situation he should never have thought him worth talking about. Lily has begun many letters to you, so that my paper case is crowded with papers commencing 'dear Tottie' but she has never had courage or industry to complete one which she thinks 'worth sending' having a salutary horror of 'blots' and respect for your critical powers. She sends her love to you. She has often wished for you here. We have had a most lovely season & have enjoyed the sea thoroughly.
>
> We leave this place next week to be nearer town. We shall go to Tunbridge Wells & stay there some weeks, so that we shall see you soon.
>
> Adieu dear.
>
> H. T.

A letter to her husband of about 1840, in which Mrs. Taylor asks for a bundle of manuscript which she left behind in town to be sent to her, 'as I am very busy writing for the printers & want to get some scraps out of that',[58] is the only indication of some literary activity of hers during that period, of the nature of which, however, we know nothing. Her health during the whole of this period seems to have been very poor. In addition to the consumptive tendencies which had shown themselves much earlier, she suffered for a time from some spinal injury suffered in a carriage accident[59] which kept her for

---

[57] King's College, Cambridge. [Hayek supplies the words in brackets. Harriet's letter is reprinted in Harriet Taylor Mill, *Complete Works*, pp. 384–85, where the editor surmises that Harriet here explains why she sent the ticket to Carlyle's lecture to Miss Gillies instead of Fox's lover, Eliza Flower.—Ed.]

[58] MTColl. XXVIII/152. The letter is dated in a later hand 'April 28, 1840', presumably from a cover now lost. [Harriet Taylor Mill, *Complete Works*, p. 451. The editor adds this note (p. 451, note 32): 'Probably written in 1842, since Harriet asks about John Taylor's mother's health. John's mother died in 1842'.—Ed.]

[59] A reference to this accident in Mill's letter to W. E. Hickson of 4 March 1859 in the Huntington Library. [See *The Later Letters of John Stuart Mill, 1849–1873*, eds. Francis E. Mineka and

long on a sofa and for the rest of her life seems to have been the cause of a recurrent paralysis or at least partial lameness. But her illness seems rarely to have been an obstacle to her travelling, or rather seems to have provided the pretext for moving about restlessly most of the time. Even while in England she appears to have been constantly on the move, not only between her cottage in Walton on Thames and the house in town, but also various places in the South of England.

Her only regular companion in this life was her daughter Helen, only ten years old in 1841, who, it would seem, never went to school,[60] but had to pick up her education from her mother, from travel and voracious reading in English, French and German. It is from the fragments of a diary[61] kept by the young girl that we get most of our information on Mrs. Taylor's mode of life during that time, and, incidentally, reflected in the mind of the precocious girl, probably also some of her opinions. The diary covers part of two Continental journeys, one in June and July 1844 to Normandy, and another during the same months of 1846 to Belgium and up the Rhine. On both these journeys Mill, who was absent from London during the periods in question,[62] may have accompanied them.

Helen Taylor's main interests at that time were the theatre and the drama. We find her constantly writing and acting plays, learning long parts, and at one stage translating Schiller's *Maria Stuart*. Her other reading is surprisingly serious for a girl of fourteen or fifteen, mainly history and religion. At thirteen and a half she complains: 'Why do not people write now? Why is there neither man nor woman who dares to say his opinions openly and so that all may know it? People fancy now that cowardice (of opinion) is prudence, and indifference philosophy'. It is probably also the mother speaking through the daughter when, two years later, Helen Taylor notes: 'Everything of the Germans seems excellent. The other books I have read are never like German full of ideas and truths which instantly light up as a new possession'. Her other great interest, which she shared with her brother Haji, was in the ritual and particularly the music of the Roman Catholic church. Even in England and still more on the Continent she rarely misses an opportunity to attend High

---

Dwight N. Lindley, vols. 14–17 (1972) of *Collected Works*, 15:602.—Ed.] It occurred probably early in May 1842, when according to Helen Taylor's diary Mr. and Mrs. Taylor were thrown out of a carriage. Mrs. Taylor was certainly very ill during the following months.

[60] See Mary Taylor in *Letters* (ed. Elliot), vol. 1, p. 43. [The essay by Mary Taylor, 'Some Notes on the Private Life of John Stuart Mill', appears at pp. 39–46. She writes on p. 43, that Helen 'had wished to go to school, that she might be prepared for taking an active part in life, but this wish was not granted'.—Ed.]

[61] MTColl. XLIV. [Hayek enters this as XLV.—Ed.]

[62] On 6 June 1844 Mill wrote in an unpublished letter to J. M. Kemble that he was '[to] going out of town for some weeks' and on 14 August to the same that he had 'just returned'. [Mill, *Earlier Letters*, vol. 13 of *Collected Works*, pp. 633 and 634, respectively.—Ed.]

Mass and at least at one stage one feels that her sympathy must have extended beyond the external forms of the service.

Haji, the younger of her two brothers, is the only other member of the family who occurs frequently in the diary. The relation of mother and daughter to Herbert, the elder, seems to have been much looser. He evidently was more attached to the father, whom he early assisted and later succeeded in the firm, and from 1846 onwards, when he went for his first long visit to America, he seems to have been overseas a good deal. There is no reference to Mill in the diary, though a few other visitors at Walton (including Carlyle in 1842 and Haji's friend George Mill) are recorded.

Only two notes of Mrs. Taylor to Mill have been preserved from this period. The first seems to be one of the few which Mill deliberately kept because of its content. It refers to his correspondence with the French philosopher Auguste Comte which had started in 1840 and continued fairly actively for about five years. Mrs. Taylor evidently had not seen it until after, in the second half of 1843, it had turned mainly on the position of women, on which the two philosophers strongly disagreed. Of this part of the correspondence Mill not only, against his usual habits, had kept the relevant parts of the drafts of his own letters, but had also copied out Comte's replies and had both sides of the discussion bound up as a volume,[63] clearly for Mrs. Taylor's use. Mill's friend, Alexander Bain, seems to have been allowed to see it before her unfavourable criticism made Mill feel 'dissatisfied with the concessions he had made to Comte' and decide that he 'would never show them to anyone again'.[64] It was probably with the following note that Mrs. Taylor returned the letters to Mill.

H. T. to J. S. M., about 1844.[65] These have greatly surprised & ~~also~~ disappointed me, & also they have pleased me, all this ~~only~~ regarding [only] *your* part in them. Comte's is what I expected—the usual partial & prejudiced view of a subject which he has little considered & on which it is probable that he is in the same state that Mr. Fox is about religion. If the truth is on the side I defend[66] I imagine C. would rather not see it. Comte is essentially *French*, in the sense in which we think French mind less admirable than English—Anti-Catholic—Anti-Cosmopolite.

---

[63] *Lettres inédites de John Stuart Mill à Auguste Comte*, ed. L. Lévy-Bruhl, (Paris: Felix Alcan, 1899), p. 296. [Mill's answer to Comte appears at pp. 295–98 and is dated 17 January 1844. It is reprinted in Mill, *Earlier Letters*, vol. 13 of *Collected Works*, pp. 619–20.—Ed.]

[64] Bain, *J. S. Mill*, p. 74. Bain's notes on the correspondence, dated 1844, are in MTColl. XLI/8. [Hayek lists these notes as XLVII/8.—Ed.]

[65] MTColl. II/327, continued on second sheet in Box III/103. [Harriet Taylor Mill, *Complete Works*, pp. 337–38. Note 43 on p. 338 concurs, 'The Comte letters were probably shown to HTM in 1844'.—Ed.]

[66] [Harriet's original, but not Hayek's reproduction, strikes out 'we': 'on the side ~~we~~ I defend'.—Ed.]

I am surprised in your letters to find your opinion undetermined where I had thought it made up—I am dissappointed at a tone more than half apologetic with which you state your opinions. & I am charmed with the exceeding nicety elegance & fineness [finesse] of your last letter.[67] Do not think that I wish you had said *more* on the subject, I only wish that what was said was in the tone of conviction, not of suggestion.

This dry sort of man is not a worthy coadjutor & scarcely a worthy opponent. with your gifts of intellect of conscience & of impartiality is it probable, or is there any ground for supposing, that there exists any man more competent to judge that question than you are?

You are in advance of your age in culture of the intellectual faculties, you would be the most remarkable man of your age if you had no other claim to be so than your perfect impartiality & your fixed love of justice. These are the two qualities of different orders which I believe to be the rarest & most difficult to human nature.

Human nature [is] essentially weak, for when it is not weak by defect of intellect it is almost inevitably weak by excess of the moral or conscientious principle, seems to me to attain its finest expression only when in addition to a high development of the powers of intellect, the moral qualities rise consciously above all—so that the being looks down on his own character with the very same feelings as on those of the rest of the world, & so desiring the qualities he thinks elevated for *themselves* wholly unmoved by considerations proper to any *portion* of the race, still less so to himself. 'To do justly, to love mercy, (generosity) & to walk humbly before all men' is very fine for the age in which it was produced, but why was it not 'before God' rather than before *all men*?

It makes the sentiment seem rather Greek than Jewish.

It appears to me that the idea which you propose in the division of the functions of men in the general Government proceeds on the supposition of the incapacity or unsuitableness of the same mind for work of active life & for work of reflection & combination: & that the same supposition is sufficient to account for the differences in the characters & apparent capacities of man & women considering that the differences of the occupations in life are just those which you say in the case of men must produce distinct characters (neither you nor Comte seem to settle the other analogous question, whether original differences of character & capacities in men are to determine to which class of workers they are to belong) & there is also to be taken into account the unknown extent of action on the physical & mental powers, of hereditary servitude.

---

[67] Probably Mill's letter of 30 October 1843, in which he extensively sums up his position on the Women question, or his letter of 8 December 1843, with which he breaks off that discussion. [Mill, *Earlier Letters*, vol. 13 of *Collected Works*, pp. 604–11 and 615–17, respectively.—Ed.]

I should like to begin the forming of a book or list of what in human beings must be individual & of in what they may be classified.

I now & then find a generous defect in your mind of yr 'method'—such is your liability to take an over large *measure* of people—sauf having to draw in afterwards—a proceeding more needful than pleasant.

Mrs. Taylor's second note from approximately the same period has survived probably by accident, but may serve as a specimen of their more ordinary correspondence.

H. T. to J. S. M.:[68] a thousand thanks & blessings dearest & kindest one. What a deal of trouble I have made you take—but you think nothing trouble for me *beloved*!

I think I had best not hope to see you to-day *dearest dearest* because Arthur[69] is coming & will be here at the time you would come—but tomorrow *certainly* for I *could not* be longer without. I will get the stupid ticket[70] & we will go for an hour & see our old friend Rhino—will you dear come [here] & take me to-morrow about five?

Yesterday I walked to Norfolk St—they were not there & then Haji and I went to mama at the old place—she was very busy & I helped her all day untill ten at night, when I came home—so you see dear all the fatigue that had gone before was little compared to this last—& if I had known what it would be I sh[d] not have gone there it was a great deal too much—but I am so perfectly & entirely happy, without one single cloud, that I shall soon get over this merely physical fatigue.

I shall hear from Herby soon & on that will depend if I go to that place again. If he is going on well I shall not go 'till next week to bring them up. So we can have Sunday if we please love & we will talk of it to-morrow.

Adieu & bless you my perfect one.

---

[68] MTColl. XXVIII/233. The letter is marked in pencil in another hand '1845?', but this is probably too late, since it suggests that Mrs. Taylor's boys were still children while in 1845 'Herby' would have been eighteen. It may well be about 1840 or even earlier. [Herby was Harriet's older son. The letter appears in Harriet Taylor Mill, *Complete Works*, pp. 335–36. Note 37 on p. 336 suggests the letter was from 1838: 'Arthur Hardy emigrated to Australia in late 1838 so this letter was probably written earlier that year'.—Ed.]

[69] Mrs. Taylor's brother.

[70] Probably the membership card of the Zoological Society, admitting to the Zoological Gardens within a few minutes' walk of the Taylors' house.

SIX

A JOINT PRODUCTION
1847–1849

In the *Autobiography* Mill says of Mrs. Taylor that

The first of my books in which her share was conspicuous was the *Principles of Political Economy*. The *System of Logic* owed little to her except in the minuter matters of composition, in which respect my writings, both great and small, have largely benefitted by her accurate and clear-sighted criticism. The chapter of the *Political Economy* which has had a greater influence on opinion than all the rest, that on 'the Probable Future of the Labouring Classes', is entirely due to her: in the first draft of the book, that chapter did not exist. She pointed out the need of such a chapter, and the extreme imperfection of the book without it: she was the cause of my writing it; and the more general part of the chapter, the statement and discussion of the two opposite theories respecting the proper condition of the labouring classes, was wholly an exposition of her thoughts, often in words taken from her [own] lips. The purely scientific part of the *Political Economy* I did not learn from her; but it was chiefly her influence that gave to the book that general tone by which it is distinguished from all previous expositions of Political Economy that had any pretension to being scientific, and which has made it so useful in conciliating minds which those previous expositions had repelled. . . . What was abstract and purely scientific was generally mine; the properly human element came from her: in all that concerned the application of philosophy to the exigencies of human society and progress, I was her pupil, alike in boldness of speculation and cautiousness of practical judgment. For, on the one hand, she was much more courageous and far-sighted than without her I should have been, in anticipations of an order of things to come, in which many of the limited generalizations now so often confounded with universal principles will cease to be applicable.[1]

---

[1] *Autobiography*, pp. 207–10. [*Autobiography and Literary Essays*, eds. John M. Robson and Jack Stillinger, vol. 1 (1981) of *The Collected Works of John Stuart Mill* [hereafter cited as *Collected Works*] (Toronto: University of Toronto Press, 1962–1991), pp. 255–61. The quoted passages appear on pp. 255 and 257.—Ed.] The whole passage is too long to quote in full, but I think it could be shown that in it Mill attributes to Mrs. Taylor's influence ideas which he demonstrably owes to the Saint-Simonians and Comte.

In Mill's hand list of his publications the *Political Economy* is described as 'a joint production with my wife'. The description of one of his publications as a 'joint production' occurs for the first time at the beginning of 1846 with regard to a newspaper article and afterwards with increasing frequency.[2] The *Autobiography* also gives an account of the incredibly short period during which the great treatise was written:

> The *Political Economy* was far more rapidly executed than the *Logic*, or indeed than anything of importance which I had previously written. It was commenced in the autumn of 1845, and was ready for the press before the end of 1847. In this period of little more than two years there was an interval of six months during which the work was laid aside, while I was writing articles in the *Morning Chronicle* (which unexpectedly entered warmly into my purpose) urging the formation of peasant properties on the waste lands of Ireland. This was during the period of the famine, the winter of 1846/47.[3]

From an unpublished letter of Mill to H. S. Chapman of 9 March 1847[4] we know that Mill had already completed the first draft, presumably the one without the chapter on 'The Futurity of the Labouring Classes', during the preceding week, that is, even before he had discontinued his intense journalistic activity which in the course of about fifteen months led him to contribute more than sixty articles to the *Morning Chronicle*. The last article of the series appeared in April and Mill then discontinued writing for the press to devote himself entirely to the final revision of the book or, as he says in the letter to

[2] MacMinn, *et al*, *Bibliography*, pp. 59 and 69. [Jack Stillinger finds seven instances where Mill uses 'joint product' or 'joint production' to refer to his work with Harriet Taylor Mill in the *Autobiography* ('Who Wrote J. S. Mill's *Autobiography*?', *Victorian Studies*, vol. 27, Autumn 1983, p. 11, note 6). Several of these appear in unpublished fragments; there are three mentions in the published version. See Mill, *Autobiography*, vol. 1 of *Collected Works*, pp. 251 (two mentions) and 257.—Ed.]

[3] *Autobiography*, p. 199. [Mill, *Autobiography*, vol. 1 of *Collected Works*, p. 243. Mill continues to provide a reason for the speed of preparation: 'when the stern necessities of the time seemed to afford a chance of gaining attention for what appeared to me the only mode of combining relief to immediate destitution with permanent improvement of the social and economical condition of the Irish people'.—Ed.]

[4] Autographed letter in possession of Mrs. Vera Eichelbaum, Wellington, New Zealand, quoted with her kind permission. [Henry S. Chapman (1803–1881) was a journalist in Canada from 1823 to 1834 who later formed an association with the *London and Westminster Review* and became a Supreme Court judge in New Zealand. See *The Earlier Letters of John Stuart Mill, 1812–1848*, ed. Francis E. Mineka, vols. 12–13 (1963) of *Collected Works*, 12:274, note 7. The letter, dated 9 March 1848, is published in Mill, *Earlier Letters*, vol. 13 of *Collected Works*, pp. 708–10. In it, Mill writes that 'I have had a book to write which will be as large a one when printed as the Logic, and which I have now, (within the last week) completed, sauf the revising, or rather rewriting, which is an indispensible part of anything which I write' (p. 708).—Ed.]

H. S. Chapman, 'rather rewriting, which is an indispensible part of anything of importance [which] I write'.

Unfortunately we have practically no documentary evidence of the part which Mrs. Taylor took in the composition of the first edition of the work. What little light the existing papers throw on the period tend on the whole to confirm Mill's account. Apart from the tour of about six weeks to the Rhine and Northern France in June and July 1846, Mrs. Taylor appears to have been in England throughout the period, living mostly at Walton, but according to her habit constantly going for short visits to Worthing, Brighton, Ryde and other places on the South Coast or the Isle of Wight, and only rarely coming to town. What time she and Mill can have spent together must have been mainly during week-ends and Mill's vacation. The first mention of the *Political Economy* in the letters of Mrs. Taylor that have been preserved occurs towards the end of 1847 when the book was practically finished.

> *H. T. to John Taylor, Walton, late 1847:*[5] I do certainly look more like a ghost [than] a living person, but I dare say I shall soon recover some better looks when we get to Brighton. I think I shall not be able to go before the end of next week being just now much occupied with the book.

A letter to her husband of only three or four weeks later refers to Mill in connexion with another matter which probably arose out of his recent journalistic activities.

> *H. T. to John Taylor, Walton (?), 18 January 1848:*[6] Mr Mill has just had an overture from Sir. J. Easthope wishing him to share the proprietorship of the Morn^g Chronicle. It seems Easthope has had a quarrel with his son in law Doyle & which he says it is impossible can be made up—nor can they go on in the same concern. The quarrel however is not about the Chroni^l but about a will. . . . Easthope says that 100,000 have been divided among the proprietors since he took it. He has 7.8^ths & Duncan the bookseller 1.8^th. He offers 3 or 4.8^th at 1700 each. He says the Daily News has made an offer to be sold to the Chronicle but they want too much. The Tory's are very eager to get it. Mr. Mill does not mean to take it as he thinks part proprietorship would not ensure the opinions he would take it solely with the object of

[5] MTColl. XXVIII/170. [*The Complete Works of Harriet Taylor Mill* [hereafter cited as *Complete Works*], ed. Jo Ellen Jacobs (Bloomington: Indiana University Press, 1998), p. 471. Note 87 states that this was 'written in March 1848, just before' the publication of the *Political Economy.*—Ed.]

[6] MTColl. XXVIII/174; Sir John Easthope, Bt., 1784–1865, was successively M.P. for St. Albans, Banbury and Leicester, and since 1834 proprietor of the *Morning Chronicle*. [The quoted passage appears in Harriet Taylor Mill, *Complete Works*, p. 467; for the entire letter, see pp. 466–67.—Ed.]

advocating—but he is very anxious to save it from the Tories. It seems Alderman Farebrother[7] has made an offer[s] for it.

Shares enough to constitute a majority would amount to a large sum. Sir J. Easthope said that La\(^y\) Easthope has one share which she would not give up. Easthope says the present sale is 3200 & that it has been done up so far by the Daily News. yet that paper seems on its last legs. I shall be very sorry if the 'rascally Times' is to become the sole representative of english liberalism!

If this was an attempt to interest Mr. Taylor in the control of the *Morning Chronicle* nothing came of it. Not much later 'the book' again appears in the correspondence between Mrs. Taylor and her husband.

H. T. to John Taylor, about February 1848.[8] I am so taken up with the Book which is near the last & has constantly something to be seen to about binding &c that I could not leave town before the beginning of April If even then.

H. T. to John Taylor, Walton, 31 March 1848.[9] The book on The Principles of Political Economy which has been the work of all this winter is now nearly ready & will be published in ten days. I am somewhat undecided whether to accept its being dedicated to me or not—dedications are not unusual even of grave books, to women, and I think it calculated to do good if short & judicious—I have a large volume of Political Economy in my hands now dedicated to Madame de Sismondi—yet I cannot quite make up my mind—what do you advise—on the whole I am inclined to think it desirable.

The reference to the dedication to Madame de Sismondi is a little disingenuous: it is evidently to the English translation of Sismondi's work which had appeared in the preceding year and which had been dedicated by the translator to the widow of the author.[10] Mr. Taylor's first reaction to this request is not preserved, nor the further note with which Mrs. Taylor followed it up, but their general character can be inferred from the more considered reply John Taylor wrote two days later.

[7] Probably Charles Farebrother, a member of the Vintner's Company and Alderman from 1826 until his death in 1858.

[8] MTColl. XXVIII/178. [Harriet Taylor Mill, *Complete Works*, pp. 473–74. Note 93 on p. 473 states that this was written in March 1848. Hayek omits a passage that is struck out in Harriet's original: 'that I have not time just now I could not leave town before the beginning of April If even then'.—Ed.]

[9] MTColl. XXVIII/179. [Harriet Taylor Mill, *Complete Works*, p. 472, note 90, dates this letter as March 1848, shortly before the publication of Mill's *Political Economy*.—Ed.]

[10] [John Charles Léonard Simonde de Sismondi,] *Political Economy and the Philosophy of Government; a series of essays selected from the Works of M. de Sismondi: with a Historical Notice of his Life and Writings* (London: John Chapman, 1847).

John Taylor to H. T.:[11] Monday 3 April 1848 / My dear Harriet, / I was so much surprised on Saturday when I received your note & found you to be inclined to have the Book dedicated to you that I could not reply until I had a little time to reflect upon the question, & this I had during a walk to Pall Mall from whence I wrote my letter.—Consideration made me decidedly think, as I did at the first moment of reading your letter, that all dedications are in bad taste, & that under our circumstances the proposed one would evince on both author's part, as well as the lady to whom the book is to be dedicated, a want of taste & tact which I could not have believed possible.—Two days have since passed & my conviction remains the same notwithstanding your letter of yesterday.

It is not only 'a few common people' who will make vulgar remarks, but all who know any of us—The dedication will revive recollections now forgotten & will create observations and talk that cannot but be extremely unpleasant to me.

I am very sorry you should be much vexed at my decided opinion. You asked me, 'what do you advise'—and feeling & thinking as I do, that the proposed dedication would be most improper, I felt bound to give my opinion in decided terms, & such as could not be mistaken. I much regret, as I always do, differing in opinions with you. But as you asked me what I advised, I have not hesitated to give my opinion.

No one would more rejoice than I should at any justice & honour done to you—and if I thought my feelings and wishes alone stood in the way of your receiving both, it would be a source of great sorrow to me. But I do not believe that either would result from anything in such bad taste as the proposed dedication would, in my opinion, shew. I can assure you that this subject has given me much anxiety & trouble these last two days,—it is never pleasant to differ with you—most of all upon questions such as this.

Yours affy

J. T.

When the *Principles of Political Economy with Some of Their Applications to Social Philosophy* appeared in April 1848, a limited number of copies had a separate sheet pasted in after the title page, marked "Gift Copy" in small print at the foot, and bearing the following dedication:[12]

[11] MTColl. XXVIII/180. [Harriet Taylor Mill, *Complete Works*, pp. 472–73.—Ed.]

[12] The dedication was repeated in a limited number of gift copies of the second edition of the *Political Economy* (1849), but omitted in the third, which appeared in 1853 after Harriet Taylor had become Mrs. Mill, because, as she explains in a letter to her brother Arthur Hardy, 'it would have been no longer appropriate' (MTColl. XXVII/50, dated 7 September 1856). [The letter is published in Harriet Taylor Mill, *Complete Works*, pp. 422–24, with the quoted sentence on p. 423.—Ed.]

TO

MRS. JOHN TAYLOR

AS THE MOST EMINENTLY QUALIFIED
OF ALL PERSONS KNOWN TO THE AUTHOR
EITHER TO ORIGINATE OR TO APPRECIATE
SPECULATIONS ON SOCIAL IMPROVEMENT,
THIS ATTEMPT TO EXPLAIN AND DIFFUSE IDEAS
MANY OF WHICH WERE FIRST LEARNED FROM HERSELF,

IS

WITH THE HIGHEST RESPECT AND REGARD
DEDICATED.

Some copies, it seems, were distributed by Mrs. Taylor herself and one of them went to the daughter of their old friend W. J. Fox.

H. T. to W. J. Fox.[13] Kent Terrace, / May 10, /1848 / Dear Mr Fox, / I am glad you like the book. It is, I think, full of good things — but I did not suppose you were interested in the subjects which most interest me in it, and I sent it to Miss Fox because when I knew her in her early youth she appeared to interest herself strongly in the cause to which for many years of my life & exertions have been devoted, justice for women. The progress of the race *waits* for the emancipation of women from their present degraded slavery to the *necessity* of marriage, or to modes of earning their living which (with the sole exception of artists) consist only of [the] poorly paid & hardly worked occupations, all the professions, mercantile clerical legal & medical, as well as all government posts being monopolised by men. Political equality would alone place women on a level with other men in these respects. I think the interested or indifferent selfishness of the low reformers would be overmastered by the real wish for greater justice for women which prevails among the upper classes of men, if but these men had *ideas* enough to perceive that society requires the infusion of the new life of the feminine element. The great practical ability of women which is now wasted on worthless trifles or sunk in the stupidities called *love* would tell with most 'productive' effect on the business of life, while their emancipation would relieve the character of men from the deadening & degrading influences of life passed in intimacy with inferiors. But *ideas* are just that needful stock in trade in which our legislators are as lamentably deficient as our chartists, who with their [one] idea of universal suffrage are too purblind to perceive or too poltron to proclaim that half the race are excluded. I cannot but dissent from an argument you for a moment turned the light of your countenance upon, the first time, I

---

[13] MTColl. XXVII/40. [Harriet Taylor Mill, *Complete Works*, pp. 390–91.—Ed.]

think, you spoke in the house—to the effect that 'who would be free themselves must strike the blow' or at all events express their desire. This argument appears to be even less appropriate to the case of women than it would have been to that of the negroes by emancipating whom, from her own sense of justice alone, England has acquired the brightest glory round any nation's name.

Domestic slaves cannot organize themselves,—each one owns a master, & this mastery which is normally passive would assert itself if they attempted it. The ~~position~~ [condition] of women is also *unique* no other slaves have . . . [14]

H. T. to W. J. Fox:[15] May 12 [1848] / Dear Mr Fox, / Your note has given me a genuine & hearty sensation of pleasure. I was going to say it is delightful to find that one has done less than justice to a friend! which you should understand but which I will change into, I am delighted to find that we agree so far.

You must not suppose that I am less interested in the other great question of our time, that of labour. The equalising among all the individuals comprising the community (varied only by variation in physical capacities) the amount of labour to be performed by them during life. But this has been so well placed on the tapis by the noble spectacle of France ('spite of Pol^l Eco^y blunders) that there is no doubt of its continuing *the* great question until the hydra-headed selfishness of the idle classes is crushed by the demands of the lower. The condition of women question goes deeper into the mental and moral characteristics of the race than the other & it is *the race* for which I am interested. God knows if only the people now living or likely to follow such progenitors were what one thought of in any exertion, both common & uncommon sense would make one as utterly and as successfully selfish (for oneself and a little band of friends) as the rest. I fear that if the suffrage is gained by *all* men before *any* women possess it, the door will be closed upon equality between the sexes perhaps for centuries. It will become a *party* question in which only the highminded of the stronger party will be interested for justice. The argument is all in the general principle—and this is neither understood nor cared for by the flood of uneducated who would be let in by the male 'universal suffrage'.

I should have said that the Ded^n. was confined to copies given to friends at my special request & to the great disappointment & regret & contrary to

---

[14] Continuation missing.
[15] King's College, Cambridge. [Hayek supplies the date in brackets. Harriet Taylor Mill, *Complete Works*, pp. 391–92.—Ed.]

the wish & opinion of the author. My reason being that opinions carry more
weight with the authority of his name alone.

Ever Truly Y^{rs}

H. T.

Of the great interest which political events abroad during 1848 must have
aroused in Mill and Mrs. Taylor we get only a slight reflection in two of her
notes written from the Isle of Wight where she was staying.

H. T. to J. S. M., Ryde, 25 July 1848:[16] It seems to me that you are the only
man with a mind & feeling in this country—certainly in public life there is
none possessing the first named requisite. Only think of *Fox* saying that he
'entirely approved & w^d do all in his power to enable the ministers to carry
the bill the earliest possible'![17] Is this place hunting or John Bullism—

I am very glad you wrote that to Crowe.[18] It is excellent & must do some
good. I only disagree in the last sentence—but that does not much matter.
How can you '*know*' that a rising c^d. not succeed—and in my opinion if it did
not succeed it might do good if it were a serious one, by exasperating & giv-
ing fire to the spirit of the people. The Irish w^d I sh^d hope not be frightened
but urged on by some loss of life. However that is entre nous & is not the
thing to say to these dowdies—the more that it might not prove true. I suppose it is *impossible* that Ireland c^d. eventually succeed & if so you are right.
I am disgusted with the mixture of impudence (in his note and marked passages) & imbecility in the article which he sends of the Reasoner[19] of this
foolish creature Holyoake. I suppose he must too be answered. What do you

[16]MTColl. L/8. [Harriet Taylor Mill, *Complete Works*, pp. 339–42. Hayek includes queries, as
follows: 'to these dowdies (?)'; 'mass of verbiage (?)'; 'their opinions touch (?) me'; and 'for having
imageried (?)' Harriet Taylor Mill, *Complete Works*, corrects 'imageried' to 'imagined' and accepts
the other queried words.]

[17]According to the Parliamentary report in the *Daily News* of 24 July 1848, which presumably Mrs. Taylor had read, W. J. Fox had said in the debate in the House of Commons on the
'Suspension of the Habeas Corpus Act (Ireland)' on 22 July 'that the sooner the bill was passed
into a law the better. He would do all in his power to aid the government in carrying it at once'.

[18]Eire Evans Crowe (1799–1868) from 1846 to 1851 editor of the *Daily News*.

[19] *The Reasoner, A Weekly Journal, Utilitarian, Republican and Communist*, edited by G. J. Holyoake, was at that time running a series of long extracts from Mill's *Political Economy*, which it
thought at the price of £1 10s. to be beyond the reach of most of its readers. The passage
quoted from *The Reasoner* later in the letter has not been traced and probably occurred in a much
earlier issue. [The extracts ran under the headings: 'Theories of Private Property and Communism', pp. 50–54; 'Theories of Private Property and Communism (II)', pp. 66–69; 'Remedies for Low Wages—Checks to Population', pp. 83–86; 'Remedies for Low Wages—Checks to
Population (II)', pp. 98–101; and 'Remedies for Low Wages—Checks to Population (III)', pp.
115–18.—Ed.]

think of the ci joint notion of an answer? I should like to see your answer before it goes if quite convenient.

I fancy I sh^d say that the morality of the reasoner appears to me as far as *any* meaning can be picked out of the mass of verbiage in which its opinions on morality are always enveloped to be as intolerant slavish & selfish as that of the religion which it attacks, and the arguments used in the reasoner against religion are even if possible more foolish & weak than ~~that~~ [those] of its opponents. None of the marked quotations against people who are afraid to acknowledge their opinions touch me, in the slightest degree I am ready to stand by my opinions but not to hear them travestied, & mixed up with what appear to me opinions founded on no principles & arguments so weak that I should dread for the furtherance of my anti religious opinions the imputation that they do not admit of being better defended.

In the very number you send me of *The Reasoner* a vulgar epithet of abuse is applied to the French for having imagined *Reason* as their head![20] You say your 'atheism does not *"negative"* (I suppose this means in English *deny*) the worship of a God to set up reason instead?' The sentence has & admits no other meaning.

The fool ought to be sharply set down by *reasons*—but he is such an *excessive* fool & so lost in self sufficiency that he will cavil & prate say what you will. But as I suppose he must have an answer the only plan is to strike hard without laying yourself open. I am glad of the quarrel with him as I am glad not to have your name and influence degraded by such a connection.

The sentence I copied above runs thus—'our atheism is not the' &c 'for it does not negative the worship of God to set up the worship of a harlot'

What does the fellow mean except by a sideblow to crush those who practise illegally what he practises legally. If he had any *principles* of morality he c^d not use such an expression. *The fact is* his irreligion like Fox's liberalism is a trade.

Will you please dear keep this note as I have put down my notions about this man.

I am as you see utterly disgusted with the adhesion to Russell[21] of Fox & that is the cause that I can for the first time in my life speak of him without the title of respect. The *tame* & stupid servility ~~If~~ [of] saying he 'would do all in his power to make Russell carry it—says "come and buy me" as plainly as words can speak for what c^d be, or be supposed to be, in *his power* beyond his vote! It was the roast pig's "come eat me"'.

[20] [Hayek omits the words Harriet struck out in her original: '*Reason* as ~~a Goddess~~ their head!'—Ed.]

[21] [Lord John Russell (1792–1861) was Prime Minister of Great Britain from 1846 to 1852 and 1865 to 1866. He was a champion of the Reform Bill of 1832 and an advocate of the repeal of the Corn Laws.—Ed.]

I was excessively amused by the top paragraph in the Daily News from Paris saying that Proudhon[22] moved that the fiction of the acknowledgement of the being of a God sh^d be erased.[23] It does one good to find one man who dares to open his mouth & say what he thinks on that subject. It did me good, & I need something for the spirits, as did also your note to Crowe— The reading that base selfish & imbecile animal Trench[24] has made my spirits faint. But the 2^d vol. is the corpus delicti. Adio caro carissimo till Sat^y when we shall talk over all these things.

Among[25] other trash did you observe Hume[26] said—'To interfere with the labour of others and to attempt to establish community of property is a direct violation of the fundamental laws of society'. What a text this would be for an article which however no paper would publish. Is not the Ten Hours' Bill an 'interference &c &c'? Is not the 'interference' with their personal freedom by this Suspension Bill a 'violation' &c, what is the meaning of 'fundamental laws of society' the very point in debate on the subject, communism, on which he professed to be speaking.

Oh English men!
English intellect!

[22] [Pierre-Joseph Proudhon (1809–1865) was a French socialist who proclaimed himself to be an anarchist. He was the author of *Qu'est-ce que la propriété? ou Recherches sur le principe du droit et du Gouvernement* (2 vols.; Paris: J. F. Brocard, 1841–1848), in which he answered the question 'what is property?' ('qu'est-ce que la propriété?') with 'property is theft' ('c'est le vol').—Ed.]

[23] In a report of their Paris correspondent on the debate of the Constituent Assembly on the Constitution in the *Daily News* of 24 July 1848 (third edition, p. 3) it was stated that 'the only event which signalized the day was the effrontery of M. Proudhon, who moved a resolution in the 4th bureau, that the fiction, as he regards it, of the acknowledgement of the existence of God, with which the preamble opens, should be erased. This proposition was of course rejected without one dissentient vote',

[24] If the correct reading of this name is 'Trench', which is not quite certain, the reference is presumably to Richard Chenevix Trench (1807–1886), Archbishop of Dublin [in 1863]. He does not appear to have published a work in two volumes and the comment therefore must refer to two distinct books of his. [Mill refers to Trench in a letter dated 1832 to John Sterling, in which he writes, 'Trench I have seen, and had some correspondence with. He seems to me to take a most gloomy view of the prospects of mankind—gloomier even than yours'. Mill, *Earlier Letters*, vol. 12 of *Collected Works*, p. 101.—Ed.]

[25] The following paragraph is on a separate sheet but seems to form a postscript to the preceding letter, although the passage quoted from Hume has not been traced in the newspapers of these days.

[26] [Joseph Hume (1777–1855) was a British politician and reformer, Radical M.P. from 1818 to 1855, and longtime friend of James Mill. He supported the Reform Act of 1832 and joined with Francis Place to improve conditions for the working classes. See Mill, *Earlier Letters*, vol. 12 of *Collected Works*, p. 5, note 3.—Ed.]

& also might it not be said that if they are justified in interfering with *personal liberty* (a fundamental law if there is any) would they not be equally justified in enacting a law that all Irish landlords whatsoever must instantly repair to Ireland? *This* w^d be in accordance with their professed principles of noble & propertied government in exchange for benefits, of *duties* accompanying *rights*—but no; troops & force—but no interference with the liberty of the propertied or extra constitutional measures for them!

H. T. to J. S. M., Ryde, 27 or 28 July 1848:[27] I am so disgusted with the French Assembly & also with the Daily News that it makes me sick to think of defending the one or helping the other. Surely the intense & disgusting vulgarity of the Daily news might be noticed ~~somewhere~~ [somehow]. Did you observe its Paris correspondants notice of Flocon's speech.[28] *Progress of liberty* forsooth advocated by a paper which applauds the Suspension of the Habeas Corpus—that is to say the suspension of the boasted freedom of the english constitution the moment ~~the~~ [any] people endeavour to profit by it. & applauds the exclusion by law of women from clubs! The last is so monstrous a fact, & involves so completely the whole principle of personal liberty or slavery for women that it seems to me a case of conscience & principle to write—specially on it. Certainly I cannot conceive publishing this[29] or any article in defence of the French revolution unless accompanied by one specially on the subject of *this act* of the chamber by such an article you would also have the means of saying out *fully* to the readers of the Daily News that in principle women ought to have votes &c. This would be in some degree pledging the Daily News still more it w^d teach many timid young or poor reformers that such an opinion is not *ridiculous*. It [is] this last that makes the *low* dread to advocate it. Look at that disgusting sentence in their Paris correspondants letter.

The French article[30] I return with some few pencil marks attached. If you follow it by one on *this* vote of the Assembly & on the true & *JUST* meaning of Universal Suffrage—on the propriety of keeping that title as best expres-

---

[27] MTColl. II/322. [Harriet Taylor Mill, *Complete Works*, pp. 342–43.—Ed.]

[28] In a letter from their Paris correspondent in the *Daily News* of 27 July 1848, on the debate of the French Assembly on the proposed Law of the Clubs, it was said that 'much amusement was produced by the ardour with which M. Flocon assailed the clause of the measure which interdicted the presence or participation of females ~~in~~ [at] the debates'.

[29] This may refer to Mill's unheaded article on French Affairs in the *Daily News* of 9 August 1848; no earlier article is traceable and no such further article on the position of women as suggested by Mrs. Taylor seems to have appeared. [Harriet Taylor Mill, *Complete Works*, p. 342, note 61, concurs with Hayek.—Ed.]

[30] This may refer to the article in the *Daily News* on 9 August, referred to before. No other article is listed in MacMinn, *et al., Bibliography*. [Harriet Taylor Mill, *Complete Works*, p. 342, note 61, concurs.—Ed.]

sive of the true & just principle instead of as some *low-minded* reformers have done merging the principle in the vulgar selfishness of 'manhood suffrage' which I perceive is quite the fashion among the active low reformers.

I confess I prefer an aristocracy of men & women together to an aristocracy of men only—for I think the *last* is far more sure to last—but all this we have often said. I sh^d be sorry this really excellent article on French affairs sh^d go unless it is to be followed by an attack on the assembly. If you think this can be done & were to do it before Sat^y we could talk it over together but you will scarcely have time—

The note to Holyoake I think is very good bring me the draft again will you? Perhaps you will think it better to leave out about Md^e d'arusmont[31] yet I long to give the rascal that retort. The pencil marks on the article are meant only as hints.[32]

I wholly disagree that the influence of Ireland on the english mind is now anti-revolutionary.

The publication of the *Political Economy* was followed by another very serious breakdown in [Mill's] health. In the summer of 1848, he had a bad accident. Inside the Kensington Grove gate of Hyde Park, there is a pump by which he used to cross in order to walk on the grass. One day he trod on a loose brick, and fell heavily on the hip. In treating the hurt, a belladonna plaster was applied. An affection of his eyes soon followed, which he had knowledge enough at once to attribute to the belladonna, and disused the plaster forthwith. For some weeks, however, he was both lame and unable to use his eyes. I never saw him in such a state of despair. Prostration of the nervous system may have aggravated his condition.[33]

Mrs. Taylor meanwhile, during the summer and autumn of 1848, was moving about in her usual manner between Walton and various places on the South Coast. A number of notes exchanged between her and her husband during these months give us a few glimpses of some of the events.

H. T. to John Taylor, Walton, 20 September 1848:[34] I must occupy myself seriously in house hunting, as we certainly must give up this nice little house

---

[31] Frances d'Arusmont, *née* Wright (1795–1852), a Scotswoman who had helped to start the Women's movement in America. She had been to England in 1847 when Holyoake got into trouble for publishing, apparently without permission, a lecture of hers in the *Reasoner*.

[32] [Harriet Taylor Mill, *Complete Works*, p. 343, states that this sentence is 'sideways' on the page and the following sentence is written 'across the edge' of the page 1.—Ed.]

[33] Alexander Bain, *J. S. Mill*, p. 90. [Hayek supplies Mill's name in brackets. —Ed.]

[34] MTColl. XXVIII/199. [The letter is published in Harriet Taylor Mill, *Complete Works*, pp. 480–81, with this passage at p. 481.—Ed.]

Harriet Taylor, *c.* 1834. Oil portrait in possession of the Author.

the sooner perhaps the better, for they have spoiled the appearance of it now from the outside by poor people's poor little places opposite—and what is another great nuisance I hear that the Austin's have taken a furnished house at Weybridge & like the place so much that they are looking out for a cottage there. I have no doubt this is to be near Claremont, & for her to make a circle of French people, the Guizots etc. as an attraction to the en-

Harriet Taylor, *c.*1844. Miniatures in the British Library of Political and Economic Science. [Mill-Taylor/Box10. Courtesy of the Library of the London School of Economics & Political Science.—Ed.]

glish already I hear [of] a number[s] of people going by the railway to call there—and I neither wish to renew the acquaintance nor to seem to avoid it.

At last, at the end of October, Mrs. Taylor settled for two months at Worthing where Mill visited her, probably only for week-ends, but long enough to write there the article in reply to Lord Brougham's attack on the French Revolution of that year, or 'the pamphlet' as he usually refers to it, since he intended to distribute a number of reprints in France. Immediately after Christmas, probably in order that Mill could use the holidays to accompany them part of the way, Mrs. Taylor and her daughter left for the South of France— somewhat to the distress of Mr. Taylor, who had been ailing for some time and, though nobody yet knew the seriousness of his condition, seems to have wished to know his wife at least in the neighbourhood. But problems arising out of the presence in London of one of her brothers on a visit from Australia made Mrs. Taylor insist.

John Taylor to H. T., 2 November 1848:[35] I hear that Geo. Mill is going to Madeira on Tuesday next. I am glad he is to go immediately—but I can-

[35] MTColl. XXVIII/203.

not believe he will derive much benefit from the change—his mind & whole morale is unhinged & unsettled.

H. T. to John Taylor:[36] Worthing Dec. 19 [1848] / My dear John, / I am very sorry to find you say *you are sorry* I am going to Pau. I can assure you I do not do it for my pleasure, but exceedingly the contrary, & only after the *most anxious* thought. Indeed I am half killed by *intense anxiety*. The near relationship to persons of the most opposite principles to my own produces excessive embarrassments.—and this spring it must be *far* worse than usual owing to the constant presence in London of A[rthur][37], whom I must either neglect (which is very disagreeable to me) or admit into a degree of intimacy which must inevitably lead to an interference on the part of Birksgate and either a rupture with them or to discussions & dissensions which I have not the strength to bear. I feel scarcely any doubt that A will not stay in England another winter & I therefore think that my going away for the next four months would *cut* the difficulties I feel about this spring, while I should return at a season (May) & in health to exert myself during the summer months—having got through by leaving England the otherwise insurmountable difficulties of those months with A. I think if you turn over in your mind my circumstances you will see how completely my going is a matter of expediency.[38] It is the alternative of a rupture with them which may thus be avoided—& it is always so undesirable to make family quarrels if it is possible to avoid them.

. . . Your saying that you are sorry I am going has given me ever since I read your note so *intense* a head-ache, that I can scarcely see to write. However it is only one of the vexations I have to bear & perhaps everybody has.

Mill probably accompanied the ladies as far as Paris, from where they proceeded slowly by *diligence* via Orleans and Bordeaux to Pau at the foot of the Pyrenees. Here they stopped for a little over three months. Although a number of Mrs. Taylor's letters from Pau to her husband and her son Algernon are preserved,[39]

---

[36] MTColl. XXVIII/217. [Harriet Taylor Mill, *Complete Works*, pp. 488–89.—Ed.]

[37] [Hayek supplies 'A[rthur]' at this point; Harriet Taylor Mill, *Complete Works*, supplies 'it' instead. According to the *Complete Works*, Harriet worried that her brother, Arthur Hardy, might discover her relationship with Mill during Arthur's visit from Australia and reveal this to her parents at Birksgate. See p. 489, note 131.—Ed.]

[38] [The original letter contains a number of strike outs that Hayek omits: 'having got through ~~the~~ by leaving England the otherwise insurmountable difficulties of ~~getting through~~ those months with A. I think if you turn over in your mind my circumstances you will see how completely my going is a matter of expediency ~~necessity~~'.—Ed.]

[39] MTColl. XXVIII/220–228 and XXVII/109–110. [Hayek lists the letters as 219–327 and 110, respectively. The letters to John Taylor are published in Harriet Taylor Mill, *Complete Works*, pp. 491–504; those to Harriet's son, Haji, are at pp. 397–401.—Ed.]

none of hers then written to Mill are extant and only six of the carefully numbered letters Mill[40] wrote to her twice a week still exist. They give, however,
the fullest information we have on the nature of the influence which Mrs.
Taylor exercised on the successive revisions of the *Political Economy* and it is
largely from them that we must draw whatever inference we can on the part
she played in the original composition of the work. The first of Mill's letters
which survives is numbered 8.

J. S. M. to H. T.[41] Saturday / 27 Jan[y] [1849] / You might well feel that the
handwriting would be 'worth having', but instead of there being 'little said'
the excessive sweetness & love in this exquisite letter makes it like something
dropt from heaven. I had been literally *pining* for it & had got into a state of
depression which I do not think I shall fall into again during this absence—
When I left you my darling & during all the journey back I was full of life &
animation & vigour of wish & purpose, because fresh from being with you,
fresh from the influence of your blessed presence & of that extreme happiness of that time which during the last week or fortnight I have hardly been
able to conceive that I ever had—much less that I ever should have again—
but this angel letter has begun to bring back happiness & spirit & I [again]
begin to feel the holiday & journey & that blessed meeting as if they would
really be—& to feel capable also of being & doing something in the meanwhile which I had entirely ceased to feel. But I am very anxious darling to
hear about the lameness & to find that it has got better.[42] I have a very strong
feeling about the obstinacy of lameness from the troublesome persistency of
this of mine—though it is certainly better—but still it does not go away, nor
allow me to take more than a very little exercise & I feel the effect a little now
in [the] general health—the sight too has not quite recovered itself [yet,]
which is an additional teaze, but I am not uneasy about it. The only piece of
news is that Austin[43] called yesterday. When he came & during all the time

[40] In Yale University Library [MS 350, Box 1, Folder 3].

[41] [Hayek numbers this note and the last one as note 33. The full letter is published at *The Later
Letters of John Stuart Mill, 1849–1873*, eds. Francis E. Mineka and Dwight N. Lindley, vols. 14–17
(1972) of *Collected Works*, 14:3–6.—Ed.]

[42] [According to *ibid*, p. 4, note 4, Harriet Taylor at this time suffered from rheumatoid pain
and a form of paralysis. The editor of Harriet Taylor Mill, *Complete Works*, suggests that she may
have contracted syphilis from her husband John Taylor; see pp. xxx–xxxii.—Ed.]

[43] [John Austin (1790–1859) was a writer on jurisprudence married to Sarah, *née* Taylor
(1793–1867). Mill had known the Austins since 1819 when they were neighbors of Jeremy Bentham and the Mills in Queen Square. Mill's letters to the Austins in Mill, *Earlier Letters*, vol. 12
of *Collected Works*, provide evidence of the long relationship. The friendship later cooled, partly
due to differing views on politics and partly due to Harriet's dislike of Sarah Austin. In addition, Mill believed that Sarah had spread stories about the relationship between Mill and Harriet. See Mill, *Earlier Letters*, vol. 12 of *Collected Works*, p. 10, note 1. See also Mill, *Later Letters*, vol.

he staid there was a Frenchman with me, a man named Guerry,[44] a statistical man whom Col. Sykes[45] brought to me—the man whose maps of France
with the dark & light colours, shewing the state of crime, instruction etc. in
each department you may remember. He was wanting[46] to show me some
other maps & tables of his & to ask me about the 'logic' of his plans so he did
not go away—& the talk was confined to general subjects, except that Austin said he was going to prepare a new edition of his book on jurisprudence
on a much enlarged plan & should wish very much to consult me on various
matters connected with the application of induction to moral science. Of
course I could not refuse & indeed saw no reason for doing so—but as this
will lead to his coming again, sending MSS. & so on it both gives an occasion
& creates a necessity of defining the relation I am to stand in with respect to
them. He said he had after much difficulty & search taken a house at Weybridge & that he liked the place, but he did not (I have no doubt purposely)
say anything about wishing that I would visit him there, or anywhere. His
talk was free & *éclairé* as it always is with me, much of it about that new publication of Guizot[47] (which I have not read) of which he spoke [very] disparagingly & defended communists & socialists against the attacks contained
in it & said he saw no real objection to socialism except the difficulty if not
impracticability of managing so great a concern as the industry of a whole
country in the way of association. Nothing was said about *her* or about the
copy of the Pol. Ec. but it is necessary to *prendre un parti*. What should it be? I
am reading Macaulay's book:[48] it is in some respects better than I expected,
& in none worse. I think the best character that can be given of it is that it
is a man without genius, who has observed what people of genius do when
they write history, & tries his very best to do the same, without the amount of

---

14 of *Collected Works*, p. 4, note 6; *ibid.*, p. 5, note 12, contains the editorial point that Mill refers
to Sarah Austin in the sentence beginning 'Nothing was said about *her* . . .'.—Ed.]

[44] André-Michel Guerry (1802–1866), French statistician, author of an *Essai sur la statistique
morale de la France* (Paris, 1833), which contains probably the identical maps to which Mill refers
and from which the author concludes that 'les départments ou l'instruction est à moins repandus
sont ceux ou il se commet le plus des crimes'. He published later a larger work: *Statistique morale
de l'Angleterre comparée avec celle de la France* (Paris: J.-B. Bailliére et fils, 1864).

[45] Lieut.-Col. William Henry Sykes, F.R.S. (1790–1872), naturalist and soldier, one of the
founders of the Royal Statistical Society, a Director of the East India Company since 1840 and
Chairman of its Court of Directors in 1856.

[46] [Mill, *Later Letters*, vol. 14 of *Collected Works*, p. 5 has this as '[wanting?]'.—Ed.]

[47] F. P. G. Guizot, *De la démocratie en France* (Janvier 1849) (Brussels: Société Typographique
Belge, 1849). [François Pierre Guillaume Guizot (1787–1874) was a historian and statesman
who had recently arrived in England as an exile. There he was befriended by the Austins, whose
acquaintance he had made during their former residence in Paris. Mill, *Later Letters*, vol. 14 of
Collected Works, p. 5, note 10.—Ed.]

[48] The first two volumes of T. B. Macaulay's *History of England* [*from the Accession of James the Second*], which had appeared in December 1848.

painful effort, & affectation, which you might expect, & which I did expect from such an attempt & such a man. I have no doubt like all his writings it will be & continue popular—it is exactly au niveau of the ideal of shallow people with a touch of the new ideas—& it is not sufficiently bad to induce anybody who knows better to take pains to lower people's estimation of it. I perceive no very bad tendency in it as yet, except that it in some degree ministers to English conceit—

From a letter by Mrs. James Mill to her children in Madeira, dated four days later, we get further information about John Mill's health.

Mrs. James Mill to Clara and George Mill, Kensington, 31 January 1849:[49] John wishes me to say that he had fully intended to write to you by this mail but that his eyes are bad from the effects of the medicine he took for his Hip, and Alexander whom he saw yesterday says that he must not use them, his hip is still bad so that he cannot walk, it is not worse he thinks, but it is not much better so that he cannot walk either way to the India House, the D[rs] say that it will require time, if he could walk he could go to the country while his eyes are bad, so that it is of no use going—I am going to Lewes[50] to see whether [if] he can recommend a Man to read to John, and to write to his dictation that he may [be][51] beginning another edition of his book as the other is almost all sold. . . . He wishes me to tell you that he will write to you as soon as he is allowed to use his eyes. We played at cards till 12 o'clock last night and between whiles he played upon the Piano without music, some of his own compositions.

John did after all add a few lines to the letter—on some problem concerning the property of his married sisters for which George acted as trustee.

The first edition of the *Political Economy* (of 1,000 copies) was in fact exhausted in less than a year and the preparation of a second edition was becoming urgent. As Mill explains in the *Autobiography*, the revolution of 1848 had made public opinion more ready to consider novelties and he and Mrs. Taylor had through it acquired a new interest in French socialism:

In the first edition the difficulties of Socialism were stated so strongly, that the tone was on the whole that of opposition to it. In the year or two which followed, much time was given to the study of the best Socialist[ic] writers

[49] MTColl. XLVII/11. [The portion added by J. S. Mill to which Hayek refers below appears in Mill, *Later Letters*, vol. 14 of *Collected Works*, pp. 6–7.—Ed.]

[50] Probably George Henry Lewes (1817–1878). [The writer Lewes later married George Eliot. See Mill, *Earlier Letters*, vol. 13 of *Collected Works*, p. 448, note 1.—Ed.]

[51] [The insertion is Hayek's.—Ed.]

on the Continent, and to meditation and discussion on the whole range of topics involved in the controversy: and the result was that most of what had been written on the subject in the first edition was cancelled, and replaced by arguments and reflexions which represent a more advanced opinion.[52]

It is this process which we can follow in part in the letters which follow. The main discussion of socialism is contained in the chapter 'On Property' at the beginning of Book II of the *Political Economy*. The first instalment of the revised proofs (probably in the type of the first edition) which contains this crucial chapter must have gone to Mrs. Mill early in February and we can gather the nature of her comments from Mill's replies.

J. S. M. to H. T.[53] 15 / Monday / 19 Febr. [1849] / I received your [dear] letter 11 on Saturday & this morning the first instalment of Pol. Ec. This last I will send again (or as much of it as is necessary) when I have been able to make up my mind about it. The objections are I think very inconsiderable as to quantity—much less than I expected—but that paragraph, p. 248, in the first edit.[54] ~~what~~ [which] you object to so strongly & totally, is what

---

[52] *Autobiography*, p. 198–99. [Mill, *Autobiography*, vol. 1 of *Collected Works*, p. 241.—Ed.] Cf. also the paragraph added to the Preface of the second edition of the *Political Economy*: 'The additions and alterations in the present edition are generally of little moment; but the increased importance which the Socialist controversy has assumed since this work was written, has made it desirable to enlarge the chapter which treats of it; the more so, as the objections therein stated to the specific schemes propounded by some Socialists, have been erroneously understood as a general condemnation of all that is commonly included under that name. A full appreciation of Socialism, and of the questions which it raises, can only be advantageously attempted in a separate work'. [John Stuart Mill, *The Principles of Political Economy with Some of Their Application to Social Philosophy*, ed. John M. Robson, vols. 2–3 (1965) of *Collected Works*, 2:xcii]

[53] Yale University Library [MS 350, Box 1, Folder 3. The letter is published in part in Mill, *Political Economy*, vol. 3 of *Collected Works*, pp. 1027–29. Hayek supplies the date in brackets.—Ed.]

[54] The passages on pp. 247–48 of vol. 1 of the first edition of the *Political Economy* which were deleted run as follows: 'Those who have never known freedom from anxiety as to the means of subsistence, are apt to overrate what is gained for positive enjoyment by the mere absence of that uncertainty. The necessaries of life, when they have always been secure for the whole of life, are scarcely more a subject of consciousness or a source of happiness than the elements. [p. 248] There is little attractive in the monotonous routine, without vicissitudes, but without excitement; a life spent in the enforced observance of an external rule, and performance of a prescribed task: in which labour would be devoid of its chief sweetener, the thought that every effort tells perceptibly on the labourer's own interests or those of some one with whom he identifies himself; in which no one could by his own exertions improve his conditions, or that of the objects of his private affections; in which no one's way of life, occupations, or movements, would depend on choice, but each would be the slave of all'.

The whole of this passage has been replaced in the second edition by the much more sympathetic account on pp. 254–56 which begins: 'On the Communistic scheme, supposing it to be successful, there would be an end to all anxiety concerning the means of subsistence; and this would be much gained for human happiness'. [The page in brackets is supplied by Hayek. For

always has seemed to me the strongest part of the argument (it is only what even Proudhon says about Communism)—& as omitting it after it has ~~ever~~ [once] been printed would imply change of opinion, it is necessary to see whether opinion has changed or not—yours has, in some respects at least, for you have marked strong dissent from the passage that 'the necessaries of life when secure of the whole of life are scarcely more a subject of conscious-ness'[55] &c. which was inserted on your proposition & very nearly in your own words. This is probably only the progress we have been always making, & by thinking sufficiently I should probably come to think the same—as is almost always the case, I believe *always* when we think long enough. But here the being unable to discuss verbally stands sadly in the way, & I am now almost convinced that as you said at first, we cannot settle this 2[d] edit. by letter. [We will try,] but [I] now ~~I~~ feel almost certain that we must adjourn the publi-cation of the 2[d] edit. to November. In the new matter one of the sentences you have cancelled is a favourite of mine, viz 'It is probable that this will finally depend upon considerations not to be measured by the coarse stan-dard which in the present state of human improvement is the only one that can be applied to it'.[56] What I meant was that whether individual agency or Socialism would be best ultimately—(*both* being necessarily very imperfect now, & *both* susceptible of immense improvement) will depend on the com-parative attractions they will hold out to human beings with all their capaci-ties, both individual & social, infinitely more developed than at present. I do not think it is English improvement only that is too backward to enable this point to be ascertained for if English character is starved in its social part I

---

the full text of these changes see Mill, *Political Economy*, vol. 3 of *Collected Works*, p. 978. The next sentence in the 1849 edition reads: 'But it is perfectly possible to realize this same advantage in a society grounded on private property; and to this point the tendencies of political specialists are rapidly converging. Supposing this attained, it is surely a vast advantage on the side of the indi-vidual system, that it is compatible with a far greater degree of personal liberty' —Ed.]

[55] See the passage from the first edition quoted in the preceding footnote; it must have been suggested by Mrs. Taylor when the first edition was written. [The quotation in the letter is not entirely accurate; compare with that in note 54 above.—Ed.]

[56] Nothing in the chapter as it stands in the second edition seems to correspond to this sen-tence, but it may well have been an earlier draft of the last paragraph which begins (p. 265): 'We are as yet too ignorant either of what individual agency in its best form, or Socialism in its best form can accomplish, to be qualified to decide which of the two will be the ultimate form of [human] society'. This replaces the paragraph in the first edition (p. 254) which relegates the 'proper sphere for collective action' to 'the things which cannot be done by individual agency' and which argues that 'where individual agency is at all suitable, it is almost always the most suit-able'. [Mill, *Political Economy*, vol. 3 of *Collected Works*, Appendix A, pp. 975–87, collates these sections of the 'Of Property' chapter in the 1849 edition with the first. This passage does not occur in any edition of the *Political Economy*. For John M. Robson's thoughts as to where Mill may have intended to place it, see *ibid.*, p. 1027, note 8. Robson notes Hayek's suggestion and offers another possibility, 49.I.254.31–255.4.—Ed.]

think Continental is as much or even more so in its individual, & Continental people incapable of entering into the feelings which make very close contacts with crowds of other people both disagreeable & mentally & morally lowering. I cannot help thinking that something like what I meant by the sentence, ought to be said though I can imagine good reasons for your disliking the way in which it is put. Then again if the sentence 'the majority would not exert themselves for anything beyond this & unless they did nobody else would &c'[57] is not tenable, then all the two or three pages of argument which precede & of which this is but a summary, are false, & there is nothing to be said against Communism at all—one would only have to turn round & advocate it—which if done would be better in a separate treatise & would be a great objection against publishing a 2ᵈ edit. until *after* such a treatise. I think I agree in all the other remarks. Fourier if I may judge by Considérant[58] is perfectly right about women both as to equality & marriage—& I suspect that Fourier himself went further than his disciple thinks prudent in the directness of his recommendations. Considérant sometimes avails himself as Mr. Fox used, of the sentimentalities & superstitions about purity, though asserting with it all the right principles. But C[onsidérant][59] says that the Fourierists are the *only* Socialists who are not orthodox about marriage—he forgets the Owenites, but I fear it is true of all the known Communist leaders in France—he says it specially of Buchez, Cabet, & what surprises one in Sand's 'guide, philosopher & friend' of Leroux.[60] This strengthens one exceedingly in one's wish to prôner[61] the Fourierists besides that their scheme of association seems to me much nearer to being practicable at present than Communism.—Your letter was delightful—it was so very pleasant to know

[57] First edition, p. 250: 'I believe that the condition of the operatives in a well-regulated manufactory, with a great reduction ~~in~~ [of] the hours of labour and a considerable variety of the kinds of it, is very ~~much~~ like what the conditions of all would be in a Socialist community. I believe the majority would not exert themselves for any thing beyond this, and that unless they did, nobody else would; and that on this basis human life would settle itself in one invariable round'. In spite of what Mill said above, the second sentence of this was omitted entirely in the second edition (p. 257), while the word 'Owenite' was substituted for 'Socialist' in the first sentence. [See Mill, *Political Economy*, vol. 3 of *Collected Works*, Appendix A, p. 980.—Ed.]

[58] [Victor-Prosper Considerant (1808–1893) was a French utopian Socialist and follower of Charles Fourier who became the leader of the Fourierist movement after Fourier's death in 1837.—Ed.]

[59] [Mill's letter has the initial; Hayek furnished the full name.—Ed.]

[60] [Pierre Leroux (1797–1871) was a journalist, philosopher, and politician. Mill, *Later Letters*, vol. 14 of *Collected Works*, p. 10, note 16. J. B. Buchez was, with P. C. Roux, coauthor of *Histoire parlementaire de la révolution* (40 vols; Paris: Picard et fils, 1833–1838). Thomas Carlyle reviewed the work. Mill, *Earlier Letters*, vol. 12 of *Collected Works*, p. 220, note 12. Etienne Cabet (1788–1856) was a French utopian socialist who founded the Icarian movement.—Ed.]

[61] [Hayek has a query here: 'in one's wish to [?] the Fourierists'. Mill, *Political Economy*, vol. 3 of *Collected Works*, p. 1028, supplies the inserted word.—Ed.]

that you were still better as to general health than I knew before, & that the lameness also improves though slowly. I am very glad I did right about Herbert—his conduct on Xmas day & his not writing even to say that he is going to America seem like ostentation of heartlessness & are only as you say to be explained by his being a very great fool (at present) & therefore influenced by some miserably petty vanities and irritabilities. Their not sending George's letter directly is very strange. The pamphlet has gone to Hickson[62]—I had thought of sending one of the separate copies to L. Blanc.[63] Whom else should it go to? To all the members of the Prov. Gov. I think, & as it will not be published till April I had better take the copies to Paris with me & send [them] when there as it saves so much uncertainty and delay. I did see that villainous thing in the Times & noticed that the American had used those words.

J. S. M. to H. T.[64] 16 / Wednesday / 21 Feb. 1849 / I despatched yesterday to the dear one an attempt at a revision of the objectionable passages. I saw on consideration that the objection to Communism on the ground of its making life a kind of dead level might admit of being weakened (though I believe it never could be taken away) consistently with the principle of Communism, though the Communistic plans now before the public could not do it. The statement of objections was moreover too vague & general. I have made it more explicit as well as more moderate; *you* will judge whether it is now sufficiently either one or the other; & altogether whether any objection can be maintained to Communism, except the amount of objection which, in the new matter I have introduced, is made to the present applicability of Fourierism. I think there can & that the objections as now stated to Communism are valid: but if *you* do not think so, I certainly will not print it, even if there were no other reason than the certainty I feel that I never should long continue of an opinion different from yours on a subject which you have fully considered. I am going on revising the book: not altering much, but in one of the purely political economy parts which occurs near the beginning, viz. the discussion as to whether buying goods made by labour gives the same employment as hiring the labourers themselves, I have added two or three pages of new explanation & illustration which I think

---

[62] W. E. Hickson, then editor of the *Westminster Review*, where the article on 'Lord Brougham and the French Revolution' appeared.

[63] [Louis Jean Joseph Charles Blanc (1811–1882), French politician and social commentator who opposed competition and advocated equality of wages, 'à chacun selon ses besoins, à chacun selon ses facultés'. He became a member of the provisional government in France after the 1848 revolution, but he fled to England and lived there in exile after its downfall.—Ed.]

[64] Yale University Library [MS 350, Box 1, Folder 3; Mill, *Later Letters*, vol. 14 of *Collected Works*, pp. 11–13.]

make the case much clearer.[65]—It is certainly an unlucky coincidence that the winter you have gone away should be so very mild a one here: on Sunday I found the cottage gardens &c. as far advanced as they often are only in the middle of April, mezereons, hepaticas, the white arabis, pyrus japonica &c. in the fullest flower, the snow ball plant very much in leaf, even periwinkles & red anemones fully out: daffodils I saw only in bud. If it is not checked it will be I think an even earlier spring than the very early one two or three years ago. I shall be able to benefit by it more than I expected in the way of country walks on Sundays although the dimness of sight, slight as it is, interferes not a little with the enjoyment of distant scenery—as I found in that beautiful Windsor Park last Sunday. If it is very fine I think I shall go some Sunday & wander about Combe—it is so full of association with all I wish & care for. As I have taken care to let my ailments be generally known at the I.H.[66] I have no doubt it will be easy to get a two or three months holiday in the spring if we like: this indeed if I return quite well would make any holiday in the after part of the year impracticable, but need not prevent me from taking two or three days at a time occasionally during a séjour at Ryde or any other place & thus making it a partial holiday there— Unless, which I do not expect, a long holiday soon should be necessary for health, the question ought to depend entirely on what would best suit you— which is quite sure to be most desirable for me—I am in hopes that parties in France are taking a more republican turn than they seemed likely to do— if Napoleon Bonaparte coalesces with Lamartine's party for election purposes there will be a much larger body of sincere republicans in the new assembly than was expected.[67] The Roman republic & the Tuscan Provisional Gov[t] I am afraid will end in nothing but a restoration by Austria & a putting down of the popular party throughout Italy. I was sorry to see in the feuilleton of the National[68] a very bad article on women in the form of a review

[65] *Principles of Political Economy* (second edition), vol. 1, pp. 102–6. [Mill, *Political Economy*, vol. 2 of *Collected Works*, note to text, pp. 84–86.—Ed.]

[66] [India House.—Ed.]

[67] [The Bonapartist Party was led by Charles Louis Napoleon Bonaparte (1808–1873), and the Republican party was led by the poet and politician Alphonse de Lamartine (1790–1869). Napoleon was at this time President of the Republic, having been elected in December 1848. Contrary to Mill's optimism, monarchists won the majority in the May 1849 Assembly elections. Mill, *Later Letters*, vol. 14 of *Collected Works*, p. 12, note 5.—Ed.]

[68] [Louis Adolphe Thiers (1797–1877) founded the newspaper, which supported liberal causes and, in 1848, endorsed Lamartine and the Democratic Republican party. Mill, *Later Letters*, vol. 14 of *Collected Works*, p. 12, note 7. For additional information regarding Mill's association with the paper in the 1830's, see Mill, *Earlier Letters*, vol. 12 of *Collected Works*, pp. 54, 194–95.—Ed.]

of a book by the M. Légouvé[69] who was so praised in La Voix des Femmes.[70] The badness consisted chiefly in laying down the doctrine very positively that women always are & must always be what men make them—just the false assumption on which the whole of the present bad constitution of the relation rests. I am convinced however that there are only two things which tend at all to shake this nonsensical prejudice: a better psychology & theory of human nature, for the few; & for the many, more & greater proofs by example of what women can do. I do not think that anything that could be written would do nearly so much good on that subject the most important of all, as the finishing of your pamphlet—or little book rather, for it should be that.[71] I do hope you are going on with it—gone on with & finished & published it *must be*, & next season too.—Do you notice that Russell in bringing forward his Jew Bill, although he is actually abolishing the old oaths & framing[72] new, still has the meanness to reinsert the words 'on the true faith of a Christian' for all persons except Jews, & justifies it by saying that the Constitution ought not avowedly to admit unbelievers into Parliament.—I have seen very little of the Chairman & Dep. Chairman[73] lately—as to avoid the long staircase I have communicated with them chiefly by [through] others but now being released from restraint I shall take an early opportunity of speaking to Galloway about Haji. I have seen nothing more of Haji any more than of Herbert.[74]

From a letter to her husband of a few days later we see that Mrs. Taylor had some real understanding of economic problems. The gold discoveries to which it refers can then only recently have become known:

[69] [Gabriel Jean Baptiste Wilfrid Légouvé (1807–1903) was a poet and dramatist. In 1847 at the Collège de France, he delivered a series of lectures, which were then published as *Cours d'histoire morale des femmes* (Paris 1848). See Mill, *Later Letters*, vol. 14 of *Collected Works*, p. 12, note 8. Hayek's rendering has a query after Légouvé's name.—Ed.]

[70] A 'political and socialist journal' started in Paris the year before to advocate the rights of all women. [It was published in Paris, between March and June 1848, and founded by the feminist author Eugénie Mouchon Niboyet (1801–1883). See Mill, *Later Letters*, vol. 14 of *Collected Works*, p. 12, note 9.—Ed.]

[71] Probably a first attempt at what two years later became the article on 'The Enfranchisement of Women'.

[72] [Hayek's text has a query after 'framing'.—Ed.]

[73] Major-General Sir Archibald Galloway (1780?–1850) and John Shepherd, in 1849 Chairman and Deputy Chairman of the East India Company respectively. [Galloway served in the army in India from 1799 to 1841 and as Director of the East India Company from 1840 to 1848. He was Chairman 1849–1850. Shepherd (1792–1859) had served as a Director of the Company since 1835. See Mill, *Later Letters*, vol. 14 of *Collected Works*, p. 13, note 12.—Ed.]

[74] The rest of the last line, about five or six words, has been cut away. [Haji and Herbert were Harriet's two sons. Hayek follows this sentence with 'Addio (?)', which the *Later Letters* version of the letter omits.—Ed.]

H. T. to John Taylor, Pau, 27 February 1849:[75] Do you suppose this Califor-
nian discovery will make any change in the value of money for some time to
come? If it continues I suppose it will lower the value of fixed incomes, but I
suppose benefit trade? If I were a young man I would go there [very] quickly.
The most probable chance is that the gold will not continue below the surface meanwhile there must be fine opportunities for *placing* goods, & especially drugs, in the *placiemento.* are you going to send out quinine.

H. T. to Algernon Taylor, Pau, 6 March 1849:[76] I have not written lately—I have
been out of spirits and therefore disinclined to enjoy or to write about the
beautiful objects and scenery which form the staple of our quiet life here.
The account I hear of George [Mill][77] and my knowledge of that insidious
disease make me very much fear for him, and I most earnestly and anxiously
wish that he may live. It is very important in writing to him to say very little
about his health, and not to seem to think of it as anything more than a common cough, because if a person thinks themselves consumptive the effect
on the spirits has the utmost possible tendency to produce or to accelerate
that fatal disease. I think he would much like to hear from you and perhaps
you have already written. You might give him a long letter about all sorts of
impersonal objects, such as politics—your review and its articles—what you
have been reading lately and your opinion thereon—our stay at his place &
its scenery, Sinnett's prospects[78]—Herbert's voyage &c.

. . . I often wish for you when I see all this beauty and feel that if we live
we will sometime see it together, and that 'Ce qui est déferé n'est pas perdu',
as the proverb says. I am very glad to hear that Papa is better on the whole
but I wish the improvement were quicker. He ought in future to pay due
respect to my medical judgement as I have twice anticipated his physician's
advice in the last few months! I do hope he will mend more quickly with the
finer weather which may be expected in April.

. . . I have not read Grote's history, I should think it must be interesting—
tho' I think that knowing his 'extreme opinions' I should think it a defect that

[75] MTColl. XXVIII/225. [According to the editor of Harriet Taylor Mill's *Complete Works*,
she may have been referring here to the discovery of gold in Placerville, California, 1848 (see p.
499, note 153). The full letter is published in *ibid.*, pp. 498–500; this passage is on p. 499.—Ed.]

[76] MTColl. XXVII/109. [Harriet Taylor Mill, *Complete Works*, pp. 397–99.—Ed.]

[77] [J. S. Mill's brother George Mill traveled to Madeira, Spain, at this time to recuperate from
tuberculosis. See Harriet Taylor Mill, *Complete Works*, p. 398, note 34. Hayek supplied the name
in brackets.—Ed.]

[78] [Frederick Sinnett (1830–1866) was an English journalist and literary critic who emigrated
to Australia in 1849. See Harriet Taylor Mill, *Complete Works*, p. 398, note 35, and for the letter to Sinnett dated 24 October 1849, see *ibid.*, pp. 399–400. Mill also corresponded with Sinnett; see the letter dated 22 October 1857 in Mill, *Later Letters*, vol. 15 of *Collected Works*, pp.
541–42.—Ed.]

he does not indicate them more clearly, as there is ample and easy room to do in treating of the Greek ~~Philosophers~~ [Philosophies]. extreme timidity is his defect, but this is a great one indeed in a public instructor. Mr. Mill was to write a review of the book in last Sunday's Spectator,[79] which you will like to see. And now dearest Haji, with love to Papa—Adieu.

The five letters which Mill wrote to Mrs. Taylor during these weeks are missing but the next three which are preserved are consecutive.

J. S. M. to H. T.[80] 22 / Wednesday / 14 March [1849] / What a nuisance it is having anything to do with printers—Though I had no reason to be particularly pleased with Harrison, I was alarmed at finding that Parker[81] had gone to another, & accordingly, though the general type of the first edition is exactly copied, yet a thing so important as the type of the headings at the top of the page cannot be got right—you know what difficulty we had before—& now the headings, & everything else which is in that type, they first gave much too close & then much too wide, & say they have not got the exact thing, unless they have the types cast on purpose. Both the things they have produced seem to me detestable & the worst is that as Parker is sole owner of this edition I suppose I have no voice in the matter at all except as a point of courtesy. I shall see Parker today & tell him that I should have much prefered waiting till another season rather than having either of these types—but I suppose it is too late now to do any good—& perhaps Parker dragged out the time in useless delays before, on purpose that all troublesome changes might be avoided by hurry now. It is as disagreeable as a thing of that sort *can* possibly be—because it is necessary that something should be decided immediately without waiting for the decision of my only guide & oracle. If the effect should be to make the book an unpleasant object to the only eyes I wish it to please, how excessively I shall regret not having put off the edition till the next season. I have had the proofs of the

---

[79] Mill's review of volumes 5 and 6 of George Grote's *History of Greece* appeared in the *Spectator* for 3 and 10 March 1849 (vol. 12, pp. 202–3 and 227–28). [An additional review of volumes 7 and 8 appeared in the *Spectator* on 16 March 1850.—Ed.]

[80] Yale University Library [MS 350, Box 2, Folder 3; the letter is published in Mill, *Later Letters*, vol. 14 of *Collected Works*, pp. 14–17. The date in brackets is Hayek's addition.—Ed.].

[81] [John William Parker (1792–1870) published Mill's *A System of Logic* in 1843 and *Political Economy* in 1848. The printers Harrison and Co., St. Martin's Lane, printed the first edition of the *Political Economy*. Mill was to receive, by arrangement with Parker, half the net profits (as was the case for *A System of Logic*). Harriet had insisted that the rights be assigned for only one edition this time. The problems with the printers and Parker were soon resolved, as the next letter from Mill reveals. See Mill, *Later Letters*, vol. 14 of *Collected Works*, pp. 17–18, and p. 14, note 2, and p. 17, note 2.—Ed.]

pamphlet,[82] all but the last few pages. There seems very little remaining in it that could be further softened without taking the sting out entirely—which would be a pity. I am rather against giving away *any* copies, at least for the present, in England—except to Louis Blanc to whom I suppose I should acknowledge authorship. He has not come near me—I see he is writing in sundry Communist papers of which there are now several in London.[83] As a heading *in the review* I have thought of 'The Revolution of February & its assailants'—it does not seem advisable to put Brougham's name at the top of the page—& 'the Revolution of February' or anything of that kind by itself would be tame, & excite no attention. There is no fresh news of George nor any incident of any kind except that Mr. Fox has send me (without any letter) four volumes of his lectures to the working classes, the last volume of which (printed this year)[84] has a preface in which he recommends to the working classes to study Polit. Economy telling them that they will see 'by the ablest book yet produced on the subject' that it is not a thing against them but for them—with some other expressions of compliment he ~~prints~~ [quotes] two ~~paragrs.~~ [passages], one of them the strongest there is in the book about independence of women, & tells them in another place though rather by inference than directly that women ought to have the suffrage. He speaks in this preface of 'failing health' & as if he did not expect either to write or to speak in public much more: this may mean little, or very much. I feel now as if the natural thing, the thing to be expected, was to hear of every one's death—as if we should outlive all we have cared for, & yet die early.

Did you notice that most bête & vulgar say by Emerson in a lecture at Boston, about the English?[85] It is hardly possible to be more stupidly wrong—& what sort of people can he have been among when here? The Austrian octroyé federal constitution seems as bad as anything pretending to be a con-

[82] [Mill, *Later Letters*, vol. 14 of *Collected Works*, p. 15, note 4 states this is 'the offprint of the article on Brougham'.—Ed.]

[83] [Mill sent the pamphlet to Louis Blanc in April 1849, and Blanc published four issues of his *Monthly Review* in London that same year. See Mill, *Later Letters*, vol. 14 of *Collected Works*, p. 15, note 5, and letter 12, pp. 23–24.—Ed.]

[84] W. J. Fox, *Lectures addressed chiefly to the Working Classes*, vol. 4 (London: Charles Fox, 1845–1849), pp. xix–xx. The paragraphs quoted there from the *Political Economy* are taken from vol. 2, pp. 525 and 526 of the first edition. [See Mill, *Political Economy*, vol. 3 of *Collected Works*, p. 953.—Ed].

[85] Ralph Waldo Emerson's lecture on England, delivered before the Boston Mercantile Library Association on 27 December 1848, was reported at considerable length in *The Times* of 14 March 1849. According to this report, 'he spoke of the steady balance of the qualities of their nature as their great characteristic, and the secret of their success. Everything in England betokens life. . . . The English surpass all others in general culture—none are so harmoniously developed. They are quick to perceive any meanness in an individual. And it is reasonable that they should have all those fastidious views which wealth and power are wont to generate'. [The article, entitled 'An American's Opinion of England', appeared on p. 8, column F of *The Times*.—Ed.]

stitution at all now dares to be—the only significant circumstances in it on the side of democracy being that there is no House of Lords nor any mention of nobility or hereditary rank.[86] Here the sort of newspaper discussion which has begun about Sterling's infidelity[87] seems to have merged into a greater scandal about a book by Froude[88]—a brother of the Froude who was the originator of Puseyism. This book was reviewed in the last Spectator I sent to you[89] & that review was the first I had heard & is all I have seen of the book—but the Herald & Standard are abusing the man in the tone of the Dominican ~~Inquisition~~ [Inquisitors] on account of the strong declarations against the inspiration of the Bible which he puts into the mouth of one of his characters, obviously as they say thinking the same himself.—It appears the Council of University College had been asked to select a schoolmaster for Hobart Town & had chosen Froude[90] from among a great many candidates & probably some rival defeated candidate has raised this stir. It all, I think, does good, but one ought to see occasionally the things that are written on such matters, in order not to forget the intensity of the vulgar bigotry, or affectation of it, that is still thought to be the thing for the Christian readers of newspapers in this precious country. The Times is quite gentlemanlike in comparison with those other papers when they get on the ground of imputed infidelity or anything approaching it. I suppose they overshoot their mark, but they would scruple nothing in any[91] such case.

The next letter is mutilated, most of the first sheet being deliberately cut away, leaving on the first page only a fragment of what was evidently a dis-

---

[86] [After withstanding the attempted revolution in 1848, the Austrian government granted a constitution for the empire. The constitution was never actualized but was instead abrogated in December 1851. Mill, *Later Letters*, vol. 14 of *Collected Works*, p. 16, note 12. Ed.]

[87] [In his Introduction to his edition of Sterling's *Essays and Tales* (London: John W. Parker, 1848), Archdeacon Julius C. Hare wrote that John Sterling, Mill's close friend for many years before Sterling's death in 1844, had 'lost his faith'. The *Record* then attacked the Sterling Club 'for bearing the heretic's name'. Mill, *Later Letters*, vol. 14 of *Collected Works*, p. 16, note 13.—Ed.]

[88] James Anthony Froude, *The Nemesis of Faith*, (London: John Chapman, 1849). The brother mentioned was Richard Hurrell Froude. [Richard Froude (1803–1836) was a Fellow of Oriel College who, with John Henry Newman, began the 'Tractarian' or 'Oxford' Movement, sometimes referred to disparagingly as the 'Puseyite' movement (after one of its leaders, Edward Pusey). The movement sought to establish that the Church of England descended directly from the Christian church of the apostles. See Mill, *Later Letters*, vol. 14 of *Collected Works*, p. 16, notes 14 and 15.—Ed.]

[89] *The Spectator* of 10 March 1849, which contained the second part of Mill's review of G. Grote's *History of Greece*.

[90] J. A. Froude had been chosen for the post by the professors of University College, London, but as a result of the attacks of the newspapers was asked to withdraw, and withdrew. [See Mill, *Later Letters*, vol. 14 of *Collected Works*, p. 16, note 18.—Ed.]

[91] [Hayek has a query here instead of 'any': 'in [?] such case'.—Ed.]

cussion of the itinerary for the joint return journey from Pau,[92] but carefully preserving the beginning of the discussion of a new paragraph on page two.

J. S. M. to H. T., 17 March 1849:[93] The bargain with Parker is a good one & that it is so is entirely your doing—all the difference between it & the last being wholly your work, as well as the best of the book itself so that you have a redoubled title to your joint ownership of it. While I am on the subject I will say that the difficulty with the printer is surmounted—both he & Parker were disposed to be accommodating & he was to have the very same type from the very same foundry today—in the meantime there has been no time lost, as they have been printing very fast without the headings, & will no doubt keep their engagement as to time. You do not say anything this time about the bit of [the] P[olitical] E[conomy][94]—I hope you did not send it during the week, as if so it has miscarried—at the rate they are printing, both volumes at once, they will soon want it.

I was wrong in expressing myself in that way about the Athenians,[95] because without due explanations it would not be rightly understood. I am always apt to get enthusiastic about those who do great things for progress & are immensely ahead of everybody else in their age—especially when like the Athenians it has been the fashion to run them down for what was best in them—& I am not always sufficiently careful to explain that the praise is *relative* to the then state & not the *now* state of knowledge & what ought to be improved feeling. I *do* think, however, even without these allowances, that an average Athenian was a far finer specimen of humanity on the whole than an average Englishman—but then unless one says how low one estimates the

---

[92] What is left of this page reads: 'the old way, or . . . has the advantage of taking . . . Toulouse, but I suspect the means of conveyance by it are much slower & more precarious, till we reach Bourges or Châteuroux where we join the railway. I think from what has been in the papers that the whole or nearly the whole of the . . .' [See Mill, *Later Letters*, vol. 14 of *Collected Works*, p. 17.—Ed.]

[93] Yale University Library [MS 350, Box 1, Folder 3]. The date of the letter itself is missing with its beginning, but as the English postmark of the cover probably belonging to it seems to be 18 March, its date is probably 16 or 17 March. [Hayek has a query after the month. The letter is published in Mill, *Later Letters*, vol. 14 of *Collected Works*, pp. 17–18, where the letter is dated 17 March 1849 and the letter is numbered 23.—Ed.]

[94] [Hayek supplies only the initials: 'about the bit of P.E'.—Ed.]

[95] In his review of volumes 5 and 6 of George Grote's *History of Greece* in the *Spectator* for 3 and 10 March 1849, in the conclusion of which he had said (p. 228): 'If there was any means by which Grecian independence and liberty could have been made a permanent thing, it would have been by the prolongation for some generations more of the organization of the larger half of Greece under the supremacy of Athens; a supremacy imposed, indeed, and upheld by force—but the mildest, the most civilizing, and, in its permanent influence on the destinies of human kind, the most brilliant and valuable, of all the usurped powers known to history'.

latter, one gives a false notion of one's estimate of the former. You are not quite right about the philosophers, for Plato *did* condemn those 'barbarisms'.

I regret much that I have *not* put in anything about Palmerston into that pamphlet—I am almost tempted to write an express article in the West[r] in order to make him the amende. As you suggested I wrote an article on Russell's piece of meanness in the Jew Bill & have sent it to Crowe from whom I have not yet any answer—there has been no time hitherto fit for its publication—the time will be when the subject is about to come on again in Parl[t]. But I fear the article even as 'from a correspondent' will be too strong meat for the Daily News, as it declares without mincing the matter, that infidels are perfectly proper persons to be in parliament. I like the article myself. I have carefully avoided anything disrespectful to Russell personally, or any of the marks, known to me, by which my writing can be recognized.

If I meet Fleming[96] again or am again assaulted on any similar point I will reply in the sort of way you recommend—I dare say the meeting with F. was accidental as it was just at the door of Somerset House where he is assistant secretary of the Poor Law Board & just at the time when he would ~~be~~ probably [be] coming out. Ever since I have kept the opposite side.

J. S. M. to H. T.: 24 / Wednesday / 21 March [1849][97] / The Pol. Ec. packet came on Monday for which a thousand thanks. I have followed to the letter every recommendation. The sentence which you objected to in toto of course has come quite out.[98] In explanation however of what I meant by it—I was not thinking of any mysterious change in human nature—but chiefly of this—that the best people now are necessarily so much cut off from sympathy with the multitudes that I should think they must have difficulty in judging how they would be affected by such an immense change in their whole circumstances as would be caused by having multitudes whom they could sympathize with—or in knowing how far the social feeling might then supply the place of that large share of solitariness & individuality which they cannot now dispense with. I meant one thing more, viz. that as, hereafter, the more obvious & coarser obstacles & objections to the ~~communist~~ [community] system will have ceased or greatly diminished, those which are less obvious & coarse will then step forward into an importance & require an attention which does not now practically belong to them & that we can

[90] Henry Fleming (d. 1876), Assistant Secretary of the Poor Law Board from its creation in 1849 and Secretary for many years from 1860. Since he had been introduced there by Charles Buller, who was the first Chairman of the Poor Law Board, it would seem probable that Mill knew him through the Buller circle.

[97] Yale University Library [MS 350, Box 1, Folder 3; Mill, *Later Letters*, vol. 14 of *Collected Works*, pp. 18–20. Hayek added the bracketed material here and below in this passage.—Ed.].

[98] See above, p. 134.

John Taylor. Miniature in the British Library of Political and Economic Science. [Mill-Taylor/Box10. Courtesy of the Library of the London School of Economics & Political Science.—Ed.]

hardly tell without trial what the result of that experience will be. I do not say that *you* cannot realize & judge of these things—but if you, & perhaps Shelley & one or two others in a generation can, I am convinced that to do so requires both great genius & great experience & I think it quite fair to say to common readers that the present race of mankind (speaking of them collectively) are not competent to it. I cannot persuade myself that you do not greatly overrate the ease of making people unselfish. Granting that in 'ten years' the children of the community might by teaching be made 'perfect' it seems to me that to do so there must be perfect people to teach them. You say 'if there were a desire on the part of the cleverer people to make them perfect it would be easy'—but how to produce that desire on the part of the cleverer people? I must say I think that if we had absolute power tomorrow,

144

John Stuart Mill, 1840. Medallion reproduced from 'The Letters of John Stuart Mill', ed. by H. S. R. Elliott.

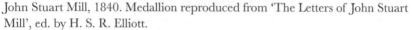

though we could do much to improve people by good laws, & could even give them a very much better education than they have ever had yet, still, for effecting in our time anything like what we aim at, all our plans would fail from the impossibility of finding fit instruments. To make people really good for much it is so necessary not merely to give them good intentions & conscientiousness but to unseal their eyes—to prevent self flattery, vanity, irritability & all that family of vices from warping their moral judgments as those of the very cleverest people are almost always warped now. But we shall have all those questions out together & they will all require to be entered into to a certain depth, at least, in the new book which I am so glad you look forward to as I do with so much interest.[99]—As for news—did you see in the Times Mrs Buller's death? I suspect it was the very day I wrote last. I have heard nothing of the manner or occasion of it, & had not supposed from anything I had heard before, that there was any likelihood of it. So that volume is

---

[99] [It is not clear to which book Mill is referring here. Mill, *Later Letters*, vol. 14 of *Collected Works*, p. 19, note 3, suggests a 'projected sequel to the Logic, never written, on "Ethology"'. Hayek supplies the brackets and contents in the passage.—Ed.]

closed now, completely.[100] I called the other day at Charles Fox's shop to ask the meaning of Mr. Fox's illness & C.F. said he has constant pains in his side which are either heart disease or merely nervous but which are made much worse by public speaking or any other excitement & that is the reason he so seldom speaks in the H.o.C.[101] It is probably mere nervous pain therefore, & not dangerous, but it shews him to be out of health. There were letters from George[102] yesterday of three weeks later date: his report is that he is neither worse nor better, he thinks that he coughs about six or seven times an hour through the 24 hours. He still writes as not at all out of spirits—one expression he uses is that he wants nothing to make him happy but to be able to go up into the mountains, & to have a better prospect of the future—I think he means better *avenir* in case he ultimately recovers—but he seems persuaded that his disease is seldom cured or stopped. I shall write to encourage him, for I am convinced it is often stopped though hardly ever cured, & I do not yet despair of his case.

Crowe's answer was 'I shall be but too happy to print the article. The Jews Bill is put off till after Easter, but if you will allow me I will insert it immediately.' There is nothing like kicking people of the D[aily] N[ews] sort it appears. I answered telling him if he thought it would be of as much use now as about the time when the bill comes on by all means to print it now. It has not yet made its appearance. The printing of the 2^d edit. goes on satisfactorily in all respects. Last Sunday I went by railway to Watford & walked from there to town, indeed more, for the direct road being by Stanmore I turned off before getting there, to Harrow, thus lengthening the walk 3 or 4 miles. I think I must have walked 20 miles, & almost all of it at a stretch, with occasional short resting on a stile. I confess however that the miles between Harrow & London were excessively long, but I felt no kind of inconvenience the next day or since from the walk. The lameness is now no obstacle at all—the only obstacle is general weakness, as compared with my state when in perfect health. The sight remains the same. I look forward to Saturday with immense pleasure because there is always a letter—adieu with every good wish.

The last of Mill's letters in this series which has been preserved is also mutilated. Almost the whole of the first half of the sheet is deliberately cut away, leaving on the second page[103] only the beginning of his reply to Mrs. Taylor's

---

[100] Mrs. Charles Buller, the mother of Mill's friend Charles Buller, had died on 13 March 1849, within ten months of the death of her husband (17 May 1848) and her eldest son Charles (29 September 1848). [Mill's friend, Charles Buller, died on 29 November 1848. See Mill, *Later Letters*, vol. 14 of *Collected Works*, p. 20, note 4.—Ed.]

[101] [House of Commons.—Ed.]

[102] [George Grote Mill, J. S. Mill's brother.—Ed.]

[103] The incomplete sentence left of the first page appears to deal merely with the weather of the preceding days.

comments on the discussion of population in the chapter on The Remedies for Low Wages towards the end of the first volume of the *Political Economy*.

J. S. M. to H. T., London, [27] / 31 March 1849:[104] The alteration I have made in ~~the~~ [that] sentence of the P.E. was instead of 'placard their intemperance' to say 'placard their enormous families'—it does not read so well, but I think it may do, especially as the previous sentence contains the words 'this sort of incontinence'—but your two sentences are so very good that as that sheet is not yet printed, get them in I must & will.[105]—Are you not amused with Peel about Ireland? He sneers down the waste lands plan,[106] two years ago, which the timid ministers, timid because without talent, give up at a single sarcasm from him, & now he has enfanté a scheme containing that & much more than was then proposed—& the Times supports him & Ireland praises him. I am extremely glad he has done it—I can see that it is working as nothing else has yet worked to break down the superstition about property—& it is the only thing happening in England which promises a step forward—a thing which one may well welcome when things are going so badly for the popular cause in Europe—not that I am discouraged by this—progress of the right kind seems to me to be quite safe now that Socialism has become *inextinguishable*. I heartily wish Proudhon dead however—there are few men whose state of mind, taken as a whole, inspires me with so much aversion, & all his influence seems to me mischievous except as a potent *dissolvent* which is good so far, but every single thing which he would substitute seems to me the worst possible in practice & mostly in principle. I have been reading another volume of Considérant lately published[107]—he has got into the *details* of Fouricrism with many large extracts from Fourier himself. It was perhaps neces-

[104] [The letter is published in Mill, *Later Letters*, vol. 14 of *Collected Works*, pp. 21–23, with a date *c.* 31 March 1849.—Ed.]

[105] *Political Economy* (first edition), vol. 1, p. 441: 'Is it not to this hour the favourite recommendation for any parochial office bestowed by popular election, to have a large family and to be unable to maintain them? Do not the candidates placard their intemperance on walls, and publish it through the town in circulars?' In the second edition, p. 457, the change mentioned in the text is made and the following footnote added which presumably contains the two sentences contributed by Mrs. Taylor: 'Little improvement can be expected in morality until the producing large families is regarded with the same feelings as overfondness for wine or any other physical excess. But while the aristocracy and clergy are foremost to set the example of incontinence, what can be expected from the poor?' [See Mill, *Political Economy*, vol. 2 of *Collected Works*, for the collated changes across editions, p. 368.—Ed.]

[106] Mill's proposal, developed in the series of [13] articles in the *Morning Chronicle* in the winter of 1846/7, advocating the creation of peasant properties on the waste lands in Ireland. [See Mill, *Newspaper Writings*, vol. 24 of *Collected Works*, pp. 879–1035.—Ed.]

[107] Probably V. P. Considerant, *Le Socialism devant le vieux monde, ou, le Vivant devant les morts* (Paris: Librairie Phalanstérienne, 1848). [Mill, *Later Letters*, vol. 14 of *Collected Works*, p. 21, note 5, concurs.—Ed.]

sary to go into details in order to make the thing look practicable, but many of the details *are*, & all *appear*, passablement ridicules. As to their system, & general mode of thought there is a great question at the root of it which must be settled before one can get a step further. Admitting the omnipotence of education, is not the very pivot & turning point of that education a *moral sense*—a feeling of duty, or conscience, or principle, or whatever name one gives it a feeling that one *ought* to do, & wish for, what is for the greatest good of all concerned. Now Fourier, & all his followers, leave this out entirely, & rely wholly on such [an] arrangements of social circumstances as without any inculcation of duty or of 'ought', will make every one, by the spontaneous action of the passions, intensely zealous[108] for all the interests of the whole. Nobody is ever to be made to do anything but act just as they like, but it is calculated that they will always, in a phalanstere, like what is best. This of course leads to the freest notions about personal relations of all sorts, but is it, in other respects, a foundation on which people would be able to live & act together. *Owen* keeps in generals & only says that education can make everybody perfect, but the Fourierists attempt to shew how, & exclude, as it seems to me, one of the most indispensable ingredients.

What a bathos[109] to turn from these speculations to pinched [&] methodistical England. It is worth while reading the articles in the newspapers about Froude & Sterling[110] to have an adequate idea of what England is. The newspaper talk on the subject having the irresistible attraction of personality still continues, & I have within this week read in shop windows leading articles of two weekly newspapers, the Church & State Gazette & the English Churchman, keeping it up. They have found the splendid mare's nest of the 'Sterling Club'.[111] I remember the foundation of the said club by Sterling himself, very many years before his death—soon after he began to live permanently out of London. Though called a club it had neither subscription nor orga-

---

[108] [Hayek has 'jealous' here instead of 'zealous'.—Ed.]

[109] The following paragraph begins on a new sheet of a different shape from that on which the preceding part of the letter is written and it is merely probable that it continues the same letter. [Mill, *Later Letters*, vol. 14 of *Collected Works*, p. 22, note 6, agrees that this is likely a continuation.—Ed.]

[110] See above, p. 141.

[111] This club was founded, as the 'Anonymous Club', by John Sterling in July 1838, a little more than six years before his death. See Sterling's letter, dated 14 July 1838, in which he informs Mill of the formation of the club, in A. K. Tuell, *John Sterling* [*A Representative Victorian*] (New York: Macmillan, 1941), p. 366, and T. Carlyle, *The Life of John Sterling* (London: Chapman and Hall: 1851), part 2, chapter 6, where a list of the original members is reproduced. The newspaper attacks on the Sterling Club were started by the *Record* on 8 March 1849, and continued throughout the year. ['Sterling and the Sterling Club' appeared in the *Church and Church Gazette* on 23 March 1949, pp. 180–81; the article in the *English Churchman* appeared on 29 March 1849, pp. 196–97. Mill, *Later Letters*, vol. 14 of *Collected Works*, p. 22, notes 7 and 8.—Ed.]

nization, but consisted in an agreement of some 12 or 20 acquaintances of Sterling, the majority resident University people, that there should be one day in the month when if any of them liked to dine at a place in Lincoln's Inn Fields he would have a chance of finding some of the others. I let them put me down as one, & went there, I think three times, with Sterling himself & at his request, in order to pass an evening in his company—the last time being, I believe, in 1838. A few weeks ago I was reminded of the existence of the thing by receiving a printed list of members, in which I was put down with many others a honorary—it has greatly increased in numbers, is composed (in more than one half) of clergymen including two bishops, Thirlwall and Wilberforce, & I suppose it has organized itself with a regular subscription, as it has removed to the Freemason's & has begun sending circulars previous to each dinner. One of these lists fell into the hands of the 'Record' newspaper & combining this with Hare's Life of Sterling it charges Hare, Maurice, Trench, these bishops, & innumerable others with founding a society to honour & commemorate an infidel, & joining for that purpose with persons strongly suspected of being no better than infidels themselves, such as Carlyle & me. It is very amusing that these people who take such care to guard their orthodoxy get nothing by it but to be more bitterly attacked. However it shews what I did not suppose, that it required some courage in a church dignitary to write about a heretic even in the guarded way that Hare did.[112]—

Yesterday Nichol[113] called on me—whom I had not seen since 1840—he is in town for some days or probably weeks & is about to publish a book on America where he has been travelling. As he is a walking man I am going to have a country walk with him tomorrow—my other Sunday walks have been alone. I ~~always~~ have [always] thought him a man of whom something might be made if one could see enough of him—I shall perhaps be able to judge now if my opinion was right, but at all events his book will shew. He has this in his favour at least which is the grand distinction now that he is intensely *forward*-looking—not at all conservative in feeling but willing to be very destructive & now adieu with every possible wish.

On Monday no doubt I shall hear again.

---

[112] Julius C. Hare had in 1848 published a memoir of the life of John Sterling as an introduction to the collected edition of the latter's *Essays and Tales*. [John Sterling, *Essays and Tales, by John Sterling, with a Memoir of His Life by Julius Hare* (London. John W. Parker, 1848). The memoir occupies pp. i–ccxxxii and is dated 1847.—Ed.]

[113] John Pringle Nichol, F.R.S., 1804–1859, since 1836 Professor of Astronomy at the University of Glasgow, contributor to the *London and Westminster Review* during Mill's editorship when he was in regular correspondence with Mill. No book of his on America seems to have appeared. [Nichol gave several series of lectures in the United States during the winter of 1848/9. Mill, *Later Letters*, vol. 14 of *Collected Works*, p. 23, notes 16 and 17.—Ed.]

In a letter from her husband received by Mrs. Taylor toward the end of March he seems to have given her a more unfavourable account of the state of his health which caused her some concern but evidently gave no idea of the real gravity of his condition.

> *H. T. to John Taylor, Pau, 30 March 1849:*[114] If I only consulted my own inclination I should come back to England immediately on the receipt of your letter in hopes of being able to be of use to you. The reason I cannot do this is that I have arranged with Mr Mill to meet me on the 20th of April when he is to have three weeks holiday on account of his health which has been the whole winter in a very precarious state, for the last two months he has been almost unable to read or write & has had to engage a man to read to him & to write from his dictation & both Clark & Alexander the occulist say that a complete change & cessation from all work is absolutely necessary to save his sight—he has had blisters & irritating applications innumerable without any effect and is indeed about half blind. They say that giving up using the eyes & mild weather will cure them as they attribute all the bad symptoms to extreme debility. I shall therefore return with him as far as Paris & I shall get back the earliest that I possibly can in the hopes of being of use to you. I have not been quite well lately having had some return of my stomach derangement, but I am getting better again & the travelling will be sure to do my health good. I feel it a duty to do all in my power for his health & it is unfortunate that he is so much required at the change of direction on 11th April that he cannot leave London before that. He does not tell even his own family *where* he goes for his holiday as I so hate all tittle-tattle. Therefore I do not mention it either except to you. I trouble you with all these particulars because I wish you to know that nothing but a feeling of right would prevent my returning at once.

Mill probably joined Mrs. Taylor and her daughter at Bagnères, where however the party cannot have stayed long since, after an excursion to Cauterets in the High Pyrénées, they were already on their way home at Toulouse on April 29[115] but appear to have spent another fortnight going north via Montauban, Limoges and Chateauroux to Orleans and Paris.

---

[114] MTColl. XXVIII/227. [Harriet Taylor Mill, *Complete Works*, pp. 501–2.]
[115] MTColl. XXVIII/229. [Harriet Taylor Mill, *Complete Works*, pp. 372–73.]

SEVEN

JOHN TAYLOR'S ILLNESS AND DEATH
1849

Either in order to avoid travelling together when they were likely to meet acquaintances, or merely because Mrs. Taylor was awaiting a calmer day for crossing the Channel, Mill returned from Paris to London a day or two in advance, with a message for Mr. Taylor that his wife was well and would arrive presently. When at last Mrs. Taylor arrived on 14 May, she found her husband much more gravely ill than she had expected—in fact, as the doctor soon gave her to understand, dying of cancer.

For two months until his death she then devoted all her strength to nursing the invalid. A long series of hastily written notes to Mill give a continuous account of her fluctuating hopes and fears. For some time she refused to accept the scarcely veiled verdict of the doctors and to submit to the inevitable. A great part of her notes to Mill during the first few weeks is concerned with the question of what other doctors to consult and with books on the disease which she studies to discover whether there is any chance of a cure. Nobody who reads the whole set of these notes[1] can doubt the genuineness of her anguish or the exclusiveness of her devotion during these last weeks, when she scarcely sees Mill, to the incessant care of her dying husband. All the following excerpts are taken from these notes to Mill, whose exact dates are mostly uncertain.

H. T. to J. S. M., 28 (?) May 1849.[2] It is extraordinary the hard work both I & L[ily] have gone through & still take each day but I have lost almost all count of the days & know not when [it] is the beginning or end of the week—the whole time passed in soothing the pain by words of sympathy or diverting it by inventing talk or actively engaged in all the incessant operation for relief. He is most patient & firm & endures with the utmost strength

---

[1] MTColl. L/9–37. From this point onwards and through the rest of the volume only selected passages from the correspondence are reproduced. [The letters are published in full in *The Complete Works of Harriet Taylor Mill* [hereafter cited as *Complete Works*], ed. Jo Ellen Jacobs (Bloomington: Indiana University Press, 1998), pp. 343–73.—Ed.]

[2] MTColl. L/16. [The letter is dated as 'probably Monday June 11' and appears in full in Harriet Taylor Mill, *Complete Works*, pp. 358–59. Hayek supplied the name in brackets.—Ed.]

& courage—but *why* sh^d he have these torments to endure! what good to anybody is *all* this—he never hurt or harmed a creature on earth. If they want the life why cant they take it—what useless torture is all this! & he is so sorry & hurt to give so much labour to me—he feels that I am the greatest good to him & feeling that no servant could do what I do for him enables me to keep up. He said 2 days since 'well if ever I *do* recover it will be entirely owing to you'. How cruel to feel that his chance is so slight—alas I feel as if he besides you is the only life I value in this wretched world. He is so thoroughly true direct honest strong & with all the realities of nice feelings, as I constantly see now. What a contrast is such a man to the vapid sentimental egotists Stirling, Carlyle, &c who let inflated conceit of their own assumed superiority run away with all strength & humility.

Early June:[3] You talk of my writing to you 'at some odd time when a change of subject of thought may be rather a relief than otherwise'! *odd time!* indeed you must be ignorant profoundly of all that *friendship* or *anxiety* means when you can use such pitiful narrow hearted expressions. The sentence appears to have come from the pen of one of the Miss Taylors. It is the puerility of thought & feeling of any utterly headless & heartless pattern of propriety old maid.

As to 'odd time' I *told* you that I have not a moment unfilled by things to be done when not actually standing by the bedside or supporting the invalid—& as to 'change of subject of thought a relief'! Good God sh^d you think it a relief to think of somebody else some acquaintance or what not while *I* was dying? If so—but I will say no more about this—only after such a mode of feeling on your part I feel it sacrilegious to enter into any account of what I feel & suffer in this most dreadful & most melancholy & most piteous case—my heart is wrung with indignation & grief.

July 6:[4] This disease seems to combine the evils of consumption with those of acute distress—all the pains of exhaustion by slow wasting away with ~~the~~ terrible local characteristics of its own. So terrible & frightful is this disease that it is something to be glad of that he remains free from pain—only those who have watched with the deep sympathy of true affection & pity can fully estimate the infinite distinction there is between freedom from pain & freedom from suffering. I am sure almost any pain is less bad (tho' not perhaps less *hard*) to bear than this which he poor poor dear calls so truly dying by inches.

[3] MTColl. L/17. [Harriet Taylor Mill, *Complete Works*, p. 359, note 107, gives a likely date as 'the second week of June'. The letter appears in full on pp. 359–60 with the quoted passage at p. 360.—Ed.]

[4] MTColl. L/28. [Harriet Taylor Mill, *Complete Works*, pp. 364–66.]

However he has hours of comparative pleasure now—& himself & those who don't hear the medical opinions seem to flatter themselves he may be going on well—but they say that tho' it is a wonderfully easy case of the kind, that others suffer so very much more than he (the truth of which is that no one I sh^d think was ever so well nursed) Yet that the result will be the same. For me after two days of feeling ill & knocked up I have now recovered again. I am now feeling scarcely tired. The certainty of being really of the greatest use & quite indispensable to him (or to any one) gives me a quantity of strength & life—so that I feel sure my health will not suffer— unless indeed the disease is contagious which I dare say it is not—if it were we three who do all for him w^d be sure of it. However never mention this idea to them.

His sisters who come to see him & others say no one w^d think there was illness in his room it is so fresh & gay—& this freshness & cheerfulness I am sure have much to do with his ease & comfort & almost complete freedom from nervous depression. Neither window nor door have been shut either day or night for a month, & the sight & scent of fresh flowers & christal iced (?) water & all sorts of nice looking things beguile him into a feeling of pleasure & cheat the low spirits.

So all this incessant attention & effort to keep up his spirits, & also the long time it is now [is], since I heard the dreadful truth, has combined to sink the deep grief & indignation I feel below the surface—but I have so much to say to you that [which] no one but you could understand.

What a duping is life & what fools are men who seem bent upon playing into the hands of the mischievous demons! One comfort & hope lies in the fact that the worst they suffer is from their own bad qualities—but the good suffer with the bad.

[I shall write a few words every few days—] Perhaps you will enclose George's letter for H[aji]^5 to me. Tell me how you are? Take care of yourself for the worlds sake.

I cannot think how you [can] have been silent all the [this] while about [the] Roman *heroism*—never equalled—& the French utter baseness. I have been longing to write myself. The only person who seems to feel it as strongly as I do is Landor & he seems half mad.

July 9.^{6} Will you send any Mag^s or Rev^s you have, for him—if you have any that is.

He has got, for July, the New Monthly & the Quarterly—

^{5} [Hayek supplies Haji's full name in brackets for his reader here.—Ed.]
^{6} MTColl. L/30. [Harriet Taylor Mill, *Complete Works*, p. 368. Note 129 states that the letter was postmarked 9 July 1849.—Ed.]

Especially I want the Edinburgh *at the earliest* possible.

Don't call again.

You have no notion what a mistake you make in saying that it could be no more contagious than a fractured skull—Any one who saw & watched this & thought so must [have] already ~~have~~ got a fractured skull. I have very little doubt that this is as often contagious as Typhus or plague—It seems very like the latter—probably all are contagious in circumstances—& to persons predisposing or predisposed. However I cannot now give my reasons for this opinion.

I have so very much to say which must wait.

What an iron despotism we live under, & who can wonder that men are bad while they take the government of this world for their model. I am glad to hear that the timid upper classes think the Romans fine—if indeed they do so—but Grote always paints his fine acquaintances couleur de rose.

That they dislike & condemn the French proceedings I have no doubt.

Tocqueville is a notable specimen of the class which includes [all] such people as the Stirlings Romillys Carlyles Austins[7]—the gentility class—weak in moral, narrow in intellect, timid, infinitely conceited, & gossiping. There are very few men in this country who can seem other than more or less respectable puppets to us.

Thus gradually, as she resigns herself to the inevitable conclusion of her husband's suffering, other topics begin to enter into Mrs. Taylor's thoughts and her correspondence. The first extraneous subject discussed, apparently still in May, was an application for money to Mill made by G. J. Holyoake to help him in an attempt to obtain a university degree. Mrs. Taylor advised '~~to~~ [I would] give but not unaccompanied with a suitable lesson on this vain & senseless affectation'[8] and Mill's draft of the reply to Holyoake is fully commented upon by her.

H. T. to J. S. M., May (?) 1849:[9] I think it *duty* when you tell him you will subscribe [~~to his~~] as he requests to tell him some of your opinion on the very

---

[7] [Alexis de Tocqueville, Anthony and John Sterling, Sir John and Caroline Romilly, Thomas and Jane Carlyle, and John and Sarah Austin. Harriet Taylor Mill, *Complete Works*, p. 368, note 128.—Ed.]

[8] MTColl. L/18. [Harriet Taylor Mill, *Complete Works*, p. 350. Note 86 suggests the letter was likely written Monday night, 21 May 1849.—Ed.]

[9] MTColl. L/I2. [Harriet Taylor Mill, *Complete Works*, pp. 349–50. Harriet's original reads, 'I [~~agreed with you~~] think it *duty*'. She also changed the following wording: 'of ~~learning~~ being "*learned*"'. Hayek supplied 'his note to Mill' in brackets. According to *ibid.*, p. 349, note 85, the founder of the Rochdale Pioneers, George Jacob Holyoake, reprinted the *Political Economy* as a serial, with an introduction depicting Mill as a militant atheist. The letter was postmarked 22 May 1849 and written the day before. *Ibid.*, p. 349, note 85.—Ed.]

false & *vicious* sort of note it [his note to Mill] is—I think, it is impossible you can agree with the humbug (even when translated into honest expressions it is humbug) that hearing men lecture at [the] London or any other University is a means of improvement of knowledge, of being '*learned*', as he so boastfully & vulgarly calls it such as can never be equalled by reading—That *lectures* & lecturers such as exist at present are means of improvement superior to all reading—Then his hypocritical cant about 'violating austere incorruptibility' either the words are a useless & therefore insincere braggadocio, or the man is 'violating &c' by his letter.

The whole thing in an honest man's language amounts to this I want to get a degree or some other University honour [in order] to try to get on in the world are you disposed to help me with a little money?

This is the whole—while his note is like all his a heap of boastful conceited vulgar insincerity & I wish that he sh[d] see or feel that you are *not* humbugged by him. And this only because it feels to me *immoral* to let falseness think itself more successful than honesty w[d] be with true & intelligent people.

Soon a more important subject arose. Captain Antony Sterling, the brother of Mill's friend John Sterling who had died not long before, was at the time preparing for publication a collection of his brother's letters. This never appeared, though it was later to serve Thomas Carlyle for his *Life of John Sterling*. Apparently Captain Sterling had applied to Mill for permission to include some of his letters to Sterling as well as some passages about him, perhaps those in the correspondence between Sterling and Carlyle which have been quoted earlier.

June:[10] I had said nothing more about those letters lately because I understood from your note a fortnight ago that it was all decided, that you meant to leave out all mention of yourself in them & also to withdraw [all] the letters addressed to you. I supposed that this had been done & that the thing was settled. I am quite sure that it ought to be done both in justice & honour and as to the difficulty you find in doing it, that does not seem to me great [even] if, what is not the case, your usual ways were exactly like those of ordinary people. In a matter of taste & one wholly concerning yourself that you should change your mind is certainly not fatally odd.

---

[10]MTColl. L/27. [Harriet Taylor Mill, *Complete Works*, pp. 362–64. Three letters concerning the publication of correspondence between Mill and John Sterling survive. The only dated letter is postmarked Saturday, 30 June. Another was written around the time of John Taylor's death (18 July), probably 8 July. The dating of this letter is less certain. Harriet Taylor Mill, *Complete Works*, p. 362, note 115, suggests 28 June as the most likely date, but if this is so, the correspondence of a fortnight earlier, referred to above, is not preserved.—Ed.]

A further note evidently refers to the letter to be sent to Captain Sterling.

June 30:[11] I think the words which I have put the pencil through are better omitted—but they might with a little alteration be placed at the end?

The *reason* I should give to Cap[t] S. if a reason is asked, is that the way in which you are mentioned in the letters is calculated to give an erroneous impression of you This is the simple truth. The words I have added at the end do not go quite right but you will make them do so. It is if possible as desirable[12] to get those passages omitted ~~as~~ [than] your own letters. Therefore something of the kind (like the words I have added) should be said.

July 7–8 (?):[13] I have had but a few moments in which to look at those extracts from S's letters. I cannot at all *understand*, & I mean this wholly *sincerely* and not at all ironically, how you could ever see with complacency or even with indifference such a quantity of misapprehension of your character to be published. I know that you place great vanity in not being vain but with me love of truth as well as vanity w[d] make repugnant to me the myself giving [to] the world an appreciation of me made by an *evident* inferior who makes it with all the air of judging from a height which is conceivable. a second thing which hurts me intensely tho' it does not surprise me is your perfect ~~madness~~ [readiness] to put your own hand & seal to the mention of your name & character soi-disant appreciatingly by a man who you perceive was weak & foolish enough to be in agreement with his correspondent in *judging* yr relations with some unknown woman in unknown circumstances. Of course the old bugbear words 'married woman' were at the bottom of this unanimity of fear & sorrow which these men honoured (or disgraced selon moi) you with. Nowadays I sh[d] have thought that with our opinion we must thoroughly despise men who have not got out of that baby morality & intellect. That you c[d] be willing to have these things printed hurts me more deeply than anything else I think c[d] do. It has disturbed my mind & feelings even amidst these trying days & nights. but if you have engaged yourself about them [I suppose] some of them must stand.

In what was probably the next note a different topic is taken up.

---

[11] MTColl. L/25. [Harriet Taylor Mill, *Complete Works*, p. 364. This is postmarked 30 June 1849. *Ibid.*, p. 364, note 118.—Ed.]

[12] [Harriet's original reads: 'It is ~~in fact~~ if possible ~~even more~~ as desirable'.—Ed.]

[13] MTColl. L/28. A sheet in J. S. M.'s hand, docketed by him 'Extracts from letters of Sterling respecting me', is in MTColl. XLIX/21, but does not contain any of the passages complained of below. [Harriet Taylor Mill, *Complete Works*, p. 367. The entry is dated as 'probably' written on 8 July 1849 and is correctly listed as MTColl. L/29.—Ed.]

July 10:[14] The enclosed paper marked A I wrote one Sunday some weeks ago but did not send it feeling [that] I had so ill expressed the fullness of my meaning. However another case which I will enclose gives so admirable an occasion for an article in the Daily News on the subject—against legalising *corporal punishment anywhere* public or private—that I think it *ought*[15] to be written.

Mark this case—how there was no *pretence* of brutality or violence in the offence that it sh^d be punished by brutal degradation (you sh^d take care to copy in the report the words *middleaged* man for tho' it adds nothing to *our* feeling it strengthens the case as against the magistrates immensely with the commonalty). Then *do* hit police magistrates in general & Secker in particular as hard as possible—all the rest of[16] the subject you will at once see as strongly & clearly as I.

How the most brutal attacks of personal violence are sentenced to *imprisonment* only—how you never see a case of that kind met by personal violence i.e. by corporal punishment—how bad & disgusting as corporal punishment is ever—if used it ought to be only for personal violence.

Enclosure A: Sunday Even^g.

My eye fell just now on the Examiner as it lay open with an account of the trial of the young man who shot at the Queen.

I see it reported that the newly revived barbarous & degrading punishment of flogging which ever since the offence the Newspapers, especially the Examiner, have been gloating over with disgusting toadying satisfaction is said to have been omitted by especial desire of the Queen—now whether this is so or not w^d it not be an excellent opportunity to treat the statement as true: to compliment [her][17] for refusing so unworthy & disgusting a tribute as the revival of a brutal degradation as punishment of offences against her. Pointing out that the offence was not of a Degraded or brutal kind but of a wicked & grave kind, and that flogging is no more fit for it than it w^d be for murder. Admiring too the *unsovereignlike* magnanimity of punishing such a serious offence only as if it had been directed against the meanest subject. In fact the punishment is not severe enough.

The second enclosure, probably a clipping from a newspaper, has not been preserved and probably was used by Mill in writing the unheaded and

---

[14] MTColl. L/31. [Harriet Taylor Mill, *Complete Works*, pp. 368–69. Note 132 on p. 369 states that the letter is postmarked 10 July 1849. During this time, Mill and Harriet were collaborating on newspaper articles concerning domestic violence.—Ed.]

[15] [Hayek supplies uppercase letters for Harriet's 'anywhere' and 'ought'.—Ed.]

[16] [Harriet Taylor Mill, *Complete Works*, strikes out 'rest of', p. 369.—Ed.]

[17] [Harriet's original reads: 'to compliment her ~~or anybody~~'.—Ed.]

unsigned article which four days later appeared in the *Daily News* of July 14 and is confirmed as Mill's by its inclusion in his hand list of his publications.[18]

Since this is the best illustration we have of the manner in which Mill expanded a brief suggestion of Mrs. Taylor's into an article which he describes as 'a joint production, very little of which was mine', it deserves a little fuller discussion. The magistrate[19] had sentenced to a fine and three months' imprisonment a man for illegally pawning another person's gold watch and had added that if the prisoner omitted to pay the fine and the estimated value of the watch 'within three days of the expiration of his imprisonment he should be once publicly whipped within the precincts of the gaol'. Mill makes this indeed the occasion for a violent onslaught on police magistrates in general and Mr. Secker in particular, but while he in general closely follows Mrs. Taylor's suggestions, he puts the main blame on the state of the law. After complaining that

> Amidst our talk of reformatory treatment we are returning to the most demoralising, the most brutalising because the most degrading of punishments, the bastinado,

he proceeds with some comments on the particular case and then continues

> If a brutal punishment can ever be appropriate, it is in a case of a brutal offence. . . . But who ever hears of corporal punishment for assault? One or two months imprisonment is all we hear of in the most atrocious cases; while, if property is in question—if pounds, shillings and pence have been tampered with, years of imprisonment, with hard labour (not to mention transportation) are almost the smallest penalty. And this is not peculiarly the fault of police magistrates. . . . It is the crime more especially of the legislators and of the superior courts. . . . Because persons in the upper and middle ranks are not subject to personal outrage, and *are* subject to having their watches stolen, the punishment of blows is revived, not for those who are guilty of blows, but for middle aged men who pawn watches. Is this to be endured?
>
> A few weeks ago, the punishment of flogging, in the case of the young man who shot at the Queen, was omitted, it is said, at the special desire of

---

[18] MacMinn, *et al.*, *Bibliography*, p. 71. The article appeared in the *Daily News*, 14 July 1849. [The article is reproduced in full in *Newspaper Writings*, eds. Ann P. Robson and John M. Robson, vols. 22–25 (1986), of *The Collected Works of John Stuart Mill* [hereafter cited as *Collected Works*] (Toronto: University of Toronto Press, 1962–1991), 25:1138–41, where it is listed as 'the seventh jointly authored by Harriet Taylor and Mill on injustice and cruelty', and in Harriet Taylor Mill, *Complete Works*, pp. 95–98.—Ed.]

[19] [Isaac Onslow Secker (1799–1861), was a barrister and the magistrate at Greenwich and Woolwich. Mill, *Newspaper Writings*, vol. 25 of *Collected Works*, p 1138.—Ed.]

the Queen herself. The forebearance was uncomplimentary to the legislatorial wisdom which had recently enacted that penalty as peculiarly fit for that particular offence: but no one can be surprised by an example of good sense, good taste, and good feeling, given by the Queen.

The crime of Hamilton was not of a degraded or brutal kind, though of a wicked and grave kind, deserving, in truth, and requiring, a severer punishment than it received. To refuse so disgusting a tribute as the revival of a brutalizing degradation as a punishment for offences against herself, was a worthy lesson to legislators and judges; and it was magnanimity, not like but most unlike a sovereign, to punish so serious an offence only as if it had been directed against the meanest subject. Would that her Majesty would take in hand this vast and vital question of the extinction of personal violence by the best and surest means—the illegalizing of corporal punishment, domestic as well as judicial, at any age. We conscientiously believe that more large and lasting good, both present and future, to the moral and social character of the whole people, would be achieved by such an act of legislation, than fifty years of legislative efforts without it would be required to supply.

A few days later all other concerns are again suspended by the obvious approach of her husband's end.

July 16.[20] Monday. I have exceedingly wanted to write about many things, but cannot find a moment.

Yesterday & to-day this sad sad tragedy seems drawing to a close in the most piteous yet most patient & calm way.

Alas poor thing what a mocking life has been to him! ending in this fierce contest in which death gains inch by inch!

The sadness & horror of Nature's daily doings exceed a million fold all the attempts of Poets! There is nothing on earth I would not do for him & there is nothing on earth which *can* be done.

Do not write.[21]

July 18.[22] Wednesday. I cannot write much now not on account of the sorrow & distress for that has been as great for weeks—but I find I am quite physically exhausted & faint after two nights & a day of most anxious and

---

[20] MTColl. L/32. [Harriet Taylor Mill, *Complete Works*, pp. 369–70. *Ibid.*, p. 369, note 133, states that this was likely written 16 July 1849, two days before John Taylor died. The final sentence is 'scribbled on the back of page'. *Ibid.*, p. 370, note 134.—Ed.]

[21] [Harriet's last sentence begins with the lowercase 'do'. Harriet Taylor Mill, *Complete Works*, p. 370.—Ed.]

[22] MTColl. L/34. [Harriet Taylor Mill, *Complete Works*, pp. 370–71. The letter is postmarked 18 July 1849. *Ibid.*, p. 370, note 138.—Ed.]

sad watching ended by his gently breathing the last without a sigh or pang at 3oclk this morning.—I must defer saying anything till this next week has passed—To me a very painful one—feeling has to remain in abeyance while the many absolutely necessary mechanical details are ordered & attended to [all] by me who never saw anything of the kind before & having no person *whatever* but the three children to advise with it is the most trying time.

I do not know *where* he should be laid—having no connection with any place—I have thought of either Kensal Green or Hampstead as not too far? Tell me what you think! Write to me[23] enclosed to Herbert at Cross Street.

There is a person here who is medisance personified & just now I w^d not have a shadow of the kind—so for a few days write to me only thus.

July 19.[24] Thursday. I want your opinion which is right & best—about coming to the funeral next Wednesday. I have no doubt your first ~~impression~~ [impulse] is like mine, to say, *of course*, yes—The grounds of all I wish done at this time are twofold—what the world thinks most respectful to him, & what he would have wished. But the latter *in this case* is I think pretty much included in the former, which is the reason I think at all of the former. I wish everything done which can be honourable & respectful to him being the last testimony of the affection I felt & feel for him & of the true & strong respect he has added too so much during this illness—& in all this I know you must truly sympathise. My *first* impression about your coming was a feeling of 'better not' grounded on the sort of distance which of late existed. But now on much consideration it seems to me in the first place that coming is certainly thought a mark of respect? Is it not? and that therefore your not doing so will be a *manque* of that. Then again the public in some degree & *his* public too have heared or are sure to hear (through Arthur[25] if no other way) of the Dedication—of our intimacy—& on the side of his relations, nor that I know of on mine, there does not appear to be any medisance. (Indeed the kindness & attention to me of all his relations is as marked as the neglect of these by mine.)

Thus all who know or care to hear anything on the subject must hear of great intimacy. Does not therefore *absence* seem much more noticeable than coming? On the other ~~hand~~ [side] nothing is more true of common world than 'out of sight out of mind' & thought about it may never occur to any one as they are principally relations or daily associates who will come. I fancy

---

[23] [Harriet's original reads, 'Write to me ~~under cover~~ enclosed to Herbert at Cross Street'. Harriet Taylor Mill, *Complete Works*, p. 371.—Ed.]

[24] MTColl. L/36. [Harriet Taylor Mill, *Complete Works*, pp. 371–72.]

[25] [According to Harriet Taylor Mill, *Complete Works*, p. 371, note 141, Harriet's brother, Arthur Hardy, received a of the *Political Economy* featuring the dedication to Harriet.—Ed.]

Herbert has like him a sort of Ostrich instinct, like morally timid people, always *not to do*—while my instinct is always to *do*.

Tell me by a note addressed here what you think or feel about this.

My first impulse was against—my present is *for*—but the reasons are so nearly balanced that an opinion of yours would turn the scale.

Write soon—I will write again too—soon—I have decided for Kensal Green. Tell me if there is *choice* as to situation there? I mean as to *niceness*, I know we can *choose*.

Do you know Gilbert Elliot? The clergyman? Is he not incumbent somewhere near here? At Kensal Green I believe one has to find ones own clergyman? Do you know? And w^d it be a suitable thing to ask him?

Every detail without exception I have to order as there is no one here but the three children. Herbert does the speaking to the people. [He (?)][26] is gone to business to-day. I thought the inserting it so soon in the Papers very ugly & unpleasant but Herbert so insisted upon it on account of his having to reply to so many enquiries, that I gave way—which I repent. Tell me if it *struck* you as indecent haste?

There is one more letter mainly about the question whether Mill should attend the funeral, on the whole more against, and it is not known whether he did. The letter concludes:

July 22.[27] Of feelings & thoughts there is far too much to be said in a note—I must see you soon—it occurs to me that it might be well to go down to Walton to spend next Sunday & that in that case you might come down for the Sunday. As there is no one there but old Mr Delarue it w^d not do for any one to sleep there but me & Lily as she is too old to do anything—but even a day would be much after such an interval

Soon after Mrs. Taylor had another severe breakdown of her health.

When John Taylor's will, made less than five months before his death, was opened, it was found that he had left to his wife a life interest in the whole of his property.

---

[26] [The paper is torn at this spot. Hayek inserts '[He]' with the query following it, and Harriet Taylor Mill, *Complete Works*, p. 371, note 142, accepts the insertion.—Ed.]

[27] MTColl. L/37. [Harriet Taylor Mill, *Complete Works*, pp. 372–73, with the quoted portion at p. 373.—Ed.]

EIGHT

MARRIAGE AND BREAK WITH MILL'S FAMILY
1851

Although nearly two years passed between John Taylor's death and Mill's marriage to Harriet Taylor, the only significant documents which we have for this period are two letters by Mill. The first of these can be dated only approximately.

> *J. S. M. to H. T., about 1850:*[1] Thanks dearest dearest angel for the note—what it contained was a really important addition to the letter & I have put it in nearly in your words, which as your impromptu words almost always are, were a hundred times better than any I could find by study. What a perfect orator you would make—& what changes might be made in the world by such a one, with such opportunities as thousands of male dunces have. But you are to me, & would be to any one who knew you, the type of Intellect—because you have all the faculties in equal perfection—you can both think, & impress the thought on others—& can both judge what ought to be done, & do it. As for me, nothing but the division of labour could make me useful—if there were not others with the capacities of intellect which I have not, where would be the use of ~~those~~ [them] I have—I am but fit to be one wheel in an engine not to be the self moving engine itself—a real majestic intellect, not to say moral nature, like yours, I can only look up to & admire—but while you can love me as you so sweetly & beautifully shewed in that hour yesterday, I have all I care for or desire for myself—& wish for nothing except not to disappoint you—& to be so happy as to be some good to you (who are all good to me) before I die. This is a graver note than I thought it would be when I began it—for the influence of that dear little hour has kept me in spirits ever since—thanks to my one only source of good.

The second letter raises the subject which during the next few months was to be the occasion for the article on the Enfranchisement of Women. Since the

---

[1] MTColl. L/39. The only evidence for assigning an approximate date to this letter is the identity of the notepaper with that of the following. [The letter is published in *The Later Letters of John Stuart Mill, 1849–1873*, eds. Francis E. Mineka and Dwight N. Lindley, vols. 14–17 (1972) of *The Collected Works of John Stuart Mill* [hereafter cited as *Collected Works*] (Toronto: University of Toronto Press, 1962–1991), 14:42–43. The date there is given as '1850?'.—Ed.]

'Women's Rights Convention' at Worcester, Massachusetts, to which it refers, took place on 23 and 24 October 1850 and was reported in the European edition of the *New York Tribune* on 29 October, it cannot be of a much later date.

J. S. M. to H. T., October/November 1850:[2] You will tell me my own dearest love, what has made you out of spirits. I have been put in spirits by what I think will put you in spirits too—you know some time ago there was a Convention of Women in Ohio to claim equal rights—(& there is to be another in May)[3] well, there has just been a Convention for the same purpose in Massachusetts—chiefly of women, but with a great number of men, including the chief slavery abolitionists Garrison, Wendell Phillips, the negro Douglass[4] &c. The New York Tribune contains a long report[5]— most of the speakers are women—& I never remember any public meetings or agitation comparable to it in the proportion which good sense bears to nonsense—while as to tone it is almost like ourselves speaking—outspoken like America, not frightened & senile [servile] like England—not the least iota of compromise—asserting the whole of the principle & claiming the whole of the consequences, without any of the little feminine concessions and reserves—the thing will evidently not drop, but will go on till it succeeds, & I really do now think that we have a good chance of living to see something decisive really accomplished on that of all practical subjects the most important—to see that will be really looking down from Pisgah on the promised land—how little I thought we should ever see it.

The days seem always short to me as they pass. The time that seems long, the time that I am often impatient of the length of, is the time till spring[6]— the time till we have a home, till we are together in our life instead of this unsatisfactory this depressing coming and going, in which all disagreeables have so much more power than belongs to them, & the atmosphere of happiness has not time to penetrate & pervade in the way I know so well even by the most imperfect experience & which then it will always——

The article which during the following winter grew out of this and finally appeared in the *Westminster Review* for July 1851 is generally described as by

[2] MTColl. I./38. [Mill, *Later Letters*, vol. 14 of *Collected Works*, pp. 49–50. The letter is dated 'After Oct. 29, 1850'.—Ed.]

[3] The two Ohio Conventions took place at Salem on 19 and 20 April 1850 and at Akron on 28 and 29 May 1851.

[4] William Lloyd Garrison (1805–1879), Wendell Phillips (1811–1884) and Frederick Douglass (1817–1895). [Hayek spells Douglass with a single 's'. All were abolitionists. The birth date of Frederick Douglass is queried in Mill, *Later Letters*, vol. 14 of *Collected Works*, p. 49, note 7.—Ed.]

[5] [*New York Tribune* for Europe, 29 October 1850.—Ed.]

[6] [Taylor and Mill planned to marry in spring.—Ed.]

Mrs. Taylor. But while this is probably true enough so far as the general argument is concerned, Mill's introduction to the reprint of the article in Volume 2 of *Dissertations and Discussions* makes one doubt how much it applies to the actual writing.[7] He describes it merely as, unlike the other 'joint productions' of the period, as 'hers in a peculiar sense, my share in it being little more than that of an editor and amanuensis'. The article must have been practically completed by the time when Mill offered it to the editor of the *Westminster Review*:

> *J. S. M. to W. E. Hickson.*[8] India House / 3rd March 1851 / Dear Hickson—If you are inclined for an article on the Emancipation of Women, a propos the Convention in Massachussets which I mentioned to you the last time I saw you, I have one nearly ready, which can be finished & sent to you within a week, which, I suppose, is in time for your April number.
>
> Very truly yours
> J. S. Mill

To Hickson this must the more have appeared as a definite statement that Mill was himself the author, as they had corresponded a year earlier about the

---

[7] At the time of publication the article appears generally to have been believed to be by Mill, and Charlotte Brontë refers to it as such in a letter dated as early as 20 September 1851, quoted in Mrs. Gaskell's *Life of Charlotte Brontë*, (Everyman edition, p. 344). Mill commented upon it in a letter, presumably to Mrs. Gaskell, saying: 'I am not the author of the article. I may claim to be its editor: and I should be proud to be identified with every thought, every sentiment and every expression in it. The writer is a woman [and the most warmhearted woman], of the largest and most genial sympathies, and the most forgetful of herself in her generous zeal to do honour to others, whom I have ever known' (*The Brontës: Their Lives, Friendships and Correspondence*, eds. T. J. Wise and J. A. Symington (Oxford: Shakespeare Head Press, 1932), vol. 3, p. 278 [note 2]). [The unsigned article appeared in the *Westminster and Foreign Quarterly Review*, 55, July 1851, pp. 289–311, with running titles 'Enfranchisement of *Women*'. It was reprinted in John Stuart Mill, *Dissertations and Discussions* (London: Longman's, Green, Reader, and Dyer, 1858 and later), 2:411–49, and as Appendix C of John Stuart Mill, *Essays on Equality, Law, and Education*, ed. John M. Robson, vol. 21 (1984) of *Collected Works*, under the title 'Harriet Taylor Mill, The Enfranchisement of Women'. In her Introduction to *The Complete Works of Harriet Taylor Mill* [hereafter cited as *Complete Works*], ed. Jo Ellen Jacobs (Bloomington: Indiana University Press, 1998), Jacobs states that this is the 'best known example of Harriet Taylor Mill's writing' (p. 30). The entire introduction to the Mill-Taylor joint products on women's rights is of interest; see *ibid.*, pp. 27–31.—Ed.]

[8] Manuscript in Huntington Library. See also the further letters to Hickson dated 10 and 19 March 1851, and of 19 March 1850, in the same collection. W. E. Hickson (1803–1870) had taken over the *Westminster Review* from Mill in June 1840. [Mill, *Later Letters*, vol. 14 of *Collected Works*, pp. 55–56. Also see the 10 March 1851 letter, p. 56, and the 19 March 1851 letter, pp. 56–57. William Edward Hickson (1803–1870) wrote about education and the labouring poor. He served as editor of the *Westminster Review*. See Mill, *Later Letters*, vol. 14 of *Collected Works*, p. 7, note 1.—Ed.]

possibility of just such an article. It would seem most unlikely that Mill should have used so definite a form of words if he had not at the time himself so regarded it. Hickson appears at first to have answered that there was not likely to be room for the article in the next issue, and when some days later he asked for the manuscript, Mill had not made enough progress and the article had to wait for the July issue.

It was thus fresh from the work on this article that Mill wrote out that formal promise never to claim any rights that the law of marriage would confer on him which has already appeared in Elliot's edition of his letters:[9]

> Being about, if I am so happy as to obtain her consent, to enter into the marriage relation with the only woman I have ever known, with whom I would have entered into that state; & the whole character of the marriage relation as constituted by law being such as both she and I entirely and conscientiously disapprove, for this amongst other reasons, that it confers upon one of the parties to the contract, legal power and control over the person, property, and freedom of action of the other party, independent of her own wishes and will; I, having no means of legally divesting myself of these odious powers (as I most assuredly would do if an engagement to that effect could be made legally binding on me), feel it my duty to put on record a formal protest against the existing law of marriage, in so far as conferring such powers; and a solemn promise never in any case or under any circumstances to use them. And in the event of marriage between Mrs. Taylor and me I declare it to be my will and intention, and the condition of the engagement between us, that she retains in all respects whatever the same absolute freedom of action, and freedom of disposal of herself and of all that does or may at any time belong to her, as if no such marriage had taken place; and I absolutely disclaim and repudiate all pretension to have acquired any *rights* whatever by virtue of such marriage.
>
> 6th March 1851[10]   J. S. Mill

About the same time Mill appears to have informed his family of the intended marriage. It must have been then that his mother and his two unmarried sisters, Clara and Harriet, with whom until then he had been living in Kensington, committed the never to be forgiven offence of not at once calling upon the lady whom until then they had not been allowed to know and to whom they had probably not even dared to allude. Very soon after Mrs.

---

[9] *Letters* (ed. Elliot), vol. 1, p. 158, giving also a facsimile reproduction. [John Stuart Mill, *The Letters of John Stuart Mill*, edited with an Introduction by Hugh S. R. Elliot, two volumes (London: Longmans, Green and Co., 1910). The letter in question appears on 1:158–59.—Ed.]

[10] [The date appears in the printed version at the top of the statement; in the facsimile, it is at the bottom of the statement.—Ed.]

Taylor seems to have left London with her younger son and her daughter for Melcombe Regis whence Mill either accompanied or soon followed them to make final arrangements for the wedding. Back in London on 11 April he acknowledged briefly but in fairly cordial terms the congratulations of his married sisters Willie and Jane.[11] 'No one ever was more to be congratulated than I am', he wrote to the latter and to both he explained that he and his wife will try to find during the summer a suitable house a little way out of London and that they did not expect to set up house before the autumn. But in a letter to his brother George in Madeira, though he provided the invalid with news of political developments at home, he made no allusion to the impending marriage.[12]

A few days later he returned to Dorsetshire for a fortnight's leave around Easter and on Easter Monday, 21 April, the ceremony was performed at the Register Office at Melcombe Regis, apparently in the presence of only Algernon and Helen Taylor, who signed as witnesses. A curious ostensible letter by Mill to his wife, of a somewhat later date, which refers to an incident at the ceremony may be inserted here.

J. S. M. to H. M., 13 July 1852:[13] My dearest wife / Though I am persuaded it is unnecessary for any practical purpose, it will be satisfactory to me to put into writing the explanation of an accidental circumstance connected with the registry of our marriage at the Superintendant Registrar's Office at Weymouth on the 21st of April 1851.—Our marriage by the Registrar Mr. Richards was perfectly regular, and was attested as such by Mr. Richards and by the Superintendant Registrar Mr. Dodson, in the presence of both of whom, as well as of the two witnesses, we signed the register. But I was not aware that it was necessary to sign my name at full length, thinking that as in most

---

[11] Draft of letter to Wilhelmina King, MTColl. XLVII/15, letter to Jane Ferraboschi, Yale University Library [MS 350, Box 1, Folder 4]. [The former appears in Mill, *Later Letters*, vol. 14 of *Collected Works*, p. 61, dated 11 April 1851; the latter bears the same date and appears in *ibid.*, p. 60. Wilhelmina Forbes ('Willie') Mill (1808–1861) was Mill's eldest sister. She married a physician, Dr. King, who soon died, leaving her a widow. See Bain, *John Stuart Mill: A Criticism with Personal Recollections* (London: Longman's, Green, and Co. 1882), p. 43; and Mill, *Later Letters*, vol. 14 of *Collected Works*, p. 61, note 1. Jane Stuart Mill (1816?–1883) was Mill's sister who lived in Paris after she married an Italian banker, Paul Ferraboschi, in 1847. See *ibid.*, p. 6, note 2.—Ed.]

[12] See George [Grote] Mill's letter to Mrs. Mill, quoted below, p. 171, and the quotation from J. S. Mill's letter given in Alexander Bain, *J. S. Mill*, p. 93. [Hayek erroneously lists George Grote Mill's letter as MTColl. XLVII/4; it is correctly XLVII/3. Mill's letter to his brother, George, is published in Mill, *Later Letters*, vol. 14 of *Collected Works*, pp. 59–60, where it is dated 8 April 1851.—Ed.]

[13] [Hayek provides no note containing the source of this letter. It is published in Mill, *Later Letters*, vol. 14 of *Collected Works*, pp. 96–97, with notes that the manuscript resides at Yale, the envelope is addressed to 'Mrs. J. S. Mill / Blackheath Park', and no such marriage ceremony occurred.—Ed.]

other legal documents, the proper signature was the ordinary one of the person signing; and my ordinary signature being J. S. Mill, I at first signed in that manner; but on being told by the Registrar that the name must be written at full length, I did the only thing which occurred to me and what I believe the Registrar suggested, that is, I filled in the remaining letters of my name. As there was not sufficient space for them, they were not only written very small and close, but not exactly in a line with the initials and the surname, and the signature consequently has an unusual appearance. The reason must be at once apparent to any one who sees it, as it is obvious that J. S. Mill was written first, and the remainder filled in afterwards. It is almost superfluous to say that this is not stated for your information—you being as well aware of it as myself, but in order that there may be a statement in existence of the manner in which the signature came to present this unusual appearance. It cannot possibly affect the legality of our marriage, which I have not the smallest doubt is as regular and valid as any marriage can be: but so long as it is possible that any doubt could for a moment suggest itself either to our own or to any other minds, I cannot feel at ease, and therefore, unpleasant as I know it must be to you, I do beg you to let us even now be married again, and this time in a [at] church, so that hereafter no shadow of a doubt on the subject can ever arise. The process is no doubt disagreeable, but I have thought much and anxiously about it, and I have quite made up my mind that however annoying the fact, it is better to undergo the annoyance than to let the matt[er][14] remain as it is. Therefore I hope you will comply with my earnest wish—and the sooner it is done the better.

Your
J. S. Mill

July 13th 1852
Mrs. J. S. Mill, / Blackheath Park

It does not seem that such a further ceremony as Mill suggested actually took place and it is to be hoped that Mrs. Mill laughed him out of his apprehensions.

Mill was back in London a week after the wedding and very soon after this engaged in reading the proofs of the article on the Enfranchisement of Women which was probably completed during the stay at Melcombe Regis.

The marriage led to the most painful episode in Mill's life, his complete break with his mother and her other children. The real cause of this is obscure and it seems to have been almost as unintelligible to his relations as

[14] Page torn. [*Ibid.*, p. 97, concurs with Hayek's choice of word.—Ed.]

to us. Twenty-two years later his sister Harriet still could only say that while 'up to the time of his marriage he had been everything to us [and] it was a frightful blow to lose him at once and for ever, without ~~even a~~ [one] word of explanation,—only in evident anger'.[15] The nearest approach to an account of what happened we get in a letter in which his youngest sister tried a few months after the marriage to remonstrate with Mill against his behaviour towards his mother and the two unmarried sisters in London. Mary Colman was then a young woman of thirty-one and since her marriage four years before was living in the country with her growing family. Her husband Charles Colman seems to have belonged to the Calvinistic sect of Plymouth Brethren and Mary herself to have been at least a devout Christian.[16]

Mary E. Colman to J. S. M.:[17] July 18th 1851 / My dear John / In thinking over the strange change which appears to have taken place in your character, which has taken place in your conduct towards your family, during the last six months whilst striving to feel indifferent towards you, I felt that even now I loved you too much for such indifference, and I trust that a worthier feeling had gained possession of me, when I determined honestly to write and remonstrate with you on your present conduct. Under these circumstances I could not help recalling the letters which you sent me immediately before my marriage, letters which first made me aware that individually I was an object of no interest to you, that you had no affection for me.

Believe me I bear you no resentment for the bitter pangs which this conviction forced on me by yourself gave me; I *never* felt the least resentfully—I thought that I had perhaps been presumptuous that the expressions of kindness which you had been in the habit of using towards me, the uniform kindness you had shown me, I had no right to suppose proceeded from love to myself, but from a *principle* of not giving others needless pain. I *had* wondered sometimes to see you (in a less degree perhaps) kind to others of whom I had heard you speak in a way which had made me know you did not respect them; I however felt assured that this was from the same principle. Although however I felt no

---

[15] Harriet I. Mill to the Rev. J. Crompton, 26 October 1873, at King's College, Cambridge. [JMK/PP/87/20A.]

[16] In a letter of about the same time (in Yale University Library [MS 350, Box 1, Folder 4], dated 27 July 1851) in which Mill's old friend and former colleague at India House, Horace Grant, congratulates him somewhat belatedly on his 'marriage with an amiable woman capable of understanding and appreciating your exertions', he also reports that 'some time ago I saw Mary & her children & thought she looked well & happy. Her exertions in the ragged schools somewhat surprized me,—as she used to be rather timid: but I dare say that the apparition of a beautiful female among a set of young thieves & vagabonds accustomed only to be cuffed about by their superiors, must have been quite that of a ministering angel, & productive of great good'.

[17] MTColl. XLVII/18. Docketed in Mill's hand: 'Mary—a reply August 14, 1851. Her rejoinder August 30'. These have not been preserved.

resentment, I felt less respect, I no longer could feel that you were unerring. I felt that you had been needlessly cruel in your *manner* of telling me this, and that however much I might have disappointed you in other respects the love I bore you even if I had been the dirt under your feet deserved it not——

On recovering a little from the *severe* 'agony' (for I *will* tell you the truth) which your letters gave me, letters which you have probably forgotten but which I have never yet had the courage to reopen, I determined that I would never again love you or any human creature to such a degree as to cause me such grief—But now when I find you acting unworthily towards others, I try to feel that your lowering yourself is nothing to me but in vain (?), and a voice within me urges me at least to endeavour to do you the only service that may ever be in my power to tell you the whole truth.

When Clara left this house December last she was congratulating herself in returning to a home, for some reasons which you know, unpleasant to her, that at least your society your kindness would compensate her for all besides. How great then was my surprise to find that you were behaving in the beginning as if she had affronted you in some way that finally after you had announced your intended marriage your behaviour became more extraordinary still, that in fact Clara was suffering intensely, the truth of which when once stated by herself no one would doubt who knew as you do how undemonstrative and uncomplaining she is by nature.

That you showed no interest in them or their concerns, these were negative, but positive acts of unkindness were not wanting. That at last your presence which used always to bring happiness, had become painful to the last degree——

I ask you now yourself if such conduct is worthy of you—If it would be well if all brothers were to act in the same way. And finally I ask you how you could act so to Clara who valued you not for your reputation or any other advantages which you could bring to her, but for yourself, thoroughly unselfishly. I tell you now and one day you may know yourself that you have cast away a pearl of great price. And for what? What has she done, what has anyone done, what do you allege. I can find nothing except that my mother did not call on your wife the day after you had announced your engagement, the propriety of which step as a matter of Etiquette remains to be settled. Anyhow however you know full well, that if you had only expressed a wish to my Mother on the subject anything would have been done. But even supposing that their behaviour had been bad which I cannot believe was that any justification for yours.

Before your marriage I trusted that anxiety and the absorbing nature of a very strong attachment might account for your appearing to forget or to be utterly indifferent to their feelings though even you must have known what a blank your mere absence would create.

But since your marriage—How bitterly cruel to refuse to see [?][18] at the India House, who if she have faults loved you enough to suffer [much] from such a refusal. Then the farce of your fashionable call, at Kensington and your evident dread lest any of your family should show the least affection for you. It was well for Clara that she felt herself unequal weakened by her passage from France, to see you without exhibiting emotion before your wife, since even I determined as I was not to let your conduct influence me in my conduct towards your wife and steeled as I fancied myself, felt a difficulty in bearing the sensation your iciness struck into me.

Again when Clara determined that your conduct should not make her behave ill to your wife called on her, how did you drive her from your door; and poor little Clara King[19] whom your wife had expressed a wish to see and who went anxious to see Hadji and Lilla about whom her Uncle George had written her. Finally your last letter, how needless an insult, and how unworthy of a man of the least sense, in the first place you knew that your sisters would not lie about your wife and if my Mother has ever erred it has been in speaking so warmly in favour of a person of whom personally she knew nothing, and with regard to the piece of mischievous gossip, which you chose to believe, I should have thought that you, who have already suffered so much from such things ought to have been the last to have given ear to them.

Do not imagine that I attribute to the influence of your wife this conduct of yours. I have none but good feelings towards her, I was no liar when I told you I wished to know her, I had long wished it, before I ever thought of her becoming your wife—Why were you not open with me, why did you not tell me when you answered my letter, that you did not wish that she should know your sisters, you would have spared yourself and your family much pain.

One word more before I close this letter, which may be the last you ever receive from me; As regards the unfortunate estrangement which has taken place between you and George now for some years, and which was increased by some occurrences which took place when I last saw you at Kensington now more than a year ago, you may remember that *I* was the only one who told you you were unjust in your judgment of him, I knew George better than you did, and I told you you were mistaken. I had known George in his unreserved moments and from childhood and although we had never spoken on the subject I felt convinced that had you not yourself destroyed your influence over him, by showing at some time or other that you were ashamed of him and thought nothing of him, did not love him, you might have led him in any direction, so great was his *respect* for you as a man. But you must have shown him that you were afraid of his disgracing *you*. From such a sway

---

[18] ['Helen' is penciled in on the original.—Ed.]
[19] The daughter of Mill's eldest sister, Wilhemina King. [See note 11 above.—Ed.]

he turned away, had you trusted him as a man, with a noble heart and as he deserved, you would never have had occasion to say he 'never had a character'. I should have told you this had I had an opportunity of being with you alone, at that time—I tell it you now because it may be my last opportunity.

And now Good Bye. I have prayed that this letter may touch your heart for we [do] differ 'as you observed' in our opinions or rather say convictions, but this difference has not made me love you less, and in striving each day to become more Christian I feel that I shall love you more really.

I finish a painful task with one last request, urging you by the only feeling that now seems remaining to you, 'your love for your wife' not to throw this from you as coming from one of a family now evidently hateful to you, but to read it through without irritation, judge from what motives it has sprung, and ask yourself if your present course is likely to conduce to her happiness.

Ever your aff^{te} Sister
Mary Elizabeth Colman

PS. If this should close all intercourse between us as I think possible it will be to me very painful, but at least the sting will be wanting of thinking that I have shrunk from the duty of honesty towards you.

Mill's reply to this and a further letter from Mary are not preserved. We may however form some conception of their tone when we see the withering replies which Mrs. Mill and Mill himself addressed to his youngest brother George in Madeira. The latter's letter which caused these retorts seems harmless enough, although we do not have the letter to Haji which accompanied it and which apparently gave the main offence.

George Grote Mill to H. M.:[20] Funchal May 20th 1851 / Dear Madam, / Though I have only heard at second hand, of your recent marriage with my brother, and know nothing certain except the bare fact, I will not pass over such an event in silence. My brother wrote to me a letter by the mail of April 9th but not a word wrote he then, had he written before, or has he written since of what I can only conclude he must have thought me either uninterested in, or undeserving to know. I don't know therefore what change your union will make in your mode of life, if any. It would give me the greatest pleasure to hear that J. was free of the tether which binds him to the City & *you* to the neighbourhood of London. Twenty-five years work at the I. House, believe me, is as much as any man can well bear. I fear his generosity in money matters, has made his leaving the office difficult, but surely with

[20] MTColl. XLVII/3. [Hayek lists this as XLVII/4.—Ed.]

171

his power of work & established reputation, he could earn enough money by writing for the press much more easily & with much greater advantage to others than by his present employment. I believe his work already published would have given him an income if he had not made such easy bargains with his publishers.

I have not heard how your health is since I saw you in person & though I then thought you looking much stronger than when I had seen you last, you complained of it: pray let me hear sometime or other. If you feel in me any part of the interest which I feel in you all, you will not leave me in entire darkness.

My own health continues pretty good. I am prosecuting the silk business, though it advances slowly towards a profitable conclusion. In the ~~meantime~~ [meanwhile] I am endeavouring to earn a little money by writing. I have a long art. in the last No. of the British Quarterly (on volcanoes & earthquakes) but there is nothing original in it.

Believe me / dear Mrs Taylor (I can't forget the old name)

Yours affect^ly
Geo G. Mill

As I don't know your present address I send this to Cross St.[21] I am writing to Hadjy. / Kind regards to Lily.

H. M. to George Grote Mill, Richmond, 5 July 1851.[22] I do not answer your letter because you deserve it—that you certainly do not—but because tho I am quite inexperienced in the best way of receiving or replying to an affront[23] I think that in this as in all things, frankness and plain speaking are the best rule, [&] as to me they are the most natural—also it is best that every one should speak for themselves. Your letters to me & to Haji must be regarded as one, being on the same subject & sent together to us. In my opinion they show want of truth modesty & justice to say little[24] of good breeding or good nature which you appear to regard as very unnecessary qualities.

Want of justice is shown in suggesting that a person has probably acted ~~in~~ without regard to their principles which principles you say you never

---

[21] The address of the firm David Taylor & Sons.

[22] Draft in MTColl. XLVII/17, dated as above and endorsed in same hand 'copied July 16 1851'. [Hayek lists this as XLVII/5. Harriet Taylor Mill, *Complete Works*, pp. 433–34, has the letter 'dated 5 July 1851', and states it is likely 'a draft response' to George.—Ed.]

[23] [Harriet strikes out 'intentional': 'to ~~intentional~~ an affront'; Harriet Taylor Mill, *Complete Works*, p. 433.—Ed.]

[24] [Harriet strikes out 'not': '~~not~~ to say little'; *ibid.*.—Ed.]

heared.[25] Want of modesty in passing judgment on a person thus far unknown to you—want of everything like truth in professing as you do [&] liking and value[26] for a person who in the same note you avoid calling[27] by their name [& say not the fancy Dear Madam so][28] using an unfriendly designation after having for years addressed[29] them in to say the least a more friendly way.[30] In fact want of truth is apparent in the whole, as your letters overflow[31] with anger & animosity about a circumstance[32] which in no way concerns you so far [as] anything you say shows & which if there was any truth in your profession of regard w^d be a subject of satisfaction to you. As to want of the good breeding which is the result of good feeling that appears to be a family failing.[33]

The only small satisfaction your letter can give is the observation that when people desert good feeling they also are deserted by good sense—your wish to make a quarrel[34] with your brother & myself because we have used[35] a right which the whole world, of whatever shade of opinion, accords to us, is as[36] absurd as unjust and wrong.

Harriet Mill

Possibly this letter was never sent and the following of Mill's dispatched instead.

J. S. M. to George Grote Mill, India House, 4 August 1851:[37] I have long ceased to be surprised at any want of good sense or good manners in what proceeds from you—you appear to be too thoughtless or too ignorant to be capable of either—but such want of good feeling, together with such arrogant assumption, as are shown in your letters to my wife & to Haji I was not prepared for. The best construction that can be put upon them is that you really

---

[25] [*Ibid.* supplies 'heared'; Hayek has a query here with no word offered.   Ed.]

[26] [*Ibid.* supplies 'and value'; Hayek has a query with no word offered.   Ed.]

[27] [*Ibid.* supplies 'you ~~impudently refuse to call~~ avoid calling'.   Ed.]

[28] [*Ibid.* supplies '~~say not the fancy Dear Madam to~~'.—Ed.]

[29] [*Ibid.* supplies 'after having ~~been in the habit of~~ for years addressed'.—Ed.]

[30] [*Ibid.* supplies 'friendly ~~designation~~ way'.—Ed.]

[31] [*Ibid.* supplies 'as ~~personally your~~ letters overflow'.—Ed.]

[32] [*Ibid.*, p. 433, supplies 'about ~~an affair~~ a circumstance'.—Ed.]

[33] [*Ibid.*, p. 433, supplies 'failing ~~and must perharps should be excused in persons who have little other family feeling to boast of~~'.   Ed.]

[34] [Hayek has a query beside 'quarrel'.—Ed.]

[35] [Harriet Taylor Mill, *Complete Works*, p. 434, supplies 'we have ~~assumed~~ used'.—Ed.]

[36] [*Ibid.* supplies 'is ~~certainly~~ as'.—Ed.]

[37] Draft in MTColl. XLVII/20. There is also another even more violent and probably earlier draft, *ibid.*, XLVII/19. [Hayek lists the draft as MTColl. XLVII/45. The letter is published in Mill, *Later Letters*, vol. 14 of *Collected Works*, pp. 73–75. See p. 75, note 3, for the draft.—Ed.]

do not know what insolence & presumption are: or you would not write such letters & seem to expect to be as well liked as before by those to whom & of whom they are written. You were 'surprised,' truly, at our marriage & do not 'know enough of the circumstances to be able to form an opinion on the subject'. Who asks you to form an opinion? An opinion on what? Do men usually when they marry consult the opinion of a brother twenty years younger than themselves? or at my age of any brother or person at all? But though you form no 'opinion' you presume to catechize Haji respecting his mother, & to call her to account before your tribunal for the conformity between her conduct & her principles—being at the same time, as you say yourself, totally ignorant what your principles are. On the part of any one who avowedly does not know what her principles are, the surmise that she may have acted contrary to them is a gratuitous impertinence. To every one who knows her it would be unnecessary to say that she has, in this as in all things, acted according to her principles. What imaginary principles are they which should prevent people who have known each other the greater part of their lives, during which her & Mr. Taylor's house has been more a home to me than any other, and who agree perfectly in all their opinions, from marrying?

You profess to have taken great offence because you knew of our intended marriage 'only at second hand'. People generally hear of marriages at 'second hand', I believe. If you mean that I did not write to you on the subject, I do not know any reason you had to expect that I should. I informed your mother & sisters who I knew would inform you—& I did not tell them of it on account of any right they had to be informed, for my relations with any of them have been always of too cool & distant a kind to give them the slightest right or reason to expect anything more than ordinary civility from me—& when I did tell them I did not receive ordinary civility in return. In the dissertation on my character with which you favour Haji, you shew yourself quite aware that it has never been my habit to talk to them about my concerns—& assuredly the feelings you have shown to me in the last two or three years have not been so friendly as to give me any cause for making an exception. As for the 'mystery' which on my father's authority you charge me with, if we are to bandy my father's sayings I could cite plenty of them about all his family except the younger ones, compared with which this is very innocent. It could be said at all but as a half joke—& every one has a right to be mysterious if they like. But I have not been mysterious, for I had never anything to be mysterious about. I have not been in the habit of talking unasked about my friends, or indeed about any other subject.

J. S. M.

A similar letter appears to have descended on George Mill from Algernon Taylor and a paragraph of his reply to it explains a little further the expressions which had given so much offence.

> *George Grote Mill to Algernon Taylor; Funchal, 27 September 1851:*[38] Believing that your mother would generally rather discourage than encourage the marriage of others I certainly was at first surprised to find her giving so deliberate an example of marriage in her own case; in which moreover there seemed to me less to be gained than in almost any marriage I could think of. I certainly took sufficient interest in both parties to wish to solve the matter in my own mind & fancied (erroneously it now appears) that I might express my feelings to you without giving offence; but you have placed yourself on stilts & decline all confidential intercourse; so the matter ends. As your letter alludes chiefly to your mother I must observe that you ought to know that I am quite incapable of being impertinent to her, a charge which I think you might leave her to make when she finds any impertinence in my letters to her.

Here this particular correspondence presumably ended and there was probably little more intercourse between J. S. Mill or his wife and young George Mill until three years later the latter put an end to his life shortly before he would inevitably have died of consumption. But his sisters Clara and Harriet in London and Mary Colman, urged on by their mother, continued their efforts at a reconciliation.

> *Clara Esther Mill to J. S. M.:*[39] Westbourne Park Villa March 3ᵈ [1852] / Dear John / I am [was] sorry to hear from my Mother that you considered I had been wanting in civility to Mʳˢ. Mill, I certainly never meant to be so, nor indeed do I think I have, though it is evident that you have had a strong impression that such was the case with the family ever since your marriage— quite erroneously however I believe. I am entirely at a loss to imagine in what my incivility has consisted. I (and I alone of those in this house) have seen your correspondence with Mary & George in which you state clearly enough your opinions of us all, and that there are some of us, myself among the rest, whom you hold in the same estimation as my father did. I [We] cannot therefore be the acquaintance of a person who 'only deserves common civility from you' which you seek for your wife, especially as you do it not on the score of relationship. What then am I to understand? You are, to use George's words 'a great and good man' and you see farther than I do. I do not therefore pretend to judge you, I only cannot understand you, but under

[38] MTColl. XLVII/21.
[39] MTColl. XLVII/22.

such circumstances to have any personal intercourse with you, could only be painful, and tho' I by no means admit that I deserve your contempt, I do not conceive that my acquaintance can be of any importance to your wife. We did not seek each other's acquaintance before her marriage nor ever should have done so—on what ground then begin it now?

This may after all not be the subject of your complaint—nor is it of much consequence, we have failed to understand each other in an apparent intimacy of 40 years it is therefore a hopeless case, and with sorrow but most decidedly I wish to give up ~~the~~ [this] appearance.

C. E. Mill

After drafting a reply to this[40] Mill seems to have confined himself to answer it and a similar note from his sister Harriet in a brief letter to his mother.

J. S. M. to Mrs. James Mill, India House, 5 March 1852:[41] My dear Mother / I received yesterday two most silly notes from Clara & Harriet filled with vague accusations. They say that when you called at the I.H. on Monday I 'complained to you of their incivility to my wife'. I did no such thing.[42] Another charge is that I repeated idle gossip in a note to you last summer— this is untrue. George Fletcher called at the I.H. a day or two before I wrote that note to you & asked after my wife saying he was sorry to hear she was not well. I asked where he had heard that; he said he was told so at Kensington, & this I mentioned in my note to you: no one else had anything to do with it. This was not 'gossip'.

I hope you are not the worse for your journey to I.H.

Y^{rs} aff^y
J. S. M.

---

[40] MTColl. XLVII/23. [Hayek lists the reply as XLVII/24 but the MTColl reports that the reply is on the reverse of 23: 'On reverse of folio 52 is an undated, and now almost obliterated draft in pencil of a letter from JSM, possibly a reply to item 22 above. Folios 53 and 54 bear a (perhaps not exact) transcription of the draft by Harriet Mill's granddaughter, Mary Taylor. ff. 52–54'.—Ed.]

[41] MTColl. XLVII/23. [The letter is published in Mill, *Later Letters*, vol. 14 of *Collected Works*, p. 83.—Ed.]

[42] [The page is torn here. Mill, *Later Letters*, vol. 14 of *Collected Works*, p. 83, supplies '[& . . . no such things]'.—Ed.]

NINE

ILLNESS
1851–1854

It was probably only after their return from a holiday in France and Belgium in September 1851 that Mill and his wife set up house together. Blackheath Park, where they had taken a house, was then still a rural district at the outskirts of London and the house itself facing 'a wide open space of rolling meadow bounded far off by a blue outline of distant hills'.[1] It was accessible from London only by railway and, although Mill made the daily train journey to the City, this placed them effectively outside the social contacts of the metropolis. The efforts of some old friends, such as Lord Ashburton,[2] to make the marriage the occasion for drawing them back into social life, proved

---

[1] *Letters of Charles Eliot Norton*, eds. Sara Norton and M. A. de Wolfe Howe (London: Constable & Co., 1913), vol. 1, p. 330.

[2] See Lord Ashburton's letter to Mill in Yale University Library [Box 1, Folder 4]:

Bath House / May 26, 51 / My dear Mill / I have promised Lady Ashburton to write to you, & I execute my promise most readily, for I should be sorry that you had reason to think, that we could overlook the occurrence in your life, which must add so much [to its repose and happiness].

We rejoice at it also on our account. We hope to gain by the change as well as yourself. We feel sure [assured] that you will live no longer [live] for your books alone, that you will allow some human sympathies to have access to your thoughts.

It is possible that you may then be forced to remember that there were once certain friends, who thought that they had a hold over you, who thought themselves as necessary to you as you are to them.

Now these friends, no wise daunted by former ill success, are very anxious to gain over M^rs. Mill to their side, and I must say that it would be most unfair if you did not give them an early opportunity of doing so. We will therefore allow you no subterfuge of any kind, no means of escape from this your destiny.

It is written that on some day this month, or an [on some] early [day] of [the] next, you will either tell us where we may call on M^rs. Mill, or you will appoint a time when you will bring M^rs. Mill to call here.

Hear and obey. The fates have willed it. / Yrs, / Ashburton.

[William Bingham Baring, 2nd Baron Ashburton (1799–1864), was a statesman. His wife, Lady Harriet, was Thomas Carlyle's friend. See *The Later Letters of John Stuart Mill, 1849–1873*, eds. Francis E. Mineka and Dwight N. Lindley, vols. 14–17 (1972) of *The Collected Works of John Stuart Mill* [hereafter cited as *Collected Works*] (Toronto: University of Toronto Press, 1962–1991), 14:203, note 5.—Ed.]

unavailing, while others appear deliberately to have omitted even the ordinary courtesy calls.[3] Their only guests, usually for weekends, seem to have been a few old friends such as W. J. Fox and his daughter or an occasional foreign scholar. Even fairly close friends of the period, such as the philosopher Alexander Bain, apparently were never asked to Blackheath Park during Mrs. Mill's life, and Mill himself never went into society, except six or seven times a year to the meetings of the Political Economy Club where he frequently opened the discussions.[4] The other members of the household were Mrs. Mill's two younger children, Algernon and Helen Taylor. Her elder son, Herbert, who had taken over his father's business, remained in town and appears to have married soon afterwards.

Of the daily routine of the life at Blackheath Park we get a glimpse in a passage of a letter by Helen Taylor to her mother written a few years later at the beginning of her first prolonged absence.

> *Helen Taylor to H. M., Newcastle, 27 November 1856:*[5] I like to think [at] about nine o'clock that you are talking with him. I feel very unhappy at three because you are at dinner and I am not there to help you. I grow impatient at five because he has not come in but at six it is pleasant to think that he is making tea and you have got my letter [which he has brought home].

A different recollection by Algernon Taylor which shows Mill in a little known role may also be given a place here:

> Mr. Mill, who used, now and then, to perform on the piano, but only when asked to do so by my mother; and then he would at once sit down to the instrument, and play music entirely of his own composition, on the spur of the moment: music of a singular character, wanting, possibly, in the finish which more practice would have imparted, but rich in feeling, vigour, and suggestiveness: the performer taking for his theme, may be, the weird grandeur of cloud and storm, the deep pathos of a dirge, the fierce onset

---

[3] See John Chapman's Diary in Gordon S. Haight, *George Eliot and John Chapman* (New Haven: Yale University Press, 1940), pp. 169–70, under the date of 24 May 1851: 'Mrs Hennell says that the lady he [Mill] has just married was a widow, her husband having been dead for a year and a half, that during the life of her former husband a "violent friendship" arose between her and him which caused him to think it desirable to go to the Continent wither she, it is said, followed him; and now (in consequence of these circumstances she presumes) Mrs Thornton Hunt declines to visit M^r and Mrs Mill'. [Hayek supplies the name in brackets.—Ed.]

[4] *Political [Economy] Club, Minutes and Proceedings*, vol. 6, Centenary Volume (London: Macmillan, 1921), pp. 65–68, from which it appears that Mill opened the discussion at six of the twenty meetings of the Club held in the years 1851–1853.

[5] MTColl. LI/[13]. [Hayek mistakenly dates this letter 23 November 1856. The phrase in brackets is Hayek's addition.—Ed.]

of the battlefield, or the triumphant, joyous time of a processional march. When he had finished, my mother would, perhaps, enquire what had been the idea running in his mind, and which had formed the theme of the improvisation—for such it was, and a strikingly characteristic one too.[6]

The quiet and retired life to which Mill and his wife had hoped to settle down did not long remain undisturbed, however. Probably even the first two years, for which we have practically no documents, were clouded by ill health. But these years were still a time of fairly normal activities. Of the very small amount of publications listed by Mill for this period it is stated of an article in the *Morning Chronicle* of 28 August 1851, on the need for protection of wives and children from brutal husbands and fathers, that 'like all my newspaper articles on similar subjects, and most of my articles on all subjects, [it] was a joint production with my wife';[7] and with regard to the small pamphlet on the same subject printed for private distribution in 1853[8] the same list says: 'In this I acted chiefly as amanuensis to my wife'. Of Mill's only major publication of these years, the article on 'Whewell's Moral Philosophy', which he contributed to the *Westminster Review,* with its strong attack on Whewell's intuitionist theory of morals, we can at least be certain that it had Mrs. Mill's full sympathy. During the seven and a half years between their marriage and Mrs. Mill's death only one other more substantial article appeared, the article on Grote's *History of Greece* to which we shall have to refer presently. Most of what he wrote then appeared only at a later date.

The first major task to which the Mills turned after commencing life at Blackheath Park was the thorough revision of the *Political Economy* for the third

[6] Algernon Taylor, *Memories of a Student,* 2nd edition enlarged (London: Simpkin, Marshall, Hamilton, Kent and Co., 1895—a first edition had been printed for private circulation only), pp. 10–11. Algernon Taylor adds that after Mill's death 'a musical paper—the "Musical Standard", if I remember right drew attention to his considerable, if little known, musical taste and capacity' [p. 12]. Later in the same volume (p. 233) mention is made of the fact that Mill also played chess well.

[7] MacMinn, *et al., Bibliography,* p. 76. [Hayek added the word in brackets. Mill describes this as 'a leading article in the Morning Chronicle of August 28th 1851, on some cases on wife murder. This, like all my newspaper articles on similar subjects, and most of my articles on all subjects, was a joint production with my wife'. The article is republished in John Stuart Mill, *Newspaper Writings,* eds. Ann P. Robson and John M. Robson, vols. 22–25 (1986) of *Collected Works,* 25:1183–86, with co-authorship assigned. It also appears in *The Complete Works of Harriet Taylor Mill* [hereafter cited as *Complete Works*], ed. Jo Ellen Jacobs (Bloomington: Indiana University Press, 1998), pp. 123–26, which assigns co-authorship.—Ed.]

[8] *Remarks on Mr. Fitzroy's Bill for the more effectual Prevention of Assaults on Women and Children.* Privately printed 1853. See MacMinn, *et al., Bibliography,* p. 79. [The pamphlet is republished in John Stuart Mill, *Essays on Equality, Law, and Education,* ed. John M. Robson, vol. 21 (1984) of *Collected Works,* pp. 101–8, with joint authorship assigned, and in Harriet Taylor Mill, *Complete Works,* pp. 126–31, where joint authorship is assigned.—Ed.]

edition which appeared in the spring of 1852. It is the most comprehensive revision the book underwent and represents a considerable further advance towards socialism. But as they were together at the time we have no documents to show us the part Mrs. Mill took in the task.

In 1853 not only Mrs. Mill's health, which had been precarious so long, was decidedly deteriorating, but Mill himself was also showing increasing signs of serious illness. Towards the end of August he took his wife to Sidmouth in Devonshire, where she stayed for a short period while Mill returned to his work at India House. Of the five of Mill's letters to her written to Sidmouth which are extant,[9] one may be given in full.

J. S. M. to H. M.: India House / Aug. 30, 1853 / This is the first time since we were married my darling wife that we have been separated & I do not like it at all—but your letters are the greatest delight & as soon as I have done reading one I begin thinking how soon I shall have another. Next to her letters the greatest pleasure I have is writing to her. I have written every day since Friday [August 26][10] except the day there was no post—I am glad the cause of your not getting Saturday's letter was the one I guessed & that you did get it at last. This time I have absolutely nothing to tell except my thoughts, & those are wholly of you. As for occupation, after I get home I read as long as I can at the thick book[11]—yesterday evening I fairly fell asleep over it, but I shall read it to the end, for I always like to get to the latest generalizations on any scientific subject & that in particular is a most rapidly progressive subject just at present & is so closely connected with the subjects of mind & feeling that there is always a chance of something practically useful turning up. I am very much inclined to take the Essay on Nature[12] again

---

[9] Four of these letters, dated 26, 29, 31 August and September 1853, are in Yale University Library and one, undated but probably of 27 August, in MTColl. II/305. All the letters by Mill to his wife quoted in this chapter are in Yale University Library [MS 350, Box 1, Folder 4]. [These are published in Mill, *Later Letters*, vol. 14 of *Collected Works*, pp. 108–13, which dates the letters 24 August 1853, 27 August 1853?, 29 August 1853, and 30 August 1853. Hayek assigned the final letter in this group, below, a 29 August date. See Mill, *Later Letters*, vol. 14 of *Collected Works*, p. 111, note 2.—Ed.]

[10] [The brackets and date are supplied by Hayek.—Ed.]

[11] Described earlier as 'the big physiology'. [Mill, *Later Letters*, vol. 14 of *Collected Works*, p. 108, note 3, states that this is likely William Benjamin Carpenter's *Principles of Human Physiology*, 4th ed. (London, 1853).—Ed.]

[12] Evidently the essay on 'Nature' published posthumously in 1874 as part of the volume *Nature, the Utility of Religion, and Theism* (London: Longmans, Green, Reader, and Dyer, 1874), but in 1853 intended to form part of a volume of essays on which Mill was working and out of which ultimately *On Liberty, Utilitarianism* and perhaps some other of his later works grew. [The essays on religion are published in John Stuart Mill, *Essays on Ethics, Religion, and Society*, ed. John M. Robson, vol. 10 (1985) of *Collected Works*, pp. 373–402.—Ed.]

in hand & rewrite it as thoroughly as I did the review of Grote[13]—that is what it wants—it is my old way of working & I do not think I have ever done anything well which was not done in that way. I am almost sorry about the engagement with Lewis[14] about India as I think it would have been a much better employment of the time to have gone on with some of our Essays. We must finish the best we have got to say, & not only that, but publish it while we are alive—I do not see what living depository there is likely to be of our thoughts, or who in this weak generation that is growing up will even be capable of thoroughly mastering & assimilating your ideas, much less of reoriginating them—so we must write them & print them, & then they can wait till there are again thinkers. But I shall never be satisfied unless you allow ou[r][15] best book, the book which is to come, to have our *two* names on the title page. It ought to be so with everything I publish, for the better half of it all is yours, but the book which will contain our best thoughts, if it has only one name to it, that should be yours. I should like everyone to know that I am the Dumont & you the originating mind, the Bentham, bless her!

I hope the weather has improved as much with you as it has here—but it does not look settled yet—with all loving thoughts & wishes

J. S. Mill

In signing this letter with his full name Mill departed for once from an almost invariable practice of himself and his wife, whose letters to each other generally lacked both the usual commencement and signature.

As Mrs. Mill's health apparently had not improved at Sidmouth and Mill's condition was getting worse, they were soon after ordered abroad by their doctor. Mill obtained leave of absence for the last three months of the year, which they spent at Nice. Although they themselves long refused to believe it, they were evidently both in fairly advanced states of consumption and this appears to have been sufficiently apparent to Mill's friends at India House to make them doubt whether they would ever see him again. At Nice Mrs. Mill had a severe hæmorrhage of which she nearly died and Mill's own symptoms continued to get worse, but he still tried to convince himself that it was not the fatal 'family disease', as he calls it in the *Autobiography*, of which his father and two of his brothers had died.[16] At the end of the year he even

---

[13] The review of volumes 9–11 of G. Grote's *History of Greece* on which Mill had spent much time during the summer in which it appeared in the *Edinburgh Review* for October.

[14] George Cornewall Lewis (1806–1863), editor of the *Edinburgh Review* from 1852 to 1855. [Lewis was a statesman and an author and, at the time of this letter, was Undersecretary of State for the Home Department, Mill, *Later Letters*, vol. 14 of *Collected Works*, p. 34, note 1.—Ed.]

[15] Page torn by seal. [Hayek supplies the brackets and completes the word.—Ed.]

[16] The youngest brother, George, actually had died a few months before in Madeira, by his own hand, thereby anticipating but a little the termination of the disease for which he had vainly

returned to London and his work at India House after he had taken Mrs. Mill to Hyères where she was to stay until the beginning of the spring. All but two of the thirty-eight carefully numbered letters written by Mill to her during this period have been preserved. They give a minute picture of the progressive deterioration of his health during the next few months. Of Mrs. Mill's penciled notes which he received in reply we have only one, because Mill burnt all the others at her request.

Mill's return to London in the middle of the winter took him almost ten days and must have put no small strain on the invalid. First by diligence to Marseilles, then by train to Avignon and again by diligence and omnibus to Lyons and Chalons, and finally with, the railroad to Paris and Boulogne; he had the extra misfortune of being snowed up in the train for twenty-four hours on the last lap of this journey. The first letter from London, written on the day of his arrival, reports on the return home and to India House.

J. S. M. to H. M., India House, 6 January 1854: [Ellice][17] as well as Hill, Thornton & others asked the questions that might be expected about your health & in a manner which shewed interest—Peacock[18] alone asked not a single question about your health & hardly about mine but struck into India House subjects & a visit he had from James.[19] Grote & Prescott[20] called together today, as they said to enquire ~~whether~~ [if] I was returned & [were] very warm, especially Grote, in their expressions of sympathy & interest about your illness. It is odd to see the sort of fragmentary manner in which news gets about—Grote had heard of you as dangerously ill but not of my being ill at all, & of your illness as a fever but not of the rupture of a bloodvessel. Grote is vastly pleased with the article in the Edinburgh—[&] a propos I found here a letter from Mrs Grote, of complimentation on the article, which though little worthy of the honour of being sent to you I may as well inclose. The impudence of writing to me at all & of writing in such a manner is only matched by the excessive conceit of the letter. Grote alluded to it saying that

---

sought a cure. [Mill refers to the 'family disease' on p. 247 of John Stuart Mill, *Autobiography and Literary Essays*, eds. John M. Robson and Jack Stillinger, vol. 1 (1981) of *Collected Works.*—Ed.]

[17] [Hayek supplies the brackets and the name.—Ed.]

[18] Russell Ellice was then Chairman of the Court of Directors and David Hill and W. T. Thornton (1813–1880) officials of the East India Company, as was also Thomas Love Peacock (1785–1866), the novelist, who from 1836 to 1856 was head of the Examiner's Department, in which post Mill succeeded him. [Ellice was a Director of the East India Company from 1831 to 1873 and Chairman from 1853 to 1854. See Mill, *Later Letters*, vol. 14 of *Collected Works*, p. 122, note 4. The full letter is published in *ibid.*, pp. 122–23.—Ed.]

[19] J. S. Mill's younger brother, recently returned from India.

[20] William George Prescott [1800–1865], George Grote's partner in the banking firm of Prescott, Grote & Co., and one of the three original members of the Utilitarian Society.

Mrs Grote had written to me after reading the article—I merely answered that I had found a note from her on arriving.

Two days later Mill commenced the 'experiment' of trying to note down in a little book 'at least one thought per day which is worth writing down'. These notes, which he continued during the whole period of his wife's absence, have been printed in full forty years ago.[21] But as some of them gain new significance and poignancy from the knowledge of the circumstances under which they were written, some passages from this 'diary' will be reproduced here together with the extracts from the letters.

J. S. M.'s Diary, 9 January 1854: What a sense of protection is given by the consciousness of being loved, and what an additional sense, over and above this, by being near the one by whom one is and wishes to be loved the best. I have experience at present of both these things; for I feel as if no really dangerous illness could actually happen to me while I have her to care for me; and yet I feel as if by coming away from her I had parted with a kind of talisman, and was more open to the attacks of the enemy than while I was with her.[22]

J. S. M. to H. M., India House, 9 January 1854:[23] The Kensington letters I inclose, as it is best you should see all that comes from that quarter—& along with them a note I have just written to my mother. I have looked through the Edinburgh Review for October—the article on Grote reads, to my mind, slighter & flimsier than I thought it would. There is another article by Greg on Parl^y reform[24] shewing that he had seen our letter to Ld Monteagle[25] (the

---

[21] *Letters* (ed. Elliot), vol. 2, pp. 357–86. [Republished in John Stuart Mill, *Journals and Debating Speeches*, ed. John M. Robson, vols. 26–27 (1988) of *Collected Works*, 27:639–68.—Ed.]

[22] [Mill, *Letters* (ed. Elliot), vol. 2, p. 357.—Ed.]

[23] [The letter is published in Mill, *Later Letters*, vol. 14 of *Collected Works*, pp. 125–26.—Ed.]

[24] 'Parliamentary Purification' in *Edinburgh Review*, vol. XCVIII/200 [October 1853], pp. 566–624, presumably by William Rathbone Greg (1809–1881), who in the preceding years had regularly written for this Review on similar subjects. [Mill, *Earlier Letters*, vol. 14 of *Collected Works*, p. 126, note 10, confirms Hayek's attribution to Greg. W. R. Greg (1809–1881) was a political economist who opposed the Corn Laws. With Francis Galton, he co-founded the eugenics movement. See Sandra J. Peart and David M. Levy, *The 'Vanity of the Philosopher': From Equality to Hierarchy in Post-Classical Economics* (Ann Arbor. University of Michigan Press, 2005).—Ed.]

[25] This letter to Lord Monteagle, dated 20 March 1853, and acknowledging his pamphlet on the Representation of Minorities, is printed in *Letters* (ed. Elliot), vol. 1, p. 173[–75]. [Thomas Spring Riche (1770–1866), first Baron Monteagle of Brandon (1839), was a contributor to the *Edinburgh Review*. From 1820 to 1839 he served as a Member of Parliament, and from 1835 to 1839 he was Chancellor of the Exchequer. Mill's letter to Monteagle is republished in Mill, *Later Letters*, vol. 14 of *Collected Works*, pp. 101–3.—Ed.]

one Marshall writes about)[26] for he has adopted nearly every idea in the letter almost in the very words, & has also said speaking of the ballot, that it is
within his knowledge that some to whom ballot was once a sine qua non, now
think it would be 'a step backward' the very phrase of the letter. He goes on
to attack the ballot with arguments some of them so exactly the same as those
in our unpublished pamphlet[27] (even to the illustrations) that one would think
he had seen that too if it had been physically possible. Though there are some
bad arguments mixed yet on the whole this diminishes my regret that ours was
not published. It is satisfactory that those letters we ~~took~~ [take] so much trouble
to write for some apparently small purpose,[28] so often turn out more useful
than we expected. Now, about reviewing Comte:[29] the reasons *pro* are evident.
Those *con* are, 1st I don't like to have anything to do with the name or with any
publication of H. Martineau. 2dly. the Westr though it will allow I dare say anything else, could not allow me to speak freely about Comte's atheism & I do
not see how it is possible to be just to him, when there is so much to attack,
without giving him praise on that ~~part~~ [point] of the subject. 3dly, as Chapman
is the publisher he doubtless wishes, & expects, an article more laudatory on
the whole, than I shd be willing to write. You dearest one will tell me what your
perfect judgment & your feeling decide.

J. S. M. to H. M., Blackheath Park, 16 January 1854:[30] About Mrs. Grote's
letter,[31] my darling is I daresay right. It did not escape me that there was
that amende, & I should have felt much more indignant if there had not.
But what was to my feelings like impudent, though impudent is not exactly
the right word, was, that after the things she has said & done respecting us,
she should imagine that a tardy sort of recognition of you, & flattery to me,

---

[26] [According to Mill, *Later Letters*, vol. 14 of *Collected Works*, pp. 101–2, note 2, the paper is
Minorities and Majorities: Their Relative Rights, A Letter to the Lord John Russell on Parliamentary Reform,
by James Garth Marshall, published later in 1854. Marshall was Lord Monteagle's son-in-
law.—Ed.]

[27] Probably the pamphlet *Thoughts on Parliamentary Reform*, published only in 1859, but according to Bain, *J. S. Mill* (p. 103), 'written some years previously'.

[28] [Hayek has a query here; the *Later Letters* republication confirms his transcription.]

[29] Among the correspondence Mill had found on his return was a request from John Chapman, then the editor of the *Westminster Review*, that Mill should review Harriet Martineau's
abridged translation of Comte's *Positive Philosophy* published by John Chapman in 1853. [See
Mill's letters to Chapman, dated 29 September 1851 and 17 October 1851, in Mill, *Later Letters*,
vol. 14 of *Collected Works*, pp. 76–77, 79.—Ed.]

[30] [The letter is published in Mill, *Later Letters*, vol. 14 of *Collected Works*, pp. 132–34.—Ed.]

[31] [Mill describes the letter from Mrs. Grote in a 6 January letter to Harriet: 'I found here a
letter from Mrs Grote, of complementation on the article, which though little worthy of the honour of being sent to you I may as well inclose. The impudence of writing to me at all & of writing in such a manner is only matched by the excessive conceit of the letter'. Mill, *Later Letters*, vol.
14 of *Collected Works*, p. 123.—Ed.]

would serve to establish some sort of relation between us & her.[32] It strikes me as déplacé to answer the letter, especially so long after it was written—but her having made this amende might make the difference of my asking how she is, at least when he mentions her. That is about as much, I think, as her good intentions deserve.—I will, dear, say to Grote what she wishes & the best opportunity will be the first time he writes a note to me in that form. I do not, and have not for years, addressed him as *Mr*—& it is very dull of him not to have taken the hint. I am getting on with India house work but the arrear will take me a long time—I worked at it at home all yesterday (Sunday) & got through a good deal. Sunday, alas, is not so different from other days as when she is here—though more so than when I am quite with her. I am reacting, in the evenings, as I said I would do, Sismondi's Italian Republics[33] which I read last in 1838, before going to Italy. Having seen many of the places since makes it very interesting.

1. H. 17th. This morning I watched the loveliest dawn & sunrise & felt that I was looking directly to where she is & that that sun came straight from her. And now here is the Friday's letter which comes from her in a still more literal sense. I am so happy that the cough is better & that she is in better spirits. How kindly she writes about the keys, never mind darling. I have bought one set of flannels since. I am glad she likes the note to Sykes. As for Chapman's request, the *pro* was the great desire I feel to atone for the overpraise I have given Comte[34] & to let it be generally known to those who know me what I think on the unfavourable side about him. The reason that the objection which you feel so strongly & which my next letter afterwards will have shown that I felt too, did not completely decide the matter with me, was that Chapman did not want a review of this particular book, but of *Comte* & I could have got rid of H. M.'s part in a sentence, perhaps without even naming her I shd certainly have put Comte's own book at the head along with hers & made all the references to *it*. But malgré cela I disliked the connexion & now I dislike it still more, & shall at once write to C. to refuse—putting the delay of an answer upon my long absence so that he may not think I hesitated.

[32] [Harriet and John believed that Mrs. Grote had spread gossip concerning them prior to their marriage. See *Later Letters*, vol. 14 of *Collected Works*, p. 133, note 4.—Ed.]

[33] [Mill, *Later Letters*, vol. 14 of *Collected Works*, p. 133, note 5, supplies J. C. L. Simonde de Sismondi, *Histoire des Républiques italiennes du moyen âge* (16 vols., Paris, 1809 1818), and notes that the English translation, *A History of the Italian Republics, Being a View of the Origin, Progress and Fall of Italian Freedom* (London, 1832), was part of *Lardner's Cabinet Encyclopedia* (133 vols., London, 1830–1849).—Ed.]

[34] [In Mill's *Logic*, Book 6, 'On the Logic of Moral Sciences', especially in the first edition. There, Mill writes of Comte: 'M. Comte alone, among the new historical school, has seen the necessity of thus connecting all our generalizations from history with the laws of human nature'. (John Stuart Mill, *A System of Logic Ratiocinative and Inductive*, ed. John M. Robson, vols. 7–8 (1974) of *Collected Works*, 7:915).—Ed.]

J. S. M.'s Diary, 19 January 1854:[35] I feel bitterly how I have procrastinated in the sacred duty of fixing in writing, so that it may not die with me, everything that I have in mind which is capable of assisting the destruction of error and prejudice and the growth of just feelings and true opinions. Still more bitterly do I feel how little I have done as an [the] interpreter of the wisdom of one whose intellect is as much profounder than mine as her heart is nobler. If I ever recover my health, this shall be amended; and even if I do not, something may, I hope, be done towards it, provided a sufficient respite is allowed me.

J. S. M. to H. M., India House, 20 January 1854:[36] I write every evening in the little book. I have been reading the Essay on Nature as I rewrote the first part of it before we left & I think it very much improved & altogether very passable. I think I could finish it equally well.

J. S. M. to H. M., 23 January 1854:[37] I too have thought very often lately about the life[38] & am most anxious that we should complete it the soonest possible. What there is of it is in a perfectly publishable state—as far as the writing goes it could be printed tomorrow—& it contains a full writing out as far as anything can write out, what you are, as far as I am competent to describe you, & what I owe to you—but, besides that until revised by you it is little better than unwritten, it contains nothing about our private circumstances, further than shewing that there was an intimate friendship for many years, & you only can decide what more is necessary or desirable to say in order to stop the mouths of enemies hereafter. The fact is that there is about as much written as I *can* write without your help & we must go through this together & add the rest to it at the very first opportunity—I have not forgotten what she said about bringing it with me to Paris.

Meanwhile Mill's health was getting constantly worse, though for a time his doctor continued to assure him that there was 'no organic disease'.

J. S. M. to H. M., 29 January 1854:[39] I have been feeling much (I must have been incapable of feeling anything if I did not) about the shortness and uncertainty of life & the wrongness of having so much of the best of what

---

[35] [The passage from Mill's diary is published in *Letters* (ed. Elliot), vol. 2, p. 361, and in Mill, *Journals and Debating Speeches*, vol. 27 of *Collected Works*, p. 644.—Ed.]

[36] [Begun on 19 January, the full letter is published in Mill, *Later Letters*, vol. 14 of *Collected Works*, pp. 135–37. The 'little book' is Mill's diary; in 1874 the essay was published posthumously in *Three Essays on Religion* (London: Longman, Greene, Reader and Dyer, 1874).—Ed.]

[37] [The full letter is published in Mill, *Later Letters*, vol. 14 of *Collected Works*, pp. 137–39.—Ed.]

[38] [Mill's *Autobiography*.—Ed.]

[39] [The full letter is published in Mill, *Later Letters*, vol. 14 of *Collected Works*, pp. 142–45.—Ed.]

we have to say, so long unwritten & in the power of chance—& I am determined to make a better use of what time we have. Two years, well employed,
would enable us I think to get most of it into a state fit for printing—if not in
the best form for popular effect, yet in the state of concentrated thought—a
sort of mental pemican, which thinkers, when there are any after us, may
nourish themselves with & then dilute for other people. The Logic & Pol.
Ec. may perhaps keep their buoyancy long enough to hold these other things
above water till there are people capable of taking up the thread of thought
& continuing it. I fancy I see one large or two small posthumous volumes
of Essays, with the Life at their head, & my heart is set on having these in a
state fit for publication quelconque, if we live so long, by Christmas 1855;
though not then to be published if we are still alive to improve & enlarge
them. The first thing to be done & which I can do immediately towards it
is to finish the paper on Nature, & this I mean to set about today, after finishing this letter—being the first Sunday that I have not thought it best to
employ in I.H. work. That paper, I mean that part of it rewritten, seems to
me on reading it to contain a great deal which we want said, said quite well
enough for the volume though not so well as we shall make it when we have
time. I hope to be able in two or three weeks to finish it equally well & then
to begin something else—but all the other subjects in our list will be much
more difficult for me even to begin upon without you to prompt me. All this
however is entirely dependent on your health continuing to go on well; for
these are not things that can be done in a state of real anxiety. In bodily ill
health they might be.

In a later part of the same letter, written on the next day, Mill returns to the
subject:

It is a pleasant coincidence that I should receive her nice say about 'Nature'
just after I have resumed it. I shall put those three beautiful sentences about
'disorder' verbatim into the essay. I wrote a large piece yesterday at intervals
(reading a bit of Sismondi whenever I was tired) & I am well pleased with it.
I don't think we should make these essays very long, though the subjects are
inexhaustible. We want a compact argument first, & if we live to expand it &
add a longer dissertation, tant mieux: there is need of both.

The 'three beautiful sentences' about disorder are probably those which
occur on pp. 30 and 31 of the posthumous edition of the essay:[40]

---

[40] [*Three Essays on Religion*, pp. 30–31. The essays are republished in Mill, *Essays on Ethics, Religion, and Society*, vol. 10 of *Collected Works*, pp. 373–489, with the passage above, from 'Nature',
on p. 386.—Ed.]

Even the love of 'order' which is thought to be a following of the ways of Nature, is in fact a contradiction of them. All which people are accustomed to deprecate as 'disorder' and its consequences, is precisely a counterpart of Nature's ways. Anarchy and the Reign of Terror are overmatched in injustice, ruin, and death, by a hurricane and a pestilence.

J. S. M. to H. M., 7 February 1854:[41] I finished the 'Nature' on Sunday as I expected. I am quite puzzled what to attempt next—I will just copy the list of subjects we made out in the confused order in which we put them down. Differences of character (nation, race, age, sex, temperament). Love. Education of tastes. Religion de l'Avenir. Plato. Slander. Foundation of morals. Utility of religion. Socialism. Liberty. Doctrine that causation is will. To these I have now added from your letter: Family, & Conventional. It will be a tolerable two years work to finish all that? Perhaps the first of them is the one I could do most to by myself, at least of those equally important.[42]

Diary, 8 February 1854:[43] I would not, for any amount of intellectual eminence, be the only one of my generation who could see the truths which I thought of most importance to the improvement of mankind. Nor would I, for anything which life could give, be without a friend from whom I could learn at least as much as I could teach. Even the merely intellectual needs of my nature suffice to make me hope that I may never outlive the companion who is the profoundest and most far-sighted and clear-sighted thinker I have ever known, as well as the most consummate in practical wisdom. I do not wish that I were so much her equal as not to be her pupil, but I would gladly be more capable than I am of thoroughly appreciating and worthily reproducing her admirable thoughts.

J. S. M. to H. M., 10 February 1854:[44] You will be surprised when I tell you that I went again to Clark[45] this morning—& I am afraid you will think I am fidgety about my ailments, but the reverse is the case, for I never was so much the opposite of nervous about my own health, & I believe whatever were to happen I should look it in the face quite calmly. But my reason for going today was one which I think would have made you wish me to go—

---

[41] [The full letter is published in Mill, *Later Letters*, vol. 14 of *Collected Works*, pp. 151–53. Hayek has a query after 'Conventional'; the *Later Letters* confirms his transcription.—Ed.]

[42] [Michael St. John Packe, *The Life of John Stuart Mill* (London: Secker and Warburg, 1954), pp. 368–69, lists Mill's works on these subjects published between 1859 and 1874.—Ed.]

[43] [The passage from the diary is published in *Letters* (ed. Elliot), vol 2, p. 369, and in Mill, *Journals and Debating Speeches*, vol. 27 of *Collected Works*, p. 652.—Ed.]

[44] [The full letter is published in Mill, *Later Letters*, vol. 14 of *Collected Works*, pp. 153–54.—Ed.]

[45] Sir James Clark, Bt., F.R.S. (1788–1870), physician in ordinary to Queen Victoria.

namely the decided & unmistakable appearance of blood in the expectoration. Clark however on my describing it to him, does not think it of any
importance, but thinks it is very likely not from the lungs, & even if it does
come from them, thinks it is from local & very circumscribed congestion not
from a generally congested state. Very glad was I to hear of anything which
diminishes the importance of bleeding in a chest case. I knew before that it
is not at all a sure sign of consumption, as it often accompanies bronchitis—
which is the real technical name of my cough, though it sounds too large &
formidable for it. I am very well convinced, since Clark thinks so, that I am
not in a consumption at present, however likely this cough is to end in that—
for it seems to resist all the usual remedies. The favourable circumstance is
that none of my ailments ever seem to yield to remedies, but after teazing
on for an unconscionable time, go away or abate of themselves—as perhaps
this will if all goes well with my dearest one. Indeed if I had belief in presen-
timents I should feel quite assured on that point, for it appears to me so completely natural that while my darling lives I should live to keep her company.
I have not begun another Essay yet, but have read through all that is written of the Life—I find it wants revision, which I shall give it—but I do not
well know what to do with some of the passages which we marked for alteration in the early part [of it] which we read together. They were mostly passages in which I had written, you thought, too much of the truth [or what I
believe to be the truth] about my own defects. I certainly do not desire to say
more about them than integrity requires, but the difficult matter is to decide
how much that is. Of course one does not, in writing a life, either one's own
or another's, undertake to tell everything—& it will be right to put something into *this* which shall prevent any one from being able to suppose or to
pretend, that we undertake to keep nothing back. Still it va sans dire that it
ought to be on the whole a fair representation. Since [Some] things appear
to me on looking at them now to be said very crudely, which does not surprise me in the [a] first draft, in which the essential was to say everything,
somehow, sauf to omit [or revise afterwards. As to matters of opinion & feel-
ing] on general subjects, I find there is a great deal of good matter written down in the Life which we have not written anywhere else, & which will
make it as valuable in that respect (apart from its main object) as the best
things we have published. But of what particularly concerns *our* life there is
nothing yet written, except the descriptions of you, & of your effect on me;
which are at all events a permanent memorial of what I know you to be, &
of (so far as it can be shewn by generalities) of what I owe to you *intellectually*.
That, though it is the smallest part of what you are to me, is the most important to commemorate, as people are comparatively willing to suppose all
the rest. But we have to consider, which we can only do together, how much
of our story it is advisable to tell, in order to make head against the repre-

sentations of enemies when we shall not be alive to add anything to it. If it was not to be published for 100 years I should say, tell all, simply & without reserve. As it is there must be care taken not to put arms into the hands of the enemy.

Mrs. Mill's reply to this is the only one of her letters from this period which has been preserved.

H. M. to J. S. M., Hyères, 14 and 15 February 1854:[46] I do not think you at all fidgetty about your illness dear, and I never should think you too much so. I never feel objections to anything you do but when I think it tends to increase an ailment. I think (you may be sure) that you were quite right to go to C.[47] about that bleeding, but I cannot help believing that the practise of looking at the expectoration in the morning, is itself in a great measure the cause of there being any expectoration at all. I cannot but think that if you tried as earnestly as I have done since Oct[r] to avoid *any* expectoration that you could lose the habit altogether as I have done. I am far more anxious about your health than about my own, and the more because I do not think a continental life would suit you. You would soon miss the stimulus and excitement of the daily intercourse with other men to which you are accustomed. However you must be the only judge on that subject & you are not likely to have to decide it at present at least. I hope you have not taken [severe] cold again— here after a cold east wind last Friday and Sat, on Monday the bright sky suddenly darkened and a snow storm more violent than we have them in England covered the whole town & country with deep snow in about an hour. Last night it froze hard & they express great fear for the olives. To-day the sun has melted the snow, tho' not in shady places, and it continues very cold. I do not feel at all the worse for the cold, but it is true it has not lasted long as yet. They say here that March is a cold windy month. After the bad days I had last week, I have been something better again, as I see I always am after an unusually bad week.

About the Essays dear, would not Religion, the Utility of Religion,[48] be one of the subjects you would have most to say on. There is to account for

---

[46] MTColl. L(i). This is a pencilled note, very faded, and some of the readings are uncertain. It is numbered 15, while Mill's letter to which it replies is his 14th. [The full letter is published in Harriet Taylor Mill, *Complete Works*, pp. 373–76, with the portion above at pp. 373–75. There it is given as MTColl. L(ii)/40. Hayek's notation is L(i) for Harriet Taylor and L(ii) for Harriet Mill.—Ed.]

[47] [Harriet Taylor Mill, *Complete Works*, p. 373, note 148, supplies the name of Mill's doctor, James Clark (1788–1870).—Ed.]

[48] The Utility of Religion became the title of the second essay contained in the posthumous volume on *Nature, the Utility of Religion, and Theism* (1874). According to Helen Taylor's Introduction to the volume it was, with the essay on Nature, written about this time.

the existence nearly universal of some religion (superstition) by the instincts of fear hope & mystery &c and throwing over all doctrines & theories, called religions, ~~and~~ [as] devices for power, to show how religion & poetry fill the same want, the craving after higher objects, the consolation of suffering, the hope of heaven for the selfish, love of God for the tender and grateful—how all this must be superseded by morality deriving its power from sympathies & benevolence & its rewards from the approbation of those we respect.

There, what a long winded sentance, which you could say ten times as well in words half the length. I feel sure dear that the Life is not half written & that half that is written will not do. Should there not be a summary of *our* relationship from its commencement in 1830—I mean given in a dozen lines—so as to preclude other and different versions of our lives at Kes[n] and Wal[n49]—our summer excursions &c This ought to be done in its genuine truth and simplicity—strong affection, intimacy of friendship, & no impropriety: It seems to me an edifying picture for those poor wretches who cannot conceive friendship but in sex—nor believe that expediency and the consideration for feelings of others can conquer sensuality. But of course this is not my reason for wishing it done. It is that every ground should be occupied by ourselves on our own subject.

I thought so exactly as you did about that trash in the Ex[r] about the Russell letters[50]—she was an amiable woman as there are, only[51] a good deal spoilt, hardened by puritanism, who was excessively in love with her husband (tho' she did not admire him much).

Will you observe dear before paying Sharpers if the Bill deli[d] you have is dated? He never has sent a bill, but I suppose if the Bill deli[d] is dated Christmas 1853 that is sufficient. Will you tell Haji on his birthday (21) that I asked you to wish him many happy returns of it for me.[52] The garden will soon want crops put in but I will write about it next time. I am very glad Kate continues satisfied and well conducted.

Adieu with all love to my kindest & dearest.

---

[49] [Kensington and Walton, where John Stuart Mill and Harriet Taylor Mill had lived. Hayek records the former as 'Kis[n]' with a query. Harriet Taylor Mill, *Complete Works*, p. 375, note 151, supplies the correction.—Ed.]

[50] A review of *Letters of Rachel, Lady Russell* (ed. J. R. [Earl Russell], 2 vols., (London: Longman, Brown, Green and Longmans, 1853), in the *Examiner* of 4 February 1854, pp. 68–69. [Hayek supplies the name in brackets. In his letter to Harriet Taylor Mill dated 7 February, Mill referred to the 'ludicrous' 'deification of Lady Russell's letters' in the review. Mill, *Later Letters*, vol. 14 of *Collected Works*, p. 152.—Ed.]

[51] [Harriet Taylor Mill, *Complete Works*, p. 375, provides a different transcription: 'she was an amiable woman as there are [hardly?] a good deal spoilt'.—Ed.]

[52] [Haji's 23rd birthday was February 21, 1854.—Ed.]

Before he received this letter Mill wrote once more about the *Autobiography* in connexion with an intended meeting at Paris.

J. S. M. to H. M., 13 February 1854:[53] I have not forgotten that I am to bring the biography with me. It *is* mentioned in the codicil, [&] placed at your absolute disposal to publish or not. But if we are not to be together this summer it is doubly important to have as much of the life written as can be written before we meet—therefore will you my own love in one of your sweetest letters give me your general notion of what we should say or imply ~~concerning~~ [respecting] our private concerns. As it is, it shews confidential friendship & strong attachment ending in marriage when you were free & ignores there having ever been any scandalous suspicions about us.

Eight days later Mrs. Mill's letter on the subject had at last reached him.

J. S. M. to H. M., 20 February 1854:[54] Your programme of an essay on [the utility of] religion is beautiful, but it requires you to fill it up—I can try, but a few paragraphs will bring me to the end of all I have got to say on the subject. What would be the use of my outliving you! I could write nothing worth keeping alive for except with your prompting. As to the Life—which I have been revising & correcting—the greater part, in bulk, of what is written consists in the history of my mind *up to* the time when your influence over it began—& I do not think there can be much objectionable in that part, even including as it does, sketches of the character of most of the people I was intimate with—if I could be said to be so with any one. I quite agree in the sort of résumé of our relationship which you suggest—but if it is to be only as you say a dozen lines, or even three or four dozen, could you not my own love write it out your darling self & send it in one of your precious letters—It is one of the many things of which the *fond* would be much better laid by you & we can add to it afterwards if we see occasion. I sent the Examiner today. I am sorry & ashamed of the spots of grease on it. The chapter of the P[olitical] E[conomy][55] I shall send by the post which takes this letter . . . I will give your 'happy returns' to Haji tomorrow. The last Sun-

---

[53] [The full letter is published in Mill, *Later Letters*, vol. 14 of *Collected Works*, pp. 157–59.—Ed.]

[54] [The full letter is published in *ibid.*, pp. 165–67.—Ed.]

[55] [Hayek supplied the words in brackets. Mill revised the chapter 'On the Probable Futurity of the Labouring Classes' for reprinting by the editor Frederick James Furnivall (1825–1910). Furnivall was a Christian Socialist who supported trade unions. See Mill's letter to Furnivall, dated 13 February 1854, *Later Letters*, vol. 14 of *Collected Works*, p. 157. For changes to Mill's *Political Economy* on this topic, see John Stuart Mill, *The Principles of Political Economy with Some of Their Application to Social Philosophy*, ed. John M. Robson, vols. 2–3 (1965) of *Collected Works*, 3:775–85.—Ed.]

day but one I took occasion in talking with him to say that you were the profoundest thinker & most consummate reasoner I had ever known—he made no remark to the point but ejaculated a strong wish that you were back here.

Two of the entries made by Mill in his 'little book' at about this time may find a place here.

Diary, 16 February, 1854:[56] Niebuhr said that he wrote only for Savigny; so I write only for her when I do not write entirely *from* her. But in my case, as in his, what is written for only one reader, that one being the most competent intellect, is likeliest to be of use to the many, readers or not, whose benefit is the object of the writing, though not the principal incentive to it.

Diary, 20 February, 1854:[57] Whenever I look back at any of my own writings of two or three years previous, they seem to me like the writings of some stranger whom I have seen and known long ago. I wish that my acquisition of power to do better had kept pace with the continual elevation of my standing point and change of my bearings towards all the great subjects of thought. But the explanation is that I owe the enlargement of my ideas and feelings to *her* influence, and that she could not in the same degree give me powers of execution.

In the letters of these weeks[58] various problems arising from the probable necessity of Mill's retirement from India House and of possibly having to live permanently on the Continent come up repeatedly. He hoped, if his health should make this necessary, to be able to retire on two-thirds of his salary, but was on the whole inclined to try to hold on for another year or so, with the help of six month's leave during the following winter on a medical certificate which he thought ought to be readily granted, considering that he had just finished all the arrears and thus 'done in two months the work of 5½'.[59] In the same connexion he explains to his wife about their income from investments that 'we are not yet at the £500 [certain] which you mention, but we are past [the] £400'.[60] The same thought had evidently been in his mind when a

[56] [Published in Mill, *Journals and Debating Speeches*, vol. 27 of *Collected Works*, pp. 654–55. The historian Barthold Georg Neibuhr (1776–1831) was the student of the historian and professor of law Friedrich Karl von Savigny (1779–1861); *ibid.*, p. 654, note 21.—Ed.]

[57] [*Ibid.*, pp. 655–56.—Ed.]

[58] 7, 13 and 15 February, and 6 March. [The full letters are published in Mill, *Later Letters*, vol. 14 of *Collected Works*, pp. 151–53, 157–59, 159–62, 176–78.—Ed.]

[59] [Mill, *Later Letters*, vol. 14 of *Collected Works*, p. 178. Hayek places the previous footnote, numbered 28 in his edition, here.—Ed.]

[60] 28 February. [The full letter is published in Mill, *Later Letters*, vol. 14 of *Collected Works*, 169–72.—Ed.]

little earlier he had expressed much pleasure about the continued favourable receipts from his books.

> *J. S. M. to H. M., 29 January 1854:* The Logic has sold 260 copies in 1853—in 1852 it sold only 206. This steady sale must proceed I think from a regular annual demand from colleges & other places of education. What is strange is that the Pol. Ec. Essays sell from 20 to 50 copies each year & bring in three or four pounds annually. This is encouraging, since if that sells, I think anything we put our name to would sell. P[arker][61] brought a cheque for £102.2.5 which with the £250, & £25 which Lewis has sent for the Grote,[62] is pretty well to have come in one year from writings of which money was not at all the object.

But doubts whether they will live to complete any of their plans creep in more and more frequently as the weeks pass on.

> *J. S. M. to H. M., 24 February 1854:*[63] Altogether I hope the best for both of us, & see nothing in the state of either to discourage the hope. I hope we shall live to write together 'all we wish to leave written' to most of which your living is quite as essential ~~than~~ [as] mine, for even if the wreck I should be could work on with undiminished faculties, my faculties at the best are not adequate to the highest subjects & have already done almost the best they are adequate to. Do not think darling that I should ever make this an excuse to myself for not doing my very best—if I survived you, & anything we much care about was not already fixed in writing, you might depend on my attempting all of it & doing my very best to make it such as you would wish, for my only rule of life *then* would be what I thought you would wish as it now is what you tell me you wish. But I *am not fit* to write on anything but the outskirts of the great questions of feeling & life without you to prompt me as well as to keep me right. So we must do what we can while we are alive—the Life being the first thing—which independent of the personal matters which it will set right when we have made it what we intend, is even now an unreserved proclamation of our opinions on religion, nature, & much else.

Apart from the suggested essay on religion on which Mill started work early in March, the main subjects discussed in the letters of the next few weeks are the proposed plans for parliamentary reform, the reconstruction of the Civil Service, and the revisions of a chapter of the *Political Economy*.

---

[61] [Hayek inserts the brackets containing the full name.—Ed.]

[62] [The review of the last three volumes of Grote's *History of Greece*; see Mill, *Later Letters*, vol. 14 of *Collected Works*, p. 142, note 3.—Ed.]

[63] [The full letter is published in Mill, *Later Letters*, vol. 14 of *Collected Works*, pp. 167–69.—Ed.]

J. S. M. to H. M., 3 March 1854:[64] The Civil Service examination plan[65] I am afraid is too good to pass. The report proposing it, by Trevelyan[66] & Northcote[67] (written no doubt by Trevelyan) has been printed in the Chronicle[68]—it is as direct, uncompromising & to the point, without reservation, as if we had written it. But even the Chronicle attacks the plan. The grand complaint is that it will bring low people into the offices! as, of course, gentlemen's sons cannot be expected to be as clever as low people. It is ominous too that the Times has said nothing on the subject lately. I should like to know who wrote the articles in the Times in support of the plan   possibly Trevelyan himself. It was somebody who saw his way to the moral & social ultimate effects of such a change. How truly you judge people—how true is what you always say that this ministry are *before* the public.

J. S. M. to H. M., 9 March 1854:[69] The other note is from Trevelyan[70] & is an appeal that I ought to respond to, but it will be difficult, & without you impossible, to write the opinion he asks for, so as to be fit to print. But he ought to be helped, for the scheme is the greatest thing yet proposed in the way of *real* reform & his report is as I said before, almost as if we had written it. I wish it were possible to delay even answering his note till I could send π [the] draft to you & receive it back but I fear that would not do.

J. S. M. to H. M., 14 March 1854:[71] I need hardly say how heartily I feel all

[64] [The full letter is published in *ibid.*, pp. 173–76.—Ed.]

[65] [Mill is referring to 'Report on the Organisation of the Permanent Civil Service, Together with a Letter from the Rev. B. Jowett', *Parliamentary Papers*, 1854, XXVII.1. Mill, *Later Letters*, vol. 14 of *Collected Works*, p. 175, note 6, describes this as 'a plan for strict qualifying examinations for civil service appointments'. The Report was dated Nov. 23, 1853.—Ed.]

[66] [Sir Charles Edward Trevelyan (1807–1886) was a statesman who held various official positions in India and later became Governor of Madras. Mill, *Later Letters*, vol. 14 of *Collected Works*, p. 175, note 7.—Ed.]

[67] [Sir Stafford Henry Northcote was a statesman who later became 1st Earl of Iddesleigh (1818–1887); *ibid.*, p. 175, note 8.—Ed.]

[68] [*Morning Chronicle*, 22 February, 1854, p. 4.—Ed.]

[69] [The full letter is published in Mill, *Later Letters*, vol. 14 of *Collected Works*, pp. 179–81.—Ed.]

[70] This letter of G. O. Trevelyan, dated 8 March 1854, and two later ones, with the draft of Mill's replies, are in the 'Hutzler Collection of Economic Classics' in Johns Hopkins University. [Trevelyan requested, in the letter dated 8 March, that 'it would be much for the public advantage if you would consider our Report, and state in writing (in a form which would admit of its being published with the opinions of other persons who have been consulted whose position & experience will cause them to be regarded with respect) what you think of the plan proposed by us, & what amendments you could recommend to be made in it'. The letters to which Hayek refers are in the special collections of the Milton S. Eisenhower Library at Johns Hopkins University.—Ed.]

[71] [The full letter is published in Mill, *Later Letters*, vol. 14 of *Collected Works*, pp. 183–87. Hayek has a query after the word 'hail'; *Later Letters* accepts his reading.—Ed.]

you say about the civil service plan & the contempt I feel for the little feeling shewn for it, not to speak of actual hostility. I give the ministers infinite credit for it—that is if they really adopt the whole plan, for as their bill is not yet brought in (it is not as you seem to think, part of the Reform Bill) we do not yet know how far they will really go; but the least they can do consistently with their speeches, will be such a sacrifice of power of jobbing as hardly a politician who ever lived, ever yet made to the sense of right, without any public demand—it stamps them as quite remarkable men for their class & country—Of course all the jobbers are ~~hard~~ [loud] against them, especially newspaper editors who all now look out for places. Yet I so share your misgiving that they cannot know how great a thing they are doing, that I am really afraid to say all I feel about it till they are fully committed, lest it should do more harm than good. This was my answer to Trevelyan.[72] 'I have not waited till now to make myself acquainted with the Report which you have done me the favour of sending to me, & to hail the plan of throwing open the civil service to competition as one of the greatest improvements in public affairs ever proposed by a government. If the examination be so contrived as to be a real test of mental superiority, it is difficult to set limits to the effect which will be produced in raising the character not only of the public service but of Society itself. I shall be most happy to express this opinion in any way in which you think it can be of the smallest use towards helping forward so noble a scheme, but as the successful working of the plan will depend principally on details into which very properly your Report does not enter, I should be unable without some time for consideration, to write anything which could have a chance of being of any service in the way of suggestion.

'I am sorry to say you are mistaken in supposing that anything bearing the remotest resemblance to what you propose, exists at the I.H. It will exist in the India Civil Service by the Act of last year'.[73]

Trevelyan's answer: 'You have done us a great service by the expression of your decided approbation of our plan for the reform of the English Civil Establishments; & as it is well known that you do not form your opinions lightly, I do not wish to trouble you to enter upon details of the subject at present. If you can suggest any improvement in the more advanced stages, we shall hope to hear from you again'. This looks as if he desired support more than criticism, but it is useful as it opens a channel by which, without obtrusiveness, we may write anything we like in the way of comment on

[72] [Mill quotes from his letter to Treveylan, published in full in *ibid.*, pp. 178–79.—Ed.]

[73] [Mill is referring to the Government of India Act, which was passed in August 1853 and conditioned admission into the Indian Civil Service on a system of examinations; *ibid.*, p. 179, note 4.—Ed.]

the bill hereafter & be sure of its being read by the government. They have already quoted me in favour of the plan.

Fortunately it was not until early in May, some time after Mrs. Mill's return, that Trevelyan asked for the substitution of another enlarged letter for the one written at first, and it was no doubt with her assistance that the Paper on the Reorganization of the Civil Service, dated 22 May, was written.[74]

The concern with the revision of the chapter on the Futurity of the Labouring Classes was caused by an application of F. J. Furnivall, 'one of the Kingsley set',[75] to reprint it: 'I did not expect the Xtian Socialists would wish to circulate the chapter as it is in the 3ᵈ edit. since it stands up for Competition, against their one-eyed attacks & denunciations of it'.[76] Mrs. Mill approved of the plan and Mill undertook not only to revise the chapter but also to translate all the French passages in it. Sheets of the chapter went to Mrs. Mill for her comment.

J. S. M. to H. M., 6 March 1854:[77] I quite agree with you about the inexpediency of adding anything like practical advice, or anything at all which alters the character of the chapter—the working men ought to see that it was not written for them—any attempt to mingle the two characters would be sure to be a failure & is not the way in which we should do the thing even if we had plenty of time & were together. This morning has come from Chapman a proposal for reprinting the article Enfranchisement of Women[78] or as he vulgarly calls it the article on Woman. How *very* vulgar all his notes are. I am glad however that it is your permission he asks. I hope the lady friend is not H. Martineau. Mrs. Gaskell perhaps?[79] you will tell me what to say.

When Mrs. Mill's comments arrived Mill wrote 'I think I agree in all your remarks & have adopted them almost all' and transcribed in the letter all the

---

[74] See also Trevelyan's letters to Mill, dated 11 and 24 May 1854, in MTColl. I/27–28.

[75] Frederick James Furnivall (1825–1910). [Charles Kingsley (1819–1875) was an English novelist, author of *Water Babies* (1863). He was sympathetic to Darwin's argument about evolution; Darwin would in the second and later editions of the *Origin of Species* refer to an unnamed Kingsley as a 'celebrated author and divine' for contributing a theological interpretation of natural selection. See Peart and Levy, '*Vanity of the Philosopher*'.—Ed.]

[76] J. S. M. to H. M., 4 February 1854. The letter in which he grants permission, dated 13 February, is printed in *Letters* (ed. Elliot), vol. 1, pp. 177–78. [The full letter is published in Mill, *Later Letters*, vol. 14 of *Collected Works*, pp. 148–50. The letter to Furnivall is also published in *ibid.*, p. 157.—Ed.]

[77] [The full letter is published in Mill, *Later Letters*, vol. 14 of *Collected Works*, pp. 176–78.—Ed.]

[78] [First published in the *Westminster Review*, July 1851.—Ed.]

[79] [The novelist Elizabeth Cleghorn Gaskell (1810–1865). Mill, *Later Letters*, vol. 14 of *Collected Works*, p. 177, note 7.—Ed.]

additions he had made to the chapter.[80] A 'saving clause' on piece work which Mrs. Mill suggests was promptly inserted before the chapter was sent to Furnivall.[81]

Early in March Mill got seriously alarmed by the progressive deterioration of his health, especially when a new symptom, night perspiration, appeared. But his doctor, Sir James Clark, at first still reassured him and Mill went away with the impression that his lungs were not even threatened.

> *J. S. M. to H. M., 11 March 1854:*[82] This being one of the great indications of consumption (though also of other ailments) it was well to find out what it meant. Clark thought it was chiefly from the sudden change of weather & said that almost everybody is complaining of night perspirations, the queen among others. Whatever he may say, it is clear to me that no weather could produce any such effect on me if there were not a strong predisposition to it.

Only a few days later the doctor had however to admit 'that there is organic disease in the lungs & that he had known this all along'.[83] Mill at first tried to keep from his wife this news, which to him seemed a fairly certain sentence of death, till he could tell it to her by word of mouth. His state of mind during the next few weeks is best shown by some of the entries in the 'little book'.[84]

---

[80] J. S. M. to H. M., 14 March 1854. [Published in Mill, *Later Letters*, vol. 14 of *Collected Works*, p. 185.—Ed.]

[81] The contemplated reprint of this chapter cannot now be traced and it is doubtful whether it ever appeared. The translations of the French passages were later used in the Popular edition of *Political Economy*, and the additions appear all in the 4th edition of 1857. The 'saving clause' inserted at Mrs. Mill's suggestion is evidently the sentence put in square brackets in the following passage as it appears on p. 350 of the 4th edition but not contained in the draft of the passage sent by Mill to his wife: 'One of the most discreditable indications of a low moral condition, given of late by the English working classes, is the opposition to piece-work. [When the payment per piece is not sufficiently high, that is a just ground for [of] objection.] But dislike of [to] piecework [in itself], except under mistaken notions, must be dislike to justice or [and] fairness; a desire to cheat, by not giving work in proportion to the pay. Piece-work is the perfection of contract; & contract, in all work, and in the most minute detail—the principle of so much pay for so much service, carried to the utmost extremity—is the system, of all others, in the present state of society [and degree of civilization], most favourable to the worker; though most unfavourable to the non-worker who wishes to be paid for being idle'. [For collations of this passage, see Mill, *Political Economy*, vol. 3 of *Collected Works*, p. 783.—Ed.]

[82] [The full letter is published in Mill, *Later Letters*, vol. 14 of *Collected Works*, pp. 181–82.—Ed.]

[83] J. S. M. to H. M., 8 April 1854. [Published in Mill, *Later Letters*, vol. 14 of *Collected Works*, p. 199.—Ed.]

[84] [These are published in *Letters* (ed. Elliot), vol. 2, pp. 379, 381–82, 383, 384, and 386; and Mill, *Journals and Debating Speeches*, vol. 27 of *Collected Works*, pp. 641–68.—Ed.]

Diary, 16 March 1854: It is part of the irony of life, and a part which never becomes the less affecting because it is so trite, that the fields, hills, and trees, the houses, really the very rooms and furniture, will look exactly the same the day after we or those we most love have died.

17 March: When we see and feel that human beings can take the deepest interest in what will befal their country or mankind long after they are dead, and in what they can themselves do while they are alive to influence that distant prospect which they are never destined to behold, we cannot doubt that if this and similar feelings were cultivated in the same manner and degree as religion they would become a religion.

25 March: The only change I find in myself from a near view of probable death is that it makes me instinctively conservative. It makes me feel, not as I am accustomed—oh, for something better!—but oh, that we could be going on as we were before. Oh, that those I love could be spared the shock of a great change! And this feeling goes with me into politics and all other human affairs, when my reason does not studiously contend against and repress it.

31 March: Apart from bodily pain, and [from] the grief for the grief of those who love us, the most disagreeable thing about dying is the intolerable ennui of it. There ought to be no slow deaths.

3 April: The effect of the bright and sunny aspects of Nature in soothing and giving cheerfulness is never more remarkable than in declining health. I look upon it as a piece of excellent good fortune to have the whole summer before one to die in.

4 April: Perhaps even the happiest of mankind would not, if it were offered, accept the privilege of being immortal. What he would ask in lieu of it is not to die until he chose.

12 April: In quitting for ever any place where one has dwelt as in a home, all the incidents and circumstances, even those which were worse than indifferent to us, appear like old friends that one is reluctant to lose. So it is in taking leave of life: even the tiresome and vexatious parts of it look pleasant and friendly, and one feels how agreeable it would be to remain among them.

As the meeting with Mrs. Mill was delayed longer than expected and she got alarmed by the partial reports, Mill has at last to break the news to her, telling her at the same time that he had placed himself in the hands of another doctor, Ramadge,[85] whose book on a new treatment of consumption had inspired him with confidence, and that he was already slightly better.[86] Two days later he has already his wife's reply from Paris.

> *J. S. M. to H. M., 10 April 1854.*[87] You will soon, darling, I know, feel calm again, for what is there that can happen to us in such a world as this that is worth being disturbed about when one is prepared for it?—except intense physical pain, but that there is no fear of in this case. I am sometimes surprised at my own perfect tranquillity when I consider how much reason I have to wish to live, but I am in my best spirits, & what I wrote even in the week after Clark's announcement before I had seen Ramadge, is written with as much spirit & I had as much pleasure in writing it as anything I ever wrote.

Indeed only a few days before he had written to her:

> I want my angel to tell me what should be the next essay written. I have done all I can for the subject she last gave me.[88]

About the same time news had reached Mill that his mother was dangerously ill. He had apparently not seen her since his return, but early exchanged some notes with her and now he learnt that she was getting worse.

> *J. S. M. to H. M., 3 April 1854.*[89] My poor mother I am afraid is not in a good way—as to health I mean. In her usual letter about receiving her pension she said: 'I have been a sufferer for nearly three months—I have only been out of doors twice' &c 'I have suffered & am still suffering great pain. I supposed the pain in my back was rheumatism, but it is not—it proceeds from the stomach, from which I suffer intense pain as well as from the back. Mr. Quain has been attending me during the time, and he & Sir Jas Clark have had a consultation and I am taking what they prescribe—I can do no more'. And again in answer to my answer 'I am just the same, but it is not rheumatism that I am suffering from, but my liver. I thought it was odd that my stomach should be so much affected from rheumatism. Sir J. Clark is coming

---

[85] Francis Hopkins Ramadge, M.D. (1793–1867), senior physician to the infirmary for asthma and consumption and other diseases of the lung, had in 1834 published a book *Consumption Curable* which went into many editions and was translated into several foreign languages.

[86] J. S. M. to H. M., 8 April 1854. [Published in Mill, *Later Letters*, vol. 14 of *Collected Works*, pp. 197–201.—Ed.]

[87] [The full letter is published in Mill, *Later Letters*, vol. 14 of *Collected Works*, pp. 201–3.—Ed.]

[88] J. S. M. to H. M., 5 April 1854. [Published in Mill, *Later Letters*, vol. 14 of *Collected Works*, pp. 196–97.—Ed.]

[89] [The full letter is published in Mill, *Later Letters*, vol. 14 of *Collected Works*, pp. 193–95.—Ed.]

here at the end of the week to have another [examination &] consultation. I cannot write much as I am so very weak'.[90] This looks very ill I fear—very like some organic disease. Mrs King she says is a little better & is probably coming to England.[91] I told her what you said a propos of Mrs King's illness. She wrote 'I hope Mrs. Mill is still going on well'.

In the last letter to his wife before her return the news about his mother is still more grave.

J. S. M. to H. M., 11 April 1854:[92] I am sorry to say darling I had two notes from Clara & Mary[93] both saying that my mother is very ill—one says that Clark & the other medical man Quain call her disease enlargement of the liver, the other tumour in the liver & they think very seriously of it though not expecting immediate danger. I need not send the notes as you will see them so soon.

It had been intended that Mill should meet his wife in Paris where she had arrived about the first of April and was stopping for some days, awaiting bet-

---

[90] The original of this letter to Mill by his mother is in the MTColl. XLVII/24. It begins: '4 Westbourne Park Villas / 29th March / My dear John / I am sorry that you did not tell me whether you had got rid of your cough, I am afraid from that you have not. As to myself . . .' and continues as quoted by Mill. It is signed 'Your [ever] Affect^e Mother / H. Mill' and has the following postscript: 'James's address is / Ullaport / North Britain / The next time you write will you tell me what Pension he has got?'

Of John Mill's letter to his brother James for which the mother supplied the address, a torn-off last page is in MTColl. XLVII/25, postmarked 31 March 1854. After an incomplete sentence about somebody's health it continues: 'I do not know how far you take interest in passing events. The time is very near when the new arrangements for the India Act will come into operation. For my part, except the throwing open the civil service to competition, all the changes appear to me to be for the worse. It is the most faulty piece of work these ministers have turned out—whom otherwise I prefer to any ministers England has yet had. / yrs aff^y / J. S. Mill'. [This partial letter is published in Mill, *Later Letters*, vol. 14 of *Collected Works*, p. 192.—Ed.]

[91] The eldest of Mill's sisters, who was living in Germany.

[92] [The full letter is published in Mill, *Later Letters*, vol. 14 of *Collected Works*, pp. 203–4.—Ed.]

[93] These notes are in MTColl. XLVII/28, 29. One may be reproduced here:

Clara E. Mill to J. S. M.: 4 Westbourne Park Villas, April 10. / Dear John / In case you should not otherwise be aware of it, I think it right to tell you that my poor Mother is very seriously ill. The doctors have pronounced her complaint to be tumour of [in] the liver, I don't think they apprehend any immediate danger, but they do not conceal the fact that at any age it would be a very serious affair, and in her case there is no doubt that her strength is decreasing. Sir James Clark saw her some 10 days ago & M^r. Quain (32 Cavendish Square) saw her on Saturday & comes twice a week at least—from either of these you can of course get any information you may wish. / My Mother does not know that I am writing. / C. E. Mill.

[The other letter, from Mary Elizabeth Coleman, is also dated 10 April 1854. See MTColl, XLVII/29.—Ed.]

ter weather for the crossing and in order to give her daughter an opportunity to see the *semaine sainte*. At first it seemed uncertain whether Mrs. Mill would be strong enough to continue the journey to England, but in the end it proved that it was Mill who was unable to come to Paris to meet her, because he had, in addition to his illness, developed a bad carbuncle, and about the middle of April the two ladies joined him at Blackheath Park.

During the next six weeks Mill's health continued to get worse so that, as he wrote a little later,[94] 'the great & rapid wasting of flesh' made him fear that he would soon be 'incapable of any bodily exertion whatever'. His doctors were urging him to go away but he delayed until the beginning of June when at last, with little hope of recovery, he set out for a tour of Brittany. But before he left it was necessary to say good-bye to his mother, who was clearly dying. Warned of the approaching end in a very formal letter of his sister Harriet,[95] he went to see his mother, and a few days later, wrote to her once more. The letter was evidently intended to convey some information to his sisters rather than for his mother, who, as he must have known, was no longer in a state to read it.

J. S. M. to Mrs. James Mill:[96] Blackheath Park, June 9, 1854 / My dear Mother—I hope ~~that~~ you are feeling better than when I saw you last week & that you continue free from pain. I write to say that I am going immediately to the Continent by the urgent recommendation of Clark who has been pressing me to do so for some time past & though I expect to return in a few weeks it will probably be to leave again soon after. I wish again to remind you in case it has not already been done how desirable it is that someone who is fixed in England should be named executor to your will, either instead of me, which I sh^d prefer, or as well as myself.

My wife sends her kindest wishes & regrets that her weak health makes it

[94] J. S. M. to H. M., St. Malo, 14 June 1854. [The full letter is published in Mill, *Later Letters*, vol. 14 of *Collected Works*, pp. 211–13, with the passage above at p. 212.—Ed.]

[95] MTColl. XLVII/32. [The letter reads: '4 Westhampton Park Villas / Friday afternoon / My dear John / Mr Quain recommends that my Mother's relatives should know she is dying. We thought she would have died last night but she has rallied again this morning and knows us generally, though she wanders a little at times. This is a great blessing that she suffers no pain. / We have found it impossible to get any changes made in her Will. Mr Wilson, as holding a partnership, is not allowed to do these things,—and she has become to weak to write for some weeks. / your aff^{ate} sister / Harriet Isabella Mill'.—Ed.]

[96] Draft in MTColl. XLVII/31. The last paragraph first ran: 'If you sh^d have occasion to write to me ~~do it~~ [direct] to my house at Blackheath and my wife will forward it. My wife sends her best wishes & regrets that her health has made it impossible for her to call on you as she much wished to have done' and the last seven words replaced first by 'would otherwise have done long before this' and then by 'much wished to have done' and finally replaced by the paragraph in the text. [The full letter is published in Mill, *Later Letters*, vol. 14 of *Collected Works*, pp. 207–8.—Ed.]

difficult for her to come to see you as she would otherwise have done. Ever my dear mother affectionately yours

J. S. M.

Mrs. James Mill died six days later, on 15 June. The news, conveyed in a letter by his brother-in-law Charles Colman, however, did not reach Mill until the 26th in Brittany. He had left on the day he had written to his mother and remained away for a little over six weeks. Again all but one of the sixteen letters he wrote to his wife during this tour have been preserved[97] and allow us to follow his daily moods and movements. After spending three days at St. Helier on the island of Jersey, he crossed to St. Malo, where he was held up by rain for a day and started writing an essay on Justice,[98] the plan of which had formed itself in his mind on the boat. But, as soon as the weather improved, he set out on his tour around the coast of Brittany, spending all day in the open, travelling only short distances by various means of conveyance but walking an astounding and, as his strength increased, rapidly increasing amount. All the time he was looking at the various towns with an eye to their suitability as places for permanent residence and reporting to his wife on the prices of food and similar items. At Morlaix he found a companion for a few excursions who, like himself, was seeking a cure for consumption.

J. S. M. to H. M., Brest, 24 June 1854:[99] I went there [from Morlaix to the central country of Brittany][100] as I said I was going to, with an Englishman who it seems is a barrister & is named Pope.[101] He turned out a pleasant person to meet, as though he does not seem to me to have any talent, he is better informed than common Englishmen—knows a good deal of French history for example, especially that of the Revolution & seems either to have already got to or to be quite ready to receive all our opinions. I tried him on religion, where I found him quite what we think right—on politics, on which he was somewhat more than a radical—on the equality of women which he seemed not to have quite dared to think of himself but seemed to adopt it at once—& to be ready for all reasonable socialism—he boggled a little at lim-

---

[97] All these letters are in Yale University Library [MS 350, Box 1, Folders 9 and 10]. [They are published in Mill, *Later Letters*, vol. 14 of *Collected Works*, pp. 208–34. Ed.]

[98] Later incorporated into *Utilitarianism*. Bain (*J. S. Mill*, p. 112) refers to a letter which suggested to him that *Utilitarianism* was written in 1854, but from the letters here quoted it seems more likely that the essays written then, though used in the composition of *Utilitarianism*, were not yet planned as a book under that title.

[99] [The full letter is published in Mill, *Later Letters*, vol. 14 of *Collected Works*, pp. 217–19.—Ed.]

[100] [Hayek supplies the brackets containing additional information here and later in the passage.—Ed.]

[101] [Mill, *Later Letters*, vol. 14 of *Collected Works*, p. 216, note 2, identifies Pope as 'Mr. Frederick Pope, a young barrister suffering from tuberculosis'.—Ed.]

iting the power of bequest which I was glad of, as it shewed that the other agreements were not mere following a lead taken. He was therefore worth talking to & I think he will have taken away a good many ideas from me. . . . From that [the French newspapers] I saw that there had been a debate on the ballot & that Palmerston had made the speech against it[102] but that was all. I reckon on leaving our opinion on that question to form part of the volume of essays, but I am more anxious to get on with other things first, since what is already written (when detached from the political pamphlet that was to have been[103]) will in the case of the worst suffice, being the essentials of what we have to say, & perhaps might serve to float the volume as the opinion on the ballot would be liked by the powerful classes, and being from a radical would be sure to be quoted by their writers, while they would detest most of the other opinions.

Six days later his wife's reply to the last passage makes him return to the subject.

J. S. M. to H. M., Lorient, 30 June 1854:[104] I wish I had seen a full report of Palmerston's speech—what was given of it in the Spectator did not at all account for your high opinion of it, ~~containing~~ [certainly] only the commonplaces I have been familiar with all my life—while the speeches *for* the ballot were below even the commonplaces. The ballot has sunk to far inferior men, the Brights[105] &c. When it was in my father's hands or even Grote's[106] such trash was not spoken as that the suffrage is a *right* &c. &c. But Palmerston's saying that a person who will not sacrifice something ~~to~~ [for] his opinion is not fit to have a vote seems to me to involve the same fallacy. It is not for his own sake that one wishes him to have a vote. It is *we* who suffer because those who would vote with us are afraid to do so. As for the suffrage being a trust, it has always been so said by the Whig & Tory opponents of the ballot & used to be agreed in by its radical supporters. I have not seen a single new argument respecting the ballot for many years except one or two of yours. I do not feel in the way you do the desirableness of writing an ar-

---

[102] [On 13 June in the House of Commons.—Ed.]

[103] Probably the *Thoughts on Parliamentary Reform*, published five years later. [Published in John Stuart Mill, *Essays on Politics and Society*, ed. John M. Robson, vols. 18–19 (1977) of *Collected Works*, 19:311–40.—Ed.]

[104] [The full letter is published in Mill, *Later Letters*, vol. 14 of *Collected Works*, pp. 221–22.—Ed.]

[105] [John Bright (1811–1889) was chief orator of the free trade movement and a renowned Quaker Member of Parliament associated with the Anti-Corn Law League and Richard Cobden. Mill was frequently critical of Bright. Mill, *Later Letters*, vol. 14 of *Collected Works*, p. 221, note 3; Peart and Levy, *'Vanity of the Philosopher'*, p. 178.—Ed.]

[106] [George Grote was a major advocate of the ballot throughout his career in Parliament (1832–1841). Mill, *Later Letters*, vol. 14 of *Collected Works*, p. 221, note 4.—Ed.]

ticle for the Ed[inburgh][107] on it. There will be plenty of people to say all that is to be said against the ballot—all it wants from us is the authority of an ancient radical & that it will have by what is already written & fit to be published as it is—but I now feel so strongly the necessity of giving the little time we are sure of to writing things which nobody could write but ourselves, that I do not like turning aside to anything else. I do not find the essay on Justice goes on well. I wrote a good long piece of it at Quimper, but it is too metaphysical, & not what is most wanted but I must finish it now in that vein & then strike into another.

In the interval between these two letters the news of his mother's death had reached him.

J. S. M. to H. M., Quimper, 26 June 1854:[108] It is a comfort that my poor mother suffered no pain—& since it was to be, I am glad that I was not in England when it happened, since what I must have done & gone through would have been very painful & wearing & would have done no good to anyone. It is on every account fortunate that another executor has been appointed. There is a matter connected with the subject which I several times intended speaking to you about, but each time forgot. Unless my memory deceives me, the property my mother inherited from her mother[109] was not left to her out & out, but was settled equally on her children. If so, a seventh part of it, being something between £100 & £500, will come to me, & I do not think we ought to take it—what do you think? Considering how they have behaved, it is a matter of pride more than of anything else—but I have a very strong feeling about it.

J. S. M. to H. M., Nantes, 1 July 1854:[110] About the matter of my mother's inheritance, of course as your feeling is so directly contrary, mine is wrong, & I give it up entirely—but it was not the vanity of 'acting on the supposition of being a man of fortune'—it was something totally different—it was wishing that they should not be able to say that I had taken [away] anything from their resources. However that is ended, & I need say no more about it.

From Nantes Mill went for a fortnight to the Vendée, again in the company of his new acquaintance, Mr. Pope, and from the southernmost point of his journey he reports continued improvement of his health.

[107] [Hayek supplies the brackets containing the full name.—Ed.]
[108] [The full letter is published in Mill, *Later Letters*, vol. 14 of *Collected Works*, pp. 219–21.—Ed.]
[109] [According to *ibid.*, p. 220, note 3, Mrs. Harriet Burrow.—Ed.]
[110] [The full letter is published in *ibid.*, pp. 223–25.—Ed.]

J. S. M. to H. M., Rochefort, 16 July 1854:[111] You may know by my taking it so leisurely that the journey continues to do me good, indeed it seems to do me more & more. I was weighed at La Rochelle & had gained two pounds more, making six pounds since St. Malo—it shews how much weight I must have lost before, [as] these six pounds make not the smallest perceptible difference to the eye. I have gained still more in strength: yesterday at Rochelle I was out from eight in the morning till nine at night *literally* with only the exceptions of breakfast & dinner—& walking all the time except an occasional sitting on a bank.

On his return to Nantes he found another letter from his brother-in-law, enclosing a letter from his mother found after her death, and asking for instructions concerning the disposal of her furniture, which she had described as belonging to Mill. He copied both letters out in full for his wife and commented:

J. S. M. to H. M., Nantes, 19 July 1854:[112] Of course we can only say that the furniture was my mother's & must be dealt with as such—*but* I cannot write the note without a consultation so unless you think it can wait for my return (as I shall be home now in little more than a week), perhaps darling you will write to Rouen what you think should be said & in what manner, both about that & the plate.

The instructions asked for promptly reached Mill and in his last letter (Rouen, 24 July)[113] he replies that he will write 'the letter to Colman exactly according to your pencil which seems to me perfectly right' and the following letter is accordingly dispatched:

J. S. M. to Charles Colman, Rouen, 24 July 1854:[114] Dear Colman, Owing to a change in my route, I did not get to Nantes till later than I originally intended. With regard to my mother's furniture, I always considered it hers, & have often told her so. I think it or its proceeds should be equally distributed among all her daughters. The plate which my mother had, also to be distributed equally in the same manner. I am,

yrs faithfully,
J. S. Mill

[111] [The full letter is published in *ibid.*, pp. 229–30, where it is dated 15 July.—Ed.]
[112] [The full letter is published in *ibid.*, pp. 230–32.—Ed.]
[113] [The full letter is published in *ibid.*, pp. 233–34.—Ed.]
[114] MTColl. XLVII/38. [The full letter is published in Mill, *Later Letters*, vol. 14 of *Collected Works*, pp. 232–33.—Ed.]

TEN

ITALY AND SICILY
1854–1855

Mill's expectation that he would have no difficulty in obtaining a medical certificate saying that he ought to go to the south for six months during the winter of 1854/5 proved only too true. About the middle of November his doctor peremptorily ordered him away for eight months. But it was not to be
the joint holiday to which he and his wife had been looking forward. Apparently Mrs. Mill was not strong enough for a long journey[1] and after taking
her to Torquay he left Blackheath Park on 8 December for an extensive tour
of France, Italy and Greece. During his absence he wrote to her almost daily,
though he could often post his letters only once a week and some of them in
consequence run to very great length. All of the 49 letters written during the
journey have been preserved[2] and if printed in full would make a fairly thick
volume. For their detailed description of the places visited, these letters, particularly those from Sicily and Greece, might deserve someday to be printed
in full. In the course of the present narrative we must, however, confine ourselves to a few extracts which throw further light on Mill's intellectual and
emotional state.

The journey began inauspiciously. A miserable crossing of the channel,
during which Mill, always a sufferer from sea-sickness, was really ill, brought
him to Boulogne hardly able 'to totter up the steps', and further upsetting

[1] Mrs. Mill at the time, it seems, was suffering from some other complaint in addition to
her lung trouble. On 30 October 1855 she wrote to her brother Arthur in Australia (MTColl.
XXVII/48): 'I have been so reduced in strength since my bad illness in 1853 when I broke a
blood vessel in the lungs and was not expected to recover for some months, and since that I have
twice undergone a surgical operation, that I have seldom had strength to write more than a few
lines at a time'. [The full letter is published in *The Complete Works of Harriet Taylor Mill*, ed. Jo Ellen
Jacobs (Bloomington: Indiana University Press, 1998), pp. 416–17; this passage appears at p.
416.—Ed.]

[2] All the letters by Mill from which passages are quoted in this and the next chapter are
in Yale University Library [MS 350, Box 1, Folders 11–16]. [The letters, dated 7 December
1854 through 18 June 1855, are published in *The Later Letters of John Stuart Mill, 1849–1873*, eds.
Francis E. Mineka and Dwight N. Lindley, vols. 14–17 (1972) of *The Collected Works of John Stuart Mill* [hereafter cited as *Collected Works*] (Toronto: University of Toronto Press, 1962–1991),
14:247–494.—Ed.]

his digestion, from which he suffered throughout the journey as much if not more than from the symptoms of his pulmonary disease. After a night in Paris he commenced his round about journey to Marseilles *via* Bordeaux and the valley of the Garonne across the whole South of France.

> *Orleans, 9 December 1854:* Yesterday in the railway I was afraid that I was getting into that half mad state which always makes me say that imprisonment would kill me—& which makes me conscious that if I let myself dwell on the idea I could get into the state of being unable to bear the impossibility of flying to the moon—it is a part of human nature I never saw described but have long known by experience—this time the occasion of it was, not being able to get to you—when I reflected that for more than six months I was to be where I could not possibly go to you in less than many days, I felt as if I *must* instantly turn back & return to you. It will require a good deal of management of myself to keep this sensation out of my nerves.[3]

On the way to Bordeaux he stopped at Libourne, and after two days at Bordeaux he started out by diligence in slow stages up the valley of the Garronne to Toulouse, Carcassonne, Narbonne and Beziers to Montpellier. Here he stopped for five days, reviving memories of the time, thirty-four years earlier, when, as a boy of fourteen, he had spent there with Sir Samuel Bentham and his family 'the six happiest months of his youth'.[4] He continued via Nîmes to Avignon where he remained for the two Christmas holidays, and where for the first time, and the only time for a long while, he felt perfectly well—as it was indeed the climate of Avignon which years later, after the sad event of his wife dying there led him to choose it as his permanent home, should at last restore to him the health which he had been vainly seeking for so long. After another miserable sea journey from Marseilles to Genoa he felt for the first time really in a foreign country.

> *Genoa, 30 December 1854:* I seem much further from my dear one than in France—any place in France if it be ever so far off seems so much a home

---

[3] [The letter is published in full in Mill, *Later Letters*, vol. 14 of *Collected Works*, pp. 248–50; this passage is at pp. 249–50.—Ed.]

[4] So described in a letter to August Comte on 12 August 1842. See *Lettres Inedités de John Stuart Mill à Auguste Comte* (Paris: F. Alcan, 1899), p. 94. [Mill wrote, 'J'ai moi-même passé dans cette ville les six mois les plus heureux de ma jeuness, ceux de l'hiver 1820/21'. *The Earlier Letters of John Stuart Mill, 1812–1848*, ed. Francis E. Mineka, vols. 12–13 (1963) of *Collected Works*, 13:540; the full letter, dated 12 August 1842, is on 13:538–40.—Ed.]

to us. I do not get on well with the Italians here not only from the badness of my Italian but of theirs, for it is a horrible patois almost as unItalian as the Venetian but without its softness. Adieu darling—love me always—a thousand dearest loves.[5]

In another letter, begun on the same evening but continued on the following two days, he commenced his more detailed descriptions of the country mixed with more general reflections. He started on his further journey in a *voiture* taken together with a number of Italians to Sestri and Spezia, and according to his usual habit walked large parts of the way.

Sestri, 31 December 1854: There is great complaint of the distress of the people here—my fellow traveller said everything had failed except olives—not only the vines but all the grain & that the propriétaires are dying of hunger. A propos I have been reading of a great & rapidly extending disease among silkworms, propagated by the eggs—it seems as if there was a conspiracy among the powers of nature to thwart human industry if it once reaches the real necessaries of life the human race may starve. The potato disease was a specimen & that was but one root: if it should reach corn? I think that should be a signal for the universal & simultaneous suicide of the whole human race, suggested by Novalis. What a number of sensible things are not done, faut de s'entendre! In the meantime let us make what we can of what human life we have got, which I am hardly doing by being away from you. I think I should feel the whole thing worthier if I were writing something but I cannot make up my mind what to write. Nothing that is not large will meet the circumstances.

Spezia, 1 January 1855: Every possible good that the new year can possibly bring to the only person living who is worthy to live, & may she have the happiest & maniest New Years that the inexorable powers allow to any of us poor living creatures.[6]

In Spezia he stopped for a day and, as everywhere, was inquiring about the suitability of the place as a permanent domicile; but better news from his wife, with whom the climate of Torquay seemed to agree at the time, made him again more doubtful whether he wanted to live abroad.

---

[5] [Mill, *Later Letters*, vol. 14 of *Collected Works*, pp. 269–70; the full letter is on pp. 268–70.—Ed.]

[6] [*Ibid.*, pp. 272–73; the full letter is on pp. 270–74.—Ed.]

Spezia, 2 January: The nuisance of England is the English: on every other account I would rather live in England passing a winter now & then abroad than live altogether anywhere else. The effect of the beauty here on me, great as it is, makes me like the beauty of English country more than I ever did before. There is such a profusion of beauty of *detail* in English country when it *is* beautiful & such a deficiency of it here & on the Continent generally & I am convinced that a week's summer tour about Dartmoor would give me as much pleasure as a week about Spezia.[7]

In Pisa he stopped for six days, because his condition for a while got seriously worse, but on the 9th he proceeded by train to Sienna and thence started on the following day a long journey by diligence to Rome, where he at last arrived on the 14th. After a short note added to the letter written during the journey and posted on arrival follows a first long letter.

Rome, 15 January: I have read up the Times at the old place, Monaldini's. There is another place of the same kind now, Piale's, also in the Piazza di Spagna, which seems more frequented, especially by English. The only thing I found noticeable was the Queen's letter[8]—was there ever such a chef d'oeuvre of feebleness—O those grandes dames how all vestige of the very conception of strength or spirit has gone out of them. Every word was evidently her own—the great baby! & it is not only the weakness but the *décousu*, the incoherence of the phrases—sentences they are

---

[7] [*Ibid.*, p. 277. The full letter begins with a date of 2 January at Spezia and continues 4 and 5 January at Pisa; see pp. 275–79.—Ed.]

[8] Apparently a letter by the Queen to Mr. Sidney Herbert, reprinted in *The Times* of 5 January 1855:

> Windsor Castle, Dec. 6, 1854. Would you tell Mrs. Herbert that I begged she would *let me see frequently* the accounts she receives from Miss Nightingale or Mrs. Bracebridge, as *I hear* no *details of the wounded*, tho' I see so many from officers, &c., about the battle-field, and naturally the former must interest *me* more than any one.
>
> Let Mrs. Herbert also know that I wish Miss Nightingale and the ladies would tell these poor noble and sick men that NO ONE *takes* a warmer interest, or feels *more* for their sufferings, or admires their courage and heroism MORE than their Queen. Day and night she thinks of her beloved troups. So does the Prince.
>
> Beg Mrs. Herbert to communicate these my words to those ladies, as I know that *our* sympathy is much valued by these noble fellows.
>
> [signed]
> Victoria.

[The letter ran with a running head 'Autographed Letter of the Queen'. Mill, *Later Letters*, vol. 14 of *Collected Works*, p. 293, note 5, states that it was to convey to Florence Nightingale the message that she should assure 'the wounded and sick soldiers in the Crimea' that the Queen 'felt deeply their suffering and admired their courage'.—Ed.]

not. No wonder such people are awed by the Times, which by the side of them looks like rude strength.—Whom should I find here, in the same inn, but Lucas[9]—not a bad rencontre to make at Rome. I left my card for him & shall no doubt see him tomorrow. Au reste, nobody else here whom I know, judging from the lists at the libraries. Hayward[10] appears to have been here in the autumn but no doubt has left. There is a Lady Duff Gordon but I suppose & hope it is the *mother* of the baronet.[11] And there are a few people whom I have just seen—Lady Langdale[12]—some of the Lyalls[13]—& others whom I forget. If Naples is like Rome I have no chance of a companion. I have found the address of Dr Deakin & shall call on him tomorrow. I have been considerably better today but think it is best to consult somebody about my stomach & my strength. I am anxious to get back the last, since at present long walks which have done me so much good hitherto, are impossible. I have not ventured to take quinine while my stomach was [at all] disordered, which it is still, a little. I see a great many English priests all about, as well as many other English. On Thursday I believe there will be fine music at St. Peter's which I will certainly hear.—There is so much to do & to see here, that it has taken off my nascent velleity of writing. On my way here cogitating thereon I came back to an idea we have talked about & thought that the best thing to write & publish at present would be a volume on

[9] Frederick Lucas, M.P., born 1812, barrister and convert to Catholicism, and friend of Carlyle, since 1840 editor of *The Tablet*. He returned to London in May 1855 and died there in the autumn of the same year. According to his biographer 'he latterly gave much time to the study of political economy, and took a special interest in the social theories of John Stuart Mill'. In 1851 Lucas and Charles Gavan Duffy had asked Mill on behalf of the Council of the Tenant League to stand for Parliament for an Irish constituency. See *Autobiography*, p. 237 [John Stuart Mill, *Autobiography and Literary Essays*, eds. John M. Robson and Jack Stillinger, vol. 1 (1981) of *Collected Works*, p. 272], and *Letters* (ed. Elliot), vol. 1, p. 159 [Mill, *Later Letters*, vol. 14 of *Collected Works*, pp. 58–59], the *Life of Frederick Lucas, M.P.* by his brother Edward Lucas, 2 vols. (London: Burns and Oates, 1886), especially vol. 2, pp. 122 and 126, and C. G. Duffy, *Conversations with Carlyle* (New York: Charles Scribner's Sons, 1892), p. 166.

[10] Probably Abraham Hayward. [Mill, *Later Letters*, vol. 14 of *Collected Works*, p. 293, note 7, adds that Hayward (1801–1884) was 'a miscellaneous writer' and, late in life, a strong critic of J. S. Mill.—Ed.]

[11] The younger Lady Duff Gordon would have been Lucie, the daughter of Sarah Austin. [Mill had known Lucie as a child but was at this time estranged from the Austins.—Ed.]

[12] [This is most likely Lady Jane Elizabeth Langdale (d. 1872), the widow of Baron Henry Bickersteth Langdale (1783–1851) and Jeremy Bentham's and James Mill's friend; see Mill, *Later Letters*, vol. 14 of *Collected Works*, p. 293, note 9.—Ed.]

[13] [The family of Alfred Lyall (1795–1865), an author and editor whose brother George (1784–1853) was a Director of the East India Company; see *ibid.*, p. 293, note 10.—Ed.]

Liberty.[14] So many things might be brought into it & nothing seems [to me] more to be needed—it is a growing need too, for opinion tends to encroach more & more on liberty, & almost all the projects of social reformers of [in] these days are really *liberticide*[15]—Comte, particularly so. I wish I had brought with me here the paper on Liberty that I wrote for our volume of Essays— perhaps my dearest will kindly read it through & tell me whether it will do as the foundation of one part of the volume in question—If she thinks so I will try to write & publish it in 1856 if my health permits as I hope it will.[16]

Most of his letters from Rome are filled with accounts of his sightseeing. He seems at first mainly to have been attracted by the sculptures.

Rome, 16 January: I went through the [Vatican] Museum,[17] catalogue in hand, today, & [now] knowing the whole, shall return often to see those I most like. It gave me quite as much & more pleasure than I expected. The celebrated Meleager[18] I do not care a rush for—I should never have guessed it to be ancient. The Apollo is fine but there is a Mercury (formerly mistaken for an Antinous) which seems to me finer & a gigantic sitting Jupiter who is magnificent. The Ariadne if such she be is most beautiful & so are many others. The Laocoon I can see deserves its reputation but it is not the sort of thing I care about. I see with very great interest the really authentic statues & busts of Roman emperors, & eminent Greeks—although as you know, not only no physiognomist but totally incapable of becoming one. But I find the pleasure which pictures & statues give me, increases with every experience, & I am acquiring strong preferences & discriminations which *with me* I think is a sign of progress.[19]

Rome, 22 January: The picture gallery at the Capitol is about equal to the Bor-

---

[14] Compare Mill's account of the conception of the book *On Liberty* in the *Autobiography*, p. 212 [Mill, *Autobiography*, vol. 1 of *Collected Works*, p. 249]: 'I had first planned and written it as a short essay, in 1854. It was in mounting the steps of the Capitol, in January 1855, that the thought first arose of converting it into a volume'.

[15] [Hayek would return to this remark in the Postscript to *The Constitution of Liberty*, 'Why I Am Not a Conservative'; see *The Constitution of Liberty: The Definitive Edition*, ed. Ronald Hamowy, vol. 17 (2011) of *The Collected Works of F. A. Hayek* (Chicago: University of Chicago Press; London: Routledge), p. 519.—Ed.]

[16] [Mill, *Later Letters*, vol. 14 of *Collected Works*, pp. 293–94. The full letter is at pp. 291–96.—Ed.]

[17] [Hayek supplied the bracketed word.—Ed.]

[18] [A statue of Meleager, hero of the Calydonian boar-hunt, with the boar's head and dog. Roman version (*c.* A.D. 150) found in the Baths of Titus, from Greek original of the 4th century B.C. Mill, *Later Letters*, vol. 14 of *Collected Works*, p. 295, note 14.—Ed.]

[19] [*Ibid.*, p. 295.—Ed.]

ghese. I liked best a Fra Bartolomeo & some Venetian portraits. The ancient sculptures are fully equal, for their number, to those at the Vatican; the Dying Gladiator perhaps superior to any. There are some reliefs of scenes in which Marcus Aurelius is introduced which appear to me [quite] wonderful & are very delightful to me from my extreme admiration of the man. The place is full too of curiosities: the brazen she wolf of Romulus which was struck by [with] lightning at the time of Julius Caesar's death: the fragments of a most curious plan of old Rome, unfortunately dug up in many small pieces: the original Fasti Consulares also fragmentary but in large fragments, going back to some of the consulships preceeding the Decemvirate. All these are believed genuine by Niebuhr & the most critical judges who have fully examined the evidence. These are much more interesting to me than the remains of Roman buildings, which with two or three exceptions are very ugly & all very much alike. Lucas says his business at Rome is coming to a crisis:[20] he came to prevail on the Pope to take off the interdict lately laid on priests against interfering in politics: if he cannot proceed in this, he & others mean to give up politics for the present. Cullen, the Archbishop, is the head of the party opposed to him & he & Cullen are to meet this week by desire of the Pope, to try if they cannot arrange matters amicably: if not, the Pope will have to decide between them. I conjecture that the interdict, so absurd in a Catholic point of view was procured by Louis Napoleon to prevent the English government from being embarrassed by Ireland during this war. Lucas thinks it is not this, but Cullen's Whiggish inclinations, & it is curious that while Cullen was supported in getting the Archbishopric on the one hand by MacHale,[21] on the other, if Lucas says true, Lord Clarendon[22] was writing the strongest letters in his support on the ground of his being a perfectly safe man: three people known to Lucas have he says seen a letter from L[d] Clarendon to the brother of More O'Ferrall to that effect. This shews skilful duplicity in Cullen at all events.[23]

---

[20] [In 1854 Lucas traveled to Rome to protest the decree, by the Archbishop of Dublin, Paul Cullen, that forbade priests from interfering in politics. Lucas had two interviews with the Pope and wrote, at his bidding, a 'Statement' about the situation of Catholics in the United Kingdom. *Ibid.*, p. 293, note 6.   Ed.]

[21] [John MacHale (1791–1881) was an Irish Archbishop and a staunch Irish nationalist. He opposed the John Henry Newman at Dublin University and disagreed with Cullen over the Catholic University. MacHale was in Rome at this time; see *ibid.*, p. 304, note 11.—Ed.]

[22] [George William Frederick Villiers, 4th Earl of Clarendon, had earlier been Lord Lieutenant of Ireland. In 1854 he was the Foreign Minister; see *ibid.*, p. 304, note 12.—Ed.]

[23] [*Ibid.*, pp. 303–4. The full letter is at pp. 301–6. Page 304, note 13, states that no letter has been found, either to Richard More O'Ferrall (1797–1880), Governor of Malta (1847–1851), or to his brother, John Lewis More O'Ferrall (1800–1881), Dublin Commissioner of Police (1836–1881).—Ed.]

Rome, 24 January: Lucas has just been here. He has had his meeting with Cullen today, finds him very hostile—no chance of an amicable arrangement—means to stay here & fight it out—but can do nothing just at present therefore thinks he shall be able to go to Naples—& if so Mr. Kyan[24] proposes to go too. So we shall be a party of three. I should have liked Lucas better without Kyan but he is not disagreeable nor much in the way. We shall see. Meanwhile they are going with me to some more pictures tomorrow.[25]

Mill's health, which had been very bad during the early part of his stay in Rome—he had lost fifteen pounds since the temporary high at Avignon, was improving sufficiently towards the end of January for him to think of further travel and finally he agreed to start for Naples on the 29th. During the last three days he made another round of galleries and churches.

Rome, 26 January: No letter today—& rather fear she did not get mine in time to write on the 16th in which case I fear I shall not hear till I get to Naples. That will be on the 31st, the places being taken for Monday, two banquettes & one coupé being the best we could do. I saw the Doria gallery today (a wet day) with Lucas & Kyne, & the Colonna & Braschi palaces by myself. The Doria disappointed me—it is a very large collection & would make a sufficient national gallery for a second rate kingdom, but most of the pictures seemed to me third rate. There is however one long corridor full of portraits by Titian, Giorgione & Rubens—in this was also a fine Francia, & (very like Francia) a Giovanni Bellini: these two & Perugino have a complete family likeness—a Leonardo which though called a portrait of the second Giovanna of Naples is vastly like his one always recurring face—& finally the Magdalen of Titian, a splendid picture, perfectly satisfactory & pleasurable in execution (conception apart) but as a Magdalen ridiculous. I have seen many Titians at Rome & they all strengthen my old feeling about him—he is of the earth earthy. At the other two palaces there were some fine pictures, the majority portraits by the Venetians—at the Braschi the so called Bella of Titian, which I don't like, & what is reckoned a chef d'oeuvre of Corregio of whom there are few good specimens here which I don't like either though I can see that it may have strong points of colouring. Lots of Gaspar Poussins[26] at all three, deadly cold, & several ambitious Salvators, to my feeling quite poor: a St John & his famous Belisarius, which seems to me inferior to the poorest even of the Bolognese painters. Evidently the culmination of painting was in the three generations of which Raphael forms

---

[24] Father Kyne, a [Roman] catholic priest who had accompanied Frederick Lucas to Rome.
[25] [Mill, *Later Letters*, vol. 14 of *Collected Works*, p. 309. The full letter is at pp. 306–11.—Ed.]
[26] [Brother-in-law of Nicolas Poussin, Dughet Gaspard, called Le Guaspre-Poussin (1615–1675). *Ibid.*, p. 312, note 3.—Ed.]

the last, Titian belonging to it also though as he lived nearly 60 years longer than Raphael one fancies him of a later date. The worship of the still earlier painters is a dandyism which will not last, even I hope in Germany: the contempt of the Bolognese eclectics who came a century after has a foundation of reason but is grossly exaggerated. Guido especially has risen greatly with me from what I have seen at Rome & so has even Domenichino[27] whose finest pictures are here: him however I do not, as a matter of taste, care the least about. But I begin to think Ruskin right about Gaspard & Salvator,[28] perhaps even Claude,[29] & to think the modern English landscape painting better than theirs. If I did not write my impressions every day I should not write them at all, for seeing so many pictures one remembrance drives out another—but they leave a total impression extremely agreeable. I never was *immersed* in pictures before, & probably never shall be again to the same degree, for at any place but Rome one hardly can be, & even at Rome with her, there would be so much greater activity of other parts of the mind that the atmosphere would be different. Even the season & the bad weather contribute by throwing me upon the indoor pleasures of the place: My dearest may well smile at my pretension of giving opinions about pictures, but as all I say about them is the expression of real feelings which they give or which they fail to give me, what I say though superficial is genuine & may go for what it is worth—it does not come from books or from other people, & I write it to her because it shews her that I have real pleasure here & have made really the most of Rome in that respects & in others.[30]

Rome, 28 January: When I have paid my bill here my journey will have cost me up to this time (deducting the fees to Deakin medicine & everything else not properly chargeable to travelling & living) as nearly as possible £50. That is for about seven weeks & a half of time, but the distance travelled is considerable. I shall post this at the moment of leaving, (seven tomorrow morning) for the diligences start from the very court yard of the post office.[31]

After a night in Terracina Mill and his two companions Lucas and Kyne arrived in Naples on 30 January. For ten days Mill, who knew Naples from

[27] [Domenichino Zampieri (1581–1641), of the Carraci School. *Ibid.*, p. 312, note 5.—Ed.]
[28] [Salvator Rosa (1615–1671), Baroque painter, printmaker, and poet. *Ibid.*, p. 312, note 4.—Ed.]
[29] [Claude Lorraine (1600–1682), French artist known for his landscape paintings. *Ibid.*, p. 312, note 6.—Ed.]
[30] [Published in *ibid.*, pp. 311–14, with the portion above on pp. 311–12.—Ed.]
[31] [This is a continuation of the letter referred to in note 30 above; see *ibid.*, p. 314.—Ed.]

his visit with Mrs. Taylor sixteen years earlier, acted mainly as cicerone to his friends, confined by bad weather mainly to the town itself except for a visit to Paestium.

Naples, 9 February 1855: The papers bring up the news to the large divisions again at the ministry & their resignation[32]—a real misfortune for it is a chance if the next is as good. I think it was foolish of them to oppose an enquiry—When such accusations are made & believed, no matter how insufficient the authority, they *ought* to be enquired into. And everything practical which is under the management of the English higher classes is always so grossly mismanaged that one can quite believe things to be very bad, though not a jot the more because it is asserted by the Times & its correspondent. How very Times like to cry out now for Lord Grey as war minister[33] after all their attacks on him in & out of office for incapacity & conceit. I shall think seriously about the book on Liberty since my darling approves of the subject. Lucas & his friend left early this morning, much delighted with his visit & said repeatedly that he had seldom enjoyed three weeks as much as since he had met me at Rome. He is really for an Englishman a well informed man—for every historical fact or Latin quotation I brought out he had one as good and he has some will & energy which distinguish him from nearly everybody now, & talks really intelligently on politics on which he & I generally agree.[34] Of course a professed Catholic could not agree with me on much else & I should have talked much more controversially with him but for the presence of his friend Kyne latterly whose priesthood imposed a restraint on us both. . . . Nothing can be more beautiful than this place. You can I dare say imagine how I enjoy the beauty when I am *not* looking at it—now in this bedroom by candlelight I am in a complete nervous state from the sensation of the beauty I am living among—While I look at it I only seem to be gathering honey which I savourer[35] the whole time afterwards. I wonder if anything in Sicily or Greece is finer.[36]

---

[32] Lord Aberdeen's Cabinet, succeeded by Lord Palmerston's first ministry, after a motion for a committee of inquiry into the mismanagement of the Crimean expedition had been passed on 29 January by 305 to 148 votes.

[33] [*The Times* leaders supported Grey on 29 and 30 January 1855.—Ed.]

[34] Edward Lucas in the biography of his brother recounts that he had 'frequently heard Father Kyne, himself a man of considerable information, dilate upon the conversation, discussions, and casual remarks of the two men [Mill and Lucas], which he said eclipsed all that he had ever heard in the way of conversation' (*The Life of Frederick Lucas, M.P.*, by his brother Edward Lucas (London: Burns and Oates, 1886), vol. 2, p. 126). [Hayek supplies the names in brackets.—Ed.]

[35] [Hayek has 'savour' followed by a query here; Mill, *Later Letters*, vol. 14 of *Collected Works*, p. 322, contains 'savourer'.—Ed.]

[36] [Published in *ibid.*, pp. 318–23, with the passage above at pp. 320, 322.—Ed.]

Gradually during the three weeks which Mill spent in and around Naples his health and strength increased and he became again able to enjoy his accustomed long walks and climbs.

Sorrento, 12 February: Here I am darling & at the same inn, La Sirena[37] which looks as pretty as possible; only I think we were not on the ground floor which I am now. By the bye I only ascertained today, by finding the number of the house in Mrs. Starke, that my inn at Naples, the Hotel des Etrangers, is the very Casa Brizzi which we were in, though not then *called* a hotel.[38]

Sorrento, 13 February: Out today from half past nine till five. I have recovered all my strength. How pleasant, once more, after 3½ hours' walking, much of it climbing, to find myself at the foot of a very steep & rather high mountain & not feel that I had rather not climb it. I did so, & when I had got to the top was not at all tired—& scarcely tired when I got back to the inn, three hours after. The mountain in question was the Punta della Campanella, or [a] promontory of Minerva, occupying the extreme end of the Peninsula of Sorrento.

Naples, 17 February: There is a fresh arrival of newspapers today, the only one for nearly a week: containing the new ministry. Palmerston will now either make or mar his reputation—which [much] will be expected from him & he will be ambitious of being remembered as the Lord Chatham of this war, I was glad to see Ld J. Russell, even at this late hour, hoping that Lord Raglan would disregard the 'ribald press'[39]—pity he never said so till he [had] felt the ribaldry of the Times against himself in its grossest form. I perceive by incidental mention that the newspaper stamp is to be given up[40]—also that the government are to bring in a bill for limited liability in partnerships.[41] My dearest one knows that I am not prone to crying out 'I did it', but I really think my evidence[42] did this—for although there are many others

---

[37] [Mill and Harriet stayed at this same inn while visiting Italy in 1839. *Ibid.*, p. 326, note 4.—Ed.]

[38] [The full letter, which includes this passage and that dated 13 February, is published in *ibid.*, pp. 323–29; the passage above is at p. 326.—Ed.]

[39] [*The Times*, 9 February 1855, p. 6: 'Lord John Russell . . . abuses the "ribald press" for what it has done, expresses his entire satisfaction with Lord Raglan'.—Ed.]

[40] [*The Times*, 13 February 1855, p. 4. Ed.]

[41] [*The Times*, 9 February 1855, p. 5.—Ed.]

[42] See 'Report from the Select Committee on Investments for the Savings of the Middle and Working Classes', ordered by the House of Commons, to be printed 5 July 1850, *Parliamentary Papers*, 1850, XIX.169 [pp. 253–66], especially Mill's answers to questions 839, 847–51 879–80, 906 and 913. [Mill's examination includes questions 835 to 961 of the evidence before the committee. This was published as 'The Savings of the Middle and Working Classes, 1850', in John

on the same side, yet there would but for me have been a great overbalance of political economy authority against it—besides I have nowhere seen the objections effectually answered except in that evidence. We have got a power of which we must try to make a good use during the few years of life we have left. The more I think of the plan of a volume on Liberty, the more likely it seems to me that it will be read & ~~will~~ make a sensation. The title itself with any known name to it would sell an edition. We must cram into it as much as possible of what we wish not to leave unsaid.—I have been reading here, for want of another book, Macaulay's Essays. He is quite a strange specimen of a man of abilities who has not even one of the ideas or impressions characteristic of this century & which will be identified with it by history—except, strangely enough, in mere literature. In poetry he belongs to the new school, & the best passage I have met with in the book is one of wonderful (for him) admiring appreciation of Shelley. But in politics, ethics, philosophy, even history, of which he knows superficially very much—he has not a single thought of either German or French origin, & that is saying enough. He is what all cockneys are, an intellectual dwarf—rounded off & stunted, full grown broad & short, without a germ or principle of further growth in his whole being. Nevertheless I think he feels rightly (what little he does feel, as my father would say) & I feel in more charity with him than I have sometimes done, & I do so the more, since Lucas told me that he has heart disease, & is told by his physician that whenever he speaks in the H. of Commons ~~it~~ is at the hazard of falling dead.[43]

Mill's spirits revived further after reaching Palermo. The dreaded crossing from Naples, on an exceptionally fine and calm day, was accomplished without the after-effect of the earlier sea-passages, and after a few days in Palermo he felt himself fitter and more energetic than he had done for a long time. Indeed his feats of walking would be remarkable in a man of perfect health and a little later (March 5) he himself observes:

> It is curious that when I am too tired or weak to do anything else I can climb mountains: that is if they are steep enough, for a long ascending slope fatigues me greatly.[44]

The first long letter from Sicily gives a full description of a tour on Monte Pelerino in which Mill grows unusually enthusiastic.

Stuart Mill, *Essays on Economics and Society*, ed. John M. Robson, vols. 4–5 (1967) of *Collected Works*, 5:405–29.—Ed.]

[43] [The letter is published in Mill, *Later Letters*, vol. 14 of *Collected Works*, pp. 330–34, with the portion above at pp. 331–32.—Ed.]

[44] [*Ibid.*, pp. 354–63, with the portion above at p. 361.—Ed.]

Palermo, 24 February: The views all the way up had been very fine but from the top was one of the most glorious I should think in the world. The whole north coast of Sicily (all mountain & bay) as far as the eye could reach, the sea studded with the little round Lipari islands, the larger island of Ustica farther west, the exquisite Vega of Palermo & the town itself spread out as in one of the bird's eye Panoramas, the amphitheatre of mountains round it—Before I had reached the top I had caught the first view of Etna, which I thought I recognized in a white dome like object that rose through & above the white clouds—& when I reached the top, the soldiers confirmed this. The day was the most perfect of summer days—the wind light & easterly, just sufficient to temper the sun's heat—the soldiers called it scirocco di levante, to distinguish it I suppose from the real African scirocco—Goodwin[45] calls it the vento Greco. After enjoying the view for some time I started down the mountain. It was 12 when I was at the top & it took an hour & a half to reach the foot. I certainly never at any time of my life could have first climbed & then descended this mountain more vigorous & fresh. I feel equal to climbing Etna itself if this were the season for it. When I got to the inn I was not even tired, except indeed my arms with the weight of plants I carried, to the edification & amidst the apostrophes of the public—who were full of questions & remarks—the most complimentary of which was one I overheard, one woman having given a shout of astonishment (all speaking here by [the] common people is shouting) when another quietly remarked to her that it was for my bella & was a galanteria. I wish indeed it had been for my bella, & a day never passes when I do not wish to bring flowers home to her.[46]

A little earlier in the same letter he reports how through the lack of a library or reading room:

I am thrown on my own books & have begun reading Goethe's Italian travels which I had in Italy formerly & read—I like them much better now—he relates impressions in so very lively a manner & they seem to me to be all true impressions—he went, too, a learner in art, & I find many of his feelings at first very like mine. I forgot, though bringing German books, to bring a German dictionary, but I get on tolerably without one. I have also Theocritus, a proper book for Sicily.

[45] The British Consul at Palermo. [John Goodwin, who died 13 December 1869; *ibid.*, p. 340, note 3.—Ed.]
[46] [The full letter, which Mill began on 22 February, is published in *ibid.*, pp. 335–43, with the portion above at pp. 340–41.—Ed.]

Palermo, 24 February: These travels of Goethe give me a number of curious feelings. I had no idea that he was so young[47] & unformed on matters of art when he went to Italy. But what strikes me most in this & in him is the grand effort of his life to make himself a Greek. He laboured at it with all his might & seemed to have a chance of succeeding—all his standards of taste & judgment were Greek—his idol was symmetry: anything either in outward objects or in characters which was great & incomplete (*exorbitant* as Balzac says of a visage d'artiste) gave him a cold shudder—he had a sort of contemptuous dislike for the northern church architecture, but I was amused (& amazed too) at this most characteristic touch—that even Greek, when it is the Greek of Palmyra, is on too gigantic a scale for him; he must have something little & perfect, & is delighted that a Greek temple he saw at Assisi was of that & not the other *monstrous* kind. He judged human character in exactly the same way. With all this he never could succeed in putting symmetry into any of his own writings, except very short ones—shewing the utter impossibility for a modern, with all the good will in the world, to tightlace himself into the dimensions of an ancient. Every modern thinker has so much wider a horizon, & there is so much deeper a soil accumulated on the surface of human nature by the ploughings it has undergone & the growths it has produced, of which soil every writer or artist of any talent turns up more or less even in spite of himself—in short the moderns have vastly more material to reduce to order than the ancients dreamt of & the secret of harmonizing it all has not yet been discovered—it is too soon by a century or two to attempt either symmetrical productions in art or symmetrical characters. We all need to be blacksmiths or ballet dancers with good stout arms or legs, useful to do what we have got to do, & useful to fight with at times—we cannot be Apollos & Venuses just yet.[48]

Continuing the same letter on the next day Mill begins to develop plans for work to be done after his return home.

Palermo, 25 February: I have been thinking darling that when I get back I should like to reprint a selection from the review articles &c. It seems desirable to do it in our lifetime, for I fancy we cannot prevent other people doing it when we are dead, & if anybody did so they would print a heap of trash which one would disown: now if *we* do it, we can exclude what we should not choose to republish, & nobody would think of reprinting what the writer had purposely rejected. Then the chance of the name selling them is as great as it

---

[47] Goethe, who in 1787 had in the course of his Italian journey made a tour of Sicily rather similar to Mill's, was thirty-seven at that time.

[48] [The letter is published in Mill, *Later Letters,* vol. 14 of *Collected Works,* pp. 343–49, with the portion above at pp. 345–46.—Ed.]

is ever likely to be—the collection would probably be a good deal reviewed, for anybody thinks he can review a miscellaneous collection but few a treatise on logic to political economy—Above all, it is not at all desirable to come before the public with two books nearly together, so if not done now it cannot be done till after some time after the volume on Liberty—but by that time, I hope there will be a volume ready of much better Essays, or something as good: In fact I hope to publish some volume almost annually for the next few years if I live as long—& I should like to get this reprint, if it is to be done at all, off my hands during the few months after I return in which India house business being in arrear will prevent me from settling properly ᴏᴨ [to] the new book. Will my dearest one think about this & tell me what her judgment & also what her feeling is.[49]

After ten days in Palermo Mill set out on March 2nd with a muleteer and two mules for a tour round Sicily from which he expects:

such a fortnight's journey for beauty & interest as I never had in my life before—& as much pleasure as I can have separated from her (March 1). [He finds his] muleteer pretty much of the same politics as myself (but in his case) turning chiefly on taxation, the excess of which is certainly one of the great evils of this government (March 2).[50]

But riding a mule proved at first much more exhausting than he expected and even seemed to make it doubtful whether he would be able to carry out his plan of going in this way all round the West and South of Sicily. He visited the ruins of Segesta and Selinus and gradually adjusted himself to the new mode of conveyance by walking great parts of the way and sitting the rest of the time on the pack-mule on the top of his luggage rather than in the saddle. But after a little more than a week of this sort of travel he was inured to the hardships and had acquired a new although, as it proved, unjustified confidence in the state of his health.

Scicca, 11 March: As we had 35 Sicilian, about 40 English, miles to go today, the guide very reasonably proposed to start at seven [from Castel Vitrano]:[51] but after I was up & ready, it was raining steadily & the sky was one mass of unbroken cloud, seeming to preclude our going any further today. However

---

[49] [*Ibid.*, pp. 348–49.—Ed.]

[50] [These passages are from two different letters. The first, begun 27 February, is published in *ibid.*, 349–54, with the closing sentence quoted by Hayek above. The second letter was begun on 2 March and is published in *ibid.*, pp. 354–63, with the quoted passage appearing on p. 356. Hayek supplies the bridging words in brackets and the material in parentheses.—Ed.]

[51] [Hayek supplied the words in brackets.—Ed.]

after I had breakfasted & read ~~the~~ [two] idyls of Theocritus & a canto of the Purgatorio of Dante (I finished the Inferno, as well as Tasso, long since) there seemed some signs of clearing, the rain ceased & we started at half past nine, the mules receiving an extra feed to enable them to do the whole distance without stopping; & they arrived here, apparently not fatigued, at half past six. Of course I had to do a considerable part of this on the mule, but I certainly walked a good deal more than half, & under such difficulties as you may suppose. I never knew before what a country without roads is. I fancied there were mule paths like those at Nice or Sorrento: but those are *made* roads as much as turnpike roads are, & as well suited for the kind of traffic they are meant for as the ground admits. Not above five miles of the forty today were made roads, & that was where the soil was so dense a clay that it would have been totally impassable unless paved in the middle. Taught by experience I now knew that in so long a day's journey there was nothing to do except to splash, not exactly through thick & thin, but through thin, reserving my efforts to avoid the thick when possible. When you consider that I had to ride on the mule for long distances with my feet in the state [this] implied, you will see that this mode of travelling would have been madness if I had been at all in the condition of a pulmonary patient. Evidently the pulmonary disease has long been arrested, & my digestion & general health are the things to be now considered, & the walk today with all its difficulties was not at all too much. I always got off the mule when my feet began to get cold.[52]

Bad weather continued to dog his way for another three days when he reached Girgenti. From there a week or more of this sort of journey in fine weather and, apart from severe attacks of indigestion and occasional struggles with fleas at the inns, tolerable comfort brought him to Syracuse and the end of the mule ride.

Syracuse, 21 March: I had the good luck to approach the town in a bright afternoon feeling & looking like the finest July day. The approach was from the side of the greater harbour, which was calm & glassy, & across it the large white buildings of the town shone brightly in the sun. You know the town is at present confined to the island, which was only one of the five large quarters in the time of Syracusan greatness: but even now it looks, & is, one of the largest towns of Sicily. I do not think there is any town, not even Athens, which I have so much feeling about as Syracuse: it is the only ancient town of which I have studied, & know & understand, the localities: so nothing was new or dark to me. I cannot look at that greater harbour which my window in the Albergo del Sole looks directly upon, without thinking of the many despairing looks which

[52] [Mill, *Later Letters*, vol. 14 of *Collected Works*, p. 369. The full letter, begun on March 7, is at pp. 363–73.—Ed.]

were cast upon the shores all round (as familiar to me as if I had known them all my life) by the armament of Nicias & Demosthenes. That event decided the fate of the world, most calamitously—If the Athenians had succeeded they would have added to their maritime supremacy all the Greek cities of Sicily & Italy, Greece must soon have become subordinate to them & the empire they formed in the only way which could have united all Greece, might have been too strong for the Romans & Carthaginians. Even if they had failed & got away safe, Athens could never have been subdued by the Peloponnesians, but would have remained powerful enough to prevent Macedonia from emerging from obscurity, or at all events to be a sufficient check on Phillip & Alexander. Perhaps the world would have been now a thousand years further advanced if freedom had thus been kept standing in the only place where it ever was or could then be powerful. I thought & felt this as I approached the town till I could have cried with regret & sympathy. . . . O the splendor of the evening view from my window. Down immediately on the greater harbor over which boats, apparently pleasure boats, were moving—the softest lights over the plain & highlands, &, to the right, Etna, which can be seen from nearly all Sicily. On enquiry finding there was a diligence (the mail) to Catania in ten hours, & that it would take my diminished luggage, I resolved to go by it & to stay in these comfortable quarters long enough thoroughly to enjoy the place. So I parted from my muleteer with great good will on my side, & apparently on his. If I go round Etna I shall miss him very much, but it would be too expensive to keep him on till then. The last six days, the fine weather part of this mule journey, have been delightful, but I am not sorry to exchange it now for going from place to place by diligence & taking walks from the places I stop at.

After three more days in Syracuse which Mill thoroughly enjoyed and on which he reported in great detail, he continued on the 25th to Catania, where he arrived somewhat exhausted and with a new attack of indigestion which, although he did not allow it seriously to interfere with his sightseeing and excursions during the next three days, somewhat diminished the pleasure of it. But continued weakness in no way diminished his enthusiasm over the beauty of the two-day journey to Messina where, after visiting Taormina, he arrived on the 30th. He found that a steamer to Corfu was due to leave on the 1st and decided to risk the long sea passage, but a delay in the arrival of the steamer kept him waiting at Messina for another three days.

Messina, 1 April.[53] I passed the rest of the day in putting in order my great accumulation of plants, & in reading Dante & the Handbook for Greece.

[53] [This letter begins on 31 March, at Messina, and continues through 7 April. The full text is at *ibid.*, pp. 399–408, with the 1 April text at p. 401; and the 2 April text at p. 403.—Ed.]

Nothing is more likely to keep off seasickness than filling my brain with an exciting conception of what I am going to~~do~~: I think I shall do in Greece the contrary of what I have done in Italy, that is, I shall take what opportunities I may have & even seek opportunities of conversing with the educated class of natives. I am curious about the mind of the leading people of Greece & feel that I have almost everything to learn about them. Doubtless my introductions to Finlay[54] & Wyse[55] will give me opportunities, & going in the first week in April I shall have a good deal of time. I am obliged to ménager the books I have with me to make them hold out. I am keeping Sophocles for Greece, Theocritus & the two [minor] Sicilian pastoral poets, Bion & Moschus, I have finished, & like the two last much better than the first, whom I think greatly overrated, & quite inferior to his imitator, Virgil.

Messina, 2 April: Messina would be on some accounts the best place in Sicily for us to live in: it is I think still more beautiful than Palermo, & there is more life in the place, more foreigners come there & it is practically much nearer to England & France owing to the English & French steamers to Malta & the Levant which do not go near Palermo: it is strange therefore that there should be but one post in a week & I suspect there must be ways of sending *via* this or that in the intervals. Oates says the Galignani reaches him, sometimes, very quickly, by the French steamers. But I do not think we should like to live in so stagnant a place as Sicily, where one falls a month behind in news if one has not one's own newspaper & meets no one who knows a single European fact.

---

[54] George Finlay (1799–1875) was a historian and the author of *A History of Greece*. He had participated in the Greek war of independence and had known Lord Byron.

[55] Sir Thomas Wyse (1791–1862), since 1849 British Minister to Athens and earlier Secretary of the Board of Control for India.

ELEVEN

GREECE
1855

After forty-eight hours spent foodless on his back in his cabin, Mill arrived at Corfu in tolerably good shape on 6 April—in 1855 Good Friday, both according to the Western and to the Greek calendar. The Ionian Islands were then still a British possession and Mill soon found agreeable company and, with an Irish botanist and a young man from Oxford, for eight days explored Corfu and finds it 'decidedly the most beautiful & agreeable little bit of our planet that I have yet seen & I do not at all expect to find anything better in Greece'.[1] He soon came to envy the post of High Commissioner there when an unexpected offer from the Colonial Secretary, Bowen, seemed almost to provide the perfect answer to his search for a place at which to live.

> *Corfu, 8 April 1855:* I breakfasted with him [Bowen][2] in his very nice rooms & took the opportunity of asking him about the eligibility of the place for living in, telling him my reason for being interested about it—that either my wife's health or my own, or both, might very possibly make it desirable for me to fix in a southern climate. He gave the greatest encouragement—said it had often surprised him that so few English settle here, that it can only be because the advantages of the place are not known. He said the common idea of the English here is that you can live as well on £600 a year here as on £1200 in England, but that quiet & economical people can

---

[1] J. S. M. to H. M., Corfu, 10 April 1855. All the letters by Mill reproduced in this chapter are in Yale University Library [MS 350, Box 1, Folders 15–16]. [The full letter, written between 7 and 12 April, is published in *The Later Letters of John Stuart Mill, 1849–1873*, eds. Francis E. Mineka and Dwight N. Lindley, vols. 14–17 (1972) of *The Collected Works of John Stuart Mill* [hereafter cited as *Collected Works*] (Toronto: University of Toronto Press, 1962–1991), 14:408–17, with the passage quoted in this paragraph appearing at p. 416, and the passage below, from 8 April, at pp. 412–13.—Ed.]

[2] [Hayek supplies the brackets and contents. George Ferguson Bowen (1821–1899), was President of the Ionian University at Corfu (1847–1851), Chief Secretary to the government of the Ionian Islands (1854), and the first Governor-in-Chief and Vice-Admiral of Queensland, Australia (1859). He received the knighthood in 1860 and later became Governor of Mauritius (1879) and Hong Kong (1882); see Mill, *Later Letters*, vol. 14 of *Collected Works*, p. 409, note 3.—Ed.]

do much better: for instance his predecessor as Colonial Secretary told him he never spent more than £500 though he had several children & kept a carriage & two or three horses. He asked me if I should like to be Resident of one of the Islands—saying that the work does not take above two hours a day to an energetic person as he has not to govern but to review the acts of the native government, all of which must be submitted to him in writing for his sanction—that the pay is £500 [a year] & a house, or rather two houses, in town & country, that the appointment is not with the Colonial office but with the Lord High Commissioner who is always eager to get better men than the officers accidentally in command of the troops, whom he is generally obliged to appoint for want of better & whose incompetence & rashness some times go near to drive him mad—that either Cephalonia or Zante will be vacant within a year; [&] that they are not bound to any representation except that they give a ball to the chief people of the island once a year on the queen's birthday & a dinner to the members of the native government about twice a year. This is tempting, now when I see how much pleasanter at least Corfu is than most of the places we could think of going to: & if Ward[3] had been going to remain I could probably have had the place for asking. The new man[4] is the son of an India director[5] but my having known him, as he died under a cloud, would not I suspect be much of a recommendation to the son. Bowen introduced me at the garrison library, the only place [here] where one can see English newspapers & periodicals—there I learnt for the first time Hume's death:[6] if all did as much good in proportion to their talents as he, what a world it would be! also that Lewis is Chancellor of the Exchequer & Vernon Smith at the India Board:[7] this last I suspect will give me a good deal of influence there.

[3] Sir H. Ward, the Lord High Commissioner for the Ionian Islands. [Sir Henry George Ward (1797–1860) was a Member of Parliament from 1837 until 1849. He became Lord High Commissioner in 1849 and later was Governor of Ceylon and of Madras; see *ibid.*, p. 407, note 12.—Ed.]

[4] Sir J. Young. [Sir John Young (1807–1876) was a politican who assumed roles in the Treasury in 1841 and 1844–1846; he became Privy Councillor in 1852, Chief Secretary for Ireland from 1852 until 1855, and Lord High Commissioner of the Ionian Islands from 1855 until 1859. See *ibid.*, p. 412, note 13.—Ed.]

[5] [Sir William Young (1773–1848), whose guilty judgment in 1847 for conspiracy to sell East India cadetships was suspended because he was ill. See *ibid.*, p. 412, note 14.—Ed.]

[6] Joseph Hume, the Radical politician, had died on 20 February 1855. [Hume (1777–1855) was a friend of James Mill since their boyhood days at school in Scotland; see *ibid.*, 413 note 15.—Ed.]

[7] On the resignation of W. E. Gladstone as Chancellor of the Exchequer and two other ministers, Sir George Cornewall Lewis had become Chancellor and R. V. Smith President of the Board of Control.

Towards the end of his stay in Corfu, and after a long and anxious pause, Mill at last received news from his wife. Apparently her health had been badly affected by the severe winter.

Corfu, 14 April.[8] Thank heaven it is over—the illness & the winter too—& though the last letter does not say how you are, the handwriting & its being in ink are encouraging. Respecting the danger of travelling in Greece, my precious one will have seen by my last letter that I am quite attentive to the subject, & shall not run any serious risks. I shall be guided by Wyse who must know the state of the country. You might well say that some other person's savoir faire was wanted 'in addition' to mine—I could not help laughing when I read those words, as if I had any savoir faire at all. . . . Bowen afterwards renewed the subject of the Residentship, said that Zante will be vacant this year: that it will be offered to Wodehouse[9] & if he takes it Cefalonia will be vacant & that he is almost sure Sir J. Young has no one to whom he wishes to give it & seemed very desirous that I should think seriously about it. I told him that I had not made up my mind to leave the India house but might very possibly be obliged to do so & that this opening would be a strong additional inducement. As one dinnering leads to another I found myself in for another dinner with Sir J. Young, yesterday: the only persons present were the Regent of Corfu (a Count something)[10] & Col. Butler.[11] I learnt a good deal & so did the Governor from the Regent, about the statistics of the island & had some talk with Sir J. Y. about the taxes. I was glad to see so much of him in case we should think in earnest about coming here. I do not believe there is a more beautiful place in the world & few more agreeable—the burthen of it to us would be that we could not (with the Residentship) have the perfectly quiet life, with ourselves & our own thoughts, which we prefer to any other, but if we have tolerable health there is not more of societyizing than would be endurable & if we have not, that would excuse us. This morning is the day for going to Athens, but the steamer has not arrived & I cannot tell when we shall get off. . . . I am impatient to get to Greece now, having seen this island thoroughly & so as never to forget it: & it has seemed to me always more & more charming. All however say that the climate is extremely variable, much

---

[8] [The letter, written between 14 and 18 April is published in Mill, *Later Letters*, vol. 14 of *Collected Works*, pp. 417–24. This passage begins at p. 417.—Ed.]

[9] Colonel Wodehouse, Resident in Ithaca. [*Ibid.*, p. 419, note 8 identifies Colonel Berkeley Wodehouse (1806–1877), who was Resident of Ithaca in 1852, Resident of Cephalonia in February 1855, Resident of Zante in June 1855, and Consul in Zante from 1864 to 1870.—Ed.]

[10] [*Ibid.*, p. 419, note 9, makes the identification: Count Candiano Roma.—Ed.]

[11] A.D.C. to the High Commissioner. [Colonel Edward C. Butler, 36th Regiment. *Ibid.*, p. 416, note 21 supplies the identification.—Ed.]

rain, a good deal of cold, & intense heat for three months. . . . Bowen tells me that Reeve[12] is editor of the Edinburgh! it is indeed fallen. Who will consent to have his writings judged of, & cut & carved by Reeve? For us it is again a complete exclusion.[13]

There is no further mention of the Residentship in Mill's letters, but from a letter written about this time by Mrs. Mill to her brother in Australia it would seem that it was probably at her wish that he did not accept the offer.

Mrs. Mill to Arthur Hardy, about April 1855:[14] M[r] Mill has the offer of a very nice place under government in one of the Greek islands, it being supposed that the climate might suit both his and my health, but tho' much tempted I do not think we shall accept it, we both dread the heat which is said to be excessive in ~~the~~ summer.

Leaving Corfu on the morning of 15 April, and after first slowly steaming along the Ionian Islands and up the Gulf of Corinth, and after a carriage drive across the Isthmus, Mill reached Athens on the evening of the 17th.

Athens, 19 April:[15] I have made good use of the two days I have been here: yesterday I saw almost all the antiquities & went today to Eleusis. I have already got quite into the feeling of the place—With regard to scenery it is hitherto rather below my expectation, very inferior to Corfu & the Corinthian Gulf, the mountains though otherwise fine being arid & bare, & very like those of the south of France, while the peculiar beauty of this place, the bright & pure atmosphere, I have not had—both these days though sunny having been extremely hazy, so that I did not see the mountains half as well as on the rainy day of my arrival. Wyse says that Lord Carlisle[16] had the same ill luck, & only

[12] Henry Reeve (1813–1895), who for fifteen years had been foreign editor of *The Times* and in 1855, when on becoming Chancellor of the Exchequer G. C. Lewis relinquished the post, succeeded him as editor of the *Edinburgh Review*, a post which he held until his death forty years later. [Reeve was a nephew of Sarah Austin. Mill had been acquainted with Reeve since boyhood; see Mill, *Later Letters*, vol. 14 of *Collected Works*, p. 421, note 10.]

[13] [Mill most likely felt he was excluded because of his strained relations with John and Sarah Austin, as well as Reeve's conservative views. He did contribute to the *Edinburgh Review* again after Harriet's death. See Mill, *Later Letters*, vol. 14 of *Collected Works*, p. 421, note 11.—Ed.]

[14] MTColl. XXVII/46. This is a copy of the concluding part of the letter with the evidently erroneous date 'March 1855' added later. [The letter, which was apparently revised several times, is published in *The Complete Works of Harriet Taylor Mill*, ed. Jo Ellen Jacobs (Bloomington: Indiana University Press, 1998), pp. 414–15. No date is provided there.—Ed.]

[15] [The full letter, written between 19 and 27 April, is published in Mill, *Later Letters*, vol. 14 of *Collected Works*, pp. 425–33.—Ed.]

[16] [George William Frederick Howard, 7th Earl of Carlisle (1802–1864), was a Member of Parliament who served for several ridings between 1826 and 1846. He served as Chief Secretary

had before his departure a few days of [the] brilliant weather. Nevertheless the view from the Acropolis was splendid. The temples [rather] surpassed my expectation ~~rather~~ than fell short of it though I had not fancied that so much of the Parthenon had perished. The beauty of it however is what no engraving can give any proper idea of, even independent of what all the buildings here owe to the excessive beauty of the Pentelicon marble they are made of. The temple of Theseus I have from my childhood been familiar with a print of. I should never be tired of looking at it. The interior has been made a museum for the sculptures they occasionally dig up & I was not at all prepared for their extreme beauty: there is one statue very like, & I think equal to, the Mercury or Antinous of the Vatican, & a number of sepulchral groups in which grace & dignity of attitude & the expression of composed grief in the faces & gestures are carried as far as I think mortal art has ever reached.

20 April: The Acropolis with its four temples, (though the Propylaea is not really a temple) combines magnificently with the hills about—& of the distant mountains, Pentelicus & the island of Ægina[17] are the finest, except the group at the Isthmus which are glorious. What light it throws on Greek history to know that the Acro Corinth is seen as a great object from all these heights — much larger & nearer looking than the Knockholt beeches[18] from home. I think that corner of the Morea must be perfectly divine. The gulf or [bay or] narrow channel between Salamis & the mainland in which the battle was fought is just under our feet but I cannot realize the history of the place while I am looking at it — all the alentours are so different. I shall do that better in our drive at dear Blackheath.

On the following, perfectly cloudless but still somewhat hazy day Mill climbed Pentelicus and was rewarded with a perfect view.

21 April: I never saw any combination of scenery so perfectly beautiful & so magnificent—& the sunset & evening lights on the innumerable mountains in front of us returning were exquisite. The haze does not so much affect the beauty of the lights when the sun is low. The more than earthly beauty of this country quite takes away from me all care or feeling about historical associations, which I had so strongly at Syracuse. *That* I shall have when I read Greek history again after becoming acquainted with the localities. I was not at all tired, except the hand which carried the plants, for the

---

for Ireland 1835–1841 and Lord-Lieutenant of Ireland 1855–1858. In the summer of 1853 he traveled to the continent. See *ibid.*, p. 426, note 5.—Ed.]

[17] [Hayek includes a query after Ægina.—Ed.]

[18] [Knockholt is between London and Dover, some twenty miles from Downe. The Beeches are to the southwest; see Mill, *Later Letters*, vol. 14 of *Collected Works*, p. 391, note 9.—Ed.]

load which Perry[19] & I brought in was quite painful to mind & body. I never felt so much the embarras des richesses. Determining them with imperfect books takes several hours in every 24: it is now past 12 & I have only determined about a third, the rest must remain in water & in the tin case till tomorrow—to be determined by day light—nor have I been able to change a single paper. I am here in the season of flowers as well as of all other beauty. It is quite true that nothing, not even Switzerland, is comparable in beauty to this—but as in all other cases, other inferior beauty will be more, not less, enjoyable in consequence. If *my* darling beauty could but see it! it is the only scenery which seems worthy of her. Even Sicily recedes quite into the background. And it is but a fortnight since I thought nothing could be finer than Messina!

After ten days in Athens Mill started on 28 April with three companions for the first of his longer excursions, to Nauplia, Argos and Corinth, which, however, he had scarcely time to describe since after only one night at Athens he starts on 2 May for a much longer excursion to the north. With one companion, a young Englishman he had met at Athens, and a guide, Mill travelled for thirteen days through Attica, Euboea and Central Greece and with his detailed daily accounts filled a letter of 22 closely written pages which he posted after his return to Athens.

Tatoe (the ancient Deceleia), 2 May:[20] I have got thus far, my angel, & am now writing in a nice room of a very pretty maison de campagne in I should think the finest situation in Attica, belonging to somebody who was minister of war during part of the revolutionary period. It stands a little way up Parnes, on the side next to Pentelicus, at a short distance from the place which the Lacedæmonians fortified in the latter part of the Peloponnesian war to take military possession of Attica. Where there are no inns, travellers are of course entertained in private houses. The owner of this is now absent. We form quite a caravan, having four horses & two mules, three for ourselves & the guide, three for [the] luggage & utensils, beds, provisions &c, also three muleteers & a cook: all this being provided for the 25 francs a day we each pay, which also includes the remuneration of the guide. . . . The commencement of the journey is auspicious. I am writing this while waiting for dinner, on a table spread as neatly as at home & I have no doubt we shall dine as well & as pleasantly as at the hotel at Athens. Our guide George Macropoulos, evidently understands this part of the [his] business, though he does not

[19] The Irish botanist whose acquaintance Mill had made at Corfu.
[20] [The full letter, written between 2 and 15 May, is published in Mill, *Later Letters*, vol. 14 of *Collected Works*, pp. 435–51.—Ed.]

know the mountains from a distance & misleads us in the most absurd manner. I have hitherto found, much to my surprise, the Greeks a remarkably stupid people—the stupidest I know, without even excepting the English. I make every allowance for the fact that they & we communicate in languages which are foreign to both & which they know very imperfectly—but they do not shew the cleverness that French, Italians, & even Germans do in making out one's meaning, & they never seem able to find out what one wants. Invariably they do the very opposite of what one tells them, ~~being~~ [very] much too conceited to say they do not understand. . . . My travelling companion Dawson is pleasant mannered & seems desirous of information but very little educated & even leaves out many an *h*—which one would not have expected from his appearance or the tones of his voice, or his general manner of expressing himself.

On the next day the party, after crossing the range of the Parnassus, descended through the valley of Tanagra, continued along the coast of the channel of Euripus, over which they finally passed to Euboea over the bridge at Chalcis, where they spent a night in the house of a local merchant. Proceeding north through the mountains in the interior of the island they made their next stop at Achmet Aga.

Achmet Aga, 4 May: a village *made* entirely by an Englishman named Noel[21] who for his reward has lately had his house actually gutted of everything worth removing, & the whole village plundered by a set of brigands. It is in his house we are lodged, quite unexpectedly, for the guide told us he had asked hospitality of a *German* named *Emile*.[22] This is exactly like the ignorance & gross inaccuracy of ~~these~~ [their] guides (this man is thought one of the best, & I have tried two others).

Continuing their way further north in the company of their host for the night, Mill's enjoyment of the beauty of the landscape steadily increased. Writing from 'a village in the north of Euboea where we are lodged very comfortably' he wrote on

5 May: It is useless attempting to describe it. Whatever one picks out as the choice bits in any other southern country compose the whole of Greece, & here we have it mixed with much of what is finest in the northern countries.

[21] [Edward Noel (*c.* 1796–*c.* 1876) was the son of Lord Wentworth's illegitimate son Thomas. Noel's cousin Lady Byron sent Noel to Switzerland for his education and bought him an estate in 1830. See *ibid.*, p. 439, note 5.—Ed.]

[22] [The German-speaking Swiss Emile Müller was Noel's partner; see *ibid.*, p. 439, note 6.—Ed.]

We often overlook[ed] the Ægean on the eastern side of the island, with Scyros apparently quite near—a long mountain ridge: & at last came in sight of the Gulf of Volo in front with Othrys & Pelion behind it & the islands of Peparethis, Sciathos & others over against its entrance—(in a clearer day we should also have seen Ossa & Olympus) making the divinest view I ever beheld. About the middle of the day we came to a large rich village where the people were assembled for the fête of their patron St. George & we saw dancing of the most barbaric kind to truly Turkish music, a drum going like strokes of a blacksmith's hammer & a sort of flute sounding like a bagpipe. There was general personal cleanliness & much fine dressing—they are an odd people like South Sea islanders I should think. Noel shewed us several of the cottages of his peasants—one large room, with an earthen floor, the fire in the middle & a hole in the roof above it for the smoke—one end of the room sometimes partitioned off, [sometimes not] for all the[ir] animals, cows, oxen & all. In the midst of one of these stood the paysanne, a neat, still handsome woman, quite finely dressed for the fête, making the oddest contrast with all that surrounded her. At the dancing nothing could exceed the polite attention we received from all the people. It is impossible to dis-like such universally good humoured & courteous people but they are almost savages. They always consider & speak of themselves as Orientals, not Euro-peans.

On the following day they reached through 'Yerochori' (Xirochorion) the channel which separates Euboea from what was then the northernmost strip of Greek mainland at Oreos and after long negotiations succeeded in hiring the only boat in the roads large enough to take horses up the gulf of Zeitun. Unfavourable winds prolonged what need have been no more than a three-hour crossing to more than twenty, including a whole night which Mill, with-out damage to his health, spent on the deck, landing at last at

Stylidha (Stylis), 7 May: Our guide wanted us to land at Molos on the south side, very near Thermopylae & not go to Lamia at all, & by this we should have saved a day, but as the dangerous part of the journey, if any, begins here, & we were told that there were only national guards at Molos, in whom we felt no confidence, we decided (as the Eparchos[23] had advised) to land at Stylidha, the port of Lamia on the north side. There we waited on the civil & military authorities, presented our ministerial order, & are to have a guard of six regular soldiers & [or] mounted gendarmes tomorrow. To this we are legally entitled: what we give to them is bakshish—a word in much use here—in which form they will cost us about a dollar a day.

[23] The *sous-préfet* of Yerochori, to whom they had had an introduction.

Topolia, 9 May: We started from Stylidha with our six guards who however were not regular soldiers: but they only went with us to Lamia, three hours off, past the head of the gulf. Here the commandant gave us two non commissioned officers & eight privates, to whom the commandant of the following station of his own accord added two more: so we are well protected. The number makes no difference in what we pay. Some of them go before us & some behind & at the commencement they threw out vedettes to right & left but they left off this when they got into the narrow ways. At the head of the gulf there is a considerable plain, & the part near Lamia is better cultivated than any other part of Greece [which] I have seen. There is however a great deal of marsh round the head, as with the Lake of Como. After crossing this ~~place~~ [plain] we entered the pass of Thermopylae, between Œta & the gulf: first crossing the Spercheius, a river of some size, the first real river I have seen in Greece. But Leonidas[24] would not know the place again, for in the 2350 years which have since passed, the Spercheius has brought down so much soil that it has converted the narrow pass into a broad flat, partly marsh, partly covered with scrub, through which the river winds its course in a very slanting direction & at last falls into the gulf. The side of Œta rises very steep, but covered with copse. The place of the ancient pass is fixed by some hot sulphurous springs which now as then gush out from the foot of the mountain, & also by the tumulus which was raised to contain the ~~slain~~ [sluice].

After a night spent at the village of Boudonitza they crossed the mountain range towards the south. The same day's entry then continues:

We were now completely in Swiss scenery. When we reached the top of the pass we looked down suddenly upon the great valley of Phocis, larger & broader than the Valais, & reaching from Boeotia to Thessaly—it lies between the range of Parnassus & that of Œta, the former of which was now spread out before us & the groups of summits more particularly known by the name of Parnassus was exactly opposite. Clouds however ~~being~~ [hung] on most of the tops & it soon began to rain & ~~it~~ rained at intervals all the rest of the day. The valley is very green at this season—the centre alone is cultivated, though the whole is evidently very fertile—the rest is waste or beautiful woods of oak & plane: several beautiful streams run down it towards Boeotia & I suppose all join ~~it~~ lower down. But a village or two of few houses, just visible in nooks of the mountain, are all that remains to represent the twenty cities of Phocis. People talk of coming to Greece to see ruins, but the whole country is one great ruin.

[24] [King of Sparta, Leonidas, who held the pass against Xerxes and the Persians in 480 B.C., see Mill, *Later Letters*, vol. 14 of *Collected Works*, p. 443, note 8.—Ed.]

From Topolia a very short day's journey of only four hours took them to Delphi.

> *Delphi, 10 May:* Delphi is one of the very few places in Greece of which the views in Wordsworth's Greece[25] give a more favourable idea than the truth: it is however fine, backed by a very precipitous cleft portion of Parnasses & looking down into the broad valley with a narrow gorge at the bottom of it, rapidly ascending from right to left. I dare say it was very imposing when it was a fine town with a magnificent temple: it seems to have been at that time [entirely] built on artificial ground supported by a solid wall along the mountain side, much of which (most splendid masonry) still remains. The Castalian spring is a humbug. The only bit of ground approaching to a level to be found near the town was also propped up by a wall & formed the stadium or racecourse for the Pythian games, the most important & celebrated in Greece next to the Olympic.

After a partial ascent of Parnassus the party almost completed their circuit of the mountain by descending to the plains of Boeotia and Lake Copias, Mill as usual noting all the places with classic associations, from the exact spot where Oedipus met his father to the scene of the tragic adventure of Philomela and of the battle of Chaeronea. The last two stages of this tour, via Livadia and Plateae, were somewhat spoiled for Mill by a more than usually severe attack of indigestion. Arriving back at Athens on 15 May, he was further disquieted by unfavourable news about his wife's health. But as a second letter gave a somewhat more reassuring account he decided to go on with his original plans, and after a short rest, he proceeded on his tour of the Peloponnesus.

> *Athens, 15 May:* I shall now take three clear days of rest before starting again for which I shall be much the better, although I am not at all done up by the journey. I have been more fatigued some days than others, but not *increasingly* fatigued: when I have been able to take a long walk before riding at all, I have hardly been tired at all—& so when the country has admitted of much trotting & [or] galloping. It is the sitting on horseback with my feet dangling that fatigues me when long continued: but I now recover myself by walking which I could not so well do in Sicily. My digestion is not quite so bad & I hope by degrees to bring it round. Probably *now* a perfectly regular life such as we have at home will agree better with it than travelling. But to all

---

[25] Christopher Wordsworth (Bishop of Lincoln), *Greece, pictorial, descriptive and historical, with upwards of three hundred and fifty engravings by Copley, Fielding etc.* (London, 1839). A new edition of this work had appeared in 1853.

appearance the pulmonary complaint has derived the greatest benefit from this holiday. I called on Wyse this morning & saw him: he agreed in all I said about the Greeks, & told me many things, shewing the same brainless stupidity, & incapacity of adapting means to ends, in the acts of their government which I had observed in the common people. I now perfectly understand all I see in Greece, but I must say I now feel little or no interest in the people. Still if they get education they may improve. Wyse thinks the stupidity is in a great measure laziness but he admits them to be stupid.

At Athens Mill parted from his companion and on 18 May started alone on his Peloponnesian journey, which on the first two days took him merely to Megara and Corinth respectively. Only the third day, his forty-ninth birthday, brings him to really new fields.

Valley of the Lake Stymphalus, 20 May:[26] This day last year I did not think I should be alive now, much less that I should pass my next birthday in Arcadia, & walk & ride nearly 14 hours of it. . . . I am [very] glad [not to] ~~I~~ have ~~not~~ missed this as it is not only of a totally different character from all else in Greece, but the mountains finer. They run into so many intersecting ranges that I have not yet got to understand them, but we do seem to have now come up to a high barrier range running east & west. We are in a village at the end of the valley of the Lake Stymphalus.

In two further long stages Mill continued south, almost the whole length of the peninsula, towards Sparta. Although he feels he is thinner than he has been before in his life, he stood the strain well.

Vurlia, 22 May: [Laconia][27] however though it would be admired anywhere else is altogether the least striking part of Greece, the forms of the mountains being more rounded than usual, & the whole ~~being~~ a complete wild with a barren arid appearance—only fine when a glimpse is caught of ~~the~~ Taygetus: but I was well rewarded at the last by the very finest view [of] ~~in~~ Greece, at least made so by the lights of ~~the~~ sunset, but it must always be one of the finest. This was in the descent to this village of Vurlia (near the site of Sellasia) which is itself very high up in the mountains on the east side of the magnificent green valley of Sparta. The opposite boundary is all formed by the range of Taygetus on which this house directly looks—& which is as fine as any part of the Alps & much finer than Parnassus or any other moun-

---

[26] [The full letter, written between 18 and 31 May, is published in Mill, *Later Letters*, vol. 14 of *Collected Works*, pp. 454–70.—Ed.]

[27] [Hayek supplies the brackets and contents.—Ed.]

tain I have seen in Greece. The highest part is something like the Dent du Midi at the head of the lake of Geneva & at present brilliant with snow like that, but from that highest part it extends in a jagged ridge or series of peaks to right & left, [falls] ~~fully~~ to the length of the Mont Blanc group of mountains. Below it glitters the Eurotas—the valley immediately under the village is hid, but above & below it glitters like an emerald, as do also the sides of the mountains & the view northward to the mountains of Western Arcadia by the sunset lights was glorious—the mountains themselves very fine, especially one like an enormous dome with smaller domes to right & left for shoulders. I shall see this valley tomorrow—unhappily time does not admit of my passing a night at Sparta & seeing the country in the way I should wish.

Khan of Georgitzi in Laconia, 23 May: I walked to Sparta after breakfast, a three hours walk. The valley, like all other scenery, loses much by the glare of ~~the~~ sunshine, but it does not disappoint the expectations ~~that~~ it raised, except that the mountains on the opposite side [of] ~~to~~ Taygetus are comparatively tame. The scale of the scenery is so great, that what seemed from above one great though uneven valley is partly made up of the buttresses of Taygetus—a range of green mountains projecting forward from the great range—behind & above these is a region of firs, & above that is the region of snow. There are besides lower hills along the middle of the valley so that the really level ground is narrow—until we reach Sparta where these intermediate hills appear to cease, & we see the mountains on both sides gradually decline into the long low ridges which form the two great southern promontories of Malea & Matapan.

Sparta itself, a new village, proved comparatively disappointing and the only impression worth recording was a visit to the local and somewhat westernized judge. Turning northward again up the valley Eurotas into the interior, the plague of vermin became serious:

Constantinos in Messenia, 25 May: I am writing in the usual great hayloft, devoured by fleas—those in Sicily were nothing to them, these are so [much more] numerous & bite so hard. The people, alas, keep their rugs &c here, which ensures what I am suffering. Since I began the last sentence I caught one in the act of getting into my nostril. They make their way up from the floor much faster than I could catch them if I did nothing else. I have two days to relate. The ways from Laconia into Messenia are two: one up a gorge of Taygetus, & through a very conspicuous gap in the ridge, to Calamata: the English at Athens all recommend[ed] this route, which is the shortest, but the most difficult. The guide however said horses could not go— mules must be taken at Sparta & the horses send round—which would cause

expense & delay, & though I suspect the difficulty is of the guide's own making, I gave up the idea. (The fleas are now attacking in columns, & firing into
many parts of my body at once.) The other way is by rounding the extreme
north end of Taygetus, & this we began on the 23rd & completed on the 24th.

The excursion into Messenia by this second somewhat roundabout route
took Mill altogether four days, with the flea plague getting worse every night:
proceeding hence north through Laconia he was gradually getting tired of
travelling, and even his final visit to Olympia on the day before reaching the
port of Pyrgos could do little to revive his flagging spirits. From Pyrgos he proceeded by boat to the British island of Zanti, his real port of embarkation.

Zanti, 29 May: Our boat was a decked one with two masts & four great oars,
& a hole below where there was just room for me to lie, & I turned in at
dark—& though the fleas in the boat or in my clothes, or both, kept running
all over me & biting me, my sleepiness made me sleep very sound though
conscious of often waking & doing battle with them. When I finally awaked
at half past five this morning we seemed almost arrived but as there had been
an almost complete calm they had had to row all night. We did not arrive
till eight. The inn here though a poor one is a perfect luxury after my late
lodgings—I made myself thoroughly clean & comfortable, then breakfasted
heartily from which I have since suffered not the smallest inconvenience, but
it is so hot here that I have been very little out except to the banker's. The air
as usual was so hazy that the coast of Greece was invisible when I landed, but
I shall perhaps see it from the castle hill which I propose climbing in the cool
of the evening. People here say the summer has set in hot all at once. The
banker here introduced me to the club where I saw the latest Galignani's:
everything both in England & the Crimea as unsatisfactory as ever.

Zanti, 30 May: I had my climb in the evening to the castle & saw the sun set
from it about 7 oclock, so much shorter are the summer days in this southern latitude. The view is very fine. The promontory of Castel Tornese in the
Morea was very distinct, & seemed quite near: the mountains behind Mes-
olonghi & those of Arcadia looked dim in the hazy distance. So goodbye
beautiful Greece—more beautiful than I ever expected, but beautiful as you
are I never wish to see you again—for I do not wish ever again to go so long
a journey without my beloved one, & the country will not be fit for her to
come to while we live.[28] What a pleasure it is to see again something looking like civilization.

[28] Mill did visit Greece again after Mrs. Mill's death and in 1862 spent some months with
Helen Taylor there and in Constantinople.

On the following day Mill boarded the steamer from Athens to Ancona and during the stop at Corfu posted the long report of his tour of the Peloponnesus to Mrs. Mill at Paris, where, as letters waiting for him informed him, she was shortly proceeding to meet him. From Ancona, where he arrived on 3 June, he started on the following day for the journey to Paris, which he did not expect to complete in much under three weeks, since he felt that he could 'not venture to travel by diligence, i.e. day & night more than a part of the way'. And although he is compelled to use right from the start the more comfortable mode of travelling by *voiture*, his apprehensions of the strain of the journey proved only too soon justified. At Florence, where reports of bandits on the direct road to Bologna led him to make a detour, renewed hæmorrhages of the lung proved how ill founded had been his hope of the disease being stopped and compelled him to consult a doctor. This and the dates of the diligences forced on him a three-day delay which he used for some sightseeing and one more long letter to Mrs. Mill.

Florence, 7 June:[29] She will not have to wait very long for me at or near Paris & I shall see her in a fortnight at farthest. I look forward to it with delight—but ah darling I had a horrible dream lately—I had come back to her & she was sweet & loving like herself at first, but presently she took a complete dislike to me saying that I was changed much for the worse—I am terribly afraid sometimes lest she should think so, not that I see any cause for it, but because I know how deficient I am in self consciousness & self observation, & how often when she sees me again after I have been even a short time absent she is disappointed—but she shall not be, she will not be so I think this time— bless my own darling, she has been all the while without intermission present to my thoughts & I shall have been all the while mentally talking with her when I have not been doing so on paper.

Florence, 8 June:[30] [I] sat a great while in the Tribune[31] full of admiration. Not of the Venus de Medici, for decidedly I do not like her: I never liked the casts of her, & I do not like the original a bit better. I think her the poorest of all the Venuses. She is neither the earthly Venus nor the Urania. Of course she is a beautifully formed woman, but the head is too *too* ridiculously small, as if to give the *idea* of having no room for brains—& they may well say she does not look immodest, for the expression of the face is complete old maidism. At least these are very strongly my impressions & I am sure they are quite spontaneous—But there is a host of most beautiful statues & pictures there, though the statues not quite equal to the Vatican. There are

[29] [The full letter is published in Mill, *Later Letters*, vol. 14 of *Collected Works*, pp. 472–78.—Ed.]
[30] [Hayek supplies the brackets and contents at the start of the passage. The full letter, written between 8 and 13 June, is published in *ibid.*, pp. 479–88.—Ed.]
[31] [Hayek has a query after 'Tribune'; *ibid.*, p. 479, accepts the transcription.—Ed.]

enough to make [one] ~~me~~ feel in an atmosphere of art—even to be among all those Roman emperors whom I have got to know like personal acquaintances. There are also so many fine statues & pictures all over Florence that I could soon get into the kind of feeling I had at Rome of being bathed in art. It is strange that the Florentines should have had so many great painters & sculptors—I suppose they are like the English, who though so unpoetical a people have had more great poets than any other country. I am convinced that the Florentines are a most unartistic, tasteless people. Who but such a people would let all the churches be masses of deformity which are a positive eyesore, and disgrace the city—like houses half built, of half burnt bricks—things in which no private person could bear to live—the only material exceptions being the Cathedral which has no front, & Santa Maria Novella which has nothing but a front. . . . The town itself is a good deal more lively now when the shops are open, & I sometimes for a moment forget that I am not in a French town. I feel [much] more in Europe than I have done at any other town of Italy. I think I could feel quite at home here if our home *was* here—but according to Wilson[32] it is a place quite unfit for pulmonary invalids, both in winter & summer.

Florence, 9 June: What I left undone yesterday I have done today, & have seen Florence itself pretty completely, though nothing of its environs. I passed a great part of the morning in the Pitti Gallery. . . . It is a very large collection, mostly of good pictures, and many chefs d'oeuvre. Those which struck me most were two of Perugino[33] which Murray in ten columns of notices does not even mention—one a descent from the Cross, which when I had only seen the print of it I thought one of the greatest pictures ever painted—all the disagreeable of the subject taken away & nothing but a beautiful dead body & the most beautiful feelings in the numerous gracefully grouped spectators. The other is an adoration of the infant Jesus by the Virgin & some children—a small thing compared to the other but quite admirable by the naturalness & natural grace of the children—the Virgin also very beautiful. There are many fine pictures by Fra Bartolomeo[34] & Andrea del Sarto[35], masters whom I admire more & more.

Another two days' travel by diligence brought Mill to the railhead at Mantua and by rail to Verona and on the following day to Milan, where from some new Galignani's he learnt about events in the world.

[32] The English doctor in Florence whom he had consulted.

[33] [Pietro Perugino (1446–1524), painter of the Umbrian School who lived and worked in Florence.—Ed.]

[34] [Fra Bartolomeo (1472–1517), also known as Baccio della Porta, an Italian Renaissance painter.—Ed.]

[35] [Andrea Del Sarto (1486–1531), another Renaissance painter, from Florence.—Ed.]

Milan, 12 June: I read Lord John Russell's disgusting speech[36] on the impossibility of doing anything for Poland & the extreme desirableness of maintaining Austria in all her possessions—I felt a strong desire to kick the rascal—it is a perfect disgrace to England that he should be tolerated as a liberal (!) minister a day after such a speech. What with our sentimental affection for one despot & our truckling to the other great enemy,[37] we are likely to have a precious character with all lovers of freedom on the Continent!

In spite of continuous spitting of blood and in spite of the warning that the road over the Gothard was not yet open for wheel carriages, and that the highest point of the pass must be crossed in sledges, Mill chose that route as the one likely to bring him quicker to his destination.

Lugano, 14 June:[38] I had the mortification of finding that I had lost my botanical tin box—which has been most useful to me, holding an apparently impossible quantity of specimens & keeping them fresh in the hottest weather for 24 hours. It must have fallen or wriggled out of my great coat pocket in the diligence or railway carriage. I am much vexed at it. I have lost nothing else of consequence in this journey—nothing beyond a pocket handkerchief which I lost on Pentelicus & an old shirt which must have been kept by some blanchisseuse—though I hardly ever failed to count the things & compare them with the note.

Airolo, 16 June: Today it rained worse than ever, but I took my place for Fluelen on the lake of Lucerne, & proceeded up the pass to the place where the sledging begins—& to my consternation found that the sledges, little things holding two persons each, were entirely open. Several passengers were as much surprised as I was, saying that on the Simplon & the Mont Cenis the sledges are covered, & that they should not have come if they had known—but to me it was out of the question going on, as I should have been thoroughly soaked & had a day in the diligence afterwards, which in my present state would have had a good chance of killing me. I had no choice, disagreeable as it was, but to get out bag & baggage, & go back to Airolo by the return diligence about an hour & a half afterwards, here to wait till the rain

---

[36] [*The Times* reported him saying that Poland's cause was 'hopeless, and therefore . . . it would be madness in England and France to take any part in promoting resistance in the country. . . . I should most sincerely lament anything which should at all weaken the power [of the Austrian Empire]'.—Ed.]

[37] [Mill, *Later Letters*, vol. 14 of *Collected Works*, pp. 488, note 18 supplies the identification 'Louis Napoleon, and Austria'.—Ed.]

[38] [The full letter, written between 14 and 16 June, is published in *ibid.*, pp. 489–92.—Ed.]

ceases, which may be by tomorrow morning, or in these mountains may not be for some time.

Fortunately the next day was fine, and Mill reached Fluelen without excessive discomfort but sufficiently tired to feel that he ought to devote the next morning to his 'real rest', a five-hour morning walk, before continuing by the steamer to Lucerne. Leaving there on the 19th for Basle and Strasbourg, he probably reached Paris and Mrs. Mill three days later.

TWELVE

LAST YEARS AND DEATH OF MRS. MILL
1856–1858

We have no documents of the winter 1855/6, which Mill and his wife spent again in England. In July and early August 1855[1] they went with Haji and Lily to Switzerland, travelling slowly to Geneva during the last week of July and visiting Chamonix later. At the end of this tour, while Mrs. Mill went on to Paris, Mill left her at Besançon to go for a week's walking tour to the French Jura. Two of his letters written from this tour[2] are extant and again testify of the prodigious feats of walking which the invalid found not only compatible with but conducive to his health.

> *J. S. M. to H. M.:* Le Pont / on the Lac de Joux [Vaux], / Wed^y, ev^g [August 13, 1855][3] / I enjoy the place ~~very~~ much & you may suppose I am very well when I say that after climbing Mont Tendre, a most beautiful mountain, one of the highest [of] ~~in~~ the Jura, which with a rest on the grass at the top & the return took six hours, I only staid half an hour to eat a crust of bread & drink a whole jug of milk, & set off again to climb another mountain & make a round which took another five hours—& I am ~~now~~ not [now] more tired than is agreeable. The views of the Alps here are splendid, especially that from the Mont Tendre—in spite of a great deal of haze towards Berne & Savoy. I saw the snowy range for a great distance, Mont Blanc tolerably & the Dent du Midi, the nearer Valais mountains & the whole lake of Geneva from end to end well, also the lake of Neuchâtel, the whole Jura, & France I should think nearly to Dijon. The evening walk was still finer: the bit of Valorbe which I descended to get to the source of the Orbe (the place where the water of the two lakes is supposed to come out) equals anything I ever saw—a narrow gorge between precipices but itself full of the richest Jura

---

[1] [Hayek misdates the tour, which occurred in 1856. See *The Later Letters of John Stuart Mill, 1849–1873*, eds. Francis E. Mineka and Dwight N. Lindley, vols. 14–17 (1972) of *The Collected Works of John Stuart Mill* [hereafter cited as *Collected Works*] (Toronto: University of Toronto Press, 1962–1991), 15:506, note 1.—Ed.]

[2] Yale University Library [MS 350, Box 1, Folder 17]. [Mill, *Later Letters*, vol. 15 of *Collected Works*, pp. 506–7 and 508–9, dates these letters 13 and 17 August 1856.—Ed.]

[3] [Hayek supplies the brackets and contents.—Ed.]

verdure of pasture & wood so high as almost to hide the precipices: & the source with its exquisite clearness & great mass of water coming out from under an amphitheatre of precipice in the heart of a wood far surpasses Vaucluse. I also went over in the rocks above a really immense cave but without any stalactites. If my beloved one was with me I could stay here with pleasure the whole week—the inn would do—a *little* below the mark of St. Martin but larger rooms. As it is I shall leave tomorrow: for quiet enjoyment one requires to be two—by oneself there is nothing but activity.

Mill appears to have joined his wife at Boulogne about a week later and to have reached London after another ten days, about the last day of August.

In the autumn of 1856 Helen Taylor at last obtained her mother's consent to her trying her luck on the stage. Her passion for the theatre, which had already shown itself when she was quite a young girl, seems never to have left her, but her mother had for years opposed her wish to become an actress. At last it was arranged through the actress Fanny Stirling,[4] who appears to have been an old acquaintance and perhaps had taught Helen Taylor, that the latter should try her powers with a provincial company which was looking for a person to act the chief parts in tragedy at their theatres in Newcastle and Sunderland. Great secrecy was to be observed and Helen Taylor not only assumed the name of 'Miss Trevor', under which alone she was known during the eighteen months or two years of her stage career, but all possible precautions were taken to prevent the reason for her absence from home becoming known or her correspondence with her mother giving any clue to her identity. Towards the end of November her brother Haji accompanied her to Newcastle and from her mother's first letter we gain some idea of the long struggle which must have preceded this decision.

H M to Helen Taylor, 24 November 1856[5] I wish you to be wholly uninfluenced by me in all your future proceedings. I would rather die than go through again your reproaches for spoiling your life. Whatever happens let your mode of life be your own free choice henceforth.

Helen Taylor's stage career, which we can follow closely in a long series of letters exchanged almost daily between mother and daughter,[6] is outside the scope of this book. It was from the beginning full of disappointments and

---

[4] [Fanny Stirling, née Mary Ann Kehl, was a well-known stage actress. See *The Complete Works of Harriet Taylor Mill* [hereafter cited as *Complete Works*], ed. Jo Ellen Jacobs (Bloomington: Indiana University Press, 1998), p. 513, note 4.—Ed.]

[5] MTColl. LI/1. [The letter, postmarked 25 November and marked LI/7, is published in Harriet Taylor Mill, *Complete Works*, pp. 513–14.—Ed.]

[6] MTColl. LI and LII. [See Harriet Taylor Mill, *Complete Works*, pp. 515–75.—Ed.]

one may well doubt whether the predominantly intellectual young woman was really suited for the stage. The letters are of course mainly concerned with Helen Taylor's practical problems, Mrs. Mill entering into the minutest details of her dresses, etc. But they also throw a good deal of light on the relation between the two hitherto inseparable women. They do not seem to have been entirely easy. Both highly strung and hyper-sensitive, the letters alternate between the most effusive professions of affection and a plaintive tone of misunderstood intentions, the mother in particular constantly feeling hurt by the apparent coolness of the daughter, who vacillates between assertion of her new independence and complete reliance on her mother's guidance.

After a joint Christmas holiday at Brighton Helen Taylor again went north to another theatre at Doncaster and later to Glasgow where her mother went to pay her a long deferred visit in February. Mill, who for a little while had again suffered from trouble with head and his eyesight, was on that account able to take a few days off and to accompany Mrs. Mill as far as Edinburgh. From the eight existing letters[7] which Mill wrote to his wife during the fortnight's absence only a few passages need be quoted.

J. S. M. to H. M., 17 February 1857:[8] It was the strangest feeling yesterday & this morning to be there & at the same time fresh from all those places. I have hardly anything running in my mind's eye but innumerable large railway stations. On Saturday night at York I slept little & dreamt much— among the rest a long dream of some speculation on animal nature, ending with my either reading or writing, just before I awoke, this Richterish[9] sentence: 'With what prospect then, until a cow is fed on broth, we can expect the truth, the whole truth & nothing but the truth to be unfolded concerning this part of nature, I leave to' &c &c. I had a still droller dream the same night. I was seated at a table like a table d'hôte, with a woman at my left hand & a young man opposite—the young man said, quoting somebody for the saying, 'there are two excellent & rare things to find in a woman, a sincere friend & a sincere Magdalen'. I answered 'the best would be to find both in one'—on which the woman said 'no, that would be *too* vain'—whereupon I broke out 'do you suppose when one speaks of what is good in itself, one must be thinking of one's own paltry self interest? no, I spoke of what is abstractedly good & admirable'. How queer to dream stupid mock mots, &

---

[7] One from York, evidently of 14 February, in MTColl. LII/125, and seven from London, probably of 16, 17, 18, 19, 24, 25 and 26 February, in Yale University Library [MS 350, Box 1, Folder 18]. [These are published in Mill, *Later Letters*, vol. 15 of *Collected Works*, pp. 521–27.—Ed.]

[8] Yale University Library [MS 350, Box 1, Folder 18].

[9] [Mill is referring to the style of German satirist Jean Paul Richter (1763–1825). See Mill, *Later Letters*, vol. 15 of *Collected Works*, p. 523, note 4.—Ed.]

of a kind totally unlike one's own ways or character. According to the usual oddity of dreams—when the man made the quotation I recognized it & thought ~~that~~ he had quoted it wrong & that the *right* words were 'an *innocent magdalen*' not perceiving the contradiction. I wonder if reading that Frenchman's book suggested the dream. These are ridiculous things to put in a letter, but perhaps they may amuse my darling.

In the following letters there are some references to his working on a revision of the *Political Economy* for the fourth edition.

J. S. M. to H. M., 19 February 1857:[10] I pass the evening always at the Pol. Economy, with now & then a little playing to rest my eyes & mind. There will be no great quantity to alter, but now & then a little thing is of importance. One page I keep for consideration when I can shew it to you. It is about the qualities of English workpeople, & of the English generally. It is not at all as I would write it now, but I do not, in reality, know how to write it.[11]

After about ten days in Glasgow Mrs. Mill fell seriously ill, probably with another hæmorrhage from the lungs.

J. S. M. to H. M., 24 February 1857:[12] It was less of a shock the first moment than I should have thought it would have been—no doubt because the *same* letter said you were better & because the sight of your beloved handwrit-

---

[10] Yale University Library [MS 350, Box 1, Folder 18].

[11] If this refers, as seems probable, to Book 1, chapter 8, § 5 of the *Political Economy*, which had been considerably revised in the previous (third) edition, no further change appears to have been made on this occasion. [John Stuart Mill, *The Principles of Political Economy with Some of Their Application to Social Philosophy*, ed. John M. Robson, vols. 2–3 (1965) of *Collected Works*, 3:1037, suggests this refers to the passage in Book 1, chapter 7 (*ibid.*, 2:102 6). Ed.]

[12] Yale University Library [MS 350, Box 1, Folder 18]. The following undated fragment, also in Yale University Library [MS 350, Box 1, Folder 18], probably belongs to the same period. It is on a single sheet which has apparently been deliberately mutilated by the lower part having been cut away, and the text of the two sides is in consequence not consecutive nor is it possible to say which part comes first. [Hayek supplies the bracketed material and ellipsis below.—Ed.]

J. S. M. to H. T., February 1857(?): if you did but know with what joy I would leave everything & live all my life in Australia if you cannot be in health anywhere else how dreadful it would be if from considerations relating to me that were left undone till it were useless.

O my beloved have pity on me & save that precious life which is the only life there is for me in this world—

[Beginning of second page] so needed, so longed to be with you—& always with you—as when you are ill. it is true I am pained by the sense of my own helplessness & uselessness in mechanical matters when they are so much needed. but your perfect love can do what . . .

ing gave me confidence—but I have been growing more anxious every hour since. Thank Heaven however we know by experience that this is not necessarily dangerous—though a warning of the danger there always is. It must have been much less bad than the former time, or you could not have written immediately. But it would be very imprudent to attempt travelling for I do not know how many days, & then it can only be by very short journeys. L[ily]'s[13] being ill at the same time is an additional misfortune. But why should I not come. I am ready to come any day & stay any time—& I do not see that your being there is ~~inconvenable~~ [inaverrable]—you are *really* on a visit, & it is nobody's concern to whom. You will judge best of everything & either you or L. will let me know—but all my wish is to be with you & to be doing my little little to help. The blessing & comfort it was & is to me to have been with you on that former occasion no words will ever express.

In another letter on the following day, addressed to Edinburgh where Mrs. Mill seems to have moved either just before or after she fell ill, her return is further discussed, but on the evening of the next, Mill, evidently on the receipt of worse news, rushes north to join her.

Mill, who in the preceding year had become head of the Examiner's Department at India House and was thus in charge of all the political relations of the Company during this year of the Indian Mutiny, must have been exceedingly busy and during the spring his wife has to go alone to Brighton to recuperate. Even their annual holiday is delayed until September. There are a few letters[14] written while they separated for four days in order that Mill should get some walking in the Lake District while Mrs. Mill and her daughter not very successfully tried their luck on the Lancashire coast.

H. M. to J. S. M., Blackpool, 16 September 1857:[15] Dearest love / We got on well to Fleetwood (luggage & all) but it is a strange place, or rather a place *meant to be* but not built. It is like a beginning of Herne Bay—roads planned but no houses—only a great staring Inn called Euston Hotel adding to the deserted look of the place—no lodgings fit to go to—so this morning we have driven over here (nine miles) & I write while we wait a few minutes which will account for a hurried note. This place is as they call it a little Brighton—a poor copy thereof except in the crowds of people so that it

---

[13] [Hayek supplies the name in brackets.—Ed.]

[14] Four letters by Mill to his wife, of 13, 16, 18 and 19 September, are in the Yale University Library [MS 350, Box 1, Folder 19]. There is only the one letter by Mrs. Mill referred to in the next footnote. [These are published in Mill, *Later Letters*, vol. 15 of *Collected Works*, pp. 535–36, 536–37, 538, and 539; and the letter from Harriet Taylor to Mill is published in Harriet Taylor Mill, *Complete Works*, p. 376.—Ed.]

[15] MTColl. XXVIII/240.

reminds me of your account of Southend. It is therefore not tempting at all, & as Lily has a great inclination to go to Lemington I decide to do so & to go on to-day. I shall order your letter to be sent on from Fleetwood but hope you will write to Post Office Lemington as soon as you get this, that I may soon know where to direct to you dear. I am so pleased at its being such a lovely day for Helvellyn that it makes me quite in spirits. my heart is with you all the time so do dearest enjoy the climbing and take good care not to slip.

I will write again to morrow Adieu now

in haste ever yrs

H. M.

J. S. M. to H. M.: Salutation, Ambleside, / September 13 [1857][16] / Dearest—I have been very fortunate in having [had] a most beautiful day for Hellvellyn. I ascended it from Patterdale having gone there by an early coach from here, & I returned here in the same way in the evening, walking up the pass so you see I was not tired. The view though there were a few clouds was splendid. It was a disappointment as to plants, as on those sunny heights everything was still more gone by than in the valleys—of all the rare plants which grow there I could only distinguish two, and those were only in leaf. But the day before I was unexpectedly successful in plants between Windermere & this place. I made a circuit & saw Mr Crosfield's cottages[17] which I will describe to you when I have the happiness of being with you again; they are not what we want; besides other objections they are in a real village or rather hamlet. I have planned a very nice round for today, and shall go to Broughton tomorrow down the Duddon, and to Lancaster, & I hope to Settle on Tuesday. I talked yesterday with people from Fleetwood & others from Blackpool & I am afraid they are but ugly places—I so hope [to hear that] you have not inflicted purgatory on yourself to give me this walk. I feel however that it will do me great good. Today the sky is gloomy—but not very threatening. Yesterday everything looked its very best. I shall write again as soon as I receive yours. Adieu my own wife from your

J. S. M.

For the second part of his walking tour Mill chose Settle in Yorkshire as his base and the remaining three letters are dated from there.

---

[16] [Hayek supplies the date in brackets.—Ed.]

[17] [According to Mill, *Later Letters*, vol. 15 of *Collected Works*, p. 536, note 2, these cottages were 'on the lands of J. Crosfield, listed as owner of Rothay Bank, a villa near Ambleside.'—Ed.]

J. S. M. to H. M., Settle, 16 September 1857: This place is a prettier country town than any in the lakes & the country about looks very pretty though the mountains have not the fine forms & beautiful arrangement of the Lakes. Please darling continue to write here, as I find it is the best centre for all I want to see—within a day's walk of everything. I have time to explore Craven between this & Sunday & I shall certainly go to Manchester on Monday & to darling on Tuesday. I saw the last Times yesterday at Lancaster. The Indian news[18] seems to me more bad than good, but not, I think, of any bad omen. I saw in a Liverpool paper an announcement from a French paper of the death of Comte.[19] It seems as if there would be no thinkers left in the world.

J. S. M. to H. M.: Settle/ Sat^y morn^g [September 19, 1857][20] / I have just got your darling letter you angel which would make me set off directly to rejoin you if I did not know that you would much rather I did not on account of the good this excursion does me. I too was feeling very sad all yesterday but for an opposite reason (partly) to yours, namely perfect beauty. It was the first *splendid* day since I have been here, & I was all day wandering over the edge of the hills having such a sun & sky as made the views both near & distant perfectly beautiful & I think that always makes one melancholy, at least when one is alone, which to me means not with you. I am now going to climb Ingleborough & see the caves, at least the principal of them, for there are multitudes all about here. I fancied Leamington would be pleasant because it has a civilized air, though very ugly—the frequented parts of the N. of E. are generally hideous as to the *human* part of them, but this Settle is a nice quiet, really pretty, very little country place, not tourified, the people of the place are civil & the few strangers one sees in the coffee room are really gentlemanly. I shall enquire at the Post Office at Manchester my own love. I will certainly look particularly at the pictures my darling liked. Adieu till Tuesday evening, and blessings from her own

J. S. M.

During the winter 1857/8 the pressure of work caused by developments in India kept the Mills in London although the state of their health would have made it advisable that they winter abroad.[21] In July 1858 we can follow Mill once more on one of his walking tours while Mrs. Mill remained at Black-

---

[18] [Regarding the Sepoy Mutiny, which had broken out in May and was proving difficult to suppress. *Ibid.*, p. 537, note 2.—Ed.]

[19] [September 5, 1857.—Ed.]

[20] [Hayek supplies the date in brackets.—Ed.]

[21] H. M. to her mother, 4 December 1857, MTColl. XXVII/83. [The letter is published in Harriet Taylor Mill, *Complete Works*, pp. 410–11.—Ed.]

heath Park. He spent a week of strenuous walking in the Peak District of Derbyshire, but neither any of his four letters to his wife nor her two letters to him[22] are of any special interest. One letter by each may serve as specimens.

H. M. to J. S. M., Blackheath, 12 July 1858: Monday Even[g] / I was quite in spirits all yesterday because you had such a nice day for the journey dearest. This morning I got your account of your day[23] which shows that all went well. It is pleasant to hear that Matlock turned out better than we expected. To-day has been very hot, tho' without bright sun & looks this evening as tho' there would be rain in the night, & already one has begun to wish for more rain. The air is so close & sultry. Among the hills no doubt you will not find it too hot. I *am* so pleased it is fine. As the people at the Inn are disagreeable you must leave it. I hope you have already, for it would much lessen the good walking may do if you are uncomfortable in the house. The Times has not yet come, but I have the Telegraph. I need not tell you things in it which will be in the Times, as you will see that, but it has a very long account of Bulwers wife[24] being seized & sent to a madhouse, which seems a *most* nefarious affair. It ought to lead to Bulwer being turned out of the ministry. I hope it will, such an incarnation of vanity & dishonesty as the man is—he could not face the ridicule of his wife talking against him on the husting. But it is a disgrace to the law that *any body* can be made prisoner & carried off on the certificate of two medical men!

If the expedition proves pleasanter than you expected, & seems to be doing you good, I do hope you will stay into the next week—It will be excessively painful to me if you come back sooner than you need, on account of what I said—or on any account. Adieu dearest if this sh[d] get lost it certainly will be no prize to the finder!

---

[22] J. S. Mill's letters from Matlock 11 and 12 July, Edensor 13 July, and Bakewell 15 July 1858, are in the Yale University Library [MS 350, Box 1, Folder 20], and Mrs. Mill's letters of 12 and 13 July in MTColl. XXVIII/236 and 237. [The letters from Mill to Harriett Taylor are published in Mill, *Later Letters*, vol. 15 of *Collected Works*, pp. 563–64, 564–65, 565–66, and 566–67; those from Harriet Taylor to Mill are published in Harriet Taylor Mill, *Complete Works*, pp. 376–77 and 377. In Harriet Taylor Mill, *Complete Works*, the third sentence reads: 'It is a pleasure to hear that Wallock turns out better than we expected'; but Hayek's transcription seems correct.—Ed.]

[23] A letter posted at Matlock Sunday evening delivered at Blackheath the next morning!

[24] Sir Edward Bulwer-Lytton (later Lord Lytton) (1803–1873), the novelist who shortly before had become Secretary for the Colonies in Lord Derby's second Cabinet. [Bulwer-Lytton had his wife, Lady Rosina Doyle Wheeler Bulwer-Lytton (1804–1882), placed in an institution against her will in June 1858. J. S. Mill wrote 'The Law of Lunacy', published in the *Daily News* on 31 July 1858, p. 4; the article is republished in John Stuart Mill, *Newspaper Writings*, eds. Ann P. Robson and John M. Robson, vols. 22–25 (1986) of *Collected Works*, 25:1198–99.—Ed.]

J. S. M. to H. M., 15 July 1858:[25] Bakewell / Thursday ev⁸. / My darling! I received her most precious letter yesterday morning and the pleasure it gave me was almost worth the absence. As to prolonging my stay, what she so kindly & sweetly writes would induce me to do it, if it were not that this excursion has not quite fulfilled our expectations or rather hopes in the matter of health. I have found no deficiency of strength, but have never been without a dry furred tongue, & never many hours without other decided sensations of indigestion, & this in spite of the greatest care, & observance of your advice in every particular. An excursion of this sort is excellent to strengthen me against indigestion, but it does not perhaps tend so much to cure it when it exists. Perhaps the regularity of home may do better. I dare say however I shall be [the] better for this *afterwards* as has so often been the case. As I shall therefore see her on Sunday morning & she will not get this till Saturday, I will keep all description for a nice talk & will only say that, contrary to my expectation, the place which seems most suitable for us to make any stay at is *Buxton* which I walked to yesterday, returning on the top of the omnibus. On consideration, I thought that Dovetale had not the étoffe of a place for more than a day, so I was driven there in a phaeton this morning from here—the place was not a disappointment but was soon seen & I have just come in from an eleven miles walk since I came back. Tomorrow morning I shall go to Castleton & shall have the greater part of tomorrow & the greater part of Saturday to spend there as I shall go from thence to Sheffield, no great distance, & return by a night train from there, arriving in town [at] about five on Sunday morning when I will rest a little & breakfast & then come home to my darling. The weather has been excellent—the last two afternoons there has been a little rain, not enough to do any harm, & tonight there has been a little since dusk, with some lightening. I found no plants on Tuesday or today, but yesterday was a splendid day for them, as I found five, of which Jacob's ladder was one.

Adieu with a thousand loves from your

J. S. M.

In the autumn of 1858 Mill was at last able to relinquish his post at East India House, which, since his appointment as Examiner a little more than two years before, had claimed more of his time than in earlier years. He took advantage of the transfer of the East India Company's functions to the Government to retire at the age of fifty-two instead of at sixty as he should otherwise have been entitled, and his thirty-five years of service were rewarded with a liberal pension of £1,500—more than his salary had been until the last promotion, when it had been raised to £2,000. Although officially his

---

[25] [The letter is published in Mill, *Later Letters*, vol. 15 of *Collected Works*, pp. 566–67.—Ed.]

connexion with the Company came to an end only at Christmas, his wife's and his own state of health urgently required that they should spend the winter outside England. They left Blackheath Park for the South of France on 11 October. Helen Taylor had been staying with them on a visit from Aberdeen, probably in order to appear on that same evening in a minor part, in a first performance of Wilkie Collins' 'The Red Vial' in the Olympic (or perhaps only to see Mrs. Stirling act in it), and Mrs. Mill's letters to her begin with a comment on the *Times*'s review of the play which still reached her at Folkestone. After another night in Boulogne Mill and his wife reached Paris on the 14th to stay there for two days. The plan was to go in easy stages to Montpellier, later to move on to Hyères, where Mrs. Mill had so well recovered four years before, and to pass the following spring in Italy. But already at Dijon Mrs. Mill's health proved unequal to the strain of the railway journey and another two days' stop became necessary. Mill himself clearly was not the best person to look after the invalid in the circumstances.

H. M. to Helen Taylor, Dijon, 18 October 1858:[26] The fact is we always get the last seats in the railway carriage, as I cannot run on quick, & if he goes on he never succeeds, I always find him running up & down & looking lost in astonishment. So I have given up trying to get any seats but those that are left.

When on the following day they arrived in Lyons, Mrs. Mill had a bad cold which rapidly developed into severe congestion of the lungs with a high fever and great general weakness. On the 21st Mill has for the first time to write to Helen Taylor in her place, but at her wish still insisting that 'there was [is] nothing to be uneasy about'.[27] Two days later she herself could report in a pencilled note that she had got up[28] and after a week's stay they were able to leave Lyons on the 26th 'in great hope—I shall by degrees get over this attack'.[29] But even the two hours' journey to Valence and the somewhat longer journey to Avignon on the next day proved too much for her strength. Although on arrival there she still hoped that 'it is all over & I shall have more cheerful letters to write',[30] and to continue at once to Montpellier, this was not

[26] MTColl. LIII/(i) 1–29, for Mrs. Mill's letters from the journey to Helen Taylor with Helen Taylor's replies; also Mrs. Mill's letter to Algernon Taylor, Paris, 15 October 1858, MTColl. XXVII/119. [The letter from which this excerpt is taken is published in Harriet Taylor Mill, *Complete Works*, pp. 580 81, with additional letters from the journey at pp. 575 87. Ed.]

[27] [*Ibid.*, p. 584; the full letter is at pp. 583–84.—Ed.]

[28] [The full letter is published in *ibid.*, pp. 584–85.—Ed.]

[29] [*Ibid.*, p. 585; the full letter is at pp. 585–86. Hayek supplies a bridging word; his text reads, 'in great hope that I shall get over the attack'.—Ed.]

[30] [*Ibid.*, p. 586; the full letter is published at pp. 586–87. Jo Ellen Jacobs notes that this is Harriet's last letter, speculates that the letter 'may have been directed to' J. S. Mill or Helen Taylor,

to be and this letter of 27 October was to be her last. On the following day Mill desperately wrote to the doctor in Nice who had saved her life four years before.

J. S. M. to Dr. Gurney at Nice:[31] Avignon, Oct. 28, 1858 / Dear Dr. Gurney / My wife is lying at the Hotel de l'Europe here, so very ill that neither she nor I have any hope but in you to save her. It is a quite sudden attack which came on at Lyons, of incessant coughing which prevents sleeping, and by the exhaustion it produces has brought her to death's door. I implore you to come immediately. I need hardly say that any expense whatever will not count for a feather in the balance. I am, dear Dr. Gurney

very truly yours

J. S. Mill

A day or two later Mill sent a hurried pencilled report to Helen Taylor, then back in Aberdeen, which is in part very difficult to read.

J. S. M. to Helen Taylor, 29 or 30 October 1858:[32] Dear Lily / Mama has had a tremendous attack of bronchitis with congestion & fever much worse than at Lyons. We have done everything possible & today for the first time she is a little better. The cough has been unceasing & most painful preventing her lying down day or night or getting any sleep besides that the intense nervous irritation caused by the congestion the fever & the fatigue made her almost out of her mind. We have had the best physician here but his prescriptions are too weak. She has taken a number of her own. On Thursday she did not think she[33] sh^d recover. She thought you w^d see by her letters from Lyons how ill she was but she did not like to alarm you. Today she is certainly better. The cough is less frequent & the head for the first time more calm. We took every precaution on the road. She was carried by the porters in a chair

---

or both, and suggests that the penultimate sentence of the letter—'We shall talk over all things when we meet'—favors the conclusion that it was directed to Helen.—Ed.]

[31] Yale University Library [MS 350, Box 1, Folder 21]. In a letter which appeared in the *Literary Guide* of 1 July 1907, Mary Taylor stated that she held a letter of Mill to Dr. Gurney offering him a fee of £1,000 for attending his wife. This would suggest that the doctor first refused to come, which is contradicted by the correspondence. Miss Taylor, however, was in a special position to know since Dr. Gurney was her uncle—her father, Algernon Taylor, had married Dr. Gurney's sister in 1860.

[32] Yale University Library [MS 350, Box 1, Folder 21]. The punctuation, mostly lacking in the original, has been interpolated. [The letter, dated 'Oct. 29 or 30? 1858', is published in Mill, *Later Letters*, vol. 15 of *Collected Works*, pp. 572–73.—Ed.]

[33] [Hayek has a query in the text here; Mill, *Later Letters*, p. 572, accepts his reading and removes the query.—Ed.]

to the railway at Lyons & we had a coupé to ourselves from Valence here but she says the whole (?) incidents of such a journey are totally unfitted for her. The excessive hardship of every part—the inability to have anything fit for a delicate stomach to eat, the tremendous noise everywhere, the coarse manners of the women, the intense fatigue of waiting in the railway rooms for at least half an hour & then the immense distance to go both to & from them. This inn is thought one of the best in France & we appear to have the best rooms yet bedrooms & sitting room are of red tiles with thin carpet over, wch she endeavoured to obviate the first day by using a footstool but in vain— but still[34] far more than all the evident fatal effect upon her of the air of the S[outh] of F[rance].[35] She dragged herself up to write to you a few words on Wed^y that you might not be anxious, hoping it w^d prove as she said—but she felt ill as she wrote & got gradually worse till at night she was very ill. She does not wish you to come to her because she thinks she has taken the turn to get better & therefore it w^d be a very great pity to break your good arrangements wch are a great pleasure to her to hear of. You shall know continually how she is going on. We have got all your letters from Monp[ellier][36] today here & continue to write here for it will probably be weeks before we leave this place. All notice of your letters must be at a future time.

She is anxious that you sh^d not think of coming to her. She w^d[37] be extremely annoyed if you did.

J. S. M.

And now she says adieu dear girl in haste.[38]

Probably even before this letter reached her a cable[39] informed Helen Taylor on 1 November that her mother was worse, and though she left Aberdeen on the following day neither she nor Dr. Gurney reached Avignon in time. Mrs. Mill died in the Hôtel de l'Europe on 3 November.

An extract from the letter to W. T. Thornton in which Mill gave to friends in England the first intimation of the event was published many years ago by A. Bain.

---

[34] [Hayek has a query in the text; Mill, *Later Letters*, p. 572, inserts 'still'.—Ed.]

[35] [Hayek supplies the brackets and contents.—Ed.]

[36] [Hayek supplies the brackets and contents.—Ed.]

[37] [Hayek supplies the full word 'would' followed by a query; Mill, *Later Letters*, supplies 'w^d'.—Ed.]

[38] [Hayek joins this sentence to the final one: 'She would (?) be extremely annoyed if you did and now she says adieu dear girl in haste'.—Ed.]

[39] Yale University Library [MS 350, Box 1, Folder 21]. Helen Taylor's reply in MTColl. LIII(i)/29. [The cable read: 'She is not better or perhaps worse have written to beg D^r G[urney] to come'. It is published in Mill, *Later Letters*, vol. 15 of *Collected Works*, p. 573.—Ed.]

J. S. M. to W. T. Thornton, Avignon, November 1858:[40] [My dear Thornton—/] The hopes with which I commenced this journey have been fatally frustrated. My Wife, the companion of all my feelings, the prompter of all my best thoughts, the guide of all my actions, is gone! She was taken ill at this place with a violent attack of bronchitis ~~and~~ [or] pulmonary congestion— the medical men here could do nothing for her, & before the physician at Nice who ~~had~~ saved her life once before could arrive, all was over.

It is doubtful if I shall ever be fit for anything public or private, again. The spring of my life is broken. But I shall best fulfil her wishes by not giving up the attempt to do something useful[, and I am not quite alone. I have with me her daughter, the one person besides myself who most loved her & whom she most loved, & we help each other to bear what is inevitable]. I am sure of your sympathy, but if you knew what she was you would feel how little any sympathy can do.

J. S. M. to the Maire of Avignon, 3 November 1858:[41] Monsieur le Maire, / Par vos fonctions officielles, vous avez eu connaissance du malheureux evénément qui a créé pour ma famille avec la ville que vous administrez un lien indissoluble. Nous croyons ne pouvoir rendre un meilleur hommage à celle que nous avons perdue qu'en faisant autant que possible les choses que, vivante, elle eût voulu faire; et comme elle n'aurait pas pu venir s'établir à Avignon sans que les malheureux de cette ville en eussent profité, nous souhaitons que, dans la triste circonstance où nous nous trouvons, ils aient encore à la remercier de quelque chose. Veuillez donc, monsieur le maire, accepter au profit de la Caisse des pauvres le don de mille francs, somme proportionnée à nos facultés plutôt qu'à nos désirs, et que nous vous prions de vouloir bien inscrire au nom de ma bien-aimée épouse, Mme Henriette Mill, née Hardy, décédée à Avignon le 3 Novembre 1858.

Agréez. . . .

J. Stuart Mill.

[40] Alexander Bain, *J. S. Mill*, p. 102. The announcement of Mrs. Mill's death, which Mill sent to Thornton with this letter, appeared in *The Times* of 13 November 1858. [The letter to Thornton, dated 9 November, is published in Mill, *Later Letters*, vol. 15 of *Collected Works*, pp. 574–75. The draft of the letter ends with the following struck-out sentence: 'The only consolation possible is the determination to live always as in her sight'. Bain's version, used by Hayek, reads: 'But I shall best fulfil her wishes by not giving up the attempt to do something useful. I am sure of your sympathy, but if you knew what she was, you would feel how little any sympathy can do'.—Ed.]

[41] Jules Véran, 'Le Souvenir de Stuart Mill à Avignon', *Revue des Deux Mondes*, 1 September 1937, p. 216. [The letter is published in Mill, *Later Letters*, vol. 15 of *Collected Works*, pp. 573–74, and dated 'after November 3, 1858'.—Ed.]

J. S. M. to Arthur Hardy, Blackheath, 5 December 1858:[42] My dear Sir / Before receiving this you will already have heard the terrible & most unexpected blow which has fallen upon us. I have not felt equal to writing to you before & now when I do, language is so utterly incapable of expressing such a loss, or what that loss is to us, that it is sickening to attempt it. But you will desire to know some of the sad details. We left England on the 12th of October, intending to pass the winter at Hyères, where she had wintered [once] before or at some other place in the south of France. For the first time we were able to do as we pleased as I had just retired from the I.H. & we were looking forward to a happy half year or year in a mild climate. She was apparently in her usual health, perhaps even better than usual, & as fit for travelling as when she set out on other much longer journeys by which her health had not suffered but benefitted. She continued pretty well up to Lyons, but when there she had a sharp feverish attack, which yielded to the usual remedies but left a good deal of cough behind it. We staid there a week, at the end of which she felt sufficiently recovered to go slowly onward, but the day after we arrived at Avignon she was again taken very ill—she was better the next day, but the improvement was not progressive—and a great shortness of breathing came on. She had the best medical men the place afforded but as usual with French physicians their remedies were not sufficiently powerful & after a few days becoming alarmed though we never suspected immediate danger, I wrote to D[r] Gurney of Nice who attended her in a dangerous illness there in 1853, asking him to come over to [&] see her. He came instantly but found all at an end! The very day before her last we thought her illness had taken a favourable turn. From the symptoms D[r] Gurney thinks the cause of death was excessive & violent[43] congestion of the lungs. She is buried in the cemetery of the town of Avignon & with her all our earthly happiness; we have henceforth no interest in life but to fulfil her wishes in all we can, & to return continually to her grave. We have bought a small house & garden near the cemetery, where we shall go early in the spring & intend to pass much of our time there until our turn comes for being buried along with her. Algernon would have written to you if I had not, but I wished to write myself if able.[44] He & Helen are pretty well, though Helen at one time broke down & had an attack of illness, but fortunately it proved short. It is useless to write more. Believe me yrs very truly

---

[42] Draft in Yale University Library [MS 350, Box 1, Folder 21]. Compare also the letters to George Grote of 28 November 1858, and to Pasquale Villari of 6 and 28 March 1859, in *Letters* (ed. Elliot), vol. 1, pp. 213, 216 and 217. [The letter is published in Mill, *Later Letters*, vol. 15 of *Collected Works*, pp. 581–82; those to George Grote and Pasquale Villari are at *ibid.*, pp. 577–78 and 603–4 and 610–12. See also the letters to Herbert Spencer (*ibid.*, pp. 576–78) and to Theodor Gomperz (*ibid.*, p. 581).—Ed.]

[43] [Hayek omits 'violent' and has a query following the ampersand.—Ed.]

[44] [Hayek omits 'if able' and has a query following 'myself'.—Ed.]

Even before Mill returned to England two or three weeks after his wife's death, he had bought the small house within sight of the cemetery in the suburb of Saint-Veran of Avignon where his wife had been buried and in which he was to spend the greater part of the rest of his life. He then at once devoted himself to the publication of the work to which they had given most of their energies during the preceding years, which was to have received its final revision during the stay on the Continent and now was to appear as it had been left on her death: *On Liberty* was published in February 1859 with the moving dedication 'to the beloved and deplored memory of her who was the inspirer, and in part the author, of all that is best in my writings'. At the same time Mill made arrangements for the republication of a collection of some of his review articles and remained in London until April to see the first two volumes of *Dissertations and Discussions* through the press. The pamphlet *Thoughts on Parliamentary Reform*, written some years earlier, and a long review article on related subjects also were brought out at about the same time, and two other major articles, probably written after he had gone with Helen Taylor to Avignon for their first long stay, appeared later in the same year. Evidently Mill tried to bury himself in intensive work.

At Avignon a monument of the finest Carrara marble was erected at great expense over the grave of his wife, bearing the inscription[45] given on the opposite page.

With this our account might well close. It cannot be the task of this study to inquire how far Mrs. Mill's ideas continued to guide her husband's work after her death. I believe that a careful study of his later development would show that in some degree he withdrew a little from the more advanced positions which he had taken under her influence and returned to views closer to those he had held in his youth. But this is an impression for which it would be impossible to give here the evidence. There is, however, one other circumstance which is of some significance for our appreciation of Mill's appraisal of his wife and which, since it is not clearly seen in the more widely read editions of the *Autobiography*, should be briefly mentioned here. After Mrs. Mill's death her daughter Helen Taylor became Mill's constant companion and devoted assistant. It had been known that he came to hold his stepdaughter in very high esteem and that he had devoted to her praise some passages in the *Autobiography* which, on Alexander Bain's urgent advice, Helen Taylor had omitted in the version published immediately after Mill's death.[46] How great Mill's

---

[45] In MTColl. XLI/11 there are several successive drafts of this inscription in Mill's hand, three of which give the date of Mrs. Mill's birth wrongly as 8 October 1808 (instead of 1807), in one instance substituting this for an earlier '1806'.

[46] Alexander Bain to Helen Taylor, 13 September 1873, MTColl. IV/17. In an earlier letter (6 September 1873, MTColl. IV/15) Bain had also unsuccessfully urged Helen Taylor to omit some of the more extravagant passages of Mill's praise of his wife. Although so far as

TO THE BELOVED MEMORY

OF

HARRIET MILL

THE DEARLY BELOVED AND DEEPLY REGRETTED

WIFE OF JOHN STUART MILL

HER GREAT AND LOVING HEART

HER NOBLE SOUL

HER CLEAR POWERFUL ORIGINAL AND

COMPREHENSIVE INTELLECT

MADE HER THE GUIDE AND SUPPORT

THE INSTRUCTOR IN WISDOM

AND THE EXAMPLE IN GOODNESS

AS SHE WAS THE SOLE EARTHLY DELIGHT

OF THOSE WHO HAD THE HAPPINESS TO BELONG TO HER

AS EARNEST FOR THE PUBLIC GOOD

AS SHE WAS GENEROUS AND DEVOTED

TO ALL WHO SURROUNDED HER

HER INFLUENCE HAS BEEN FELT

IN MANY OF THE GREATEST

IMPROVEMENTS OF THE AGE

AND WILL BE IN THOSE STILL TO COME

WERE THERE BUT A FEW HEARTS AND INTELLECTS

LIKE HERS

THIS EARTH WOULD ALREADY BECOME

THE HOPED-FOR HEAVEN

SHE DIED

TO THE IRREPARABLE LOSS OF THOSE WHO SURVIVE HER

AT AVIGNON

NOV. 3 1858

257

admiration for her had grown[47] became apparent however only when the suppressed passages were restored from the manuscript in a recent complete edition of the *Autobiography*.[48] The most characteristic of these passages in which Helen Taylor is placed on the same pedestal with his wife will form a fitting conclusion.

> Though the inspirer of my best thoughts was no longer with me, I was not alone: she had left a daughter—my stepdaughter, Miss Helen Taylor, the inheritor of much of her wisdom, and of all her nobleness of character, whose ever growing and ripening talents from that day to this have been devoted to the same great purposes, and have already made better and more widely known than was that of her mother, though far less so than I predict that if she lives, it is destined to become. Of the value of her direct coopera-

---

the passages referring to herself were concerned, Helen Taylor at least in part followed Bain's advice; she left instructions that the complete manuscript was 'to be published without alterations or omissions within one year after my death'. These instructions were not carried out and complete publication had to wait until the 1924 edition quoted in the note 48. [Here is the passage to which Hayek refers in Bain's 6 September 1873 letter to Helen Taylor: 'But I greatly doubt the propriety of your printing those sentences where he declared her to be a greater poet than Carlyle, and a greater thinker than himself—and again, a greater leader (that is, if you have accepted his offer) for America'. Alan Ryan, in the Introduction to *Mill: Texts and Commentary* (New York: Norton, 1975), opines that 'nobody other than Mill has thought that she was superior in poetic sensibility to Carlyle and intellectually his own superior in all matters of technical detail' (p. xvii).—Ed.]

[47] The following description by an American visitor of Mill's relation to Helen Taylor towards the end of his life is of interest in this connexion:

> *C. E. Norton to Chauncey Wright, 13 September 1870:* I doubt whether Mill's interest in the cause of woman is serviceable to him as a thinker. It has a tendency to develop the sentimental part of his intelligence, which is of immense force, and has only been kept in due subjection by his respect for his own reason. This respect diminishes under the powerful influence of his daughter, Miss Taylor, who is an admirable personage doubtless, but is what, were she of the sex that she regards as inferior, would be called decidedly priggish. Her self-confidence, which embraces her confidence in Mill, is tremendous, and Mill is overpowered by it. Her words have an oracular value for him,—something more than their just weight; and her unconscious flattery, joined with the very direct flattery of many other prominent leaders of the great female army, have a not unnatural effect on his tender, susceptible and sympathetic nature. In putting the case so strongly I perhaps define it with too great a force, but you can make the needful allowance for the over-distinctness of words. (*Letters of Charles Eliot Norton* (London: Constable & Co, 1913), vol. 1, p. 400) [The full letter is at pp. 398–402.—Ed.]

[48] *Autobiography of John Stuart Mill*, published for the first time without alterations or omissions from the original manuscript in the possession of Columbia University with a preface by John Jacob Coss (New York: Columbia University Press, 1924). The passage quoted occurs on pp. 184–85. [John Stuart Mill, *Autobiography and Literary Essays*, eds. John M. Robson and Jack Stillinger, vol. 1 (1981) of *Collected Works*, pp. 264–65.—Ed.]

tion with me, something will be said hereafter: of what I owe in the way of instruction to her great powers of original thought and soundness of practical judgment, it would be [a] vain [attempt] to give an adequate idea. Surely no one ever before was so fortunate, as, after such a loss as mine, to draw another [such] prize in the lottery of life—another companion, stimulator, adviser, and instructor of the rarest quality. Whoever, either now or hereafter, may think of me and of the work I have done, must never forget that it is the product not of one intellect and conscience but of three, the least considerable of whom, and above all the least original, is the one whose name is attached to it.

POEMS
By Harriet Taylor

I

Written at Daybreak[1]

Hushed are all sounds, the sons of toil and pain,
The poor and wealthy [all] are all one again;
Sleep closes o'er the high and lowly head,
And makes the living fellows with the dead.
The clouds of night roll sullenly away,
Humbly obedient to th'approach of day;
The fragrant flowers unfold their scented heads,
The birds with gladness leave their leafy beds—
But unperceived at first the orb of day,
Sending alone a faint and trembling ray;
The glowing east, streaming with floods of gold
The fleeing clouds a thousand hues unfold.
At last he comes majestically slow
Pouring bright radiance on the world below,
And springing upwards from th'embrace of night
Gilding the heavn's with beams of orient light
O beauteous hour to minds of feeling giv'n
Filling the heart with thoughts and hopes of heav'n.
Lofty and noble purposes arise
[Giving] ~~And give~~ the soul communion with the skies;
To Nature's God our highest hopes ascend
The bounding heart paints joys which cannot end—
Oh, if to mortals it could e'er be given,
To chuse the path the spirit takes to Heav'n;

---

[1] MTColl., Box III/206, and other drafts of the same poem, *ibid.*, 204, 207 and 208, the last dated 1828. [The drafts are published in *The Complete Works of Harriet Taylor Mill* [hereafter cited as *Complete Works*], ed. Jo Ellen Jacobs (Bloomington: Indiana University Press, 1998), pp. 209–13, with this version at pp. 211–12.—Ed.]

Guided by him, from whom my doating heart
Not opening heav'n itself could tempt to part,
Mind ~~would~~ [should] ascend, on such a morn as this
On wings of glorious light to realms of bliss
And he whose love illumes this world of care[2]
Should dwell with me in all the transports there.

II

To the Summer Wind[3]

Whence comest thou, sweet wind?
Didst take thy phantom form
'Mid the depth of forest trees?
    Or spring, new born,
    Of the fragrant morn,
'Mong the far-off Indian seas?

Where speedest thou, sweet wind?
Though little heedest, I trow—
Dost thou sigh for some glancing star?
    Or cool [the] brow
    Of the dying now,
As they pass to their home afar?

What mission is thine, O wind?
Say for what thou yearnest—
That, like the wayward mind,
    Earth thou spurnest,
    Heaven-ward turnest,
And rest canst nowhere find!

---

[2] [The draft of the poem has the following line struck out: 'Would double all the joys which wait us there'. 'Awaiting' is supplied as an alternative to 'wait'.—Ed.]

[3] *Monthly Repository* (new series), vol. 6, September 1832, p. 617. [Republished in Harriet Taylor Mill, *Complete Works*, pp. 218–19.—Ed.]

III

Nature[4]

Manifold cords, invisible or seen
Present or past, or only hoped for, bind
All to our mother earth.—No step-dame she,
Coz'ning with forced fondness, but a fount,
Rightly pursued, of never-failing love.—
True, that too oft we lose ourselves 'mong thorns
That tear and wound.—But why impatient haste
From the smooth path our fairest mother drew?
'Tis man, not nature, works the general ill,
By folly piled on folly, till the heap
Hides every natural feeling, save alone
Great Discontent, upraised to ominous height,
And keeping drowsy watch o'er buried wishes.

---

[4] *Monthly Repository* (new series), vol. 6, September 1832, p. 636. [Republished in Harriet Taylor Mill, *Complete Works*, p. 219.—Ed.].

AN EARLY ESSAY
By Harriet Taylor[1]

More than two hundred years ago, Cecil[2] said 'Tenderness & sympathy are not enough cultivated by any of us; no one is kind enough, gentle enough, forbearing and forgiving enough'. In this two centuries in how many ways have we advanced and improved, yet could the speaker of those words now 'revisit the glimpses of the moon', he would find us but at the point he left us on the ground of toleration: his lovely lament is to the full as applicable now, as it was in the days of the hard-visaged and cold-blooded Puritans. Our faults of uncharitableness have rather changed their objects than their degree. The root of all intolerance, the spirit of conformity, remains; and not until that is destroyed, will envy hatred and all uncharitableness, with their attendant hypocrisies, be destroyed too. Whether it ~~would~~ be religious conformity, Political conformity, moral conformity or Social conformity, no matter which the species, the spirit is the same: all kinds agree in this one point, of hostility to individual character, and individual character if it exist at all, can rarely declare itself openly while there is, on all topics of importance a standard of conformity raised by the indolent minded many and guarded by a fasces[3] of opinion which, though composed individually of the weakest twigs, yet makes up collectively a mass which is not to be resisted with impunity.

[1] MTColl., Box III/78, on pages watermarked '1832'. [This essay is published in *The Complete Works of Harriet Taylor Mill* [hereafter cited as *Complete Works*], ed. Jo Ellen Jacobs (Bloomington: Indiana University Press, 1998), pp. 137–42, under the title 'Sources of Conformity'. The reader will note some similarities to the discussion of eccentricity in chapter 3 of Mill's 1859 *On Liberty* in *Essays on Politics and Society*, ed. John M. Robson, vols. 18–19 (1977) of *The Collected Works of John Stuart Mill* (Toronto: University of Toronto Press, 1962–1991), 18:260–75. Similar passages appear in Harriet Taylor's essay 'Laconicisms' in *Complete Works*, pp. 143–48.—Ed.]

[2] [William Cecil (1520–1598) was an English statesman who advised Queen Elizabeth for forty years. He was Secretary of State from 1550 to 1553 and 1558 to 1572 and Lord High Treasurer from 1572 until 1598. See *Oxford Dictionary of National Biography*, *s.v.* 'Cecil, William, first Baron Burghley', by Wallace T. MacCaffrey, accessed 20 May 2014, http://www.oxforddnb.com/view/article/4983.—Ed.]

[3] [Hayek has a query here; 'fasces'—a Roman symbol of authority—is supplied by the editor of Harriet Taylor Mill, *Complete Works*, p. 138, note 3.—Ed.]

What is called the opinion of Society is a phantom power, yet as is often the case with phantoms, of more force over the minds of the unthinking than all the flesh and blood arguments which can be brought to bear against it. It is a combination of the many weak, against the few strong; an association of the mentally listless to punish any manifestation of mental independance. The remedy is, to make all strong enough to stand alone; and whoever has once known the pleasure of self-dependance, will be in no danger of relapsing into subserviency. Let people once suspect that their leader is a phantom, the next step will be, to cease to be led altogether and each mind guide itself by the light of as much knowledge as it can acquire for itself by means of unbiased experience.

We have always been an aristocracy-ridden people, which may account for the fact of our being so peculiarly a propriety-ridden people. The aim of our life seems to be, not our own happiness, not the happiness of others unless it happens to come in as an accident of our great endeavour to attain some standard of right or duty erected by some or other of the sets into which society is divided like a net to catch gudgeons.

Who are the people who talk most about doing their duty? always those who for their life could give no intelligible theory of duty? What are called people of principle, are often the most unprincipled people in the world, if by principle is intended the only useful meaning of the word, accordance of the individual's conduct with the individual's self-formed opinion. Grant this to be the definition of principle, then eccentricity should be prima facie evidence for the existence of principle. So far from this being the case, 'it is odd' therefore it is wrong is the feeling of society; while they whom it distinguishes par excellence as people of principle, are almost invariably the slaves of some dicta or other. They have been taught to think, and accustomed to think, so and so right—others think so and so right—therefore it must be right. This is the logic of the world's good sort of people; and if, as is often the case their right should prove indisputable wrong, they can but plead those good intentions which make a most slippery and uneven pavement.

To all such we would say, think for yourself, and act for yourself, but whether you have strength to do either the one or the other, attempt not to impede, much less to resent the genuine expression[4] of the others.

---

[4] [At this point Harriet inserts a ' | '. Later, the following paragraph appears after another ' | ': 'Toleration can not even rank with those strangely named qualities, a "negative virtue" while we can be conscious that we tolerate there must remain some vestige of *intolerance*—not being virtuous it is possible also not to be vicious: not so in this—not to be charitable is to be uncharitable'. In another version of the essay, the passage proceeds without the addition, as above. The text reproduced above follows that in Harriet Taylor Mill, *Complete Works*, p. 139; as noted below, in note 5, Hayek's version includes this omitted passage.]

Were the spirit of toleration abroad, the name of toleration would be unknown.[5] [It is[6] one of those strangely named qualities, a 'negative virtue'.][7]

[It represents at best but the absence of vices, and under the shadow of whose respectable name many sins of omission pass.] To tolerate is to abstain from unjust interference, a quality which will surely one day not need a place in any catalogue of virtues. Now, alas, its spirit is not even comprehended by many, 'The quality of mercy is strained', and by the education for its opposite which most of us receive becomes if ever it be attained, a praiseworthy faculty, instead of an unconscious and almost intuitive state.

'Evil-speaking, lying and slandering' as the catechism formulary has it, is accounted a bad thing by every one. Yet how many do not hesitate about the evil-speaking as long as they avoid the lying and slandering—making what they call Truth a mantel to cover a multitude of injuries. 'Truth must not be spoken at all times' is the vulgar maxim. We would have the Truth, and if possible all the Truth, certainly nothing but the Truth said and acted universally. But we would never lose sight of the important fact that what is truth to one mind is often not truth to another. That no human being ever did or ever will comprehend the whole mind of any other human being. It would perhaps not be possible to find two minds accustomed to think for themselves whose thoughts on any identical subject should take in their expression the same form of words. Who shall say that the very same order of ideas is conveyed to another mind, by those words which to him perfectly represent his thought? It is probable that innumerable shades of variety, modify in each instance, the conception of every expression of thought; for which variety the imperfections of language offer no measure, and the differences of organization no proof. To an honest mind what a lesson of tolerance is included in this knowledge. To such not a living heart and brain but is like the planet 'whose worth's unknown although his height *be* taken',[8] and feeling that 'one touch of nature makes the

---

[5] [Hayek's version follows this with: 'The name implies the existence of its opposites. Toleration can not even rank with those strangely named qualities a "negative virtue"; while we can be conscious that we tolerate there must remain some vestige of *intolerance*—not being virtuous it is possible also not to be vicious: not so in this—not to be charitable is to be uncharitable'. Harriet later added in another color of ink: 'as the existence of a sense can be known only by its exercise the name implies the existence of its opposite. it speaks of a province of the mind in wh there can be no neutral ground'. Harriet Taylor Mill, *Complete Works*, p. 139.—Ed.]

[6] [Harriet Taylor Mill, *Complete Works*, p. 139, note 8, states that 'Toleration is' was 'added later in another ink'.—Ed.]

[7] [Another draft inserts 'than which phrase a more complete contradiction in terms is not to be found' (MTColl., Box III/86). See Harriet Taylor Mill, *Complete Works*, p. 139, for collations.—Ed.]

[8] [Harriet Taylor Mill, *Complete Works*, p. 140, note 11, attributes 'Let me not to the marriage of true minds' to one of Shakespeare's sonnets.—Ed.]

whole world kin'[9] finds something that is admirable in all, and something to interest and respect in each. In this view we comprehend that

All thoughts, all creeds, all dreams are true,
All visions wild and strange—[10]

to those who believe them, for after all we must come to that fine saying of the poet-philosopher,[11]

Man is the measure of all Truth
Unto himself

of the same signification is that thought, as moral as profound, which has been often in different ways expressed, yet which the universal practice of the world disproves its comprehension of, 'Toute la moralité de nos actions est dans le jugement que nous portons nousmême'[12]—'dangerous' may exclaim the blind follower of that sort of conscience, which is the very opposite of consciousness: would but people give up that sort of conscience which depends on conforming they would find the judgement of an enlightened consciousness proved by its results the voice of God:

Our acts our angels are, or good or ill,
Our fatal shadows that walk by us still[13]

and to make them pleasant companions we must get rid, not only of error, but of the moral sources from which it springs.

As the study of the mind of others is the only way in which effectually to improve our own, the endeavour to approximate as nearly as possible towards a complete knowledge of, and sympathy with another mind, is the spring and the food of all fineness of heart and mind. There seems to be this great distinction between physical and moral science; That while the degree of perfection which the first has attained is marked by the progressive completeness and exactness of its rules, that of the latter is in the state most favourable to, and

---

[9] [From Shakespeare's *Troilus and Cressida*, Act 3, Scene 3.—Ed.]

[10] [The first stanza of Tennyson's *Poems, Chiefly Lyrical* (1830) begins with these lines. Harriet Taylor Mill, *Complete Works*, p. 140, note 13.   Ed.]

[11] [Protagoras.—Ed.]

[12] ['All the morality of our actions is in the judgment we pass on them ourselves'. Translation provided by Harriet Taylor Mill, *Complete Works*, p. 140, note 14.—Ed.]

[13] [From 'Epilogue to Beaumont and Fletcher's Honest Man's Fortune'. According to Harriet Taylor Mill, *Complete Works*, p. 141, note 15, Harriet very likely took this from the beginning of Emerson's essay 'Self-Reliance'.—Ed.]

most showing healthfulness as it advances beyond all classification except on the widest and most universal principles. The science of morals should rather be called an art: to do something towards its improvement is in the power of every one, for every one may at least show truly their own page in the volume of human history, and be willing to allow that no two pages of it are alike.

Were everyone to seek only the beauty and the good which might be found in every object, and to pass by defect lightly where it could not but be evident, if evil would not cease to exist, it would surely be greatly mitigated, for half the ~~power~~ [force] of outward ill may be destroyed by inward strength, and half the beauty of outward objects is shown by the light within. The admiring state of mind is like a refracting surface which while it receives the rays of light, and is illuminated by them gives back an added splendour; the critical state is the impassive medium which cannot help.[14]

The sun's beams, but can neither transmit nor increase them. It is indeed much easier to discern the errors and blemishes of things than their good, for the same reason that we observe more quickly privation than enjoyment. Suffering is the exception to the extensive rule of good, and so stands out distinctly and vividly. It should be remembered by the critically-minded, that the habit of noting deficiencies before we observe beauties, does really for themselves lessen the amount of the latter.

Whoever notes a fault in the right spirit will surely find some beauty too. He who appreciates the one is the fittest judge of the other also. The capability of even serious error, proves the capacity for proportionate good. For if anything may be called a principle of nature this seems to be one, that force of any kind has an intuitive tendency towards good.

We believe that a child of good physical organization who were never to hear of evil, would not know from its own nature that evil existed in the mental or moral world. We would place before the minds of children no examples but of good and beautiful, and our strongest efforts should be, to prevent individual emulation. The spirit of Emulation in childhood and of competition in manhood are the fruitful sources of selfishness and misery. They are a part of the conformity plan, making each person's idea of goodness and happiness a thing of comparison with some received mode of being good and happy. But this is not the Creed of Society, for Society abhors individual character. It asks the sacrifice of body heart and mind. This is the summary of its cardinal virtues[15] would that such virtues were as nearly extinct as the dignitaries who are their namesakes.

[14] A gap left in the manuscript for one word later to be filled in. [Hayek continues after the gap, marked by square brackets in his text, followed by 'the sun's beams'. Harriet Taylor Mill, *Complete Works*, p. 141, has a full stop and begins a new paragraph. Note 16 on p. 141 states that a 'long space' exists in the manuscript.—Ed.]

[15] [Hayek inserts a comma here, which Harriet Taylor Mill, *Complete Works*, p. 142, omits, following Harriet's original.—Ed.]

At this present time the subject of social morals is in a state of most lamentable neglect. It is a subject so deeply interesting to all, yet so beset by prejudice, that the mere approach to it is difficult, if not dangerous. Yet there are 'thunders heared afar' by quick senses, and we firmly believe that many years will not pass before the clearest intellects of the time will expound, and the multitude have wisdom to receive reverently the exposition of the great moral paradoxes with which Society is hemmed in on all sides. Meanwhile they do something who in ever so small a circle or in ever so humble a guise, have[16] courage to declare the evil they see.

---

[16] [In the manuscript, Harriet struck out 'the' before 'courage'; see Harriet Taylor Mill, *Complete Works*, p. 142.—Ed.]

APPENDIX III. FAMILY TREES

1. MILL

James Mill
6.4.1773–23.6.1836 m. 5.6.1805   Harriet Burrow
d. 15.6.1854

John Stuart	Wilhelmina Forbes	Clara Esther	Harriet Isabella	James Bentham	Jane Stuart	Henry (Derry)	Mary Elizabeth	George Grote
20.5.1806 –7.5.1873*	1808–1861	1810–1886	1812–1897	1814–1862	1816?–1883	1820– 4.4.1840	1822– 15.1.1913	c. 1825– 15.7.1853
m. 21.4.1851 at Melcombe Regis Weymouth	m.	m. 28.4.1860 at Brighton			m. 28.9.1847 at Kensington		m. 23.8.1847 at Abergavenny	
Harriet Taylor, *née* Hardy (*q.v.* under Hardy below)	Dr. King	John Stephen Digweed			Marcus Paul Feraboschi		Charles Frederick Colman	

* The date of John Stuart Mill's death is almost invariably given as 8 May 1873. Professor Emile Thouverez in his brochure *Stuart Mill* (Paris, Bloud & Cie, 4th edition, 1908, p. 23) reproduces the official entry in the Registres de l'Etat civil d'Avignon from which it appears that Mill died at 7 o'clock in the morning of 7 May 1873.

2. HARDY

Thomas Hardy
c. 1775–3.6.1849 m.   Harriet Hurst
(order of children uncertain)

Thomas	Alfred	William	Harriet	Caroline	Edward	Arthur
13.11.1803–c. 1829	m. at Hartley Bank (Australia)	m. at Naples	8.10.1807–3.11.1858 m.	m.	10.10.1811	m. at Adelaide
	Louisa ———	Emilia ———	1. John Taylor (*q.v.* under Taylor below) 2. J. S. Mill (*q.v.* under Mill above)	Arthur Ley		Martha ———

3. TAYLOR

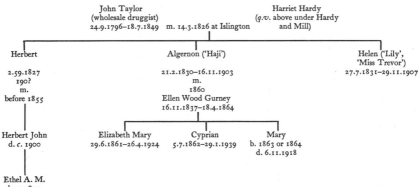

John Taylor
(wholesale druggist)
24.9.1796–18.7.1849 m. 14.3.1826 at Islington   Harriet Hardy
(*q.v.* above under Hardy and Mill)

Herbert	Algernon ('Haji')	Helen ('Lily', 'Miss Trevor')
2.59.1827 190? m. before 1855	21.2.1830–16.11.1903 m. 1860 Ellen Wood Gurney 16.11.1837–18.4.1864	27.7.1831–29.11.1907

Herbert John d. c. 1900	Elizabeth Mary 29.6.1861–26.4.1924	Cyprian 5.7.1862–29.1.1939	Mary b. 1863 or 1864 d. 6.11.1918

Ethel A. M.
b. c. 1875

PART TWO
RELATED WRITINGS

THIRTEEN

JOHN STUART MILL AT THE AGE OF TWENTY-FIVE[1]

I

It is a mistake that we all at times make to think of the great men of the past as 'representative' of their age or country. The temptation to do so is particularly strong in regard to our near intellectual forebears, the men who have to a large extent fashioned our own outlook. As their contributions to thought become commonplace, we notice in their work mainly the peculiar garb of their time, the points where they were not ahead of their contemporaries; and a period label becomes the great bar to their appreciation.

To our generation it is the men of the Victorian age who are suffering the temporary eclipse through which the reputation of every generation seems to pass and from which it recovers only when it is seen in a longer perspective. The time has not yet come, as it surely will, when we shall naturally think of the great figures of the middle of the nineteenth century as those Revolutionary Victorians who prepared the changes through which we are now passing. But it is not too early to attempt to distinguish those men and women of the period who should be regarded rather as precursors of our age than as typical of their own. Among them John Stuart Mill occupies no mean place.

John Stuart Mill may not have been an original thinker of the very first rank. But he was certainly not, as is now sometimes suggested, merely a late representative of a once powerful school whose thought he summarized at the height of its popular influence. Any suggestion of this sort completely misjudges Mill the mature thinker and confuses him with the boy writer who

---

[1] [Published as 'John Stuart Mill at the Age of Twenty-Five', Introductory Essay to John Stuart Mill, *The Spirit of the Age* (Chicago: University of Chicago Press, 1942), pp. v–xxxiii. For a fine review of the monograph including remarks on Hayek's Introduction, see C. B. Macpherson, *Canadian Journal of Economics and Political Science*, vol. 9, May 1943, pp. 267–68. The reader will note some overlap between this essay and Hayek's later essay 'John Stuart Mill, Mrs. Taylor, and Socialism' (this volume, pp. 298–312). Hayek's 'The Counter-Revolution of Science', in *Studies on the Abuse and Decline of Reason*, ed. Bruce Caldwell, vol. 13 (2010) of *The Collected Works of F. A. Hayek* (Chicago: University of Chicago Press; London: Routledge), pp. 167–281, was written at the same time as this study of the young Mill.—Ed.]

had been the mere expositor of the ideas of his elders. Mill the man was less than most men the exponent of the views of any school or sect or country. There was little that was typical of anything about the man who has been well described as 'an alien among men of his own class in English society'[2] and whose catholicity of mind enabled him to draw from the widest possible range of sources. It would indeed be less unjust to call him an eclectic than to regard him as the representative of any one school. And he is representative of his age only because his rare capacity of absorbing new ideas made him a kind of focus in which most of the significant changes of thought of his time combined. Though he built on the foundation of a strong English tradition, the new structure that he erected upon it added more that derived from foreign than from native sources. In fact, if one may speak of prejudices of so singularly candid a mind, there can be little doubt that Mill had acquired something like prejudice and even contempt not only for English society, which he little knew, but also for contemporary development of English thought and especially of English political economy, which he neglected to a surprising extent.

This character of the mature work of one whose unique education had been designed, and for a period had succeeded, in steeping him exclusively in the doctrines of one school makes the period in which this young but fully trained mind discovered entirely new intellectual worlds an unusually fascinating chapter of biography. The young Mill in the years when he had just broken away from inherited views and in the enthusiasm of his discoveries went much further than sober reflection would allow him to remain is in many ways a more attractive figure than the zealous sectarian of his early days or the austere and balanced philosopher of mature years. His essay on 'The Spirit of the Age' derives its peculiar interest from the fact that it shows Mill almost at the height of his reaction against his earlier views.

[2] Sir Leslie Stephen, *The English Utilitarians*, vol. 3: *John Stuart Mill* (London: Duckworth and Co., 1900), p. 16. This is the only satisfactory biography of J. S. Mill, though for the period in which we are here mainly interested, Emery Neff's *Carlyle and Mill: An Introduction to Victorian Thought*, 2nd ed. (New York: Columbia University Press, 1926), may also be usefully consulted. A suggestive summary of Mill's views which is less known than it deserves will be found in James Bonar, *The Tables Turned* (London: Macmillan and Co., 1931), pp. 79–132. The main source for Mill's life, his *Autobiography* (London: Longmans, Green, Reader, and Dyer, 1873), we shall quote from the edition in 'The World's Classics' (Oxford: Oxford University Press, 1924), which has the great advantage of an index. [Quotations from Mill's *Autobiography* have been standardized to *Autobiography and Literary Essays*, eds. John M. Robson and Jack Stillinger, vol. 1 (1981) of *The Collected Works of John Stuart Mill* [hereafter cited as *Collected Works*] (Toronto: University of Toronto Press, 1962–1991).—Ed.]

II

These pages are not likely to be read by anybody who does not know, at least in outline, the story of Mill's extraordinary education; and there is, therefore, no need for retelling it. A warning, however, may be necessary, not only against overstressing the influence of this education on his later views but also against overestimating the length of the period during which he remained completely under the sway of the views he had been taught. It is sometimes difficult to remember that the extensive literary activity and the participation in the various debating groups between 1822 and 1828 were all the work of a young man between sixteen and twenty-two years of age. Mill himself, by devoting more than forty percent of his *Autobiography* to the first twenty-two years of his life, gives a rather misleading impression. The 'reasoning machine' as which he appears there, the 'made man'[3] as which he was known to his contemporaries, was, after all, little more than a boy, carefully trained, and continuing to train himself, as an instrument of propaganda of the views of his unquestioned intellectual masters. It would probably not be unjust to say that he was then rather less original or independent in thought than many a brilliant young man of the same age. The picture of John Mill of the 'Utilitarian Society' period which we owe to his friend John Roebuck is probably not far from the truth. He says that in 1824 or 1825 Mill (then about nineteen years of age), 'although possessed of much learning, and thoroughly acquainted with the state of the political world, was, as might have been expected, the mere exponent of other men's ideas, those men being his father and Bentham; and that he was utterly ignorant of what is called society; that of the world, as it worked around him, he knew nothing; and, above all, of *woman*, he was [as] a child. He had never played with boys; in his life he had never known any, and we, in fact, who were now his associates, were the first companions he had ever mixed with'.[4]

---

[3] [In the *Autobiography* Mill wrote: 'I conceive that the description so often given of a Benthamite, as a mere *reasoning* machine, though extremely inapplicable to most of those who have been designated by that title, was during two or three years of my life not altogether untrue of me. It was perhaps as applicable to me as it can well be to any one just entering into life, to whom the common objects of desire must in general have at least the attraction of novelty' (*Autobiography*, vol. 1 of *Collected Works*, p. 110). In the early draft of the *Autobiography*, he remarked: 'In after conversations with Sterling, he told me how he and others had been accustomed to look upon me as a "made" or manufactured man' (*ibid.*, pp. 160, 162).—Ed.]

[4] *Life and Letters of John Arthur Roebuck: With Chapters of Autobiography*, ed. R. E. Leader (London: Edward Arnold, 1897), p. 28. One feels grateful to Roebuck for transmitting to us, in addition to this not over-attractive description of Mill, the charming picture of how on their long country excursions young Mill 'would fill his pockets with sweet violet seed, and scatter it in the hedges as he went along' (*ibid.*, p. 29).

It is not surprising that this period in Mill's life should have ended in that deep mental depression from which he suffered between his twentieth and his twenty-second year and which he describes in the *Autobiography*. It is from the recovery from that depression toward the end of 1828 that we must probably date the beginning of his career as an independent thinker. During the three or four years which followed, a great variety of new ideas crowded upon him under the influence of which he moved rapidly away from his initial position.[5]

Mill himself connects his recovery from the depression with his introduction to the poetry of Wordsworth. This seems to have made him receptive to the ideas of what he was later to call the Germano-Coleridgian school of thinkers, with which he became acquainted through his friends Frederick Maurice and John Sterling. A perhaps even more important link to German thought were [sic] John Austin, with whom Mill had read law in 1820–1821, and his wife, then freshly returned from Germany. Mill attended in 1828 and 1829 Austin's lectures on jurisprudence; and from Mrs. Austin, who as a writer and translator was then one of the most active interpreters of German thought in England and whom Mill invariably addressed, in the German term, as his *Mutter*, he seems to have acquired a fairly extensive acquaintance with German literature.[6] During 1829 also occurred his introduction to the ideas of the Saint-Simonians and the early Comte, which we shall presently have to consider more fully. And it was in the same year that Macaulay's celebrated essay on James Mill's theory of government[7] administered a severe shock to the beliefs of the younger Mill.

But John Mill remained by no means purely receptive. It was during the same period that he not only conceived, but actually wrote, some of his most original work. Early in 1830 he sketches his first ideas on Logic, and in the same year, if not before, he begins to write his first and most original work on economics, the *Essays on Some Unsettled Questions of Political Economy*.[8]

---

[5] It is, perhaps, also significant that his maturity was recognized in the same year (1828) by the East India Company, which he had entered five years before as a clerk at a salary of £30 a year, promoting him over the heads of all the clerks to the position of assistant examiner at £600 a year.

[6] On John Austin's 'strong distaste for the general meanness of English life' and his admiration for Germany, see *Autobiography*, pp. 150–51. Cf. also Mill to Carlyle, April 11 and 12, 1833 (*Letters of John Stuart Mill*, ed. Hugh Elliot (London and New York: Longmans, Green and Co., 1910), vol. 1, p. 46), where Mill says that the Austins 'seem to have almost resolved to emigrate into Germany this autumn'. On Mrs. Austin see the article in the *Dictionary of National Biography*, s.v. 'Sarah Austin'. [See Mill, *Autobiography*, vol. 1 of *Collected Works*, p. 185. For Mill's letter, see *The Earlier Letters of John Stuart Mill, 1812–1848*, ed. Francis E. Mineka, vols. 12–13 (1963) of *Collected Works*, 12:151–52.—Ed.]

[7] [Thomas Babington Macaulay, 'Mill's *Essay on Government*: Utilitarian Logic and Politics', *Edinburgh Review*, vol. 49, March 1829, pp. 159–89; see note 50, p. 34 above.—Ed.]

[8] [John Stuart Mill, *Essays on Economics and Society*, ed. John M. Robson, vols. 4–5 (1967) of *Collected Works*, 4:229–339. Subsequent brackets in this note indicate additional editorial

Either in 1830 or in 1831 Mill also made the acquaintance of Mrs. Taylor, who was twenty years later to become Mrs. Mill. This acquaintance seems very rapidly to have grown into a close friendship which, whatever may have been its true significance for Mill's intellectual development, certainly had the effect that he entirely withdrew from social life and became the recluse he remained for the rest of his life.[9]

Already at the end of 1829 he had withdrawn from the London Debating Society, to which, apart from his acquaintance with Maurice and Sterling, he owed also a new friend whom we shall presently meet. This withdrawal seems to mark a definite separation from those who had so far been his closest associates. Mill himself, in a letter written some years later, gives 1829 as the date when his political differences with them became apparent. As this letter is written to the editor of the journal in which 'The Spirit of the Age' appeared, and as it evidently refers generally to the period in which the two men closely collaborated, it may be worthwhile to quote from it at some length:

> What is the meaning of *your* insisting upon identifying me with Grote or Roebuck or the rest? Do you in your conscience think that my opinions are at all like theirs? Have you forgotten, what I am sure you once knew, that my opinion of their philosophy is & has for years been *more* unfavourable by far than your own? & that my radicalism is of a school the most remote from theirs, at all points, which exists? *They* knew this as long ago as 1829, since which time the variance has been growing wider & wider. . . . In the face of this it is rather hard to be accused of ascribing all wisdom & infallibility to a set from whose opinions I differ more than from the Tories.[10]

---

commentary.—Ed.] First published in 1844, except for the last essay ['On the Definition of Political Economy and on the Method of Investigation Proper to It'], which had appeared before [in *London and Westminster Review*, IV and XXXVI, October 1836, pp. 1–29]. While, in the Preface, Mill says that the *Essays* were written in 1829 and 1830 [*Essays on Economics and Society*, vol. 4. of *Collected Works*, p. 231], he gives in the *Autobiography* [vol. 1 of *Collected Works*, p. 189] the years 1830 and 1831, though the context of an earlier reference to it (*ibid.*, p. 102) suggests a rather earlier date. From a brief passage in a letter to Sterling (*Letters*, ed. Elliot, vol. 1, p. 9 [republished in Mill, *Earlier Letters*, vol. 12 of *Collected Works*, p. 79]) it would appear that he 'put the finishing hand' to them in October, 1831.

[9] [Hayek's 1962 Introduction to Mill's *On Representative Government*, however, provides compelling evidence that Mill was extraordinarily productive after Harriet Mill's death; see this volume, p. 319.—Ed.]

[10] This is a quotation from a letter to A. Fonblanque written in January, 1838, given in *The Life and Labours of Albany Fonblanque*, ed. by his nephew, Edward Barrington de Fonblanque (London: R. Bentley and Son, 1874), p. 32. Cf. also *John Stuart Mill: Notices of His Life and Works*, reprinted from the *Examiner* (London: E. Dallow, 1873), p. 9. [The full letter is republished in Mill, *Earlier Letters*, vol. 13 of *Collected Works*, pp. 370–71. Hayek's rendition of the third and fourth sentences reads: 'Have you forgotten what I am? How you once knew that my opinion of their philosophy is . . .'—Ed.]

In spite of this growing divergence in the underlying philosophy, John Mill continued, however, to collaborate with his old group on the great political issues of the day. And these years of intense intellectual activity were at the same time the years of his most passionate participation in the political struggle of the day. Catholic emancipation was rapidly followed by the bitter and long-drawn-out struggle for parliamentary reform. And as for the Radicals[11] generally, so it was also for him the news of the July revolution in France which in 1830 brought the long-existing tension to a head. But his relations to France will require a fuller account.

III

John Mill had already as a boy of fourteen spent more than a year in France with the family of Sir Samuel Bentham, the brother of Jeremy.[12] To this he owed not only a ready command of the language and a general acquaintance with French literature but also

> a strong and permanent interest in Continental Liberalism, of which I ever afterwards kept myself *au courant*, as much as of English politics: a thing not at all usual in those days with Englishmen, and which had a very salutary influence on my development, keeping me free from the error always prevalent in England, and from which even my father with all his superiority to prejudice was not exempt, of judging universal questions by a merely English standard.[13]

This contact with French thought was considerably strengthened after 1828 by a new friend who was to have a much greater influence on Mill than the single reference to him in the *Autobiography* would suggest. Gustave d'Eichthal, the young visitor from France whom one of Mill's friends brought on May 30, 1828, to a meeting of the London Debating Society and who could later claim that it had been 'I who in a certain measure had opened France to him

---

[11] [The Philosophical Radicals included like-minded English political radicals inspired by Bentham, James Mill, and Malthus such as Francis Place, George Grote, John Arthur Roebuck, Charles Buller, John Stuart Mill, and Edward John Telawny. Mill wrote that they were Malthusians in a qualified sense: 'This great doctrine, originally brought forward as an argument against the indefinite improvability of human affairs, we took up with ardent zeal in the contrary sense, as indicating the sole means of realizing that improvability by securing full employment at high wages to the whole labouring population through a voluntary restriction of the increase of their numbers' (Mill, *Autobiography*, vol. 1 of *Collected Works*, pp. 107 and 109).—Ed.]

[12] [See this volume, p. 208.—Ed.]

[13] *Autobiography*, p. 51 [Mill, *Autobiography*, vol. 1 of *Collected Works*, p. 63.—Ed.].

[Mill] as he [Mill] had opened England to me',[14] is a sufficiently interesting figure to justify a few words about him. Born in 1804 and thus by two years Mill's senior, he had in 1824 become the enthusiastic first disciple of Auguste Comte, then still fresh from his collaboration with Saint-Simon. Later (1824–1825) he had traveled for two years in Germany, studying philosophy, one of the first to spread the early forms of positivism in that country and at the same time communicating to Comte his impressions of German philosophy. After a year or two of commercial apprenticeship in France he came early in 1828 for the rest of that year to England to study her industrial development.

In one of the notes published by his son, Gustave d'Eichthal records how at the first meeting of the London Debating Society which he attended he was greatly impressed by the speech of 'a young man of great merit, Mr. Mill, whose acquaintance I made, who spoke last, and, who took up, one after another, all the points on which the discussion had touched, even those most remote from the subject, and gave in a few words his opinions on these points with a restraint, good sense, and knowledge of the subject which were altogether astonishing'.[15]

---

[14] [Hayek supplies Mill's name in brackets.—Ed.] 'Unpublished Letters of John Stuart Mill to Gustave d'Eichthal, edited by Eugène d'Eichthal', in *Cosmopolis: An International Monthly Review*, vol. 6, London and New York, April, 1897, p. 20. Further installments of this series appeared in the May issue of the same volume and in two issues of vol. 9 (February and March, 1898). These letters (the early ones, originally written and first published in English, in French translations) were republished by E. d'Eichthal together with some letters by his father and by Mill's friend Eyton Tooke in *J. S. Mill: Correspondance inédite avec Gustave d'Eichthal (1828–1842)–(1864–1871)*, translated, with an Introduction, by Eugène d'Eichthal (Paris: F. Alcan, 1898). Cf. also Pierre Lahtte, 'Correspondance d'Auguste Comte et de Gustave d'Eichthal', *Revue occidentale*, vol. 12, 2nd series, Paris, 1891; 'Conditions de la classe ouvrière en Angletere (1828): Notes de voyage de Gustave d'Eichthal', *Revue historique*, vol. 74, 1902; and Eugène d'Eichthal, 'Carlyle et le Saint Simonisme', *Revue historique*, vol. 82, 1910.

[15] *Correspondance inédite*, p. vi. It seems from another account (*Revue historique*, vol. 74, p. 83) which d'Eichthal gave of what must have been the same meeting that the subject had been the law against cruelty to animals and that the speaker introducing it had taken the opportunity to discuss the purposes of government in general and that he had opposed to the 'greatest happiness principle' the principle of the 'preservation of society'. After five other speakers had ranged from the position of the church, the theory of punishment, and the effectiveness of education to the meaning of the word 'cruelty' and the rights of animals, Mill spoke last: 'He admitted in principle the appropriateness of the law but regarded its application as impracticable because it was often impossible to decide to what point a certain amount of ill-treatment was more or less necessary. But Mr. Mill did not confine himself to basing his opinions on these reasonable grounds. He took up in turn all the points raised in the course of the evening, even those which had only a remote bearing on the subject, and commented on each full of appropriate good sense and free from all absolute considerations. Thus he reviewed what had been said about the rights of animals, the rights of men over them, the effects of punishment, the changes in morals and legislation, etc. Never have I heard a speech in which I had less desire to change anything'.

This acquaintance, renewed at another meeting of the society a fortnight later, seems rapidly to have grown into a friendship. Kept up through Gustave d'Eichthal's younger brother Adolphe, the banker, who followed Gustave with a visit to England, it led to an extensive correspondence which is one of the most important, though little-known, sources of our knowledge of Mill's intellectual development during these years. A year or so after his return to France, Gustave joined the Saint-Simonian group (from which Comte had by then separated), at that time at the height of its activity, and he became one of its most ardent and active apostles. And henceforth he spared no pains to convert his young English friends to the new creed.

He seems either to have left with Mill, or sent to him soon after his return, copies of Comte's early *Système de politique positive* (1824, first published in 1822 as part of Saint-Simon's *Catéchisme des industriels*)[16] and of Saint-Simon's *Opinions littéraires, philosophiques, et industriels*; and perhaps also some numbers of the Saint-Simonian journal *Producteur*.[17] But it was only in the summer or autumn of 1829[18] that Mill began to study these works. And while he writes that he was perfectly astonished at the shallowness of the *Opinions littéraires*, he was immediately impressed by Comte's work:

When, however, I read Comte's 'Traité [*sic*] de Politique positive' I was no longer surprised at the high opinion which I had heard you express of the book, & the writer, and was even seduced by the plausibility of his manner

---

[16] [Comte's 'Plan des travaux scientifiques nécessaires pour réorganiser la société' was published in Saint-Simon's 1822 *Du contrat social.*—Ed.]

[17] [Claude Henri, Comte de Saint-Simon, *Catéchisme des industriels* (Paris: Imprimerie de sétier, 1823–1824); Auguste Comte, *Système de politique positive* (Paris: Chez les principaux libraires, 1824); Claude Henri, Comte de Saint-Simon, *Opinions litteraires, philosophiques et industrielles* (Paris: Galerie de Bossange, 1825); *Le Producteur: Journal philosophique de l'industrie, des sciences et des beaux-arts* (Paris: Chez Sautelet et Cie., 1825–1826).—Ed.]

[18] More precisely between May 15 and October 8, 1829. In a letter to d'Eichthal under the former date he says: 'I am only now about to read the work of Mr. Comte which you ~~have~~ [so strongly] recommended to me'. [The full letter to d'Eichthal dated October 8, 1829, is published in Mill, *Earlier Letters*, vol. 12 of *Collected Works*, pp. 34–38. Mill was evidently referring here to Comte's *Système de politique positive*. The full letter dated May 15 is published in Mill, *Earlier Letters*, vol. 12 of *Collected Works*, pp. 30–34.—Ed.] Mill seems later himself not too clearly to have remembered either the date when he first read Comte or the gradualness with which his influence operated. In his first letters to Comte (November 8, 1841; see L. Lévy-Bruhl, ed., *Lettres inédites de John Stuart Mill à Auguste Comte* (Paris: F. Alcan, 1899), p. 2), he writes: 'C'est dans l'année 1828, Monsieur, que j'ai lu pour la première fois votre petit Traité de *Politique Positive*; et cette lecture a donné à toutes mes idées une forte secousse, qui, avec d'autres causes, mais beaucoup plus qu'elles, a déterminé ma sortie définitive de la section benthamiste de l'école révolutionnaire, dans laquelle je fus élevé, et même je puis presque dire dans laquelle je naquis'. [Mill's letter to Comte is republished in Mill, *Earlier Letters*, vol. 13 of *Collected Works*, p. 488–90, with the quoted text at p. 489.—Ed.]

into forming a higher opinion of the doctrines which he delivers, than on reflexion they appear to me at all entitled to.[19]

This, however, still leads Mill to a most thoroughgoing criticism of the whole of Comte's theoretical and political views in which he uses the lesson recently learned from Macaulay about the danger of the use in politics of deductive arguments on the lines of mathematics. And it is interesting that in this first reaction he immediately laid his fingers on one of the most vulnerable spots in Comte's political doctrines:

> The very first and fundamental principle of the whole system, that government and the social union exist for the purpose of concentrating and directing all the forces of *society to some one end*. He cannot mean that government should exist for more than one purpose, or that this one purpose should be the direction of the united force of society to more than one end. What a foundation for a system of political science this is! Government exists for all purposes whatever that are *for man's good*: and the highest & most important of these purposes is, the improvement of man himself as a moral and intelligent being, which is an end not included in M. Comte's category at all. *The united forces of society* never were, nor can be, directed to one single end, nor is there, so far as I can perceive, any reason for desiring that they should. Men do not come into the world to fulfil one single end, and there is *no single end which if fulfilled* even in the most complete manner *would make them happy*.[20]

But Gustave d'Eichthal, who in the meantime had become a member of the innermost circle of the Saint-Simonian sect, spares no effort to meet all criticism. In two impassionate letters of great length he endeavors to persuade Mill to become a member of the school and informs him fully of its doctrine and organization.[21] And in the course of the lively correspondence extending over the next two years we can watch how Mill gradually approaches to the views of the Saint-Simonians, although he never fails to stress that in no circumstances would he become a member and repeatedly expresses his hor-

---

[19] Mill to d'Eichthal, October 8, 1829 (*Cosmopolis*, vol. 6, p. 29). [The quoted text is at p. 35 of Mill, *Earlier Letters*, vol. 12 of *Collected Works*. Hayek supplies the addition in brackets.—Ed.]

[20] *Ibid.*, p. 30. [The full letter is published in Mill, *Earlier Letters*, vol. 12 of *Collected Works*, pp. 34–38; the quoted text appears at p. 36 and reads: 'forces of society never were, never can be directed to one single end'. The emphasis in the quoted passage is Hayek's. The reader will be reminded of Hayek's concern with single goals in *Road to Serfdom*; see *The Road to Serfdom: Texts and Documents—The Definitive Edition*, ed. Bruce Caldwell, vol. 2 (2007) of *The Collected Works of F. A. Hayek*, pp. 100–111; and Sandra J. Peart and David M. Levy, 'F. A. Hayek and the "Individualists"', in *F. A. Hayek and the Modern Economy: Economic Organization and Activity*, eds. Sandra J. Peart and David M. Levy (New York: Palgrave Macmillan, 2013), pp. 29–56.—Ed.]

[21] D'Eichthal to Mill, November 23 and December 1, 1829 (*Correspondence inédite*, pp. 39–89).

ror of all sectarianism. Already, in February, 1830, he concedes that being completely 'cured of those *habitudes critiques*, which, you seem to suppose, are the only obstacle to my adopting the entire doctrine of your school' is a debt which he owes 'partly though not entirely to the St Simonian school: I had much changed from what I was, before I read any of their publications; but it was their works which gave order and system to the ideas which I had already imbibed from intercourse with others, and derived from my own reflexions'.[22] He even expressly retracts now some of 'the objections I formerly urged against the St Simonian school, as some of the points which I objected to, appeared from a perusal of the *Producteur* (every word of which I have read with as great care and interest as any book I ever saw) never to have been held by [them] him in the sense in which I thought them objectionable, & as you informed me in answer to my two letters the other points had been given up'.[23] The continued refusal formally to collaborate with the Saint-Simonian society is now based largely on the ground that it appears to him 'utterly hopeless and chimerical to suppose that the regeneration of mankind can ever be wrought by means of working on their opinions', particularly in England, where 'Englishmen habitually distrust the most obvious truths, if the person who advances them is suspected of having any general views'.[24]

A year later, after referring to the unsuccessful attempt of two other Saint-Simonian emissaries to convert him, he adds: 'But if you are sufficiently catholic, in the original & correct sense of the word, to rejoice at any progress which does not bring [any] proselytes within your pale, I think you will be pleased with two or three articles of mine in the Examiner, headed "The Spirit of the Age", which Adolphe is so kind as to take charge of for you'. And, after reporting how he has been helping to spread information about the Saint-Simonian doctrine, he concludes: 'In short, although I am not a St Simonist nor at all likely to become one, *je tiens bureau de St-Simonisme chez moi*'.[25]

Mill's approach toward Saint-Simonian continued after this date. At the end of November of the same year he writes that

> the daily reading of the Globe, combined with various other causes, has brought me much nearer to many of your opinions than I was before; and I regard you as decidedly *à la tête de la civilisation*.

---

[22] [The full text of the letter from Mill to d'Eichthal, dated February 9, 1830, is republished in Mill, *Earlier Letters*, vol. 12 of *Collected Works*, pp. 44–49; the quoted text above appears at p. 45—Ed.]

[23] [*Ibid.*, p. 47.—Ed.]

[24] Mill to d'Eichthal, February 9, 1830 (*Cosmopolis*, vol. 6, pp. 350–53). [Mill, *Earlier Letters*, vol. 12 of *Collected Works*, pp. 47, 48.—Ed.]

[25] Mill to d'Eichthal, March 1, 1831 (*ibid.*, pp. 355–56). [Mill, *Earlier Letters*, vol. 12 of *Collected Works*, p. 71.—Ed.]

> I am now inclined to think that your social organisation, under some modification or other, which experience, no doubt, will one day suggest to yourselves, is likely to be the final and permanent condition of the human race.[26]

Long before this, however, and during the long break in the correspondence from February, 1830, to January, 1831, Mill had himself been in Paris and made contact with the Saint-Simonians, including their leaders, Enfantin and Bazard.[27] He hurried to Paris immediately the news of the 'three days of July' (July 27–29, 1830) arrived and, in the company of some of his friends, seems to have spent some little time there, studying the state of the political parties and taking the greatest interest in the doings of the younger men and the common people.[28]

IV

About the time of Mill's return from Paris an old member of the Mill circle, Albany Fonblanque, had taken over the entire management of the weekly *Examiner*, a journal with 'the reputation as the chief organ of high-class intel-

---

[26] Mill to d'Eichthal, November 30, 1831 (*ibid.*, p. 356). Toward the end of the same year we find Mill in another letter (December 6 (*ibid.*, pp. 358–61)) giving detailed advice on the people in England likely to be interested in Saint-Simonian literature; and the last letter of the series which falls into the period of the activity of the Saint-Simonians (May 30, 1832) refers to a letter of his in the Saint-Simonian *Globe*, which, according to a footnote in the French edition of the *Correspondance*, appeared in the issue of April 18, 1832, but which in the present (i.e., wartime) circumstances I have not been able to consult. [For the November 30, 1831, December 6, 1831, and May 30, 1832, letters, see Mill, *Earlier Letters*, vol. 12 of *Collected Works*, pp. 88, 90–93, and 107–9, respectively. Hayek's reference here, written in the middle of World War II, is correct. The letter in question, entitled 'Comparison of the Tendencies of French and English Intellect', appears on p. 433 of the April 18, 1832, issue of *Le Globe*, now published in John Stuart Mill, *Newspaper Writings*, eds. Ann P. Robson and John M. Robson, vols. 22–25 (1986) of *Collected Works*, 23:442–47.—Ed.]

[27] [Saint Amand Bazard (1791–1832) and Barthelémy Prosper Enfantin (1796–1864) were leaders of the Saint-Simonians until 1831, when Bazard broke off in disagreement with Enfantin's views about the relation between the sexes. Bazard died shortly thereafter and Enfantin formed a sect of his own. Mill, *Earlier Letters*, vol. 12 of *Collected Works*, p. 71, note 5. For Mill's remarks on Bazard and Enfantin, see *Autobiography*, vol. 1 of *Collected Works*, p. 173.—Ed.]

[28] The enthusiasm with which Mill entered into the spirit of the revolution may be gathered from the story in Roebuck's *Life* that 'on the occasion of Louis Philippe's first visit to the opera these young Englishmen (apparently including Mill) happened to be present, and they presently began to shout for "La Marseillaise", in which the house joined; and [then] they shouted: "Debout, debout", until the whole audience, including the King himself, actually stood up during the playing of the revolutionary tune' (p. 30).

lectual radicalism'.[29] This paper was in general appearance and character very much like the corresponding political weeklies of our own day. It had been founded in 1808 by John and Leigh Hunt,[30] and, with Byron, Shelley, Keats, and William Hazlitt among its occasional contributors, had rapidly established a foremost position among the journals of its day. Its circulation, however, seems to have remained limited.[31]

When Fonblanque took control of the paper, Mill soon became one of the most frequent contributors to whom Fonblanque later gave (together with W. J. Fox) 'the chief credit for the exertions in accomplishing the end in view'.[32] Mill, in the *Autobiography*, says that Fonblanque himself contributed to the *Examiner*

> at least three-fourths of all the original writing contained in it: but of the remaining fourth I contributed during those years a much larger share than any one else. I wrote nearly all the articles on French subjects, including a weekly summary of French politics, often extending to considerable length; together with many leading articles on general politics, commercial and financial legislation, and any miscellaneous subjects in which I felt interested, and which were suitable to the paper, including occasional reviews of books.[33]

This work for the *Examiner* seems to fall mainly in the years from 1831 to 1833. There is little clear evidence that Mill was already a regular contributor in 1830, though in August and September of that year the *Examiner* printed six letters from Paris 'from two gentlemen whose knowledge, ability, and exalted principles induce us to attach great value to all their opinions and statements', some of which, at least, clearly seem to be from J. S. Mill's pen.[34] It would

[29] See the article by R. Garnett on Albany Fonblanque in the *Dictionary of National Biography*.

[30] [James Henry Leigh Hunt (1784–1859); see note 23, p. 25 above.—Ed.]

[31] In a letter to Carlyle, dated December 22, 1833 (*Letters*, ed. Elliot, vol. 1, p. 82), Mill explains that 'the sale of the Examiner does not much exceed 3000 copies. This is as you say a scandalous symptom, yet there are many causes that contribute to it besides the scandalous ones that first suggest themselves. Of course it can only expect buyers (*readers* are quite another matter) from radicals: ~~and~~ [now] of [these] ~~them~~ the more vulgar sort find as much radicalism in [other] ~~the~~ papers, of a more direct and [palpable] ~~popular~~ kind'. [Mill, *Earlier Letters*, vol. 12 of *Collected Works*, p. 200.—Ed.]

[32] In an unpublished letter from which this passage is quoted in the article on Fonblanque in the *Dictionary of National Biography*.

[33] *Autobiography*, p. 147 [Mill, *Autobiography*, vol. 1 of *Collected Works*, pp. 179 and 181.—Ed.].

[34] Particularly the second and third letters of the series, dated August 20 and 21, in the *Examiner* for August 29, 1830, which bear an unmistakable resemblance to the fragment of a letter by John Mill to his father, dated August 13, given by A. Bain (*J. S. Mill: A Criticism* (London: Longmans, Green, and Co., 1882), pp. 41–42). [For the August 20 and 51 letters, see Mill, *Earlier Letters*, vol. 12 of *Collected Works*, pp. 55–63; and for the August 13 letter, see *ibid.*, pp. 54–55.—Ed.].

seem, therefore, that Mill's work on the paper commenced more or less with the articles on 'The Spirit of the Age', although the continuation of the passage in the *Autobiography* just quoted would suggest the contrary:

> Mere newspaper articles on the occurrences or questions of the moment gave no opportunity for the development of any general mode of thought; but I attempted, in the beginning of 1831, to embody in a series of articles, headed 'The Spirit of the Age', some of my new opinions, and especially to point out in the character of the present age, the anomalies and evils characteristic of the transition from a system of opinions which had worn out, to another only in process of being formed. These articles were, I fancy, lumbering in style, and not lively or striking enough to be at any time acceptable to newspaper readers; but had they been far more attractive, still, at that particular moment, when great political changes were impending, and engrossing all minds, these discussions were ill timed, and missed fire altogether. The only effect which I know to have been produced by them, was that Carlyle, then living in a secluded part of Scotland, read them in his solitude, and saying to himself (as he afterwards told me) 'here is a new Mystic', enquired on coming to London that autumn respecting their authorship; an enquiry which was the immediate cause of our becoming personally acquainted.[35]

The articles on 'The Spirit of the Age' began to appear in the *Examiner* over the signature 'A.B.' on January 6, 1831, and continued at intervals, sometimes of considerable length, until May 29.[36]

The series of seven articles on 'The Prospects of France', beginning in the *Examiner* for September 19, 1830, and signed 'S-' do not suggest to me Mill's hand. [These fragments are, however, now thought to be by Mill. See Mill, *Newspaper Writings*, eds. Ann P. Robson and John M. Robson, vols. 22–25 (1986) of *Collected Works*, 22:128–63, 184–202.—Ed.] I have also been unable to find the 'notice of the St. Simonians' to which reference is made in a passage in Mill's letter to d'Eichthal of January, 1831 (*Cosmopolis*, vol. 6, p. 355, but not reproduced in the French edition of the *Correspondance*). [The letter is in fact January 30, 1832. See Mill, *Earlier Letters*, vol. 12 of *Collected Works*, p. 96. The notice is in an article in the *Examiner*, January 29, 1832, in Mill, *Newspaper Writings*, vol. 23 of *Collected Works*, pp. 401–3.—Ed.]

[35] *Autobiography*, pp. 147–48. [See Mill, *Autobiography*, vol. 1 of *Collected Works*, p. 181.—Ed.] Cf. also Mill to John Sterling, October 20–22, 1831 (*Letters*, ed. Elliot, vol. 1, p. 17): 'He [Carlyle] is a great hunter-out of acquaintances; he hunted me out, or rather hunted out the author of certain papers in the Examiner (the first, as he said, which he had ever seen in a newspaper, hinting that the age was not the best of all possible ages): & his acquaintance is the only substantial good I have yet derived from writing those papers, & a much greater one than I expected when I wrote them'. [Hayek supplies the brackets and contents. Mill, *Earlier Letters*, vol. 12 of *Collected Works*, pp. 85–86.—Ed.]

[36] The second section appeared in the issue of the *Examiner* of January 23; the third, in two parts, in the issues of February 6 and March 13; the fourth on April 3; and the fifth, again divided into two installments, on May 15 and 29. [The first article appeared on January 9, 1831.

V

Very little need now be added on the essay itself. Mill takes from Comte and the Saint-Simonians his leading ideas and several details, but he uses them for his own ends.[37] What he takes are characteristic aspects of their philosophy of history which probably appealed to him the more for its obvious resemblance to certain German strands of thought with which he had recently become acquainted. The conception of his age as an age of transition, the central theme of the essay, pervades the whole of the work of the Saint-Simonians. The idea of the 'necessary stage in the ~~process~~ [progress] of civilization', the description of the existing 'intellectual anarchy',[38] and the discussion of the significance of the 'exercise of private judgement',[39] with its emphasis on the different role of private judgement in the natural sciences as compared with the discussion of social problems, are taken straight from Comte.[40] Mill's contrast between the 'natural' and the 'transitional'[41] states of society is the same as that between the 'organic' and 'critical' phases of social evolution in the philosophy of Comte and the Saint-Simonians. Obvious also is the influence of the Saint-Simonian discussion of the

See Mill, *Newspaper Writings*, vol. 22 of *Collected Works*, pp. 227–34, 238–45, 252–58, 278–82, 289–95, 304–7, 312–16.—Ed.]

[37] The two works by Comte and the Saint-Simonians in which all the relevant ideas can be found are, in the first instance, Comte's essay of 1822, which we already know to have made a deep impression on Mill, and, second, the celebrated *Doctrine de Saint-Simon: Exposition: premiére année*, 1829 (rev. ed., with an Introduction and notes, by C. Bouglé and Elie Halévy (Paris: Mr. Rivière, 1924)), the most important and most influential work of the school—a course of lectures in which Bazard in 1828–1829 had expounded the Saint-Simonian ideas in the form given to them mainly by Enfantin. Although we have no direct evidence that Mill knew the *Exposition*, there could be no real doubt about it, even if he had not told us that he 'read nearly everything they [the Saint-Simonians] wrote' (*Autobiography*, p. 141). [Mill, *Autobiography*, vol. 1 of *Collected Works*; p. 173. Hayek supplies the words in brackets.—Ed.] The *Exposition* is also largely a restatement of ideas developed by Enfantin in 1825 and 1826 in the Saint-Simonian journal *Producteur*, which we know Mill to have studied carefully. Of Comte's essay, there is a convenient English edition available in Auguste Comte, *Early Essays on Social Philosophy*, H. D. Hutton, trans., with an Introduction by F. Harrison ('New Universal Library' (London: E. P. Dutton and Co., 1911)). This contains also two earlier essays of Comte (which Mill is not likely to have known) and two later ones which Mill is almost certain to have seen in the *Producteur*. For a fuller summary of the history of the Saint-Simonian movement and its doctrines see the present writer's series of articles on 'The Counter-Revolution of Science', in *Economica*, February–August 1941. ['The Counter-Revolution of Science', in *Studies on the Abuse and Decline of Reason*, vol. 13 of *The Collected Works of F. A. Hayek*, pp. 167–281.—Ed.].

[38] [Mill, *Newspaper Writings*, vol. 22 of *Collected Works*, p. 233.—Ed.]

[39] [*Ibid.*, p. 239.—Ed.]

[40] There is no space here for detailed documentation of the sources of these ideas, but the opening sentence of Comte's essay of 1822 may be given to indicate the general similarity of his approach to Mill's: 'A social system in its decline, a New System arrived at maturity—such is the fundamental character which the general progress of Civilisation has assigned to the present epoch' (*Early Essays on Social Philosophy*, p. 88).

[41] [Mill, *Newspaper Writings*, vol. 22 of *Collected Works*, p. 252.—Ed.]

relations between the spiritual and the temporal powers in the different stages of evolution, which occupies much space in their discussions. But beyond this there is not much resemblance in the detail of the argument, however similar the phraseology. It is significant that, beyond a strong awareness of what in the *Autobiography* Mill was to call 'the very limited and temporary value of the old political economy, which assumes private property and inheritance as indefeasible facts, and freedom of production and exchange as the *dernier mot* of social improvement',[42] there is nothing in the essay of the concrete socialist proposals for reform. Mill indeed, while sympathizing with the ultimate aims of socialism, disagreed to the end with the concrete suggestions for the abolition of private property, and particularly never ceased, as he put it in the *Political Economy*, 'utterly [to] dissent from the most conspicuous and vehement part of their teaching, their declamations against competition'.[43]

His argument leads him to an interesting distinction, which I believe in this form is his own, 'between the[se] two states of society, that in which capacity raises men to power, and that in which power calls forth their capacity'[44] from time to time, in ages of transition like his own, it happens, however, that 'power, and fitness for power, have altogether ceased to correspond'.[45] The aristocracy is no longer fit to exercise the power which it still possesses, and the crisis can be resolved only by admitting to power the classes which in the new circumstances are best qualified to govern. Thus the argument is made directly to apply to the burning question of the reform of parliamentary representation.

Mill's essay is now readily available to the reader, and there can be no use in further summarizing his argument. But two more quotations may be of interest which curiously illustrate the spirit in which the essay was written. The first is from a letter Mill wrote to the editor of the *Examiner* in the year when the essay appeared:

> The people, to be in the best state, should appear to be ready and impatient to break out into outrage, *without actually breaking out*. The Press, which is our only instrument, has at this moment the most delicate and the most exalted functions to discharge that any power has yet had to perform in this country. It has at once to raise the waves and to calm them; to say, like the Lord, 'Hitherto shalt thou go and no further'. With such words ringing in their ears, Ministers cannot waver [even] if they would . . .[46]

[42] *Autobiography*, p. 141. [Mill, *Autobiography*, vol. 1 of *Collected Works*, p. 175. Ed.]

[43] *Principles of Political Economy*, Book 4, chap. 7, sec. 7 (ed. Ashley, p. 792). [John Stuart Mill, *The Principles of Political Economy with Some of Their Application to Social Philosophy*, ed. John M. Robson, vols. 2–3 of *Collected Works*, 3:794. Hayek supplies the word in brackets.—Ed.]

[44] [Mill, *Newspaper Writings*, vol. 22 of *Collected Works*, p. 254.—Ed.]

[45] [*Ibid.*, p. 255.—Ed.]

[46] *The Life and Labours of Albany Fonblanque*, p. 29. [Hayek placed 'even' in brackets.—Ed.]

The other, from the *Autobiography*, refers to the period during which the essay was written and explains that Mill then

> earnestly hoped that Owenite, St. Simonian, and all other anti-property doctrines might spread widely among the poorer classes; not that I thought those doctrines true, or desired that they should be acted on, but in order that the higher classes might be made to see that they had more to fear from the poor when uneducated, than when educated.[47]

As the articles stand, there is no real conclusion to the argument. The series is, in fact, unfinished. Mill genuinely meant, as he says in the concluding paragraph, to 'resume [his] subject as early as possible after the passing of the Reform Bill'.[48] As late as October, 1831, he still mentions this intention.[49] But another year was to pass before the bill finally became law. Eighteen months is a long time during a period of such rapid intellectual development as that through which Mill was then passing. When the time came, he seems no longer to have been able to put himself back into the state of mind in which the articles had been written. The continuation of his thought we must seek in his later writings on representative government.

Mill himself did not regard the essay on 'The Spirit of the Age' as part of his mature work. Not only did he not include it in his *Dissertations and Discussions*, which begin with a paper written a year later, but he says explicitly in the *Autobiography* that 'in the whole mass of what I wrote previous to these, there is nothing of sufficient permanent value to justify reprinting'.[50] We have already quoted his harsh judgment on the 'lumbering style' of the essay, which, I think, the reader will not share, though, it must be admitted, it has been endorsed by no less an authority than Sir Leslie Stephen.[51] But the importance of the essay lies not in its style or in any permanent contribution to knowledge but in the light it throws on one of the most interesting phases in the development of a great figure of the past century. As such it deserves to be rescued from the oblivion in which it has rested for over a hundred years.

---

[47] *Autobiography*, p. 146. [Mill, *Autobiography*, vol. 1 of *Collected Works*, p. 179.—Ed.]

[48] [Mill, *Newspaper Writings*, vol. 22 of *Collected Works*, p. 316.—Ed.]

[49] Mill to Sterling, October 20–22, 1831 (*Letters*, ed. Elliot, vol. 1, p. 10). [Mill, *Earlier Letters*, vol. 12 of *Collected Works*, p. 80.—Ed.]

[50] *Autobiography*, p. 154–55. [Mill, *Autobiography*, vol. 1 of *Collected Works*, vol. 1, p. 191.—Ed.] Mill had, however, earlier made an exception for the *Essays on Some Unsettled Questions of Political Economy* written at least in part before 'The Spirit of the Age'.

[51] [Stephen, *The English Utilitarians*,] p. 26n.

FOURTEEN

J. S. MILL'S CORRESPONDENCE[1]

When in 1910 Mr. Hugh S. R. Elliot edited his two volumes of *The Letters of John Stuart Mill*[2] he had before him rough drafts of 'many thousands' of letters, comprising probably the greater part of all the letters written by Mill during the last twenty-six years of his life. From this wealth of material Mr. Elliot published a selection which might well satisfy us so far as this part of Mill's life is concerned. But for the period till 1847, the year in which Mill reached his forty first year and completed his second *magnum opus*, the *Principles of Political Economy*, no such drafts seem to have been available. Mr. Elliot was fortunate enough to secure for this earlier period three series of hitherto unpublished letters, to Thomas Carlyle, John Sterling, and Edward Bulwer; and a selection from these is included in his volumes. Yet, interesting as these are, they represent only a few sides of Mill's intellectual development during the formative and the most productive time of his life which was also the period in which in many ways he took a much more active part in public affairs than he did later. Not only many of his varied interests, but also fairly long intervals of his life are entirely unrepresented in Mr. Elliot's collection.

Scattered Letters

How important many of Mill's other letters of this early period are, not only for the understanding of his own development, but for the intellectual history of the time in general, is shown by the numerous smaller collections and single letters which have been published at various dates. They include, apart from the comparatively well-known collections of his correspondence with Auguste Comte and Gustave d'Eichthal, many others, no less interesting, which have fallen in undeserved oblivion. Indeed, for the period till 1847, for which Mr.

[1] [Published as 'J. S. Mill's Correspondence', *Times Literary Supplement*, February 1943, issue 2141, p. 84. Typographical errors and inconsistencies in formatting have been corrected silently in what follows; additional bibliographical information is provided in brackets.—Ed.]

[2] [John Stuart Mill, *The Letters of John Stuart Mill*, ed. Hugh S. R. Elliot (London: Longmans, Green & Co., 1910).—Ed.]

Elliot's two volumes contain forty-six letters, certainly more than 160 letters (or fragments of letters) by Mill had already been printed before 1910 and at least another twenty-five have been published since: yet only one of the previously published letters was included in Mr. Elliot's collection, it seems because a copy which d'Eichthal had made for Mill forty years after it had been first written was found among Mill's papers. As not even a complete list of these published letters appears to exist in print, the following summary, including in chronological order all the other published letters by Mill, written prior to 1848, may be of interest:

(1) A[lexander] Bain, *John Stuart Mill[: A Criticism with Personal Recollections* (London: Longman's, Green, and Co. 1882)]: three letters written by Mill as a boy and fifteen fragments of letters to members of Mill's family or to Bain.

(2) Eugène d'Eichthal, 'Letters of John Stuart Mill to Gustave d'Eichthal', *Cosmopolis, An International Monthly Review* (London and New York), vol. 6, April and May, 1897, and vol. 9, February and March, 1898: twenty letters written 1829–1842 (and eleven further letters written in French 1864–1871). These letters (those of the earlier period in French translations), together with some of the replies and a few additional letters by Mill of the later period, were republished in J. S. Mill, *Correspondance inédite avec Gustave d'Eichthal, 1828–1842; 1864–1871*, Paris[: F. Alcan], 1898.

(3, 4) E. B. de Fonblanque, *The Life and Labours of Albany Fonblanque*, [London: R. Bentley and Son,] 1874; and J. S. Mill, Notices of his Life and Work', reprinted from the *Examiner*, 1873: ten substantial and partly overlapping fragments of letters to Albany Fonblanque, 1831–1841.

(5) Richard Garnett, *The Life of W. J. Fox*, edited by Edward Garnett, [London: John Lane Co.,] 1910: thirteen letters to W. J. Fox, 1832–1837.

(6) William Knight, 'Letters of J. S. Mill to Prof. John Nicholl', *Fortnightly Review*, vol. 61, May, 1897: twelve letters to John Nicholl, 1833–1848 (mainly 1833–1835).

(7) *The Life of Edward Bulwer, First Lord Lytton*, by his grandson the Earl of Lytton, [London: Macmillan and Co.,] 1913: three letters to Bulwer, 1836–1838.

(8) Harriet Grote, *The Philosophical Radicals of 1832*, [London: Saville and Co.,] 1866: one fragment of a letter to Mrs. Grote, 1837.

(9) R. E. Leader, *Life and Letters of John Arthur Roebuck*, [London: E. Arnold,] 1897: one fragment of a letter to Francis Place, 1837 (apparently the same letter is also referred to with a brief quotation in Graham Wallas, *The Life of Francis Place*, [London: Longmans, Green and Co.,] 1908.

(10) G. D. M. Towers, 'John Stuart Mill and the London and Westminster Review', *Atlantic Monthly*, vol. 69, 1892: twenty-one letters to John Robertson, 1837–1839.

(11) Mrs. Fawcett, *The Life of the Right Hon. Sir William Molesworth, Bart.*, [London: Macmillan and Co., 1901]: two letters and two fragments of letters to Molesworth, 1838–1840.

(12) *Letters of Thomas Carlyle to John Stuart Mill, John Sterling and Robert Browning,* edited by A. Carlyle, [New York: Frederick A. Stokes Company,] 1923: one fragment of a letter to Carlyle, 1839.

(13) A. T. Kitchel, *George Lewes and George Eliot,* [New York: J. Day & Co.,] 1933: nine letters to G. H. Lewes, 1840–1842.

(14) Caroline Fox, *Memories of Old Friends,* second edition, [edited] by H. N. Pym, [London: Smith, Elder and Co.,] 1882: fifteen letters to Robert Barclay Fox, 1840–1843.

(15) *Selections from the Correspondence of the late Macvey Napier, Esq.,* [London: Macmillan and Co.,] 1879: nine letters to McV. Napier, 1840–1846.

(16) J. Drummond and C. B. Upton, *The Life and Letters of James Martineau,* [New York: Dodd, Mead and Company,] 1902: two letters to James Martineau, 1835 and 1841.

(17) *Lettres Inédites de John Stuart Mill à Auguste Comte,* edited by L. Lèvy-Bruhl, Paris[: F. Akan], 1899: forty-four letters to Comte, 1841–1847.

(18) Janet Ross, *Three Generations of English Women,* [London: John Murray,] 1888: one letter to Sarah Austin (Mrs. John Austin), 1845.

(19) *Posthumous Papers . . . by the late George Grote,* edited (for private circulation) by Mrs. Grote, [London: Clowes,] 1874: one letter to George Grote and one to Mrs. Grote, 1846.

(20) Joseph McCabe, *Life and Letters of George Jacob Holyoake,* [London: Watts and Co.,] 1908: one fragment of a letter, 1847.

(21) *Letters of the Right Hon. Sir George Cornewall Lewis, Bart.,* edited by Sir Gilbert F. Lewis, Bart., [London: Longmans, Green, and Co.,] 1870: one letter to Sir Alexander Duff Gordon, 1847.

Those who have read these widely spread letters will have no doubt that merely to have them collected would be of considerable interest. But probably an even greater number, and some of them of still greater interest than those which have reached publication, often more or less by accident, seem to be still in existence in manuscript. There is a fair number in various public libraries in this country, particularly in the British Museum, the National Library for Scotland, in Leeds, and in the Library of the London School of Economics. An even greater number is probably distributed between numerous public and university libraries in the United States where most of the Mill letters seem to have gone which have passed through the sales-room in recent years. And it is likely that there are many more in the hands of private collectors or still in the possession of the descendants of Mill's correspondents.

Proposed Publication

The London School of Economics, which some years ago acquired a substantial part of the papers left behind by Mill, has conducted a preliminary survey of existing material with a view to the publication after the war of a new collection of his letters. Whether this collection will in the main confine itself to the earlier part of Mill's life, so imperfectly represented by the existing one, or whether it will ultimately extend to the whole of his life and aim at a definite edition of the whole of his correspondence, will have to be decided at a later date. Some letters of the later period which have already come to light suggest some doubt whether the set of drafts from which Mr. Elliot was able to choose was really as complete or, perhaps, whether his selection was always as judicious as one might wish. A new collection of Mill's letters up to 1847 is, however, in a state of active preparation, though publication will have to wait till after the war. While only time which would not otherwise be available for more immediately important purposes can be devoted to this work, it has yet been felt that the task, which is made more difficult by every year that passes, should not be indefinitely postponed. Efforts are being made to trace as many of the existing autograph letters of John Stuart Mill as possible. These efforts can, however, hardly be successful without spontaneous cooperation from the numerous private owners of such autograph letters. The London School of Economics will therefore greatly appreciate any offers of the loan of such letters or communications of information which may help in tracing such letters (including references to published letters not listed above or to the originals of already published letters).[3]

---

[3] Communications should be addressed to The Chairman, Economic Research Division, London School of Economics, The Hostel, Peterhouse, Cambridge. Autograph letters should not be sent unless by registered post. [Hayek was then at the wartime quarters of the London School of Economics in Cambridge.—Ed.]

FIFTEEN

THE DISPERSAL OF THE BOOKS AND PAPERS OF JOHN STUART MILL[1]

At least the greater part of Mill's books and papers appear at the time of his death to have been at his cottage at Avignon which passed into the possession of his step-daughter Helen Taylor who later made it her permanent residence till 1904. In March of that year her niece Mary Taylor (daughter of Algernon T.), who, together with a friend ('Molly' or 'Marian'), had a year or two earlier come to live with her as a companion, succeeded in rescuing the old and apparently somewhat senile lady from the clutches of designing French servants and to take her to England. In February 1905 'Molly' together with friends (a Mr. and Mrs. Joll) went to Avignon to liquidate the household. They did there 'the work of three months in three weeks. Half a ton of letters to be sorted, all manner of rubbish to be separated from useful things, books to be dusted and selected from, arrangements to be made for sale, and 18 boxes to be packed' (Mary Taylor's diary in L.S.E. collection).

It appears that at least some of the books were sold to an Avignon bookseller Romanille, though the account given by Jules Véran (*Revue des deux mondes*, September 1937)[2] according to which these books were bought by the poet Mariéton and to have been left by him to the Library in Avignon does not seem altogether correct. At least when Mr. Sraffa, some years ago, went to Avignon he was unable to trace these books or to find the 'liassé d'autographes' which in the same article Mme Romanille was said to possess. These are, however, probably identical with the volume of Mill MSS (containing the Review of Grote's *Aristotle*, sections of the Inaugural Address, of 'England and Ireland', of a speech on the 'Enlargement of Franchise' and various others) which were bought from Romanille by Professor George

---

[1] [This previously-unpublished essay by Hayek, dated July 1944, constitutes the starting point for his 1963 Introduction to *The Earlier Letters of John Stuart Mill, 1812–1848*, ed. Francis E. Mineka, vols. 12–13 (1963) of *The Collected Works of John Stuart Mill* (Toronto: University of Toronto Press, 1962–1991), 12:xv–xxiv.—Ed.]

[2] [Jules Véran, 'Le Souvenir de Stuart Mill à Avignon', *Revue des deux mondes*, vol. 41, September 1937, pp. 211–12.—Ed.]

Herbert Palmer (of Harvard?)[3] and are now in the Houghton Library of Harvard University.

In the autumn of 1905 Miss Mary Taylor disposed on behalf of her aunt Helen Taylor of Mill's books and furniture stored in the Pantechnicon in London, but it is not clear whether this is the material brought from Avignon or whether it was stored there since the dissolution of the London home of Mill and Helen Taylor. On September 21, 1905, Mary Taylor, on behalf of her aunt and on the advice of John Morley, offered the Library to Sommerville College, Oxford, (one of the Women's Colleges) which accepted. Miss Taylor retained a few books and Sommerville College was to be entitled to dispose of what they do not want, and in the course of 1906 sold a number of books. A full list of the books which had been stored in the Pantechnicon is preserved and it seems that nearly all of them are now in Sommerville College. It is evidently not the whole of Mill's Library and contains in particular surprisingly few books on economics. (There are, however, among them a few interesting volumes of pamphlets, originally belonging to James Mill, including one pamphlet by Blake with very full notes by Ricardo to be printed by Sraffa,[4] and a copy of Ricardo's 'Essay on the Influence of a Low Price of Corn' etc. with notes by James Mill). There is a rumour that some other books of Mill were at the same time presented to Morlay College (a workingman's college in London); but though the Library of that institution escaped when the main building was completely destroyed by bombs, no books of that kind are now preserved there; it is possible however that they were among a quantity of old books which had been stored in the main building.

After Helen Taylor's death in Torquay on November 29, 1907, some of Mill's effects (possibly only furniture) were disposed of in a sale at Torquay. Soon after that date Mary Taylor placed the editing of the Mill Letters in the hands of Mr. Elliot. There are various curious stories current about that connection. The late Sir Frederic Chapman, in a letter to an American correspondent (Mr. McCrimmon of Toledo)[5] reports that Miss Mary Taylor men-

---

[3] [George Herbert Palmer (1842–1933) was an American scholar and author. He graduated from Harvard in 1864 and was the Alford Professor of Natural Religion, Moral Philosophy, and Civil Polity there from 1889 to 1913. See Hayek's Introduction to the *Earlier Letters*, below, note 9, p. 326.—Ed.]

[4] ['On Blake's "Observations on the Effects Produced by the Expenditure of Government", 1823', followed by 'Notes on Blake's . . . with Blake's Replies', in *The Works and Correspondence of David Ricardo*, ed. Piero Sraffa, vol. 4, *Pamphlets and Papers, 1815–1823* (Cambridge: Cambridge University Press, 1951), pp. 323–52. In his introductory note, Sraffa credits Hayek with the discovery of the manuscript (p. 326).—Ed.]

[5] [James McNab McCrimmon. With Ney Macminn and J. R. Hainds, he edited the *Bibliography of the Published Writings of John Stuart Mill*, Northwestern University Studies in the Humanities No. 12 (Evanston, IL: Northwestern University, 1945). Hayek reviewed this in *Economica*, n.s., vol. 12, no. 47, August 1945, pp. 183–84. He quotes more extensively from the letter in the Introduction to *Earlier Letters* (this volume, p. 328).—Ed.]

tioned to him 'another fact that seemed very curious to me. She had placed the whole of the copies of Mr. Mill's correspondence at the disposal of Mr. Elliot when assisting him in the preparation of the published letters. When he had made his selection he induced her to destroy the rest save only what she termed the "intimate letters" which she intended to embody in another book'. From the letters so far recovered it appears that this statement is certainly not correct. Many of the drafts from which Elliot worked as well as many he omitted have been preserved, and whether any destruction at all took place at that time (whatever may have happened in 1905 in Avignon) seems uncertain.

In the L.S.E. collection, there is an instructive letter by Mr. Elliot to Lord Courtney (dated May 8, 1910) in which, after some reference to the Carlyle letters, he continues:

As to the private letters of Mill to his wife & daughter, we hesitated for a very long time about them; but Miss Taylor, who is a lady of very peculiar ideas and habits, did not wish them to be published. She has it in her mind to bring out another volume in a few years' time, consisting exclusively of Mill's letters to his wife, daughter, and sisters; but wants to delay this until the last of Mill's sisters is dead [i.e., Mrs. Mary Colman, who died only on January 15, 1913].[6] Whether it will ever be done I cannot say. She guards the letters very jealously; and it was only after much pressure and persuasion that I was allowed to see them at all.

As to her published introduction, following mine in the book, it was entirely an afterthought. In the study of the private letters, I formed a very unfavourable opinion both of Mrs. Mill and of Miss Helen Taylor. It appeared to me that they were both selfish and somewhat conceited women, and that Mill (who must have been a very poor judge of character) was largely deceived with regard to them. Of course I could not state my views openly in a book which is published by Miss Mary Taylor at her own expense. But in my original introduction I found it impossible to allude to the women without unconsciously conveying into my language some suggestion of what I thought. To this Miss Mary Taylor took the strongest possible exception. I reconsidered the whole matter, but found myself unable to speak more favourably of them than I had done. For some days Miss Taylor declined even to see me, and we were completely at a deadlock; but at last it was agreed that I should omit all mention of Mill's private life and that Miss Taylor should herself write a second introduction (for which I took no responsibility) and say what she liked. I did not greatly care for her contribution, but it was a necessary compromise. Myself, however, I entertain no sort of doubt that Miss Taylor is right in her main belief that there was no 'guilty' intrigue. . . .

[6] [The bracket and contents were added by Hayek.—Ed.]

At a later date there recur renewed references to Miss Mary Taylor's intention to prepare the further volume of family letters, and at the beginning of 1918, apparently with the assistance of a Miss Lee (sister of Sir Sidney Lee) she seems to have completed a typescript and was negotiating through Messrs. A. P. Watts, literary agents, with Longmans about publication. But before these were concluded Mary Taylor suffered a 'nervous breakdown' and was removed to a mental asylum where she died on November 6, 1918. Efforts to trace the typescript have been unsuccessful, though Mr. C. A. Watts, one of the partners of A. P. Watts (now 86) well remembers the 'irresponsible Miss Mary Taylor' (and his negotiations with her).

Mary Taylor's sister, Elizabeth, died in Victoria, British Columbia, on April 26, 1924, when the winding up of Mary Taylor's estate was not yet completed. Her only brother, Cyprian, lived till January 29, 1939, when he died in the mental home which he had inhabited for forty years.

In her Will Mary Taylor had left 'all copyrights and letters and correspondence referring to J. S. Mill and Helen Taylor to the National Provincial Bank', who were also Executors. As part of the files of the National Provincial Bank and the whole of the files of the solicitors engaged and of the publishers concerned (Messrs. Longmans) were destroyed by enemy action, the information about precisely what happened is a little incomplete. The following account is based mainly on the remaining files of the N.P.B. and partly on the catalogues of Messrs. Sotheby's sales.

According to the inventory of Miss Taylor's estate there were found in 'a gun-powder-proof safe': 'Public letters from J. S. Mill, A to Z' and 'Mill's Executorship under his father's Will' and (separately?) a parcel of family letters. A Mr. P. W. Sergeant (who cannot now be traced) was called in to value the letters, but his report has not been preserved. As a result it was decided to put all the letters except the intimate letters (which apparently did not include those to Mrs. Mill but only those to the Mill family) up for sale by auction. A first sale was held at Messrs. Sotheby's on March 29, 1922, which (according to the N.P.B. files) produced a gross amount of £276.19.–, of which £200 was given for the letters by Carlyle (soon after published by Mr. Alexander Carlyle). The Mill material in this sale consisted of 21 lots, including many notebooks (mostly botanical), and the greater part was sold to various booksellers, few of whom are now able to trace the ultimate buyer. It was from one of these booksellers that in 1926 the L.S.E. acquired a large collection, consisting however mainly of material not readily saleable. It is probable that most of the material in the American Libraries (certainly that at Northwestern) as well as that in Leeds and Edinburgh (?) derives from this sale. Other material has been traced to private owners, such as Professor Laski and Lord Keynes.

It is not clear why a second sale was held at Sotheby's five years later on June 27, 1927,[7] as there is a gap in the files of the N.P.B. But the 14 lots then sold were also described as 'The Property of Miss Mary Taylor, dec.' The buyers were again mostly booksellers, including B. F. Stevens & Brown, who is known to have resold some of the material he bought at the earlier sale to 'a Boston bookseller' and who on this occasion bought three lots, the contents of the first of which I have not noted, the second of which (No. 668) was described as 'upwards of 132 AL' to his wife and the third (No. 670) simply as 'large correspondence'. It would appear that this must be the material now at Yale University Library. (I cannot at present consult the annotated sales catalogue in the British Museum for further detail.)

The National Provincial Bank seems to have retained only the small collection of letters by Mill to his family and a few portraits, both of which have recently been presented by them to the L.S.E.[8]

The only item which was sent to the heirs of Miss Elisabeth Taylor in British Columbia, a large portrait of Mrs. Mill, has been traced and acquired and ought now to be on the way to Harvard, to be temporarily deposited in the Baker Library.

---

[7] [Hayek lists the sale as July 27, 1827. The date has been corrected in the text above.—Ed.]

[8] [In 1943 the National Provincial Bank gave the remaining collection, consisting of correspondence between Mill and his brothers and sisters and a few family documents and portraits, to the London School of Economics for inclusion in the Mill-Taylor collection. See the Introduction to *Earlier Letters*, this volume, p. 330.—Ed.]

SIXTEEN

J. S. MILL, MRS. TAYLOR, AND SOCIALISM[1]

How far it is always justified to pry into the intimate life of the great man of the past is a question on which opinions will probably differ. But in the case of John Stuart Mill the connection which bound him for over twenty years to Mrs. Taylor, before she became at last for seven short years his wife, is undoubtedly of peculiar and legitimate interest. If what Mill himself has told us about Mrs. Taylor's gifts and the influence she exerted on him is anywhere near the objective truth, she would not only be one of the most remarkable women who ever lived but also have played a decisive part in shaping the opinions which govern our own time. Up till now Mill's own estimate of her was almost the only basis for judgment. The extravagance of his claims on her behalf have with some reason led to considerable doubts whether so far as she was concerned he was not completely deprived of his critical faculties. As early as 1848, while Mrs. Taylor's first husband was still alive, he had printed in a number of gift copies of the first edition of his *Political Economy* a dedication to Mrs. Taylor in which he described her 'as the most eminently qualified of all persons known to the author either to originate or to appreciate speculations on social improvements'.[2] After her death, in the dedication of his famous *On Liberty*, in the inscription on her tomb, and finally in the *Autobiography*, Mill's panegyrics were even more unrestricted. 'Were I [but] capable of interpreting to the world one half of the great thoughts and noble feelings which are buried in her grave', he wrote in *On Liberty*, 'I should be the medium of a greater benefit to it, than is ever likely to arise from anything that I can write, unprompted and unassisted by her all but unrivalled wisdom'.[3] And in the *Autobiography* in many pages of praise she is compared to Shelley who

[1] [This manuscript was discovered by Bruce Caldwell in the study of Hayek's son, Laurence Hayek, after Laurence's death. See Caldwell 'Hayek on Mill', *History of Political Economy*, vol. 40, Winter 2008, p. 697. It is published here with the permission of the Estate of F. A. Hayek. While Hayek's published views are on the whole consistent with the essay, *John Stuart Mill and Harriet Taylor: Their Friendship and Subsequent Marriage* presents a richer portrait of Harriet's influence on Mill. Hayek included in his Mill-Taylor book many of the letters from which he presents excerpts in this essay. Cross-references to the present volume highlight these connections.—Ed.]

[2] [Hayek included the full dedication as well as a discussion of the controversy it created in *John Stuart Mill and Harriet Taylor*; see this volume, p. 119.—Ed.]

[3] [Hayek supplies 'would' instead of 'should' in this passage. It is republished in *Essays on Politics and Society*, ed. John M. Robson, vols. 18–19 (1977) of *The Collected Works of John*

'in thought and intellect so far as his powers were developed in his short life was but a child with what she ultimately became',[4] and represented as greatly superior to both Carlyle and Mill himself, because she was 'more a poet than he and more of a thinker than I'.[5]

There is a great deal more in the same strain, and Mill's friend the historian George Grote, was not far wrong when he said that 'only John Mill's reputation could survive such displays'.[6] Others evidently did not think too much of the lady. Goldwin Smith[7] remarked that 'Mill's hallucination as to his wife's genius deprived him of all authority wherever that came in', and T. Carlyle, who knew Mrs. Taylor well, thought that concerning her Mill 'had got possessed of an idea, or, indeed, a series of ideas which were altogether absurd and unsupportable'.[8]

Yet, however heavily we discount Mill's own statement there remain certain facts which make us want more information about Mrs. Taylor. Whatever she was, there is no reason to doubt that she had great influence on some of Mill's work, that she had closely collaborated with him in writing his famous, and in many ways his finest book, *On Liberty*, and that she is in some measure responsible for Mill's gradual movement towards socialism. For good or bad she has thus taken some part in the development of modern ideas. But on the question of how much of an original thinker she was and precisely what influence she had on Mill we have so far had little means of judging.

In the course of the preparation of an edition of Mill's correspondence I have recently come across some of the letters exchanged between Mill and Mrs. Taylor, both before and after their marriage, which for the first time

---

Stuart Mill [hereafter cited as *Collected Works*] (Toronto: University of Toronto Press, 1962–1991), 18:213.—Ed.]

[4] [The full passage reads: 'In general spiritual characteristics, as well as in temperament and organisation, I have often compared her, as she was at this time, to Shelley: but in thought and intellect, Shelley, so far as his powers were developed in his short life, was but a child compared with what she ultimately became'. It appears in Mill, *Autobiography and Literary Essays*, eds. John M. Robson and Jack Stillinger, vol. 1 (1981) of *Collected Works*, p 195. See this volume, p. 10.—Ed.]

[5] ['I never presumed to judge [Carlyle] with any definiteness, until he was interpreted to me by one greatly the superior of us both—who was more a poet than he, and more a thinker than I—whose own mind and nature included his, and inifinitely more'. Mill, *Autobiography*, vol. 1 of *Collected Works*, p. 182.—Ed.]

[6] [Grote's remark is quoted in Alexander Bain, *John Stuart Mill* (London: Longmans, Green and Co., 1882), p. 167.—Ed.]

[7] [Quoted in *ibid.*, p. 171. Goldwin Smith (1823–1910) was a historian and publicist who published a series of letters in the *Daily News* in 1862 and 1863 advocating independence for mature colonies. He opposed Mill's views on marriage; see 'Female Suffrage', *Macmillan's Magazine*, vol. 30, June 1874, p. 140. Perhaps because he came to learn of Smith's anti-Jewish positions, Hayek omitted reference to Smith in *John Stuart Mill and Harriet Taylor*.—Ed.]

[8] [Sir Charles G. Duffy, *Conversations and Correspondence with Carlyle*, (New York: Charles Scribner's Sons, 1892), p. 167; Thomas Carlyle to John A. Carlyle, 29 March 1851, *The Collected Letters of Thomas and Jane Welsh Carlyle*, 26:51–53, doi:10.1215/lt-18510329-TC-JAC-01.—Ed.]

throw real light on the whole relation. There is a good deal more material in existence which I have not yet seen and it will be some time until it is ready for publication. But it is possible now to give a provisional sketch of the picture which emerges.

When Mill and Mrs. Taylor first met in 1830 he was 24 and she 23, married for four years to John Taylor, a wholesale merchant twelve years her senior, and already mother of two boys and soon to become mother of her third and last child, Helen Taylor, who in many ways was to continue her work. Her husband was evidently a pleasant and amiable man, 'the pink of social hospitality', as Carlyle described him,[9] politically a Radical like Mill and not without intellectual interests, or, as Mill describes him in the *Autobiography* 'a most upright, brave and honourable man, of liberal opinions and good education, but without the intellectual or artistic tastes which would have made him a companion for her'.[10]

Mill at the age of 24 was of course very far from being an ordinary young man. Although most of you will probably be familiar with the extraordinary story of his education and youth, it is so important for what follows that I must briefly recall it. Even the most attentive reader of the *Autobiography* may be excused if he has forgotten, when he is nearly about half-way through the book and has read of an amount of work which might well fill half a life-time, that the man he is reading about is still the young man of 24. Most readers will remember the earliest and somewhat pathetic part of this story, of the boy whom his father began to teach Greek at the age of three, who at the age of eight had read most of the Greek classics, including six of the Dialogues of Plato (of only one of which he ventures to suggest in the *Autobiography* that 'it had better been omitted, as it was totally impossible that I should understand it'),[11] and an enormous amount of general history, and who was ready to begin a similar course in Latin and Higher Mathematics, who at the age of eleven and twelve wrote a History of Roman Government and soon turned to 'more advanced subjects' like Logic and Political Economy and at the age of fourteen had completed what to all intents and purposes was a respectable University education, and was ready to be sent for a year's finishing course to France. Probably Mill's observation on this that all this achievement is solely

---

[9] [Thomas Carlyle to Dr. John Carlyle, 15 August 1834. The letter appears in J. A. Froude, *Thomas Carlyle, A History of the First Forty Years of His Life* (London: Longman's, Green, and Co., 1882 edition), vol. 2, pp. 447–50, with the quoted passage at p. 448. See this volume, p. 75.—Ed.]

[10] [Mill, *Autobiography and Literary Essays*, vol. 1 *Collected Works*, p. 193. For an extended discussion of this quote, see this volume, p. 20.—Ed.]

[11] [The passage reads: 'I also read in 1813 the first six *dialogues* of Plato (in the common arrangement) from the *Euthyphron* to the *Theætetus* inclusive, which last dialogue had been better omitted, as it was utterly impossible I should understand it'. Mill, *Autobiography*, vol. 1 of *Collected Works*, p. 8.—Ed.]

due to the teaching of his father and that in all natural gifts he was rather below than above par and that what he could do could assuredly be done by any boy or girl of average capacity and healthy physical 'constitution' will also have stuck in your memory.[12] I should like to add that this estimate after a good deal of study of his early letters, strikes me as at least less exaggerated in one direction than the judgment of some recent American psychologist who has represented Mill as the greatest child prodigy that ever lived. There was in fact nothing of a Gauss in him.[13]

That the young man of fifteen who, as he later himself said, never had been a boy, never had played cricket or even mixed with a companion of his age, entered upon his career as a writer as a 'thinking machine' or a 'made man',[14] that he became the zealous apostle of that utilitarian philosophy which his father had intended him to make, and that for a time he devoted himself to ardent propaganda for such causes as birth control, which at one point seems to have brought him before a police court, is not surprising. Nor is it unexpected to find that even two or three years later he is described as totally inexperienced in the practical affairs of life and particularly as a complete child in his relations to women.[15] But while there were still many totally blind spots in his spiritual and emotional make-up, the essentially soft and almost femininely receptive nature of John Mill was even then by no means entirely suppressed. It is pleasant to imagine him, as he has been described by one of his friends, as filling his pockets with violet seeds for his regular Sunday walks, so that he could throw them under the hedges and along the paths as he went along.[16]

But the tremendous strain of his intense and purely intellectual education led soon to that severe intellectual crisis which is fully described in the *Autobiography*. Between the ages of 20 and 22 he passed through a period of acute depression and dejection, and it was in the end not new thought, but an emotional relief in music and poetry which brought his recovery. After the poems of Wordsworth had opened to him a new world he gave himself with all his personality to new influences. What he later called the Germano-Coleridgian

---

[12] [Mill, *Autobiography*, vol. 1 of *Collected Works*, p. 182.—Ed.]

[13] [Catherine Morris Cox, *The Early Mental Traits of Three Hundred Geniuses*, vol. 2 of *Genetic Studies of Genius*, ed. Lewis Madison Terman (Stanford, CA: Stanford University Press, 1926). See also Alan Ryan's Introduction to *Mill: Texts and Commentaries*, ed. Alan Ryan, (New York: Norton, 1975), p. xii, note 6: 'Psychologists who try to guess what the measured IQ of distinguished figures from the past might have been usually place Mill at the top of the chart with a guessed IQ of 192'.—Ed.]

[14] [In the *Autobiography*, Mill writes, 'In after conversations with Sterling, he told me how he and others had been accustomed to look upon me as a "made" or manufactured man'. Mill, *Autobiography*, vol. 1 of *Collected Works*, pp. 160 and 162.—Ed.]

[15] [John Roebuck, *Life and Letters of John Arthur Roebuck with Chapters of Autobiography*, ed. Robert Eadon Leader (London and New York: Edward Arnold, 1897), pp. 28, 29.—Ed.]

[16] [*Ibid.*, p. 29.—Ed.]

School, the Saint-Simonians, Carlyle and finally Auguste Comte took successively the place of the dominating influence which his father had exercised over his early youth. But the most important of these influences was of course Mrs. Taylor.

It was only two years after the emergence from his mental crisis that John Mill and Harriet Taylor met. Mill was introduced to the Taylors by W. J. Fox, a Unitarian minister to whose congregation they belonged. In Fox's circle there were two remarkable girls, Sarah and Eliza Flower, one a composer and the other a poetess, who were among Mrs. Taylor's closest friends. Mrs. Taylor herself contributed occasionally to the journal which Fox edited, the *Monthly Repository*, and one or two of her poems which appeared there show real poetic gifts.[17] She must undoubtedly have been a very attractive young woman and a portrait of her painted only a few years later, when she was about 27 shows a striking face with incredibly large eyes and finely chiseled delicate and yet somewhat hard features.[18] Carlyle's description of her as he knew her a few years later, as a 'very will o' the wispish irridescence of a creature . . . pale and passionate and sad-looking, a living romance heroine of the royalist volition and questionable destiny',[19] although written only long after, is probably not very far from the truth.

The two young people seem at once to have been attracted to each other and the friendship to have grown soon into love. We know little about the first two or three years beyond that Mr. Taylor, naturally alarmed, demanded from his wife that she should 'renounce sight' of Mill, which she refused outright.[20] There seems to have been a good deal of unpleasantness even before, early in Sep-

[17] [See 'To the Summer Wind' and 'Nature', printed in this volume on pp. 262–63.—Ed.]

[18] [For this portrait, see this volume, p. 126.—Ed.]

[19] [Hayek here merged Carlyle's remarks from *Reminiscences by Thomas Carlyle*, ed. J. A. Froude (New York: Harper and Brothers, 1881), and J. A. Froude, *Thomas Carlyle, The First Forty Years*. Froude reproduces extracts from Carlyle's journal dated 8 September 1834: 'Mrs. Taylor with her husband make their appearance, walking; pale she, and passionate and sad looking: really felt a kind of interest in her' (*Thomas Carlyle, The First Forty Years*, vol. 2, p. 466). The description of Mrs. Taylor as 'very will o' wispish irridescence of a creature' is from a letter dated 22 July 1834 from Thomas Carlyle to Dr. John Carlyle (*Reminiscences*, p. 409), and Hayek reproduces it partially in the Mill-Taylor volume with the original spelling (see this volume, p. 74).—Ed.]

[20] [In *John Stuart Mill and Harriet Taylor*, Hayek includes a lengthy letter from Mill to W. J. Fox dated 5 or 6 November 1833 (this volume, pp. 51–52). There, Mill writes that Harriet had 'decided nothing except what has always been decided—not to renounce the liberty of sight' and refers to how 'she *never* had decided upon anything except not to give up either the feeling, or the power of communication with me—unless she did so, it was *Mr. Taylor's* wish'. The words 'renounce sight' do not appear in the Mill-Taylor book, but Michael St. John Packe, who perhaps read the aforementioned letter from Mill to Fox or Hayek's essay, uses them without attribution in *The Life of John Stuart Mill* (London: Secker and Warburg, 1954), p. 139, writing that Taylor 'advised her reasonably enough, as much for Mill's sake as for her own peace of mind and her duty to her household, to "renounce sight"'.—Ed.]

tember 1833, things came to a crisis. Mill at last seems to have declared himself more fully than before; on the sixth of September Mrs. Taylor writes to him:[21]

> I am glad you have said it—I am *happy* that you have—no one with any fineness and beauty of character but must feel compelled to say *all* to the being they really *love*, or rather with any *permanent* reservation it is *not* love—while there is reservation, however little of it, the love is just *so much* imperfect. There has never, *yet*, been entire confidence around us. The difference between you and me in that respect is, that *I* have always *yearned* to have *your* confidence with an intensity which has *often*, for a time, swallowed up the naturally stronger feeling—the affection itself—you have not given it, not that you wished to reserve—but that you did not *need* to give—but not having that need of course you had no perception that I had it and so you have discouraged confidence from me 'til the habit of *checking first thoughts* has become so strong that when in your presence timidity has become almost a *disease* of the nerves. It would be absurd, only it is so painful to notice in myself that every word I ever speak to you is detained a second before it is said 'til I am quite sure I am not by implication asking your confidence. It is true that the only being who has ever called forth my faculties of affection is the only in whose presence I ever felt constraint.

The letter is too long to quote in full, and I will read only a few more sentences which occur towards its end:

> If I did not know them to be false, how heartily I should scorn such expressions as 'I have ceased to will'! Then to wish? for does not wish with the power to fulfill constitute will?
>
> It is false that 'your strength is not equal to the circumstances in which you have placed' yourself—It is quite another thing to be guided by a judgment on which you can rely and which is better placed for judgment than yourself.
>
> Would you let yourself 'drift with the tide whether it flow or ebb' if in one case every wave took yourself further from me? Would you not put what strength you have in resisting it? Would you not wish to resist it, would you not *will* to resist it? Tell me—for if you would not, how happens it that you will to love me.[22]

Developments after this seem to have been fairly rapid. Mr. Taylor was persuaded to agree on an experimental separation for six months, and Mrs.

[21] [Harriet Taylor to John Stuart Mill, 6 September 1833, this volume, pp. 49–50. It is published in *The Complete Works of Harriet Taylor Mill* [hereafter cited as *Complete Works*], ed. Jo Ellen Jacobs (Bloomington: Indiana University Press, 1998), pp. 326–27.—Ed.]

[22] [*Ibid.*—Ed.]

Taylor left for Paris with a view to the possibility of remaining there permanently separated from her husband, and about the middle of October Mill joined her there for some five weeks. Mill seems to have found it more difficult to face the practical obstacles than Mrs. Taylor. Shortly before she left he wrote to their common friend Fox[23] that 'if she is ever out of spirits it is always something amiss in *me* that is the cause—it is so now—it is because she sees that what ought to be so much easier to me than to her, is in reality more difficult—costs harder struggle—to part company with the opinion of the world, and with my former mode of doing good in it, however thank heaven, she does not doubt that I can do it'.

When Mill had gone to Paris he had expected that Mrs. Taylor's separation from her husband would become permanent and that sooner or later she and Mill would start a new life together, probably overseas—Australia is mentioned on a later occasion. But that was not to be. As Mill reported from Paris to Fox:[24]

> When the separation had actually taken place the result did as you say seem certain—not because we had willed to make it so, but because it seemed the necessary consequence of the new circumstances if the feelings of all continued the same. This was the sole cause and I think cause enough for the hopefulness and happiness which I felt. . . . Her affection for him, which has always been the principal, is now the sole obstacle to our being together— for the present there seems absolutely no prospect of that obstacle's being got over. She believes . . . that it would be the breaking-up of his whole future life—*that* she is determined never to be the cause of.

Eventually a compromise was arrived at and Mrs. Taylor returned to London even sooner than had been planned, but apparently, at least for some time, to a home of her own. There were renewed crises but the *modus vivendi* then arrived at and under which Mrs. Taylor lived much away from her husband and even when at his home was given regular opportunities to spend at least an evening a week with Mill without her husband was maintained till Mr. Taylor died fourteen years later.

It seems that almost since Mill knew her Mrs. Taylor was invalid, suffering not only, as Mill himself, from consumption, of which she ultimately died, but also of attacks of severe lameness. This was the cause or excuse for her living much of the time in the country near London, or abroad, where Mill visited her regularly. Once or twice they seem also to have travelled together with Mrs.

[23] [Mill to W. J. Fox, Saturday, 7 September 1833, this volume, p. 51. The full letter is published in *The Earlier Letters of John Stuart Mill, 1812–1848*, ed. Francis E. Mineka, vols. 12–13 (1963) of *Collected Works*, 12:177–78.—Ed.]

[24] [*Ibid.*—Ed.]

Taylor's children and some of Mill's young brothers and sisters. Although I am convinced that the relationship was purely platonic, it is not surprising that from 1834 onwards, when the story became generally known, it caused a good deal of scandal. Mill's family and particularly his father, who died only in 1836, were seriously disturbed, and Mill himself withdrew increasingly from his old circle of friends and altogether broke with some who had dared to remonstrate with him. Only very few, especially the Carlyles, were allowed to make Mrs. Taylor's acquaintance. Some of you will remember the story of the accidental destruction of the manuscript of the first volume of Carlyle's *French Revolution*, which incidentally occurred in Mrs. Taylor's house to whom Mill had passed on the precious bundle entrusted to him by Carlyle for an opinion.[25] 'Gracious Providence, he has gone off with Mrs. Taylor'[26] is Carlyle's recorded exclamation as he saw a carriage containing Mill and Mrs. Taylor draw up before his door when they came with the sad story of the loss of the manuscript.

That Mill was at that time completely under Mrs. Taylor's dominance and that she proved to be the much stronger character of the two is shown beyond doubt by the letters we have. Often she would lecture him severely on his lack of self-confidence and energy. In one of her letters which is particularly revealing she writes:[27]

> Good heaven, have *you* at last arrived at fearing to be '*obscure and insignificant*'! What *can* I say to that but 'by all means pursue your brilliant and important career!' Am *I* one to be the cause that the person I love feels himself reduced to 'obscure and insignificant'! Good God what has the love of two equals to do with making obscure and insignificant. If ever you *could* be obscure and insignificant you *are* so whatever happens and certainly a person who did not feel contempt at the very idea the words create is not one to brave the world. I never before (for years) knew you to have mesquin feelings. . . . There seems a touch of Common Place rarity in that dread of being obscure and insignificant—you will never be that—and still more surely I am not a person who in any event could give you cause to feel that *I* made you so. Whatever you think I could never be either of those words.

Most of the other correspondence between them which has been preserved from the early years, and indeed till shortly before Mr. Taylor's death, are of the nature of short informal notes which show little more than that they were and continued to be deeply in love and that the difficulty of their position

[25] [For a full description of the episode, see this volume, p. 77.—Ed.]

[26] [Recorded in Duffy, *Conversations and Correspondence with Carlyle*, p. 169; see this volume, p. 77.—Ed.]

[27] [For the full letter, watermarked 1835, see this volume, pp. 94–96; the full letter is republished in Harriet Taylor Mill, *Complete Works*, pp. 332–33.—Ed.]

and the recurrent anxiety about each other's health often put a great strain on them. But while there are many indirect signs that Mrs. Taylor took to an increasing extent part in Mill's intellectual activities, the only real insight we get into this part of their relationship is for a comparatively late date, the beginning of 1849.

Mill was then revising his *Principles of Political Economy*, published in the preceding year, for a second edition. Mrs. Taylor had at Christmas 1848 gone to Pan in the Pyrenees and Mill was sending to her successive instalments of the proofs of the second edition. Mrs. Taylor's comments on these have not been preserved, but a series of letters of Mill's in which he replies to them and which are probably the most interesting and significant of all the newly discovered letters. As they numbered their letters it appears that they wrote each other a long letter every second or third day for three months. The first of these,[28] dated February 19th, and like all their letters without formal address or signature, begins

> I received your dear letter 11 on Saturday and this morning the first instalment of the Pol. Ec. This last I will send again (or as much of it as is necessary) when I have been able to make up my mind about it. The objections are I think very inconsiderable as to quantity—much less than I expected—but that paragraph, p. 248, in the first edit. what you object to so strongly and totally, is what has always seemed to me the strongest part of the argument (it is only what even Proudhon says about Communism)—and as omitting it after it has ever been printed would imply change of opinion, it is necessary to see whether opinion has changed or not—yours has, in some respects at least, for you have marked strong dissent from the passage that "the necessaries of life when secure for the whole of life are scarcely more a subject of consciousness" which was inserted on your proposition and very nearly in your words. This is probably only the progress we have been always making, and by thinking sufficiently I should probably come to think the same—as is almost always the case, I believe always when we think long enough.

Later in the same letter Mill defends a passage in which he had argued about conditions in 'a Socialist community' that 'the majority would not exert themselves for anything beyond [what the conditions of operatives are in a well-regulated manufactory with a great reduction in in the hours of labour] and that, unless they did, nobody else would do; and that on this basis human

---

[28] [Mill to Taylor, 19 February 1849, this volume, pp. 132–35. The letter is published in full in *The Later Letters of John Stuart Mill, 1849–1873*, eds. Francis E. Mineka and Dwight N. Lindley, vols. 14–17 (1972) of *Collected Works*, 14:8–10. Hayek supplies the words in brackets.—Ed.]

life would settle in one invariable round'. In defence of this he writes to Mrs. Taylor that if this 'is not tenable, then all the two or three pages of argument which precede and of which this is but the summary, are false and there is nothing to be said against Communism at all—one would have to turn round and advocate it—which if done would be better in a separate treatise and would be a great objection to publishing a second edition until after such a treatise'. Yet this single sentence disappeared in the second edition, without alterations in the preceding two or three pages of which it was but the summary.

Two days later he wrote again on the same subject:[29]

> I despatched yesterday to the dear one an attempt at a revision of the objectionable passages. I saw on consideration that the objection to Communism on the ground of its making a kind of dead level might admit of being weakened (though I believe it never can be taken away) consistently with the principle of Communism, though the Communistic plans now before the public could not do it. The statement of objections was moreover too vague and general. I have made it more explicit as well as more moderate; you will judge whether it is now sufficiently either one or the other; and altogether whether any objection can be maintained to Communism, except the amount of objection which, in the new matter I have introduced is made to the present applicability of Fourierism. I think there can—and that the objections as now stated to Communism are valid: but if you do not think so, I certainly will not print it, even if there were no other reason than the certainty I feel that I never should long continue of an opinion different from yours on a subject which you have fully considered.

One more letter of exactly one month later deserves to be quoted in part:[30]

> The Pol. Ec. Packet came on Monday for which a thousand thanks. I have followed to the letter every recommendation. The sentence which you objected to in toto of course has come quite out. In explanation however of what I meant by it—I was not thinking of any mysterious change in human nature—but chiefly of this—that the best people now are necessarily so much cut off from sympathy with the multitude that I should think they must have difficulty in judging how they would be affected by such an immense change in their whole circumstances as would be caused by having multitudes whom they could sympathize with or in knowing how far the social feeling might then

[29] [Mill to Taylor, 21 February 1849, is published in Mill, *Later Letters*, vol. 14 of *Collected Works*, pp. 11–13; this volume, pp. 135–37.—Ed.]

[30] [Mill to Taylor, 21 March 1849, *ibid.*, pp. 18–20; and this volume, pp. 143–46.—Ed.]

supply the place of that large share of solitariness and individuality which they cannot now dispense with. I meant one thing more, viz. that as, hereafter, the more obvious and coarser obstacles and objections to the community system will have ceased or greatly diminished, those which are less obvious and coarse will then step forwards into an importance and require an attention which does not now practically belong to them and that we can hardly tell without trial what the result of that experience will be. I do not say that you cannot realise and judge of these things—but if you and perhaps Shelley and one or two others in a generation can, I am convinced that to do so requires both great genius and great experience and I think it quite fair to say to common readers that the present race of mankind (speaking of them collectively) are not competent to it. I cannot persuade myself that you do not greatly overrate the ease of making people unselfish. Granting that in 'ten years' the children of a community might by teaching be made 'perfect' it seems to me that to do so there must be perfect people to teach them. You say 'if there were a desire on the part of the cleverer people to make them perfect it will be easy'—but how to produce that desire on the part of the cleverer people?

This exchange of letters ends when towards the end of March 1849 Mill joins Mrs. Taylor for a six weeks' holiday in France. The circumstances of this visit are somewhat tragic. Mr. Taylor, who had been ailing for some time, had been urging Mrs. Taylor to return. In reply Mrs. Taylor explained that Mr. Mill, who was in serious danger of losing his eyesight, was dependent on assistance for reading and writing and ordered to take immediate rest, was coming out to join her and that in consequence she could not return before the beginning of May. When she did at last return at that time, she found Mr. Taylor desperately ill, in fact, as soon appeared, dying of cancer. There follow ten weeks during which in an increasingly hopeless struggle, devotedly she nurses her husband day and night, scarcely ever leaving his bedside, reporting almost daily in short scribbled notes her hopes and anxieties to Mill, asking his advice about the specialists to be consulted or new medical discoveries which might help. To anyone who reads these notes there can be no doubt how genuinely and desperately she was anxious to save the life of the husband who for many years cannot have been more to her than a dear friend. On one occasion even Mill becomes the object of her bitterest reproaches for not fully appreciating the exclusiveness of her devotion to the needs of the invalid. But all is in vain and on July 18, 1849, John Taylor dies at the age of 54.

A little less than two years later, on April 21, 1851, Mill and Mrs. Taylor were quietly married at Weymouth in Dorsetshire. Two weeks before the ceremony Mill wrote out and signed a document in which he formally disclaimed and repudiated all pretence to have acquired any rights which the then existing matrimonial law gave him over his wife-to-be or her property.

As already earlier Mrs. Taylor had been the cause of the ending of many of Mill's friendships so the marriage led to a complete estrangement from his mother and his sisters. Apparently the family did not show sufficient enthusiasm or did not rapidly enough pay their respects to the new Mrs. Mill; at any rate contact with the Mill family ceased almost entirely and very few of Mill's other friends were admitted to the new home which he now established at Blackheath. We have for obvious reasons letters only for a few periods of their married life, and many of those which exist I have not yet seen. But that Mrs. Mill's influence on his work increased further is clearly shown by the further and decisive advance towards socialism noticeable in the third edition of the *Political Economy* which appeared not long after their marriage. It was largely in the form which the relevant chapters of the *Political Economy* were given at that time that they went through the many editions and exerted that great influence to which no less a person than Sidney Webb (or Lord Passfield) has paid eloquent tribute as one of the main causes which assisted the growth of socialism in England. If that is true, there can be no doubt now that it was Mrs. Mill rather than John Stuart Mill to whom this is due.

How great Mrs. Mill's influence on Mill's work was also in other respects will be seen from the fragment of a letter of hers to him of about 1854 from which I will briefly quote:[31]

> About the Essays dear would not Religion, the Utility of Religion be one of the subjects you would have most to say on—there is to account for the existence nearly universal of some religion (superstition) by the instincts of fear hope and mystery &c and throwing over all doctrines and theories called religious as devices for power, to show how religion and poetry fill the same want, the craving after higher objects, the consolation of suffering, by hopes of heaven for the selfish, love of God for the tender and grateful—how all this must be superseded by morality deriving its power from sympathies and benevolence and its rewards from the approbation of those we respect. There what a longwinded sentence, which you would say ten times as well in words half the length. I feel sure dear that the Life is not half written and that half that is written will not do. Should there not be a summary of our relationship from its commencement in 1830—I mean given in a dozen lines—so as to preclude other and different versions of our lives at Kesn (?) and Watr (?)—our summer excursions &c. This ought to be done in its genuine truth and simplicity—strong affection—intimacy of friendship and no impropriety. It seems to me an edifying picture for those poor wretches who cannot conceive friendship but in sex—nor believe that expediency consid-

[31] [Harriet Taylor Mill to Mill, 14 and 15 February 1854, this volume, pp. 190–91; the full letter is published in Harriet Taylor Mill, *Complete Works*, pp. 373–76.—Ed.]

erations for the feelings of others can conquer sensuality. But of course this is not my reason for wishing it done. It is that every ground should be occupied by ourselves on our own subject.

That after their marriage Mrs. Mill's influence on Mill increased further and even determined in a large measure his interests is quite clear. That Mill devoted thereafter much of his energies to what Mrs. Taylor had in 1848 (in a letter to Fox)[32] described as 'the cause to which for many years my life and exertions have been devoted, justice for women. The progress of the race *waits* for the emancipation of women from their present degraded slavery to the necessity of marriage'. It is the only subject on which she had published an independent essay, and Mill's later book on *The Subjection of Women* is avowedly largely her work.[33] The feelings which prompted this book, which has had such profound influence on the feminist movement of all countries may be illustrated by one more quotation from a letter by Mill.[34] It was written to Mrs. Taylor during the interval between her husband's death and their marriage:

> Thanks dearest dearest angel for the note—what it contained was a really important addition to the letter and I have put it in nearly in your word, which as your impromptu words almost always are, were a hundred times better than any I could find by study. What a perfect orator you would make—and what changes might be made in the world by such a one, with such opportunities as thousands of male dunces have. But you are to me, and would be to any one who knew you, the type of Intellect—because you have all the faculties in equal perfection—you can both think and impress the thought on others—and can both judge what ought to be done, and do it. As for me, nothing but the division of labour could make me useful if there were not others with the capacities of intellect which I have not, where would be the use of those I have. I am but fit to be one wheel in an engine not to be the self-moving engine itself—a real majestic intellect, not to say moral nature like yours. I can only look and admire.

Since I have yet seen only a small part of the correspondence during their married life which has been preserved, I will say no more about this period. It was tragically short. In 1858, just after Mill, still only 52, had retired after 33 years of service from the East India Company, they set out together for a jour-

---

[32] [Mill to Fox, 10 May 1848, this volume, p. 119; the full letter is published in Harriet Taylor Mill, *Complete Works*, pp. 390–93.—Ed.]

[33] [*John Stuart Mill and Harriet Taylor*, however, demonstrates that Mill's views were fully consistent at an early age with those of his wife; see above, pp. 57–71.—Ed.]

[34] [Mill to Taylor, about 1850, this volume, p. 162. It is published in Mill, *Later Letters*, vol. 14 of *Collected Works*, pp. 42–43.—Ed.]

ney to Italy and the Mediterranean. But on the way out they were stopped by another severe attack of Mrs. Mill's old disease, of which she died in Avignon on February 2, 1858.

Mill never quite recovered from this blow of fate. He bought a cottage in Avignon where he spent the greater part of the remaining fifteen years of his life to be near her grave, and his work henceforth was largely devoted to her memory and to work for the ideals which they had shared.[35] Immediately on Mrs. Mill's death her daughter, Helen Taylor, who had started on a career of an actress and at the time had been touring with a company in the North of England joined him in Avignon and became his steady companion for his remaining years. Indeed in the course of time she began gradually to fill the void which his wife had left and became almost as much of an idol to Mill as Mrs. Mill had been. In a revealing passage of the *Autobiography* of which Helen Taylor had discreetly suppressed the more extravagant parts when she first published it from Mill's manuscript, but which has recently become available in the complete American edition of that work, Mill says of her that[36]

> though the inspirer of my best thought was no longer with me, I was not alone: she had left a daughter, my step-daughter, Miss Helen Taylor, the inheritor of much of her wisdom and of all her nobleness of character whose ever growing and ripening talents from that day to this have been devoted to the same great purposes, and have already made her name better and more widely known than was that of her mother, though far less so than I predict that if she lives it is destined to become. Surely no one ever before was so fortunate, as, after such a loss as mine, to draw another prize in the lottery of life—another companion, stimulator and instructor of the rarest quality.

I believe this passage goes far to solve the riddle which Mill's relation to his wife presents. We still do not know enough about her to say with assurance how much Mill must have overestimated her. But we know enough of Helen Taylor to be fairly certain that, although in her way quite a remarkable woman, she was nothing like as extraordinary a person as this passage suggests. It seems to me to confirm what one would even without it be inclined to suspect: that probably by the education given him by his father in his early youth Mill's character was so formed that he stood in need of someone whom he could adore and to whom he could ascribe all possible perfection. Behind the hard shell of complete self-control and strictly rational behavior there was

---

[35] [Hayek came to a different assessment in *John Stuart Mill and Harriet Taylor*. There he writes that 'evidently Mill tried to bury himself in intensive work', and rightly recognized Mill's substantial accomplishments after his wife's death. See above, p. 256.—Ed.]

[36] [Mill, *Autobiography*, vol. 1 of *Collected Works*, p. 264; see above p. 258.—Ed.]

a core of a very soft and almost feminine sensitivity,[37] a craving for a strong person on whom he could lean, and on whom he could concentrate all his affection and admiration. No doubt Mrs. Mill was an unusual person. But the picture Mill has given us of her is throughout determined by his own character and tells us probably more of him than of her.

[37] [As noted in the Editor's Introduction, there is a long history of associating Mill with feminine causes and characteristics (see this volume, p. xxiii).—Ed.]

SEVENTEEN

PORTRAITS OF J. S. MILL[1]

Sir,—John Stuart Mill's appearance is generally known only from portraits taken very late in his life. The only known early portraits are the Daguerreotype reproduced as frontispiece to Volume 1, and the cameo or medallion reproduced opposite page 322 of H. S. R. Elliot's edition of the *Letters of John Stuart Mill* (1910).[2] The latter is undoubtedly the earlier and almost certainly identical with, or at least derived from, a portrait of Mill done by an artist named Cunningham in Falmouth in April, 1940, when Mill was in his thirty-fourth year. It is mentioned in Caroline Fox's *Memories of Old Friends*, and referred to as a medallion in an unpublished letter by John Sterling to Mill of the same year.

The present whereabouts of the originals of both these portraits are unknown. They were almost certainly in the possession of the late Miss Mary Taylor, the granddaughter of Mrs. J. S. Mill, who died in 1918, but no portrait of Mill described as such can be traced among the effects which were sold after her death. It is to be feared that they were not recognized as portraits of Mill, and are lost, but it may not yet be too late to recover them for some national collection where they clearly belong. At the moment I am anxious to trace the medallion for reproduction in an edition of the correspondence between Mill and Harriet Taylor, which is almost ready to go to press. I should be most grateful to any of your readers who might be able to help me in this or in identifying the artist.

---

[1] [Published as a letter to the editor under Hayek's signature in the *Times Literary Supplement*, November 1949, issue 2493, p. 733.—Ed.]

[2] [*The Letters of John Stuart Mill*, ed. Hugh S. R. Elliot (London: Longmans, Green, and Co. 1910). For the medallion, see this volume, p. 145. As mentioned in note 31 on p. 28 above, Hayek used 'medaillon' instead of 'medallion'.—Ed.]

EIGHTEEN

PREFACE TO *THE LIFE OF JOHN STUART MILL*[1]

There are few other eminent figures in the intellectual life of the nineteenth century about whom some unusual facts are so widely known, and yet of whose whole character and personality we know so little, as John Stuart Mill. Perhaps in no other instance can we see how misleading an impression even the most honest of autobiographies can give. Mill's account of his own life is of course a document of such psychological interest that its very popularity was bound to discourage others from attempting to draw a fuller picture. This alone, however, does not adequately explain why, for eighty years after his death, no satisfactory biography of Mill has been available. In many ways, the unique value of his own description of his intellectual development has increased rather than diminished the need for a more comprehensive account of the setting against which it ought to be seen.

Until recently, the material on which such a picture could be based was not available. For fifty years Mill's papers had been closely guarded, first by his step-daughter and later by her niece. When the latter died, they were offered for public auction, and were widely dispersed over two continents, at a time when Mill's reputation was passing through that eclipse which, a generation or two after a man's death, most reputations seem to suffer. Only during the last twenty years, as interest in the nineteenth century gradually revived, did it become apparent how much information could be brought to light by patient search. Most of the dispersed material has since been traced, much of it collected together, and some of the more important documents have been published.

The time was therefore just about ripe when a few years ago Mr. Packe set out on a new attempt to write Mill's life. It has been my privilege to watch his progress during part of that period, and occasionally to help on particular points when I happened to be specially familiar with the material. Yet even though I had seen a good deal of the new information, it was something of a

---

[1] [Published as the Preface to Michael St. John Packe, *The Life of John Stuart Mill* (London: Secker and Warburg, 1954), pp. xi–xii. As noted in the Editor's Introduction, the appearance of Hayek's *John Stuart Mill and Harriet Taylor* allowed for a 'new era' of Mill scholarship to begin, including Packe's biography of Mill (see this volume, p. xix).—Ed.]

surprise to me to see how complete and rounded a picture Mr. Packe has been able to draw by carefully fitting together all the evidence. Hitherto, we have had occasional glimpses of the human being concealed behind what was, it must be admitted, a somewhat forbidding appearance: now, for the first time, Mr. Packe has resurrected a whole personality with all its failings and achievements. Though the emphasis of the book is on John Stuart Mill the man, rather than on the philosopher and economist, the nature of his influence upon the intellectual life of his time stands out all the more clearly against the background of his whole life. There may still be details to be filled in here and there; but on the whole I feel that Mr. Packe has given us the definitive biography of Mill for which we have so long been waiting.

NINETEEN

REVIEW OF *MILL AND HIS EARLY CRITICS*[1]

The title of this little brochure hardly indicates its main subject or interest. In a sense the topic is even narrower than the title suggests, since 'early' is used entirely with reference to John Stuart Mill's essay *On Liberty* (1859). But though the survey of the reception accorded to this classic work is both useful and interesting, the main merit of the study is its cautious, yet, to the reviewer, convincing demonstration that an essay published under Mill's name in 1907 under the title *On Social Freedom*[2] and reprinted in book form in 1941 is *not* by Mill. Apparently what happened is that a paper submitted to Mill for criticism in 1862 by a Mr. E. R. Edger and commented upon by Mill in his published correspondence was found among Mill's papers at Avignon by Mrs. Mill's granddaughter, Mary Taylor. It is not known who was responsible for its original publication in the *Oxford and Cambridge Review*. If one did not know that Miss Mary Taylor's judgment was, to put it mildly, somewhat erratic and that whoever published the essay in the review may never have seen the original manuscript, one might seriously doubt the good faith of that publication.

Rees has had an opportunity to examine the original manuscript, and it proves not to be in the hand of either Mill or his stepdaughter Helen Taylor (who often acted as his secretary). It also contains a further twelve pages of outline notes for an intended continuation which were not published with the completed part but which should have made it evident to any tolerably competent person that it could not possibly be by Mill. Rees gives enough information about the contents of those unpublished leaves to exclude, to my mind, every possibility that they could have been written by Mill. Surely, Mill could never have seriously proposed uniformity of dress for social classes or occupational groups! Even after the 1941 publication, this presumed addendum to Mill's works was universally disregarded; the editor on that occasion, Miss Dorothy Fosdick, remaining nearly alone

---

[1] [Published as a review of J. C. Rees, *Mill and His Early Critics* (Leicester, UK: University College of Leicester, 1956), in *Journal of Modern History*, vol. 29, June 1957, p. 184.—Ed.]

[2] [*On Social Freedom: Or the Necessary Limits of Individual Freedom Arising Out of the Conditions of Our Social Life*, ed. Dorothy Fosdick (New York: Columbia University Press, 1941).—Ed.]

in discovering in it 'a marked advance in Mill's thinking'.[3] Miss Fosdick cannot be much blamed for accepting an essay which seemed to have fairly good credentials, though she might have been warned by the fact that what she regarded as its significance had been overlooked for thirty-four years.

[3] [*Ibid.*, p. 43.—Ed.]

TWENTY

REVIEW OF *JOHN MILL'S BOYHOOD VISIT TO FRANCE*[1]

This is a welcome publication of one of the most important documents from John Stuart Mill's boyhood, together with some hitherto unknown supplementary material which considerably enhances the value of the whole. The chief document is the 'journal' the boy sent to his father during the early part of the stay in France for which he had left a few days before his fourteenth birthday. The great influence of this experience on his later outlook and thought is well known, and the document has been extensively used by Mill's first biographer, Alexander Bain, and occasionally been consulted by later writers. It would have deserved publication *in extenso* even if the present editor had not been so fortunate as to discover a manuscript book containing the rough notes from which part of the 'journal' was written and extending considerably beyond the date at which the 'journal' stops.

In the slim volume now published the more important parts of this material are presented with great competence and excellent judgment. There is a brief but illuminating introduction which contains some of the most perceptive observations on Mill as a boy known to me; some additional helpful matter is given in appendixes, of which Mill's notes of one of the lectures on Logic which he attended at Montpellier and the excerpts from the diary of George Bentham covering the same events as does Mill's deserve special mention. Though one is at first disappointed to learn that even this publication should give only part of the existing manuscript and substitutes summaries where the editor did not feel publication in full justified, Dr. Mill makes a good case for this decision, and my distant recollection of part of the material tends to confirm her judgment.

At any rate, the result of this skillful editing is that the present text makes good reading and that probably everything in the manuscript that is really important for our understanding of the formation of Mill's personality is now readily available in print. The task Dr. Mill has undertaken was well worth while, and I believe that even those most familiar with the details of the extraordinary story of John Mill's development will find that this presentation of the documents throws new light on it.

---

[1] [Review of Anna Jean Mill, ed., *John Mill's Boyhood Visit to France: Being a Journal and Notebook Written by John Stuart Mill in France, 1820–21* (Toronto: University of Toronto Press, 1960), published in the *Journal of Political Economy*, vol. 69, no. 1, February 1961, pp. 103–4.—Ed.]

TWENTY-ONE

INTRODUCTION TO *CONSIDERATIONS ON REPRESENTATIVE GOVERNMENT*[1]

The masterly and mature exposition of opinions held by a small group in advance of their time will sometimes have a formative influence over the mind of succeeding generations greater than the thought of an original thinker of the first rank. This is most likely to happen when the opinions so aptly expressed appear to the young as the next step in an already recognizable direction of progress. Indeed the influence of such a radical system may be such that its expositor will come to be regarded by posterity as representative of his generation.

John Stuart Mill belongs to this class. He was at the height of his powers, though close to the end of his most productive years, when in 1861, at the age of 55, he published his chief contribution to political philosophy. Unlike his more famous and more brilliant *On Liberty*, published two years earlier, the *Considerations on Representative Government* is not a brief essay written to stress a single point, but a systematic survey of the chief problems of political organization. It is weightier, more carefully considered, and much more comprehensive than *On Liberty* which had been rapidly written and not further revised after death deprived Mill of the wife who had counseled him in writing it. If less widely known, *Considerations on Representative Government* had at least as great an influence on serious political thought as the more celebrated work.

When he published *Considerations on Representative Government*, Mill was already a famous man. This is not the place to retell the story of the extraordinary education and variety of activities through which he had passed when at the age of 37, Mill became known as one of the leading thinkers of his time by the publication of his *System of Logic*. Only five years later, in 1848, Mill established himself as the first authority in another field through his *Principles of Political Economy with Some of Their Applications to Social Philosophy*, not so much an original work as a most successful piece of exposition leading far beyond the traditional limits of the subject. To both these works it was given to dominate their field for over half a century as is true of few comparable treatises.

---

[1] [First published as the Introduction to John Stuart Mill, *Considerations on Representative Government* (Chicago: Henry Regnery Company, 1962), pp. ix–xiii.—Ed.]

John Stuart Mill occupied a unique position for so long because he was not merely the heir and developer of a set of ideas which were in the ascendancy, but was also capable of absorbing and learning from most of the other worthwhile ideas of his age. He started as the product and most faithful disciple of his father who was the most active and forceful expositor of Benthamite utilitarianism. He had behind him years of literary activity as an orthodox utilitarian when, at the age twenty-two, he broke away from all orthodoxy and, after a hard struggle and a severe mental crisis, established himself as an independent thinker. Though utilitarianism would continue to provide the general mental framework of his thought, Mill incorporated into it suggestions derived from Saint-Simonian socialism and Comtean positivism over the following years. These elements were derived from Burke and German idealism through Coleridge and Carlyle, much of the French liberal thought of the period leading up to the 1848 revolution and—most important for the understanding of the development of his political philosophy—Alexis de Tocqueville. To this should be added an often forgotten factor, his continued interest in ancient philosophy, especially Plato.[2]

Mill's preparation for writing the work now reprinted was, however, by no means purely philosophical and literary. Ever since as a very young man he had lived through the exciting events leading up to the reform bill of 1832, Mill had kept in close contact with current politics. Though his position as an employee of the East India Company made it impossible for him to enter politics actively, he was for five years, as the *de facto* editor of the *London and Westminster Review*, the guiding spirit of an effort to create a new radical party in [the] English parliament. Though this attempt failed and he gave up regular political journalism, Mill had in the meantime risen to a leading position in the Company which made him in effect one of the chief persons in London directing the affairs of the distant Indian empire. Only four years before the publication of the present work Mill retired from this post when the Company was taken over by the government and from that time was able to devote himself entirely to his studies.

On Liberty,[3] the first fruit of this leisure, was rapidly followed by *Thoughts on Parliamentary Reform.*[4] Another work, *Utilitarianism*[5] appeared in the same year

---

[2] See his translation of *Four Dialogues of Plato*, edited, with an Introductory Essay, by Ruth Borchardt (London: Watts & Co., 1946).

[3] [Republished in *Essays on Politics and Society*, ed. John M. Robson, vols. 18–19 (1977) of *The Collected Works of John Stuart Mill* [hereafter cited as *Collected Works*] (Toronto: University of Toronto Press, 1962–1991), 18:213–310.—Ed.]

[4] [Republished in *ibid.*, 19:311–39.—Ed.]

[5] [Republished in John Stuart Mill, *Essays on Ethics, Religion, and Society*, ed. John M. Robson, vol. 10 (1985) of *Collected Works*, pp. 203–58.—Ed.]

as *Representative Government* as a series of articles.[6] (Two years later it was published as a book.) In some respects it should be regarded as an important complement to the former. The publication in 1865 of Mill's biggest and least read philosophical work, *An Examination of Sir W. Hamilton's Philosophy*[7] concluded this period of great productivity, perhaps because of his election to Parliament in that year.

The reader who wishes to know more about Mill as a person will first turn to his famous *Autobiography*,[8] written largely during the period we have just considered though published only after his death. More than is true of most works of a similar nature this account of his intellectual development needs to be supplemented by a more complete picture of the man. However, there now exists a full and reliable *Life of John Stuart Mill* by Michael St. John Packe (1954)[9] and a much shorter but very perceptive account *John Stuart Mill the Man* by Ruth Borchardt (1957).[10] The first part of a complete edition of his letters is also to appear shortly[11] and a collected edition of his works is now in preparation. After a period of comparative neglect, in recent years there has been a great revival of interest in Mill. This interest has resulted in numerous publications of some of his writings and of works about him and various aspects of this thought. The prevalence of adequate library catalogues makes a bibliography of such works unnecessary here.

It cannot be the task of a brief introduction to give a summary of the contents of a book. In the present case, the carefully worded headings of the chapters and the detailed Table of Contents give a fully adequate outline of the steps in the argument.

The reader will find that in this field most of the problems which Mill discussed a hundred years ago are still with us—in some respects his discussions are even strikingly topical and prophetic.

---

[6] [Republished in Mill, *Essays on Politics and Society*, vol. 19 of *Collected Works*, pp. 203–61.—Ed.]

[7] [See John Stuart Mill, *An Examination of Sir William Hamilton's Philosophy and of the Principal Philosophical Questions Discussed in His Writings*, ed. John M. Robson, vol. 9 (1979) of *Collected Works*.—Ed.]

[8] [John Stuart Mill, *Autobiography and Literary Essays*, eds. John M. Robson and Jack Stillinger, vol. 1 (1981) of *Collected Works*, pp. 1–290.—Ed.]

[9] [See Hayek's Preface to Michael St. John Packe, *The Life of John Stuart Mill* (London: Secker and Warburg, 1954), pp. xi–xii (reprinted in this volume, pp. 314–15).—Ed.]

[10] [Ruth Borchardt, *John Stuart Mill the Man* (London: Watts, 1957).—Ed.]

[11] [See Hayek's Introduction to *The Earlier Letters of John Stuart Mill, 1812–1848*, ed. Francis E. Mineka, vols. 12–13 (1963) of *Collected Works*, 12:xv–xxiv (reprinted in this volume, pp. 322–31).—Ed.]

TWENTY-TWO

INTRODUCTION TO *THE EARLIER LETTERS OF JOHN STUART MILL, 1812–1848*[1]

John Stuart Mill has not been altogether fortunate in the manner in which his memory was served by those most concerned and best authorized to honour it. It is true that his stepdaughter, heir, and literary executor, Helen Taylor, promptly published the *Autobiography*, which chiefly determined the picture posterity formed of Mill, and that the only other manuscript ready for publication was also rapidly printed. But during the next forty years, while Mill's fame persisted undiminished, little was done either to make his literary work more readily accessible or his other activities better known. There are few figures of comparable standing whose works have had to wait nearly a hundred years for a collected edition in English to be published. Nor, while his reputation was at its height, did any significant information become available that would have enabled another hand to round off the somewhat angular and fragmentary picture Mill had given of himself. He had been quite aware that his more public activities would be of interest to later generations and had begun to mark some of the copies of his letters which he had kept as suitable for publication. But Helen Taylor appears increasingly to have been more concerned to prevent others from encroaching upon her proprietary rights than to push on with her own plans for publication. It was only when the material so jealously guarded by her finally passed to one of Mrs. Mill's granddaughters, Mary Taylor, that an outsider was called in to publish some of the more readily accessible correspondence. Again, however, Mary Tay-

---

[1] [Published as the Introduction to *The Earlier Letters of John Stuart Mill, 1812–1848*, ed. Francis E. Mineka, vols. 12–13 (1963) of *The Collected Works of John Stuart Mill* [hereafter cited as *Collected Works*] (Toronto: University of Toronto Press, 1962–1991), 12:xv–xxiv. © 1963 by University of Toronto Press. Reprinted with permission of the publisher. In a letter dated December 11, 1952, Francis Mineka proposed that Hayek be co-editor of the collection; Hayek responded in a letter dated December 30, 1952, 'If you were to mention in the Preface that I had carried the collection of the material up to a certain point, this should be all that I expect' (Box 38, Folder 20, Hoover Institution Archives). Upon reading the letters, Lionel Robbins in a letter dated May 22, 1964, wrote to Hayek, 'I have read the letters now from beginning to end and my only complaint is that your name is not on the title page as joint editor with Mineka; for, surely, whatever he has done would have been utterly impossible if you had not done all the pioneer work' (Box 46, Folder 25, Hoover Institution Archives).—Ed.]

lor reserved to herself part of the task which she was hardly qualified to carry out and in fact did not bring to completion. When at last after her death the papers in her possession became generally accessible, interest in Mill seems to have been at a low point and those papers were allowed to be widely dispersed. Nothing illustrates better the temporary eclipse of his fame than that some of the institutions which then acquired important parts of these papers did not trouble to catalogue them for another fifteen years.

It would seem that at least in his native country, during the period between the two great wars, Mill was regarded as one of those outmoded figures of the recent past whose ideas have ceased to be interesting because they have become commonplace. Most of the battles he fought had been won and to many of those who knew his name he probably appeared as a somewhat dim figure whose *On Liberty* they had been made to read at school but whose 'Victorian' outlook had lost most of its appeal. There was, perhaps, also some suspicion that his reputation had been somewhat exaggerated and that he had not been a great original genius but rather an honest, hardworking, and lucid expositor of ideas that other and greater minds had originated. He even came to be regarded, very unjustly, as the last of the 'orthodox' tradition in economics and politics. In fact, however, few men have done more to create the intellectual climate in which most of what he stood for was finally taken for granted.

The gradual but steady revival of the interest in John Stuart Mill in the course of the last twenty years is based on a truer understanding of the significance of his work.[2] Though nothing could be more misleading than to represent him as a 'typical' Victorian or a 'typical' Englishman (he certainly was neither), he was one of the most representative figures of the changes of thought that were germinating during his lifetime. During the forty years after his death he governed liberal thought as did no other man, and as late as 1914 he was still the chief source of inspiration of the progressive part of the intellectuals of the West—of the men whose dream of an indefinitely peaceful progress and expansion of Western civilization was shattered by the cataclysms of war and revolution. But even to that development Mill had unquestionably contributed by his sympathies for the rising aspirations of national self-determination and of socialism. His reputation declined with the confidence in the steady advance of civilization in which he had believed, and for a time the kind of minds who had believed in him were attracted by more revolutionary thinkers.

It must probably still be admitted that it is not so much for the originality of his thinking as for its influence on a world now past that Mill is chiefly of

[2] This new interest is by no means confined to the Western world. A bibliography of John Stuart Mill, published in *Keizai Ronshu, The Economic Review of Kansai University* (Osaka), 6, no. 7 (Nov., 1956), lists, in addition to about 350 works about Mill in European languages, over 180 in the Japanese language alone!

importance today. We may still discover that he is a better guide to many of our present problems than is generally appreciated. But there can be no question that his influence is such that to the historian of thought all information we have about Mill's activities, his contacts, and about the channels through which ideas reached him and through which he acted upon others is nearly as important as his published work. This is particularly true of a man like Mill who strove to keep his mind open to new ideas but upon whom accident and personal idiosyncrasies nevertheless acted to decide in some measure what would and what would not enter his system of thought.

The present volume contains some of the most important sources of information we have on all the different spheres of Mill's activities. The work on the collection of these letters started about the same time as the new interest in Mill began to make itself felt, but for reasons presently to be explained, publication has been long delayed. Some of the early results of these efforts have however already been used in various contributions to our knowledge of Mill which have appeared during this period, particularly in Mr. Michael Packe's vivid *Life of John Stuart Mill* (1954). The following brief account of the circumstances which led to the present edition may be found useful.

Although more than fifty years ago there were published two volumes of *Letters of John Stuart Mill*, edited by Hugh S. R. Elliot, these were in the main confined to the last twenty-five years of Mill's life. Of the earlier and most productive period the edition contained only three series of letters which happened to have been returned to Mill or his heirs. Many more belonging to this period have been published in some thirty different places, while an even larger number of unpublished letters was found to be dispersed among many private and public collections.

This unsatisfactory state of affairs, of which every student of nineteenth-century ideas must soon become aware, induced me nearly twenty years ago to attempt to bring together the main body of Mill's early correspondence as a supplement to the existing collection. This soon proved a much bigger task than I had anticipated and a task, moreover, which in one sense I had started too late and in another sense too early. Eighteen or even thirteen years earlier I should still have found together all or at least part of Mill's own papers which in the meanwhile had been dispersed; and as it soon appeared, much important information had been destroyed by fire during the bombing of London only a few months before I started my work. On the other hand, wartime conditions in England made inaccessible for the next five years some of the material that had to be examined. In the circumstances I carried the task of collection as far as was then possible, but had in the late forties to postpone its completion, first temporarily and then, consequent upon my move from London to Chicago, indefinitely. By then I had completed the editing of one rather special set of Mill's letters which, for reasons explained in the Introduction to the edition published in 1951 (*John Stuart Mill and Harriet Taylor: Their Friendship and Subsequent Marriage* [London and Chicago, 1951]),[3] seemed to demand separate treatment. That experience taught me that if I was not for years to abandon all my other work I could not adequately perform the same task for the complete collection. I was therefore only too grateful when not long after, an expert in the field, Professor Francis E. Mineka of Cornell University, agreed to assume responsibility for that arduous task. The editing of the present volume is entirely his and in the course of this work he has also been able to add to the collection of transcripts I had assembled over sixty additional hitherto unpublished letters by Mill.

It may be useful if, before commenting on the character of the present volumes, I give a brief account of the fate of the books and papers which were in Mill's possession at the time of his death, so far as this became known in the course of the search for his letters. Mill died on May 7, 1873, at Avignon, where for the preceding fifteen years he had spent much of his time in the house he had bought to be near his wife's grave.[4] His stepdaughter and sole heir, Helen Taylor, continued to live there most of the time for another thirty years, jealously guarding her exclusive rights to all of Mill's literary remains and steadfastly refusing requests for permission to publish any of his letters. The draft of a letter of hers written not long after Mill's death (on the back of a letter addressed to her, dated July 30, 1873) shows that she was then contemplating publication of some of his letters:

> I have all my dear stepfather's letters, preserved, looked through from time to time by himself, arranged in order by myself, and left by him in my hands with directions, verbal and written, to deal with them according to my judgement. When the more pressing task of the publication of his MSS. is completed, I shall, if I live, occupy myself with his correspondence, if I do not live it will be for my literary Executors to decide what to do with it.[5]

It seems that by 'all [her] dear stepfather's letters'[6] she meant no more than the drafts he had begun to keep from about 1848 or 1849. But she did make

---

[3] [Hayek supplies the words in brackets.—Ed.]

[4] As I am revising this Introduction for publication (January, 1962), I learn that last autumn this house, visited by so many admirers of John Stuart Mill, was torn down, the operations actually beginning while a committee formed to assure its preservation and conversion into a museum was holding its first meeting!

[5] The Mill-Taylor Collection, British Library of Political and Economic Science (London School of Economics), vol. 53.

[6] [Hayek supplies the word in brackets.—Ed.]

some efforts to recover from the heirs of his correspondents sets of earlier letters in exchange for those written to him and it was probably in this manner that the letters to Sterling and Bulwer included in the Elliot edition came to be among the Mill papers.

Nothing came of Helen Taylor's plans for publication and the Mill papers rested at the Avignon cottage until 1904, when Helen Taylor's niece Mary Taylor (the younger daughter of Mrs. Mill's son Algernon) succeeded in persuading the old lady, who at seventy-three appears to have been somewhat peculiar and senile, to return to England. Early in 1905 a friend of Mary Taylor's (Mary Ann Trimble, who earlier had spent some time at Avignon with Mary Taylor) returned to Avignon and, with the assistance of a married couple who had accompanied her from England, (according to a diary Mary Taylor kept at the time) did there 'the work of three months in three weeks. Half a ton of letters to be sorted, all manner of rubbish to be separated from useful things, books to be dusted and selected from, arrangements to be made for sale, and 18 boxes to be packed'.[7]

A considerable part of Mill's library and at least some of his papers were disposed of at a sale held at Avignon from May 21 to 28, 1905.[8] Some of the manuscripts were acquired by a local bookseller, Romanille, from whom at least one bound volume was bought by an American scholar,[9] while a London clergyman bought a manuscript entitled 'On Social Freedom' which he published (reputedly with the consent of Helen Taylor, who had died a few months before it appeared) as a posthumous work of Mill in the *Oxford and Cambridge Review* of June, 1907, and which was republished in book form under Mill's name as late as 1941, though it now appears that it was not a work by Mill but a manuscript sent to Mill for his opinion by one of his admirers.[10]

On their return to England Helen Taylor had been taken by her niece to Devon, where she died at Torquay on January 29, 1907. As she appears, in the words of the younger woman, long before that time to have 'lost her mem-

---

[7] *Ibid.*, vol. 58.

[8] The manuscripts mentioned in the two following notes which are known to derive from this sale bear a printed label inside the front cover which states 'De la bibliothèque de / John Stuart Mill / Vendue à Avignon / les 21, 23, 24, 26, 27, 28 Mai 1905'. Some at least of the books are reported to have been bought by the poet Paul Mariéton and to have been left by him to the library at Avignon (see Jules Véran, 'Le Souvenir de Stuart Mill à Avignon', *Revue des deux mondes*, vol. 41, septembre 1937[, pp. 211–12]), but attempts by several persons to find them there have failed.

[9] This volume of manuscripts of various minor published works by Mill was bought by Professor George Herbert Palmer of Harvard University and given by him to the library of his University where it is now preserved in the Houghton Library, classed as 'MS Eng 1105'.

[10] See this article by Jules Véran cited in note 8 above, and, for the evidence showing that the manuscript is not by Mill, J. C. Rees, *Mill and His Early Critics* (Leicester: University College, 1956). [Hayek's review of Rees is included in this volume, pp. 316–17.—Ed.]

ory to a great extent', all business, even the signing of legal documents, was conducted on her behalf by Mary Taylor. One of the first steps taken by the latter soon after the return to England was, on the advice of John Morley, to give that part of Mill's and Helen Taylor's library which had been stored in London to Somerville College (one of the women's colleges at Oxford). Miss Taylor retained a few books and Somerville College was to be entitled to dispose of what it did not want and in the course of 1906 actually sold some of the books.[11]

It seems that shortly after Helen Taylor's death Mary Taylor placed the collection of Mill's correspondence in the hand of Mr. Hugh S. R. Elliot. Little is known about him or the authority he was given and the fragments of information we have about the proceedings are somewhat puzzling. There is extant an account by Mr. Elliot of his relations to Mary Taylor[12] from which the following passages may be quoted:

> As to the private letters of Mill to his wife & daughter, we hesitated for a very long time about them; but Miss Taylor, who is a lady of very peculiar ideas and habits, did not wish them to be published. She has it in her mind to bring out another volume in a few years' time, consisting exclusively of Mill's letters to his wife, daughter, and sisters; but wants to delay this until the last of Mill's sisters[13] is dead. Whether it will ever be done I cannot say. She guards the letters very jealously; and it was only after much pressure and persuasion that I was allowed to see them at all.
>
> As to her published introduction, following mine in the book, it was entirely an afterthought. In the study of the private letters, I formed a very unfavourable opinion both of Mrs. Mill and of Miss Helen Taylor. It appeared to me that they were both selfish and somewhat conceited women, and that Mill (who must have been a very poor judge of character) was largely deceived with regard to them. Of course I could not state my views openly in a book which is published by Miss Mary Taylor at her own expense. But in my original introduction, I found it impossible to allude to the women without unconsciously conveying into my language some suggestion of what I thought. To this Miss Mary Taylor took the strongest possible exception. I reconsidered the

[11] There was also a story current in London twenty years ago that some of Mill's books had been given at some time to Morley College (a workingmen's college in the South of London); but though the library of that institution escaped when the main building was destroyed by bombs, no such books can be traced now, and unless they were among a quantity of books stored in the destroyed main building the story is probably incorrect. On the whole it seems that all the books, except 'a box' returned to Mary Taylor, stored in the Pantechnicon in 1905, were given to Somerville College, which still has the original list.

[12] In a letter by Hugh Elliot to Lord Courtney, dated May 8, 1910. MS at London School of Economics.

[13] Mrs. Mary Colman, who died on January 15, 1913.

whole matter, but found myself unable to speak any more favourably of them than I had done. For some days Miss Taylor declined even to see me, and we were completely at a deadlock; but at last it was agreed that I should omit all mention of Mill's private life and that Miss Taylor should herself write a second introduction (for which I took no responsibility) and say what she liked. I did not greatly care for her contribution, but it was a necessary compromise. Myself, however, I entertain no sort of doubt that Miss Taylor is right in her main belief that there was no 'guilty' intrigue. . . .

There is, on the other hand, an account which the late Sir Frederick R. Chapman gave twenty-five years ago in a letter to an American scholar:

> Miss Mary [Taylor] mentioned another fact that seemed very strange to me. She had placed the whole of the copies of Mr. Mill's correspondence at the disposal of Mr. Elliot when assisting him in the preparation of the published letters. When he had made his selection he induced her to destroy the rest save only what she termed the 'intimate letters' which she intended to embody in another book. I understand that the book has never appeared.
>
> Assuming that she has told me the actual facts I should say that her weakness is as remarkable as Mr. Elliot's meaningless advice or request to destroy the balance of the letters which must have been very numerous.[14]

Though Sir Frederick's recollection was no doubt correct, there is every reason to doubt Miss Taylor's account of the events and it is by no means certain that any destruction of letters did take place at that time (whatever may have happened at Avignon in 1905). Not only most of the letters which Mr. Elliot published but so many others are known to have been preserved that I am on the whole inclined to think that nothing was destroyed then.

Mary Taylor appears to have proceeded with her plan of preparing a further volume of family letters and it seems that by the beginning of 1918 she had, with the assistance of Miss Elizabeth Lee (sister of Sir Sidney Lee and author of the article on Helen Taylor in the *Dictionary of National Biography*), completed a typescript and was negotiating through a literary agent (Mr. A. P. Watts) with Messrs. Longmans, Green & Co. concerning publication. Since the files of all parties involved (the literary agent, the publishers, Miss Mary Taylor's solicitors and, at least in part, her literary executors) were destroyed by fire during the London 'Blitz' in December, 1940, it is now impossible to

[14] A letter by Sir Frederick R. Chapman to Professor J. M. McCrimmon, now of the University of Illinois, Urbana, Illinois, dated July 26, 1935. I wish to thank Professor McCrimmon for letting me have the text of this letter and permitting me to reprint it. The episode is briefly discussed on p. vi of Professor McCrimmon's doctoral dissertation in Northwestern University Library. [Hayek supplies the name in brackets.—Ed.]

say with certainty why it was not published. But some letters of Mary Taylor together with the recollections of one of the partners of the literary agents (Mr. C. A. Watts, who in his old age still distinctly remembered the 'irresponsible Miss Mary Taylor') show that after a period of irresolution Miss Taylor suffered a 'nervous breakdown', accompanied by insomnia and illusions. After certification she was in March, 1918, taken to an institution in London where she died on November 6, 1918.

In her will Mary Taylor had left all copyrights and letters and correspondence referring to John Stuart Mill and Helen Taylor to the National Provincial Bank Ltd. as residuary legatees and literary executors who were to be free to use this material in any way they saw fit. An inventory of her possessions mentions among the contents of 'a gunpowder proof safe', a collection of 'Public Letters to and from J. S. Mill A to Z', and a packet of private letters. The former together with various other manuscript material the Bank decided, on the report of a Mr. P. W. Sergeant who had been asked to value them, to sell by auction, while it was thought that 'the intimate letters relating to the family quarrel . . . could not be offered for sale publicly'.

A first sale was accordingly held at Sotheby's of London on March 29, 1922, which produced a gross amount of £276.19.–. Of this, however, £200 were paid on behalf of the Trustees of the Carlyle House Memorial Trust for a set of seventy-seven letters by Thomas Carlyle to Mill (which in the following year were published by Mr. Alexander Carlyle in *Letters of Thomas Carlyle to John Stuart Mill, John Sterling and Robert Browning* [London: T. Fisher Unwin, 1923]).[15] The twenty-one lots of Mill manuscripts proper seem all to have been bought by various London booksellers and altogether to have fetched no more than £76.19. . They appear to have contained numerous notebooks, mostly botanical, and miscellaneous correspondence. Most of the Mill manuscripts now in various American libraries derive from this sale.[16] Quantitatively the largest part (although much of it of a kind not readily salable otherwise) was in 1926 sold by one of the booksellers to the Library of the London School of Economics, where it constitutes the nucleus of the Mill-Taylor Collection, since much enriched by many additions.

Because of the loss of part of the relevant files of the National Provincial Bank, we do not know why the sale of a large part of the papers was postponed for five years. But on June 27, 1927, Sotheby's sold another fourteen lots described as 'The Property of Miss Mary Taylor, dec.', containing mostly letters to Mill, but also one lot containing 'upwards of 132 autograph letters to his wife on literary work and travel'. It seems that both the material now at Yale University Library and that acquired by Lord Keynes and

---

[15] [Hayek supplies the words in brackets.—Ed.]
[16] See the annotated catalogues of this and the second sale in the British Museum Library.

now at King's College, Cambridge, derive from this sale. The National Provincial Bank apparently retained only the small collection of correspondence exchanged between Mill and his brothers and sisters and a few family documents and portraits, all of which were in 1943 presented by the Bank to the London School of Economics for inclusion in the Mill-Taylor Collection.

Although it seemed appropriate to use this occasion to give an account of what happened to Mill's own books and papers, the material deriving from them could in fact make little contribution to the present edition. This is intended to cover the period up to 1849, which, because Mill did not then keep copies of his letters, is so little represented in Elliot's edition of his letters, which was based on his papers. In so far as the present collection was to go beyond bringing together the considerable number of earlier letters that had been published in a great variety of places and a few unpublished ones known to be preserved in libraries, the main effort had to be directed towards tracing descendants of Mill's correspondents in the hope that some of their papers might be preserved. This indeed absorbed the greater part of the time I was able to devote to the project, yet the results were not great. Even in England, where in general family papers are preserved perhaps longer than anywhere else, two wars have led to the destruction of much of the extraordinary quantity of manuscript material which had accumulated by 1914. It was not so much destruction by enemy action as the appeal for old paper for salvage and the insistence of air-raid wardens that lofts should be cleared of all inflammable matter which caused most of the loss. In more than one instance it seemed at least likely that what I was searching for had only a short while before left the place where it had rested undisturbed for two or three generations. I should add that wherever I succeeded in tracing descendants of Mill's correspondents, my inquiries were invariably met with the greatest courtesy and helpfulness. I can of course not claim that I have exhausted even all the likely leads and no doubt in the course of time further letters by Mill will turn up by accident. But while I do not feel that further systematic search in England would be likely to produce much, there may well be such opportunities on the Continent and particularly in France which, during the greater part of the time I was engaged on this work, was inaccessible to me. If, for instance, good fortune had somewhere preserved the letters which for some years after his visit to France as a boy Mill wrote to his 'first friend' Antoine Jérôme Balard,[17] later a distinguished chemist, these would probably tell us more about his early development than any document which might still be found in England.

[17] Cf. the reference to Balard in Mill's letter to Auguste Comte dated August 12, 1842—Letter 367 in the present collection. [Mill, *Earlier Letters*, vol. 13 of *Collected Works*, p. 540.—Ed.]

There are various obligations I have incurred in the work on the material now published in this volume and which I wish to acknowledge in this place. All the work I did on the collection was done while I held a professorship at the London School of Economics and Political Science and I have received all sorts of assistance from the Economic Research Division of that institution, including the provision of assistance and of some funds for various incidental expenditures. Dr. Ruth Borchardt and Miss Dorothy Salter (now Mrs. F. H. Hahn) in succession helped me for long periods of the work. I must also especially mention the Library of the London School of Economics, or the British Library of Political and Economic Science as it is officially called, which as custodian of the Mill-Taylor Collection not only has provided much of the material of this book but also has often helped by buying at my suggestion documents to which I otherwise might not have obtained access. It was in these circumstances very generous of the authorities of the School to give first to me and then to Professor Mineka permission to use the material collected in any way we thought best. Of the many others who in various ways have helped I ought to single out the National Provincial Bank Ltd. which, after so many years conscientiously watching over the interests of Mill's heirs, finally decided to hand over to the uses of scholarship what the bombs had spared of the papers of the late Mary Taylor.[18]

The chief credit for the appearance of this edition, however, belongs of course to the editor. Only those who have tried their hands at this kind of task at least on small scale will appreciate the amount of painstaking care and ingenuity that has to be devoted to an edition of the size of the present one before the reader can use it with the implicit trust and ease which a good editor's work assures. I am the more indebted to Professor Mineka because he was prepared to take over the more burdensome part of the task I had half-playfully commenced. The tracing of unpublished manuscripts is the kind of detective work which most people will enjoy doing as a recreation in their spare time. But while the pleasure of the hunt was largely mine, the solid hard work to which the reader owes this edition is entirely Professor Mineka's.

F.A.H.
University of Chicago
January, 1962

---

[18] [For a different perspective on this, however, see Hayek's February 12, 1944, letter to Jacob Viner; this volume, p. 343.—Ed.]

TWENTY-THREE

RELATED CORRESPONDENCE[1]

December 7, 1941

Dr. F. A. v. Hayek
8, Turner Close
London, N.W.11, England

Dear Hayek:

I have just finished reading your 'The Counter-Revolution of Science' and want to tell you how much I enjoyed it. Most of the contents were wholly new to me, and you have handled a great mass of difficult material in masterly manner. In so far as you reveal a position, I feel that I probably would be in close agreement with you.

I regretted the absence of a fuller account of the Saint-Simon-Comteau influence on English thought, and hope that in your book you will expand here. I missed mention of Frederick Harrison, and of the *Fortnightly Review*. Re J. S. Mill, you should read his series of essays, 'The Spirit of the Age', in the *Examiner*, running through 1831 from January 9 on, which seem to me strongly Saint-Simonian. There are also some letters of Mill to d'Eichthal, not published elsewhere, in *Cosmopolis*, 6 and 7 (1897), which may have material of use to you—although my notes on these letters do not indicate it. For Mill letters to Saint-Simonians, unpublished and I fear unavailable, see Cat. gén. des manuscrits des Bibliothèques Publiques de France, series 4, vol. 43: Bibliothèque de l'Arsenal, p. 7 (item 7605) letter of J.S.M. to *Globe*?; p. 66, item 7759, J.S.M. to Enfantin. Also, you might find something (although once more my notes do not indicate it) in Mlle. M. Apchié, *Les sources francaises de certains aspects de la pensée economique de John Stuart Mill*, p. 1931.

---

[1] [The correspondence provides additional evidence of the enormity of the task before Hayek as he set out to collect the materials eventually published in 1951. More than this, we learn of the important role of Jacob Viner in Hayek's endeavor. The letters further reveal collegiality and warmth that extended across political affiliations. Finally, they provide glimpses into life during World War II as recorded by Hayek and his colleagues.—Ed.]

P. 318, 'George Lewis' is, I take it, a misprint for George Lewes.

Could you spare me another reprint for my colleague, Ronald Crane (in the English Department here) who is a student of the history of ideas and has shown very much interest in what I have told him of your essays? I am lending him my copy to read, but he would very much like one to keep.

While I write this, the newspaper boys are calling out the news of the Japanese commencement of hostilities against us. I think this means that at last we really are going to put our shoulders to the common task for all decent people of crushing the dictators.

Cordially,
Jacob Viner[2]

February 1st, 1942

Dear Viner,

Many thanks for your kind letter of December 7th, which, delivered at my now empty London House, reached me even later than would otherwise have been the case. I am naturally very pleased by what you say about my article and some of your suggestions will be very useful.—I did not really try to deal adequately with English Positivism, but you are perfectly right that in the end my few references to it have become unduly patchy. I had glanced through Mill's articles in the *Examiner* and gained the same impression as you, but then postponed closer study for later. Since I have got a girl to work on the general influence of Comte and Saint-Simon on J. S. Mill and the first thing I made her do was of course a careful analysis of these articles. I don't know yet whether she will produce a useful thesis, but in any case I am learning a good deal in helping her. You may be interested, incidentally, that there is a very full treatment of the English Positivist movement in R. Metz, *A Hundred Years of British Philosophy*, Allen & Unwin (New York: Macmillan) 1938, pp. 171–83.

The reason why I did not go further into the influence of S.S. and Comte on English writers is that I hope, after I have dealt with the 'German Phase' (about 1842–1880) of the strand of thought with which I am dealing, to follow up with two more sections on England and the U.S.A. But this is of course a very slow affair and in the present circumstances it is impossible to predict

<hr>

[2] [Jacob Viner (1892–1970) was a Canadian-born economist who is well known for his work on international trade. His papers may be found at http://findingaids.princeton.edu/collections/MC138; the correspondence below demonstrates his deep and broad knowledge of the nineteenth-century literature in economics as well as his influence on Hayek's project of collecting J. S. Mill's correspondence.—Ed.]

with any degree of certainty when or whether I shall be able to execute my plans. So far my life has been little affected by the war, apart from the move to Cambridge and the somewhat increased amount of work caused by the absence of most of my colleagues on war service. But I find that I make even slower progress with my own work than usual—and particularly historical work is made much more difficult by the reduced library facilities.

I need not tell you what a relief it has been to all of us here to know that the United States are now definitely in the war. It has outweighted all the setbacks suffered since and one can look once more to the future with a measure of confidence. But although I am fairly optimistic about the war, I am by no means so about the peace, or rather about the economic regime that will follow the war. But as, in my position, I am forced to watch events almost purely as a spectator, there is not much use getting worked up about it.

One of my main problems at the moment is to keep *Economica* going. I am now practically alone responsible for it and the great difficulty is to get decent contributions. The number of economists here who are masters of their time has by now dwindled to a handful and I doubt from issue to issue whether I shall be able to fill it. If you could help me with an occasional contribution I should be exceedingly grateful. I believe *Economica* has never yet had an article from you!

I am sending you under separate cover another offprint of my last article for your colleague Crane.

Very cordially yours,
F. A. Hayek

September 22, 1942

Professor F. A. Hayek
The London School of Economics
New Court
Peterhouse, Cambridge
England

Dear Hayek:

Your introduction to the John Stuart Mill essay was perfect for its purpose. I have already read galley proof on it, and there were very few corrections to make. We checked up on your longer quotations, and have made some corrections in them, but otherwise your text has been left practically unchanged.

I am very glad indeed to hear that somebody is at last getting to work on the collection of the Mill correspondence. As you say, it is huge. I have no doubt that there are hundreds of unpublished John Stuart Mill letters scattered about the United States. I have one letter myself and know of others. I am enclosing a location list for uncollected Mill letters, including only such items as I happened to note and put in my file. I have deliberately excluded the most obvious sources. You of course know that Laski[3] has a good many Mill letters.

The volume of Mill correspondence is so great that I fear the usual practice for locating uncollected items of putting a request in the appropriate periodicals would not do in this case. It would not be altogether reasonable to ask the aid of the public unless there were some way of letting them know what had already been collected.

I am going to be at Yale University during the next academic year as a visiting professor. I will be practically on a research basis, with almost no teaching obligations. It will be convenient for me to be in the East, as it will save me a good deal of the time on the railway which my frequent trips East from Chicago involve. This is of increasing importance as travelling conditions become less pleasant. Also it will help to keep our family somewhat together, as my daughter Ellen is at nearby Smith College, and my son Arthur is about to enter cadet training for naval (Coast Guard) service at a nearby Coast Guard training college.

I will drop all my *Journal of Political Economy* responsibilities during the year, and therefore will not pursue any further the question of exchange of reviews.

Cordially yours,
Jacob Viner

February 16th, 1943

Dear Viner,

Is [*sic*] has now been very much longer than I meant it to be till I answered your kind letter of September 22 with all the very helpful information it brought. But I meant to enclose the attached note with it, and it has taken me much longer than I had expected first to complete it and then to get it published. You will see that we are getting on with our project concerning the Mill letters and that we have already done a fair amount of work. I have no doubt now that at least so far as the early period of Mill's life is concerned it was very well worth undertaking and is certain to produce an interesting volume.

Though we have already traced a fair number of unpublished letters (I think nearly a hundred belonging to the early period) this is, of course, very

[3] [Harold Laski, professor at the London School of Economics until his death in 1950.—Ed.]

slow work. It seems that for quite a long period nearly all the Mill letters which have gone through the sales rooms went to America, and it seems usually to be impossible to trace the buyers. We have, however, traced a number, largely through Mr. McCrimmon, Professor Emery Neff, Mr. N. Himes, Professor MacMinn and others, whose addresses we partly owe to you. But we have not yet succeeded to establish any contacts with Yale which seems to be a very likely place to possess such letters. An inquiry which the young person who is doing most of the work has some months ago directed to the University Librarian of Yale, and which perhaps has not been very felicitously worded, has so far remained without reply. I do not like now to write again without knowing precisely to whom to address my inquiry and I wonder whether we might ask for your help by either directly inquiring at likely places in Yale or letting us know whom we ought to write to.

In your letter you also mention one Mill letter in your own possession. This is now probably difficult for you to get; but may we hope that whenever you conveniently can you will be willing to let us have a copy?

Except for a continuous increase in the amount of my duties—entirely of a 'peace' kind—there is little change in our life here and Cambridge is not a bad place to live in war-time.—Is there no prospect of seeing you over here? I hope that in that case you will let me know so I don't hear only afterwards that you have been in London as has been the case with some of my other American Friends.

Yours sincerely,
F. A. Hayek

April 14, 1943

Professor F. A. Hayek
The Hostel, Peterhouse
Cambridge, England

Dear Hayek:

I cannot remember the name of your assistant and therefore cannot locate in my files, which are arranged alphabetically, the previous letter I wrote. I am thus not sure that I have not already sent you some of the information given below. I take it from your *Times Literary Supplement* note that you are for the present interested primarily in letters prior to 1848. Yale Library will write you direct about its J. S. Mill letters. Professor James Osborne here has about a dozen letters, which I have seen, some of them of real economic interest, but they are post-1848. On a recent visit to Chicago I looked up my own files, and I find I have two Mill letters, dated in the 1860's, copies of which I enclose.

The following items may give you clues as to the location of letters prior to 1848:

/_W. A._/ Knight, *Memoir of John Nichol*, Glasgow, 1896, p. xiii, says that John Pringle Nichol (father of John N.) corresponded with J.S.M. from 1833 to his death.

The successive editions of the *Catalogue of Additions to the MSS in the British Museum* list a number of pre-1848 letters.

National Library of Scotland, *MSS Catalogue*, 1, 1938, index, lists some pre-1848 letters.

Herman Finer's brother, who has in manuscript a biography of Edwin Chadwick, refers therein to at least one J.S.M. letter.

R. Garnett, *Edward Gibbon Wakefield*, L[ondon]. 1898, Pref. XVI–XVII, a Mill letter Ca. 1848.

Letters to Pasqual Villari (See *Notes and Queries*, 14th ser. 160 (1931) 101.)

See Elkin Mathews Ltd. Cat. 86, 1941, pp. 18–19.

B. W. Richardson, *Health of Nations*, 1:lxviii–lxix. A letter to Edwin Chadwick (post-1848, I think)

A biography of (a collection of letters by and to) George Lewes (George Eliot's husband) to which I do not have the exact reference at the moment, contains half a dozen or so Mill letters of the early 1840's.

If you wish references to post 1848 letters, or wish me to negotiate with Osborne for copies of his post-1848 letters, please let me know and I will do what I can.

Cordially yours,
Jacob Viner

May 28th, 1943

Dear Viner,

Many thanks for your letter of April 14th and the copy of the let. of the Yale Librarian of April 15th, which both arrived within the last two or three days. Special thanks also for the copies of your two Mill letters. Most of the information you had already given in your letter to me of September 22nd of last year, but one or two items were new. I understand that the young lady here (Dr. Borchardt),[4] who is doing most of the actual work, has not written to you, so your reference to an assistant in the first sentence of your letter cannot refer to anyone over here. I wonder whether Dr. Norman Himes of Baltimore, who has appointed himself, somewhat to our embarrassment, our agent in the United States, has written to you on our behalf. He seems to be full of good intentions, but seems to be very busy with other things—and so far the only result of his activities has been that in one or two instances we received replies that the people to whom we had written had already given all the information to Dr. Himes, who had inquired on our behalf! But we have only much later had a first letter from him promising to send more definite contributions in the future. I am a little unhappy about this situation, but do not want to appear ungrateful for what is evidently done with the best of intentions— though there is just a shade of a suggestion in his letter that J. S. Mill is really his private property.

As regards Professor Osborne, I have already written to him, not as a presumptive owner of Mill letters, but with respect to 'Works in Progress' of which I understand he is the Editor, asking him to insert a brief announcement in our plans. Since I wrote to him only on March 14th, nearly a month after my last letter to you, I could hardly yet have a reply. If you will be good enough to inquire whether Professor Osborne would be prepared to let us have copies of his letters, I should be most grateful.

As regard the post 1848 period the position is simply that 1) that will probably have to come later, and 2) while I want to make the earlier collection definitely a complete one, I am afraid to commit us in this respect for the post 1848 period. The available material seems to be so enormous that a complete edition may be impracticable and it may prove wiser merely to supplement Elliot than to reprint his letters—though, as our work proceeds, I get more and more doubtful even of his reliability. But we are trying to collect *all* Mill letters we can get hold of.

Cordially yours,
F. A. Hayek

P.S. I am writing at the same time to the Yale University Librarian.

---

[4] [See Hayek's acknowledgement of Dr. Ruth Borchardt's assistance above on p. 331.—Ed.]

November 22, 1943

Professor F. A. Hayek
The Hostel
Peterhouse
Cambridge, England

Dear Hayek:

This is a further report on Mill correspondence.

I have gone through hastily the Yale collection. I am under the impression that it must be a part of the Helen Taylor collection (now at the London School?) and that it got separated and into a bookseller's hands by some accident. Yale acquired it from an American bookseller in 1930. The latter has no record of where he acquired it. It consists of some four or five hundred items, of which a fraction is of wholly unimportant correspondence by Helen Taylor herself and the bulk of the remainder consists of correspondence after 1848, including many letters by J.S.M. to Mrs. Taylor (and later to Mrs. Mill) herself. None of the letters in the Yale collection, I believe, is in the Elliott [sic] volumes, but I have not made a careful check. There are perhaps 30 items antedating 1848, of which the most important are probably J.S.M.'s letter to W. J. Fox re Mrs. Taylor, to which Mary Taylor refers on page xlii of Elliott's [sic] edition of the letters, Mrs. James Mill's farewell letter to J.S.M. just before her death, and John Sterling's farewell letter to J.S.M., written a few days before the former's death. There are also several letters from Bentham to James Mill, one of which relates to J.S.M. (J.B.'s offer to act as guardian of J.S.M. if James M. should die.)

Also important is a substantial memorandum by J.S.M., indicating in quite specific terms the extent and nature of Mrs. Taylor's influence with reference to the *Principles* and a letter of Roebuck to a third party (post-1848), giving an intellectual appraisal of J.S.M. Dr. Osborne of Yale has another manuscript appraisal of J.S.M. by Roebuck.

Yale Library is finally proceeding to a detailed listing of the contents of the collection and a copy of the list will be sent to you as soon as it is completed. I have agreed to write up the collection in a brief article for the *Yale Library Gazette* as soon as the list is available.

I find that a friend of mine, Joseph H. Schaffner, Washington, D.C., has about a dozen J.S.M. letters. He will shortly send me a list and then I will arrange to have copies made for you of the items you are interested in. At the moment these letters are in storage, but the owner will soon have them at hand. I doubt whether any of them are pre-1848.

I have a copy of a sale catalogue of J. Pearson & Company, 5 Pall Mall Place, London, item 153, of which is a collection of 33 J.S. Mill letters, most of them pre-1848. The letters are described in some detail and seem important. Many of them are to W. J. Fox; others to Molesworth. The whole collection is described as 'inlaid to a uniform size and bound in red morocco extra. Royal 4to'. It was listed at £84! The catalogue is unnumbered and undated. The title (on outside cover) reads: '*A Highly Important Collection of Original Holograph Manuscripts and Original Holograph Correspondences* . . . Part II.' Perhaps you can trace this collection.

Sincerely,
Jacob Viner

February 7th, 1944

Mr. James T. Babb
Acting Librarian
Yale University Library

Dear Mr. Babb,

Thank you very much for your letter of December 30th with the attached list of the Mill letters, which has just arrived, though the copy of the letter sent by air-mail has not yet done so.

I believe I cannot now tell you with a fair degree of certainty where your collection comes from; in the second sale of letters of J. S. Mill, at Messrs. Sotheby's, from the property of Miss Mary Taylor, dec. (a grandchild of Mrs. Mill) three lots, including one (no. 668) described as 'upwards of 132 AL to his wife' and another (no. 668) were sold to the London booksellers of B. F. Stevens & Brown, who are known to have resold Mill letters bought at the earlier sale to 'a Boston bookseller'. The dates of the two Mill sales at Sotheby's are March 29, 1922, and July 27, 1927, and the lots which, according to the annotated catalogue in the British Museum, were sold to B. F. Stevens were (according to my notes taken at an earlier occasion and not strictly reliable) nos. 724 (letters by Emerson, etc) at the first sale and lots 666, 668, and 670 at the second sale. That the first of these lots was sold to 'a Boston bookseller' was ascertained by a friend of mine several years ago. When I recently called at the firm they declared to be unable to trace any records of the transaction.

The magnitude of your collection is of course such that probably it would hardly be possible for you in the present circumstances to supply us with copies, nor could we raise the funds for the expenses involved. But I am rather anxious to obtain, if possible copies of those letters by and to Mill which belong to the relatively early period on which alone, for the time being, we are seriously working. They are the following, in the order of your list:

p. 1: 2 letters to (Charles?) Austin, Dec. 1844
     letter to Mrs. Austin, Jan. 9, 1836
     Dft. of reply to Jeremy Bentham, 1827?
p. 2: 3 letters to W. J. Fox, Oct. 18, 1832, Nov. 7, 1833, Nov. 22?, 1833
p. 4 letter to John Taylor, Sept. 1, 1832
p. 5 4 letters to Mrs. Taylor, about 1834
    6 letters to Mrs. Taylor, about 1849
p. 6: 1 letter by John Austin, Dec. 25, 1844
p. 7: 4 letters by Jeremy Bentham, 1827
p. 8: letter by Sir John Herschel, July 13th, 1845
p. 9: letter by John Sterling, Sept. 8, 1844

If it were possible for you to let us have photostat copies of these letters (made at our expense) and to give us permission to include the letters by Mill in our proposed collection, this is as much as we should wish till better times return and we shall both be in a better position to contemplate the larger task presented by the letters belonging to the later part of Mill's life. We do, of course, in general, not propose to publish letters *to* Mill, except possibly as part of the explanatory text or footnotes. But the few letters to Mill for copies of which I am asking are of the kind which are likely to throw light on letters by Mill which we either already have or are likely to obtain.

According to our experience there does not seem to be any difficulty about sending photostat copies in small quantities, so long as they are packed like printed matter (preferably in a cardboard roll); while if sent in parcels the customs require all kinds of irritating formalities.

I shall be writing in a day or two to Professor Viner and enclose a somewhat fuller statement about what I know concerning the history of the dispersal of the Mill papers, which he might care to use in connection with the note I understand he is writing about your collection.

With renewed thanks for all the courtesy shown,
I am, yours very truly,
F. A. Hayek

Professor Jacob Viner,
Department of Economics,
University of Chicago

February 12th, 1944

Dear Viner,

Your two letters of November 22nd and 24th have, of course, been in my hands for some time. What has kept me from replying earlier was still the same cause as that which prevented me from writing to you (and incidentally to Frank Knight)[5] for nearly a year: my bad conscience about the review of Graham's book which I had promised, and the constant vain hope that in another week's time I might be able to send it. But I must not let this delay this letter any longer and I will only briefly explain what the position is about that review. It is not that I do not like the book—far from it—but I find it exceedingly difficult to review and I have now so little time that I have never been able to get the few days of quiet work which it would require. My difficulty is that I agree so much with the general approach and disagree with so many of the details. My first attempt at a review resulted in the article in the *E*[*conomic*] *J*[*ournal*][6] which I sent you and which would certainly not have been suitable as a review and which you probably did not particularly like. I have made several attempts since and I go on hoping that before long I shall be able to send you a review, if you still want it, but I feel a little discouraged. Don't hesitate to explain the position to Graham should occasion arise.

Before your first letter I had heard only indirectly from Sraffa about the extent of the collection in Yale, but I have since received the fulle [*sic*] list from Yale and replied to ask in the first instance for photostate [*sic*] copies of the few but interesting letters belonging to the early period. I also explained to the Librarian what I knew about the probably [*sic*] origin of their collection and I am including with this letter a somewhat fuller sketch of the history of the dispersal of the Mill material. I had hoped to let you have this more promptly so that there might be a chance of your using it in the article on the Yale collection, but my not being able to get down to write it has been another rea-

---

[5] [Frank Knight, Chicago School economist in the 'Old Chicago School' tradition and author of *Risk, Uncertainty and Profit* (Boston: Houghton Mifflin, 1921). On the 'Old Chicago School', see Ekkehard Köhler and Stefan Kolev, 'The Conjoint Quest for a Liberal Positive Program: "Old Chicago", Freiburg, and Hayek', in *F. A. Hayek and the Modern Economy: Economic Organization and Activity*, eds. Sandra J. Peart and David M. Levy (New York: Palgrave Macmillan, 2013), pp. 211–29.—Ed.]

[6] [Hayek, 'A Commodity Reserve Currency', *Economic Journal*, 53, June–September 1943, pp. 176–84.—Ed.]

son for the delay of this letter; and I fear it will now be too late. I also hoped to include with this letter a list of all the letters before 1848 which we have so far collected, but the only one I have has now so may ink insertion that it has to be copied and with that I would rather wait till a few more letters that are known to be in the post have arrived.

I should very much like to see your article in the *Yale Library Gazette* when it comes out. I am thinking of writing in the not too distant future a brief survey of the Mill material in the various Public Libraries and to offer it to some American Library Journal as a means of tracing other collections which we have not yet found. So far as we have yet discovered (I am writing from memory) there seem to be substantial collections in Northwestern, the Huntington Library, the Morgan Library and an apparently very large collection, the contents of which we do not yet know, in Johns Hopkins. A few letters have also turned up in the various Harvard Libraries and one very interesting early one (from Paris in 1830) in the University of Rochester.—also a few in Columbia. Over here, apart from the L.S.E., B.M., and Edinburgh collections there appears to be a substantial one in Leeds on which our assistant is working at the moment and on which I am expecting a report any day. It seems to derive from the same sale as the L.S.E. and Yale collections.—The way in which the National Provincial Bank as Literary executors of Mary Taylor allowed all the papers to be dispersed is really disgusting—and as they were now rather helpful, I shant [*sic*] even be able to speak my mind publicly about it.

Of later material we have obtained a great deal, the most important from descendants of Mill's correspondents, including complete sets of his letters to Cairnes, Fawcett, and T. Hare—and I have some hope of still tracing those to W. T. Thornton.

I am looking forward to hear from you about the letters owned by J. H. Schaffner and I have been very interested in what you say about the item in the sales catalogue of J. Pearson & Company. Unfortunately the firm no longer exists; both partners died shortly before the war and I have not been able to trace the clerk who liquidated the business or even to find a copy of the catalogue in any Library. It seems likely to be a most important collection and I suspect it is that which is known to have been in the Molesworth family but cannot now be found. There are many such collections we know to have existed but cannot now trace or get access to; the most important are those of Alexander Bain (apparently lost) and of Sarah Austin (probably in private hands in Florence). In general it is fairly clear now that we must not publish before we have had an opportunity of searching the continental sources fairly thoroughly. There ought, e.g., be important letters to de Tocqueville.

There is, unfortunately, a little doubt whether our work shall not have to be interrupted because of lack of funds, as so far the grant out of which the School financed it has not yet been renewed. But I hope that will be avoided.

As regards publication, as I had to explain in reply to an inquiry from your University Press which I gather was due to a suggestion of yours, the whole work was undertaken by the School with the intention to make it part of a new series of publication to be issued by the School after the war, possibly even by a new separate Press which we may start. The plans are all still in a state of flux and the assistant whom the School has engaged to prepare the Mill collection is the only definite step which as yet been taken. But in the circumstances I (who am merely supervising the work on behalf of the School) am clearly not free to make any arrangements. But there is one point to which I could not more than hint in my reply to the Chicago University Press, but on which I should like to have your opinion. Our present plan is to get one of the big publishers here to issue all School publications on commission and under the imprint of the School. But it is rather doubtful whether they would be able to handle the American side of the business and we are naturally anxious to have all our publications come into the American market. Do you think the Chicago University Press might be interested in this? I have no authority to raise the matter, but I am sure that our publications committee would be very interested if I could report that such a possibility existed. I should add that all these plans may come to nothing if the renewed efforts to create a London University Press should succeed; the obstacle for many years past has been that there is a firm with this name but which has no connection with the University.

A few days ago I learnt to my great satisfaction that the Chicago University Press will bring out the American edition of my book on the political consequences of 'planning' (*The Road to Serfdom*) which, in spite of its briefness (and together with the series of articles which will be concluded in the forthcoming *Economica*) has taken up almost all the little time I could spare for literary work during the past three years. Though it is directed very much to the English public, I hope it will not be entirely irrelevant so far as American conditions are concerned.

In conclusion I want to make a suggestion which I should be particularly glad if you could accept. You will probably know that on the occasion of the 250th anniversary of its foundation the Bank of England will issue in June a 2 volume history by Sir John Clapham. Do you think you would care to review it for *Economica*, preferably in the form of an article? If you were willing I think I could get an advance copy (probably sheets) to send to you by air mail some time before publication (the printing seems nearly completed)—you would, of course, get the bound copy later. The August number of *Economica* will contain two articles on the occasion of the centenary of the 1844 act and it would be particularly welcome if we could have an article of yours on Clapham's history at the same time—though that may prove impracticable. But even if either your time or postal communications should make this impossible, I should still rather have an article of yours than by anybody else.

With regard to your second letter, I had had a vague recollection that some-body somewhere had already refered [sic] to Senior's comments on Rae, but could not recollect where. I am sorry I did not then remember your review in the *E. J.* (of course not in *Economica* as you say), but I am glad now to have the source of your statement.

Yours very sincerely,
F. A. Hayek.

March 13, 1944

Professor F. A. Hayek
New Court
Peterhouse
Cambridge, England

Dear Hayek:

Thank you for your letter of February 12, with all its interesting contents. First, re Mill letters. I am enclosing a copy of the material in the Pearson cat-alogue; even if you can't locate the letters, the information given in the cat-alogue may be of use to you. I learned sometime ago of the Johns Hopkins collection of Mill letters, and Professor C. H. Evans has just sent me a list of its contents. I presume he has also sent you a copy of this list. This collection was bought from an American bookseller in 1922 who in turn had bought it at Sotheby's sale. It is quite extensive, but has almost no early material. I will see to it that you get a list of the letters owned by J. H. Schaffner before long—they are still not accessible. You are probably wise in postponing publication until the end of the war makes it possible to canvas the Continent for letters. I am not doing my article for the *Yale Library Gazette* until next summer, when I will be at Yale again and thus have easy access to the letters. I hope it will not interfere with your plans if I make some brief quotations from a few of the letters of special personal interest—the quotations I would most want to make would be from letters *to* Mill.

I will make some discreet inquiries as to the possibility of an arrangement of the kind you suggest with the University of Chicago Press. It does not seem to me to be at all out of the question.

I know something about the Clapham history of the Bank of England, and in fact I have already received from him a few of the sheets dealing with a

345

phase of the Bank's 18th century history which I had brought to his attention through a friend at the Bank. I would be glad to undertake a review of it for *Economica*, but I am afraid I could not undertake it in time to have it appear in the August number. I already have urgent publication commitments which will take me until at least August to liquidate, and I am still—though to a much less degree than formerly—subject to sudden Washington calls which disrupt all my carefully-laid plans. I don't recall offhand how often *Economica* appears each year, but if you have a later issue in 1944 than the August one, I feel reasonably sure I could meet that. If you do not insist on my making the August number, then get me the sheets as soon as possible, and I will try at least to finish my review in time for that number. May I suggest that Keynes might be able—or Robertson—to get the sheets to me by diplomatic air pouch, which would speed the process very much.

Do send me a list of the Mill letters you have located as soon as you can, as it may help me to find additional ones.

Cordially yours,
Jacob Viner

April 28th, 1944

Professor Jacob Viner
Department of Economics
University of Chicago.

Dear Viner,

Thank you for your letter of March 13 and the trouble you have taken in having the entry from the Pearson catalogue copied for me. It has, in fact, proved very instructive. From Part 1 of the catalogue which I have at last traced in the Bodleian[7] it proves that it was published as long ago as 1916, and from what seem to be earlier catalogues of Pearson's containing some of the same letters separately it appears that they must have made up the volume themselves. The letters to Robertson are indeed those used and largely reprinted by Towers in the *Atlantic Monthly* 1892, and the letters to W. J. Fox are those used by R. Garnett in Fox's *Life* (1910). The quotations given in the catalogue help us in one or two instances to date letters and even to add a few sentences. The other letters, particularly those to Mrs. Austin, are unknown to me. It is evidently not, as I had first thought, the Molesworth collection, which may still turn up in the family.

---

[7] [Hayek's spelling is 'Bodleyan'.—Ed.]

I am very glad that you are willing to review Clapham. I have not yet had the sheets, but as soon as I receive them, which ought to be within the next few weeks, I shall see that they are sent to you by the quickest means available. I shan't expect your review for the August issue, but if I could have it for the November issue, which would mean early in October, that would be very welcome. But I shall wait longer if necessary. If you wish to make it an article, please do.

The publishers with whom we are negotiating about the future School series are now offering to arrange also the American side of the business and it seems certain that it will all be settled together. So if you have not yet done so, please do not trouble further about it.

I enclose a list of all the dateable Mill letters up to 1848 which we have so far traced. Apart from those in the collections not now accessible we have a few more which clearly belong to this period but for which I do not know even an approximate date and which for that reason I have not inserted.

I also enclose at last my review of Graham. I don't know if you still want it or whether you have not made other arrangements in the long interval. It is not a good review anyhow and if you prefer not to publish it at this late date, I shall be quite happy.

To go back for a moment to the Mill letters: as you will see from the enclosed list, we have no information yet about the contents of the Johns Hopkins collection, but expect we shall receive it in due course. There is, of course, no reason why in your article [you] should not quote some of the Yale letters. And if you could mention that we are preparing and [*sic*] edition and suggest that any owner of other Mill letters communicate with us, that would be of considerable help.

Yours very sincerely,
F. A. Hayek

February 7, 1948

Dear Viner,

As you will probably have heard already from both Director and Morgenstern[8], I am planning another short visit to the States and I understand that I may hope to see you already during the first part of this visit in Chicago.

According to my present plans I ought to arrive in New York about March 25th and to go on to Chicago after two or three days. When I have done my

---

[8] [Oskar Morgenstern, Princeton faculty member who, with John von Neuman, published *Theory of Games and Economic Behavior* (Princeton, NJ: Princeton University Press, 1944). See note 9 below.—Ed.]

main work there I have promised to go to Detroit for one or two lectures and hope then still to have ten or twelve days before I sail again on April 22. I have promised to go to Baltimore and Chapel Hill and on the way there hope to make a brief stop in Princeton. This, according to my present vague ideas should be about April 11–13. I hope very much that you will then be at Princeton and that there will be an opportunity for a quiet talk.

Morgenstern I believe is trying to arrange some sort of lecture for me and although with the short time I shall have at my disposal I shall mainly want to see people and should probably not be able to prepare any formal lecture, I must be grateful for anything which will help me to finance the second half of my stay. But as I have definite invitation to Baltimore and Chapel Hill I hope that they will relieve me of that concern and I should certainly prefer in Princeton to talk informally to some small group rather than to give any formal lecture. I have suggested to Morgenstern (partly thinking of you) that there might be in Princeton some groups interested in a paper on Mill and Mrs. Taylor (on which I have now all the material together) and you will certainly be in the best position to judge whether this would be a suitable subject. Perhaps you will be good enough to advise Morgenstern on what to do.

With the very best regards,

yours cordially
F. A. Hayek

February 17, 1948

Professor F. A. Hayek
London School of Economics
Houghton Street, Aldwych
London, W.C.2, England

Dear Hayek:

I have just this morning heard from Director[9] about the Chicago meeting for the first time. I won't be able to go because of another engagement. We are not at all equipped here with lecture funds, but Oskar tells me he is working on it. I would, of course, be delighted if you could come to Princeton. Your

---

[9] [Aaron Director, the influential force in establishing the law and economics field of study. See Robert Van Horn, 'Aaron Director', *The Elgar Companion to the Chicago School of Economics*, ed. Ross Emmett (Cheltenham, MA: Edward Elgar, 2010), pp. 265–69.—Ed.]

dates are suitable to me and I would be very happy to put you up. I would be entranced at hearing you on Mill and Mrs. Taylor, especially as I have read, or rather looked through hastily, all the Yale material. As 1948 is a sort of a J. S. Mill centennial, I think that would add to the appropriateness of the subject.

Looking forward to seeing you, I am,
Warmly yours,
Jacob Viner

October 2nd, 1948.

Mr. E. A. G. Robinson, C.M.G., O.B.E.,
Secretary, Royal Economic Society,
Marshall Library, Downing Street,
Cambridge.

Dear Robinson,

As you know I have now been engaged for about six years in my spare time in bringing together the material for an edition of J. S. Mill's letters of the period up to 1848, i.e. the more interesting part of his life which is almost unrepresented in Elliot's edition of his letters. The material I have got together has proved to be much more voluminous than I had expected and the task of editing and publishing it raises problems which I hope the R.E.S. might be willing to take an interest.

I have got together well over 400 letters by Mill belonging to the period, some of these very interesting and throwing much light on his development and the politics of the times. Of these only some thirty have been published by Elliot, about 200 have been published in some thirty other places, while the rest are unpublished. I have now a complete set of transcriptions ready and, with one exception (Mill's letters to de Tocqueville which are probably in the de Tocqueville archives which have not yet again become accessible since the war and which might prove very interesting), I do not expect that further material will turn up except by accident.

Now the question of editing arises and in this connection I have been forced to a decision which, so far as the main body of the letters is concerned, precludes that I could undertake it in the reasonably near future. In the course of my work I have also come across a good deal of correspondence between Mill and the famous Mrs. Taylor who was ultimately to become Mrs. Mill. For a number of reasons these letters are not suitable for inclusion in a straightforward edition of his letter[s]: both sides of the correspondence must be given, a good deal of it is unsuitable for publication because it deals with ordinary household matters or contains interminable discussions of their health, a great deal of explanatory text is required, and the series extend far beyond the year 1848 beyond with (in view of the Elliot volumes) a re-editing of his general correspondence could hardly be justified. I have therefore decided to take this part of the correspondence out of the general collection and to make a separate book of it on which I am now working.

This leaves far the greater part of the correspondence (I should say at least 95 per cent in quantity) to the general edition. I neither want to commit myself for such a long period ahead nor do I see any chance that I shall ever be able to complete the task of editing it in my spare time. There are probably two years of solid work in it, not counting the period of the actual printing, and if the task is ever to be completed what is wanted is somebody who can give the greater part of his time to the task of editing the edition and seeing it through the press. While I shall be very glad to assist with my advice in this and (if that were wished) to appear as co-editor, I don't think I can or ought to undertake the task myself.

I have nobody in mind for the job, but there did not seem to be any point in looking about for somebody until there seemed to exist a chance that the task can be financed. There is a technical problem connected with it: it is desirable that before this work is taken in hand the precise form of publication is decided upon; not only because the question will arise how much of the material can or ought to be published (I have on the whole come to the conclusion that it ought to be printed in its entirety) but also because for this kind of work it is infinitely easier if the editor can work on printed galley-proofs rather than on typescripts, which would involve double checking with the originals.

What I should like to see done is that the R.E.S. undertakes the task of publishing the collection of Mill's letters and that it appoint a person as editor for a period of two or three years who can devote to it at least the greater part of his time. The costs to the Society, apart from the actual printing, would be the salary of the editor and possibly of a part-time typist. If I knew that the R.E.S. were willing to undertake this I should try to find a suitable person, and if he is appointed hand over to him all my material and remain after that available for advice whenever needed, but leave the task of editing entirely to him. (I should, perhaps, mention that I have of course done already a fair amount of work preparatory to the actual editing and also experimentally edited a small portion of the letters.)

Since L.S.E. had during the first two years of my work supplied me with a research assistant and had therefore a prior claim on the results, I have raised the matter with the authorities of L.S.E. who have expressly waived all claims and have authorized me to make whatever arrangements I can for the publication of the results.

If you think this is worth putting up to the Council, please do so. Any further information you want I shall be glad to supply, and I shall of course be available for any explanations the Council may want.

Yours sincerely,
F. A. Hayek

P.S. I enclose an earlier printed description of my plans which may on some points supplement the above.

19th October 1948

My dear Hayek,

I have just had your letter about the great edition of the Mill letters on which you have been working for so long. In goes back, of course, to an earlier conversation that we had about it. I think you know my mind in the matter. I am quite convinced myself that this is just the sort of thing on which some of the capital balances of the R.E.S., built up by rather inadvertent surpluses of income over the expenditure permitted by our limited paper supplies, ought to be spent. And I think the proper use of your talents is that you should exercise a general direction rather than be a slave. I shall be delighted, therefore, to put it on the next agenda. There is not much immediate business, and I would not expect a meeting before December, when I shall be back in London. My one doubt is whether your present proposals are not a little too self-effacing. We shall want to feel that your eagle eye is still available, and that the editor, whoever he may be, will follow out your policies.

What I think we ought to do is to refer your proposal with certain others to a small committee which should be made to advise on these general problems of R.E.S. publications.[10] I have a number of things which should, I think, be considered together. First, there is Ricardo. Sraffa has persuaded Dobb to take a hand, and Dobb is pushing it along very effectively. But we must think about how we handle the financial problems, including a proper recog-

---

[10] [Robinson reported on 'progress made with the forthcoming publications of the Society', including Bentham, Ricardo, Guillebaud, Marshall, and Mill, at the January 27, 1949 meeting. At that time a committee comprised of Robinson, Robertson, Harrod, and Robbins was formed 'to make recommendations to the Council as to its future policy with regard to these and other publications'. Correspondence of Austin Robinson, including some minutes 1945–1948, Royal Economic Society Additional Material, RES/16/4, London School of Economics Library's Collections.—Ed.]

nition of Dobb's services.[11] Second, there is Bentham. Stark's Man[uscript] is approaching completion, and he and I have had discussions with Sir Stanley Unwin about problems of printing and publication.[12] Third, there is Guillebaud's edition of Marshall which may raise a number of problems of assistance and publication rather similar to those about which you have written to me.[13] Finally, there are the problems you raise of the Mill letters.

My personal view is that, spread over several years, as they must be, these projects together do not represent more than we can afford to undertake. But clearly that needs thinking about. I have been wondering whether it would not be best (as I indicated above) to refer the whole group of problems to a committee composed, perhaps, of D.H.R. [D. H. Robertson] (as President), L.R. [Lionel Robbins], R.F.H. [R. F. Harrod], H.C.B.M. [H. C. B. Mynors] (as Treasurer) and myself. As at present advised that is the suggestion I shall make to D.H.R. What do you think?

Yours,

E. A. G. Robinson

P.S. You may like to show this to Lionel to save my writing.

October 15, 1951

Professor Friedrich A. Hayek
Committee on Social Thought
Social Science Building
University of Chicago
Chicago 37, Illinois

Dear Hayek:

Belated thanks for your Mill-Taylor book. You did an excellent job—as I expected—and I found it very interesting reading, indeed. I have no emen-

---

[11] [When Ricardo's works were published for the Royal Economic Society, Maurice Dobb's role was explicitly recognized; see *The Works and Correspondence of David Ricardo*, ed. Pierro Sraffa with the collaboration of M. H. Dobb, 11 vols. (Cambridge: Cambridge University Press, 1951– 1973). On Dobb's role, see Brian H. Pollitt, 'The Collaboration of Maurice Dobb in Sraffa's edition of Ricardo', *Cambridge Journal of Economics*, vol. 12 (1), 1988, pp. 55–65.—Ed.]

[12] [Eventually published for the Royal Economic Society as *Jeremy Bentham's Economic Writings*, ed. Werner Stark, 3 vols. (New York: Bert Franklin, 1952–1954).—Ed.]

[13] [Guillebaud's variorum edition of Marshall's *Principles* was published for the Royal Economic Society in 1961; Alfred Marshall, *Principles of Economics*, 9th ed., ed. C. W. Guillebaud (London: Macmillan, 1961)].—Ed.]

dations to suggest, except that I seem to remember reading once a quite flattering appraisal of Harriet Taylor in some Bunbury biography to which you have no reference. In one of the Yale J.S.M. letters, he makes an acknowledgment of intellectual partnership with Helen Taylor which as far as it goes is quite in keeping with his tributes to Harriet Taylor (to D. McLaren, Edinburgh, Jan. 3, 1869).

In 1865 J.S.M. wrote to a correspondent that he had written a contribution to his father's memory which he intended for posthumous publication. Has this turned up in any of the collections of his papers?

Cordially yours,
Jacob Viner

INDEX OF NAMES

INDEX OF SUBJECTS

Note on abbreviations used: J.S.M. is John Stuart Mill, H.T. is Harriet Taylor prior to her marriage to Mill, and H.M. is Harriet Mill after her marriage to Mill.